STUDENT SUPPLEMENTS

Essentials of Corporate Finance, *The Wall Street Journal Edition*, ISBN 0-256-20017-3. The price of this version of the student text includes a 10-week subscription to *The Wall Street Journal*, the leading business daily newspaper. The *Journal's* coverage of financial topics, both domestic and global, is unparalleled by any other business periodical. To activate the subscription, students simply complete and return the postage paid card bound into each text of *The Wall Street Journal* Edition. Irwin is pleased to offer this as part of the Ross/Westerfield/Jordan package.

Student Problem Manual for use with Essentials of Corporate Finance, ISBN 0-256-16987-X, prepared by Dr. Thomas Eyssell, University of Missouri-St. Louis. This valuable resource provides students additional problems for practice. Each chapter begins with *Concepts for Review*, followed by *Chapter Highlights*. These reemphasize the key terms and concepts in that chapter. A short *Concept Test*, averaging 10 questions and answers, appears next. Each chapter concludes with additional problems for the students to review. Answers to these problems appear at the end of the Student Problem Manual.

Financial Analysis with an Electronic Calculator, Second Edition, ISBN 0-256-15210-1, prepared by Dr. Mark White, University of Virginia-McIntyre School of Commerce. The information and procedures in this supplementary text enable students to master the use of financial calculators and develop a working knowledge of financial mathematics and problem-solving. Complete instructions are included for solving all major problem types on three common models: Hewlett-Packard HP-10B, Sharp Electronics EL-733-A, and Texas Instruments BA II Plus. Forty hands-on problems with detailed solutions allow students to practice the skills outlined in the text and obtain instant reinforcement. *Financial Analysis with an Electronic Calculator* is a self-contained supplement to the introductory financial management course.

Ready Notes for use with Essentials of Corporate Finance, ISBN 0-256-21678-9-0. This is an inexpensive note-taking system that contains a reduced copy of every transparency in the transparency-acetate package. With a copy of each transparency in front of them, students can listen and record your comments about each point – instead of hurriedly copying the transparency into their notebooks.

Inside the back cover of the AIE and in the student text, you will find a detailed explanation of the functional use of color for this edition.

ESSENTIALS OF CORPORATE FINANCE

• • •

ANNOTATED INSTRUCTOR'S EDTION

Irwin Series in Finance

Consulting Editor Stephen A. Ross
Sterling Professor of Economics and Finance
Yale University

FINANCIAL MANAGEMENT

Block and Hirt
Foundations of Financial Management
Seventh Edition

Brooks
PC Fingame: *The Financial Management Decision Game*
Version 2.0

Bruner
Case Studies in Finance: *Managing for Corporate Value Creation*
Second Edition

Fruhan, Kester, Mason, Piper and Ruback
Case Problems in Finance
Tenth Edition

Harrington
Corporate Financial Analysis: *Decisions in a Global Environment*
Fourth Edition

Helfert
Techniques of Financial Analysis
Eighth Edition

Higgins
Analysis for Financial Management
Fourth Edition

Kallberg and Parkinson
Corporate Liquidity: *Management and Measurement*

Nunnally and Plath
Cases in Finance

Ross, Westerfield and Jaffe
Corporate Finance
Fourth Edition

Ross, Westerfield and Jordan
Essentials of Corporate Finance

Ross, Westerfield and Jordan
Fundamentals of Corporate Finance
Third Edition

Schary
Cases in Financial Management

Stonehill and Eiteman
Finance: *An International Perspective*

White
Financial Analysis with an Electronic Calculator
Second Edition

INVESTMENTS

Bodie, Kane and Marcus
Essentials of Investments
Second Edition

Bodie, Kane and Marcus
Investments
Third Edition

Cohen, Zinbarg and Zeikel
Investment Analysis and Portfolio Management
Fifth Edition

Hirt and Block
Fundamentals of Investment Management
Fifth Edition

Lorie, Dodd and Kimpton
The Stock Market: *Theories and Evidence*
Second Edition

Morningstar, Inc. and Remaley
U.S. Equities OnFloppy
Annual Edition

Shimko
The Innovative Investor
Version 3.0

FINANCIAL INSTITUTIONS AND MARKETS

Rose
Commercial Bank Management: *Producing and Selling Financial Services*
Third Edition

Rose
Money and Capital Markets: *The Financial System in an Increasingly Global Economy*
Fifth Edition

Rose
Reading on Financial Institutions and Markets
1995 - 1996 Edition

Rose and Kolari
Financial Institutions: *Understanding and Managing Financial Services*
Fifth Edition

Saunders
Financial Institutions Management: *A Modern Perspective*

REAL ESTATE

Berston
California Real Estate Principles
Seventh Edition

Berston
California Real Estate Practice
Sixth Edition

Brueggeman and Fisher
Real Estate Finance and Investments
Tenth Edition

Smith and Corgel
Real Estate Perspectives: *An Introduction to Real Estate*
Second Edition

FINANCIAL PLANNING AND INSURANCE

Allen, Melone, Rosenbloom and VanDerhei
Pension Planning: *Pensions, Profit-Sharing, and Other Deferred Compensation Plans*
Seventh Edition

Crawford
Law and the Life Insurance Contract
Seventh Edition

Crawford
Life and Health Insurance Law
LOMA Edition

Hirsch
Casualty Claim Practice
Sixth Edition

Kapoor, Dlabay and Hughes
Personal Finance
Fourth Edition

Kellison
Theory of Interest
Second Edition

Rokes
Human Relations in Handling Insurance Claims
Revised Edition

ESSENTIALS OF CORPORATE FINANCE

ANNOTATED INSTRUCTOR'S EDTION

STEPHEN A. ROSS
Yale University

RANDOLPH W. WESTERFIELD
University of Southern California

BRADFORD D. JORDAN
University of Missouri–Columbia

IRWIN
Chicago • Bogotá • Boston • Buenos Aires • Caracas
London • Madrid • Mexico City • Sydney • Toronto

Senior sponsoring editor:	*James M. Keefe*
Project editor:	*Rebecca Dodson*
Production supervisor:	*Bette K. Ittersagen*
Assistant manager, graphics:	*Charlene R. Breeden*
Cover designer:	*Maureen McCutcheon*
Cover illustrator:	*Skip Baker*
Interior designer:	*Maureen McCutcheon*
Art studio:	*Electronic Publishing Services, Inc.*
Compositor:	*Beacon Graphics Corp.*
Typeface:	*10.5/12 Times Roman*
Printer:	*Von Hoffmann Press, Inc.*

Library of Congress Cataloging-in-Publication Data

Ross, Stephen A.
Essentials of corporate finance/Stephen A. Ross, Randolph W. Westerfield, Bradford D. Jordan
p. cm.
Includes index.
ISBN 0-256-16986-1
ISBN 0-256-20018-1 (annotated instructor's ed.)
ISBN 0-256-20017-3 (*Wall Street Journal* ed.)
1. Corporations—Finance. I. Westerfield, Randolph. II. Jordan, Bradford D. III. Title.
HG4026.R675 1996
658.15—dc20 95–35439

Printed in the United States of America

1 2 3 4 5 6 7 8 9 0 VH 2 1 0 9 8 7 6 5

To our families and friends with love and gratitude

S. A. R. R.W.W. B. D. J.

About the Authors

• • •

Stephen A. Ross, Yale University

Stephen A. Ross has held the position of Sterling Professor of Economics and Finance at Yale University since 1985. One of the most widely published authors in finance and economics, Professor Ross is recognized for his work in developing the Arbitrage Pricing Theory. He has also made substantial contributions to the discipline through his research in signalling, agency theory, options, and the theory of the term structure of interest rates. Previously the president of the American Finance Association, he serves as an associate editor of the *Journal of Finance* and the *Journal of Economic Theory.* He is cochairman of Roll and Ross Asset Management Corporation, a trustee of Cal Tech, a director of CREF, and a director of GenRe.

Randolph W. Westerfield, University of Southern California

Randolph W. Westerfield is Dean of the University of Southern California School of Business Administration and holder of the Robert R. Dockson Dean's Chair of Business Administration. The USC School of Business Administration, founded in 1920, is the oldest business school in Southern California.

From 1988 to 1993 Professor Westerfield served as the chairman of the School's finance and business economics department and the Charles B. Thornton Professor of Finance. He came to USC from the Wharton School, University of Pennsylvania, where he was the chairman of the finance department and member of the finance faculty for 20 years. He was the senior research associate at the Rodney L. White Center for Financial Research at Wharton. His areas of expertise include corporate financial policy, investment management and analysis, mergers and acquisitions, and stock market price behavior.

Professor Westerfield has served as a member of the Continental Bank trust committee, supervising all activities of the trust department. He has been consultant to a number of corporations, including AT&T, Mobil Oil and Pacific Enterprises, as well as to the United Nations, the U.S. Department of Justice and Labor, and the State of California.

Bradford D. Jordan, University of Missouri–Columbia

Bradford D. Jordan is Associate Professor of Finance at the University of Missouri. He has a longstanding interest in both applied and theoretical issues in corporate finance, and he has extensive experience teaching all levels of corporate finance and financial management policy. Professor Jordan has published numerous articles on issues such as cost of capital, capital structure, and the behavior of security prices.

Preface

We wrote this book because so many of you told us of changes taking place in your introductory finance classes. What we have learned, both from comments and discussions we have had with you and from our own classes, is that this course is increasingly the only finance course a majority of students enrolled will ever take. In addition, a growing percentage of students in introductory finance classes do not have traditional pre-business backgrounds. Finally, time pressure during the term and the desire to integrate other materials increasingly mean that only a limited number of chapters can be covered.

So what did we do about it?

We have always maintained that the subject of corporate finance can be viewed as the working of a few very powerful intuitions. Based on the gratifying market feedback we have received over the last several years from our first text, *Fundamentals of Corporate Finance,* many of you agree. We therefore decided to try and distill the subject down to its bare essentials (hence, the name of this book), while retaining the same modern approach to finance. Our goal was to produce a text that conveys the most important concepts and principles at a level that is approachable for the widest possible audience in a package that realistically can be covered in a single term.

To accomplish our goal, we assembled a diverse panel of our colleagues currently teaching introductory finance courses. We asked them to tell us what should and what should not be included. Based on their feedback, we eliminated some chapters on more specialized subjects altogether. We then went through every remaining page, paring back where recommended and eliminating material not absolutely essential. We very consciously tried to hold computation and mathematical formulations to the minimum needed to convey key financial principles. This process led us to condense several subject treatments, such as capital budgeting, to single chapters. As a result, *Essentials* provides a thorough survey in only 18 chapters.

Of course, we didn't just cut and combine in producing *Essentials.* For example, we learned from our reviewers (and our own teaching experience) that a single chapter on time value of money just contains too much number crunching and too many new concepts for a large percentage of students. We therefore wrote two chapters on time value for *Essentials* to break the subject into more manageable size and promote a building block approach. The first chapter considers only the basics of compounding and discounting. With these principles firmly in place, the second chapter expands to cover annuities and other financial instruments. For similar reasons, we provide two chapters on risk and return because the subject is so important and contains so many new and novel ideas.

Beyond this, to motivate various subjects and to illustrate the wide applicability and relevance of topics covered in the text, we created a new running series of boxes called *Principles in Action.* These appear in almost every chapter throughout the text and discuss current subjects as diverse as the recent attempted takeover of Chrysler to Shaquille O'Neill's salary.

The Underlying Philosophy

As the 21st century approaches, the challenge of financial management is greater than ever. In recent years, we have seen fundamental changes in financial markets and instruments, and the practice of corporate finance continues to evolve rapidly. Often, what was yesterday's state of the art is commonplace today, and it is essential that our finance courses and finance texts do not get left behind.

Rapid and extensive change place new burdens on those teaching corporate finance. It becomes much more difficult to keep materials up to date. Further, the permanent must be distinguished from the temporary to avoid following what is merely the latest fad. Our approach is to stress the modern fundamentals of finance and make the subject come alive with contemporary examples.

From our survey of existing introductory textbooks, this commonsense approach seems to be the exception rather than the rule. All too often, the beginning student views corporate finance as a collection of unrelated topics which are unified by virtue of being bound together between the covers of one book. In many cases, this perception is only natural because the subject is treated in a way that is both topic oriented and procedural. Commonly, emphasis is placed on detailed and specific "solutions" to certain narrowly posed problems. How often have we heard students exclaim that they could solve a particular problem if only they knew which formula to use?

We think this approach misses the forest for the trees. As time passes, the details fade, and what remains, if we are successful, is a sound grasp of the underlying principles. This is why our overriding concern, from the first page to the last, is with the basic logic of financial decision making.

Distinctive Features

Our general philosophy is apparent in the following ways:

An Emphasis on Intuition We are always careful to separate and explain the principles at work on an intuitive level before launching into any specifics. The underlying ideas are discussed first in very general terms and then by way of examples that illustrate in more concrete terms how a financial manager might proceed in a given situation.

A Unified Valuation Approach Many texts pay only lip service to net present value (NPV) as the basic concept of corporate finance and stop short of consistently integrating this important principle. The most basic notion, that

NPV represents the excess of market value over cost, tends to get lost in an overly mechanical approach to NPV that emphasizes computation at the expense of understanding. Every subject covered in *Essentials of Corporate Finance,* from capital budgeting to capital structure, is firmly rooted in valuation, and care is taken throughout to explain how particular decisions have valuation effects.

A Managerial Focus Students won't lose sight of the fact that financial management concerns management. Throughout the text, the role of the financial manager as decision maker is emphasized, and the need for managerial input and judgment is stressed. "Black box" approaches to finance are consciously avoided.

In *Essentials of Corporate Finance,* these three themes work together to provide a consistent treatment, a sound foundation, and a practical, workable understanding of how to evaluate financial decisions. Because *Essentials* is not a "me-too" book, we have, with extensive help from our colleagues across the country, taken a hard look at what is really relevant and important for an introductory class. This process led us to take a fresh, modern approach to many traditional subjects. Along the way, we downplay purely theoretical issues and associated mathematical formulations, and we avoid the use of elaborate computations to illustrate points that are either intuitively obvious or of limited practical use.

Intended Audience

This text is designed and developed explicitly for a first course in business or corporate finance. The typical student will not have previously taken a course in finance, and no previous knowledge of finance is assumed. Since this course is frequently part of a common business core, the text is intended for majors and nonmajors alike. In terms of background or prerequisites, the book is nearly self-contained. Some familiarity with basic accounting principles is helpful, but even these are reviewed very early on. As a result, students with very different backgrounds will find the text very accessible.

Attention to Pedagogy

In addition to illustrating pertinent concepts and presenting up-to-date coverage, *Essentials of Corporate Finance* strives to present the material in a way that makes it coherent and easy to understand. To meet the varied needs of the intended audience, *Essentials of Corporate Finance* is rich in valuable learning tools and support, including:

1. **Pedagogical Use of Color.** Throughout *Essentials*, color is used as a functional element in the discussion. In almost every chapter, color plays an important, largely self-evident role. An example of the pedagogical use of color follows.

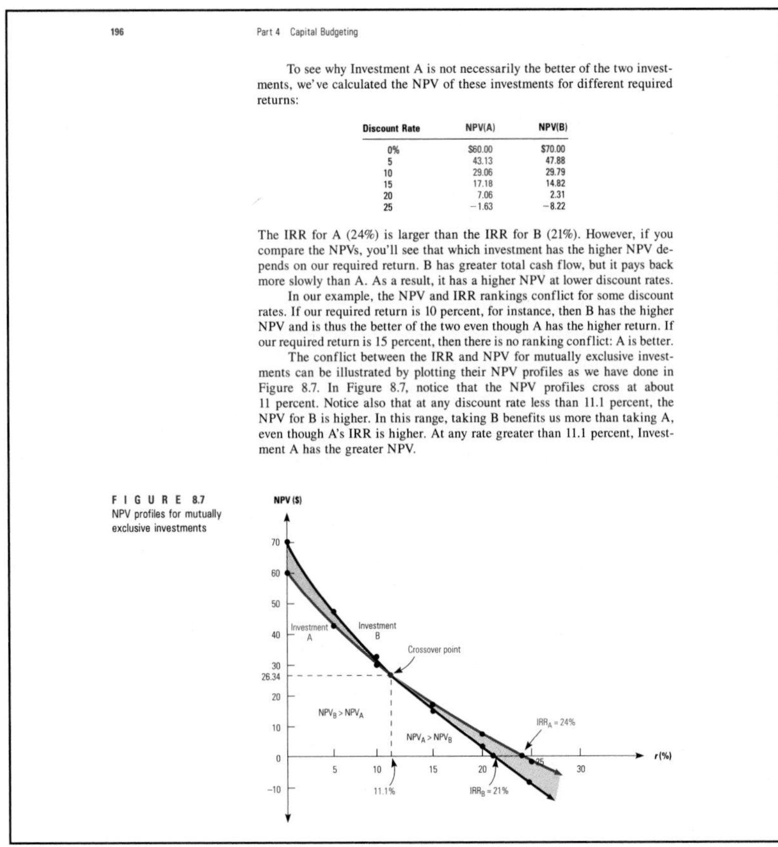

To see why Investment A is not necessarily the better of the two investments, we've calculated the NPV of these investments for different required returns:

Discount Rate	NPV(A)	NPV(B)
0%	$60.00	$70.00
5	43.13	47.88
10	29.06	29.79
15	17.18	14.82
20	7.06	2.31
25	−1.63	−8.22

The IRR for A (24%) is larger than the IRR for B (21%). However, if you compare the NPVs, you'll see that which investment has the higher NPV depends on our required return. B has greater total cash flow, but it pays back more slowly than A. As a result, it has a higher NPV at lower discount rates.

In our example, the NPV and IRR rankings conflict for some discount rates. If our required return is 10 percent, for instance, then B has the higher NPV and is thus the better of the two even though A has the higher return. If our required return is 15 percent, then there is no ranking conflict: A is better.

The conflict between the IRR and NPV for mutually exclusive investments can be illustrated by plotting their NPV profiles as we have done in Figure 8.7. In Figure 8.7, notice that the NPV profiles cross at about 11 percent. Notice also that at any discount rate less than 11.1 percent, the NPV for B is higher. In this range, taking B benefits us more than taking A, even though A's IRR is higher. At any rate greater than 11.1 percent, Investment A has the greater NPV.

FIGURE 8.7
NPV profiles for mutually exclusive investments

2. ***Principles in Action* Boxes.** This unique series of boxes appears throughout the text. Each box takes a particular chapter issue and shows how it is being used right now in everyday financial decision-making.
3. **Concept Building.** Chapter sections are intentionally kept short to promote a step-by-step, building block approach to learning. Each section is then followed by a series of short concept questions that highlight the key ideas just presented. Students use these questions to make sure they can identify and understand the most important concepts as they read.
4. **Summary Tables.** These tables succinctly restate key principles, results, and equations. They appear whenever it is useful to emphasize and summarize a group of related concepts.

Principles in Action

Was Chrysler's Cash Flow to Stockholders Too Small?

In April 1995, financier Kirk Kerkorian and former Chrysler chairman Lee A. Iacocca stunned the financial world by offering to buy the common stock of Chrysler Corporation for $55 a share. The purchase was to be financed primarily with debt, but the offer had a novel twist. They also planned to use $5.5 billion of Chrysler's own cash to finance the purchase. Their offer increased the level of debate over how large a cash balance is appropriate for a corporation and just how the financial managers of a corporation should go about maximizing shareholder wealth.

At the time of the offer, Chrysler had amassed a cash balance in excess of $7 billion. Chrysler's board of directors argued the company needed about $7.5 billion in cash to survive the next recession, a goal clearly in the best interest of the stockholders. However, Chrysler's largest stockholder, Kirk Kerkorian, who at that time owned just under 10 percent of Chrysler's outstanding stock (an investment valued at $1.5 billion), disagreed. He believed Chrysler's cash balance was excessive and should be reduced by returning the cash to its owners, the stockholders.

To understand Kerkorian's perspective, it is crucial to determine who the cash of the corporation belongs to. Each quarter, Chrysler's corporate directors decide what to do with any excess cash generated from operations. The cash can be paid out to stockholders in the form of a dividend or it can be retained in the business. If a dividend is paid, it is a cash flow to stockholders. If, however, the cash is retained in the corporation, the money still belongs to the stockholders, but the directors have effectively reinvested the shareholder's money in the corporation itself by increasing net working capital.

At issue is whether or not the investment in net working capital provides an adequate return to the stockholders. Chrysler's directors argued that the cash lessened the chance of financial distress, a benefit to stockholders. However, from Kerkorian's perspective, while Chrysler's cash balance grew, its stock price did not. In late 1994, Kerkorian convinced Chrysler's board to use some of its excess cash to boost its dividend by 60 percent and initiate a $1 billion stock-buyback program, each of which is a cash flow to stockholders. Despite these actions, Chrysler's cash balance continued to rise in early 1995 while the stock price languished. Kerkorian argued that accumulating cash was not enhancing shareholder wealth, and a better way to do so was to allow the stockholders to reinvest it themselves.

How the struggle for control between Kerkorian and Chrysler is ultimately played out will not solve the more general issue of how much cash a corporation should hold, and Chrysler isn't the only company with large amounts of cash. In April 1995, *The Wall Street Journal* reported that Chrysler had a cash balance equal to about 30 percent of the market value of its stock, Ford had cash equal to 22 percent of its value, Intel had 9 percent, United Healthcare had 33 percent, and Apple Computer held about 25 percent. These corporations have reinvested substantial sums of money for their stockholders. Corporations such as these who accumulate large cash balances may ultimately need to defend their actions to an important and sometimes vocal group: their stockholders.

Source: "Chrysler Boosts Dividend, Sets Buyback of Stock in Effort to Mollify Kerkorian," *The Wall Street Journal*, December 2, 1994, p. A3; "Rich and Richer: How Much Cash a Firm Should Keep Is an Issue in Wake of Chrysler Bid," *The Wall Street Journal*, April 20, 1995, p. A1; "At the Factory Gate: Kerkorian and Iacocca Make a Run at Chrysler: Motives Are Unclear," *The Wall Street Journal*, April 13, 1995, p. A1.

• • •

As we have seen in this section, estimating NPV is one way of assessing the profitability of a proposed investment. It is certainly not the only way profitability is assessed, and we now turn to some alternatives. As we will see, when compared to NPV, each of the ways of assessing profitability that we examine is flawed in some key way; so NPV is the preferred approach in principle, if not always in practice.

CONCEPT QUESTIONS

8.1a What is the net present value rule?

8.1b If we say an investment has an NPV of $1,000, what exactly do we mean?

TABLE 4.9
Summary of internal and sustainable growth rates

I. Internal Growth Rate

$$\text{Internal growth rate} = \frac{\text{ROA} \times b}{1 - \text{ROA} \times b}$$

where

ROA = Return on assets = Net income/Total assets
b = Plowback (retention) ratio
= Addition to retained earnings/Net income

The internal growth rate is the maximum growth rate that can be achieved with no external financing of any kind.

II. Sustainable Growth Rate

$$\text{Sustainable growth rate} = \frac{\text{ROE} \times b}{1 - \text{ROE} \times b}$$

where

ROE = Return on equity = Net income/Total equity
b = Plowback (retention) ratio
= Addition to retained earnings/Net income

The sustainable growth rate is the maximum growth rate that can be achieved with no external equity financing while maintaining a constant debt/equity ratio.

5. **Numbered Examples.** Separate numbered and titled examples are extensively integrated into the chapters as indicated below. These examples provide detailed applications and illustrations of the text material in a step-by-step format. Each example is completely self-contained so that students don't have to search for additional information. Based on our classroom testing, these examples are among the most useful learning aids because they provide both detail and explanation. A small color icon signals the end of each example.

EXAMPLE 17.2 What's the Rate?

Ordinary tiles are often sold 3/30, net 60. What effective annual rate does a buyer pay by not taking the discount? What would the APR be if one were quoted?

Here we have 3 percent discount interest on 60 − 30 = 30 days' credit. The rate per 30 days is .03/.97 = 3.093%. There are 365/30 = 12.17 such periods in a year, so the effective annual rate is:

$$\text{EAR} = (1.03093)^{12.17} - 1 = 44.9\%$$

The APR, as always, would be calculated by multiplying the rate per period by the number of periods:

$$\text{APR} = .03093 \times 12.17 = 37.6\%$$

An interest rate calculated like this APR is often quoted as the cost of the trade credit, and, as this example illustrates, can seriously understate the true cost. ...

6. **Key Terms.** These are contained in each chapter and are printed in teal the first time they appear. These terms are defined within the text and also in the marginal definitions.

Average versus Marginal Tax Rates

In making financial decisions, it is frequently important to distinguish between average and marginal tax rates. Your **average tax rate** is your tax bill divided by your taxable income, in other words, the percentage of your income that goes to pay taxes. Your **marginal tax rate** is the extra tax you would pay if you earned one more dollar. The percentage tax rates shown in Table 2.3 are all marginal rates. Put another way, the tax rates in Table 2.3 apply to the part of income in the indicated range only, not all income.

average tax rate
Total taxes paid divided by total taxable income.

marginal tax rate
Amount of tax payable on the next dollar earned.

7. **Key Equations.** These are called out in the text and identified by equation numbers. The list in Appendix B shows the key equations by chapter.
8. **Highlighted Phrases.** Throughout the text important ideas are presented separately and printed in teal. Printing these phrases in color not only draws attention to them, but also indicates their importance to the students.

Given our observations, it follows that the financial manager acts in the shareholders' best interests by making decisions that increase the value of the stock. The appropriate goal for the financial manager in a corporation can thus be stated quite easily:

The goal of financial management in a corporation is to maximize the current value per share of the existing stock.

The goal of maximizing the value of the stock avoids the problems associated with the different goals we discussed above. There is no ambiguity in the criterion, and there is no short-run versus long-run issue. We explicitly mean that our goal is to maximize the *current* stock value.

9. Chapter Summary and Conclusion. These paragraphs review the chapter's key points and provide closure to the chapter.

14.9 SUMMARY AND CONCLUSIONS

The ideal mixture of debt and equity for a firm—its optimal capital structure—is the one that maximizes the value of the firm and minimizes the overall cost of capital. If we ignore taxes, financial distress costs, and any other imperfections, we find that there is no ideal mixture. Under these circumstances, the firm's capital structure is simply irrelevant.

If we consider the effect of corporate taxes, we find that capital structure matters a great deal. This conclusion is based on the fact that interest is tax deductible and thus generates a valuable tax shield. Unfortunately, we also find that the optimal capital structure is 100 percent debt, which is not something we observe for healthy firms.

We next introduced costs associated with bankruptcy, or, more generally, financial distress. These costs reduce the attractiveness of debt financing. We concluded that an optimal capital structure exists when the net tax saving from an additional dollar in interest just equals the increase in expected financial distress costs. This is the essence of the static theory of capital structure.

10. Chapter Review Problems and Self-Tests. Review and self-test problems appear after the chapter summaries. Detailed answers to the self-test problems immediately follow. These questions and answers allow students to test their abilities in solving key problems related to the content of the chapter.

Chapter Review Problems and Self-Test

14.1 **EBIT and EPS** Suppose the GNR Corporation has decided in favor of a capital restructuring that involves increasing its existing $5 million in debt to $25 million. The interest rate on the debt is 12 percent and is not expected to change. The firm currently has 1 million shares outstanding, and the price per share is $40. If the restructuring is expected to increase the ROE, what is the minimum level for EBIT that GNR's management must be expecting? Ignore taxes in your answer.

Answers to Self-Test Problems

14.1 To answer, we can calculate the break-even EBIT. At any EBIT above this, the increased financial leverage will increase EPS. Under the old capital structure, the interest bill is $5 million × .12 = $600,000. There are 1 million shares of stock, so, ignoring taxes, EPS is (EBIT − $600,000)/1 million.

Under the new capital structure, the interest expense will be $25 million × .12 = $3 million. Furthermore, the debt rises by $20 million. This amount is sufficient to repurchase $20 million/$40 = 500,000 shares of stock, leaving 500,000 outstanding. EPS is thus (EBIT − $3 million)/500,000.

Now that we know how to calculate EPS under both scenarios, we set them equal to each other and solve for the break-even EBIT:

$$(\text{EBIT} - \$600{,}000)/1 \text{ million} = (\text{EBIT} - \$3 \text{ million})/500{,}000$$
$$(\text{EBIT} - \$600{,}000) = 2 \times (\text{EBIT} - \$3 \text{ million})$$
$$\text{EBIT} = \$5{,}400{,}000$$

Check that, in either case, EPS is $4.80 when EBIT is $5.4 million.

14.2 According to M&M Proposition II (no taxes), the cost of equity is:

$$\begin{aligned} R_E &= R_A + (R_A - R_D) \times (D/E) \\ &= 20\% + (20\% - 12\%) \times 2 \\ &= 36\% \end{aligned}$$

11. **End-of-Chapter Questions and Problems.** We have found that many students learn better when they have plenty of opportunity to practice. We therefore provide extensive end-of-chapter questions and problems. The end-of-chapter support we provide greatly exceeds what is typical in an introductory textbook. The questions and problems are generally segregated into two levels—Basic and Intermediate. All problems are fully annotated so that students and instructors can readily identify particular types. Throughout the text, we have worked to supply interesting problems that illustrate real world applications of chapter material. Answers to selected end-of-chapter questions appear in Appendix C.

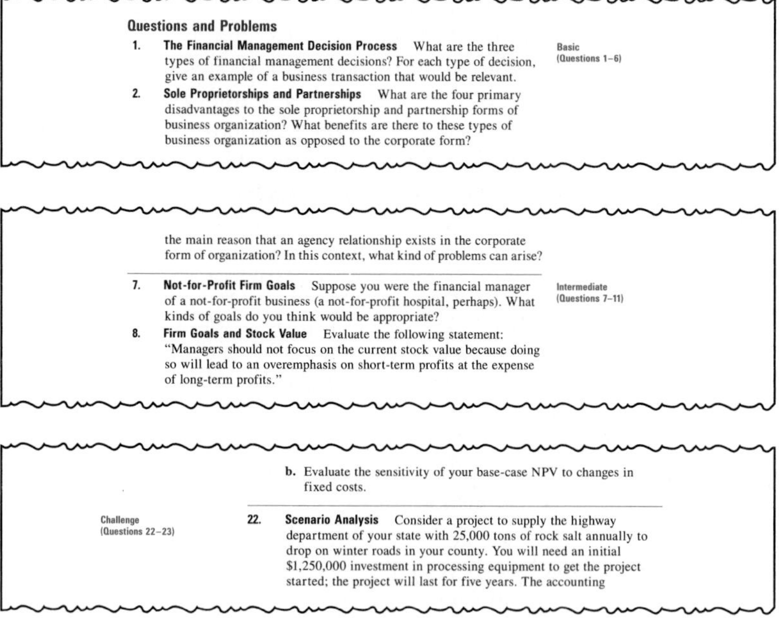

Questions and Problems

Basic (Questions 1–6)

1. **The Financial Management Decision Process** What are the three types of financial management decisions? For each type of decision, give an example of a business transaction that would be relevant.
2. **Sole Proprietorships and Partnerships** What are the four primary disadvantages to the sole proprietorship and partnership forms of business organization? What benefits are there to these types of business organization as opposed to the corporate form?

the main reason that an agency relationship exists in the corporate form of organization? In this context, what kind of problems can arise?

Intermediate (Questions 7–11)

7. **Not-for-Profit Firm Goals** Suppose you were the financial manager of a not-for-profit business (a not-for-profit hospital, perhaps). What kinds of goals do you think would be appropriate?
8. **Firm Goals and Stock Value** Evaluate the following statement: "Managers should not focus on the current stock value because doing so will lead to an overemphasis on short-term profits at the expense of long-term profits."

b. Evaluate the sensitivity of your base-case NPV to changes in fixed costs.

Challenge (Questions 22–23)

22. **Scenario Analysis** Consider a project to supply the highway department of your state with 25,000 tons of rock salt annually to drop on winter roads in your county. You will need an initial $1,250,000 investment in processing equipment to get the project started; the project will last for five years. The accounting

12. **Indexes.** This edition is divided into three types—name, equation, and subject indexes.

Organization of the Text

We have found that the phrase "so much to do, so little time" accurately describes an introductory finance course. For this reason, we designed *Essentials of Corporate Finance* to be as flexible and modular as possible. There are a total of eight parts, and, in broad terms, the instructor is free to decide the particular sequence. Further, within each part, the first chapter generally contains an overview and survey. Thus, when time is limited, subsequent chapters can be omitted. Finally, the sections placed early in each chapter are generally the most important, and later sections frequently can be omitted without loss of continuity. For these reasons, the instructor has great control over the topics covered, the sequence in which they are covered, and the depth of coverage.

Essentials has a total of 18 chapters. The average chapter length is well under 30 pages, so it is quite possible to cover the vast majority of the text in a single term. Based on our experience, covering every single chapter in depth might be a bit of a stretch, although it can certainly be done. However, we have found that it is not difficult to cover all but one or two.

Part One of the text contains two chapters. Chapter 1 considers the goal of the corporation, the corporate form of organization, the agency problem, and, briefly, financial markets. Chapter 2 succinctly discusses cash flow versus accounting income, market value versus book value, and taxes. It also provides a useful review of financial statements.

After Part One, either Part Two, on financial statements analysis, long-range planning, and corporate growth, or Part Three, on time value and stock and bond valuation, follows naturally. Part Two can be omitted entirely if desired. After Part Three, most instructors will probably want to move directly into Part Four, which covers net present value, discounted cash flow valuation, and capital budgeting.

Part Five contains two chapters on risk and return. The first one, on market history, is designed to give students a feel for typical rates of return on risky assets. The second one discusses the expected return/risk tradeoff, and it develops the security market line in a highly intuitive way that bypasses much of the usual portfolio theory and statistics.

Part Six contains four chapters on long-term financing. The first covers cost of capital. The second chapter describes ways businesses raise capital. Venture capital, the role of investment banks, and the costs of going public are emphasized. Because this chapter contains a good deal of descriptive material, it can be assigned as outside reading if time is tight. The third chapter covers leverage and capital structure. It also contains a brief discussion of the bankruptcy process. The final chapter in Part Six covers dividends and dividend policy.

Part Seven contains two chapters on short-term financial management. The first is an introduction to the subject that emphasizes the cash cycle and the need for short-term planning. The second chapter provides greater detail, covering essentials of cash, inventory, and receivables management. The second chapter can be omitted as time constraints dictate.

Finally, Part Eight has a single chapter on international financial management. Because of the importance of this subject, we felt it should be included. We designed the chapter to be a stand-alone treatment so that it can be covered at almost any point in the term, not necessarily at the very end. For example, it would come very naturally after discussing risk and return or after covering long-term financing.

Acknowledgments

To borrow a phrase, writing an introductory finance textbook is easy—all you do is sit down at a word processor and open a vein. We never would have completed any of our books without the incredible amount of help and support we received from literally dozens of our colleagues, students, editors, family members, and friends. We would like to thank, without implicating, all of you.

Clearly, our greatest debt is to our many colleagues (and their students) around the world who, like us, wanted to try an alternative to what they were using and made the switch to our first book, *Fundamentals of Corporate Finance.* In the six years since we first launched *Fundamentals,* we have been through three U. S. editions. With various coauthors, we have developed country-specific Australian, Canadian, and South African editions. There's an international edition, and the book has even been translated into Chinese and Spanish. Needless to say, without this support, we would not be writing another book!

Our plan for developing *Essentials* revolved around the detailed feedback we received from eight of our colleagues who had an interest in the book and regularly teach the introductory course. These brave souls, to whom we are very grateful, are:

Anand Desai, *Kansas State University*
Glenn Pettingill, *Emporia State University*
Wallace Davidson, *Southern Illinois University*
E. Bruce Frederickson, *Syracuse University*
Alan Robert Jung, *San Francisco State University*
Karlyn Mitchell, *North Carolina State University*
Reinhold Lamb, *University of North Carolina–Charlotte*
Bill Francis, *University of North Carolina–Charlotte*

Randy D. Jorgensen of the University of Southern Maine worked closely with us to develop the Principles in Action boxes. We think these turned out great, so we would like to particularly thank Randy for his efforts. We also thank Robert C. Higgins of the University of Washington, Clifford Smith, Jr. of the University of Rochester, and Samuel Weaver of Hershey Foods for contributing to the Principles boxes.

We owe a special, and continuing, debt to Thomas H. Eyssell of the University of Missouri. As he has done with our other books, Tom did yeoman's work getting the many supplements to this text ready. Tom also worked with us to develop the Annotated Instructor's Edition of the text, which, along with Instructor's Manual, contains a wealth of lecture tips, teaching notes, international notes, and ethics notes. Between the Instructor's Manual, Study Guide, Testbank, Transparencies, and Ready Notes, there are many more pages of supplemental material than there are pages in the book, so we are especially appreciative of Tom's efforts.

The following University of Missouri doctoral students did outstanding work on this edition of *Essentials:* Barbara Lippincott, Michael Sleight, and David Kuipers. To them fell the unenviable task of technical proofreading and, in particular, of carefully checking each calculation throughout the text.

Finally, in every phase of this project, we have been privileged to have had the complete and unwavering support of two great organizations: Richard D. Irwin, Inc. and Times Mirror. We are deeply grateful to the select group of professionals who served as our development team. They are: John Black, Mike Junior, Jim Keefe, Beth Kessler, Ron Bloecher, Bette Ittersagen, Michael Warrell, Becky Dodson, and Heather Burbridge. Others at Irwin, too numerous to list here, have improved the book in countless ways.

Throughout the development of this edition, we have taken great care to discover and eliminate errors. Our goal is to provide the best textbook available on the subject. We want to ensure that future editions are error free, and, to that end, we will gladly offer $10 per arithmetic error to the first individual reporting it as a modest token of our appreciation. More than this, we would like to hear from instructors and students alike. Please write and tell us how to make this a better text. Forward your comments to: Dr. Brad Jordan, c/o Irwin Editorial–Finance, Richard D. Irwin, Inc., 1333 Burr Ridge Parkway, Burr Ridge, IL 60521.

Stephen A. Ross
Randolph W. Westerfield
Bradford D. Jordan

Brief Contents

Contents

ESSENTIALS OF CORPORATE FINANCE

Part One

OVERVIEW OF FINANCIAL MANAGEMENT

We begin our study of business finance by describing the role of the financial manager and the goal of financial management. We describe the various forms of business organization and the advantages and disadvantages of each.

In our second chapter, we discuss the basic financial statements used by financial managers. We focus closely on the critical differences between cash flow and accounting income. In a similar vein, we emphasize that the accounting value and market (or economic) value can be very different and we explain why this occurs.

OUTLINE

Chapter One

Introduction to Financial Management

After studying this chapter, you should have a good understanding of:

. . .

The basic types of financial management decisions and the role of the financial manager.

. . .

The goal of financial management.

. . .

The financial implications of the different forms of business organization.

. . .

The conflicts of interest that can arise between managers and owners.

Trans. 1.1
Chapter Outline

To begin our study of financial management, we address two central issues. First, what is business finance and what is the role of the financial manager? Second, what is the goal of financial management?

1.1 THE FINANCIAL MANAGER

We begin by defining business finance and the financial manager's job.

What Is Business Finance?

Imagine you were to start your own business. No matter what type you started, you would have to answer the following three questions in some form or another:

1. What long-term investments should you take on? That is, what lines of business will you be in and what sorts of buildings, machinery, and equipment will you need?
2. Where will you get the long-term financing to pay for your investment? Will you bring in other owners or will you borrow the money?

3. How will you manage your everyday financial activities such as collecting from customers and paying suppliers?

These are not the only questions, but they are among the most important. Business finance, broadly speaking, is the study of ways to answer these three questions. We'll be looking at each of them in the chapters ahead.

The Financial Manager

The financial management function is usually associated with a top officer of the firm, often called the chief financial officer (CFO) or vice president of finance. Figure 1.1 is a simplified organizational chart that highlights the finance activity in a large firm. As shown, the vice president of finance coordinates the activities of the treasurer and the controller. The controller's office handles cost and financial accounting, tax payments, and management information systems. The treasurer's office is responsible for managing the firm's cash and credit, its financial planning, and its capital expenditures. These treasury activities are all related to the three general questions raised above, and the chapters ahead deal primarily with these issues. Our study thus bears mostly on activities usually associated with the treasurer's office. In a smaller firm, the treasurer and controller might be the same person, and there would be only one office.

Problem 4

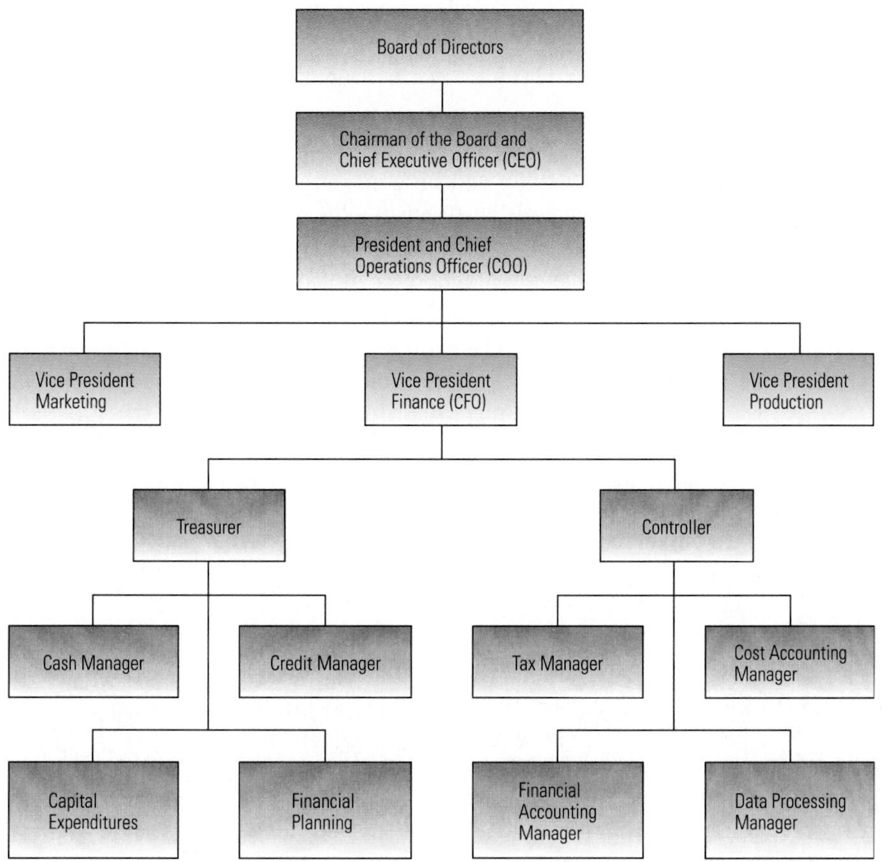

FIGURE 1.1
A simplified organizational chart. The exact titles and organization differ from company to company.

Trans. 1.2

Financial Management Decisions

Problem 1

As our discussion above suggests, the financial manager must be concerned with three basic types of questions. We consider these in greater detail next.

Concept Q Answer 1.1a

capital budgeting The process of planning and managing a firm's long-term investments.

Capital Budgeting The first question concerns the firm's long-term investments. The process of planning and managing a firm's long-term investments is called **capital budgeting.** In capital budgeting, the financial manager tries to identify investment opportunities that are worth more to the firm than they cost to acquire. Loosely speaking, this means that the value of the cash flow generated by an asset exceeds the cost of that asset.

Regardless of the specific investment under consideration, financial managers must be concerned with how much cash they expect to receive, when they expect to receive it, and how likely they are to receive it. Evaluating the *size, timing,* and *risk* of future cash flows is the essence of capital budgeting. In fact, whenever we evaluate a business decision, the size, timing, and risk of the cash flows will be, by far, the most important things we will consider.

capital structure The mixture of debt and equity maintained by a firm.

Concept Q Answer 1.1b

Capital Structure The second question for the financial manager concerns how the firm obtains the financing it needs to support its long-term investments. A firm's **capital structure** (or financial structure) refers to the specific mixture of long-term debt and equity the firm uses to finance its operations. The financial manager has two concerns in this area. First, how much should the firm borrow? Second, what are the least expensive sources of funds for the firm?

In addition to deciding on the financing mix, the financial manager has to decide exactly how and where to raise the money. The expenses associated with raising long-term financing can be considerable, so different possibilities must be carefully evaluated. Also, businesses borrow money from a variety of lenders in a number of different ways. Choosing among lenders and among loan types is another job handled by the financial manager.

working capital A firm's short-term assets and liabilities.

Working Capital Management The third question concerns **working capital** management. The phrase *working capital* refers to a firm's short-term assets, such as inventory, and its short-term liabilities, such as money owed to suppliers. Managing the firm's working capital is a day-to-day activity that ensures the firm has sufficient resources to continue its operations and avoid costly interruptions. This involves a number of activities related to the firm's receipt and disbursement of cash.

Concept Q Answer 1.1c

Some questions about working capital that must be answered are: (1) How much cash and inventory should we keep on hand? (2) Should we sell on credit? (3) How will we obtain any needed short-term financing? If we borrow short-term, how and where should we do it? This is just a small sample of the issues that arise in managing a firm's working capital.

The three areas of corporate financial management we have described—capital budgeting, capital structure, and working capital management—are very broad categories. Each includes a rich variety of topics, and we have indicated only a few of the questions that arise in the different areas. The chapters ahead contain greater detail.

CONCEPT QUESTIONS

1.1a What is the capital budgeting decision?

1.1b What do you call the specific mixture of long-term debt and equity that a firm chooses to use?

1.1c Into what category of financial management does cash management fall?

1.2 FORMS OF BUSINESS ORGANIZATION

Large firms in the United States, such as IBM and Exxon, are almost all organized as corporations. We examine the three different legal forms of business organization—sole proprietorship, partnership, and corporation—to see why this is so.

Concept Q Answer 1.2a

Trans. 1.3 Forms of Organization

Problems 2, 3

Sole Proprietorship

A **sole proprietorship** is a business owned by one person. This is the simplest type of business to start and is the least regulated form of organization. For this reason, there are more proprietorships than any other type of business, and many businesses that later become large corporations start out as small proprietorships.

sole proprietorship
A business owned by a single individual.

The owner of a sole proprietorship keeps all the profits. That's the good news. The bad news is that the owner has *unlimited liability* for business debts. This means that creditors can look to the proprietor's personal assets for payment. Similarly, there is no distinction between personal and business income, so all business income is taxed as personal income.

Concept Q Answer 1.2b

The life of a sole proprietorship is limited to the owner's life span, and, importantly, the amount of equity that can be raised is limited to the proprietor's personal wealth. This limitation often means that the business cannot exploit new opportunities because of insufficient capital. Ownership of a sole proprietorship may be difficult to transfer since this requires the sale of the entire business to a new owner.

Partnership

A **partnership** is similar to a proprietorship, except that there are two or more owners (partners). In a *general partnership,* all the partners share in gains or losses, and all have unlimited liability for *all* partnership debts, not just some particular share. The way partnership gains (and losses) are divided is described in the *partnership agreement.* This agreement can be an informal oral agreement, such as "let's start a lawn mowing business," or a lengthy, formal written document.

partnership
A business formed by two or more individuals or entities.

In a *limited partnership,* one or more *general partners* will run the business and have unlimited liability, but there will be one or more *limited partners* who do not actively participate in the business. A limited partner's liability for business debts is limited to the amount that she contributes to the partnership. This form of organization is common in real estate ventures, for example.

Concept Q Answer 1.2c

The advantages and disadvantages of a partnership are basically the same as those for a proprietorship. Partnerships based on a relatively informal

Concept Q Answer 1.2b

agreement are easy and inexpensive to form. General partners have unlimited liability for partnership debts, and the partnership terminates when a general partner wishes to sell out or dies. All income is taxed as personal income to the partners, and the amount of equity that can be raised is limited to the partners' combined wealth. Ownership by a general partner is not easily transferred because a new partnership must be formed. A limited partner's interest can be sold without dissolving the partnership, but finding a buyer may be difficult.

Because a partner in a general partnership can be held responsible for all partnership debts, having a written agreement is very important. Failure to spell out the rights and duties of the partners frequently leads to misunderstandings later on. Also, if you are a limited partner, you must not become deeply involved in business decisions unless you are willing to assume the obligations of a general partner. The reason is that if things go badly, you may be deemed to be a general partner even though you say you are a limited partner.

Based on our discussion, the primary disadvantages of sole proprietorships and partnerships as forms of business organization are (1) unlimited liability for business debts on the part of the owners, (2) limited life of the business, and (3) difficulty of transferring ownership. These three disadvantages add up to a single, central problem: The ability of such businesses to grow can be seriously limited by an inability to raise cash for investment.

Corporation

corporation
A business created as a distinct legal entity composed of one or more individuals or entities.

The **corporation** is the most important form (in terms of size) of business organization in the United States. A corporation is a legal "person" separate and distinct from its owners, and it has many of the rights, duties, and privileges of an actual person. Corporations can borrow money and own property, can sue and be sued, and can enter into contracts. A corporation can even be a general partner or a limited partner in a partnership, and a corporation can own stock in another corporation.

Not surprisingly, starting a corporation is somewhat more complicated than starting the other forms of business organization. Forming a corporation involves preparing *articles of incorporation* (or a charter) and a set of *bylaws.* The articles of incorporation must contain a number of things, including the corporation's name, its intended life (which can be forever), its business purpose, and the number of shares that can be issued. This information must normally be supplied to the state in which the firm will be incorporated. For most legal purposes, the corporation is a "resident" of that state.

The bylaws are rules describing how the corporation regulates its own existence. For example, the bylaws describe how directors are elected. The bylaws may be amended or extended from time to time by the stockholders.

In a large corporation, the stockholders and the managers are usually separate groups. The stockholders elect the board of directors, who then select the managers. Management is charged with running the corporation's affairs in the stockholders' interests. In principle, stockholders control the corporation because they elect the directors.

As a result of the separation of ownership and management, the corporate form has several advantages. Ownership (represented by shares of stock) can be readily transferred, and the life of the corporation is therefore not limited. The corporation borrows money in its own name. As a result, the stockholders in a corporation have limited liability for corporate debts. The most they can lose is what they have invested.

The relative ease of transferring ownership, the limited liability for business debts, and the unlimited life of the business are the reasons why the corporate form is superior when it comes to raising cash. If a corporation needs new equity, it can sell new shares of stock and attract new investors. The number of owners can be huge; larger corporations have many thousands or even millions of stockholders. For example, AT&T has about 3 million stockholders and General Motors has about 2 million.

Concept Q Answer 1.2d

The corporate form has a significant disadvantage. Since a corporation is a legal "person," it must pay taxes. Moreover, money paid out to stockholders in the form of dividends is taxed again as income to those stockholders. This is *double taxation,* meaning that corporate profits are taxed twice: at the corporate level when they are earned and again at the personal level when they are paid out.

Lecture Tip: IM 1.2 provides a discussion of the S corporation. The main advantage of this hybrid form is that it allows firm profits to be taxed only at the individual level.

A Corporation by Another Name . . .

The corporate form has many variations around the world. Exact laws and regulations differ, of course, but the essential features of public ownership and limited liability remain. These firms are often called *joint stock companies, public limited companies,* or *limited liability companies.*

Table 1.1 gives the names of a few well-known international corporations, their country of origin, and a translation of the abbreviation that follows the company name.

Lecture Tip: See IM 1.2 for a discussion of an increasingly popular new organizational form—the limited liability company (LLC), which is a hybrid of the partnership and the corporation.

CONCEPT QUESTIONS

1.2a What are the three forms of business organization?

1.2b What are the primary advantages and disadvantages of sole proprietorships and partnerships?

1.2c What is the difference between a general and a limited partnership?

1.2d Why is the corporate form superior when it comes to raising cash?

TABLE 1.1 International corporations

Company	Country of Origin	Type of Company	Translation
Porsche AG	Germany	Aktiengesellschaft	Corporation
Bayerische Moteren Werke (BMW) AG	Germany	Aktiengesellschaft	Corporation
Dornier GmBH	Germany	Gesellshaft mit Beschraenkter Haftung	Cooperative with limited liability
Rolls-Royce PLC	United Kingdom	Public limited company	Public limited company
Shell UK LTD	United Kingdom	Limited	Corporation
Unilever NV	Netherlands	Naamloze Vennootschap	Limited liability company
Fiat SpA	Italy	Societa per Azioni	Public limited company
Volvo AB	Sweden	Aktiebolag	Joint stock company
Peugeot SA	France	Sociedad Anonima	Joint stock company

1.3 THE GOAL OF FINANCIAL MANAGEMENT

Problem 5

To study financial decision making, we first need to understand the goal of financial management. Such an understanding is important because it leads to an objective basis for making and evaluating financial decisions.

Profit Maximization

Concept Q Answer 1.3b

Profit maximization would probably be the most commonly cited business goal, but this is not a very precise objective. Do we mean profits this year? If so, then actions such as deferring maintenance, letting inventories run down, and other short-run, cost-cutting measures will tend to increase profits now, but these activities aren't necessarily desirable.

The goal of maximizing profits may refer to some sort of "long-run" or "average" profits, but it's unclear exactly what this means. First, do we mean something like accounting net income or earnings per share? As we will see, these numbers may have little to do with what is good or bad for the firm. Second, what do we mean by the long run? As a famous economist once remarked, in the long run, we're all dead! More to the point, this goal doesn't tell us the appropriate trade-off between current and future profits.

The Goal of Financial Management in a Corporation

The financial manager in a corporation makes decisions for the stockholders of the firm. Given this, instead of listing possible goals for the financial manager, we really need to answer a more fundamental question: From the stockholders' point of view, what is a good financial management decision?

If we assume stockholders buy stock because they seek to gain financially, then the answer is obvious: Good decisions increase the value of the stock, and poor decisions decrease it.

Given our observations, it follows that the financial manager acts in the shareholders' best interests by making decisions that increase the value of the stock. The appropriate goal for the financial manager in a corporation can thus be stated quite easily:

Trans. 1.4 The Goal of Financial Management

The goal of financial management in a corporation is to maximize the current value per share of the existing stock.

The goal of maximizing the value of the stock avoids the problems associated with the different goals we discussed above. There is no ambiguity in the criterion, and there is no short-run versus long-run issue. We explicitly mean that our goal is to maximize the *current* stock value.

A More General Financial Management Goal

Given our goal as stated above (maximize the value of the stock), an obvious question comes up: What is the appropriate goal when the firm has no traded stock? Corporations are certainly not the only type of business, and the stock in many corporations rarely changes hands, so it's difficult to say what the value per share is at any given time.

Concept Q Answer 1.3a

As long as we are dealing with for-profit businesses, only a slight modification is needed. The total value of the stock in a corporation is simply equal to the value of the owners' equity. Therefore, a more general way of stating our goal is:

Maximize the market value of the existing owners' equity.

With this goal in mind, it doesn't matter whether the business is a proprietorship, a partnership, or a corporation. For each of these, good financial decisions increase the market value of the owners' equity and poor financial decisions decrease it.

Finally, our goal does not imply that the financial manager should take illegal or unethical actions in the hope of increasing the value of the equity in the firm. What we mean is that the financial manager best serves the owners of the business by identifying goods and services that add value to the firm because they are desired and valued in the free marketplace.

Lecture Tip: You may wish to emphasize the general applicability of the principles of finance by reminding students that "maximizing the value of owners' equity" in a not-for-profit organization is equivalent to maximizing the benefits available to those served. (Example: Policyholders in a Blue Cross/Blue Shield organization.)

CONCEPT QUESTIONS

1.3a What is the goal of financial management?

1.3b What are some shortcomings of the goal of profit maximization?

1.4 THE AGENCY PROBLEM AND CONTROL OF THE CORPORATION

We've seen that the financial manager in a corporation acts in the best interests of the stockholders by taking actions that increase the value of the stock. However, we've also seen that in large corporations ownership can be spread over a huge number of stockholders. This dispersion of ownership arguably means that management effectively controls the firm. In this case, will management necessarily act in the best interests of the stockholders? Put another way, might not management pursue its own goals at the stockholders' expense? We briefly consider some of the arguments below.

Problem 6

Trans. 1.5
The Agency Problem

✯ **Ethics Note:** See IM 1.4 for a look at the agency problem using the case of Gillette.

Agency Relationships

The relationship between stockholders and management is called an *agency relationship.* Such a relationship exists whenever someone (the principal) hires another (the agent) to represent her interests. For example, you might hire someone (an agent) to sell a car that you own while you are away at school. In all such relationships, there is a possibility of conflict of interest between the principal and the agent. Such a conflict is called an **agency problem.**

Concept Q
Answer 1.4a

Suppose you hire someone to sell your car and you agree to pay her a flat fee when she sells the car. The agent's incentive in this case is to make the sale, not necessarily to get you the best price. If you paid a commission of, say, 10 percent of the sales price instead of a flat fee, then this problem might not exist. This example illustrates that the way an agent is compensated is one factor that affects agency problems.

agency problem
The possibility of conflict of interest between the owners and management of a firm.

Management Goals

To see how management and stockholder interests might differ, imagine that a corporation is considering a new investment. The new investment is expected to favorably impact the share value, but it is also a relatively risky venture. The owners of the firm will wish to take the investment (because the

Concept Q
Answer 1.4b

Principles in Action

Clifford W. Smith, Jr. on Market Incentives for Ethical Behavior

Ethics is a topic that has been receiving increased interest in the business community. Much of this discussion has been led by philosophers and has focused on moral principles. Rather than review these issues, I want to discuss a complementary (but often ignored) set of issues from an economist's viewpoint. Markets impose potentially substantial costs on individuals and institutions that engage in unethical behavior. These market forces thus provide important incentives which foster ethical behavior in the business community.

At its core, economics is the study of making choices. I thus want to examine ethical behavior simply as one choice facing an individual. Economic analysis suggests that in considering an action, you identify its expected costs and benefits. If the estimated benefits exceed the estimated costs, you take the action; if not, you don't. To focus this discussion, let's consider the following specific choice: Suppose you have a contract to deliver a product of a specified quality. Would you cheat by reducing quality to lower costs in an attempt to increase profits?

Economics implies that the higher the expected costs of cheating, the more likely ethical actions will be chosen. This simple principle has several implications.

First, the higher the probability of detection, the less likely an individual is to cheat. This implication helps us understand numerous institutional arrangements for monitoring in the marketplace. For example, a company agrees to have its financial statements audited by an external public accounting firm. This periodic professional monitoring increases the probability of detection, thereby reducing any incentive to misstate the firm's financial condition.

Second, the higher the sanctions imposed if detected, the less likely an individual is to cheat. Hence, a business transaction that is expected to be repeated between the same parties faces a lower probability of cheating because the lost profits from the foregone stream of future sales provide powerful incentives for contract compliance. However, if continued corporate existence is more uncertain, so are the expected costs of foregone future sales. Therefore firms in financial difficulty are more likely to cheat than financially healthy firms. Firms thus have

• • •

stock value will rise), but management may not because there is the possibility that things will turn out badly and management jobs will be lost. If management does not take the investment, then the stockholders may have lost a valuable opportunity. This is one example of an *agency cost.*

Concept Q Answer 1.4b

Lecture Tip: See IM 1.4 for two examples of how the agency problem is manifested in the classroom.

It is sometimes argued that, left to themselves, managers would tend to maximize the amount of resources over which they have control or, more generally, business power or wealth. This goal could lead to an overemphasis on business size or growth. For example, cases where management is accused of overpaying to buy up another company just to increase the size of the business or to demonstrate corporate power are not uncommon. Obviously, if overpayment does take place, such a purchase does not benefit the owners of the purchasing company.

Our discussion indicates that management may tend to overemphasize organizational survival to protect job security. Also, management may dislike outside interference, so independence and corporate self-sufficiency may be important goals.

Do Managers Act in the Stockholders' Interests?

Whether managers will, in fact, act in the best interests of stockholders depends on two factors. First, how closely are management goals aligned with incentives to adopt financial policies that help credibly bond against cheating. For example, if product quality is difficult to assess prior to purchase, customers doubt a firm's claims about product quality. Where quality is more uncertain, customers are only willing to pay lower prices. Such firms thus have particularly strong incentives to adopt financial policies that imply a lower probability of insolvency. Therefore such firms should have lower leverage, fewer leases, and engage in more hedging.

Third, the expected costs are higher if information about cheating is rapidly and widely distributed to potential future customers. Thus information services like Consumer Reports, which monitor and report on product quality, help deter cheating. By lowering the costs for potential customers to monitor quality, the expected costs of cheating are raised.

Finally, the costs imposed on a firm that is caught cheating depend on the market's assessment of the ethical breach. Some actions viewed as clear transgressions by some might be viewed as justifiable behavior by others. Ethical standards also vary across markets. For example, a payment that if disclosed in the U.S. would be labeled a bribe, might be viewed as a standard business practice in a third-world market. The costs imposed will be higher the greater the consensus that the behavior was unethical.

Establishing and maintaining a reputation for ethical behavior is a valuable corporate asset in the business community. This analysis suggests that a firm concerned about the ethical conduct of its employees should pay careful attention to potential conflicts among the firm's management, employees, customers, creditors, and shareholders. Consider Sears, the department store giant that was found to be charging customers for auto repairs of questionable necessity. In an effort to make the company more service oriented (in the way that competitors like Nordstrom are), Sears initiated an across-the-board policy of commission sales. But what works in clothing and housewares does not always work the same way in the auto repair shop. A customer for a man's suit knows as much as the salesperson about the product. But many auto repair customers know little about the inner workings of their cars and thus are more likely to rely on employee recommendations in deciding on purchases. Sears's compensation policy resulted in recommendations of unnecessary repairs to customers. Sears would not have had to deal with its repair shop problems and the consequent erosion of its reputation had it anticipated that its commission sales policy would encourage auto shop employees to cheat its customers.

Clifford W. Smith, Jr. is the Clarey Professor of Finance at the University of Rochester's Simon School of Business Administration. He is an editor of the Journal of Financial Economics. His research focuses on corporate financial policy and the structure of financial institutions.

• • •

stockholder goals? This question relates to the way managers are compensated. Second, can management be replaced if they do not pursue stockholder goals? This issue relates to control of the firm. As we will discuss, there are a number of reasons to think that, even in the largest firms, management has a significant incentive to act in the interests of stockholders.

Managerial Compensation Management will frequently have a significant economic incentive to increase share value for two reasons. First, managerial compensation, particularly at the top, is usually tied to financial performance in general and oftentimes to share value in particular. For example, managers are frequently given the option to buy stock at a bargain price. The more the stock is worth, the more valuable is this option. The second incentive managers have relates to job prospects. Better performers within the firm will tend to get promoted. More generally, those managers who are successful in pursuing stockholder goals will be in greater demand in the labor market and thus command higher salaries.

Concept Q Answer 1.4c

Lecture Tip: See IM 1.4 for a discussion of recent examples and empirical evidence on the use of executive stock options to align the incentives of management and stockholders to mitigate agency problems.

Control of the Firm Control of the firm ultimately rests with stockholders. They elect the board of directors, who, in turn, hire and fire management. The mechanism by which unhappy stockholders can act to replace existing management is called a *proxy fight.* A proxy is the authority to vote someone else's stock. A proxy fight develops when a group solicits proxies in order to replace the existing board, and thereby replace existing management.

Another way that management can be replaced is by takeover. Those firms that are poorly managed are more attractive as acquisitions than well-managed firms because a greater profit potential exists. Thus, avoiding a takeover by another firm gives management another incentive to act in the stockholders' interests.

The available theory and evidence are consistent with the view that stockholders control the firm and that stockholder wealth maximization is the relevant goal of the corporation. Even so, there will undoubtedly be times where management goals are pursued at the expense of the stockholders, at least temporarily.

Agency problems are not unique to corporations; they exist whenever there is a separation of ownership and management. This separation is most pronounced in corporations, but it certainly exists in partnerships and proprietorships as well.

Lecture Tip: See IM 1.4 for a business press article that provides one CEO's views on stakeholder interests.

stakeholder
Someone other than a stockholder or creditor who potentially has a claim on the cash flows of the firm.

Ethics Note: Classical approaches to ethical decision-making vis-à-vis the stakeholder model are described in IM 1.4.

Video Note: Discussions of the difficulties in balancing the concerns of the firm, the stakeholders, and society appear in the first video supplied with this text.

Stakeholders Our discussion thus far implies that management and stockholders are the only parties with an interest in the firm's decisions. This is an oversimplification, of course. Employees, customers, suppliers, and even the government all have a financial interest in the firm.

Taken together, these various groups are called **stakeholders** in the firm. In general, a stakeholder is someone other than a stockholder or creditor who potentially has a claim on the cash flows of the firm. Such groups will also attempt to exert control over the firm, perhaps to the detriment of the owners.

CONCEPT QUESTIONS

1.4a What is an agency relationship?

1.4b What are agency problems and how do they come about? What are agency costs?

1.4c What incentives do managers in large corporations have to maximize share value?

1.5 SUMMARY AND CONCLUSIONS

This chapter has introduced you to some of the basic ideas in business finance. In it, we saw that:

1. Business finance has three main areas of concern:
   a. Capital budgeting. What long-term investments should the firm take?
   b. Capital structure. Where will the firm get the long-term financing to pay for its investments? In other words, what mixture of debt and equity should we use to fund our operations?
   c. Working capital management. How should the firm manage its everyday financial activities?

2. The goal of financial management in a for-profit business is to make decisions that increase the value of the stock or, more generally, increase the market value of the equity.
3. The corporate form of organization is superior to other forms when it comes to raising money and transferring ownership interests, but it has the significant disadvantage of double taxation.
4. There is the possibility of conflicts between stockholders and management in a large corporation. We called these conflicts agency problems and discussed how they might be controlled and reduced.

Of the topics we've discussed thus far, the most important is the goal of financial management. Throughout the text, we will be analyzing many different financial decisions, but we always ask the same question: How does the decision under consideration affect the value of the equity in the firm?

Questions and Problems

Basic (Questions 1–6)

1. **The Financial Management Decision Process** What are the three types of financial management decisions? For each type of decision, give an example of a business transaction that would be relevant.
2. **Sole Proprietorships and Partnerships** What are the four primary disadvantages to the sole proprietorship and partnership forms of business organization? What benefits are there to these types of business organization as opposed to the corporate form?
3. **Corporate Organization** What is the primary disadvantage of the corporate form of organization? Name at least two of the advantages of corporate organization.
4. **Corporate Finance Organizational Structure** In a large corporation, what are the two distinct groups that report to the chief financial officer? Which group is the focus of corporate finance?
5. **The Goal of Financial Management** What goal should always motivate the actions of the firm's financial manager?
6. **Corporate Agency Issues** Who owns a corporation? Describe the process whereby the owners control the firm's management. What is the main reason that an agency relationship exists in the corporate form of organization? In this context, what kind of problems can arise?

Intermediate (Questions 7–11)

7. **Not-for-Profit Firm Goals** Suppose you were the financial manager of a not-for-profit business (a not-for-profit hospital, perhaps). What kinds of goals do you think would be appropriate?
8. **Firm Goals and Stock Value** Evaluate the following statement: "Managers should not focus on the current stock value because doing so will lead to an overemphasis on short-term profits at the expense of long-term profits."
9. **Firm Goals and Ethics** Can our goal of maximizing the value of the stock conflict with other goals, such as avoiding unethical or illegal behavior? In particular, do you think subjects like customer and

employee safety, the environment, and the general good of society fit in this framework, or are they essentially ignored? Try to think of some specific scenarios to illustrate your answer.

10. **Firm Goals and Multinational Firms** Would our goal of maximizing the value of the stock be different if we were thinking about financial management in a foreign country? Why or why not?

11. **Agency Issues and Corporate Control** Suppose you own stock in a company. The current price per share is $25. Another company has just announced that it wants to buy your company and will pay $35 per share to acquire all the outstanding stock. Your company's management immediately begins fighting off this hostile bid. Is management acting in the shareholders' best interests? Why or why not?

Chapter Two

2

Financial Statements, Taxes, and Cash Flow

After studying this chapter, you should have a good understanding of:

. . .

The difference between accounting value (or "book" value) and market value.

. . .

The difference between accounting income and cash flow.

. . .

The difference between average and marginal tax rates.

. . .

How to determine a firm's cash flow from its financial statements.

In this chapter, we examine financial statements, taxes, and cash flow. Our emphasis is not on preparing financial statements. Instead, we recognize that financial statements are frequently a key source of information for financial decisions, so our goal is to briefly examine such statements and point out some of their more relevant features. We pay special attention to some of the practical details of cash flow.

Trans. 2.1
Chapter Outline

As you read, pay particular attention to two important differences: (1) the difference between accounting value and market value, and (2) the difference between accounting income and cash flow. These distinctions will be important throughout the book.

2.1 THE BALANCE SHEET

The **balance sheet** is a snapshot of the firm. It is a convenient means of organizing and sumarizing what a firm owns (its *assets*), what a firm owes (its *liabilities*), and the difference between the two (the firm's *equity*) at a given point in time. Figure 2.1 illustrates how the balance sheet is constructed. As shown, the left-hand side lists the assets of the firm, and the right-hand side lists the liabilities and equity.

balance sheet
Financial statement showing a firm's accounting value on a particular date.

Problems 1, 5, 16, 23

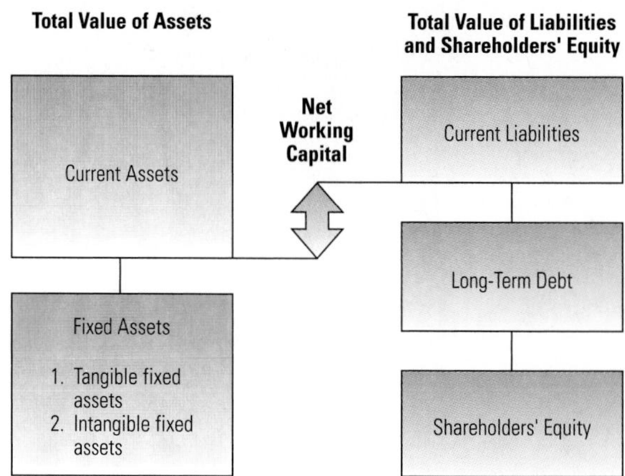

FIGURE 2.1
The balance sheet. Left side: total value of assets. Right side: total value of liabilities and shareholders' equity.

Trans. 2.2

Assets: The Left-Hand Side

Assets are classified as either *current* or *fixed.* A fixed asset is one that has a relatively long life. Fixed assets can either be *tangible,* such as a truck or a computer, or *intangible,* such as a trademark or patent. A current asset has a life of less than one year. This means that the asset will convert to cash within 12 months. For example, inventory would normally be purchased and sold within a year and is thus classified as a current asset. Obviously, cash itself is a current asset. Accounts receivable (money owed to the firm by its customers) is also a current asset.

Liabilities and Owners' Equity: The Right-Hand Side

The firm's liabilities are the first thing listed on the right-hand side of the balance sheet. These are classified as either *current* or *long-term.* Current liabilities, like current assets, have a life of less than one year (meaning they must be paid within the year) and are listed before long-term liabilities. Accounts payable (money the firm owes to its suppliers) is one example of a current liability.

A debt that is not due in the coming year is classified as a long-term liability. A loan that the firm will pay off in five years is one such long-term debt. Firms borrow long term from a variety of sources. We will tend to use the terms *bond* and *bondholders* generically to refer to long-term debt and long-term creditors, respectively.

Finally, by definition, the difference between the total value of the assets (current and fixed) and the total value of the liabilities (current and long-term) is the *shareholders' equity,* also called *common equity* or *owners' equity.* This feature of the balance sheet is intended to reflect the fact that, if the firm were to sell all of its assets and use the money to pay off its debts, then whatever residual value remains belongs to the shareholders. So, the balance sheet "balances" because the value of the left-hand side always equals the value of the right-hand side. That is, the value of the firm's assets is equal to the sum of its liabilities and shareholders' equity:[1]

$$\text{Assets} = \text{Liabilities} + \text{Shareholders' equity} \quad [2.1]$$

Concept Q Answer 2.1a

This is the balance sheet identity or equation, and it always holds because shareholders' equity is defined as the difference between assets and liabilities.

Net Working Capital

As shown in Figure 2.1, the difference between a firm's current assets and its current liabilities is called **net working capital.** Net working capital is positive when current assets exceed current liabilities. Based on the definitions of current assets and current liabilities, this means that the cash that will become available over the next 12 months exceeds the cash that must be paid over that same period. For this reason, net working capital is usually positive in a healthy firm.

net working capital Current assets less current liabilities.

EXAMPLE 2.1 Building the Balance Sheet

A firm has current assets of $100, net fixed assets of $500, short-term debt of $70, and long-term debt of $200. What does the balance sheet look like? What is shareholders' equity? What is net working capital?

Lecture Tip: IM 2.1 links balance sheet values and the decisions made by financial managers.

In this case, total assets are $100 + 500 = $600 and total liabilities are $70 + 200 = $270, so shareholders' equity is the difference: $600 − 270 = $330. The balance sheet would thus look like:

Assets		**Liabilities and Shareholders' Equity**	
Current assets	$100	Current liabilities	$ 70
Net fixed assets	500	Long-term debt	200
		Shareholders' equity	330
Total assets	$600	Total liabilities and shareholders' equity	$600

Lecture Tip: See IM 2.1 for tips on explaining the concepts of shareholders' equity and retained earnings.

Net working capital is the difference between current assets and current liabilities, or $100 − 70 = $30. • • •

Table 2.1 shows a simplified balance sheet for the fictitious U.S. Corporation. There are three particularly important things to keep in mind when examining a balance sheet: liquidity, debt versus equity, and market value versus book value.

Liquidity

Liquidity refers to the speed and ease with which an asset can be converted to cash. Gold is a relatively liquid asset; a custom manufacturing facility is not.

Concept Q Answer 2.1b

[1] The terms *owners' equity, shareholders' equity,* and *stockholders' equity* are used interchangeably to refer to the equity in a corporation. The term *net worth* is also used. Variations exist in addition to these.

TABLE 2.1
Balance sheets for U.S. Corporation

U.S. CORPORATION
Balance Sheets as of December 31, 1994 and 1995
($ in millions)

	1994	1995		1994	1995
Assets			**Liabilities and Owners' Equity**		
Current assets			Current liabilities		
Cash	$ 104	$ 160	Accounts payable	$ 232	$ 266
Accounts receivable	455	688	Notes payable	196	123
Inventory	553	555	Total	$ 428	$ 389
Total	$1,112	$1,403			
Fixed assets					
Net plant and equipment	$1,644	$1,709	Long-term debt	$ 408	$ 454
			Owners' equity		
			Common stock and paid-in surplus	600	640
			Retained earnings	1,320	1,629
			Total	$1,920	$2,269
Total assets	$2,756	$3,112	Total liabilities and owners' equity	$2,756	$3,112

Liquidity really has two dimensions: ease of conversion versus loss of value. Any asset can be converted to cash quickly if we cut the price enough. A highly liquid asset is therefore one that can be quickly sold without significant loss of value. An illiquid asset is one that cannot be quickly converted to cash without a substantial price reduction.

Assets are normally listed on the balance sheet in order of decreasing liquidity, meaning that the most liquid assets are listed first. Current assets are relatively liquid and include cash and those assets that we expect to convert to cash over the next 12 months. Accounts receivable, for example, represents amounts not yet collected from customers on sales already made. Naturally, we hope these will convert to cash in the near future. Inventory is probably the least liquid of the current assets, at least for many businesses.

Fixed assets are, for the most part, relatively illiquid. These consist of tangible things such as buildings and equipment that don't convert to cash at all in normal business activity (they are, of course, used in the business to generate cash). Intangible assets, such as a trademark, have no physical existence but can be very valuable. Like tangible fixed assets, they won't ordinarily convert to cash and are generally considered illiquid.

Concept Q Answer 2.1b

Liquidity is valuable. The more liquid a business is, the less likely it is to experience financial distress (that is, difficulty in paying debts or buying needed assets). Unfortunately, liquid assets are generally less profitable to hold. For example, cash holdings are the most liquid of all investments, but they sometimes earn no return at all—they just sit there. There is therefore a trade-off between the advantages of liquidity and forgone potential profits.

Lecture Tip: See IM 2.1 for tips on helping students conceptualize the opportunity costs of excessively high levels of cash.

Debt versus Equity

To the extent that a firm borrows money, it usually gives first claim to the firm's cash flow to creditors. Equity holders are only entitled to the residual value, the portion left after creditors are paid. The value of this residual portion is the shareholders' equity in the firm, which is just the value of the firm's assets less the value of the firm's liabilities:

Shareholders' equity = Assets − Liabilities

This is true in an accounting sense because shareholders' equity is defined as this residual portion. More importantly, it is true in an economic sense: If the firm sells its assets and pays its debts, whatever cash is left belongs to the shareholders.

The use of debt in a firm's capital structure is called *financial leverage.* The more debt a firm has (as a percentage of assets), the greater is its degree of financial leverage. As we discuss in later chapters, debt acts like a lever in the sense that using it can greatly magnify both gains and losses. So financial leverage increases the potential reward to shareholders, but it also increases the potential for financial distress and business failure.

Concept Q Answer 2.1c

Market Value versus Book Value

The values shown on the balance sheet for the firm's assets are *book values* and generally are not what the assets are actually worth. Under **Generally Accepted Accounting Principles (GAAP),** audited financial statements in the United States generally show assets at *historical cost.* In other words, assets are "carried on the books" at what the firm paid for them, no matter how long ago they were purchased or how much they are worth today.

Generally Accepted Accounting Principles (GAAP)
The common set of standards and procedures by which audited financial statements are prepared.

★ **Ethics Note:** It is often useful to remind students here of the degree of latitude in GAAP. Ethical accountants can arrive at different asset and liability values. However, ethical accountants will seek to most fairly represent the firm's financial condition.

For current assets, market value and book value might be somewhat similar since current assets are bought and converted into cash over a relatively short span of time. In other circumstances, they might differ quite a bit. Moreover, for fixed assets, it would be purely a coincidence if the actual market value of an asset (what the asset could be sold for) were equal to its book value. For example, a railroad might own enormous tracts of land purchased a century or more ago. What the railroad paid for that land could be hundreds or thousands of times less than it is worth today. The balance sheet would nonetheless show the historical cost.

Concept Q Answer 2.1d

Managers and investors will frequently be interested in knowing the value of the firm. This information is not on the balance sheet. The fact that balance sheet assets are listed at cost means that there is no necessary connection between the total assets shown and the value of the firm. Indeed, many of the most valuable assets that a firm might have—good management, a good reputation, talented employees—don't appear on the balance sheet at all.

Lecture Tip: IM 2.1 discusses additional ways to emphasize the difference between historical cost and market value.

Video Note: "Valuing the Stock Market" discusses the calculation and uses of book value per share, as well as its implications for, and relationship to, market value.

Similarly, the owners' equity figure on the balance sheet and the true value of the equity need not be related. For financial managers, then, the accounting value of the equity is not an especially important concern; it is the market value that matters. Henceforth, whenever we speak of the value of an asset or the value of the firm, we will normally mean its *market value.* So, for

Lecture Tip: See IM 2.1 for hints on helping students understand why book values are below market values in Example 2.2.

example, when we say the goal of the financial manager is to increase the value of the stock, we mean the market value of the stock.

Lecture Tip: See IM 2.1 for an extension of this example to the case where fixed assets have a market value less than cost.

EXAMPLE 2.2 Market versus Book Values

The Klingon Corporation has fixed assets with a book value of $700 and an appraised market value of about $1,000. Net working capital is $400 on the books, but approximately $600 would be realized if all the current accounts were liquidated. Klingon has $500 in long-term debt, both book value and market value. What is the book value of the equity? What is the market value?

We can construct two simplified balance sheets, one in accounting (book value) terms and one in economic (market value) terms:

KLINGON CORPORATION
Balance Sheets
Market Value versus Book Value

	Book	Market		Book	Market
Assets			**Liabilities and Shareholders' Equity**		
Net working capital	$ 400	$ 600	Long-term debt	$ 500	$ 500
Net fixed assets	700	1,000	Shareholders' equity	600	1,100
	$1,100	$1,600		$1,100	$1,600

Lecture Tip: See IM 2.1 for a discussion of the practice of "marking-to-market."

In this example, shareholders' equity is actually worth almost twice as much as what is shown on the books. The distinction between book and market values is important precisely because book values can be so different from true economic value. • • •

CONCEPT QUESTIONS

2.1a What is the balance sheet identity?

2.1b What is liquidity? Why is it important?

2.1c What do we mean by financial leverage?

2.1d Explain the difference between accounting value and market value. Which is more important to the financial manager? Why?

2.2 THE INCOME STATEMENT

income statement
Financial statement summarizing a firm's performance over a period of time.

The **income statement** measures performance over some period of time, usually a quarter or a year. The income statement equation is:

$$\text{Revenues} - \text{Expenses} = \text{Income} \qquad [2.2]$$

Concept Q Answer 2.2a

Problems 2, 3, 4, 15

Lecture Tip: See IM 2.2 for tips on relating the income statement to financial managers' decisions.

If you think of the balance sheet as a snapshot, then you can think of the income statement as a video recording covering the period between a before and an after picture. Table 2.2 gives a simplified income statement for U.S. Corporation.

The first thing reported on an income statement would usually be revenue and expenses from the firm's principal operations. Subsequent parts include, among other things, financing expenses such as interest paid. Taxes paid are reported separately. The last item is *net income* (the so-called bottom line). Net income is often expressed on a per share basis and called *earnings per share (EPS).*

As indicated, U.S. paid cash dividends of $103. The difference between net income and cash dividends, $309, is the addition to retained earnings for

TABLE 2.2
Income statement for U.S. Corporation

U.S. CORPORATION 1995 Income Statement ($ in millions)		
Net sales		$1,509
Cost of goods sold		750
Depreciation		65
Earnings before interest and taxes		$ 694
Interest paid		70
Taxable income		$ 624
Taxes		212
Net income		$ 412
Addition to retained earnings	$309	
Dividends	103	

the year. This amount is added to the cumulative retained earnings account on the balance sheet. If you'll look back at the two balance sheets for U.S. Corporation, you'll see that retained earnings did go up by this amount, $1,320 + 309 = $1,629.

EXAMPLE 2.3 Earnings and Dividends per Share

Suppose U.S. had 200 million shares outstanding at the end of 1995. Based on the income statement above, what was EPS? What were dividends per share?

From the income statement, U.S. had a net income of $412 million for the year. Total dividends were $103. Since 200 million shares were outstanding, we can calculate earnings per share (EPS) and dividends per share as follows:

$$\text{Earnings per share (EPS)} = \text{Net income/Total shares outstanding}$$
$$= \$412/200 = \$2.06 \text{ per share}$$
$$\text{Dividends per share} = \text{Total dividends/Total shares outstanding}$$
$$= \$103/200 = \$0.515 \text{ per share}$$

When looking at an income statement, the financial manager needs to keep three things in mind: GAAP, cash versus noncash items, and time and costs.

Concept Q Answer 2.2b

GAAP and the Income Statement

Trans. 2.3 GAAP vs. Cash Flow Time Line (Supplemental)

An income statement prepared using GAAP will show revenue when it accrues. This is not necessarily when the cash comes in. The general rule (the realization principle) is to recognize revenue when the earnings process is virtually complete and the value of an exchange of goods or services is known or can be reliably determined. In practice, this principle usually means that revenue is recognized at the time of sale, which need not be the same as the time of collection.

Expenses shown on the income statement are based on the matching principle. The basic idea here is to first determine revenues as described above and then match those revenues with the costs associated with producing them. So, if we manufacture and then sell a product on credit, the revenue is realized at the time of sale. The production and other costs associated with the sale of that product would likewise be recognized at that time. Once again, the actual cash outflows may have occurred at some very different time.

As a result of the way revenues and expenses are reported, the figures shown on the income statement may not be at all representative of the actual cash inflows and outflows that occurred during a particular period.

Noncash Items

noncash items
Expenses charged against revenues that do not directly affect cash flow, such as depreciation.

Concept Q Answer 2.2c

Lecture Tip: See IM 2.2 for a discussion of economic life, useful life, and GAAP.

A primary reason that accounting income differs from cash flow is that an income statement contains **noncash items.** The most important of these is *depreciation.* Suppose a firm purchases an asset for $5,000 and pays in cash. Obviously, the firm has a $5,000 cash outflow at the time of purchase. However, instead of deducting the $5,000 as an expense, an accountant might depreciate the asset over a five-year period.

If the depreciation is straight-line and the asset is written down to zero over that period, then $5,000/5 = $1,000 would be deducted each year as an expense.[2] The important thing to recognize is that this $1,000 deduction isn't cash—it's an accounting number. The actual cash outflow occurred when the asset was purchased.

The depreciation deduction is simply another application of the matching principle in accounting. The revenues associated with an asset would generally occur over some length of time. So the accountant seeks to match the expense of purchasing the asset with the benefits produced from owning it.

As we will see, for the financial manager, the actual timing of cash inflows and outflows is critical in coming up with a reasonable estimate of market value, so we need to learn how to separate the cash flows from the noncash accounting entries.

Time and Costs

It is often useful to think of the future as having two distinct parts: the short run and the long run. These are not precise time periods. The distinction has to do with whether costs are fixed or variable. In the long run, all business costs are variable. Given sufficient time, assets can be sold, debts can be paid, and so on.

If our time horizon is relatively short, however, some costs are effectively fixed—they must be paid no matter what (property taxes, for example). Other costs such as wages to laborers and payments to suppliers are still variable. As a result, even in the short run, the firm can vary its output level by varying expenditures in these areas.

Lecture Tip: See IM 2.2 for more distinctions between fixed and variable costs.

The distinction between fixed and variable costs is important, at times, to the financial manager, but the way costs are reported on the income statement is not a good guide as to which costs are which. The reason is that, in practice, accountants tend to classify costs as either product costs or period costs.

[2] By "straight-line," we mean that the depreciation deduction is the same every year. By "written down to zero," we mean that the asset is assumed to have no value at the end of five years. Depreciation is discussed in more detail in Chapter 9.

Product costs include such things as raw materials, direct labor expense, and manufacturing overhead. These are reported on the income statement as costs of goods sold, but they include both fixed and variable costs. Similarly, period costs are incurred during a particular time period and might be reported as selling, general, and administrative expenses. Once again, some of these period costs may be fixed and others may be variable. The company president's salary, for example, is a period cost and is probably fixed, at least in the short run.

CONCEPT QUESTIONS

2.2a What is the income statement equation?

2.2b What are the three things to keep in mind when looking at an income statement?

2.2c Why is accounting income not the same as cash flow?

2.3 TAXES

Problems 6, 7, 18

Trans. 2.4
Taxes (Supplemental)

Taxes can be one of the largest cash outflows that a firm experiences. The size of the tax bill is determined through the tax code, an often amended and changed set of rules. In this section, we examine corporate tax rates and how taxes are calculated. Taxes for partnerships and proprietorships are computed using the personal income tax schedules; we don't discuss these here, but the general procedures are the same.

If the various rules of taxation seem a little bizarre or convoluted to you, keep in mind that the tax code is the result of political, not economic, forces. As a result, there is no reason why it has to make economic sense.

Lecture Tip: A good example of the convolutions of the tax code is the "Case of the Vanishing (and Reappearing) Investment Tax Credit." See IM 2.3 for a discussion of the record of changes in the ITC.

Corporate Tax Rates

Corporate tax rates in effect for 1995 are shown in Table 2.3. A peculiar feature is that corporate tax rates are not strictly increasing. As shown, corporate tax rates rise from 15 percent to 39 percent, but they drop back to 34 percent on income over $335,000. They then rise to 38 percent and subsequently fall to 35 percent.

According to the originators of the current tax rules, there are only four corporate rates: 15 percent, 25 percent, 34 percent, and 35 percent. The 38

TABLE 2.3
Corporate tax rates

Corporate Tax Rates	
Taxable Income	Tax Rate
$ 0– 50,000	15%
50,001– 75,000	25
75,001– 100,000	34
100,001– 335,000	39
335,001–10,000,000	34
10,000,001–15,000,000	35
15,000,001–18,333,333	38
18,333,334+	35

and 39 percent brackets arise because of "surcharges" applied on top of the 34 and 35 percent rates. A tax is a tax is a tax, however, so there are really six corporate tax brackets, as we have shown.

Average versus Marginal Tax Rates

average tax rate
Total taxes paid divided by total taxable income.

marginal tax rate
Amount of tax payable on the next dollar earned.

Concept Q Answer 2.3a

Problem 18

In making financial decisions, it is frequently important to distinguish between average and marginal tax rates. Your **average tax rate** is your tax bill divided by your taxable income, in other words, the percentage of your income that goes to pay taxes. Your **marginal tax rate** is the extra tax you would pay if you earned one more dollar. The percentage tax rates shown in Table 2.3 are all marginal rates. Put another way, the tax rates in Table 2.3 apply to the part of income in the indicated range only, not all income.

The difference between average and marginal tax rates can best be illustrated with a simple example. Suppose our corporation has a taxable income of $200,000. What is the tax bill? From Table 2.3, we can figure our tax bill as:

.15($ 50,000)	= $ 7,500
.25($ 75,000 − 50,000) =	6,250
.34($100,000 − 75,000) =	8,500
.39($200,000 − 100,000) =	39,000
	$61,250

Our total tax is thus $61,250.

In our example, what is the average tax rate? We had a taxable income of $200,000 and a tax bill of $61,250, so the average tax rate is $61,250/200,000 = 30.625%. What is the marginal tax rate? If we made one more dollar, the tax on that dollar would be 39 cents, so our marginal rate is 39 percent.

EXAMPLE 2.4 Deep in the Heart of Taxes

Algernon, Inc., has a taxable income of $85,000. What is its tax bill? What is its average tax rate? Its marginal tax rate?

From Table 2.3, the tax rate applied to the first $50,000 is 15 percent; the rate applied to the next $25,000 is 25 percent, and the rate applied after that up to $100,000 is 34 percent. So Algernon must pay .15 × $50,000 + .25 × $25,000 + .34 × ($85,000 − 75,000) = $17,150. The average tax rate is thus $17,150/85,000 = 20.18%. The marginal rate is 34 percent since Algernon's taxes would rise by 34 cents if it had another dollar in taxable income. • • •

Trans. 2.5 Marginal v. Average Corporate Tax Rates (Supplemental)

Lecture Tip: See IM 2.3 for situations in which the application of marginal versus average tax rates is relevant.

Concept Q Answer 2.3b

Table 2.4 sumarizes some different taxable incomes, marginal tax rates, and average tax rates for corporations. Notice how the average and marginal tax rates come together at 35 percent.

With a *flat rate* tax, there is only one tax rate, and this rate is the same for all income levels. With such a tax, the marginal tax rate is always the same as the average tax rate. As it stands now, corporate taxation in the United States is a modified flat rate tax, becoming a true flat rate for the highest incomes.

In looking at Table 2.4, notice that the more a corporation makes, the greater is the percentage of taxable income paid in taxes. Put another way, under current tax law, the average tax rate never goes down, even though the

TABLE 2.4
Corporate taxes and tax rates

(1) Taxable Income	(2) Marginal Tax Rate	(3) Total Tax	(3)/(1) Average Tax Rate
$ 45,000	15%	$ 6,750	15.00%
70,000	25	12,500	17.86
95,000	34	20,550	21.63
250,000	39	80,750	32.30
1,000,000	34	340,000	34.00
17,500,000	38	6,100,000	34.86
50,000,000	35	17,500,000	35.00
100,000,000	35	35,000,000	35.00

marginal tax rate does. As illustrated, for corporations, average tax rates begin at 15 percent and rise to a maximum of 35 percent.

It will normally be the marginal tax rate that is relevant for financial decision making. The reason is that any new cash flows will be taxed at that marginal rate. Since financial decisions usually involve new cash flows or changes in existing ones, this rate will tell us the marginal effect on our tax bill.

There is one last thing to notice about the tax code as it affects corporations. It's easy to verify that the corporate tax bill is just a flat 35 percent of taxable income if our taxable income is more than $18.33 million. Also, for the many midsize corporations with taxable incomes in the $335,000–$10,000,000 range, the tax rate is a flat 34 percent. Since we will often be talking about large corporations, you can assume that the average and marginal tax rates are 35 percent unless we explicitly say otherwise.

CONCEPT QUESTIONS

2.3a What is the difference between a marginal and an average tax rate?

2.3b Do the wealthiest corporations receive a tax break in terms of a lower tax rate? Explain.

2.4 CASH FLOW

Self-Test Problem 2.1
Problems 8, 9, 10, 13, 14, 16, 17, 19, 20–22

At this point, we are ready to discuss perhaps one of the most important pieces of financial information that can be gleaned from financial statements: *cash flow*. By cash flow, we simply mean the difference between the number of dollars that came in and the number that went out. For example, if you were the owner of a business, you might be very interested in how much cash you actually took out of your business in a given year. How to determine this amount is one of the things we discuss next.

There is no standard financial statement that presents this information in the way that we wish. We will therefore discuss how to calculate cash flow for U.S. Corporation and point out how the result differs from standard financial statement calculations. There is a standard financial accounting statement called the *statement of cash flows*, but it is concerned with a somewhat different issue and should not be confused with what is discussed in this section. The accounting statement of cash flows is discussed in Chapter 3.

Trans. 2.6
Cash Flow Example
(Supplemental)

Concept Q
Answer 2.4a

From the balance sheet identity, we know that the value of a firm's assets is equal to the value of its liabilities plus the value of its equity. Similarly, the cash flow from the firm's assets must equal the sum of the cash flow to creditors plus the cash flow to stockholders (or owners if the business is not a corporation):

$$\text{Cash flow from assets} = \text{Cash flow to creditors} + \text{Cash flow to stockholders} \qquad [2.3]$$

This is the cash flow identity. What it reflects is the fact that a firm generates cash through its various activities, and that cash is either used to pay creditors or else it is paid out to the owners of the firm. We discuss the various things that make up these cash flows next.

Cash Flow from Assets

cash flow from assets
The total of cash flow to creditors and cash flow to stockholders, consisting of the following: operating cash flow, capital spending, and additions to net working capital.

operating cash flow
Cash generated from a firm's normal business activities.

Cash flow from assets involves three components: operating cash flow, capital spending, and additions to net working capital. **Operating cash flow** refers to the cash flow that results from the firm's day-to-day activities of producing and selling. Expenses associated with the firm's financing of its assets are not included since they are not operating expenses.

In the normal course of events, some portion of the firm's cash flow is reinvested in the firm. *Capital spending* refers to the net spending on fixed assets (purchases of fixed assets less sales of fixed assets). Finally, *additions to net working capital* is the amount spent on net working capital. It is measured as the change in net working capital over the period being examined and represents the net increase in current assets over current liabilities. The three components of cash flow are examined in more detail below.

Operating Cash Flow To calculate operating cash flow (OCF), we want to calculate revenues minus costs, but we don't want to include depreciation since it's not a cash outflow, and we don't want to include interest because it's a financing expense. We do want to include taxes, because taxes are, unfortunately, paid in cash.

If we look at U.S. Corporation's income statement (Table 2.2), earnings before interest and taxes (EBIT) are $694. This is almost what we want since it doesn't include interest paid. We need to make two adjustments. First, recall that depreciation is a noncash expense. To get cash flow, we first add back the $65 in depreciation since it wasn't a cash deduction. The other adjustment is to subtract the $212 in taxes since these were paid in cash. The result is operating cash flow:

Concept Q
Answer 2.4b

U.S. CORPORATION
1995 Operating Cash Flow

Earnings before interest and taxes	$694
+ Depreciation	65
− Taxes	212
Operating cash flow	$547

U.S. Corporation thus had a 1995 operating cash flow of $547.

Operating cash flow is an important number because it tells us, on a very basic level, whether or not a firm's cash inflows from its business operations are sufficient to cover its everyday cash outflows. For this reason, a negative operating cash flow is often a sign of trouble.

There is an unpleasant possibility for confusion when we speak of operating cash flow. In accounting practice, operating cash flow is often defined as net income plus depreciation. For U.S. Corporation, this would amount to $412 + 65 = $477.

The accounting definition of operating cash flow differs from ours in one important way: Interest is deducted when net income is computed. Notice that the difference between the $547 operating cash flow we calculated and this $477 is $70, the amount of interest paid for the year. This definition of cash flow thus considers interest paid to be an operating expense. Our definition treats it properly as a financing expense. If there were no interest expense, the two definitions would be the same.

Concept Q Answer 2.4c

To finish our calculation of cash flow from assets for U.S. Corporation, we need to consider how much of the $547 operating cash flow was reinvested in the firm. We consider spending on fixed assets first.

Capital Spending Net capital spending is just money spent on fixed assets less money received from the sale of fixed assets. At the end of 1994, net fixed assets for U.S. Corporation (Table 2.1) were $1,644. During the year, we wrote off (depreciated) $65 worth of fixed assets on the income statement. So, if we didn't purchase any new fixed assets, net fixed assets would have been $1,644 − 65 = $1,579 at year's end. The 1995 balance sheet shows $1,709 in net fixed assets, so we must have spent a total of $1,709 − 1,579 = $130 on fixed assets during the year:

Ending net fixed assets	$1,709
− Beginning net fixed assets	1,644
+ Depreciation	65
Net investment in fixed assets	$ 130

This $130 is our net capital spending for 1995.

Could net capital spending be negative? The answer is yes. This would happen if the firm sold off more assets than it purchased. The *net* here refers to purchases of fixed assets net of any sales of fixed assets.

Additions to Net Working Capital In addition to investing in fixed assets, a firm will also invest in current assets. For example, going back to the balance sheet in Table 2.1, we see that, at the end of 1995, U.S. had current assets of $1,403. At the end of 1994, current assets were $1,112, so, during the year, U.S. invested $1,403 − 1,112 = $291 in current assets.

As the firm changes its investment in current assets, its current liabilities will usually change as well. To determine the additions to net working capital, the easiest approach is just to take the difference between the beginning and ending net working capital (NWC) figures. Net working capital at the end of 1995 was $1,403 − 389 = $1,014. Similarly, at the end of 1994, net working capital was $1,112 − 428 = $684. So, given these figures, we have:

Ending NWC	$1,014
− Beginning NWC	684
Additions to NWC	$ 330

Net working capital thus increased by $330. Put another way, U.S. Corporation had a net investment of $330 in NWC for the year.

Cash Flow from Assets Given the figures we've come up with, we're ready to calculate cash flow from assets. The total cash flow from assets is given by operating cash flow less the amounts invested in fixed assets and net working capital. So, for U.S., we have:

U.S. CORPORATION
1995 Cash Flow from Assets

Operating cash flow	$547
− Net capital spending	130
− Additions to NWC	330
Cash flow from assets	$ 87

From the cash flow identity above, this $87 cash flow from assets equals the sum of the firm's cash flow to creditors and cash flow to stockholders. We consider these next.

It wouldn't be at all unusual for a growing corporation to have a negative cash flow. As we shall see below, a negative cash flow means that the firm raised more money by borrowing and selling stock than it paid out to creditors and stockholders that year.

Cash Flow to Creditors and Stockholders

cash flow to creditors
A firm's interest payments to creditors less net new borrowings.

cash flow to stockholders
Dividends paid out by a firm less net new equity raised.

Problems 11, 12

The cash flows to creditors and stockholders represent the net payments to creditors and owners during the year. They are calculated in a similar way. **Cash flow to creditors** is interest paid less net new borrowing; **cash flow to stockholders** is dividends paid less net new equity raised.

Cash Flow to Creditors Looking at the income statement in Table 2.2, U.S. paid $70 in interest to creditors. From the balance sheets in Table 2.1, long-term debt rose by $454 − 408 = $46. So, U.S. Corporation paid out $70 in interest, but it borrowed an additional $46. Net cash flow to creditors is thus:

U.S. CORPORATION
1995 Cash Flow to Creditors

Interest paid	$70
− Net new borrowing	46
Cash flow to creditors	$24

Cash flow to creditors is sometimes called *cash flow to "bondholders"*; we will use these terms interchangeably.

Cash Flow to Stockholders From the income statement, dividends paid to stockholders amount to $103. To get net new equity raised, we need to look at the common stock and paid-in surplus account. This account tells us how much stock the company has sold. During the year, this account rose by $40, so $40 in net new equity was raised. Given this, we have:

U.S. CORPORATION
1995 Cash Flow to Stockholders

Dividends paid	$103
− Net new equity raised	40
Cash flow to stockholders	$ 63

The cash flow to stockholders for 1995 was thus $63.

TABLE 2.5
Cash flow summary

Trans. 2.7

I. The cash flow identity
Cash flow from assets = Cash flow to creditors (bondholders)
+ Cash flow to stockholders (owners)

II. Cash flow from assets
Cash flow from assets = Operating cash flow
− Net capital spending
− Additions to net working capital (NWC)

where:
Operating cash flow = Earnings before interest and taxes (EBIT)
+ Depreciation − Taxes

Net capital spending = Ending net fixed assets − Beginning net fixed assets
+ Depreciation

Additions to NWC = Ending NWC − Beginning NWC

III. Cash flow to creditors (bondholders)
Cash flow to creditors = Interest paid − Net new borrowing

IV. Cash flow to stockholders (owners)
Cash flow to stockholders = Dividends paid − Net new equity raised

The last thing that we need to do is to check that the cash flow identity holds to be sure that we didn't make any mistakes. From above, cash flow from assets is $87. Cash flow to creditors and stockholders is $24 + 63 = $87, so everything checks out. Table 2.5 contains a summary of the various cash flow calculations for future reference.

The relationship between a firm's cash flow from assets and its cash flows to creditors and stockholders highlights an important issue. As the accompanying *Principles in Action* box shows, whenever a firm such as Chrysler chooses to build up its cash reserves, it chooses, in effect, *not* to increase its cash flow to stockholders. As Chrysler learned the hard way, stockholders may or may not approve of management's decisions in this regard.

As our discussion indicates, it is essential that a firm keep an eye on its cash flow. The following serves as an excellent reminder of why doing so is a good idea, unless the firm's owners wish to end up in the "Po'" house.

Quoth the Banker, "Watch Cash Flow"[3]

Once upon a midnight dreary as I pondered weak and weary
Over many a quaint and curious volume of accounting lore,
Seeking gimmicks (without scruple) to squeeze through
some new tax loophole,
Suddenly I heard a knock upon my door,
Only this, and nothing more.

Then I felt a queasy tingling and I heard the cash a-jingling
As a fearsome banker entered whom I'd often seen before.
His face was money-green and in his eyes there could be seen
Dollar-signs that seemed to glitter as he reckoned up the score.
"Cash flow," the banker said, and nothing more.

I had always thought it fine to show a jet black bottom line.
But the banker sounded a resounding, "No.

[3] Reprinted from the January 13, 1975, issue of *Publishers Weekly*, published by R. R. Bowker, a Xerox company. Copyright © 1975 by the Xerox Corporation.

Principles in Action

Was Chrysler's Cash Flow to Stockholders Too Small?

In April 1995, financier Kirk Kerkorian and former Chrysler chairman Lee A. Iacocca stunned the financial world by offering to buy the common stock of Chrysler Corporation for $55 a share. The purchase was to be financed primarily with debt, but the offer had a novel twist. They also planned to use $5.5 billion of Chrysler's own cash to finance the purchase. Their offer increased the level of debate over how large a cash balance is appropriate for a corporation and just how the financial managers of a corporation should go about maximizing shareholder wealth.

At the time of the offer, Chrysler had amassed a cash balance in excess of $7 billion. Chrysler's board of directors argued the company needed about $7.5 billion in cash to survive the next recession, a goal clearly in the best interest of the stockholders. However, Chrysler's largest stockholder, Kirk Kerkorian, who at that time owned just under 10 percent of Chrysler's outstanding stock (an investment valued at $1.5 billion), disagreed. He believed Chrysler's cash balance was excessive and should be reduced by returning the cash to its owners, the stockholders.

To understand Kerkorian's perspective, it is crucial to determine who the cash of the corporation belongs to. Each quarter, Chrysler's corporate directors decide what to do with any excess cash generated from operations. The cash can be paid out to stockholders in the form of a dividend or it can be retained in the business. If a dividend is paid, it is a cash flow to stockholders. If, however, the cash is retained in the corporation, the money still belongs to the stockholders, but the directors have effectively reinvested the shareholder's money in the corporation itself by increasing net working capital.

At issue is whether or not the investment in net working capital provides an adequate return to the stockholders. Chrysler's directors argued that the cash lessened the chance of financial distress, a benefit to stockholders. However, from Kerkorian's perspective, while Chrysler's cash balance grew, its stock price did not. In late 1994, Kerkorian convinced Chrysler's board to use some of its excess cash to boost its dividend by 60 percent and initiate a $1 billion stock-buyback program, each of which is a cash flow to stockholders. Despite these actions, Chrysler's cash balance continued to rise in early 1995 while the stock price languished. Kerkorian argued that accumulating cash was not enhancing shareholder wealth, and a better way to do so was to allow the stockholders to reinvest it themselves.

How the struggle for control between Kerkorian and Chrysler is ultimately played out will not solve the more general issue of how much cash a corporation should hold, and Chrysler isn't the only company with large amounts of cash. In April 1995, *The Wall Street Journal* reported that Chrysler had a cash balance equal to about 30 percent of the market value of its stock, Ford had cash equal to 22 percent of its value, Intel had 9 percent, United Healthcare had 33 percent, and Apple Computer held about 25 percent. These corporations have reinvested substantial sums of money for their stockholders. Corporations such as these who accumulate large cash balances may ultimately need to defend their actions to an important and sometimes vocal group: their stockholders.

Source: "Chrysler Boosts Dividend, Sets Buyback of Stock in Effort to Mollify Kerkorian," *The Wall Street Journal,* December 2, 1994, p. A3; "Rich and Richer: How Much Cash a Firm Should Keep Is an Issue in Wake of Chrysler Bid," *The Wall Street Journal,* April 20, 1995, p. A1; "At the Factory Gate: Kerkorian and Iacocca Make a Run at Chrysler: Motives Are Unclear," *The Wall Street Journal,* April 13, 1995, p. A1.

Your receivables are high, mounting upward toward the sky;
Write-offs loom. What matters is cash flow."
He repeated, "Watch cash flow."

Then I tried to tell the story of our lovely inventory
Which, though large, is full of most delightful stuff.
But the banker saw its growth, and with a mighty oath
He waved his arms and shouted, "Stop! Enough!
Pay the interest, and don't give me any guff!"

Next I looked for noncash items which could add ad infinitum
To replace the ever-outward flow of cash,
But to keep my statement black I'd held depreciation back,
And my banker said that I'd done something rash.
He quivered, and his teeth began to gnash.

When I asked him for a loan, he responded, with a groan,
That the interest rate would be just prime plus eight,
And to guarantee my purity he'd insist on some security—
All my assets plus the scalp upon my pate.
Only this, a standard rate.

Though my bottom line is black, I am flat upon my back,
My cash flows out and customers pay slow.
The growth of my receivables is almost unbelievable:
The result is certain—unremitting woe!
And I hear the banker utter an ominous low mutter,
"Watch cash flow."

Herbert S. Bailey, Jr.

To which we can only add: "Amen."

An Example: Cash Flows for Dole Cola

This extended example covers the various cash flow calculations discussed in the chapter. It also illustrates a few variations that may arise.

Operating Cash Flow During the year, Dole Cola, Inc., had sales and costs of goods sold of $600 and $300, respectively. Depreciation was $150 and interest paid was $30. Taxes were calculated at a straight 34 percent. Dividends were $30. (All figures are in millions of dollars.) What was operating cash flow for Dole? Why is this different from net income?

The easiest thing to do here is to go ahead and create an income statement. We can then pick up the numbers we need. Dole Cola's income statement is given below.

DOLE COLA
1995 Income Statement

Net sales		$600
Cost of goods sold		300
Depreciation		150
Earnings before interest and taxes		$150
Interest paid		30
Taxable income		$120
Taxes		41
Net income		$ 79
Addition to retained earnings	$49	
Dividends	30	

Net income for Dole was thus $79. We now have all the numbers we need. Referring back to the U.S. Corporation example and Table 2.5, we have:

DOLE COLA
1995 Operating Cash Flow

Earnings before interest and taxes	$150
+ Depreciation	150
− Taxes	41
Operating cash flow	$259

As this example illustrates, operating cash flow is not the same as net income, because depreciation and interest are subtracted out when net income is calculated. If you recall our earlier discussion, we don't subtract these out in computing operating cash flow because depreciation is not a cash expense and interest paid is a financing expense, not an operating expense.

Net Capital Spending Suppose beginning net fixed assets were $500 and ending net fixed assets were $750. What was the net capital spending for the year?

From the income statement for Dole, depreciation for the year was $150. Net fixed assets rose by $250. Dole thus spent $250 along with an additional $150, for a total of $400.

Change in NWC and Cash Flow from Assets Suppose Dole Cola started the year with $2,130 in current assets and $1,620 in current liabilities. The corresponding ending figures were $2,260 and $1,710. What was the addition to NWC during the year? What was cash flow from assets? How does this compare to net income?

Net working capital started out as $2,130 − 1,620 = $510 and ended up at $2,260 − 1,710 = $550. The addition to NWC was thus $550 − 510 = $40. Putting together all the information for Dole we have:

DOLE COLA
1995 Cash Flow from Assets

Operating cash flow	$259
− Net capital spending	400
− Additions to NWC	40
Cash flow from assets	−$181

Dole had a cash flow from assets of −$181. Net income was positive at $79. Is the fact that cash flow from assets was negative a cause for alarm? Not necessarily. The cash flow here is negative primarily because of a large investment in fixed assets. If these are good investments, then the resulting negative cash flow is not a worry.

Cash Flow to Creditors and Stockholders We saw that Dole Cola had cash flow from assets of −$181. The fact that this is negative means that Dole raised more money in the form of new debt and equity than it paid out for the year. For example, suppose we know that Dole didn't sell any new equity for the year. What was cash flow to stockholders? To creditors?

Since it didn't raise any new equity, Dole's cash flow to stockholders is just equal to the cash dividend paid:

DOLE COLA
1995 Cash Flow to Stockholders

Dividends paid	$30
− Net new equity	0
Cash flow to stockholders	$30

Now, from the cash flow identity, the total cash paid to creditors and stockholders was −$181. Cash flow to stockholders is $30, so cash flow to creditors must be equal to −$181 − 30 = −$211:

Cash flow to creditors + Cash flow to stockholders	=	−$181
Cash flow to creditors + $30	=	−$181
Cash flow to creditors	=	−$211

Since cash flow to creditors is −$211 and interest paid is $30 (from the income statement), we can now determine net new borrowing. Dole must have borrowed $241 during the year to help finance the fixed asset expansion:

Trans 2.8, 2.9, 2.10
Hermetic, Inc., Example (Supplemental)

DOLE COLA
1995 Cash Flow to Creditors

Interest paid	$ 30
− Net new borrowing	− 241
Cash flow to creditors	−$211

CONCEPT QUESTIONS

2.4a What is the cash flow identity? Explain what it says.

2.4b What are the components of operating cash flow?

2.4c Why is interest paid not a component of operating cash flow?

2.5 SUMMARY AND CONCLUSIONS

This chapter has introduced you to some of the basics of financial statements, taxes, and cash flow. In it we saw that:

1. The book values on an accounting balance sheet can be very different from market values. The goal of financial management is to maximize the market value of the stock, not its book value.
2. Net income as it is computed on the income statement is not cash flow. A primary reason is that depreciation, a noncash expense, is deducted when net income is computed.
3. Marginal and average tax rates can be different, and it is the marginal tax rate that is relevant for most financial decisions.
4. The marginal tax rate paid by the corporations with the largest incomes is 35 percent.
5. There is a cash flow identity much like the balance sheet identity. It says that cash flow from assets equals cash flow to creditors and stockholders.

The calculation of cash flow from financial statements isn't difficult. Care must be taken in handling noncash expenses, such as depreciation, and in not confusing operating costs with financing costs. Most of all, it is important not to confuse book values with market values and accounting income with cash flow.

Chapter Review Problem and Self-Test

2.1 **Cash Flow for Rasputin Corporation** This problem will give you some practice working with financial statements and figuring cash flow. Based on the following information for Rasputin Corporation, prepare an income statement for 1995 and balance sheets for 1994 and 1995. Next, following our U.S. Corporation examples in the chapter, calculate cash flow from assets for Rasputin, cash flow to creditors, and cash flow to stockholders for 1995. Use a 34 percent tax rate throughout. You can check your answers below.

	1994	1995
Sales	$3,790	$3,990
Cost of goods sold	2,043	2,137
Depreciation	975	1,018
Interest	225	267
Dividends	200	225
Current assets	2,140	2,346
Net fixed assets	6,770	7,087
Current liabilities	994	1,126
Long-term debt	2,869	2,956

Answer to Self-Test Problem

2.1 In preparing the balance sheets, remember that shareholders' equity is the residual. With this in mind, Rasputin's balance sheets are as follows:

RASPUTIN CORPORATION
Balance Sheets as of December 31, 1994 and 1995

	1994	1995		1994	1995
Current assets	$2,140	$2,346	Current liabilities	$ 994	$1,126
Net fixed assets	6,770	7,087	Long-term debt	2,869	2,956
			Equity	5,047	5,351
Total assets	$8,910	$9,433	Total liabilities and shareholders' equity	$8,910	$9,433

The income statement is straightforward:

RASPUTIN CORPORATION
1995 Income Statement

Sales		$3,990
Cost of goods sold		2,137
Depreciation		1,018
Earnings before interest and taxes		$ 835
Interest paid		267
Taxable income		$ 568
Taxes (34%)		193
Net income		$ 375
Addition to retained earnings	$150	
Dividends	225	

Notice that we've used a flat 34 percent tax rate. Also notice that the addition to retained earnings is just net income less cash dividends.

We can now pick up the figures we need to get operating cash flow:

RASPUTIN CORPORATION
1995 Operating Cash Flow

Earnings before interest and taxes	$ 835
+ Depreciation	1,018
− Current taxes	193
Operating cash flow	$1,660

Next, we get the capital spending for the year by looking at the change in fixed assets, remembering to account for the depreciation:

Ending fixed assets	$7,087
− Beginning fixed assets	6,770
+ Depreciation	1,018
Net investment in fixed assets	$1,335

After calculating beginning and ending NWC, we take the difference to get the additions to NWC:

Ending NWC	$1,220
− Beginning NWC	1,146
Additions to NWC	$ 74

We now combine operating cash flow, net capital spending, and the additions to net working capital to get the total cash flow from assets:

RASPUTIN CORPORATION
1995 Cash Flow from Assets

Operating cash flow	$1,660
− Net capital spending	1,335
− Additions to NWC	74
Cash flow from assets	$ 251

To get cash flow to creditors, notice that long-term borrowing increased by $87 during the year and that interest paid was $267, so:

RASPUTIN CORPORATION
1995 Cash Flow to Creditors

Interest paid	$267
− Net new borrowing	87
Cash flow to creditors	$180

Finally, dividends paid were $225. To get net new equity, we have to do some extra calculating. Total equity was up by $5,351 − 5,047 = $304. Of this increase, $150 was from additions to retained earnings, so $154 in new equity was raised during the year. Cash flow to stockholders was thus:

RASPUTIN CORPORATION
1995 Cash Flow to Stockholders

Dividends paid	$225
− Net new equity	154
Cash flow to stockholders	$ 71

As a check, notice that cash flow from assets ($251) does equal cash flow to creditors plus cash flow to stockholders ($180 + 71 = $251).

Questions and Problems

Basic (Questions 1–13)

1. **Building a Balance Sheet** Green Day, Inc., has current assets of $1,000, net fixed assets of $4,500, current liabilities of $500, and long-term debt of $1,200. What is the shareholders' equity account for this firm? How much is net working capital?

Equity = $3,800
NWC = $500

Net income = $46,200

2. **Building an Income Statement** Kuipers Manufacturing Co. has sales of $300,000, costs of $175,000, depreciation expense of $25,000, interest expense of $30,000, and a tax rate of 34 percent. What is the net income for this firm?

See Answer Key, page AK-1

3. **Dividends and Retained Earnings** Suppose the firm in Problem 2 paid out $20,000 in cash dividends. What is the addition to retained earnings?

EPS = $1.54
DPS = $0.67

4. **Per Share Earnings and Dividends** Suppose the firm in Problem 3 had 30,000 shares of common stock outstanding. What is the earnings per share (EPS) figure? What is the dividends per share figure?

Book value = $2.5M
Market value = $3.2M

5. **Market Values and Book Values** Klingon Widgets, Inc., purchased new machinery three years ago for $3 million. The machinery can be sold to the Romulans today for $2 million. Klingon's current balance sheet shows net fixed assets of $1.5 million, current liabilities of $500,000, and net working capital of $500,000. If all the current accounts were liquidated today, the company would receive $1.2 million cash. What is the book value of Klingon's assets today? What is the market value?

$37,850
Trans. 2.11

6. **Calculating Taxes** The Stowe Co. had $140,000 in 1995 taxable income. Using Table 2.3 in the chapter, calculate the company's actual 1995 taxes paid.

Average tax rate = 27.04%
Marginal tax rate = 39%

7. **Tax Rates** In Problem 6, what is the average tax rate? What is the marginal tax rate?

OCF = $1,545

8. **Calculating OCF** Cyclone Water Works, Inc., has sales of $5,000, costs of $3,000, depreciation expense of $450, and interest expense of $250. If the tax rate is 35 percent, what is the operating cash flow (OCF)?

Net capital spending = $500,000

9. **Calculating Net Capital Spending** The Maxwell Hammer Co.'s December 31, 1994, balance sheet showed net fixed assets of $3.4 million, and the December 31, 1995, balance sheet showed net fixed assets of $3.5 million. The company's 1995 income statement showed a depreciation expense of $400,000. What was Maxwell's net capital spending for 1995?

Addition to NWC = $50

10. **Calculating Additions to NWC** Jordan and Jordan Manufacturing, Inc.'s December 31, 1994, balance sheet showed current assets of $500 and current liabilities of $400. The December 31, 1995, balance sheet showed current assets of $600 and current liabilities of $450. What was the company's 1995 addition to net working capital (NWC)?

Cash flow to creditors = −$325,000

Trans. 2.12

11. **Cash Flow to Creditors** ABC, Inc.'s December 31, 1994, balance sheet showed long-term debt of $5 million, and the December 31, 1995, balance sheet showed long-term debt of $5.9 million. The 1995 income statement showed an interest expense of $575,000. What was ABC's cash flow to creditors during 1995?

Cash flow to stockholders = $150,000

12. **Cash Flow to Stockholders** ABC, Inc.'s December 31, 1994, balance sheet showed $300,000 in the common stock account, and $5,700,000 in the additional paid-in surplus account. The December 31, 1995, balance sheet showed $325,000 and $5,975,000 in the same two accounts. If the company paid out $450,000 in cash dividends during 1995, what was the cash flow to stockholders for the year?

13. **Calculating Total Cash Flows** Given the information for ABC, Inc., in Problems 11 and 12, suppose you also know that the firm made $750,000 in new capital spending investments during 1995, and that the firm reduced its net working capital investment by $75,000. What was ABC, Inc.'s 1995 operating cash flow (OCF)?

OCF = $500,000

Intermediate (Questions 14–23)

14. **Calculating Total Cash Flows** Bliss, Inc., shows the following information on its 1995 income statement: sales = $50,000; costs = $30,000; other expenses = $2,500; depreciation expense = $2,500; interest expense = $5,000; taxes paid = $3,400; dividends paid = $3,200. In addition, you're told that the firm issued $500 in new equity during 1995, and repaid $1,000 in outstanding long-term debt.

a. What is the 1995 cash flow from operations?
b. What is the 1995 cash flow to creditors?
c. What is the 1995 cash flow to stockholders?
d. If net fixed assets increased by $2,900 during the year, what were the additions to NWC?

a. OCF = $14,100
b. Cash flow to creditors = $6,000
c. Cash flow to stockholders = $2,700
d. Additions to NWC = $0

15. **Using Income Statements** Given the following information, calculate the depreciation expense: sales = $10,000; costs = $6,000; additions to retained earnings = $1,000; dividends paid = $625; interest expense = $500; tax rate = 35 percent.

Depreciation = $1,000

16. **Preparing a Balance Sheet** Prepare a balance sheet for the Nimby Corp. as of December 31, 1995, based on the following information: cash = $110,000; patents and copyrights = $750,000; accounts payable = $200,000; accounts receivable = $300,000; tangible net fixed assets = $2,000,000; inventory = $400,000; notes payable = $300,000; accumulated retained earnings = $2,500,000; long-term debt = $175,000.

Common stock = $385,000

17. **Residual Claims** OnTheBrink, Inc., is obligated to pay its creditors $1,700 during the year. What is the value of the shareholders' equity if assets equal $1,800? What if assets equal $1,500?

Equity = $100
Equity = $0

18. **Marginal versus Average Tax Rates** (Refer to Table 2.3.) Corporation X has $80,000 in taxable income, and Corporation Y has $800,000 in taxable income.

a. What is the tax bill for each firm?
b. Suppose both firms have identified a new project that will increase taxable income by $10,000. How much in additional taxes will each firm pay? Why is this amount the same?

a. X: $15,450
Y: $272,000
b. $3,400

19. **OCF and Net Income** During 1995, My Money, Inc., had sales of $750,000. Cost of goods sold, administrative and selling expenses, and depreciation expenses were $500,000, $150,000, and $50,000, respectively. In addition, the company had an interest expense of $75,000 and a tax rate of 35 percent. (Ignore any tax loss carry-back or carry-forward provisions.)

a. What is My Money's net income for 1995?
b. What is its operating cash flow?
c. Explain your results in (*a*) and (*b*).

a. Net income = −$25,000
b. OCF = $100,000

Net new long-term debt = $0

20. **Accounting Values versus Cash Flows** In Problem 19, suppose My Money, Inc., paid out $25,000 in cash dividends. Is this possible? If no new investments were made in capital spending or net working capital, and if no new stock was issued during the year, what do you know about the firm's long-term debt account?

a. Net income = $462
b. OCF = $1,762
c. Cash flow from assets = −$338
d. Cash flow to creditors = $300
Cash flow to stockholders = −$638

21. **Calculating Cash Flows** Tiger Paw Corporation had the following operating results for 1995: sales = $4,000; cost of goods sold = $2,000; depreciation expense = $1,000; interest expense = $300; dividends paid = $250. At the beginning of the year, net fixed assets were $3,000, current assets were $2,000, and current liabilities were $1,000. At the end of the year, net fixed assets were $3,600, current assets were $2,750, and current liabilities were $1,250. The tax rate for 1995 was 34 percent.

a. What is net income for 1995?
b. What is the operating cash flow for 1995?
c. What is the cash flow from assets for 1995? Is this possible? Explain.
d. If no new debt was issued during the year, what is the cash flow to creditors? What is the cash flow to stockholders? Explain and interpret the positive and negative signs of your answers in (*a*) through (*d*).

22. **Calculating Cash Flows** Consider the following abbreviated financial statements for Jumbo, Inc.:

Jumbo, Inc.
Partial Balance Sheets as of December 31, 1994 and 1995

Assets	1994	1995	Liabilities and Owners' Equity	1994	1995
Current assets	$ 354	$ 465	Current liabilities	$ 171	$ 205
Net fixed assets	1,800	1,995	Long-term debt	1,150	1,190

Jumbo, Inc.
1995 Income Statement

Sales	$5,125
Costs	1,478
Depreciation	540
Interest	259

a. Equity 1994: $833
Equity 1995: $1,065
b. Addition to NWC = $77
c. Fixed assets sold = $265
Cash flow from assets = $1,838.20
d. Debt retired = $60
Cash flow to creditors = $219

a. What is owners' equity for 1994 and 1995?
b. What is the addition to net working capital for 1995?
c. In 1995, Jumbo purchased $1,000 in new fixed assets. How much in fixed assets did Jumbo sell? What is the cash flow from assets for the year? (The tax rate is 35 percent.)
d. During 1995, Jumbo raised $100 in new long-term debt. How much long-term debt must Jumbo have paid off during the year? What is the cash flow to bondholders?

23. **Liquidity** What does liquidity measure? Explain the trade-off the firm faces between high liquidity and low liquidity levels.

Part Two

FINANCIAL STATEMENTS AND LONG-TERM FINANCIAL PLANNING

• • •

We extend our discussion of uses of financial statement information by examining how the accounting statement of cash flows is constructed and how financial statements can be standardized for comparison purposes. We develop a number of useful financial ratios, focusing on how they are interpreted and potential pitfalls that can arise. We present the famous Du Pont identity, which is an especially useful means of analyzing accounting-based financial performance.

In Chapter 4 we examine the basics of long-term financial planning. We show how financial statements can be used as a basis for examining future investment and financing needs. We introduce and develop the concept of sustainable growth, a very useful tool in financial anaylsis and planning.

OUTLINE

Chapter Three

3

Working with Financial Statements

After studying this chapter, you should have a good understanding of:

Sources and uses of cash and the accounting statement of cash flows.

How to standardize financial statements for comparison purposes.

How to compute and interpret some important financial ratios.

Some of the problems and pitfalls in financial statements analysis.

Trans. 3.1
Chapter Outline

In Chapter 2, we discussed some of the essential concepts of financial statements and cash flows. Part 2, this chapter and the next, continues where our earlier discussion left off. Our goal here is to expand your understanding of the uses (and abuses) of financial statement information.

A good working knowledge of financial statements is desirable simply because such statements, and numbers derived from those statements, are the primary means of communicating financial information both within the firm and outside the firm. In short, much of the language of business finance is rooted in the ideas we discuss in this chapter.

In the best of all worlds, the financial manager has full market value information about all of the firm's assets. This will rarely (if ever) happen. So the reason we rely on accounting figures for much of our financial information is that we almost always cannot obtain all (or even part) of the market information that we want. The only meaningful yardstick for evaluating business decisions is whether or not they create economic value (see Chapter 1). However, in many important situations, it will not be possible to make this judgment directly because we can't see the market value effects.

Lecture Tip: See IM 3.1 for a brief discussion of the importance of both accounting and market value data.

We recognize accounting numbers are often just pale reflections of economic reality, but they frequently are the best available information. For privately held corporations, not-for-profit businesses, and smaller firms, for example, very little direct market value information exists at all. The accountant's reporting function is crucial in these circumstances.

Clearly, one important goal of the accountant is to report financial information to the user in a form useful for decision making. Ironically, the information frequently does not come to the user in such a form. In other words, financial statements don't come with a user's guide. This chapter and the next are first steps in filling this gap.

3.1 CASH FLOW AND FINANCIAL STATEMENTS: A CLOSER LOOK

In this section, we continue to examine the subject of cash flow by taking a closer look at the cash events during the year that lead to the total cash flow figures we discussed in Chapter 2.

Sources and Uses of Cash

Those activities that bring in cash are called **sources of cash.** Those activities that involve spending cash are called **uses** (or applications) **of cash.** What we need to do is to trace the changes in the firm's balance sheet to see how the firm obtained its cash and how the firm spent its cash during some time period.

sources of cash
A firm's activities that generate cash.

uses of cash
A firm's activities in which cash is spent. Also called applications of cash.

To get started, consider the balance sheets for the Prufrock Corporation in Table 3.1. Notice that we have calculated the changes in each of the items on the balance sheet.

TABLE 3.1

PRUFROCK CORPORATION
Balance Sheets as of December 31, 1994 and 1995
($ in millions)

	1994	1995	Change
Assets			
Current assets			
Cash	$ 84	$ 98	+$ 14
Accounts receivable	165	188	+ 23
Inventory	393	422	+ 29
Total	$ 642	$ 708	+$ 66
Fixed assets			
Net plant and equipment	$2,731	$2,880	+$149
Total assets	$3,373	$3,588	+$215
Liabilities and Owners' Equity			
Current liabilities			
Accounts payable	$ 312	$ 344	+$ 32
Notes payable	231	196	− 35
Total	$ 543	$ 540	−$ 3
Long-term debt	$ 531	$ 457	−$ 74
Owners' equity			
Common stock and paid-in surplus	$ 500	$ 550	+$ 50
Retained earnings	1,799	2,041	+ 242
Total	$2,299	$2,591	+$292
Total liabilities and owners' equity	$3,373	$3,588	+$215

Trans. 3.2
Hermetic, Inc., Balance Sheet (Supplemental)

Looking over the balance sheets for Prufrock, we see quite a few things changed during the year. For example, Prufrock increased its net fixed assets by $149 and its inventory by $29. Where did the money come from? To answer this and related questions, we need to first identify those changes that used up cash (uses) and those that brought cash in (sources).

A little common sense is useful here. A firm uses cash by either buying assets or making payments. So, loosely speaking, an increase in an asset account means the firm, on a net basis, bought some assets, a use of cash. If an asset account went down, then, on a net basis, the firm sold some assets. This would be a net source. Similarly, if a liability account goes down, then the firm has made a net payment, a use of cash.

Lecture Tip: See IM 3.1 for hints on helping students conceptualize an increase in the cash balance as a *use* of cash.

Given this reasoning, there is a simple, albeit mechanical, definition you may find useful. An increase in a left-hand side (asset) account or a decrease in a right-hand side (liability or equity) account is a use of cash. Likewise, a decrease in an asset account or an increase in a liability (or equity) account is a source of cash.

Looking again at Prufrock, we see inventory rose by $29. This is a net use since Prufrock effectively paid out $29 to increase inventories. Accounts payable rose by $32. This is a source of cash since Prufrock effectively has borrowed an additional $32 by the end of the year. Notes payable, on the other hand, went down by $35, so Prufrock effectively paid off $35 worth of short-term debt—a use of cash.

Based on our discussion, we can summarize the sources and uses from the balance sheet as follows:

Sources of cash:	
Increase in accounts payable	$ 32
Increase in common stock	50
Increase in retained earnings	242
Total sources	$324
Uses of cash:	
Increase in accounts receivable	$ 23
Increase in inventory	29
Decrease in notes payable	35
Decrease in long-term debt	74
Net fixed asset acquisitions	149
Total uses	$310
Net addition to cash	$ 14

The net addition to cash is just the difference between sources and uses, and our $14 result here agrees with the $14 change shown on the balance sheet.

This simple statement tells us much of what happened during the year, but it doesn't tell the whole story. For example, the increase in retained earnings is net income (a source of funds) less dividends (a use of funds). It would be more enlightening to have these reported separately so we could see the breakdown. Also, we have only considered net fixed asset acquisitions. Total or gross spending would be more interesting to know.

Trans. 3.3
Hermetic, Inc., Income Statement (Supplemental)

To further trace the flow of cash through the firm during the year, we need an income statement. For Prufrock, the results for the year are shown in Table 3.2.

Notice here that the $242 addition to retained earnings we calculated from the balance sheet is just the difference between the net income of $363 and the dividend of $121.

TABLE 3.2

PRUFROCK CORPORATION 1995 Income Statement ($ in millions)		
Sales		$2,311
Cost of goods sold		1,344
Depreciation		276
Earnings before interest and taxes		$ 691
Interest paid		141
Taxable income		$ 550
Taxes (34%)		187
Net income		$ 363
Addition to retained earnings	$242	
Dividends	121	

TABLE 3.3

PRUFROCK CORPORATION 1995 Statement of Cash Flows ($ in millions)	
Cash, beginning of year	$ 84
Operating activity	
Net income	363
Plus:	
Depreciation	276
Increase in accounts payable	32
Less:	
Increase in accounts receivable	− 23
Increase in inventory	− 29
Net cash from operating activity	$619
Investment activity	
Fixed asset acquisitions	−$425
Net cash from investment activity	−$425
Financing activity	
Decrease in notes payable	−$ 35
Decrease in long-term debt	− 74
Dividends paid	− 121
Increase in common stock	50
Net cash from financing activity	−$180
Net increase in cash	$ 14
Cash, end of year	$ 98

The Statement of Cash Flows

There is some flexibility in summarizing the sources and uses of cash in the form of a financial statement. However it is presented, the result is called the **statement of cash flows.**

statement of cash flows
A firm's financial statement that summarizes its sources and uses of cash over a specified period.

We present a particular format in Table 3.3 for this statement. The basic idea is to group all the changes into one of three categories: operating activities, financing activities, and investment activities. The exact form differs in detail from one preparer to the next.

Trans. 3.4
Statement of Cash Flows (Supplemental)

Trans. 3.5
Hermetic, Inc., Statement of Cash Flows (Supplemental)

Don't be surprised if you come across different arrangements. The types of information presented will be very similar; the exact order can differ. The key thing to remember in this case is we started out with $84 in cash and ended up with $98, for a net increase of $14. We're just trying to see what events led to this change.

Going back to Chapter 2, there is a slight conceptual problem here. Interest paid should really go under financing activities, but unfortunately that's not the way the accounting is handled. The reason, you may recall, is interest is deducted as an expense when net income is computed. Also, as shown, notice our net purchase of fixed assets was $149. Since we wrote off $276 worth (the depreciation), we must have actually spent a total of $149 + 276 = $425 on fixed assets.

Once we have this statement, it might seem appropriate to express the change in cash on a per-share basis, much as we did for net income. Ironically, despite the interest we might have in some measure of cash flow per share, standard accounting practice expressly prohibits reporting this information. The reason is accountants feel that cash flow (or some component of cash flow) is not an alternative to accounting income, so only earnings per share are to be reported.

Now that we have the various cash pieces in place, we can get a good idea of what happened during the year. Prufrock's major cash outlays were fixed asset acquisitions and cash dividends. They paid for these activities primarily with cash generated from operations.

Prufrock also retired some long-term debt and increased current assets. Finally, current liabilities were not greatly changed, and a relatively small amount of new equity was sold. Altogether, this short sketch captures Prufrock's major sources and uses of cash for the year.

CONCEPT QUESTIONS

3.1a What is a source of cash? Give three examples.

3.1b What is a use or application of cash? Give three examples.

3.2 STANDARDIZED FINANCIAL STATEMENTS

Self-Test Problem 3.2
Problem 17

The next thing we might want to do with Prufrock's financial statements is to compare them to those of other, similar companies. We would immediately have a problem, however. It's almost impossible to directly compare the financial statements for two companies because of differences in size.

Concept Q Answer 3.2a

For example, Ford and GM are obviously serious rivals in the auto market, but GM is much larger (in terms of assets), so it is difficult to compare them directly. For that matter, it's difficult to even compare financial statements from different points in time for the same company if the company's size has changed. The size problem is compounded if we try to compare GM and, say, Toyota. If Toyota's financial statements are denominated in yen, then we have a size *and* a currency difference.

Concept Q Answer 3.2b

common-size statement A standardized financial statement presenting all items in percentage terms. Balance sheets are shown as a percentage of assets and income statements as a percentage of sales.

To start making comparisons, one obvious thing we might try to do is to somehow standardize the financial statements. One very common and useful way of doing this is to work with percentages instead of total dollars. The resulting financial statements are called **common-size statements.** We consider these next.

Common-Size Balance Sheets

To construct a common-size balance sheet, we express each item as a percentage of total assets. Prufrock's 1994 and 1995 common-size balance sheets are shown in Table 3.4.

TABLE 3.4

PRUFROCK CORPORATION Common-Size Balance Sheets December 31, 1994 and 1995	1994	1995	Change
Assets			
Current assets			
Cash	2.5%	2.7%	+ .2%
Accounts receivable	4.9	5.2	+ .3
Inventory	11.7	11.8	+ .1
Total	19.1	19.7	+ .6
Fixed assets			
Net plant and equipment	80.9	80.3	− .6
Total assets	100.0%	100.0%	0
Liabilities and Owners' Equity			
Current liabilities			
Accounts payable	9.2%	9.6%	+ .4%
Notes payable	6.8	5.5	−1.3
Total	16.0	15.1	− .9
Long-term debt	15.7	12.7	−3.0
Owners' equity			
Common stock and paid-in surplus	14.8	15.3	+ .5
Retained earnings	53.3	56.9	+3.6
Total	68.1	72.2	+4.1
Total liabilities and owners' equity	100.0%	100.0%	0

Notice some of the totals don't check exactly because of rounding errors. Also notice the total change has to be zero since the beginning and ending numbers must add up to 100 percent.

In this form, financial statements are relatively easy to read and compare. For example, just looking at the two balance sheets for Prufrock, we see current assets were 19.7 percent of total assets in 1995, up from 19.1 percent in 1994. Current liabilities declined from 16.0 percent to 15.1 percent of total liabilities and equity over that same time. Similarly, total equity rose from 68.1 percent of total liabilities and equity to 72.2 percent.

Trans. 3.6
Hermetic, Inc., Common-Size Balance Sheet (Supplemental)

Overall, Prufrock's liquidity, as measured by current assets compared to current liabilities, increased over the year. Simultaneously, Prufrock's indebtedness diminished as a percentage of total assets. We might be tempted to conclude that the balance sheet has grown "stronger."

Common-Size Income Statements

A useful way of standardizing the income statement is to express each item as a percentage of total sales, as illustrated for Prufrock in Table 3.5.

Trans. 3.7
Hermetic, Inc., Common-Size Income Statement (Supplemental)

This income statement tells us what happens to each dollar in sales. For Prufrock, interest expense eats up $.061 out of every sales dollar and taxes take another $.081. When all is said and done, $.157 of each dollar flows through to the bottom line (net income), and that amount is split into $.105 retained in the business and $.052 paid out in dividends.

Lecture Tip: Further discussion of the use of standardized financial statements can be found in *Fundamentals of Corporate Finance* by Ross, Westerfield, and Jordan.

These percentages are very useful in comparisons. For example, a very relevant figure is the cost percentage. For Prufrock, $.582 of each $1.00 in

TABLE 3.5

PRUFROCK CORPORATION Common-Size Income Statement 1995		
Sales		100.0%
Cost of goods sold		58.2
Depreciation		11.9
Earnings before interest and taxes		29.9
Interest paid		6.1
Taxable income		23.8
Taxes (34%)		8.1
Net income		15.7%
Addition to retained earnings	10.5%	
Dividends	5.2	

sales goes to pay for goods sold. It would be interesting to compute the same percentage for Prufrock's main competitors to see how Prufrock stacks up in terms of cost control.

CONCEPT QUESTIONS

3.2a Why is it often necessary to standardize financial statements?

3.2b Describe how common-size balance sheets and income statements are formed.

3.3 RATIO ANALYSIS

financial ratios
Relationships determined from a firm's financial information and used for comparison purposes.

Another way of avoiding the problem of comparing companies of different sizes is to calculate and compare **financial ratios.** Such ratios are ways of comparing and investigating the relationships between different pieces of financial information. We cover some of the more common ratios next, but there are many others that we don't touch on.

One problem with ratios is that different people and different sources frequently don't compute them in exactly the same way, and this leads to much confusion. The specific definitions we use here may or may not be the same as ones you have seen or will see elsewhere. If you are ever using ratios as a tool for analysis, you should be careful to document how you calculate each one, and, if you are comparing your numbers to another source, be sure you know how their numbers are computed.

We will defer much of our discussion of how ratios are used and some problems that come up with using them to the next section. For now, for each of the ratios we discuss, several questions come to mind:

Trans. 3.8
Things to Consider: Financial Ratios (Supplemental)

1. How is it computed?
2. What is it intended to measure, and why might we be interested?
3. What is the unit of measurement?
4. What might a high or low value be telling us? How might such values be misleading?
5. How could this measure be improved?

Financial ratios are traditionally grouped into the following categories:

1. Short-term solvency or liquidity ratios.
2. Long-term solvency or financial leverage ratios.
3. Asset management or turnover ratios.
4. Profitability ratios.
5. Market value ratios.

Concept Q Answer 3.3a

Trans. 3.9 Categories of Financial Ratios (Supplemental)

We will consider each of these in turn. In calculating these numbers for Prufrock, we will use the ending balance sheet (1995) figures unless we explicitly say otherwise. Also notice the various ratios are color-keyed to indicate which numbers come from the income statement and which come from the balance sheet.

Lecture Tip: See IM 3.3 for tips on helping students conceptualize these categories of financial ratios.

Short-Term Solvency or Liquidity Measures

As the name suggests, short-term solvency ratios as a group are intended to provide information about a firm's liquidity, and these ratios are sometimes called *liquidity measures.* The primary concern is the firm's ability to pay its bills over the short run without undue stress. Consequently, these ratios focus on current assets and current liabilities.

Lecture Tip: See IM 3.3 for some useful tips for emphasizing the characteristics of liquidity.

For obvious reasons, liquidity ratios are particularly interesting to short-term creditors. Since financial managers are constantly working with banks and other short-term lenders, an understanding of these ratios is essential.

One advantage of looking at current assets and liabilities is their book values and market values are likely to be similar. Often (but not always), these assets and liabilities just don't live long enough for the two to get seriously out of step. On the other hand, like any type of near-cash, current assets and liabilities can and do change fairly rapidly, so today's amounts may not be a reliable guide to the future.

Current Ratio One of the best known and most widely used ratios is the *current ratio.* As you might guess, the current ratio is defined as:

$$\text{Current ratio} = \frac{\text{Current assets}}{\text{Current liabilities}} \qquad [3.1]$$

For Prufrock, the 1995 current ratio is:

$$\text{Current ratio} = \frac{\$708}{\$540} = 1.31 \text{ times}$$

Because current assets and liabilities are, in principle, converted to cash over the following 12 months, the current ratio is a measure of short-term liquidity. The unit of measurement is either dollars or times. So, we could say Prufrock has $1.31 in current assets for every $1 in current liabilities, or we could say Prufrock has its current liabilities covered 1.31 times over.

To a creditor, particularly a short-term creditor such as a supplier, the higher the current ratio, the better. To the firm, a high current ratio indicates liquidity, but it also may indicate an inefficient use of cash and other short-term assets. Absent some extraordinary circumstances, we would expect to see a current ratio of at least 1, because a current ratio of less than 1 would mean

Lecture Tip: See IM 3.3 for more on why a high current ratio is not always favorable for a company.

that net working capital (current assets less current liabilities) is negative. This would be unusual in a healthy firm, at least for most types of businesses.

The current ratio, like any ratio, is affected by various types of transactions. For example, suppose the firm borrows long term to raise money. The short-run effect would be an increase in cash from the issue proceeds and an increase in long-term debt. Current liabilities would not be affected, so the current ratio would rise.

Finally, note that an apparently low current ratio may not be a bad sign for a company with a large reserve of untapped borrowing power.

EXAMPLE 3.1 Current Events

Suppose a firm were to pay off some of its suppliers and short-term creditors. What would happen to the current ratio? Suppose a firm buys some inventory. What happens in this case? What happens if a firm sells some merchandise?

The first case is a trick question. What happens is the current ratio moves away from 1. If it is greater than 1 (the usual case), it will get bigger, but if it is less than 1, it will get smaller. To see this, suppose the firm has $4 in current assets and $2 in current liabilities for a current ratio of 2. If we use $1 in cash to reduce current liabilities, then the new current ratio is ($4 − $1)/($2 − $1) = 3. If we reverse this to $2 in current assets and $4 in current liabilities, the current ratio would fall to 1/3 from 1/2.

The second case is not quite as tricky. Nothing happens to the current ratio because cash goes down while inventory goes up—total current assets are unaffected.

In the third case, the current ratio would usually rise because inventory is normally shown at cost and the sale would normally be at something greater than cost (the difference is the markup). The increase in either cash or receivables is therefore greater than the decrease in inventory. This increases current assets, and the current ratio rises. • • •

The Quick (or Acid-Test) Ratio Inventory is often the least liquid current asset. It's also the one for which the book values are least reliable as measures of market value since the quality of the inventory isn't considered. Some of it may later turn out to be damaged, obsolete, or lost.

More to the point, relatively large inventories are often a sign of short-term trouble. The firm may have overestimated sales and overbought or overproduced as a result. In this case, the firm may have a substantial portion of its liquidity tied up in slow-moving inventory.

To further evaluate liquidity, the *quick* or *acid-test ratio* is computed just like the current ratio, except inventory is omitted:

$$\text{Quick ratio} = \frac{\text{Current assets} - \text{Inventory}}{\text{Current liabilities}} \qquad [3.2]$$

Notice that using cash to buy inventory does not affect the current ratio, but it reduces the quick ratio. Again, the idea is inventory is relatively illiquid compared to cash.

For Prufrock, this ratio in 1995 was:

$$\text{Quick ratio} = \frac{\$708 - 422}{\$540} = .53 \text{ times}$$

Lecture Tip: See IM 3.3 for more on why the interaction among ratios is important to consider at this point.

The quick ratio here tells a somewhat different story from the current ratio, because inventory accounts for more than half of Prufrock's current assets.

To exaggerate the point, if this inventory consisted of, say, unsold nuclear power plants, then this is a cause for concern.

The Cash Ratio A very short-term creditor might be interested in the *cash ratio:*

$$\text{Cash ratio} = \frac{\text{Cash}}{\text{Current liabilities}} \quad [3.3]$$

You can verify this works out to be .18 times for Prufrock.

Long-Term Solvency Measures

This group of ratios is intended to address the firm's long-run ability to meet its obligations or, more generally, its financial leverage. These are sometimes called *financial leverage ratios* or just *leverage ratios.* We consider three commonly used measures and some variations.

Lecture Tip: See IM 3.3 for hints on helping students understand the nature of the ratios in this category.

Total Debt Ratio The *total debt ratio* takes into account all debts of all maturities to all creditors. It can be defined in several ways, the easiest of which is:

$$\begin{aligned} \text{Total debt ratio} &= \frac{\text{Total assets} - \text{Total equity}}{\text{Total assets}} \\ &= \frac{\$3{,}588 - 2{,}591}{\$3{,}588} = .28 \text{ times} \end{aligned} \quad [3.4]$$

Concept Q Answer 3.3d

In this case, an analyst might say Prufrock uses 28 percent debt.[1] Whether this is high or low or whether it even makes any difference depends on whether or not capital structure matters, a subject we discuss in Part 7.

Prufrock has \$.28 in debt for every \$1 in assets. Therefore, there is \$.72 in equity (\$1 − \$.28) for every \$.28 in debt. With this in mind, we can define two useful variations on the total debt ratio, the *debt/equity ratio* and the *equity multiplier:*

$$\begin{aligned} \text{Debt/Equity ratio} &= \text{Total debt/Total equity} \\ &= \$.28/\$.72 = .39 \text{ times} \end{aligned} \quad [3.5]$$

$$\begin{aligned} \text{Equity multiplier} &= \text{Total assets/Total equity} \\ &= \$1/\$.72 = 1.39 \text{ times} \end{aligned} \quad [3.6]$$

The fact that the equity multiplier is 1 plus the debt/equity ratio is not a coincidence:

$$\begin{aligned} \text{Equity multiplier} &= \text{Total assets/Total equity} = \$1/\$.72 = 1.39 \\ &= (\text{Total equity} + \text{Total debt})/\text{Total equity} \\ &= 1 + \text{Debt/Equity ratio} = 1.39 \text{ times} \end{aligned}$$

The thing to notice here is that given any one of these three ratios, you can immediately calculate the other two, so they all say exactly the same thing.

[1] Total equity here includes preferred stock (discussed in Chapter 12 and elsewhere), if there is any. An equivalent numerator in this ratio would be (Current liabilities + Long-term debt).

Times Interest Earned Another common measure of long-term solvency is the *times interest earned* (TIE) *ratio.* Once again, there are several possible (and common) definitions, but we'll stick with the most traditional:

$$\text{Times interest earned ratio} = \frac{\text{EBIT}}{\text{Interest}} = \frac{\$691}{\$141} = 4.9 \text{ times} \qquad [3.7]$$

As the name suggests, this ratio measures how well a company has its interest obligations covered, and it is often called the interest coverage ratio. For Prufrock, the interest bill is covered 4.9 times over.

Cash Coverage A problem with the TIE ratio is that it is based on EBIT, which is not really a measure of cash available to pay interest. The reason is that depreciation, a noncash expense, has been deducted out. Since interest is most definitely a cash outflow (to creditors), one way to define the *cash coverage ratio* is:

Lecture Tip: It is useful to point out that the numerator of the cash coverage ratio, EBDIT, is often used as a measure of cash flow to meet obligations.

$$\text{Cash coverage ratio} = \frac{\text{EBIT + Depreciation}}{\text{Interest}} = \frac{\$691 + 276}{\$141} = \frac{\$967}{\$141} = 6.9 \text{ times} \qquad [3.8]$$

Lecture Tip: For more on coverage ratios, see IM 3.3.

The numerator here, EBIT plus depreciation, is often abbreviated EBDIT (earnings before depreciation, interest, and taxes). It is a basic measure of the firm's ability to generate cash from operations, and it is frequently used as a measure of cash flow available to meet financial obligations.

Asset Management or Turnover Measures

We next turn our attention to the efficiency with which Prufrock uses its assets. The measures in this section are sometimes called *asset utilization ratios.* The specific ratios we discuss can all be interpreted as measures of turnover. What they are intended to describe is how efficiently or intensively a firm uses its assets to generate sales. We first look at two important current assets, inventory and receivables.

Inventory Turnover and Days' Sales in Inventory During the year, Prufrock had a cost of goods sold of $1,344. Inventory at the end of the year was $422. With these numbers, *inventory turnover* can be calculated as:

Concept Q Answer 3.3b

$$\text{Inventory turnover} = \frac{\text{Cost of goods sold}}{\text{Inventory}} = \frac{\$1{,}344}{\$422} = 3.2 \text{ times} \qquad [3.9]$$

Lecture Tip: See IM 3.3 for some examples showing that inconsistent methods of ratio computation may exist across industries.

In a sense, we sold off or turned over the entire inventory 3.2 times. As long as we are not running out of stock and thereby forgoing sales, the higher this ratio is, the more efficiently we are managing inventory.

If we turned our inventory over 3.2 times during the year, then we can immediately figure out how long it took us to turn it over on average. The result is the average *days' sales in inventory:*

$$\text{Days' sales in inventory} = \frac{365 \text{ days}}{\text{Inventory turnover}} = \frac{365}{3.2} = 114 \text{ days} \qquad [3.10]$$

This tells us that, roughly speaking, inventory sits 114 days on average before it is sold. Alternatively, assuming we used the most recent inventory and cost figures, it will take about 114 days to work off our current inventory.

For example, we frequently hear things like "Majestic Motors has a 60 days' supply of cars. Thirty days is considered normal." This means that, at current daily sales, it would take 60 days to deplete the available inventory. We could also say we have 60 days of sales in inventory.

Receivables Turnover and Days' Sales in Receivables Our inventory measures give some indication of how fast we can sell product. We now look at how fast we collect on those sales. The *receivables turnover* is defined in the same way as inventory turnover:

$$\text{Receivables turnover} = \frac{\text{Sales}}{\text{Accounts receivable}} = \frac{\$2{,}311}{\$188} = 12.3 \text{ times} \qquad [3.11]$$

Concept Q Answer 3.3b

Loosely speaking, we collected our outstanding credit accounts and reloaned the money 12.3 times during the year.[2]

This ratio makes more sense if we convert it to days, so the *days' sales in receivables* is:

$$\text{Days' sales in receivables} = \frac{365 \text{ days}}{\text{Receivables turnover}} = \frac{365}{12.3} = 30 \text{ days} \qquad [3.12]$$

Therefore, on average, we collect on our credit sales in 30 days. For this reason, this ratio is very frequently called the *average collection period* (ACP).

Also note that if we are using the most recent figures, we could also say that we have 30 days' worth of sales currently uncollected. We will learn more about this subject when we study credit policy in a later chapter.

Lecture Tip: See IM 3.3 for useful tips on emphasizing the "red flag" aspects of ratio analysis in the context of the average collection period ratio.

EXAMPLE 3.2 Payables Turnover

Here is a variation on the receivables collection period. How long, on average, does it take for Prufrock Corporation to pay its bills? To answer, we need to calculate the accounts payable turnover rate using cost of goods sold. We will assume that Prufrock purchases everything on credit.

---

[2] Here we have implicitly assumed that all sales are credit sales. If they are not, then we would simply use total credit sales in these calculations, not total sales.

The cost of goods sold is $1,344, and accounts payable are $344. The turnover is therefore $1,344/$344 = 3.9 times. So payables turned over about every 365/3.9 = 94 days. On average, then, Prufrock takes 94 days to pay. As a potential creditor, we might take note of this fact. • • •

Total Asset Turnover Moving away from specific accounts like inventory or receivables, we can consider an important "big picture" ratio, the *total asset turnover* ratio. As the name suggests, total asset turnover is:

$$\text{Total asset turnover} = \frac{\text{Sales}}{\text{Total assets}} = \frac{\$2,311}{\$3,588} = .64 \text{ times} \quad [3.13]$$

In other words, for every dollar in assets, we generated $.64 in sales.

EXAMPLE 3.3 More Turnover

Suppose you find a particular company generates $.40 in sales for every dollar in total assets. How often does this company turn over its total assets?

Lecture Tip: See IM 3.3 for caveats concerning the use of turnover ratios.

The total asset turnover here is .40 times per year. It takes 1/.40 = 2.5 years to turn them over completely. • • •

Profitability Measures

Concept Q Answer 3.3c

The three measures we discuss in this section are probably the best known and most widely used of all financial ratios. In one form or another, they are intended to measure how efficiently the firm uses its assets and how efficiently the firm manages its operations. The focus in this group is on the bottom line, net income.

Profit Margin Companies pay a great deal of attention to their *profit margin:*

$$\text{Profit margin} = \frac{\text{Net income}}{\text{Sales}} = \frac{\$363}{\$2,311} = 15.7\% \quad [3.14]$$

This tells us Prufrock, in an accounting sense, generates a little less than 16 cents in profit for every dollar in sales.

All other things being equal, a relatively high profit margin is obviously desirable. This situation corresponds to low expense ratios relative to sales. However, we hasten to add that other things are often not equal.

For example, lowering our sales price will usually increase unit volume, but profit margins will normally shrink. Total profit (or more importantly, operating cash flow) may go up or down; so the fact that margins are smaller isn't necessarily bad. After all, isn't it possible that, as the saying goes, "Our prices are so low that we lose money on everything we sell, but we make it up in volume!"?[3]

[3] No, it's not.

Return on Assets *Return on assets* (ROA) is a measure of profit per dollar of assets. It can be defined several ways, but the most common is:

$$\text{Return on assets} = \frac{\text{Net income}}{\text{Total assets}} = \frac{\$363}{\$3{,}588} = 10.12\% \qquad [3.15]$$

Lecture Tip: ROA is often referred to as ROI (return on investment) since it relates net income to dollars invested in firm assets.

Return on Equity *Return on equity* (ROE) is a measure of how the stockholders fared during the year. Since benefiting shareholders is our goal, ROE is, in an accounting sense, the true bottom-line measure of performance. ROE is usually measured as:

$$\text{Return on equity} = \frac{\text{Net income}}{\text{Total equity}} = \frac{\$363}{\$2{,}591} = 14\% \qquad [3.16]$$

Lecture Tip: You may want to emphasize that ROE is a very important indication of management's achievement of the shareholder valuation objective. The Du Pont identity described in Section 3.4 decomposes ROE to allow more detailed analysis of managerial decisions.

For every dollar in equity, therefore, Prufrock generated 14 cents in profit, but, again, this is only correct in accounting terms.

Because ROA and ROE are such commonly cited numbers, we stress that it is important to remember they are accounting rates of return. For this reason, these measures should properly be called *return on book assets* and *return on book equity*. In addition, ROE is sometimes called *return on net worth*. Whatever it's called, it would be inappropriate to compare the result to, for example, an interest rate observed in the financial markets. In fact, as the accompanying *Principles in Action* box indicates, what constitutes a "good" ROE appears to have changed through time.

The fact that ROE exceeds ROA reflects Prufrock's use of financial leverage. We will examine the relationship between these two measures in more detail below.

Market Value Measures

Our final group of measures is based, in part, on information not necessarily contained in financial statements—the market price per share of the stock. Obviously, these measures can only be calculated directly for publicly traded companies.

We assume that Prufrock has 33 million shares outstanding and the stock sold for $88 per share at the end of the year. If we recall Prufrock's net income was $363 million, then its earnings per share (EPS) were:

$$\text{EPS} = \frac{\text{Net income}}{\text{Shares outstanding}} = \frac{\$363}{33} = \$11$$

Price/Earnings Ratio The first of our market value measures, the *price/earnings* (P/E) *ratio* (or multiple), is defined as:

$$\text{P/E ratio} = \frac{\text{Price per share}}{\text{Earnings per share}} = \frac{\$88}{\$11} = 8 \text{ times} \qquad [3.17]$$

In the vernacular, we would say Prufrock shares sell for 8 times earnings, or we might say Prufrock shares have or "carry" a P/E multiple of 8.

International Note: See IM 3.3 for a business press article concerning the differences in the P/E ratio in the United States and Japan.

Principles in Action

An Exclusive Club Lowers Its Admission Standards

Return on equity, or ROE, has long been used by investment analysts to assess the health of a firm. Historically, the ROE of the average S&P 500 company has hovered in the low teens for many years and an ROE in excess of 20 percent placed a company in the ranks of the elite. However, for the first quarter of 1995, the ROE for the *average* S&P 500 company was 20.1 percent, outstanding by historical standards. So are firms more profitable than ever in 1995, or is it suddenly easier for firms to achieve the once lofty standard of a 20 percent ROE?

ROE is viewed by many as an important intrinsic measure of profitability. It measures how much income a firm generates for each dollar stockholders have invested. From 1978 through the end of 1994, the market-wide average ROE ranged from a low of around 9 percent to a high of just under 20 percent, averaging about 14.5 percent over the period. The trend in ROE has been increasing since 1991, when it was about 10 percent.

The problem with corporate performance measures such as ROE is that the accounts used as inputs to the ratio can be subject to variation from year to year. For example, if a company writes off an obsolete asset, such as an outdated manufacturing facility, its book value of equity declines permanently. Since equity is in the denominator of the ROE ratio, ROE goes up. The S&P 500 companies took numerous such write-offs during the early 1990s, thereby increasing ROE. Book values are also subject to changes in accounting practices. Equity book values declined in 1992 when companies changed the way they account for health benefits for future retirees. Combined, these accounting changes increase ROE but do not necessarily signal greater profitability for a firm. In fact, such changes make it difficult to make clear comparisons of ROE from one year to the next.

All of this leads back to the basic question: Was the first quarter of 1995 a period of truly unusual profitability for S&P 500 firms? It is a certainty that not all of the recent increases in ROE are due solely to changing accounting practices. However, given the changes to equity book value that occurred during the early 1990s, the once lofty goal of a 20 percent ROE may at least temporarily be easier to achieve than it used to be.

Source: "The 20% Club No Longer Is Exclusive," *The Wall Street Journal,* May 4, 1995, p. C1.

Since the P/E ratio measures how much investors are willing to pay per dollar of current earnings, higher P/Es are often taken to mean the firm has significant prospects for future growth. Of course, if a firm had no or almost no earnings, its P/E would probably be quite large; so, as always, care is needed in interpreting this ratio.

Market-to-Book Ratio A second commonly quoted measure is the *market-to-book ratio:*

Video Note: The long-term relationship between market value and book value is discussed extensively in Video 2, "Valuing the Stock Market."

$$\text{Market-to-book ratio} = \frac{\text{Market value per share}}{\text{Book value per share}} = \frac{\$88}{(\$2{,}591/33)} = \frac{\$88}{\$78.5} = 1.12 \text{ times} \quad [3.18]$$

Notice that book value per share is total equity (not just common stock) divided by the number of shares outstanding.

Lecture Tip: See IM 3.3 for an exercise to help students gain a better understanding of the market-to-book ratio.

Since book value per share is an accounting number, it reflects historical costs. In a loose sense, the market-to-book ratio therefore compares the market value of the firm's investments to their cost. A value less than 1 could mean the firm has not been successful overall in creating value for its stockholders.

TABLE 3.6 Common financial ratios **Trans. 3.10**

I. Short-Term Solvency or Liquidity Ratios

$$\text{Current ratio} = \frac{\text{Current assets}}{\text{Current liabilities}}$$

$$\text{Quick ratio} = \frac{\text{Current assets} - \text{Inventory}}{\text{Current liabilities}}$$

$$\text{Cash ratio} = \frac{\text{Cash}}{\text{Current liabilities}}$$

II. Long-Term Solvency or Financial Leverage Ratios

$$\text{Total debt ratio} = \frac{\text{Total assets} - \text{Total equity}}{\text{Total assets}}$$

Debt/equity ratio = Total debt/Total equity

Equity multiplier = Total assets/Total equity

$$\text{Times interest earned ratio} = \frac{\text{EBIT}}{\text{Interest}}$$

$$\text{Cash coverage ratio} = \frac{\text{EBIT} + \text{Depreciation}}{\text{Interest}}$$

III. Asset Utilization or Turnover Ratios

$$\text{Inventory turnover} = \frac{\text{Cost of goods sold}}{\text{Inventory}}$$

$$\text{Days' sales in inventory} = \frac{\text{365 days}}{\text{Inventory turnover}}$$

$$\text{Receivables turnover} = \frac{\text{Sales}}{\text{Accounts receivable}}$$

$$\text{Days' sales in receivables} = \frac{\text{365 days}}{\text{Receivables turnover}}$$

$$\text{Total asset turnover} = \frac{\text{Sales}}{\text{Total assets}}$$

IV. Profitability Ratios

$$\text{Profit margin} = \frac{\text{Net income}}{\text{Sales}}$$

$$\text{Return on assets (ROA)} = \frac{\text{Net income}}{\text{Total assets}}$$

$$\text{Return on equity (ROE)} = \frac{\text{Net income}}{\text{Total equity}}$$

$$\text{ROE} = \frac{\text{Net income}}{\text{Sales}} \times \frac{\text{Sales}}{\text{Assets}} \times \frac{\text{Assets}}{\text{Equity}}$$

V. Market Value Ratios

$$\text{Price/earnings ratio} = \frac{\text{Price per share}}{\text{Earnings per share}}$$

$$\text{Market-to-book ratio} = \frac{\text{Market value per share}}{\text{Book value per share}}$$

This completes our definitions of some common ratios. We could tell you about more of them, but these are enough for now. We'll leave it here and go on to discuss some ways of using these ratios instead of just how to calculate them. Table 3.6 summarizes the ratios we've discussed.

Lecture Tip: Recent empirical evidence suggests that the market-to-book ratio may be a good measure of future performance.

CONCEPT QUESTIONS

3.3a What are the five groups of ratios? Give two or three examples of each kind.

3.3b Turnover ratios all have one of two figures as numerators. What are they? What do these ratios measure? How do you interpret the results?

3.3c Profitability ratios all have the same figure in the numerator. What is it? What do these ratios measure? How do you interpret the results?

3.3d Given the total debt ratio, what other two ratios can be computed? Explain how.

3.4 THE DU PONT IDENTITY

Self-Test Problem 3.4
Problems 11, 12, 16, 22, 23, 26

Trans. 3.11
The Du Pont Identity (Supplemental)

As we mentioned in discussing ROA and ROE, the difference between these two profitability measures is a reflection of the use of debt financing or financial leverage. We illustrate the relationship between these measures in this section by investigating a famous way of decomposing ROE into its component parts.

To begin, let's recall the definition of ROE:

$$\text{Return on equity} = \frac{\text{Net income}}{\text{Total equity}}$$

If we were so inclined, we could multiply this ratio by Assets/Assets without changing anything:

$$\text{Return on equity} = \frac{\text{Net income}}{\text{Total equity}} = \frac{\text{Net income}}{\text{Total equity}} \times \frac{\text{Assets}}{\text{Assets}}$$
$$= \frac{\text{Net income}}{\text{Assets}} \times \frac{\text{Assets}}{\text{Total equity}}$$

Notice we have expressed the ROE as the product of two other ratios—ROA and the equity multiplier:

$$\text{ROE} = \text{ROA} \times \text{Equity multiplier} = \text{ROA} \times (1 + \text{Debt/Equity ratio})$$

Looking back at Prufrock, for example, the debt/equity ratio was .39 and ROA was 10.12 percent. Our work here implies that Prufrock's ROE, as we previously calculated, is:

$$\text{ROE} = 10.12\% \times 1.39 = 14\%$$

We can further decompose ROE by multiplying the top and bottom by total sales:

$$\text{ROE} = \frac{\text{Sales}}{\text{Sales}} \times \frac{\text{Net income}}{\text{Assets}} \times \frac{\text{Assets}}{\text{Total equity}}$$

If we rearrange things a bit, ROE is:

Concept Q Answers 3.4a, 3.4b

$$\text{ROE} = \underbrace{\frac{\text{Net income}}{\text{Sales}} \times \frac{\text{Sales}}{\text{Assets}}}_{\text{Return on assets}} \times \frac{\text{Assets}}{\text{Total equity}} \qquad [3.19]$$
$$= \text{Profit margin} \times \text{Total asset turnover} \times \text{Equity multiplier}$$

What we have now done is to partition ROA into its two component parts, profit margin and total asset turnover. This last expression is called the **Du Pont identity**, after the Du Pont Corporation, which popularized its use.

Du Pont identity
Popular expression breaking ROE into three parts: operating efficiency, asset use efficiency, and financial leverage.

We can check this relationship for Prufrock by noting that the profit margin was 15.7 percent and the total asset turnover was .64. ROE should thus be:

$$\begin{aligned}\text{ROE} &= \text{Profit margin} \times \text{Total asset turnover} \times \text{Equity multiplier}\\ &= 15.7\% \times .64 \times 1.39\\ &= 14\%\end{aligned}$$

This 14 percent ROE is exactly what we had before.

The Du Pont identity tells us that ROE is affected by three things:

1. Operating efficiency (as measured by profit margin).
2. Asset use efficiency (as measured by total asset turnover).
3. Financial leverage (as measured by the equity multiplier).

Weakness in either operating or asset use efficiency (or both) will show up in a diminished return on assets, which will translate into a lower ROE.

Considering the Du Pont identity, it appears the ROE could be leveraged up by increasing the amount of debt in the firm. It turns out this will only happen if the firm's ROA exceeds the interest rate on the debt. More importantly, the use of debt financing has a number of other effects, and, as we discuss at some length in later chapters, the amount of leverage a firm uses is governed by its capital structure policy.

The decomposition of ROE we've discussed in this section is a convenient way of systematically approaching financial statement analysis. If ROE is unsatisfactory by some measure, then the Du Pont identity tells you where to start looking for the reasons.

Lecture Tip: Notice that the Du Pont identity reflects the three categories of decisions made by financial managers: investment (asset use efficiency); financing (financial leverage); and those involving the day-to-day finances of the firm (operating efficiency).

CONCEPT QUESTIONS

3.4a Return on assets (ROA) can be expressed as the product of two ratios. Which two?

3.4b Return on equity (ROE) can be expressed as the product of three ratios. Which three?

3.5 USING FINANCIAL STATEMENT INFORMATION

Our last task in this chapter is to discuss in more detail some practical aspects of financial statement analysis. In particular, we will look at reasons for doing financial statement analysis, how to go about getting benchmark information, and some of the problems that come up in the process.

Why Evaluate Financial Statements?

As we have discussed, the primary reason for looking at accounting information is we don't have, and can't reasonably expect to get, market value information. It is important to emphasize that, whenever we have market information, we would use it instead of accounting data. Also, if there is a conflict between accounting and market data, market data should be given precedence.

Lecture Tip: See IM 3.5 for some insight into how financial statement analysis has evolved in economic history.

Financial statement analysis is essentially an application of "management by exception." In many cases, such analysis will boil down to comparing ratios for one business with some kind of average or representative ratios. Those ratios that seem to differ the most from the averages are tagged for further study.

Internal Uses Financial statement information has a variety of uses within a firm. Among the most important of these is performance evaluation. For example, managers are frequently evaluated and compensated on the basis of accounting measures of performance such as profit margin and return on equity. Also, firms with multiple divisions frequently compare the performance of those divisions using financial statement information.

Concept Q Answer 3.5a

Another important internal use that we will explore in the next chapter is planning for the future. As we will see, historical financial statement information is very useful for generating projections about the future and for checking the realism of assumptions made in those projections.

Lecture Tip: You may wish to emphasize here the importance of comparability of ratios across firms (as well as across industries). Accountants have a significant amount of latitude within GAAP.

External Uses Financial statements are useful to parties outside the firm, including short-term and long-term creditors and potential investors. For ex-

Concept Q Answer 3.5a

ample, we would find such information quite useful in deciding whether or not to grant credit to a new customer.

We would also use this information to evaluate suppliers, and suppliers would use our statements before deciding to extend credit to us. Large customers use this information to decide if we are likely to be around in the future. Credit-rating agencies rely on financial statements in assessing a firm's overall creditworthiness. The common theme here is that financial statements are a prime source of information about a firm's financial health.

We would also find such information useful in evaluating our main competitors. We might be thinking of launching a new product. A prime concern would be whether the competition would jump in shortly thereafter. In this case, we would be interested in our competitors' financial strength to see if they can afford the necessary development.

Finally, we might be thinking of acquiring another firm. Financial statement information would be essential in identifying potential targets and deciding what to offer.

Choosing a Benchmark

Given that we want to evaluate a division or a firm based on its financial statements, a basic problem imediately comes up. How do we choose a benchmark or a standard of comparison? We describe some ways of getting started in this section.

Time-Trend Analysis One standard we could use is history. Suppose we found the current ratio for a particular firm is 2.4 based on the most recent financial statement information. Looking back over the last 10 years, we might find this ratio has declined fairly steadily over that period.

Concept Q Answer 3.5c

Based on this, we might wonder if the liquidity position of the firm has deteriorated. It could be, of course, the firm has made changes that allow it to more efficiently use its current assets, the nature of the firm's business has changed, or business practices have changed. If we investigate, these are all possible explanations. This is an example of what we mean by management by exception—a deteriorating time trend may not be bad, but it does merit investigation.

Trans. 3.12 Ratio Comparison Across Business Types (Supplemental)

Peer Group Analysis The second means of establishing a benchmark is to identify firms similar in the sense that they compete in the same markets, have similar assets, and operate in similar ways. In other words, we need to identify a *peer group.* There are obvious problems with doing this since no two companies are identical. Ultimately, the choice of which companies to use as a basis for comparison is subjective.

Standard Industry Classification (SIC) code
U.S. government code used to classify a firm by its type of business operations.

One common way of identifying potential peers is based on **Standard Industry Classification (SIC) codes.** These are four-digit codes established by the U.S. government for statistical reporting purposes. Firms with the same SIC code are frequently assumed to be similar.

Concept Q Answer 3.5b

The first digit in a SIC code establishes the general type of business. For example, firms engaged in finance, insurance, and real estate have SIC codes beginning with 6. Each additional digit narrows down the industry. So, companies with SIC codes beginning with 60 are mostly banks and banklike

TABLE 3.7
Selected two-digit SIC codes

Agriculture, Forestry, and Fishing	Transportation, Communication, Electric, Gas, and Sanitary Service
01 Agriculture production—crops	45 Transportation by air
08 Forestry	49 Electric, gas, and sanitary services
Mining	Retail Trade
10 Metal mining	54 Food stores
13 Oil and gas extraction	55 Auto dealers and gas stations
Construction	58 Eating and drinking places
15 Building construction	Finance, Insurance, and Real Estate
16 Construction other than building	60 Banking
Manufacturing	63 Insurance
28 Chemicals and allied products	65 Real estate
29 Petroleum refining	Services
35 Machinery, except electrical	78 Motion pictures
37 Transportation equipment	80 Health services
	82 Educational services

businesses, those beginning with 602 are mostly commercial banks, and SIC code 6025 is assigned to national banks that are members of the Federal Reserve system. Table 3.7 is a list of selected two-digit codes (the first two digits of the four-digit SIC codes) and the industries they represent.

SIC codes are far from perfect. For example, suppose you were examining financial statements for Wal-Mart, the largest retailer in the United States. The relevant SIC code is 5310, Department Stores. After a quick scan of the nearest financial database, you would find about 20 large, publicly owned corporations with this same SIC code, but you might not be too comfortable with some of them. Kmart would seem to be a reasonable peer, but Neiman-Marcus also carries the same industry code. Are Wal-Mart and Neiman-Marcus really comparable?

As this example illustrates, it is probably not appropriate to blindly use SIC-code-based averages. Instead, analysts often identify a set of primary competitors and then compute a set of averages based on just this group. Also, we may be more concerned with a group of the top firms in an industry, not the average firm. Such a group is called an *aspirant group,* because we aspire to be like them. In this case, a financial statement analysis reveals how far we have to go.

With these caveats about SIC codes in mind, we can now take a look at a specific industry. Suppose we are in the retail furniture business. Table 3.8 contains some condensed common-size financial statements for this industry from Robert Morris Associates, one of many sources of such information. Table 3.9 contains selected ratios from the same source.

There is a large amount of information here. On the right in Table 3.8 we have current information reported for different groups based on sales. Within each sales group, common-size information is reported. For example, firms with sales in the \$10 million to \$25 million range have Cash & Equivalents equal to 7.7 percent of total assets. There are 50 companies in this group out of 592 in all.

On the left we have three years' worth of summary historical information for the entire group. For example, Operating Expenses fell from 38.1 percent of sales to 37.3 percent over that time.

Table 3.9 contains some selected ratios, again reported by sales groups on the right and time period on the left. To see how we might use this infor-

TABLE 3.8 Selected financial statement information

RETAILERS - FURNITURE. SIC# 5712

Comparative Historical Data				Current Data Sorted By Sales					
		8	**# Postretirement Benefits**	1	3	1	1	1	1
			Type of Statement						
59	67	65	Unqualified	4	4	6	3	16	32
169	154	130	Reviewed	10	41	23	37	13	6
272	241	251	Compiled	63	120	31	27	8	2
6	15	27	Tax Returns	12	10	2		3	
113	98	119	Other	25	42	16	17	10	9
4/1/90-3/31/91	4/1/91-3/31/92	4/1/92-3/31/93		257(4/1-9/30/92)			335(10/1/92-3/31/93)		
TOTAL	TOTAL	TOTAL		0-1MM	1-3MM	3-5MM	5-10MM	10-25MM	25MM & OVER
619	575	592	**NUMBER OF STATEMENTS**	114	217	78	84	50	49
%	%	%	**ASSETS**	%	%	%	%	%	%
6.6	6.4	6.7	Cash & Equivalents	7.2	6.3	6.4	6.0	7.7	8.1
19.4	17.7	18.8	Trade Receivables - (net)	19.2	16.9	20.4	18.5	18.8	24.2
51.8	51.6	50.5	Inventory	48.8	53.9	50.7	53.5	50.8	34.1
1.5	1.3	1.1	All Other Current	.9	1.1	1.4	1.2	.9	1.2
79.3	77.0	77.1	Total Current	76.0	78.2	78.9	79.2	78.2	67.6
14.8	16.8	16.4	Fixed Assets (net)	16.2	16.3	15.2	14.9	15.6	22.3
1.0	.9	1.1	Intangibles (net)	2.2	.8	.7	.6	.6	1.6
4.9	5.3	5.4	All Other Non-Current	5.6	4.7	5.2	5.2	5.6	8.5
100.0	100.0	100.0	Total	100.0	100.0	100.0	100.0	100.0	100.0
			LIABILITIES						
12.4	12.4	10.1	Notes Payable-Short Term	9.8	9.2	9.7	12.2	11.9	9.8
3.8	3.6	3.1	Cur. Mat.-L/T/D	4.0	3.2	2.6	2.7	2.4	2.3
17.9	17.7	18.8	Trade Payables	18.6	17.6	18.6	22.6	21.5	15.6
.6	.5	.4	Income Taxes Payable	.3	.3	.4	.7	.5	.2
12.0	12.1	13.2	All Other Current	10.8	13.5	14.2	13.1	15.0	14.1
46.8	46.3	45.5	Total Current	43.5	43.8	45.7	51.2	51.4	41.9
14.1	15.0	14.3	Long Term Debt	19.8	14.0	14.4	9.3	7.1	18.4
.2	.2	.2	Deferred Taxes	.1	.2	.3	.1	.2	.4
3.5	2.8	3.2	All Other Non-Current	3.1	3.1	3.2	4.1	3.9	2.2
35.4	35.7	36.8	Net Worth	33.6	38.9	36.4	35.2	37.5	37.0
100.0	100.0	100.0	Total Liabilities & Net Worth	100.0	100.0	100.0	100.0	100.0	100.0
			INCOME DATA						
100.0	100.0	100.0	Net Sales	100.0	100.0	100.0	100.0	100.0	100.0
40.2	39.9	39.6	Gross Profit	41.7	39.3	37.2	39.0	40.6	39.6
38.1	37.8	37.3	Operating Expenses	39.8	36.9	34.4	37.1	38.0	37.0
2.1	2.2	2.3	Operating Profit	1.9	2.4	2.7	1.8	2.6	2.6
.7	.7	.5	All Other Expenses (net)	.8	.4	.5	.3	.6	−.1
1.4	1.5	1.9	Profit Before Taxes	1.1	2.0	2.2	1.5	2.1	2.7
4,402,965M	5,608,844M	6,129,816M	Net Sales ($)	70,883M	395,823M	295,845M	576,217M	829,752M	3,961,296M
2,444,149M	3,213,247M	3,341,580M	Total Assets ($)	39,739M	199,100M	132,270M	227,903M	353,467M	2,389,101M

M = $thousand MM = $million

See Pages 1 through 15 for Explanation of Ratios and Data

Lecture Tip: Students are often unsure about the degree of precision necessary when computing financial ratios. Professionals rarely find it useful to carry computations past one or two decimal places.

mation, suppose our firm has a current ratio of 2. Based on these ratios, is this value unusual?

Looking at the current ratio for the overall group (third column from the left), three numbers are reported. The one in the middle, 1.8, is the median, meaning that half of the 592 firms had current ratios that were lower and half had bigger current ratios. The other two numbers are the upper and lower quartiles. So, 25 percent of the firms had a current ratio larger than 2.8 and 25 percent had a current ratio smaller than 1.3. Our value of 2 falls comfortably within these bounds, so it doesn't appear too unusual. This comparison illustrates how knowledge of the range of ratios is important in addition to knowledge of the average. Notice how stable the current ratio has been for the last three years.

EXAMPLE 3.4 More Ratios

Take a look at the numbers reported for Sales/Receivables and EBIT/Interest in Table 3.9. What are the overall median values? What are these ratios?

Lecture Tip: See IM for a brief case involving Compaq Computer that can be handed out with this chapter.

If you look back at our discussion, these are the receivables turnover and the times interest earned (TIE) ratios. The median value for receivables turnover for the entire group is 24.6 times. So, the days in receivables is 365/24.6 = 15, which is the bold-faced number reported. The median for the TIE is 2.3 times. The number in parentheses indicates the calculation is meaningful for, and therefore based on, only 531 of the 592 companies. In this case, the reason is probably that only 531 companies paid any significant amount of interest. • • •

TABLE 3.9 Selected ratios

RETAILERS - FURNITURE. SIC# 5712

Comparative Historical Data				Current Data Sorted By Sales					
		8	**# Postretirement Benefits**	1	3	1	1	1	1
			Type of Statement						
59	67	65	Unqualified	4	4	6	3	16	32
169	154	130	Reviewed	10	41	23	37	13	6
272	241	251	Compiled	63	120	31	27	8	2
6	15	27	Tax Returns	12	10	2		3	
113	98	119	Other	25	42	16	17	10	9
4/1/90-3/31/91	4/1/91-3/31/92	4/1/92-3/31/93		257(4/1-9/30/92)			335(10/1/92-3/31/93)		
TOTAL	TOTAL	TOTAL		0-1MM	1-3MM	3-5MM	5-10MM	10-25MM	25MM & OVER
619	575	592	**NUMBER OF STATEMENTS**	114	217	78	84	50	49
			RATIOS						
2.7	2.6	2.8		3.6	3.0	2.8	2.4	2.2	2.6
1.8	1.7	1.8	Current	1.9	1.9	1.8	1.5	1.5	1.7
1.3	1.2	1.3		1.2	1.4	1.3	1.2	1.2	1.2
1.0	.9	1.0		1.3	1.0	1.1	.8	.8	1.6
(617) .5	(574) .4	(589) .5	Quick	(113) .5	(215) .5	.5	.4	.4	.8
.2	.2	.2		.2	.2	.2	.1	.2	.4
3 129.5	2 151.6	3 131.1		4 83.0	3 139.8	3 113.5	2 242.1	2 228.5	2 148.0
16 22.2	14 25.4	15 24.6	Sales/Receivables	15 23.6	14 26.3	17 22.0	12 31.7	9 42.1	21 17.2
42 8.6	40 9.1	42 8.6		54 6.8	35 10.3	40 9.2	41 8.8	41 8.8	118 3.1
89 4.1	81 4.5	83 4.4		85 4.3	94 3.9	69 5.3	69 5.3	76 4.8	69 5.3
130 2.8	126 2.9	122 3.0	Cost of Sales/Inventory	146 2.5	140 2.6	111 3.3	122 3.0	101 3.6	99 3.7
174 2.1	192 1.9	183 2.0		203 1.8	192 1.9	174 2.1	159 2.3	146 2.5	135 2.7
22 16.6	21 17.3	22 16.6		19 19.0	22 16.5	21 17.6	22 16.3	25 14.6	29 12.4
38 9.7	37 9.9	38 9.7	Cost of Sales/Payables	39 9.4	37 9.9	33 10.9	40 9.1	38 9.7	43 8.4
59 6.2	55 6.6	59 6.2		79 4.6	58 6.3	54 6.7	57 6.4	59 6.2	58 6.3
4.3	4.3	4.0		3.1	3.8	4.1	5.2	5.5	3.6
8.3	8.5	7.2	Sales/Working Capital	6.0	6.4	7.2	12.5	18.7	7.2
20.0	24.0	22.4		22.4	14.5	18.9	32.3	29.1	30.0
4.9	3.6	5.3		4.3	5.3	5.0	5.3	9.5	8.5
(551) 1.9	(537) 1.8	(531) 2.3	EBIT/Interest	(97) 1.8	(194) 2.4	(69) 2.6	(79) 2.2	(47) 3.0	(45) 2.6
.8	.8	1.2		.4	1.2	1.2	1.2	1.3	1.6
4.1	3.6	4.9		3.6	4.1	4.8	4.4	7.7	7.6
(273) 1.5	(230) 1.5	(218) 2.0	Net Profit + Depr., Dep., Amort./Cur. Mat. L/T/D	(20) 1.0	(87) 1.6	(32) 2.9	(34) 2.5	(25) 3.1	(20) 3.2
.2	.2	.6		.5	.3	.7	.8	.9	1.3
.1	.2	.1		.1	.1	.1	.2	.2	.3
.3	.4	.4	Fixed/Worth	.3	.3	.3	.4	.4	.6
.9	1.1	1.0		1.7	.9	1.0	.8	.8	1.1
.8	.8	.8		.8	.7	1.1	1.0	.7	1.0
1.9	1.9	1.7	Debt/Worth	1.8	1.4	1.9	1.9	2.3	1.7
4.7	4.3	4.0		6.7	3.9	3.7	4.3	4.1	3.1
24.9	23.7	26.6		29.2	20.6	29.4	24.3	34.6	32.6
(567) 9.3	(534) 8.1	(546) 11.2	% Profit Before Taxes/Tangible Net Worth	(96) 6.4	(198) 10.4	(74) 14.2	(81) 10.6	(49) 14.9	(48) 19.3
.2	.3	2.4		−1.4	2.0	3.9	3.1	3.8	7.4
9.0	8.2	8.9		9.2	8.1	10.5	7.8	10.5	11.8
3.2	2.8	3.9	% Profit Before Taxes/Total Assets	2.6	4.0	4.0	3.8	4.4	6.2
−.7	−.6	.5		−2.6	.5	1.0	.6	1.3	2.6
53.6	45.2	51.1		81.9	58.2	54.8	52.1	43.6	17.9
26.5	22.3	24.1	Sales/Net Fixed Assets	24.3	25.3	29.6	24.1	25.2	9.7
12.1	10.0	10.4		8.6	11.6	10.1	13.7	14.9	5.3
3.3	3.3	3.4		3.0	3.2	3.5	3.7	4.4	3.2
2.5	2.5	2.5	Sales/Total Assets	2.1	2.4	2.7	2.9	3.1	2.1
1.7	1.7	1.7		1.3	1.7	2.0	2.0	1.8	1.2
.6	.6	.6		.6	.5	.5	.5	.6	1.0
(553) .9	(524) 1.0	(538) .9	% Depr., Dep., Amort./Sales	(87) 1.2	(204) .9	(72) .8	(77) .8	.8	(48) 1.4
1.5	1.5	1.4		1.9	1.4	1.2	1.1	1.3	2.0
2.7	2.7	2.6		4.5	3.1	1.7	1.9	1.4	.9
(306) 4.8	(291) 4.5	(287) 4.4	% Officers', Directors', Owners' Comp/Sales	(57) 7.0	(122) 4.7	(36) 3.5	(41) 2.8	(21) 2.0	(10) 2.1
7.5	6.8	7.3		11.0	7.3	7.5	5.3	3.5	6.5
4,402,965M	5,608,844M	6,129,816M	Net Sales ($)	70,883M	395,823M	295,845M	576,217M	829,752M	3,961,296M
2,444,149M	3,213,247M	3,341,580M	Total Assets ($)	39,739M	199,100M	132,270M	227,903M	353,467M	2,389,101M

M = $thousand MM = $million

See Pages 1 through 15 for Explanation of Ratios and Data

Problems with Financial Statement Analysis

We close out our chapter on financial statements by discussing some additional problems that can arise in using financial statements. In one way or another, the basic problem with financial statement analysis is there is no underlying theory to help us identify which quantities to look at and to guide us in establishing benchmarks.

As we discuss in other chapters, there are many cases where financial theory and economic logic provide guidance in making judgments about

Concept Q Answer 3.5d

value and risk. Very little such help exists with financial statements. This is why we can't say which ratios matter the most and what a high or low value might be.

One particularly severe problem is that many firms are conglomerates, owning more-or-less unrelated lines of business. The consolidated financial statements for such firms don't really fit any neat industry category. Going back to department stores, for example, Sears has a SIC code of 6710 (Holding Offices) because of its diverse financial and retailing operations. More generally, the kind of peer group analysis we have been describing is going to work best when the firms are strictly in the same line of business, the industry is competitive, and there is only one way of operating.

Another problem that is becoming increasingly common is major competitors and natural peer group members in an industry may be scattered around the globe. The automobile industry is an obvious example. The problem here is that financial statements from outside the United States do not necessarily conform at all to GAAP. The existence of different standards and procedures makes it very difficult to compare financial statements across national borders.

Trans. 3.13
A Brief Case History of Hermetic, Inc. (Supplemental)

Even companies that are clearly in the same line of business may not be comparable. For example, electric utilities engaged primarily in power generation are all classified in the same group (SIC 4911). This group is often thought to be relatively homogeneous. However, utilities generally operate as regulated monopolies, so they don't compete with each other. Many have stockholders, and many are organized as cooperatives with no stockholders. There are several different ways of generating power, ranging from hydroelectric to nuclear, so their operating activities can differ quite a bit. Finally, profitability is strongly affected by regulatory environment, so utilities in different locations can be very similar but show very different profits.

★ **Ethics Note:** IM 3.5 discusses an additional problem faced by the analyst—reporting results unfavorable to the firm being analyzed.

Lecture Tip: See IM 3.5 for a "Spot the Potential Problems" example involving Hermetic, Inc.

Several other general problems frequently crop up. First, different firms use different accounting procedures for inventory, for example. This makes it difficult to compare statements. Second, different firms end their fiscal years at different times. For firms in seasonal businesses (such as a retailer with a large Christmas season), this can lead to difficulties in comparing balance sheets because of fluctuations in accounts during the year. Finally, for any particular firm, unusual or transient events, such as a one-time profit from an asset sale, may affect financial performance. In comparing firms, such events can give misleading signals.

CONCEPT QUESTIONS

3.5a What are some uses for financial statement analysis?

3.5b What are SIC codes and how might they be useful?

3.5c Why do we say that financial statement analysis is "management by exception"?

3.5d What are some of the problems that can come up with financial statement analysis?

3.6 SUMMARY AND CONCLUSIONS

This chapter has discussed aspects of financial statement analysis:

1. Sources and uses of cash. We discussed how to identify the ways businesses obtain and use cash, and we described how to trace the

flow of cash through the business over the course of the year. We briefly looked at the statement of cash flows.

2. Standardized financial statements. We explained that differences in size make it difficult to compare financial statements, and we discussed how to form common-size statements to make comparisons easier.
3. Ratio analysis. Evaluating ratios of accounting numbers is another way of comparing financial statement information. We therefore defined and discussed a number of the most commonly reported and used financial ratios. We also discussed the famous Du Pont identity as a way of analyzing financial performance.
4. Using financial statements. We described how to establish benchmarks for comparison purposes and discussed some of the types of information that are available. We then examined some of the potential problems that can arise.

After you study this chapter, we hope that you will have some perspective on the uses and abuses of financial statements. You should also find that your vocabulary of business and financial terms has grown substantially.

Chapter Review Problems and Self-Test

3.1 Sources and Uses of Cash Consider the following balance sheets for the Wildhack Corporation. Calculate the changes in the various accounts and, where applicable, identify the change as a source or use of cash. What were the major sources and uses of cash? Did the company become more or less liquid during the year? What happened to cash during the year?

WILDHACK CORPORATION
Balance Sheets as of December 31, 1994 and 1995
($ in millions)

	1994	1995
Assets		
Current assets		
Cash	$ 120	$ 88
Accounts receivable	224	192
Inventory	424	368
Total	$ 768	$ 648
Fixed assets		
Net plant and equipment	$5,228	$5,354
Total assets	$5,996	$6,002
Liabilities and Owners' Equity		
Current liabilities		
Accounts payable	$ 124	$ 144
Notes payable	1,412	1,039
Total	$1,536	$1,183
Long-term debt	$1,804	$2,077
Owners' equity		
Common stock and paid-in surplus	300	300
Retained earnings	2,356	2,442
Total	$2,656	$2,742
Total liabilities and owners' equity	$5,996	$6,002

3.2 Common-Size Statements Below is the most recent income statement for Wildhack. Prepare a common-size income statement based on this information. How do you interpret the standardized net income? What percentage of sales goes to cost of goods sold?

WILDHACK CORPORATION
1995 Income Statement
($ in millions)

Sales		$3,756
Cost of goods sold		2,453
Depreciation		490
Earnings before interest and taxes		$ 813
Interest paid		613
Taxable income		$ 200
Taxes (34%)		68
Net income		$ 132
Addition to retained earnings	$86	
Dividends	46	

3.3 Financial Ratios Based on the balance sheets and income statement in the previous two problems, calculate the following ratios for 1995:

Current ratio ________
Quick ratio ________
Cash ratio ________
Inventory turnover ________
Receivables turnover ________
Days' sales in inventory ________
Days' sales in receivables ________
Total debt ratio ________
Times interest earned ratio ________
Cash coverage ratio ________

3.4 ROE and the Du Pont Identity Calculate the 1995 ROE for the Wildhack Corporation and then break down your answer into its component parts using the Du Pont identity.

Answers to Self-Test Problems

3.1 We've filled in the answers below. Remember, increases in assets and decreases in liabilities indicate that we spent some cash. Decreases in assets and increases in liabilities are ways of getting cash.

WILDHACK CORPORATION
Balance Sheets as of December 31, 1994 and 1995
($ in millions)

	1994	1995	Change	Source/Use of Cash
Assets				
Current assets				
Cash	$ 120	$ 88	−$ 32	
Accounts receivable	224	192	− 32	Source
Inventory	424	368	− 56	Source
Total	$ 768	$ 648	−$120	
Fixed assets				
Net plant and equipment	$5,228	$5,354	+$126	Use
Total assets	$5,996	$6,002	+$ 6	

WILDHACK CORPORATION *(Continued)*

	1994	1995	Change	Source/Use of Cash
Liabilities and Owners' Equity				
Current liabilities				
Accounts payable	$ 124	$ 144	+$ 20	Source
Notes payable	1,412	1,039	− 373	Use
Total	$1,536	$1,183	−$353	
Long-term debt	$1,804	$2,077	+$273	Source
Owners' equity				
Common stock and paid-in surplus	300	300	+ 0	—
Retained earnings	2,356	2,442	+ 86	Source
Total	$2,656	$2,742	+$ 86	
Total liabilities and owners' equity	$5,996	$6,002	+$ 6	

Wildhack used its cash primarily to purchase fixed assets and to pay off short-term debt. The major sources of cash to do this were additional long-term borrowing, and, to a larger extent, reductions in current assets and additions to retained earnings.

The current ratio went from $768/$1,536 = .5 to $648/$1,183 = .55; so the firm's liquidity appears to have improved somewhat, primarily because of the large reduction in short-term debt. Overall, however, the amount of cash on hand declined by $32.

3.2 We've calculated the common-size income statement below. Remember that we simply divide each item by total sales.

WILDHACK CORPORATION
1995 Common-Size Income Statement

Sales		100.0%
Cost of goods sold		65.3
Depreciation		13.0
Earnings before interest and taxes		21.6
Interest paid		16.3
Taxable income		5.3
Taxes (34%)		1.8
Net income		3.5%
Addition to retained earnings	2.3%	
Dividends	1.2	

Net income is 3.5 percent of sales. Since this is the percentage of each sales dollar that makes its way to the bottom line, the standardized net income is the firm's profit margin. Cost of goods sold is 65.3 percent of sales.

3.3 We've calculated the ratios below based on the ending figures. If you don't remember a definition, refer back to Table 3.6.

Current ratio	$648/$1,183	= .55 times
Quick ratio	$280/$1,183	= .24 times
Cash ratio	$88/$1,183	= .07 times
Inventory turnover	$2,453/$368	= 6.7 times
Receivables turnover	$3,756/$192	= 19.6 times
Days' sales in inventory	365/6.7	= 54.5 days
Days' sales in receivables	365/19.6	= 18.6 days

Total debt ratio	\$3,260/\$6,002	= 54.3%
Times interest earned ratio	\$813/\$613	= 1.33 times
Cash coverage ratio	\$1,303/\$613	= 2.13 times

3.4 The return on equity is the ratio of net income to total equity. For Wildhack, this is \$132/\$2,742 = 4.8%, which is not outstanding.

Given the Du Pont identity, ROE can be written as:

$$\begin{aligned} \text{ROE} &= \text{Profit margin} \times \text{Total asset turnover} \times \text{Equity multiplier} \\ &= \$132/\$3{,}756 \times \$3{,}756/\$6{,}002 \times \$6{,}002/\$2{,}742 \\ &= 3.5\% \times .626 \times 2.19 \\ &= 4.8\% \end{aligned}$$

Notice that return on assets, ROA, is 3.5% × .626 = 2.2%.

Questions and Problems

Basic
(Questions 1–19)

1. **Changes in the Current Ratio** What effect would the following actions have on a firm's current ratio? Assume that net working capital is positive.
   a. Inventory is purchased.
   b. A supplier is paid.
   c. A short-term bank loan is repaid.
   d. A long-term debt is paid off early.
   e. A customer pays off a credit account.
   f. Inventory is sold at cost.
   g. Inventory is sold for a profit.

2. **Liquidity and Ratios** In recent years, Dixie Co. has greatly increased its current ratio. At the same time, the quick ratio has fallen. What has happened? Has the liquidity of the company improved?

3. **Current Ratio** Explain what it means for a firm to have a current ratio equal to 0.50. Would the firm be better off if the current ratio was 1.50? What if it was 15.0? Explain your answers.

4. **Interpreting Financial Ratios** Explain the kind of information the following financial ratios provide about a firm:
   a. Quick ratio
   b. Cash ratio
   c. Total asset turnover
   d. Equity multiplier
   e. Times interest earned ratio
   f. Profit margin
   g. Return on assets
   h. Return on equity
   i. Price/earnings ratio

Current ratio = 1.28 times
Quick ratio = 0.94 times

5. **Calculating Liquidity Ratios** A firm has net working capital of \$500, current liabilities of \$1,800, and inventory of \$600. What is the current ratio? What is the quick ratio?

Trans. 3.14
Net income = \$550,000
ROA = 6.11%
ROE = 9.17%

6. **Calculating Profitability Ratios** A firm has sales of \$5 million, total assets of \$9 million, and total debt of \$3 million. If the profit margin is 11 percent, what is net income? What is ROA? What is ROE?

Receivables turnover = 6.95 times

7. **Calculating the Average Collection Period** Fred's Print Shop has a current accounts receivable balance of \$13,565. Credit sales for the

year just ended were $94,300. What is the receivables turnover? The days' sales in receivables? How long did it take on average for credit customers to pay off their accounts during the past year?

Days' sales in receivables = 52.51 days
Average collection period = 52.51 days

8. **Calculating Inventory Turnover** Mary's Print Shop has a current inventory of $46,325, and cost of goods sold for the year just ended was $147,750. What is the inventory turnover? The days' sales in inventory? How long on average did a unit of inventory sit on the shelf before it was sold?

Inventory turnover = 3.19 times
Days' sales in inventory = 114.44 days
Average inventory period = 114.44 days

9. **Calculating Leverage Ratios** A firm has a total debt ratio of 0.60. What is its debt/equity ratio? What is its equity multiplier?

Debt/equity ratio = 1.50
Equity multiplier = 2.50

10. **Calculating Market Value Ratios** MegaWidgets Co. had additions to retained earnings for the year just ended of $170,000. The firm paid out $80,000 in cash dividends and it has total equity of $4 million. If MegaWidgets currently has 120,000 shares of common stock outstanding, what is earnings per share? Dividends per share? Book value per share? If the stock currently sells for $50 per share, what is the market-to-book ratio? The price/earnings ratio?

EPS = $2.08
DPS = $0.67
BVPS = $33.33
Market-to-book ratio = 1.50 times
P/E ratio = 24.0 times

11. **Du Pont Identity** If a firm has an equity multiplier of 2.0, total asset turnover of 1.25, and a profit margin of 8 percent, what is its ROE?

ROE = 20%

12. **Du Pont Identity** Smith Manufacturing has a profit margin of 9 percent, total asset turnover of 1.5, and ROE of 20.25 percent. What is this firm's debt/equity ratio?

Debt/equity ratio = 0.50 times

13. **Sources and Uses of Cash** Based only on the following information for SemiPhonics Corp., did cash go up or down? By how much? Classify each event as a source or use of cash.

Cash decreased by $825
Trans.3.15

Decrease in inventory	$350
Decrease in accounts payable	175
Decrease in notes payable	400
Increase in accounts receivable	600

14. **Calculating Average Payables Period** For 1995, DRK, Inc., had cost of goods sold of $8,325. At the end of the year, the accounts payable balance was $1,100. How long on average did it take the company to pay off its suppliers last year? What might a large value for this ratio imply?

Average payables period = 48.23 days

15. **Cash Flow and Capital Spending** For the year just ended, AWOI Co. shows an increase in its net fixed assets account of $370. The company took $130 in depreciation expense for the year. How much did AWOI spend on new fixed assets? Is this a source or use of cash?

New fixed assets = $500

16. **Equity Multiplier and Return on Equity** Folker Fried Chicken Company has a debt/equity ratio of 1.10. Return on assets is 6.5 percent, and total equity is $210,000. What is the equity multiplier? Return on equity? Net income?

Equity multiplier = 2.10 times
ROE = 13.65%
Net income = $28.665

Montana Dental Floss Corporation reports the following balance sheet information for 1994 and 1995. Use this information to work Problems 17 through 21.

MONTANA DENTAL FLOSS CORPORATION
Balance Sheets as of December 31, 1994 and 1995

	1994	1995
Assets		
Current assets		
Cash	$ 9,320	$ 10,050
Accounts receivable	29,720	31,525
Inventory	58,500	66,710
Total	$ 97,540	$108,285
Fixed assets		
Net plant and equipment	248,060	269,460
Total assets	$345,600	$377,745
Liabilities and Owners' Equity		
Current liabilities		
Accounts payable	$ 56,250	$ 51,900
Notes payable	26,200	30,000
Total	$ 82,450	$ 81,900
Long-term debt	$ 50,000	$ 35,000
Owners' equity		
Common stock and paid-in surplus	$ 62,600	$ 62,600
Accumulated retained earnings	150,550	198,245
Total	$213,150	$260,845
Total liabilities and owners' equity	$345,600	$377,745

17. **Preparing Standardized Financial Statements** Prepare the 1994 and 1995 common-size balance sheets for Montana Dental Floss.

18. **Sources and Uses of Cash** For each account on this company's balance sheet, show the change in the account during 1995 and note whether this change was a source or use of cash. Do your numbers add up and make sense? Explain your answer for total assets compared to your answer for total liabilities and owners' equity.

19. **Calculating Financial Ratios** Based on the balance sheets given for Montana Dental Floss, calculate the following financial ratios for each year:
    - **a.** Current ratio
    - **b.** Quick ratio
    - **c.** Cash ratio
    - **d.** Debt/equity ratio and equity multiplier
    - **e.** Total debt ratio

Intermediate
(Questions 20–33)

20. **Using Standardized Financial Statements** What types of information do common-size financial statements reveal about the firm? What is the best use for these common-size statements?

21. **Using Financial Ratios** Explain what peer group analysis means. As a financial manager, how could you use the results of peer group analysis to evaluate the performance of your firm? How is a peer group different from an aspirant group?

22. **Interpreting the Du Pont Identity** Why is the Du Pont identity a valuable tool for analyzing the performance of a firm? Discuss the types of information it reveals compared to the ROE ratio considered by itself.

Net income = $22.50

23. **Using the Du Pont Identity** A firm has sales of $500, total assets of $300, and a debt/equity ratio of 1.00. If its return on equity is 15 percent, what is its net income?

24. **Sources and Uses of Cash** If accounts payable on the balance sheet increase by $4,000 from the beginning of the year to the end of the year, is this a source or a use of cash? Explain your answer.

Source of cash

25. **Profit Margin** In response to complaints about high prices, a grocery store chain runs the following advertising campaign: "If you pay your child 75 cents to go buy $25 worth of groceries, then your child makes twice as much on the trip as we do." You've collected the following information from the grocery chain's financial statements:

Sales	$225 million
Net income	$3.375 million
Total assets	$40 million
Total debt	$17 million

Evaluate the grocery chain's claim. What is the basis for the statement? Is this claim misleading? Why or why not?

Child: Profit margin = 3%
Store: Profit margin = 1.5%
ROE = 14.67%

26. **Using the Du Pont Identity** The Jordan Company has net income of $47,500. There are currently 16.60 days' sales in receivables. Total assets are $527,000, total receivables are $61,000, and the debt/equity ratio is 0.85. What is Jordan's profit margin? Its total asset turnover? Its ROE?

Profit margin = 3.54%
Total asset turnover = 2.55 times
ROE = 16.67%

27. **Calculating the Cash Coverage Ratio** Iskandar, Inc.'s net income for the most recent year was $4,950. The tax rate was 34 percent. The firm paid $1,200 in total interest expense and deducted $1,300 in depreciation expense. What was Iskandar's cash coverage ratio for the year?

Cash coverage ratio = 8.33 times

28. **Calculating the Times Interest Earned Ratio** For the most recent year, a firm had sales of $110,000, cost of goods sold of $45,000, depreciation expense of $15,000, and additions to retained earnings of $12,800. The firm currently has 5,000 shares of common stock outstanding, and last year dividends per share were $1.40. What was the times interest earned ratio? Assume a 34 percent tax rate.

TIE ratio = 2.50 times

29. **Ratios and Foreign Companies** The London Bridge Company PLC had 1995 net income of £6,211 on sales of £479,650 (both in thousands of pounds). What was the company's profit margin? Does the fact that these figures are quoted in a foreign currency make any difference? Why? In thousands of dollars, sales were $767,440. What was net income in dollars?

Profit margin = 1.29%
Net income = $9,937,000
Trans. 3.16

Some recent financial statements for Kuipers Enterprises are given below. Use this information to work Problems 30 through 33.

KUIPERS ENTERPRISES
1995 Income Statement

Sales		$9,000
Cost of goods sold		4,500
Depreciation		700
EBIT		$3,800
Interest paid		600
Taxable income		$3,200
Taxes (34%)		1,088
Net income		$2,112
Addition to retained earnings	$1,512	
Dividends	600	

KUIPERS ENTERPRISES
Balance sheets ending December 31, 1994 and 1995

	1994	1995		1994	1995
Assets			**Liabilities and Owners' Equity**		
Current assets			Current liabilities		
Cash	$ 404	$ 247	Accounts payable	$ 650	$ 679
Receivables	1,115	1,616	Notes payable	375	400
Inventory	2,870	4,225	Other	219	250
Total	4,389	6,088	Total	1,244	1,329
Fixed assets			Long-term debt	3,400	3,150
Net plant and equipment	8,452	8,100	Owners' equity		
			Common stock	500	500
			Capital surplus	1,300	1,300
			Retained earnings	6,397	7,909
			Total	8,197	9,709
Total	$12,841	$14,188	Total	$12,841	$14,188

Current ratio: 3.53 times; 4.58 times
Quick ratio: 1.22 times; 1.40 times
Cash ratio: 0.33 times; 0.19 times
Total assets turnover: 0.634 times
Inventory turnover: 1.07 times
Receivables turnover: 5.57 times
Debt ratio: 0.36 times; 0.32 times
D/E ratio: 0.57 times; 0.46 times
Equity multiplier: 1.57 times; 1.46 times
TIE ratio: 6.33 times
Cash coverage ratio: 7.50 times
Profit margin: 23.47%
ROA: 14.89%
ROE: 21.75%

30. **Calculating Financial Ratios** Find the following financial ratios for Kuipers Enterprises:

Short-term solvency ratios

Current ratio __________
Quick ratio __________
Cash ratio __________

Asset management ratios

Total asset turnover __________
Inventory turnover __________
Receivables turnover __________

Long-term solvency ratios

Debt ratio __________
Debt/equity ratio __________
Equity multiplier __________
Times interest earned ratio __________
Cash coverage ratio __________

Profitability ratios

Profit margin __________
Return on assets __________
Return on equity __________

ROE = 21.75%

31. **Du Pont Identity** Construct the Du Pont identity for Kuipers Enterprises.

32. **Statement of Cash Flows** Prepare the 1995 statement of cash flows for Kuipers Enterprises.

P/E ratio = 9.85 times
DPS = $1.50
Market-to-book ratio = 2.14 times

33. **Market Value Ratios** Kuipers has 400 shares of common stock outstanding, and the market price for a share of stock at the end of 1995 is $52.00. What is the price/earnings ratio? What are dividends per share? What is the market-to-book ratio at the end of 1995?

Long-Term Financial Planning and Growth

After studying this chapter, you should have a good understanding of:

. . .

Why financial planning is important and what it can accomplish.

. . .

How to prepare a long-range financial plan using the percentage of sales approach.

. . .

The determinants of growth for a firm.

A lack of effective long-range planning is a commonly cited reason for financial distress and failure. As we will develop in this chapter, long-range planning is a means of systematically thinking about the future and anticipating possible problems before they arrive. There are no magic mirrors, of course, so the best we can hope for is a logical and organized procedure for exploring the unknown. As one member of GM's board was heard to say, "Planning is a process that at best helps the firm avoid stumbling into the future backwards."

Trans. 4.1 Chapter Outline

Financial planning establishes guidelines for change and growth in a firm. It normally focuses on the "big picture." This means it is concerned with the major elements of a firm's financial and investment policies without examining the individual components of those policies in detail.

A key lesson from this chapter is that the firm's investment and financing policies interact and thus cannot truly be considered in isolation from one another. The types and amounts of assets the firm plans on purchasing must be considered along with the firm's ability to raise the necessary capital to fund those investments.

There are direct connections between the growth a company can achieve and its financial policy. In the sections below, we show how financial planning models can be used to better understand how growth is achieved. We also show how such models can be used to establish the limits on possible growth.

4.1 WHAT IS FINANCIAL PLANNING?

Financial planning formulates the way financial goals are to be achieved. A financial plan is thus a statement of what is to be done in the future. Most decisions have long lead times, which means they take a long time to implement. In an uncertain world, this requires that decisions be made far in advance of their implementation. If a firm wants to build a factory in 1998, for example, it might have to begin lining up contractors and financing in 1996, or even earlier.

Growth as a Financial Management Goal

Because the subject of growth will be discussed in various places in this chapter, we need to start out with an important warning: Growth, by itself, is *not* an appropriate goal for the financial manager. As we discussed in Chapter 1, the appropriate goal is increasing the market value of the owners' equity. Of course, if a firm is successful in doing this, then growth will usually result.

Growth may thus be a desirable consequence of good decision making, but it is not an end unto itself. We discuss growth simply because growth rates are so commonly used in the planning process. As we will see, growth is a convenient means of summarizing various aspects of a firm's financial and investment policies. Also, if we think of growth as growth in the market value of the equity in the firm, then goals of growth and increasing the market value of the equity in the firm are not all that different.

What Can Planning Accomplish?

Concept Q Answer 4.1a

Because the company is likely to spend a lot of time examining the different scenarios that will become the basis for the company's financial plan, it seems reasonable to ask what the planning process will accomplish.

Interactions As we discuss in greater detail below, the financial plan must make explicit the linkages between investment proposals for the different operating activities of the firm and the financing choices available to the firm. In other words, if the firm is planning on expanding and undertaking new investments and projects, where will the financing be obtained to pay for this activity? As the accompanying *Principles in Action* box illustrates, failure to understand the linkage between, for example, sales growth and production needs can lead to financial disaster.

Options The financial plan provides the opportunity for the firm to develop, analyze, and compare many different scenarios in a consistent way. Various investment and financing options can be explored, and their impact on the firm's shareholders can be evaluated. Questions concerning the firm's future lines of business and questions of what financing arrangements are optimal are addressed. Options such as marketing new products or closing plants might be evaluated.

Lecture Tip: Some emphasize this as the most important aspect of financial planning. Committing a plan to paper forces managers to think seriously about the future and to anticipate the effects of future events.

Avoiding Surprises Financial planning should identify what may happen to the firm if different events take place. In particular, it should address what actions the firm will take if things go seriously wrong or, more generally, if assumptions made today about the future are seriously in error. Thus, one of

Principles in Action

Growing for Broke

It's not often that firms fail because their product is too successful, but it happened to the Grandmother Calendar Company. The demise of this company illustrates the importance of careful coordination between sales growth and production capacity, and what can happen to firms with significant external financing needed: They may grow broke!

The Grandmother Calendar Company began selling personalized photo calendar kits in 1992. Customers send the kit, along with photos and special instructions, to the company. The company then scans the photos into their computers and arranges a custom-designed, personalized calendar to the customer's specifications. The downfall of the company wasn't that it failed to produce sales. On the contrary—the founder of the company was an excellent salesman. He signed on numerous suppliers, including one that sells to Kmart Corp. The kits were priced about 20 percent below those of competitors, despite the fact that the Grandmother calendars were more detailed and allowed for more custom design by purchasers.

The demise of the company is a classic tale of a mismatch between sales and production capacity. The kits were a hit with customers and sales sharply exceeded forecasts. The rush of orders created a huge backlog of calendars to be produced. The company leased more space and expanded capacity, yet it could not keep up with demand. The equipment failed from overuse and quality suffered. Working capital was drained, partially to expand production and partially as customers paid for extra options for their calendars with credit cards. The credit card companies wouldn't pay Grandmother until the product was shipped. Thus, the company had to shoulder the burden of all production costs until the calendar was finally delivered. The company was unable to deliver on its huge backlog of orders and the cash-strapped company's employee paychecks began to bounce. Finally, out of cash, the company ceased operations entirely in January 1995.

Successful business planning requires a realistic assessment of the interactions between sales levels and asset needs, and assessment of the feasibility and internal consistency of goals and projections. The Grandmother Calendar Company expanded its capacity to fill orders, but increasing sales does not always result in increased cash, particularly if accounts receivable and work-in-progress inventory also increase. The sales increase resulted in external financing needed, apparently beyond the levels the firm could acquire. Careful planning is crucial, for as this case illustrates, if a company runs out of cash, it is out of business, regardless of the popularity of its product.

Source: "Picture This! A Firm Failing From Too Much Success," *The Wall Street Journal*, March 17, 1995, p. B1.

the purposes of financial planning is to avoid surprises and develop contingency plans.

Feasibility and Internal Consistency Beyond a general goal of creating value, a firm will normally have many specific goals. Such goals might be couched in terms of market share, return on equity, financial leverage, and so on. At times, the linkages between different goals and different aspects of a firm's business are difficult to see. Not only does a financial plan make explicit these linkages, but it also imposes a unified structure for reconciling differing goals and objectives. In other words, financial planning is a way of checking that the goals and plans made with regard to specific areas of a firm's operations are feasible and internally consistent. Conflicting goals will often exist. To generate a coherent plan, goals and objectives will therefore have to be modified, and priorities will have to be established.

For example, one goal a firm might have is 12 percent growth in unit sales per year. Another goal might be to reduce the firm's total debt ratio from 40 percent to 20 percent. Are these two goals compatible? Can they be accomplished simultaneously? Maybe yes, maybe no. As we discuss below, financial planning is a way of finding out just what is possible, and, by implication, what is not possible.

Concept Q Answer 4.1b

The fact that planning forces management to think about goals and to establish priorities is probably the most important result of the process. In fact, conventional business wisdom holds that financial plans don't work, but financial planning does. The future is inherently unknown. What we can do is establish the direction we want to travel and take some educated guesses at what we will find along the way. If we do a good job, then we won't be caught off guard when the future rolls around.

CONCEPT QUESTIONS

4.1a What are some of the things financial planning can accomplish?

4.1b Why should firms draw up financial plans?

4.2 FINANCIAL PLANNING MODELS: A FIRST LOOK

Problems 1, 2

Just as companies differ in size and products, the financial planning process will differ from firm to firm. In this section, we discuss some common elements in financial plans and develop a basic model to illustrate these elements. What follows is just a quick overview; later sections will take up the various topics in more detail.

A Financial Planning Model: The Ingredients

Trans. 4.2 Financial Planning Model Ingredients

Concept Q Answer 4.2a

Most financial planning models require the user to specify some assumptions about the future. Based on those assumptions, the model generates predicted values for a large number of other variables. Models can vary quite a bit in terms of their complexity, but almost all will have the elements that we discuss next.

Sales Forecast Almost all financial plans require an externally supplied sales forecast. In our models below, for example, the sales forecast will be the "driver," meaning that the user of the planning model will supply this value and most other values will be calculated based on it. This arrangement would be common for many types of business; planning will focus on projected future sales and the assets and financing needed to support those sales.

Frequently, the sales forecast will be given as the growth rate in sales rather than as an explicit sales figure. These two approaches are essentially the same since we can calculate projected sales once we know the growth rate. Perfect sales forecasts are not possible, of course, because sales depend on the uncertain future state of the economy. To help a firm come up with such projections, some businesses specialize in macroeconomic and industry projections.

As we discussed above, we frequently will be interested in evaluating alternative scenarios, so it isn't necessarily crucial that the sales forecast be accurate. In such cases, our goal is to examine the interplay between investment and financing needs at different possible sales levels, not to pinpoint what we expect to happen.

Pro Forma Statements A financial plan will have a forecasted balance sheet, income statement, and statement of cash flows. These are called *pro forma statements,* or *pro formas* for short. The phrase *pro forma* literally means "as a matter of form." In our case, this means the financial statements are the form we use to summarize the different events projected for the future. At a minimum, a financial planning model will generate these statements based on projections of key items such as sales.

Asset Requirements The plan will describe projected capital spending. At a minimum, the projected balance sheet will contain changes in total fixed assets and net working capital. These changes are effectively the firm's total capital budget.

Financial Requirements The plan will include a section on the necessary financing arrangements. This part of the plan should discuss dividend policy and debt policy. Sometimes firms will expect to raise cash by selling new shares of stock or by borrowing. In this case, the plan will have to consider what kinds of securities have to be sold and what methods of issuance are most appropriate.

The "Plug" After the firm has a sales forecast and an estimate of the required spending on assets, some amount of new financing will often be necessary because projected total assets will exceed projected total liabilities and equity. In other words, the balance sheet will no longer balance.

Concept Q Answer 4.2b

Since new financing may be necessary to cover all of the projected capital spending, a financial "plug" variable must be selected. The plug is the designated source or sources of external financing needed to deal with any shortfall (or surplus) in financing and thereby bring the balance sheet into balance.

For example, a firm with a great number of investment opportunities and limited cash flow may have to raise new equity. Other firms with few growth opportunities and ample cash flow will have a surplus and thus might pay an extra dividend. In the first case, external equity is the plug variable. In the second, the dividend is used.

Economic Assumptions The plan will have to state explicitly the economic environment in which the firm expects to reside over the life of the plan. Among the more important economic assumptions that will have to be made are the level of interest rates and the firm's tax rate.

A Simple Financial Planning Model

We can begin our discussion of long-term planning models with a relatively simple example. The Computerfield Corporation's financial statements from the most recent year are as follows:

Trans. 4.3 Example: A Simple Financial Planning Model (Supplemental)

COMPUTERFIELD CORPORATION
Financial Statements

Income Statement	
Sales	$1,000
Costs	800
Net income	$ 200

Balance Sheet			
Assets	$500	Debt	$250
		Equity	250
Total	$500	Total	$500

Lecture Tip: You might point out that the goal of a planning model is to highlight relationships that need to be considered—not necessarily to develop an exact financial plan.

Unless otherwise stated, the financial planners at Computerfield assume all variables are tied directly to sales and current relationships are optimal. This means all items will grow at exactly the same rate as sales. This is obviously oversimplified; we use this assumption only to make a point.

Suppose sales increase by 20 percent, rising from $1,000 to $1,200. Planners would then also forecast a 20 percent increase in costs, from $800 to $800 × 1.2 = $960. The pro forma income statement would thus be:

Pro Forma Income Statement

Sales	$1,200
Costs	960
Net income	$ 240

The assumption that all variables will grow by 20 percent will enable us to easily construct the pro forma balance sheet as well:

Pro Forma Balance Sheet

Assets	$600 (+100)	Debt	$300 (+ 50)
		Equity	300 (+ 50)
Total	$600 (+100)	Total	$600 (+100)

Notice we have simply increased every item by 20 percent. The numbers in parentheses are the dollar changes for the different items.

Now we have to reconcile these two pro formas. How, for example, can net income be equal to $240 and equity increase by only $50? The answer is that Computerfield must have paid out the difference of $240 − 50 = $190, possibly as a cash dividend. In this case, dividends are the plug variable.

Suppose Computerfield does not pay out the $190. In this case, the addition to retained earnings is the full $240. Computerfield's equity will thus grow to $250 (the starting amount) + $240 (net income) = $490, and debt must be retired to keep total assets equal to $600.

With $600 in total assets and $490 in equity, debt will have to be $600 − 490 = $110. Since we started with $250 in debt, Computerfield will have to retire $250 − 110 = $140 in debt. The resulting pro forma balance sheet would look like this:

Pro Forma Balance Sheet

Assets	$600 (+100)	Debt	$110 (−140)
		Equity	490 (+240)
Total	$600 (+100)	Total	$600 (+100)

In this case, debt is the plug variable used to balance out projected total assets and liabilities.

This example shows the interaction between sales growth and financial policy. As sales increase, so do total assets. This occurs because the firm must invest in net working capital and fixed assets to support higher sales levels. Since assets are growing, total liabilities and equity, the right-hand side of the balance sheet, will grow as well.

The thing to notice from our simple example is that the way the liabilities and owners' equity change depends on the firm's financing policy and its dividend policy. The growth in assets requires that the firm decide on how to finance that growth. This is strictly a managerial decision. Also, in our example the firm needed no outside funds. This won't usually be the case, so we explore a more detailed situation in the next section.

CONCEPT QUESTIONS

4.2a What are the basic components of a financial plan?

4.2b Why is it necessary to designate a plug in a financial planning model?

4.3 THE PERCENTAGE OF SALES APPROACH

Self-Test Problem 4.1
Problems 2–5, 10, 11, 12, 18

In the previous section, we described a simple planning model in which every item increased at the same rate as sales. This may be a reasonable assumption for some elements. For others, such as long-term borrowing, it probably is not, because the amount of long-term borrowing is something set by management, and it does not necessarily relate directly to the level of sales.

Concept Q
Answer 4.3a

In this section, we describe an extended version of our simple model above. The basic idea is to separate the income statement and balance sheet accounts into two groups, those that do vary directly with sales and those that do not. Given a sales forecast, we will then be able to calculate how much financing the firm will need to support the predicted sales level.

Lecture Tip: Throughout this chapter we assume that the firm is operating at full capacity. A discussion of the effects of financial planning for firms operating at less-than-full capacity can be found in *Fundamentals of Corporate Finance* by Ross, Westerfield, and Jordan.

An Illustration of the Percentage of Sales Approach

The financial planning model we describe next is based on the **percentage of sales approach.** Our goal here is to develop a quick and practical way of generating pro forma statements.

percentage of sales approach
Financial planning method in which accounts are varied depending on a firm's predicted sales level.

The Income Statement We start out with the most recent income statement for the Rosengarten Corporation, as shown in Table 4.1. Notice we have still simplified things by including costs, depreciation, and interest in a single cost figure.

Rosengarten has projected a 25 percent increase in sales for the coming year, so we are anticipating sales of $\$1{,}000 \times 1.25 = \$1{,}250$. To generate a pro forma income statement, we assume total costs will continue to run at $\$800/\$1{,}000 = 80\%$ of sales. With this assumption, Rosengarten's pro forma income statement is as shown in Table 4.2. The effect here of assuming costs are a constant percentage of sales is to assume the profit margin is constant.

Trans. 4.4
The Percentage of Sales Approach (Supplemental)

TABLE 4.1

ROSENGARTEN CORPORATION Income Statement		
Sales		$1,000
Costs		800
Taxable income		$ 200
Taxes (34%)		68
Net income		$ 132
Addition to retained earnings	$88	
Dividends	44	

TABLE 4.2

ROSENGARTEN CORPORATION Pro Forma Income Statement	
Sales (projected)	$1,250
Costs (80% of sales)	1,000
Taxable income	$ 250
Taxes (34%)	85
Net income	$ 165

To check this, notice the profit margin was $132/$1,000 = 13.2%. In our pro forma, the profit margin is $165/$1,250 = 13.2%; so it is unchanged.

Next, we need to project the dividend payment. This amount is up to Rosengarten's management. We will assume Rosengarten has a policy of paying out a constant fraction of net income in the form of a cash dividend. From the most recent year, the **dividend payout ratio** was:

dividend payout ratio
Amount of cash paid out to shareholders divided by net income.

$$\begin{aligned}\text{Dividend payout ratio} &= \text{Cash dividends/Net income} \\ &= \$44/\$132 = 33\ 1/3\%\end{aligned} \qquad [4.1]$$

We can also calculate the ratio of the addition to retained earnings to net income as:

$$\text{Addition to retained earnings/Net income} = \$88/\$132 = 66\ 2/3\%.$$

retention ratio
Addition to retained earnings divided by net income. Also called the plowback ratio.

This ratio is called the **retention ratio** or **plowback ratio,** and it is equal to 1 minus the dividend payout ratio because everything not paid out is retained. Assuming that the payout and retention ratios are constant, the projected dividends and addition to retained earnings will be:

$$\begin{aligned}\text{Projected addition to retained earnings} &= \$165 \times 2/3 = \$110 \\ \text{Projected dividends paid to shareholders} &= \$165 \times 1/3 = \underline{\ \ 55} \\ &\qquad\qquad\qquad\ \ \underline{\underline{\$165}}\end{aligned}$$

The Balance Sheet To generate a pro forma balance sheet, we start with the most recent statement, as shown in Table 4.3.

Trans. 4.5
Pro Forma Statements (Supplemental)

On our balance sheet, we assume some of the items vary directly with sales while others do not. For those items that do vary with sales, we express each as a percentage of sales for the year just completed. When an item does not vary directly with sales, we write "n/a" for "not applicable."

Concept Q
Answer 4.3b

For example, on the asset side, inventory is equal to 60 percent of sales ($600/$1,000) for the year just ended. We assume this percentage applies to the coming year, so for each $1 increase in sales, inventory will rise by $.60. More generally, the ratio of total assets to sales for the year just ended is $3,000/$1,000 = 3, or 300%.

capital intensity ratio
A firm's total assets divided by its sales, or the amount of assets needed to generate $1 in sales.

This ratio of total assets to sales is sometimes called the **capital intensity ratio.** It tells us the assets needed to generate $1 in sales; so the higher the ratio is, the more capital intensive is the firm. Notice also this ratio is just the reciprocal of the total asset turnover ratio we defined in the last chapter.

For Rosengarten, assuming this ratio is constant, it takes $3 in total assets to generate $1 in sales (apparently Rosengarten is in a relatively capital

TABLE 4.3

ROSENGARTEN CORPORATION Balance Sheet	($)	(%)		($)	(%)
Assets			**Liabilities and Owners' Equity**		
Current assets			Current liabilities		
Cash	$ 160	16%	Accounts payable	$ 300	30%
Accounts receivable	440	44	Notes payable	100	n/a
Inventory	600	60	Total	$ 400	n/a
Total	$1,200	120%			
			Long-term debt	$ 800	n/a
Fixed assets			Owners' equity		
Net plant and equipment	$1,800	180%	Common stock and paid-in surplus	$ 800	n/a
			Retained earnings	1,000	n/a
			Total	$1,800	n/a
Total assets	$3,000	300%	Total liabilities and owners' equity	$3,000	n/a

intensive business). Therefore, if sales are to increase by $100, then Rosengarten will have to increase total assets by three times this amount, or $300.

On the liability side of the balance sheet, we show accounts payable varying with sales. The reason is that we expect to place more orders with our suppliers as sales volume increases, so payables will change "spontaneously" with sales. Notes payable, on the other hand, represent short-term debt such as bank borrowing. These will not vary unless we take specific actions to change the amount, so we mark them as "n/a."

Lecture Tip: See IM 4.3 for further discussion of spontaneous and non-spontaneous financing.

Similarly, we use "n/a" for long-term debt because it won't automatically change with sales. The same is true for common stock and paid-in surplus. The last item on the right-hand side, retained earnings, will vary with sales, but it won't be a simple percentage of sales. Instead, we will explicitly calculate the change in retained earnings based on our projected net income and dividends.

We can now construct a partial pro forma balance sheet for Rosengarten. We do this by using the percentages we calculated above wherever possible to calculate the projected amounts. For example, net fixed assets are 180 percent of sales; so, with a new sales level of $1,250, the net fixed asset amount will be $1.80 \times \$1,250 = \$2,250$, an increase of $\$2,250 - 1,800 = \$450$ in plant and equipment. Importantly, for those items that don't vary directly with sales, we initially assume no change and simply write in the original amounts. The result is shown in Table 4.4. Notice the change in retained earnings is equal to the $110 addition to retained earnings we calculated above.

Inspecting our pro forma balance sheet, we notice assets are projected to increase by $750. However, without additional financing, liabilities and equity will only increase by $185, leaving a shortfall of $\$750 - 185 = \$565$. We label this amount *external financing needed* (EFN).

Lecture Tip: See IM 4.3 for an example that integrates the various issues presented in Chapters 1–4.

A Particular Scenario Our financial planning model now reminds us of one of those good news/bad news jokes. The good news is we're projecting a

TABLE 4.4

	Present Year	Change from Previous Year		Present Year	Change from Previous Year
ROSENGARTEN CORPORATION Partial Pro Forma Balance Sheet					
Assets			**Liabilities and Owners' Equity**		
Current assets			Current liabilities		
Cash	$ 200	$ 40	Accounts payable	$ 375	$ 75
Accounts receivable	550	110	Notes payable	100	0
Inventory	750	150	Total	$ 475	$ 75
Total	$1,500	$300	Long-term debt	$ 800	$ 0
Fixed assets			Owners' equity		
Net plant and equipment	$2,250	$450	Common stock and paid-in surplus	800	0
			Retained earnings	1,110	110
			Total	$1,910	$110
Total assets	$3,750	$750	Total liabilities and owners' equity	$3,185	$185
			External financing needed	$ 565	$565

Lecture Tip: In more concise terms, EFN = (A × *g*) − [S(1 + *g*) × PM × *b*], where A = assets, *g* = growth rate, S = sales, PM = profit margin, and *b* = retention ratio. Note, however, that this formula assumes no liabilities vary spontaneously with sales.

Trans. 4.6
The Percentage of Sales Approach: A Financing Plan (Supplemental)

Lecture Tip: You may wish to take this opportunity to mention the importance of issuance costs, market rates, and agency issues in making external financing decisions. Doing so provides a link between this chapter and Chapters 1, 7, 12, and 13.

Lecture Tip: Prudent forecasters will analyze the pro forma statements using techniques such as those described in Chapter 3 in order to assess both the feasibility of the results and implications for liquidity, leverage, and asset management.

25 percent increase in sales. The bad news is this isn't going to happen unless we can somehow raise $565 in new financing.

This is a good example of how the planning process can point out problems and potential conflicts. If, for example, Rosengarten had a goal of not borrowing any additional funds and not selling any new equity, then a 25 percent increase in sales is probably not feasible.

If we take the need for $565 in new financing as given, Rosengarten has three possible sources: short-term borrowing, long-term borrowing, and new equity. The choice of a combination among these three is up to management; we will illustrate only one of the many possibilities.

Suppose Rosengarten decides to borrow the needed funds. In this case, they might choose to borrow some short-term and some long-term. For example, current assets increased by $300 while current liabilities rose by only $75. Rosengarten could borrow $300 − 75 = $225 in short-term notes payable and leave total net working capital unchanged. With $565 needed, the remaining $565 − 225 = $340 would have to come from long-term debt. Table 4.5 shows the completed pro forma balance sheet for Rosengarten.

We have used a combination of short- and long-term debt as the plug here, but we emphasize this is just one possible strategy; it is not necessarily the best one by any means. There are many other scenarios we could (and should) investigate. The various ratios we discussed in Chapter 3 come in very handy here. For example, with the scenario we have just examined, we would surely want to examine the current ratio and the total debt ratio to see if we are comfortable with the new projected debt levels.

Now that we have finished our balance sheet, we have all of the projected sources and uses of cash. We could finish off our pro formas by drawing up the projected statement of cash flows along the lines discussed in Chapter 3. We will leave this as an exercise and instead investigate the connection between growth and financing needed.

TABLE 4.5

ROSENGARTEN CORPORATION
Pro Forma Balance Sheet

	Present Year	Change from Previous Year		Present Year	Change from Previous Year
Assets			**Liabilities and Owners' Equity**		
Current assets			Current liabilities		
Cash	$ 200	$ 40	Accounts payable	$ 375	$ 75
Accounts receivable	550	110	Notes payable	325	225
Inventory	750	150	Total	$ 700	$300
Total	$1,500	$300	Long-term debt	$1,140	$340
Fixed assets			Owners' equity		
Net plant and equipment	$2,250	$450	Common stock and paid-in surplus	800	0
			Retained earnings	1,110	110
			Total	$1,910	$110
Total assets	$3,750	$750	Total liabilities and owners' equity	$3,750	$750

CONCEPT QUESTIONS

4.3a What is the basic idea behind the percentage of sales approach?

4.3b What is the capital intensity ratio? What does it tell us?

4.4 EXTERNAL FINANCING AND GROWTH

Self-Test Problem 4.2
Problems 7–9, 13–17, 22, 23

Lecture Tip: IM 4.4 discusses the relative importance of external financing and growth to firms in the early stages of their life cycles.

External financing needed and growth are obviously related. All other things the same, the higher the rate of growth in sales or assets, the greater will be the need for external financing. In the previous section, we took a growth rate as given, and then we determined the amount of external financing needed to support that growth. In this section, we turn things around a bit. We will take the firm's financial policy as given and then examine the relationship between that financial policy and the firm's ability to finance new investments and thereby grow.

Once again, we emphasize that we are focusing on growth not because growth is an appropriate goal; instead, for our purposes, growth is simply a convenient means of examining the interactions between investment and financing decisions.

EFN and Growth

Trans. 4.7
Growth and External Financing (Supplemental)

The first thing we need to do is establish the relationship between EFN and growth. To do this, we introduce the simplified income statement and balance sheet for the Hoffman Company in Table 4.6. Notice we have simplified the balance sheet by combining short-term and long-term debt into a single total debt figure. Effectively, we are assuming that none of the current liabilities vary spontaneously with sales. This assumption isn't as restrictive as it sounds. If any current liabilities (such as accounts payable) vary with sales, we can assume they have been netted out in current assets. Also, we continue to combine depreciation, interest, and costs on the income statement.

TABLE 4.6

HOFFMAN COMPANY
Income Statement and Balance Sheet

Income Statement

Sales		$500
Costs		400
Taxable income		$100
Taxes (34%)		34
Net income		$ 66
Addition to retained earnings	$44	
Dividends	22	

Balance Sheet

	($)	(% of sales)		($)	(% of sales)
Assets			**Liabilities and Owners' Equity**		
Current assets	$200	140%	Total debt	$250	n/a
Net fixed assets	300	60	Owners' equity	250	n/a
Total assets	$500	100%	Total liabilities and owners' equity	$500	n/a

TABLE 4.7

HOFFMAN COMPANY
Pro Forma Income Statement and Balance Sheet

Income Statement

Sales		$600.0
Costs (80% of sales)		480.0
Taxable income		$120.0
Taxes (34%)		40.8
Net income		$ 79.2
Addition to retained earnings	$52.8	
Dividends	26.4	

Balance Sheet

	($)	(% of sales)		($)	(% of sales)
Assets			**Liabilities and Owners' Equity**		
Current assets	$240.0	140%	Total debt	$250.0	n/a
Net fixed assets	360.0	60	Owners' equity	302.8	n/a
Total assets	$600.0	100%	Total liabilities and owners' equity	$552.8	n/a
			External financing needed	$ 47.2	

Suppose the Hoffman Company is forecasting next year's sales level at $600, a $100 increase. Notice the percentage increase in sales is $100/$500 = 20%. Using the percentage of sales approach and the figures in Table 4.6, we can prepare a pro forma income statement and balance sheet as in Table 4.7. As Table 4.7 illustrates, at a 20 percent growth rate, Hoffman needs $100 in new assets. The projected addition to retained earnings is $52.8, so the external financing needed (EFN) is $100 − 52.8 = $47.2.

TABLE 4.8
Growth and projected EFN for the Hoffman Company

Projected Sales Growth	Increase in Assets Required	Addition to Retained Earnings	External Financing Needed (EFN)	Projected Debt/Equity Ratio
0%	$ 0	$44.0	−$44.0	.70
5	25	46.2	− 21.2	.77
10	50	48.4	1.6	.84
15	75	50.6	24.4	.91
20	100	52.8	47.2	.98
25	125	55.0	70.0	1.05

Notice the debt/equity ratio for Hoffman was originally (from Table 4.6) equal to $250/$250 = 1.0. We will assume the Hoffman Corporation does not wish to sell new equity. In this case, the $47.2 in EFN will have to be borrowed. What will the new debt/equity ratio be? From Table 4.7, total owners' equity is projected at $302.8. The new total debt will be the original $250 plus $47.2 in new borrowing, or $297.2 total. The debt/equity ratio thus falls slightly from 1.0 to $297.2/$302.8 = .98.

Table 4.8 shows EFN for several different growth rates. The projected addition to retained earnings and the projected debt/equity ratio for each scenario are also given (you should probably calculate a few of these for practice). In determining the debt/equity ratios, we assumed any needed funds were borrowed, and we also assumed any surplus funds were used to pay off debt. Thus, for the zero growth case, the debt falls by $44, from $250 to $206. In Table 4.8, notice the increase in assets required is simply equal to the original assets of $500 multiplied by the growth rate. Similarly, the addition to retained earnings is equal to the original $44 plus $44 times the growth rate.

Table 4.8 shows that for relatively low growth rates, Hoffman will run a surplus, and its debt/equity ratio will decline. Once the growth rate increases to about 10 percent, however, the surplus becomes a deficit. Furthermore, as the growth rate exceeds approximately 20 percent, the debt/equity ratio passes its original value of 1.0.

Figure 4.1 illustrates the connection between growth in sales and external financing needed in more detail by plotting asset needs and additions to retained earnings from Table 4.8 against the growth rates. As shown, the need for new assets grows at a much faster rate than the addition to retained earnings, so the internal financing provided by the addition to retained earnings rapidly disappears.

Lecture Tip: A handout providing an additional EFN example appears at the end of Chapter 4 in the IM.

Financial Policy and Growth

Based on our discussion just above, there is a direct link between growth and external financing. In this section, we discuss two growth rates particularly useful in long-range planning.

The Internal Growth Rate The first growth rate of interest is the maximum growth rate that can be achieved with no external financing of any kind. We will call this the **internal growth rate** because this is the rate the firm can maintain with internal financing only. In Figure 4.1, this internal growth rate is the point where the two lines cross. At this point, the required increase in assets is exactly equal to the addition to retained earnings, and EFN is

internal growth rate
The maximum growth rate a firm can achieve without external financing of any kind.

F I G U R E 4.1
Growth and financing needed for the Hoffman Company

Trans. 4.9

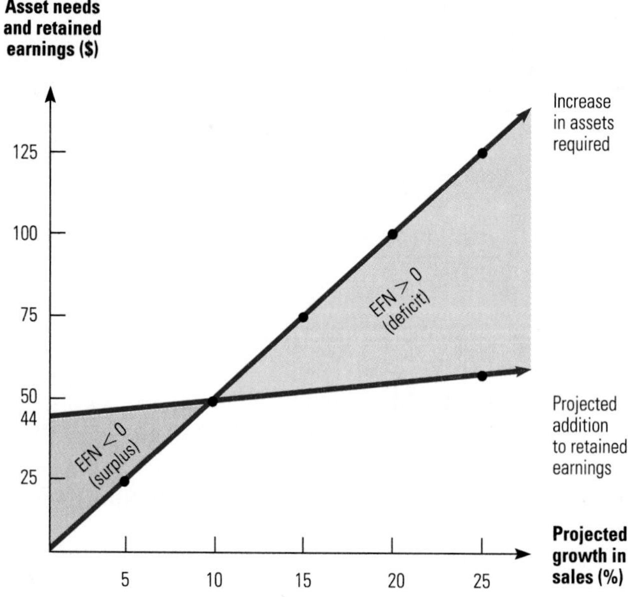

therefore zero. We have seen that this happens when the growth rate is slightly less than 10 percent. With a little algebra we find this growth rate more precisely as:

$$\text{Internal growth rate} = \frac{\text{ROA} \times b}{1 - \text{ROA} \times b} \quad [4.2]$$

where ROA is the return on assets we discussed in Chapter 3, and b is the plowback or retention ratio defined earlier in this chapter.

For the Hoffman Company, net income was $66 and total assets were $500. ROA is thus $66/$500 = 13.2%. Of the $66 net income, $44 was retained, so the plowback ratio, b, is $44/$66 = 2/3. With these numbers, we can calculate the internal growth rate as:

$$\begin{aligned}\text{Internal growth rate} &= \frac{\text{ROA} \times b}{1 - \text{ROA} \times b} \\ &= \frac{.132 \times (2/3)}{1 - .132 \times (2/3)} \\ &= 9.65\%\end{aligned}$$

Lecture Tip: In other words, if sales increase by 9.65% (to $548.25), the increase in assets required is $48.25 ($500 × .0965), which equals the addition to retained earnings.

Thus, the Hoffman Company can expand at a maximum rate of 9.65 percent per year without external financing.

Trans. 4.9
Sustainable Growth Rate (Supplemental)

The Sustainable Growth Rate We have seen that if the Hoffman Company wishes to grow more rapidly than 9.65 percent per year, then external financing must be arranged. The second growth rate of interest is the maximum growth rate a firm can achieve with no external *equity* financing while it maintains a constant debt/equity ratio. This rate is commonly called the

sustainable growth rate because it is the maximum rate of growth a firm can maintain without increasing its financial leverage.

sustainable growth rate
The maximum growth rate a firm can achieve without external equity financing while maintaining a constant debt/equity ratio.

There are various reasons why a firm might wish to avoid equity sales. For example, as we discuss in Chapter 13, new equity sales can be very expensive. Alternatively, the current owners may not wish to bring in new owners or contribute additional equity. Why a firm might view a particular debt/equity ratio as optimal is discussed in a later chapter; for now, we will take it as given.

Lecture Tip: Reasons for wishing to avoid issuing external equity appear in IM 4.4.

Based on Table 4.8, the sustainable growth rate for Hoffman is approximately 20 percent because the debt/equity ratio is near 1.0 at that growth rate. The precise value can be calculated as:

$$\text{Sustainable growth rate} = \frac{\text{ROE} \times b}{1 - \text{ROE} \times b} \quad [4.3]$$

Concept Q Answer 4.4b

This is identical to the internal growth rate except ROE (return on equity) is used instead of ROA.

For the Hoffman Company, net income was \$66 and total equity was \$250; ROE is thus \$66/\$250 = 26.4 percent. The plowback ratio, *b*, is still 2/3, so we can calculate the sustainable growth rate as:

$$\begin{aligned}\text{Sustainable growth rate} &= \frac{\text{ROE} \times b}{1 - \text{ROE} \times b} \\ &= \frac{.264 \times (2/3)}{1 - .264 \times (2/3)} \\ &= 21.36\%\end{aligned}$$

Thus, the Hoffman Company can expand at a maximum rate of 21.36 percent per year without external equity financing.

EXAMPLE 4.1 Sustainable Growth

Suppose Hoffman grows at exactly the sustainable growth rate of 21.36 percent. What will the pro forma statements look like?

At a 21.36 percent growth rate, sales will rise from \$500 to \$606.8. The pro forma income statement will look like this:

HOFFMAN COMPANY
Pro Forma Income Statement

Sales		\$606.8
Costs (80% of sales)		485.4
Taxable income		\$121.4
Taxes (34%)		41.3
Net income		\$ 80.1
Addition to retained earnings	\$53.4	
Dividends	26.7	

We construct the balance sheet just as we did above. Notice, in this case, owners' equity will rise from \$250 to \$303.4 because the addition to retained earnings is \$53.4.

HOFFMAN COMPANY
Pro Forma Balance Sheet

	($)	(% of sales)		($)	(% of sales)
Assets			**Liabilities and Owners' Equity**		
Current assets	$242.7	40%	Total debt	$250.0	n/a
Net fixed assets	364.1	60	Owners' equity	303.4	n/a
Total assets	$606.8	100%	Total liabilities and owners' equity	$553.4	n/a
			External funds needed	$ 53.4	

As illustrated, EFN is $53.4. If Hoffman borrows this amount, then total debt will rise to $303.4, and the debt/equity ratio will be exactly 1.0, thereby verifying our earlier calculation. At any other growth rate, something would have to change. • • •

Determinants of Growth In the last chapter, we saw the return on equity (ROE) could be decomposed into its various components using the Du Pont identity. Since ROE appears so prominently in the determination of the sustainable growth rate, the factors important in determining ROE are also important determinants of growth.

From Chapter 3, we know ROE can be written as the product of three factors:

$$\text{ROE} = \text{Profit margin} \times \text{Total asset turnover} \times \text{Equity multiplier}$$

If we examine our expression for the sustainable growth rate, anything that increases ROE will increase the sustainable growth rate by making the top bigger and the bottom smaller. Increasing the plowback ratio will have the same effect.

Putting it all together, what we have is that a firm's ability to sustain growth depends explicitly on the following four factors:

Concept Q Answer 4.4a

1. Profit margin. An increase in profit margin will increase the firm's ability to generate funds internally and thereby increase its sustainable growth.
2. Total asset turnover. An increase in the firm's total asset turnover increases the sales generated for each dollar in assets. This decreases the firm's need for new assets as sales grow and thereby increases the sustainable growth rate. Notice increasing total asset turnover is the same thing as decreasing capital intensity.
3. Financial policy. An increase in the debt/equity ratio increases the firm's financial leverage. Since this makes additional debt financing available, it increases the sustainable growth rate.
4. Dividend policy. A decrease in the percentage of net income paid out as dividends will increase the retention ratio. This increases internally generated equity and thus increases sustainable growth.

The sustainable growth rate is a very useful planning number. What it illustrates is the explicit relationship between the firm's four major areas of concern: its operating efficiency as measured by profit margin, its asset use efficiency as measured by total asset turnover, its financial policy as mea-

Principles in Action

Robert C. Higgins on Sustainable Growth

Most financial officers know intuitively that it takes money to make money. Rapid sales growth requires increased assets in the form of accounts receivable, inventory, and fixed plant, which, in turn, require money to pay for assets. They also know that if their company does not have the money when needed, it can literally "grow broke." The sustainable growth equation states these intuitive truths explicitly.

Sustainable growth is often used by bankers and other external analysts to assess a company's credit worthiness. They are aided in this exercise by several sophisticated computer software packages that provide detailed analyses of the company's past financial performance, including its annual sustainable growth rate.

Bankers use this information in several ways. Quick comparison of a company's actual growth rate to its sustainable rate tells the banker what issues will be at the top of management's financial agenda. If actual growth consistently exceeds sustainable growth, management's problem will be where to get the cash to finance growth. The banker thus can anticipate interest in loan products. Conversely, if sustainable growth consistently exceeds actual, the banker had best be prepared to talk about investment products, because management's problem will be what to do with all the cash that keeps piling up in the till.

Bankers also find the sustainable growth equation useful for explaining to financially inexperienced small business owners and overly optimistic entrepreneurs that, for the long-run viability of their business, it is necessary to keep growth and profitability in proper balance.

Finally, comparison of actual to sustainable growth rates helps a banker understand why a loan applicant needs money and for how long the need might continue. In one instance, a loan applicant requested $100,000 to pay off several insistent suppliers and promised to repay in a few months when he collected some accounts receivable that were coming due. A sustainable growth analysis revealed that the firm had been growing at four to six times its sustainable growth rate and that this pattern was likely to continue in the foreseeable future. This alerted the banker that impatient suppliers were only a symptom of the much more fundamental disease of overly rapid growth, and that a $100,000 loan would likely prove to be only the down payment on a much larger, multiyear commitment.

Robert C. Higgins is Professor of Finance at the University of Washington. He pioneered the use of sustainable growth as a tool for financial analysis.

sured by the debt/equity ratio, and its dividend policy as measured by the retention ratio.

Given values for all four of these, there is only one growth rate that can be achieved. This is an important point, so it bears restating:

If a firm does not wish to sell new equity and its profit margin, total asset turnover (or capital intensity), financial policy, and dividend policy are all fixed, then there is only one possible growth rate.

As we described early in this chapter, one of the primary benefits of financial planning is to ensure internal consistency among the firm's various goals. The sustainable growth rate captures this element nicely. Also, we now see how a financial planning model can be used to test the feasibility of a planned growth rate. If sales are to grow at a rate higher than the sustainable growth rate, the firm must increase profit margins, increase total asset turnover, increase financial leverage, increase earnings retention, or sell new shares.

Lecture Tip: See IM 4.4 for other factors to take into account in undertaking sales growth as a goal of the firm.

The two growth rates, internal and sustainable, are summarized in Table 4.9.

TABLE 4.9
Summary of internal and sustainable growth rates

I. Internal Growth Rate

$$\text{Internal growth rate} = \frac{\text{ROA} \times b}{1 - \text{ROA} \times b}$$

where

ROA = Return on assets = Net income/Total assets
b = Plowback (retention) ratio
= Addition to retained earnings/Net income

The internal growth rate is the maximum growth rate that can be achieved with no external financing of any kind.

II. Sustainable Growth Rate

$$\text{Sustainable growth rate} = \frac{\text{ROE} \times b}{1 - \text{ROE} \times b}$$

where

ROE = Return on equity = Net income/Total equity
b = Plowback (retention) ratio
= Addition to retained earnings/Net income

The sustainable growth rate is the maximum growth rate that can be achieved with no external equity financing while maintaining a constant debt/equity ratio.

EXAMPLE 4.2 Profit Margins and Sustainable Growth

The Sandar Co. has a debt/equity ratio of .5, a profit margin of 3 percent, a dividend payout of 40 percent, and a capital intensity ratio of 1.0. What is its sustainable growth rate? If Sandar desires a 10 percent sustainable growth rate and plans to achieve this goal by improving profit margins, what would you think?

ROE is $.03 \times 1.0 \times 1.5 = 4.5$ percent. The retention ratio is $1.0 - .40 = .60$.

Sustainable growth is thus $.045(.60)/[1.0 - .045(.60)] = 2.77$ percent.

To achieve a 10 percent growth rate, the profit margin will have to rise. To see this, assume that sustainable growth is equal to 10 percent and then solve for profit margin, PM:

$$.10 = \text{PM}(1.0)(1.5)(.6)/[1 - \text{PM}(1.0)(1.5)(.6)]$$
$$\text{PM} = .1/.99 = 10.1\%$$

For the plan to succeed, the necessary increase in profit margin is substantial, from 3 percent to about 10 percent. This may not be feasible. • • •

CONCEPT QUESTIONS

4.4a What are the determinants of growth?

4.4b How is a firm's sustainable growth related to its accounting return on equity (ROE)?

4.5 SOME CAVEATS OF FINANCIAL PLANNING MODELS

Concept Q Answer 4.5a

Financial planning models do not always ask the right questions. A primary reason is they tend to rely on accounting relationships and not financial relationships. In particular, the three basic elements of firm value tend to get left out, namely, cash flow size, risk, and timing.

Because of this, financial planning models sometimes do not produce output that gives the user many meaningful clues about what strategies will lead to increases in value. Instead, they divert the user's attention to questions concerning the association of, say, the debt/equity ratio and firm growth.

The financial model we used for the Hoffman Company was simple, in fact, too simple. Our model, like many in use today, is really an accounting statement generator at heart. Such models are useful for pointing out inconsistencies and reminding us of financial needs, but they offer very little guidance concerning what to do about these problems.

In closing our discussion, we should add that financial planning is an iterative process. Plans are created, examined, and modified over and over. The final plan will be a negotiated result between all the different parties to the process. In fact, long-term financial planning in most corporations relies on what might be called the Procrustes approach.[1] Upper-level management has a goal in mind, and it is up to the planning staff to rework and ultimately deliver a feasible plan that meets that goal.

The final plan will therefore implicitly contain different goals in different areas and also satisfy many constraints. For this reason, such a plan need not be a dispassionate assessment of what we think the future will bring; it may instead be a means of reconciling the planned activities of different groups and a way of setting common goals for the future.

Lecture Tip: It should be noted that financial planning models of the type described here also do not replace the cash budget for forecasting cash inflows and outflows. Cash budgeting is discussed in Chapter 16.

Concept Q Answer 4.5b

Video Note: Some of the difficulties inherent in starting a business are described in the video supplement, "Financial Reality and the Entrepreneur."

Lecture Tip: Although our focus is on the investment and financing implications of growth, the impact of management on growth should not be underestimated.

Lecture Tip: See IM 4.5 and Trans. 4.10 for a list of questions a forecaster may wish to consider in interpreting the results of a financial planning exercise.

CONCEPT QUESTIONS

4.5a What are some important elements that are often missing in financial planning models?

4.5b Why do we say planning is an iterative process?

4.6 SUMMARY AND CONCLUSIONS

Financial planning forces the firm to think about the future. We have examined a number of features of the planning process. We describe what financial planning can accomplish and the components of a financial model. We go on to develop the relationship between growth and financing needs, and we discuss how a financial planning model is useful in exploring that relationship.

Corporate financial planning should not become a purely mechanical activity. If it does, it will probably focus on the wrong things. In particular, plans all too often are formulated in terms of a growth target with no explicit linkage to value creation, and they frequently are overly concerned with accounting statements. Nevertheless, the alternative to financial planning is "stumbling into the future."

Chapter Review Problems and Self-Test

4.1 Calculating EFN Based on the following information for the Corwin Company, what is EFN if sales are predicted to grow by 20 percent? Use the percentage of sales approach. The payout ratio is constant.

[1] In Greek mythology, Procrustes is a giant who seizes travelers and ties them to an iron bed. He stretches them or cuts off their legs as needed to make them fit the bed.

CORWIN COMPANY
Financial Statements

Income Statement	
Sales	$2,750
Cost of sales	2,400
Tax (34%)	119
Net income	$ 231
Dividends	$ 77

Balance Sheet			
Current assets	$ 600	Long-term debt	$ 200
Net fixed assets	800	Equity	1,200
Total	$1,400	Total	$1,400

4.2 **Sustainable Growth** Based on the information in Problem 4.1, what growth rate can Corwin maintain if no external financing is used? What is the sustainable growth rate?

Answers to Self-Test Problems

4.1 We can calculate EFN by preparing the pro forma statements using the percentage of sales approach. Note that sales are forecast to be $2,750 × 1.2 = $3,300.

CORWIN COMPANY
Financial Statements
Pro Forma Income Statement

Sales	$3,300.0	Forecast
Cost of sales	2,880.0	87.27% of sales
Tax (34%)	142.8	
Net income	$ 277.2	
Dividends	$ 92.4	33.33% of net income

Pro Forma Balance Sheet

Current assets	$ 720	21.81% of sales	Long-term debt	$ 200.0	n/a
Net fixed assets	960	29.09% of sales	Equity	1,384.8	n/a
Total	$1,680	50.90% of sales	Total	$1,584.8	n/a
			EFN	$ 95.2	

4.2 Corwin retains $b = (1 - .33) = .67$ of net income. Return on assets is $231/$1,400 = 16.5%. The internal growth rate is

$$\frac{(\text{ROA} \times b)}{(1 - \text{ROA} \times b)} = \frac{(.165 \times .67)}{(1 - .165 \times .67)}$$
$$= 12.36\%$$

Return on equity for Corwin is $231/$1,200 = 19.25%, so we can calculate the sustainable growth rate as

$$\frac{(\text{ROE} \times b)}{(1 - \text{ROE} \times b)} = \frac{(.1925 \times .67)}{(1 - .1925 \times .67)}$$
$$= 14.81\%$$

Questions and Problems

Basic
(Questions 1–17)

1. **Pro Forma Statements** Consider the following simplified financial statements for the Goldfinch Corporation:

Income Statement			Balance Sheet			
Sales	$7,000	Assets	$3,500	Debt	$1,750
Costs	6,000			Equity	1,750
Net income	$1,000	Total	$3,500	Total	$3,500

Dividends = $850

Goldfinch has predicted a sales increase of 20 percent. It has also predicted that every item on the balance sheet will increase by 20 percent as well. Create the pro forma statements and reconcile them. What is the plug variable here?

2. **Pro Forma Statements and EFN** In the previous question, assume Goldfinch pays out half of net income in the form of a cash dividend. Costs and assets vary with sales, but debt and equity do not. Prepare the pro forma statements and determine the external financing needed. EFN = $100

3. **Calculating EFN** The most recent financial statements for Gletglen Co. are shown below. EFN = −$572.50

Income Statement		Balance Sheet			
Sales	$2,000	Assets	$5,000	Debt	$3,000
Costs	850			Equity	2,000
Net income	$1,150	Total	$5,000	Total	$5,000

Assets and costs are proportional to sales. Debt is not. No dividends are paid. Next year's sales are projected to be $2,300. What is the external financing needed (EFN)?

4. **EFN** The most recent financial statements for REM Co. are shown below. EFN = $6,080

Income Statement		Balance Sheet			
Sales	$10,000	Assets	$40,000	Debt	$15,000
Costs	4,000			Equity	25,000
EBIT	$ 6,000	Total	$40,000	Total	$40,000
Taxes	2,400				
Net income	$ 3,600				

Assets and costs are proportional to sales. Debt is not. A dividend of $2,000 was paid, and REM wishes to maintain a constant payout. Next year's sales are projected to be $12,000. What is the external financing needed (EFN)?

5. **EFN** The most recent financial statements for Aprostate Co. are shown below. EFN = $692.80

Income Statement		Balance Sheet			
Sales	$2,500	Current assets	$2,000	Current liabilities	$ 800
Costs	2,000	Fixed assets	4,000	Long-term debt	1,200
Taxes	200			Equity	4,000
Net income	$ 300	Total	$6,000	Total	$6,000

Assets, costs, and current liabilities are proportional to sales. Long-term debt is not. Aprostate maintains a constant 60 percent dividend payout. Next year's sales are projected to be $2,900. What is the external financing needed (EFN)?

Internal growth rate = 2.41%

6. **Calculating Internal Growth** The most recent financial statements for Piltdown Co. are shown below.

Income Statement		Balance Sheet			
Sales	$4,750	Current assets	$ 5,500	Debt	$20,000
Costs	2,900	Fixed assets	27,500	Equity	13,000
Taxes	740	Total	$33,000	Total	$33,000
Net income	$1,110				

Assets and costs are proportional to sales. Debt is not. Piltdown maintains a constant 30 percent dividend payout. No equity external financing is possible. What is the internal growth rate?

Sustainable growth rate = 6.36%

7. **Calculating Sustainable Growth** For the company in the previous problem, what is the sustainable growth rate?

8. **Growth as a Firm Goal** Explain why growth by itself is not an appropriate goal for financial management. In particular, describe a scenario under which the goals of growth and owner wealth maximization could be in conflict.

Maximum sales increase = $837.78
Trans. 4.11

9. **Sales and Growth** The most recent financial statements for Fiddich Co. are shown below.

Income Statement		Balance Sheet			
Sales	$19,000	Net working capital	$17,475	Long-term debt	$55,820
Costs	14,700	Fixed assets	75,000	Equity	36,655
Taxes	1,720	Total	$92,475	Total	$92,475
Net income	$ 2,580				

Assets and costs are proportional to sales. Fiddich maintains a constant 40 percent dividend payout and a constant debt/equity ratio. What is the maximum increase in sales that can be sustained assuming no new equity is issued?

Addition to retained earnings = $1,702

10. **Calculating Retained Earnings from Pro Forma Income** Consider the following income statement for the Folker Corporation:

FOLKER CORPORATION
Income Statement

Sales		$9,000
Costs		6,000
Taxable income		$3,000
Taxes (34%)		1,020
Net income		$1,980
Dividends	$500	

A 15 percent growth rate in sales is projected. Prepare a pro forma income statement assuming costs vary with sales and the dividend payout ratio is constant. What is the projected addition to retained earnings?

11. **Applying Percentage of Sales** The balance sheet for the Folker Corporation is shown below. Based on this information and the income statement in the previous problem, supply the missing information using the percentage of sales approach. Assume that

accounts payable vary with sales while notes payable do not. Put "n/a" where needed.

FOLKER CORPORATION
Balance Sheet

	($)	(%)		($)	(%)
Assets			**Liabilities and Owners' Equity**		
Current assets			Current liabilities		
Cash	$ 1,500	______	Accounts payable	$ 3,000	______
Accounts receivable	3,000	______	Notes payable	2,000	______
Inventory	3,000	______	Total	$ 5,000	______
Total	$ 7,500	______	Long-term debt	3,000	______
Fixed assets			Owners' equity		
Net plant and equipment	10,000	______	Common stock and paid-in surplus	$ 2,500	______
			Retained earnings	7,000	______
			Total	$ 9,500	______
Total assets	$17,500	______	Total liabilities and owners' equity	$17,500	______

12. **EFN and Sales** From the previous two questions, prepare a pro forma balance sheet showing EFN, assuming a 15 percent increase in sales and no new external debt or equity financing. EFN = $473

13. **Calculating ROA and ROE** From the previous question, what is the projected ROA? ROE? ROA = 11.31% ROE = 20.33%

14. **Internal Growth** If a firm has a 12 percent ROA and a 60 percent payout ratio, what is its internal growth rate? Internal growth rate = 5.04%

15. **Sustainable Growth** If a firm has a 25 percent ROE and a 45 percent payout ratio, what is its sustainable growth rate? Sustainable growth rate = 15.94%

16. **Sustainable Growth** Based on the following information, calculate the sustainable growth rate: Sustainable growth rate = 19.33% ROE = 21.6% **Trans. 4.12**

$$\begin{aligned} \text{Profit margin} &= 6\% \\ \text{Capital intensity ratio} &= 0.5 \\ \text{Debt/equity ratio} &= 0.8 \\ \text{Net income} &= \$20{,}000 \\ \text{Dividends} &= \$5{,}000 \end{aligned}$$

What is the ROE here?

17. **Sustainable Growth** Assuming the following ratios are constant, what is the sustainable growth rate? Sustainable growth rate = 7.53%

$$\begin{aligned} \text{Total asset turnover} &= 1.0 \\ \text{Profit margin} &= 4\% \\ \text{Equity multiplier} &= 2.5 \\ \text{Payout ratio} &= 30\% \end{aligned}$$

Intermediate (Questions 18–25)

18. **Percentage of Sales Issues** What are the advantages and disadvantages of the percentage of sales approach? In particular, is the assumption that many of the firm's costs and assets are directly proportional to sales a reasonable assumption? Does your answer depend on the time horizon being considered?

Profit margin = 12.28%

19. **Growth and Profit Margin** A firm wishes to maintain a growth rate of 12 percent a year, a debt/equity ratio of 0.6, and a dividend payout of 40 percent. The ratio of total assets to sales is constant at 1.1. What profit margin must the firm achieve?

D/E ratio = 2.49 times

20. **Growth and Debt/Equity Ratio** A firm wishes to maintain a growth rate of 15 percent and a dividend payout of 30 percent. The ratio of total assets to sales is constant at 1.5, and profit margin is 8 percent. If the firm also wishes to maintain a constant debt/equity ratio, what must it be?

TAT = 1.89 times

21. **Growth and Assets** A firm wishes to maintain a growth rate of 6 percent and a dividend payout of 70 percent. The current profit margin is 10 percent and the firm uses no external financing sources. What must the current total asset turnover be?

Sustainable growth rate = 9.89%
ROA = 6%

22. **Sustainable Growth** Based on the following information, calculate the sustainable growth rate:

Profit margin = 5%
Total asset turnover = 1.2
Total debt ratio = 0.6
Payout ratio = 40%

What is ROA here?

Sustainable growth rate = 1.52%
New borrowing = $457
Internal growth rate = 0.86%

23. **Sustainable Growth and Outside Financing** You've collected the following information about the Wutzup Corporation:

Sales = $25,000
Net income = $1,000
Dividends = $400
Total debt = $30,000
Total equity = $40,000

What is the sustainable growth rate for Wutzup? If they do grow at this rate, how much borrowing will take place in the coming year? What rate could be supported with no outside financing at all?

EFN = $14,315

24. **Calculating EFN** The most recent financial statements for Hi Grow, Inc., are shown below. 1995 sales are projected to grow by

25 percent. Depreciation expense and interest expense will remain constant; the tax rate and the payout rate will also remain constant. Costs, other expenses, assets, and accounts payable increase spontaneously with sales. If no new debt or equity is issued, what is the external financing needed (EFN) to support the 25 percent growth rate in sales?

HI GROW, INC
1994 Income Statement

Sales	$600,000
Costs	450,000
Other expenses	25,000
EBDIT	$125,000
Depreciation	25,000
EBIT	$100,000
Interest	10,000
Taxable income	$ 90,000
Taxes (34%)	30,600
Net income	$ 59,400
Dividends	$ 12,500
Retained earnings	46,900

HI GROW, INC.
Balance Sheet as of December 31, 1994

Assets		Liabilities and Owners' Equity	
Current assets		Current liabilities	
Cash	$ 10,000	Accounts payable	$ 40,000
Accounts receivable	40,000	Notes payable	10,000
Inventory	50,000	Total	$ 50,000
Total	$100,000	Long-term debt	75,000
Fixed assets		Total liabilities	$125,000
Net plant and equipment	250,000	Owners' equity	
		Common stock and paid-in surplus	$ 25,000
		Retained earnings	200,000
		Total	$225,000
Total assets	$350,000	Total liabilities and owners' equity	$350,000

25. **Calculating EFN** In Problem 24, suppose the firm wishes to keep its debt/equity ratio constant. What is EFN now? EFN = −$10,788

Part Three

3

VALUATION OF FUTURE CASH FLOWS

A core question in finance is: What is the value today of cash flows to be received at a later date? This question will occupy our attention for many chapters. This part of our text introduces some of the basic procedures used. Chapter 5 considers the value of a single cash flow to be received at some future date, and it develops the basic present value equation, a key result.

In Chapter 6, we expand on the basic present value equation to value multiple cash flows. We also consider a number of related topics, including loan valuation, calculation of loan payments, and determination of rates of return.

Chapter 7 shows how the valuation principles developed can be applied to stock and bond valuation. We also describe essential features of stocks and bonds and how their prices are reported in the financial press.

OUTLINE

Chapter Five

Introduction to Valuation: The Time Value of Money

After studying this chapter, you should have a good understanding of:

How to determine the future value of an investment made today.

How to determine the present value of cash to be received at a future date.

How to find the return on an investment.

Trans. 5.1
Chapter Outline

Lecture Tip: See IM 5.1 for a slightly different presentation of time value of money.

One of the basic problems faced by the financial manager is how to determine the value today of cash flows expected in the future. For example, the jackpot in a PowerBall™ lottery drawing was \$110 million. Does this mean the winning ticket was worth \$110 million? The answer is no because the jackpot was actually going to pay out over a 20-year period at a rate of \$5.5 million per year. How much is the ticket worth then? The answer depends on the time value of money, the subject of this chapter.

In the most general sense, the phrase *time value of money* refers to the fact that a dollar in hand today is worth more than a dollar promised at some time in the future. On a practical level, one reason for this is that you could earn interest while you waited; so a dollar today would grow to more than a dollar later. The trade-off between money now and money later thus depends on, among other things, the rate you can earn by investing. Our goal in this chapter is to explicitly evaluate this trade-off between dollars today and dollars at some future time.

A thorough understanding of the material in this chapter is critical to understanding material in subsequent chapters, so you should study it with particular care. We will present a number of examples in this chapter. In many problems, your answer may differ from ours slightly. This can happen because of rounding and is not a cause for concern.

5.1 FUTURE VALUE AND COMPOUNDING

future value (FV)
The amount an investment is worth after one or more periods.

The first thing we will study is future value. **Future value (FV)** refers to the amount of money an investment will grow to over some period of time at some given interest rate. Put another way, future value is the cash value of an investment some time in the future. We start out by considering the simplest case, a single period investment.

Concept Q Answer 5.1a

Self-Test Problem 5.1 Problem 2

Investing for a Single Period

Suppose you were to invest \$100 in a savings account that pays 10 percent interest per year. How much will you have in one year? You would have \$110. This \$110 is equal to your original *principal* of \$100 plus \$10 in interest that you earn. We say that \$110 is the future value of \$100 invested for one year at 10 percent, and we simply mean that \$100 today is worth \$110 in one year, given that 10 percent is the interest rate.

In general, if you invest for one period at an interest rate of r, your investment will grow to $(1 + r)$ per dollar invested. In our example, r is 10 percent, so your investment grows to $(1 + .10) = 1.1$ dollars per dollar invested. You invested \$100 in this case, so you ended up with $\$100 \times (1.10) = \$110$.

Investing for More than One Period

Lecture Tip: See IM 5.1 for an example to further enhance students' intuition of the impact of interest on interest.

Concept Q Answer 5.1b

Going back to our \$100 investment, what will you have after two years, assuming the interest rate doesn't change? If you leave the entire \$110 in the bank, you will earn $\$110 \times .10 = \$11$ in interest during the second year, so you will have a total of $\$110 + 11 = \$121$. This \$121 is the future value of \$100 in two years at 10 percent. Another way of looking at it is that one year from now you are effectively investing \$110 at 10 percent for a year. This is a single period problem, so you'll end up with \$1.1 for every dollar invested or $\$110 \times 1.1 = \$121$ total.

This \$121 has four parts. The first part is the \$100 original principal. The second part is the \$10 in interest you earned in the first year along with another \$10 (the third part) you earn in the second year, for a total of \$120. The last \$1 you end up with (the fourth part) is interest you earn in the second year on the interest paid in the first year: $\$10 \times .10 = \$1$.

This process of leaving your money and any accumulated interest in an investment for more than one period, thereby *reinvesting* the interest, is called **compounding.** Compounding the interest means earning **interest on interest,** so we call the result **compound interest.** With **simple interest,** the interest is not reinvested, so interest is earned each period only on the original principal.

compounding
The process of accumulating interest in an investment over time to earn more interest.

interest on interest
Interest earned on the reinvestment of previous interest payments.

compound interest
Interest earned on both the initial principal and the interest reinvested from prior periods.

simple interest
Interest earned only on the original principal amount invested.

EXAMPLE 5.1 Interest on Interest

Suppose you locate a two-year investment that pays 14 percent per year. If you invest \$325, how much will you have at the end of the two years? How much of this is simple interest? How much is compound interest?

At the end of the first year, you will have $\$325 \times (1 + .14) = \$370.50$. If you reinvest this entire amount, and thereby compound the interest, you will have $\$370.50 \times 1.14 = \$422.37$ at the end of the second year. The total interest you earn is thus $\$422.37 - 325 = \$97.37$. Your \$325 original principal earns $\$325 \times .14 = \$45.50$ in interest each year, for a two-year total of \$91 in simple interest. The remaining $\$97.37 - 91 = \$6.37$ results from compounding. You can check this by noting that the interest earned in the first year is \$45.50. The interest on interest earned in the second year thus amounts to $\$45.50 \times .14 = \$6.37$, as we calculated. • • •

Trans. 5.2 FV for a Lump Sum (Supplemental)

We now take a closer look at how we calculated the \$121 future value. We multiplied \$110 by 1.1 to get \$121. The \$110, however, was \$100 also multiplied by 1.1. In other words:

$$\begin{aligned}\$121 &= \$110 \times 1.1 \\ &= (\$100 \times 1.1) \times 1.1 \\ &= \$100 \times (1.1 \times 1.1) \\ &= \$100 \times 1.1^2 \\ &= \$100 \times 1.21\end{aligned}$$

At the risk of belaboring the obvious, let's ask: How much would our \$100 grow to after three years? Once again, in two years, we'll be investing \$121 for one period at 10 percent. We'll end up with \$1.1 for every dollar we invest, or \$121 × 1.1 = \$133.1 total. This \$133.1 is thus:

$$\begin{aligned}\$133.1 &= \$121 \times 1.1 \\ &= (\$110 \times 1.1) \times 1.1 \\ &= (\$100 \times 1.1) \times 1.1 \times 1.1 \\ &= \$100 \times (1.1 \times 1.1 \times 1.1) \\ &= \$100 \times 1.1^3 \\ &= \$100 \times 1.331\end{aligned}$$

Concept Q Answer 5.1c

You're probably noticing a pattern to these calculations, so we can now go ahead and state the general result. As our examples suggest, the future value of \$1 invested for t periods at a rate of r per period is:

$$\text{Future value} = \$1 \times (1 + r)^t \qquad [5.1]$$

The expression $(1 + r)^t$ is sometimes called the *future value interest factor* (or just *future value factor*) for \$1 invested at r percent for t periods and can be abbreviated as FVIF(r, t).

In our example, what would your \$100 be worth after five years? We can first compute the relevant future value factor as:

$$(1 + r)^t = (1 + .10)^5 = 1.1^5 = 1.6105$$

Your \$100 will thus grow to:

$$\$100 \times 1.6105 = \$161.05$$

The growth of your \$100 each year is illustrated in Table 5.1. As shown, the interest earned in each year is equal to the beginning amount multiplied by the interest rate of 10 percent.

In Table 5.1, notice the total interest you earn is \$61.05. Over the five-year span of this investment, the simple interest is \$100 × .10 = \$10 per year, so you accumulate \$50 this way. The other \$11.05 is from compounding.

Trans. 5.3 Interest on Interest Illustration (Supplemental)

Figure 5.1 illustrates the growth of the compound interest in Table 5.1. Notice how the simple interest is constant each year, but the compound interest you earn gets bigger every year. The size of the compound interest keeps increasing because more and more interest builds up and there is thus more to compound.

Future values depend critically on the assumed interest rate, particularly for long-lived investments. Figure 5.2 illustrates this relationship by

TABLE 5.1
Future value of $100 at 10 percent

Trans. 5.4

Year	Beginning Amount		Interest Earned	Ending Amount
1	$100.00		$10.00	$110.00
2	110.00		11.00	121.00
3	121.00		12.10	133.10
4	133.10		13.31	146.41
5	146.41		14.64	161.05
		Total interest	$61.05	

FIGURE 5.1
Future value, simple interest, and compound interest

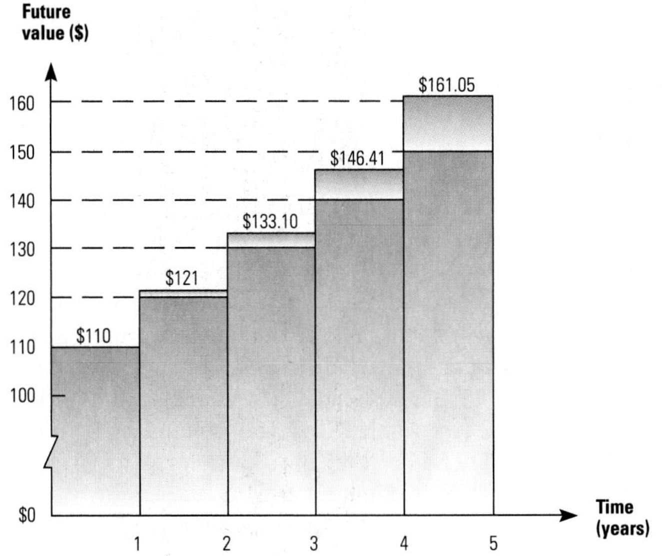

Growth of $100 original amount at 10% per year. Blue shaded area represents the portion of the total that results from compounding of interest.

FIGURE 5.2
Future value of $1 for different periods and rates

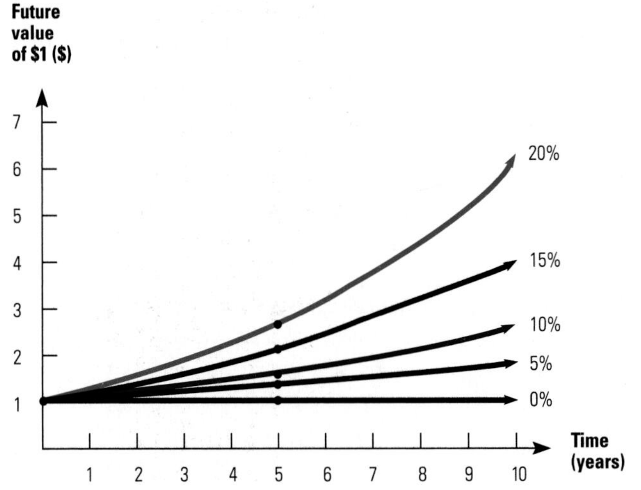

TABLE 5.2
Future value interest factors

Number of Periods	Interest Rate 5%	10%	15%	20%
1	1.0500	1.1000	1.1500	1.2000
2	1.1025	1.2100	1.3225	1.4400
3	1.1576	1.3310	1.5209	1.7280
4	1.2155	1.4641	1.7490	2.0736
5	1.2763	1.6105	2.0114	2.4883

plotting the growth of \$1 for different rates and lengths of time. Notice the future value of \$1 after 10 years is about \$6.20 at a 20 percent rate, but it is only about \$2.60 at 10 percent. In this case, doubling the interest rate more than doubles the future value.

To solve future value problems, we need to come up with the relevant future value factors. There are several different ways of doing this. In our example, we could have multiplied 1.1 by itself 5 times. This will work just fine, but it would get to be very tedious for, say, a 30-year investment.

Fortunately, there are several easier ways to get future value factors. Most calculators have a key labeled "y^x." You can usually just enter 1.1, press this key, enter 5, and press the "=" key to get the answer. This is an easy way to calculate future value factors because it's quick and accurate.

Alternatively, you can use a table that contains future value factors for some common interest rates and time periods. Table 5.2 contains some of these factors. Table A.1 in the Appendix at the end of the book contains a much larger set. To use the table, find the column that corresponds to 10 percent. Then look down the rows until you come to five periods. You should find the factor that we calculated, 1.6105.

Tables such as 5.2 are not as common as they once were because they predate inexpensive calculators and are only available for a relatively small number of rates. Interest rates are often quoted to three or four decimal points, so the size of tables needed to deal with these accurately would be quite large. As a result, the "real world" has moved away from using them. We will emphasize the use of a calculator in this chapter.

These tables still serve a useful purpose. To make sure you are doing the calculations correctly, pick a factor from the table and then calculate it yourself to see that you get the same answer. There are plenty of numbers to choose from.

EXAMPLE 5.2 Compound Interest

You've located an investment that pays 12 percent. That rate sounds good to you, so you invest \$400. How much will you have in three years? How much will you have in seven years? At the end of seven years, how much interest have you earned? How much of that interest results from compounding?

Based on our discussion, we can calculate the future value factor for 12 percent and three years as:

$$(1 + r)^t = 1.12^3 = 1.4049$$

Your \$400 thus grows to:

$$\$400 \times 1.4049 = \$561.97$$

After seven years, you would have:

$$\$400 \times 1.12^7 = \$400 \times 2.2107 = \$884.27$$

Thus, you will more than double your money over seven years.

Since you invested \$400, the interest in the \$884.27 future value is \$884.27 − 400 = \$484.27. At 12 percent, your \$400 investment earns \$400 × .12 = \$48 in simple interest every year. Over seven years, the simple interest thus totals 7 × \$48 = \$336. The other \$484.27 − 336 = \$148.27 is from compounding. • • •

The effect of compounding is not great over short time periods, but it really starts to add up as the horizon grows. To take an extreme case, suppose one of your more frugal ancestors had invested \$5 for you at a 6 percent interest rate 200 years ago. How much would you have today? The future value factor is a substantial $(1.06)^{200} = 115{,}125.91$ (you won't find this one in a table), so you would have \$5 × 115,125.91 = \$575,629.53 today. Notice that the simple interest is just \$5 × .06 = \$.30 per year. After 200 years, this amounts to \$60. The rest is from reinvesting. Such is the power of compound interest!

EXAMPLE 5.3 How Much for That Island?

To further illustrate the effect of compounding for long horizons, consider the case of Peter Minuit and the Indians. In 1626, Minuit bought all of Manhattan Island for about \$24 in goods and trinkets. This sounds cheap, but the Indians may have gotten the better end of the deal. To see why, suppose the Indians had sold the goods and invested the \$24 at 10 percent. How much would it be worth today?

Roughly 370 years have passed since the transaction. At 10 percent, \$24 will grow by quite a bit over that time. How much? The future value factor is approximately:

$$(1 + r)^t = 1.1^{370} \approx 2{,}000{,}000{,}000{,}000{,}000$$

That is, 2 followed by 15 zeroes. The future value is thus on the order of 24 × 2 quadrillion or about 48 *quadrillion* dollars (give or take a few hundreds of trillions).

Well, \$48 quadrillion is a lot of money. How much? If you had it, you could buy the United States. All of it. Cash. With money left over to buy Canada, Mexico, and the rest of the world, for that matter.

Lecture Tip: Additional real-world examples of the effects of compound interest appear in IM 5.1.

This example is something of an exaggeration, of course. In 1626, it would not have been easy to locate an investment that would pay 10 percent every year without fail for the next 370 years. • • •

CONCEPT QUESTIONS

5.1a What do we mean by the future value of an investment?

5.1b What does it mean to compound interest? How does compound interest differ from simple interest?

5.1c In general, what is the future value of \$1 invested at *r* per period for *t* periods?

5.2 PRESENT VALUE AND DISCOUNTING

Self-Test Problem 5.2
Problems 3, 10, 28

When we discuss future value, we are thinking of questions like "What will my \$2,000 investment grow to if it earns a 6.5 percent return every year for the next six years?" The answer to this question is what we called the future value of $2,000 invested at 6.5 percent for six years (check that the answer is about $2,918).

Lecture Tip: It is often useful to emphasize that, as this example points out, the appropriate discount rate is really an "opportunity rate"; i.e., the return one could earn on other investments of similar risk.

There is another type of question that comes up even more often in financial management which is obviously related to future value. Suppose you need to have $10,000 in 10 years, and you can earn 6.5 percent on your money. How much do you have to invest today to reach your goal? You can verify that the answer is $5,327.26. How do we know this? Read on.

Trans. 5.5
PV for a Lump Sum (Supplemental)

The Single Period Case

present value (PV)
The current value of future cash flows discounted at the appropriate discount rate.

We've seen that the future value of $1 invested for one year at 10 percent is $1.10. We now ask a slightly different question: How much do we have to invest today at 10 percent to get $1 in one year? In other words, we know the future value here is $1, but what is the **present value (PV)**? The answer isn't too hard to figure out. Whatever we invest today will be 1.1 times bigger at the end of the year. Since we need $1 at the end of the year:

$$\text{Present value} \times 1.1 = \$1$$

Or, solving for the present value:

$$\text{Present value} = \$1/1.1 = \$.909$$

Concept Q
Answers 5.2a, 5.2b

discount
Calculate the present value of some future amount.

In this case, the present value is the answer to the following question: "What amount, invested today, will grow to $1 in one year if the interest rate is 10 percent?" Present value is thus just the reverse of future value. Instead of compounding the money forward into the future, we **discount** it back to the present.

Lecture Tip: See IM 5.2 for more regarding the relationship between present and future value interest factors.

EXAMPLE 5.4 Single Period PV

Suppose you need $400 to buy textbooks next year. You can earn 7 percent on your money. How much do you have to put up today?

We need to know the PV of $400 in one year at 7 percent. Proceeding as above:

$$\text{Present value} \times 1.07 = \$400$$

We can now solve for the present value:

$$\text{Present value} = \$400 \times (1/1.07) = \$373.83$$

Thus, $373.83 is the present value. Again, this just means that investing this amount for one year at 7 percent will result in your having a future value of $400. • • •

From our examples, the present value of $1 to be received in one period is generally given as:

$$\text{PV} = \$1 \times [1/(1 + r)] = \$1/(1 + r)$$

We next examine how to get the present value of an amount to be paid in two or more periods into the future.

Trans. 5.6
PV of $1 for Different Periods and Rates

Present Values for Multiple Periods

Suppose you needed to have $1,000 in two years. If you can earn 7 percent, how much do you have to invest to make sure that you have the $1,000 when you need it? In other words, what is the present value of $1,000 in two years if the relevant rate is 7 percent?

Based on your knowledge of future values, you know the amount invested must grow to $1,000 over the two years. In other words, it must be the case that:

$$\begin{aligned}\$1{,}000 &= \text{PV} \times 1.07 \times 1.07 \\ &= \text{PV} \times 1.07^2 \\ &= \text{PV} \times 1.1449\end{aligned}$$

Given this, we can solve for the present value:

$$\text{Present value} = \$1{,}000/1.1449 = \$873.44$$

Therefore, $873.44 is the amount you must invest in order to achieve your goal.

EXAMPLE 5.5 Saving Up

You would like to buy a new automobile. You have about $50,000 or so, but the car costs $68,500. If you can earn 9 percent, how much do you have to invest today to buy the car in two years? Do you have enough? Assume the price will stay the same.

What we need to know is the present value of $68,500 to be paid in two years, assuming a 9 percent rate. Based on our discussion, this is:

$$\text{PV} = \$68{,}500/1.09^2 = \$68{,}500/1.1881 = \$57{,}655.08$$

You're still about $7,655 short, even if you're willing to wait two years. • • •

Concept Q Answer 5.2d

As you have probably recognized by now, calculating present values is quite similar to calculating future values, and the general result looks much the same. The present value of $1 to be received t periods in the future at a discount rate of r is:

$$\text{PV} = \$1 \times [1/(1 + r)^t] = \$1/(1 + r)^t \qquad [5.2]$$

Concept Q Answer 5.2c

The quantity in brackets, $1/(1 + r)^t$, goes by several different names. Since it's used to discount a future cash flow, it is often called a *discount factor.* With this name, it is not surprising that the rate used in the calculation is often called the **discount rate.** We will tend to call it this in talking about present values. The quantity in brackets is also called the *present value interest factor* (or just *present value factor*) for $1 at r percent for t periods and is sometimes abbreviated as PVIF(r, t). Finally, calculating the present value of a future cash flow to determine its worth today is commonly called **discounted cash flow (DCF)** valuation.

discount rate
The rate used to calculate the present value of future cash flows.

discounted cash flow (DCF)
Valuation calculating the present value of a future cash flow to determine its value today.

To illustrate, suppose you need $1,000 in three years. You can earn 15 percent on your money. How much do you have to invest today? To find out, we have to determine the present value of $1,000 in three years at 15 percent. We do this by discounting $1,000 back three periods at 15 percent. With these numbers, the discount factor is:

$$1/(1 + .15)^3 = 1/1.5209 = .6575$$

The amount you must invest is thus:

$$\$1{,}000 \times .6575 = \$657.50$$

We say that $657.50 is the present or discounted value of $1,000 to be received in three years at 15 percent.

Lecture Tip: IM 5.2 provides an interesting real-world application of multi-period discounting.

There are tables for present value factors just as there are tables for future value factors, and you use them in the same way (if you use them at all). Table 5.3 contains a small set. A much larger set can be found in Table A.2 in the book's Appendix.

TABLE 5.3
Present value interest factors

Number of Periods	Interest Rate 5%	10%	15%	20%
1	.9524	.9091	.8696	.8333
2	.9070	.8264	.7561	.6944
3	.8638	.7513	.6575	.5787
4	.8227	.6830	.5718	.4823
5	.7835	.6209	.4972	.4019

In Table 5.3, the discount factor we just calculated, .6575, can be found by looking down the column labeled 15% until you come to the third row.

EXAMPLE 5.6 Deceptive Advertising

Recently, some businesses have been advertising things like "Come try our product. If you do, we'll give you $100 just for coming by!" If you read the fine print, what you find out is that they will give you a savings certificate that will pay you $100 in 25 years or so. If the going interest rate on such certificates is 10 percent per year, how much are they really giving you today?

What you're actually getting is the present value of $100 to be paid in 25 years. If the discount rate is 10 percent per year, then the discount factor is:

$$1/1.1^{25} = 1/10.8347 = .0923$$

This tells you that a dollar in 25 years is worth a little more than nine cents today, assuming a 10 percent discount rate. Given this, the promotion is actually paying you about .0923 × $100 = $9.23. Maybe this is enough to draw customers, but it's not $100. • • •

Lecture Tip: See IM 5.2 for more regarding the impact of varied interest rates on a given future value.

As the length of time until payment grows, present values decline. As Example 5.6 illustrates, present values tend to become small as the time horizon grows. If you look out far enough, they will always get close to zero. Also, for a given length of time, the higher the discount rate is, the lower is the present value. Put another way, present values and discount rates are inversely related. Increasing the discount rate decreases the PV and vice versa.

The relationship between time, discount rates, and present values is illustrated in Figure 5.3. Notice that by the time we get to 10 years, the present values are all substantially smaller than the future amounts.

FIGURE 5.3
Present value of $1 for different periods and rates

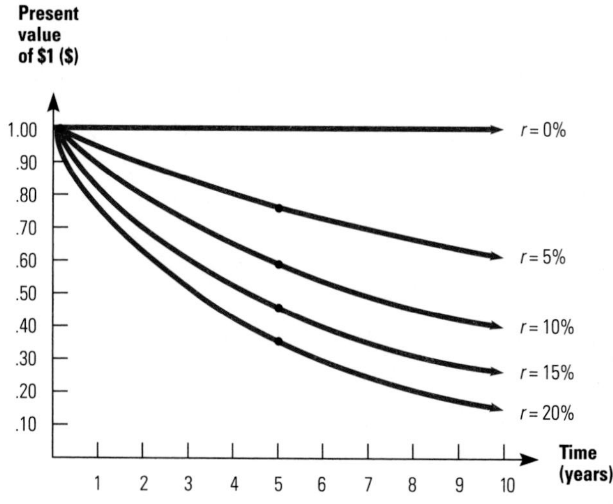

CONCEPT QUESTIONS

5.2a What do we mean by the present value of an investment?

5.2b The process of discounting a future amount back to the present is the opposite of doing what?

5.2c What do we mean by discounted cash flow or DCF valuation?

5.2d In general, what is the present value of $1 to be received in *t* periods, assuming a discount rate of *r* per period?

5.3 MORE ON PRESENT AND FUTURE VALUES

If you look back at the expressions we came up with for present and future values, you will see there is a very simple relationship between the two. We explore this relationship and some related issues in this section.

Problems 3, 12, 14, 15

Present versus Future Value

What we called the present value factor is just the reciprocal of (that is, 1 divided by) the future value factor:

$$\text{Future value factor} = (1 + r)^t$$
$$\text{Present value factor} = 1/(1 + r)^t$$

In fact, the easy way to calculate a present value factor on many calculators is to first calculate the future value factor and then press the "1/x" key to flip it over.

If we let FV_t stand for the future value after *t* periods, then the relationship between future value and present value can be written very simply as one of the following:

$$PV \times (1 + r)^t = FV_t$$
$$PV = FV_t/(1 + r)^t = FV_t \times [1/(1 + r)^t] \quad [5.3]$$

Concept Q Answer 5.3a, 5.3c

This last result we will call the *basic present value equation.* We will use it throughout the text. There are a number of variations that come up, but this simple equation underlies many of the most important ideas in finance.

Lecture Tip: The important notion of cash-flow equivalence is discussed in IM 5.3.

EXAMPLE 5.7 Evaluating Investments

To give you an idea of how we will be using present and future values, consider the following simple investment. Your company proposes to buy an asset for $335. This investment is very safe. You will sell off the asset in three years for $400. You know you could invest the $335 elsewhere at 10 percent with very little risk. What do you think of the proposed investment?

This is not a good investment. Why not? Because you can invest the $335 elsewhere at 10 percent. If you do, after three years it will grow to:

$$\begin{aligned} \$335 \times (1 + r)^t &= \$335 \times 1.1^3 \\ &= \$335 \times 1.331 \\ &= \$445.89 \end{aligned}$$

Since the proposed investment only pays out $400, it is not as good as other alternatives we have. Another way of saying the same thing is to notice that the present value of $400 in three years at 10 percent is:

$$\$400 \times [1/(1 + r)^t] = \$400/1.1^3 = \$400/1.331 = \$300.53$$

This tells us that we only have to invest about $300 to get $400 in three years, not $335. We will return to this type of analysis later on. • • •

Trans. 5.7
The Basic PV Equation
(Supplemental)

Determining the Discount Rate

It will turn out that we will frequently need to determine what discount rate is implicit in an investment. We can do this by looking at the basic present value equation:

$$PV = FV_t/(1 + r)^t$$

Lecture Tip: See IM 5.3 for a suggestion on alerting students to simplified logic of solving for "*r*."

There are only four parts to this equation: the present value (PV), the future value (FV_t), the discount rate (r), and the life of the investment (t). Given any three of these, we can always find the fourth.

EXAMPLE 5.8 Finding *r* for a Single Period Investment

You are considering a one-year investment. If you put up $1,250, you will get back $1,350. What rate is this investment paying?

First, in this single period case, the answer is fairly obvious. You are getting a total of $100 in addition to your $1,250. The implicit rate on this investment is thus $100/1,250 = 8 percent.

More formally, from the basic present value equation, the present value (the amount you must put up today) is $1,250. The future value (what the present value grows to) is $1,350. The time involved is one period, so we have:

$$\begin{aligned} \$1{,}250 &= \$1{,}350/(1 + r)^1 \\ (1 + r) &= \$1{,}350/1{,}250 = 1.08 \\ r &= 8\% \end{aligned}$$

In this simple case, of course, there was no need to go through this calculation, but, as we describe below, it gets a little harder when there is more than one period. • • •

To illustrate what happens with multiple periods, we might be offered an investment that costs us $100 and will double our money in eight years. To compare this to other investments, we would like to know what discount rate is implicit in these numbers. This discount rate is called the *rate of return* or sometimes just *return* on the investment. In this case, we have a present value of $100, a future value of $200 (double our money), and an eight-year life. To calculate the return, we can write the basic present value equation as:

$$\begin{aligned} PV &= FV_t/(1 + r)^t \\ \$100 &= \$200/(1 + r)^8 \end{aligned}$$

It could also be written as:

$$(1 + r)^8 = \$200/100 = 2$$

We now need to solve for r. There are three ways we could do it:

1. Use a financial calculator.
2. Solve the equation for $1 + r$ by taking the eighth root of both sides. Since this is the same thing as raising both sides to the power of ⅛ or .125, this is actually easy to do with the "y^x" key on a calculator. Just enter 2, then press "y^x," enter .125, and press the

" = " key. The eighth root should be about 1.09, which implies that r is 9 percent.

3. Use a future value table. The future value factor after eight years is equal to 2. If you look across the row corresponding to eight periods in Table A.1, you will see that a future value factor of 2 corresponds to the 9 percent column, again implying that the return here is 9 percent.

Lecture Tip: More generally, r is equal to $(FV/PV)^{1/t} - 1$.

Actually, in this particular example, there is a useful "back of the envelope" means of solving for r—the Rule of 72. For reasonable rates of return, the time it takes to double your money is given approximately by $72/r\%$. In our example, this is $72/r\% = 8$ years, implying that r is 9 percent as we calculated. This rule is fairly accurate for discount rates in the 5 percent to 20 percent range.

Concept Q Answer 5.3b

EXAMPLE 5.9 Double Your Fun

You have been offered an investment that promises to double your money every 10 years. What is the approximate rate of return on the investment?

From the Rule of 72, the rate of return is approximately $72/r\% = 10$, so the rate is approximately $72/10 = 7.2\%$. Check that the exact answer is 7.177 percent. • • •

A slightly more extreme example involves money bequeathed by Benjamin Franklin, who died on April 17, 1790. In his will, he gave 1,000 pounds sterling to Massachusetts and the city of Boston. He gave a like amount to Pennsylvania and the city of Philadelphia. The money was paid to Franklin when he held political office, but he believed that politicians should not be paid for their service (it appears that this view is not widely shared by modern-day politicians).

Trans. 5.8
An Example: A Penny Saved

Franklin originally specified that the money should be paid out 100 years after his death and used to train young people. Later, however, after some legal wrangling, it was agreed that the money would be paid out in 1990, 200 years after Franklin's death. By that time, the Pennsylvania bequest had grown to about \$2 million; the Massachusetts bequest had grown to \$4.5 million. The money was used to fund the Franklin Institutes in Boston and Philadelphia. Assuming that 1,000 pounds sterling was equivalent to 1,000 dollars, what rate of return did the two states earn (the dollar did not become the official U.S. currency until 1792)?

For Pennsylvania, the future value is \$2 million and the present value is \$1,000. There are 200 years involved, so we need to solve for r in the following:

$$\$1000 = \$2 \text{ million}/(1 + r)^{200}$$
$$(1 + r)^{200} = 2{,}000$$

Solving for r, the Pennsylvania money grew at about 3.87 percent per year. The Massachusetts money did better; check that the rate of return in this case was 4.3 percent. Small differences can add up!

For some recent examples of rates of return on collectibles, see the accompanying *Principles in Action* box. Be sure to verify some of the calculations underlying the claimed returns.

Principles in Action

'R' Toys '4' Us?

Christie's International PLC, perhaps best known for their art auctions, recently sold some toys at auction. Not just any toys, mind you, but collectibles including the action figure G. I. Joe and "Hot Wheels" cars, tiny metal cars from the late 60s and early 70s. The most visible form of collectible is probably the baseball trading card, but virtually anything of sentimental value from days gone by is considered collectible, and more and more they are being viewed as investments. Art and collectibles typically provide no cash flows, except when sold, and condition and buyer sentiment are the major determinants of value. The rate of return on such investments can be staggering at times.

A Schwinn Deluxe Tornado boy's bicycle cost $49.95 when it was new in 1959, and it was a beauty. Assuming it is still in like-new condition in 1995, it would be worth $500, ten times its original cost. While this looks to the untrained eye like a 1,000 percent return, the actual return on investment is only about 6.6 percent per year for the 36-year life of the investment. In contrast, a typical share of common stock earned, on average, a return of about 11.5 percent over the same period. Then there's the problem of storing the bike and keeping it in like-new condition, hardly a small detail.

Hot Wheels cars are a little easier to store. They cost about 75 cents each in their heyday of the mid 70s, and if not removed from their original package, they might be worth about $100 in 1995, a heady return of 27.7 percent per year. The problem is that in order to achieve this return, you would have had to purchase the toy when it was new and store it for all those years. The corresponding problem is in predicting what the future value of the toy will be. You can earn a positive return on investment only if the market value of your asset rises above the purchase price at some point. That, of course, is not always assured.

Art is another form of collectible, but the prices of the paintings of famous artists put this type of collector in a whole different category. In early 1995, a painting by the famous artist William de Kooning was offered at auction. The highest bid of $1.95 million for the painting "Untitled" was rejected by the seller who had paid $3.52 million for it back in 1989, the height of prices in the art market. If the seller had accepted the bid, his return would have been a negative 9.4 percent per year for the period he owned the painting.

Of these investments, the bike did okay, the Hot Wheels generated the highest return, and the art did terribly. So how can a mass-produced child's toy earn a greater return as an investment than a one-of-a-kind painting by a famous artist? Well, the condition of a collectible, whether it be art or toys, is a major key to its value. Most collectibles are virtually worthless if in poor condition. Also, items in short supply are typically more valuable than those that aren't. Picassos are one-of-a-kind and are extremely valuable. As for toys, most youngsters play with their toys and wear them out, thereby reducing the supply of those left as collectibles. Ultimately, however, the market value of any collectible depends on one and only one thing: what a buyer is willing to pay for it.

Sources: "'Hot Wheels' Take a Spin at Christie's," *The Wall Street Journal,* November 17, 1994, p. C1; "So Buying Action Figures Is Good, But Playing with Them Is Bad," *The Wall Street Journal,* July 29, 1994, p. B1; "Surprisingly, the Spring Auctions of Art Are Suitable for Framing," *The Wall Street Journal,* May 12, 1995, p. C1.

EXAMPLE 5.10 Saving for College

You estimate that you will need about $80,000 to send your child to college in eight years. You have about $35,000 now. If you can earn 20 percent per year, will you make it? At what rate will you just reach your goal?

If you can earn 20 percent, the future value of your $35,000 in eight years will be:

$$FV = \$35{,}000 \times (1.20)^8 = \$35{,}000 \times 4.2998 = \$150{,}493.59$$

So you will make it easily. The minimum rate is the unknown r in the following:

$$FV = \$35{,}000 \times (1 + r)^8 = \$80{,}000$$

$$(1 + r)^8 = \$80{,}000/35{,}000 = 2.2857$$

Therefore, the future value factor is 2.2857. Looking at the row in Table A.1 that corresponds to eight periods, our future value factor is roughly halfway between the ones shown for 10 percent (2.1436) and 12 percent (2.4760), so you will just reach your goal if you earn approximately 11 percent. To get the exact answer, we could use a financial calculator or we can solve for r:

$$(1 + r)^8 = \$80{,}000/35{,}000 = 2.2857$$
$$(1 + r) = 2.2857^{(1/8)} = 2.2857^{.125} = 1.1089$$
$$r = 10.89\%$$

• • •

EXAMPLE 5.11 Only 18,262.5 Days to Retirement

You would like to retire in 50 years as a millionaire. If you have $10,000 today, what rate of return do you need to earn to achieve your goal?

The future value is $1,000,000. The present value is $10,000, and there are 50 years until payment. We need to calculate the unknown discount rate in the following:

$$\$10{,}000 = \$1{,}000{,}000/(1 + r)^{50}$$
$$(1 + r)^{50} = 100$$

The future value factor is thus 100. You can verify that the implicit rate is about 9.65 percent. • • •

Finding the Number of Periods

Trans. 5.9 The Basic PV Equation—Revisited (Supplemental)

Suppose we were interested in purchasing an asset that costs $50,000. We currently have $25,000. If we can earn 12 percent on this $25,000, how long until we have the $50,000? The answer involves solving for the last variable in the basic present value equation, the number of periods. You already know how to get an approximate answer to this particular problem. Notice that we need to double our money. From the Rule of 72, this will take about 72/12 = 6 years at 12 percent.

To come up with the exact answer, we can again manipulate the basic present value equation. The present value is $25,000, and the future value is $50,000. With a 12 percent discount rate, the basic equation takes one of the following forms:

$$\$25{,}000 = \$50{,}000/(1.12)^t$$
$$\$50{,}000/25{,}000 = (1.12)^t = 2$$

We thus have a future value factor of 2 for a 12 percent rate. We now need to solve for t. If you look down the column in Table A.1 that corresponds to 12 percent, you will see that a future value factor of 1.9738 occurs at six periods. It will thus take about six years as we calculated. To get the exact answer, we have to explicitly solve for t (or use a financial calculator). If you do this, the answer is 6.1163 years, so our approximation was quite close in this case.

Lecture Tip: In general, $t = \ln(FV/PV)/\ln(1 + r)$.

EXAMPLE 5.12 Waiting for Godot

You've been saving up to buy the Godot Company. The total cost will be $10 million. You currently have about $2.3 million. If you can earn 5 percent on your money, how long will you have to wait? At 16 percent, how long must you wait?

TABLE 5.4
Summary of time value calculations

Trans. 5.10

I. Symbols:

PV = Present value, what future cash flows are worth today
FV_t = Future value, what cash flows are worth in the future
r = Interest rate, rate of return, or discount rate per period—typically, but not always, one year
t = Number of periods—typically, but not always, the number of years
C = Cash amount

II. Future value of C invested at r percent per period for t periods:

$$FV_t = C \times (1 + r)^t$$

The term $(1 + r)^t$ is called the *future value factor.*

III. Present value of C to be received in t periods at r percent per period:

$$PV = C/(1 + r)^t$$

The term $1/(1 + r)^t$ is called the *present value factor.*

IV. The basic present value equation giving the relationship between present and future value is:

$$PV = FV_t/(1 + r)^t$$

At 5 percent, you'll have to wait a long time. From the basic present value equation:

$$\$2.3 = \$10/(1.05)^t$$
$$1.05^t = 4.35$$
$$t = 30 \text{ years}$$

At 16 percent, things are a little better. Check for yourself that it will take about 10 years. • • •

This example finishes our introduction to basic time value of money concepts. Table 5.4 summarizes present value and future value calculations for future reference.

CONCEPT QUESTIONS

5.3a What is the basic present value equation?

5.3b What is the Rule of 72?

5.4 SUMMARY AND CONCLUSIONS

This chapter has introduced you to the basic principles of present value and discounted cash flow valuation. In it, we explain a number of things about the time value of money, including:

1. For a given rate of return, the value at some point in the future of an investment made today can be determined by calculating the future value of that investment.
2. The current worth of a future cash flow or series of cash flows can be determined for a given rate of return by calculating the present value of the cash flow(s) involved.

3. The relationship between present value (PV) and future value (FV) for a given rate r and time t is given by the basic present value equation:

$$PV = FV_t/(1 + r)^t$$

As we have shown, it is possible to find any one of the four components (PV, FV_t, r, t) given the other three.

The principles developed in this chapter will figure prominently in the chapters to come. The reason for this is that most investments, whether they involve real assets or financial assets, can be analyzed using the discounted cash flow (DCF) approach. As a result, the DCF approach is broadly applicable and widely used in practice. Before going on, however, you might want to do some of the problems below.

Chapter Review Problems and Self-Test

5.1 **Calculating Future Values** Assume you deposit $1,000 today in an account that pays 8 percent interest. How much will you have in four years?

5.2 **Calculating Present Values** Suppose you have just celebrated your 19th birthday. A rich uncle set up a trust fund for you that will pay you $100,000 when you turn 25. If the relevant discount rate is 11 percent, how much is this fund worth today?

5.3 **Calculating Rates of Return** You've been offered an investment that will double your money in 12 years. What rate of return are you being offered? Check your answer using the Rule of 72.

5.4 **Calculating the Number of Periods** You've been offered an investment that will pay you 7 percent per year. If you invest $10,000, how long until you have $20,000? How long until you have $30,000?

Answers to Self-Test Problems

5.1 We need to calculate the future value of $1,000 at 8 percent for four years. The future value factor is:

$$1.08^4 = 1.3605$$

The future value is thus $1,000 × 1.3605 = $1,360.50.

5.2 We need the present value of $100,000 to be paid in six years at 11 percent. The discount factor is:

$$1/1.11^6 = 1/1.8704 = .5346$$

The present value is thus about $53,460.

5.3 Suppose you invest, say, $100. You will have $200 in 12 years with this investment. So, $100 is the amount you have today, the present value, and $200 is the amount you will have in 12 years, or the future value. From the basic present value equation, we have:

$$\$200 = \$100 \times (1 + r)^{12}$$
$$2 = (1 + r)^{12}$$

From here, we need to solve for r, the unknown rate. As in the chapter, there are several different ways to do this. We will take the twelfth root of 2 (by raising 2 to the power of 1/12):

$$2^{(1/12)} = (1 + r)$$
$$1.0595 = 1 + r$$
$$r = 5.95\%$$

Using the Rule of 72, we have $72/t = r\%$, or $72/12 = 6\%$, so our answer looks good (remember that the Rule of 72 is only an approximation).

5.4 The basic equation is:

$$\$20{,}000 = \$10{,}000 \times (1 + .07)^t$$
$$2 = (1 + .07)^t$$

If we solve for t, we get that $t = 10.24$ years. Using the Rule of 72, we get $72/7 = 10.29$, so, once again, our answer looks good. To get \$30,000, check for yourself that you will have to wait 16.24 years.

Questions and Problems

Basic (Questions 1–10)

$1,958.56

1. **Simple Interest versus Compound Interest** 1st Simpleton Bank pays 5 percent simple interest on its savings account balances, while 1st Complexity Bank pays 5 percent interest compounded annually. If you made a \$10,000 deposit in each bank, how much additional money would you earn from your 1st Complexity Bank account at the end of 12 years?

$2,076.22
$39,573.12
$85,887.46
$325,431.71

2. **Calculating Future Values** For each of the following, compute the future value:

Present Value	Years	Interest Rate	Future Value
\$ 570	15	9%	
\$ 8,922	9	18%	
\$ 61,133	3	12%	
\$219,850	10	4%	

$260.79
$3,517.62
$3,363.82
$83,205.57

3. **Calculating Present Values** For each of the following, compute the present value:

Future Value	Years	Interest Rate	Present Value
\$ 349	5	6%	
\$ 5,227	20	2%	
\$ 48,950	12	25%	
\$612,511	7	33%	

6.67%
13.96%
8.25%
4.09%

4. **Calculating Interest Rates** Solve for the unknown interest rate in each of the following:

Present Value	Years	Interest Rate	Future Value
\$ 475	4		\$ 615
\$ 7,350	7		\$ 18,350
\$27,175	11		\$ 65,000
\$93,412	19		\$200,000

5. **Calculating the Number of Periods** Solve for the unknown number of years in each of the following:

Present Value	Years	Interest Rate	Future Value
$ 1,200		8%	$ 2,550
$ 16,310		12%	$ 21,225
$ 75,000		3%	$175,000
$183,650		29%	$912,475

9.79 years
2.32 years
28.66 years
6.30 years

6. **Calculating Interest Rates** Assume the total cost of a college education will be $50,000 when your child enters college in 18 years. You presently have $5,000 to invest. What rate of interest must you earn on your investment to cover the cost of your child's college education?

13.65%
Trans. 5.11

7. **Calculating the Number of Periods** At 9 percent interest, how long does it take to double your money? To triple?

8.04 years
12.75 years

8. **Calculating Interest Rates** You are offered an investment that requires you to put up $4,000 today in exchange for $10,000 eight years from now. What is the rate of return on this investment?

12.14%

9. **Calculating the Number of Periods** You're trying to save to buy a new $20,000 speedboat to take to the lake. You have $16,000 today that can be invested at your bank. The bank pays 6 percent annual interest on its accounts. How long will it be before you have enough to buy the speedboat?

3.83 years

10. **Calculating Present Value** Rarely Prudent, Inc., has an unfunded pension liability of $225 million that must be paid in 17 years. To assess the value of the firm's stock, financial analysts want to discount this liability back to the present. If the relevant discount rate is 8.5 percent, what is the present value of this liability?

$56.22 million
Trans. 5.12

Intermediate (Questions 11–15)

11. **Calculating Future Values** You have an investment that will pay you 2 percent per month. How much will you have per dollar invested in one year? In two years?

$1.27; $1.61

12. **Calculating the Number of Periods** You have $200 today. You need $230. If you earn 0.5 percent per month, how many months will you wait?

28 months

13. **Calculating Rates** Suppose an investment offers to quadruple your money in 18 months (don't believe it). What rate per six months are you being offered?

58.7% per six months

14. **Calculating Future Values** You are scheduled to receive $6,000 in three years. When you receive it, you will invest it for six more years at 8 percent per year. How much will you have in nine years?

$9,521.25

15. **Calculating the Number of Periods** You are scheduled to receive $8,500 in five years. You plan on investing it at 6 percent until you have $12,500. How long will you wait in all?

6.62 additional years

Chapter Six

Discounted Cash Flow Valuation

After studying this chapter, you should have a good understanding of:

. . .

How to determine future and present value of investments with multiple cash flows.

. . .

How loan payments are calculated and how to find the interest rate on a loan.

. . .

How loans are amortized or paid off.

. . .

How interest rates are quoted (and misquoted).

Trans. 6.1

In our previous chapter, we covered the basics of discounted cash flow valuation. However, so far, we have only dealt with single cash flows. In reality, most investments have multiple cash flows. For example, if Sears is thinking of opening a new department store, there will be a large cash outlay in the beginning and then cash inflows for many years. In this chapter, we begin to explore how to value such investments.

When you finish this chapter, you should have some very practical skills. For example, you will know how to calculate your own car payments or student loan payments. You will also be able to determine how long it will take to pay off a credit card if you make the minimum payment each month (a practice we do not recommend). We will show you how to compare interest rates to determine which are the highest and which are the lowest, and we will also show you how interest rates can be quoted in different, and at times deceptive, ways.

6.1 FUTURE AND PRESENT VALUES OF MULTIPLE CASH FLOWS

Self-Test Problems 6.1, 6.2
Problems 1, 3–9

Thus far, we have restricted our attention to either the future value of a lump-sum present amount or the present value of some single future cash flow. In this section, we begin to study ways to value multiple cash flows. We start with future value.

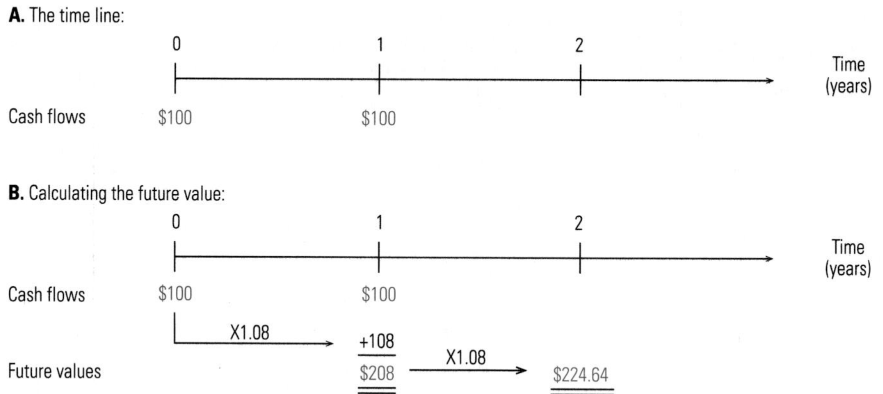

FIGURE 6.1
Drawing and using a time line

Future Value with Multiple Cash Flows

Concept Q Answer 6.1a

Suppose you deposit \$100 today in an account paying 8 percent. In one year, you will deposit another \$100. How much will you have in two years? This particular problem is relatively easy. At the end of the first year, you will have \$108 plus the second \$100 you deposit for a total of \$208. You leave this \$208 on deposit at 8 percent for another year. At the end of this second year, it is worth:

$$\$208 \times 1.08 = \$224.64$$

Figure 6.1 is a *time line* that illustrates the process of calculating the future value of these two \$100 deposits. Figures such as this one are very useful for solving complicated problems. Anytime you are having trouble with a present or future value problem, drawing a time line will usually help you to see what is happening.

In the first part of Figure 6.1, we show the cash flows on the time line. The most important thing is that we write them down where they actually occur. Here, the first cash flow occurs today, which we label as Time 0. We therefore put \$100 at Time 0 on the time line. The second \$100 cash flow occurs one year from today, so we write it down at the point labeled as Time 1. In the second part of Figure 6.1, we calculate the future values one period at a time to come up with the final \$224.64.

EXAMPLE 6.1 Saving Up Revisited

You think you will be able to deposit \$4,000 at the end of each of the next three years in a bank account paying 8 percent interest. You currently have \$7,000 in the account. How much will you have in three years? In four years?

At the end of the first year, you will have:

$$\$7{,}000 \times (1.08) + \$4{,}000 = \$11{,}560$$

At the end of the second year, you will have:

$$\$11{,}560 \times (1.08) + \$4{,}000 = \$16{,}484.80$$

Repeating this for the third year gives:

$$\$16{,}484.80 \times (1.08) + \$4{,}000 = \$21{,}803.58$$

Therefore, you will have $21,803.58 in three years. If you leave this on deposit for one more year (and don't add to it), at the end of the fourth year you'll have:

$$\$21{,}803.58 \times (1.08) = \$23{,}547.87$$ • • •

Lecture Tip: The value of compounding is well-illustrated by the recent news story of a retired priest who, despite never having earned more than $6,000 per year, amassed a stock portfolio valued at $1.3 million by saving and investing wisely.

When we calculated the future value of the two $100 deposits, we simply calculated the balance as of the beginning of each year and then rolled that amount forward to the next year. We could have done it another, quicker way. The first $100 was on deposit for two years at 8 percent, so its future value is:

$$\$100 \times (1.08)^2 = \$100 \times 1.1664 = \$116.64$$

The second $100 was on deposit for one year at 8 percent, and its future value is thus:

$$\$100 \times 1.08 = \$108.00$$

The total future value, as we previously calculated, is equal to the sum of these two future values:

$$\$116.64 + 108 = \$224.64$$

Based on this example, there are two ways to calculate future values for multiple cash flows: (1) compound the accumulated balance forward one year at a time or (2) calculate the future value of each cash flow first and then add them up. Both give the same answer, so you can do it either way.

To illustrate the two different ways of calculating future values, consider the future value of $2,000 invested at the end of each of the next five years. The current balance is zero, and the rate is 10 percent. We first draw a time line in Figure 6.2.

On the time line, notice that nothing happens until the end of the first year when we make the first $2,000 investment. This first $2,000 earns interest for the next four (not five) years. Also notice that the last $2,000 is invested at the end of the fifth year, so it earns no interest at all.

Figure 6.3 illustrates the calculations involved if we compound the investment one period at a time. As illustrated, the future value is $12,210.20.

Figure 6.4 goes through the same calculations, but the second technique is used. Naturally, the answer is the same.

FIGURE 6.2
Time line for $2,000 per year for five years

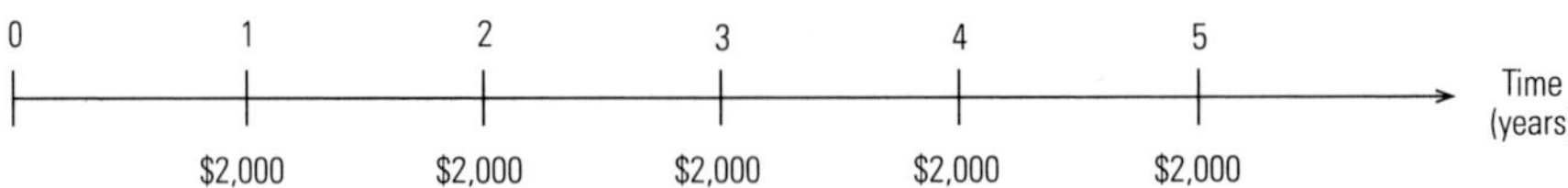

FIGURE 6.3 Future value calculated by compounding forward one period at a time **Trans. 6.2**

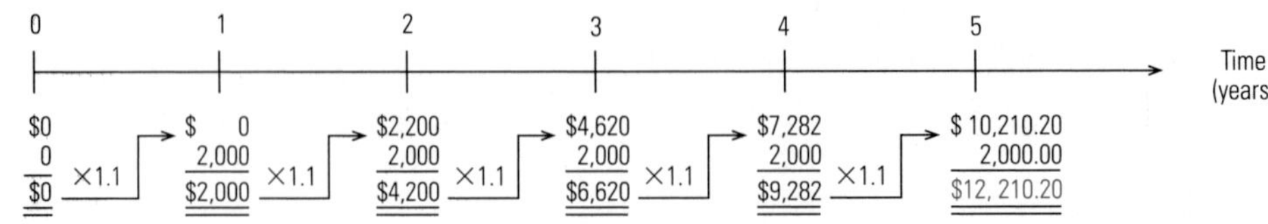

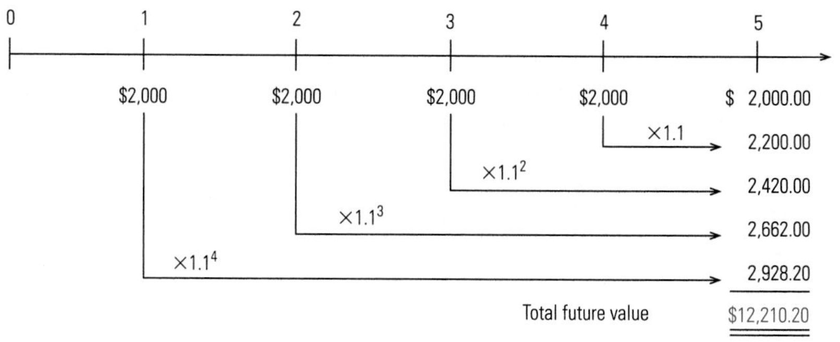

FIGURE 6.4 Future value calculated by compounding each cash flow separately

Trans. 6.2

EXAMPLE 6.2 Saving Up Once Again

If you deposit \$100 in one year, \$200 in two years, and \$300 in three years, how much will you have in three years? How much of this is interest? How much will you have in five years if you don't add additional amounts? Assume a 7 percent interest rate throughout.

We will calculate the future value of each amount in three years. Notice that the \$100 earns interest for two years, and the \$200 earns interest for one year. The final \$300 earns no interest. The future values are thus:

$$\begin{aligned} \$100 \times 1.07^2 &= \$114.49 \\ \$200 \times 1.07 &= 214.00 \\ + \$300 &= \underline{300.00} \\ \text{Total future value} &= \underline{\underline{\$628.49}} \end{aligned}$$

The future value is thus \$628.49. The total interest is:

$$\$628.49 - (\$100 + 200 + 300) = \$28.49$$

How much will you have in five years? We know that you will have \$628.49 in three years. If you leave that in for two more years, it will grow to:

$$\$628.49 \times (1.07)^2 = \$628.49 \times 1.1449 = \$719.56$$

Notice that we could have calculated the future value of each amount separately. Once again, be careful about the lengths of time. As we previously calculated, the first \$100 earns interest for only four years, the second deposit earns three years' interest, and the last earns two years' interest:

$$\begin{aligned} \$100 \times (1.07)^4 &= \$100 \times 1.3108 = \$131.08 \\ \$200 \times (1.07)^3 &= \$200 \times 1.2250 = 245.01 \\ + \$300 \times (1.07)^2 &= \$300 \times 1.1449 = \underline{343.47} \\ \text{Total future value} &= \underline{\underline{\$719.56}} \end{aligned}$$

Present Value with Multiple Cash Flows

It will turn out that we will very often need to determine the present value of a series of future cash flows. As with future values, there are two ways we can do it. We can either discount back one period at a time, or we can just calculate the present values individually and add them up.

Concept Q Answer 6.1b

Suppose you needed \$1,000 in one year and \$2,000 more in two years. If you can earn 9 percent on your money, how much do you have to put up today to exactly cover these amounts in the future? In other words, what is the present value of the two cash flows at 9 percent?

The present value of \$2,000 in two years at 9 percent is:

$$\$2{,}000/1.09^2 = \$1{,}683.36$$

The present value of \$1,000 in one year is:

$$\$1{,}000/1.09 = \$917.43$$

Therefore, the total present value is:

$$\$1{,}683.36 + 917.43 = \$2{,}600.79$$

To see why \$2,600.79 is the right answer, we can check to see that after the \$2,000 is paid out in two years, there is no money left. If we invest \$2,600.79 for one year at 9 percent, we will have:

$$\$2{,}600.79 \times 1.09 = \$2{,}834.86$$

We take out \$1,000, leaving \$1,834.86. This amount earns 9 percent for another year, leaving us with:

$$\$1{,}834.86 \times 1.09 = \$2{,}000$$

This is just as we planned. As this example illustrates, the present value of a series of future cash flows is simply the amount that you would need today in order to exactly duplicate those future cash flows (for a given discount rate).

An alternative way of calculating present values for multiple future cash flows is to discount back to the present one period at a time. To illustrate, suppose we had an investment that was going to pay \$1,000 at the end of every year for the next five years. To find the present value, we could discount each \$1,000 back to the present separately and then add them up. Figure 6.5 illustrates this approach for a 6 percent discount rate.

As Figure 6.5 shows, the answer is \$4,212.37 (ignoring a small rounding error).

Alternatively, we could discount the last cash flow back one period and add it to the next-to-the-last cash flow:

$$\$1{,}000/1.06 + 1{,}000 = \$943.40 + 1{,}000 = \$1{,}943.40$$

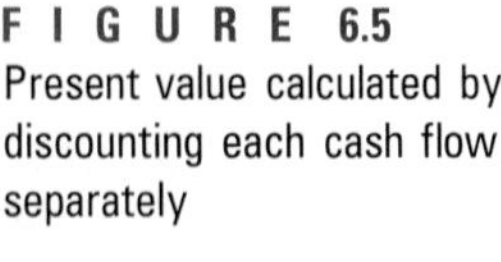

FIGURE 6.5
Present value calculated by discounting each cash flow separately

Trans. 6.3

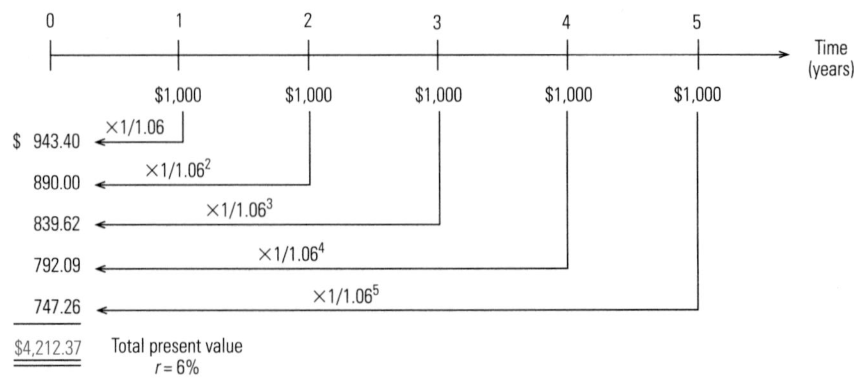

Principles in Action

Big Dog versus the Shaq Attack

The signing of big-name professional athletes to new, long-term contracts is usually accompanied by great fanfare and large headlines. Glenn "Big Dog" Robinson, who played basketball at Purdue University, was the most sought-after player in the 1994 NBA draft, so it came as no surprise when the Milwaukee Bucks made him the first player chosen. What did come as a surprise, particularly to the owners of the Bucks, was the amount of money Robinson was demanding: he wanted a 13-year contract worth a total of $100 million. In short, he wanted big bucks from the Bucks.

Robinson's goal was to be paid more than any other rookie in NBA history, including Shaquille "Shaq" O'Neal, the number one pick in 1992. O'Neal, who was drafted by the Orlando Magic, signed a 7-year contract with estimated total payments of $40 million. The precise terms were not disclosed, but it was reported that Shaq would receive a salary of $3 million in his first year, with raises of $900,000 each year thereafter.

Robinson eventually met his goal of being paid more than O'Neal, but he didn't quite get $100 million. Instead, he signed for only $68 million to be paid over 10 years. His contract calls for $2.9 million the first year with raises of $870,000 in each subsequent year. Thus, in year 10 of the contract, Robinson will receive $10.7 million.

The $68 million cited in news reports of the signing substantially overstates the value of Robinson's contract because it ignores the time value of money. For example, assuming a discount rate of 12 percent, the $10.7 million to be received in 10 years had a present value of only $3.5 million at the time of signing. While this is still a lot of money, the payment is worth only about one-third of the publicized value. Using the same assumptions, the total present value of the contract was $34 million when it was signed, barely half the $68 million widely quoted and not even close to the $100 million originally requested.

Finally, there is the question of whether Robinson's contract was more valuable than O'Neal's. Clearly, on the face of things, Big Dog's $68 million contract was more lucrative than Shaq's $40 million contract. If Shaq's cash flows are discounted at 12 percent, his deal was worth about $24 million at the time the contract was signed, so Big Dog came out well ahead. Of course, Big Dog is a *much* better free throw shooter.

Sources: "Bucks Make Robinson Richest NBA Rookie," *Washington Post,* November 4, 1994, p. D:1:1; "Touch of Magic to O'Neal Signing," *Boston Globe,* August 8, 1992, p. 67:1.

We could then discount this amount back one period and add it to the Year 3 cash flow:

$$\$1,943.40/1.06 + 1,000 = \$1,833.39 + 1,000 = \$2,833.40$$

This process could be repeated as necessary. Figure 6.6 illustrates this approach and the remaining calculations.

As the accompanying *Principles in Action* box shows, calculating present values is a vital step in comparing alternative cash flows. We will have much more to say on this subject in our next chapter.

FIGURE 6.6 Present value calculated by discounting back one period at a time **Trans. 6.3**

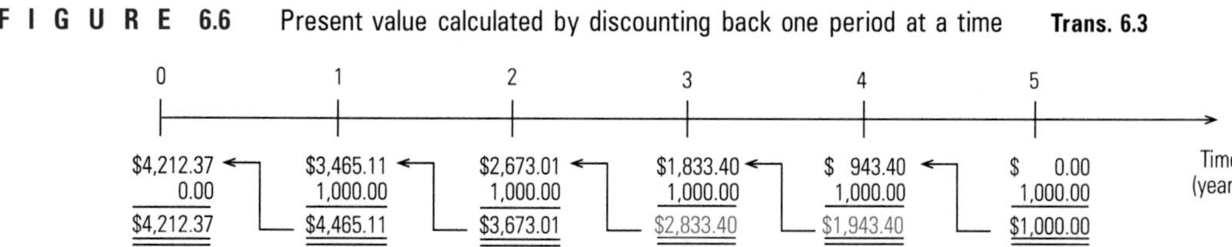

EXAMPLE 6.3 How Much Is It Worth?

You are offered an investment that will pay you \$200 in one year, \$400 the next year, \$600 the next year, and \$800 at the end of the next year. You can earn 12 percent on very similar investments. What is the most you should pay for this one?

We need to calculate the present value of these cash flows at 12 percent. Taking them one at a time gives:

$$\begin{aligned} \$200 \times 1/1.12^1 &= \$200/1.1200 = \$\ \ 178.57 \\ \$400 \times 1/1.12^2 &= \$400/1.2544 = \quad 318.88 \\ \$600 \times 1/1.12^3 &= \$600/1.4049 = \quad 427.07 \\ + \$800 \times 1/1.12^4 &= \$800/1.5735 = \underline{\$\ \ 508.41} \\ \text{Total present value} &= \underline{\underline{\$1{,}432.93}} \end{aligned}$$

If you can earn 12 percent on your money, then you can duplicate this investment's cash flows for \$1,432.93, so this is the most you should be willing to pay. • • •

EXAMPLE 6.4 How Much Is It Worth? Part 2

You are offered an investment that will make three \$5,000 payments. The first payment will occur four years from today. The second will occur in five years, the third will follow in six years. If you can earn 11 percent, what is the most this investment is worth today? What is the future value of the cash flows?

We will answer the questions in reverse order to illustrate a point. The future value of the cash flows in six years is:

$$\begin{aligned} \$5{,}000 \times (1.11)^2 + 5{,}000 \times (1.11) + 5{,}000 &= \$6{,}160.50 + 5{,}550 + 5{,}000 \\ &= \$16{,}710.50 \end{aligned}$$

The present value must be:

$$\$16{,}710.50/1.11^6 = \$8{,}934.12$$

Let's check this. Taking them one at a time, the PV of the cash flows is:

$$\begin{aligned} \$5{,}000 \times (1/1.11^6) &= \$5{,}000/1.8704 = \$2{,}673.20 \\ \$5{,}000 \times (1/1.11^5) &= \$5{,}000/1.6851 = \$2{,}967.26 \\ + \$5{,}000 \times (1/1.11^4) &= \$5{,}000/1.5181 = \underline{\$3{,}293.65} \\ \text{Total present value} &= \underline{\underline{\$8{,}934.12}} \end{aligned}$$

This is as we previously calculated. The point we want to make is that we can calculate present and future values in any order and convert between them using whatever way seems most convenient. The answers will always be the same as long as we stick with the same discount rate and are careful to keep track of the right number of periods. • • •

A Note on Cash Flow Timing

Concept Q Answer 6.1c

In working present and future value problems, cash flow timing is critically important. In almost all such calculations, it is implicitly assumed that the cash flows occur at the *end* of each period. In fact, all the formulas we have discussed, all the numbers in a standard present value or future value table, and, very importantly, all the preset (or default) settings on a financial calculator assume that cash flows occur at the end of each period. Unless you are very explicitly told otherwise, you should always assume that this is what is meant.

As a quick illustration of this point, suppose you are told that a three-year investment has a first year cash flow of $100, a second-year cash flow of $200, and a third-year cash flow of $300. You are asked to draw a time line. Without further information, you should always assume that the time line looks like this:

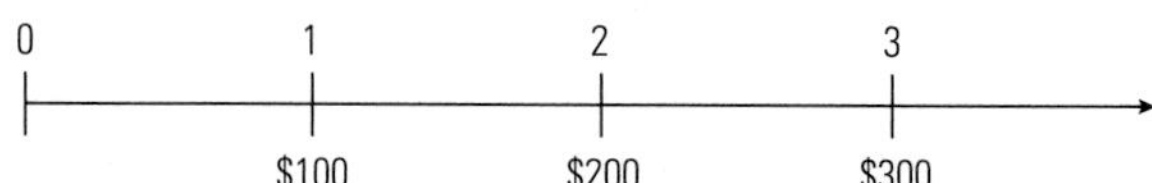

On our time line, notice how the first cash flow occurs at the end of the first period, the second at the end of the second period, and the third at the end of the third period.

CONCEPT QUESTIONS

6.1a Describe how to calculate the future value of a series of cash flows.

6.1b Describe how to calculate the present value of a series of cash flows.

6.1c Unless we are explicitly told otherwise, what do we always assume about the timing of cash flows in present and future value problems?

6.2 VALUING LEVEL CASH FLOWS: ANNUITIES AND PERPETUITIES

Self-Test Problem 6.3
Problems 3–11, 26, 33, 34

We will frequently encounter situations where we have multiple cash flows that are all the same amount. For example, a very common type of loan repayment plan calls for the borrower to repay the loan by making a series of equal payments for some length of time. Almost all consumer loans (such as car loans) and home mortgages feature equal payments, usually made each month.

More generally, a series of constant or level cash flows that occurs at the end of each period for some fixed number of periods is called an ordinary **annuity,** or, more correctly, the cash flows are said to be in ordinary annuity form. Annuities appear very frequently in financial arrangements, and there are some useful shortcuts for determining their values. We consider these next.

annuity
A level stream of cash flows for a fixed period of time.

Present Value for Annuity Cash Flows

Trans. 6.4
Annuities and Perpetuities (Supplemental)

Suppose we were examining an asset that promised to pay $500 at the end of each of the next three years. The cash flows from this asset are in the form of a three-year, $500 annuity. If we wanted to earn 10 percent on our money, how much would we offer for this annuity?

Trans. 6.5
Annuities and Perpetuities—Examples (Supplemental)

Trans. 6.6
A 0% Financing Example (Supplemental)

From the previous section, we can discount each of these $500 payments back to the present at 10 percent to determine the total present value:

$$\begin{aligned}\text{Present value} &= \$500/1.1^1 + 500/1.1^2 + 500/1.1^3\\ &= \$500/1.10 + 500/1.21 + 500/1.331\\ &= \$454.55 + 413.22 + 375.66\\ &= \$1{,}243.43\end{aligned}$$

This approach works just fine. However, we will often encounter situations where the number of cash flows is quite large. For example, a typical home mortgage calls for monthly payments over 30 years, for a total of 360 payments. If we were trying to determine the present value of those payments, it would be useful to have a shortcut.

Concept Q Answer 6.2a

Lecture Tip: See IM 6.2 for a demonstration of the annuity approach as a shortcut alternative for calculating the PV of a constant cash flow stream.

Since the cash flows on an annuity are all the same, we can come up with a very useful variation on the basic present value equation. It turns out that the present value of an annuity of C dollars per period for t periods when the rate of return or interest rate is r is given by:

$$\begin{aligned}\text{Annuity present value} &= C \times \left[\frac{1 - \text{Present value factor}}{r}\right] \\ &= C \times \left[\frac{1 - \{1/(1 + r)^t\}}{r}\right]\end{aligned} \tag{6.1}$$

The term in square brackets is sometimes called the present value interest factor for annuities and abbreviated PVIFA(r, t).

The expression for the annuity present value may look a little complicated, but it isn't difficult to use. Notice that the term in curly braces, $\{1/(1 + r)^t\}$, is the same present value factor we've been calculating. In our example just above, the interest rate is 10 percent and there are three years involved. The usual present value factor is thus:

$$\text{Present value factor} = 1/1.1^3 = 1/1.331 = .75131$$

To calculate the annuity present value factor, we just plug this in:

$$\begin{aligned}\text{Annuity present value factor} &= (1 - \text{Present value factor})/r \\ &= (1 - .75131)/.10 \\ &= .248685/.10 = 2.48685\end{aligned}$$

Just as we calculated before, the present value of our \$500 annuity is then:[1]

$$\text{Annuity present value} = \$500 \times 2.48685 = \$1{,}243.43$$

EXAMPLE 6.5 How Much Can You Afford?

After carefully going over your budget, you have determined you can afford to pay \$632 per month towards a new sports car. You call up your local bank and find out that the going rate is 1 percent per month for 48 months. How much can you borrow?

---

[1] To solve this problem on a common type of financial calculator, you would need to do the following:

1. Enter the "payment" of C = \$500 and press "PMT."
2. Enter the "interest rate" of r = 10 percent as 10 (not .10) and press "i."
3. Enter the number of periods as 3 and press "n."
4. Ask the calculator for the PV by pressing the "compute" or "solve" key and then pressing PV. The answer may come out with a negative sign.

Here is a useful tip: Many financial calculators have the feature of "constant memory." As a practical matter, what this can mean is that the calculator will remember your mistakes, even if you turn it off. You need to be sure and press the appropriate key(s) to clear out the calculator's memory before you begin. If you make a mistake, it is usually better to clear the memory and start over. Otherwise, you may learn the hard way what "GIGO" stands for (it stands for "garbage in, garbage out").

To determine how much you can borrow, we need to calculate the present value of \$632 per month for 48 months at 1 percent per month. The loan payments are in ordinary annuity form, so the annuity present value factor is:

$$\begin{aligned} \text{Annuity PV factor} &= (1 - \text{Present value factor})/r \\ &= [1 - (1/(1.01)^{48})]/.01 \\ &= (1 - .6203)/.01 = 37.9740 \end{aligned}$$

With this factor, we can calculate the present value of the 48 payments of \$632 each as:

$$\text{Present value} = \$632 \times 37.9740 = \$24{,}000$$

Therefore, \$24,000 is what you can afford to borrow and repay. • • •

Annuity Tables Just as there are tables for ordinary present value factors, there are tables for annuity factors as well. Table 6.1 contains a few such factors; Table A.3 in the Appendix to the book contains a larger set. To find the annuity present value factor we just calculated, look for the row corresponding to three periods and then find the column for 10 percent. The number you see at that intersection should be 2.4869 (rounded to 4 decimal places), as we calculated. Once again, try calculating a few of these factors yourself and compare your answers to the ones in the table to make sure you know how to do it. If you are using a financial calculator, just enter \$1 as the payment and calculate the present value; the result should be the annuity present value factor.

Lecture Tip: Although amortization tables are no longer prepared by hand, their preparation is a good exercise and foreshadows such topics as interest tax shields. A brief amortization example appears in the IM.

Finding the Payment Suppose you wished to start up a new business that specializes in the latest of health food trends, frozen yak milk. To produce and market your product, the Yakkee Doodle Dandy, you need to borrow \$100,000. Because it strikes you as unlikely that this particular fad will be long-lived, you propose to pay off the loan quickly by making five equal annual payments. If the interest rate is 18 percent, what will the payment be?

In this case, we know the present value is \$100,000. The interest rate is 18 percent, and there are five years. The payments are all equal, so we need to find the relevant annuity factor and solve for the unknown cash flow:

Lecture Tip: Perhaps one of the most useful applications of present value analysis is in solving loan problems. IM 6.3 provides an extended mortgage loan problem, along with some "tips and tricks."

$$\begin{aligned} \text{Annuity present value} = \$100{,}000 &= C \times (1 - \text{Present value factor})/r \\ \$100{,}000 &= C \times (1 - 1/1.18^5)/.18 \\ &= C \times (1 - .4371)/.18 \\ &= C \times (3.1272) \\ C &= \$100{,}000/3.1272 = \$31{,}977 \end{aligned}$$

Therefore, you'll make five payments of just under \$32,000 each.

TABLE 6.1
Annuity present value interest factors

Number of Periods	Interest Rate			
	5%	10%	15%	20%
1	.9524	.9091	.8696	.8333
2	1.8594	1.7355	1.6257	1.5278
3	2.7232	2.4869	2.2832	2.1065
4	3.5460	3.1699	2.8550	2.5887
5	4.3295	3.7908	3.3522	2.9906

EXAMPLE 6.6 Finding the Number of Payments

You ran a little short on your spring break vacation, so you put \$1,000 on your credit card. You can only afford to make the minimum payment of \$20 per month. The interest rate on the credit card is 1.5 percent per month. How long will you need to pay off the \$1,000?

What we have here is an annuity of \$20 per month at 1.5 percent per month for some unknown length of time. The present value is \$1,000 (the amount you owe today). We need to do a little algebra (or else use a financial calculator):

$$\begin{aligned} \$1{,}000 &= \$20 \times (1 - \text{Present value factor})/.015 \\ (\$1{,}000/20) \times .015 &= 1 - \text{Present value factor} \\ \text{Present value factor} &= .25 = 1/(1 + r)^t \\ (1.015)^t &= 1/.25 = 4 \end{aligned}$$

At this point, the problem boils down to asking the question "How long does it take for your money to quadruple at 1.5 percent per month?" Based on our previous chapter, the answer is about 93 months:

$$1.015^{93} = 3.99 \approx 4$$

It will take you about 93/12 = 7.75 years at this rate. If you use a financial calculator for problems like this one, you should be aware that some automatically round up to the next whole period. • • •

Finding the Rate The last question we might want to ask concerns the interest rate implicit in an annuity. For example, an insurance company offers to pay you \$1,000 per year for 10 years if you will pay \$6,710 up front. What rate is implicit in this 10-year annuity?

In this case, we know the present value (\$6,710), we know the cash flows (\$1,000 per year), and we know the life of the investment (10 years). What we don't know is the discount rate:

$$\begin{aligned} \$6{,}710 &= \$1{,}000 \times (1 - \text{Present value factor})/r \\ \$6{,}710/1{,}000 &= 6.71 = [1 - \{1/(1 + r)^{10}\}]/r \end{aligned}$$

So, the annuity factor for 10 periods is equal to 6.71, and we need to solve this equation for the unknown value of r. Unfortunately, this is mathematically impossible to do directly. The only way to do it is to use a table or trial and error to find a value for r.

If you look across the row corresponding to 10 periods in Table A.3, you will see a factor of 6.7101 for 8 percent, so we see right away that the insurance company is offering just about 8 percent. Alternatively, we could just start trying different values until we get very close to the answer. Using this trial-and-error approach can be a little tedious, but, fortunately, machines are good at that sort of thing.[2]

To illustrate how to find the answer by trial and error, suppose a relative of yours wants to borrow \$3,000. She offers to repay you \$1,000 every year for four years. What interest rate are you being offered?

---

[2] Financial calculators rely on trial and error to find the answer. That's why they sometimes appear to be "thinking" before coming up with the answer. Actually, it is possible to directly solve for r if there are less than five periods, but it's usually not worth the trouble.

The cash flows here have the form of a four-year, \$1,000 annuity. The present value is \$3,000. We need to find the discount rate, *r*. Our goal in doing so is primarily to give you a feel for the relationship between annuity values and discount rates.

We need to start somewhere, so 10 percent is probably as good a place as any to begin. At 10 percent, the annuity factor is:

$$\text{Annuity present value factor} = (1 - 1/1.10^4)/.10 = 3.1699$$

The present value of the cash flows at 10 percent is thus:

$$\text{Present value} = \$1{,}000 \times 3.1699 = \$3{,}169.90$$

You can see that we're already in the right ballpark.

Is 10 percent too high or too low? Recall that present values and discount rates move in opposite directions: Increasing the discount rate lowers the PV and vice versa. Our present value here is too high, so the discount rate is too low. If we try 12 percent:

$$\text{Present value} = \$1{,}000 \times (1 - 1/1.12^4)/.12 = \$3{,}037.35$$

Now we're almost there. We are still a little low on the discount rate (because the PV is a little high), so we'll try 13 percent:

$$\text{Present value} = \$1{,}000 \times (1 - 1/1.13^4)/.13 = \$2{,}974.47$$

This is less than \$3,000, so we now know that the answer is between 12 percent and 13 percent, and it looks to be about 12.5 percent. For practice, work at it for a while longer and see if you find that the answer is about 12.59 percent.

Lecture Tip: See IM for how you might simplify and summarize the various valuation problems.

Future Value for Annuities

On occasion, it's also handy to know a shortcut for calculating the future value of an annuity. As you might guess, there are future value factors for annuities as well as present value factors. In general, the future value factor for an annuity is given by:

Concept Q Answer 6.2a

Lecture Tip: See IM for the impact of an annuity stream on FV when the initial payment is made at t_0 rather than t_1.

$$\begin{aligned}\text{Annuity FV factor} &= (\text{Future value factor} - 1)/r \\ &= [\{(1 + r)^t\} - 1]/r\end{aligned} \qquad [6.2]$$

To see how we use annuity future value factors, suppose you plan to contribute \$2,000 every year into a retirement account paying 8 percent. If you retire in 30 years, how much will you have?

The number of years here, *t*, is 30, and the interest rate, *r*, is 8 percent, so we can calculate the annuity future value factor as:

$$\begin{aligned}\text{Annuity FV factor} &= (\text{Future value factor} - 1)/r \\ &= (1.08^{30} - 1)/.08 \\ &= (10.0627 - 1)/.08 \\ &= 113.2832\end{aligned}$$

The future value of this 30-year, \$2,000 annuity is thus:

$$\begin{aligned}\text{Annuity future value} &= \$2{,}000 \times 113.28 \\ &= \$226{,}566.4\end{aligned}$$

A Note on Annuities Due

So far, we have only discussed ordinary annuities. These are the most important, but there is a variation that is fairly common. Remember that with an ordinary annuity, the cash flows occur at the end of each period. When you take out a loan with monthly payments, for example, the first loan payment normally occurs one month after you get the loan. However, when you lease an apartment, the first lease payment is usually due immediately. The second payment is due at the beginning of the second month, and so on. A lease is an example of an **annuity due.** An annuity due is an annuity for which the cash flows occur at the beginning of each period. Almost any type of arrangement in which we have to prepay the same amount each period is an annuity due.

annuity due
An annuity for which the cash flows occur at the beginning of the period.

There are several different ways to calculate the value of an annuity due. With a financial calculator, you simply switch it into "due" or "beginning" mode. It is very important to remember to switch it back when you are done! Another way to calculate the present value of an annuity due can be illustrated with a time line. Suppose an annuity due has five payments of $400 each, and the relevant discount rate is 10 percent. The time line looks like this:

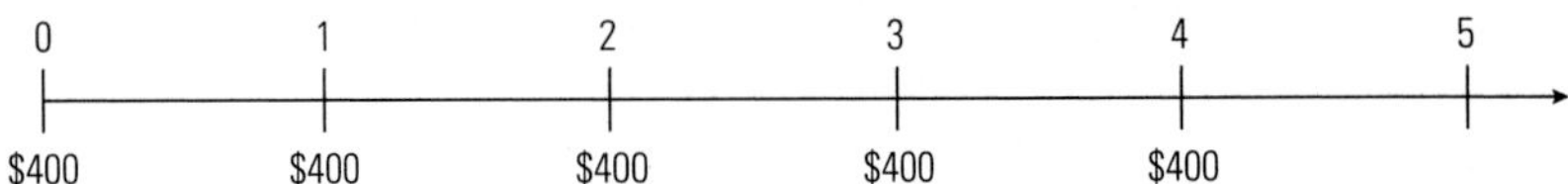

Notice how the cash flows here are the same as those for a *four*-year ordinary annuity, except that there is an extra $400 at Time 0. For practice, check that the value of a four-year ordinary annuity at 10 percent is $1,267.95. If we add on the extra $400, we get $1,667.95, which is the present value of this annuity due.

Lecture Tip: The annuity material is summarized in three "GURFs"—Great Underlying Rules of Finance—in the IM.

There is an even easier way to calculate the present or future value of an annuity due. If we assume cash flows occur at the end of each period when they really occur at the beginning, then we discount each one by one period too many. We could fix this by simply multiplying our answer by $(1 + r)$, where r is the discount rate. In fact, the relationship between the value of an annuity due and an ordinary annuity is just:

$$\text{Annuity due value} = \text{Ordinary annuity value} \times (1 + r) \qquad [6.3]$$

This works for both present and future values, so calculating the value of an annuity due involves two steps: (1) calculate the present or future value as though it were an ordinary annuity, and (2) multiply your answer by $(1 + r)$.

Perpetuities

We've seen that a series of level cash flows can be valued by treating those cash flows as an annuity. An important special case of an annuity arises when the level stream of cash flows continues forever. Such an asset is called a **perpetuity** since the cash flows are perpetual. Perpetuities are also called **consols,** particularly in Canada and the United Kingdom. See Example 6.7 for an important example of a perpetuity.

perpetuity
An annuity in which the cash flows continue forever.

consol
A type of perpetuity.

Since a perpetuity has an infinite number of cash flows, we obviously can't compute its value by discounting each one. Fortunately, valuing a per-

TABLE 6.2
Summary of annuity and perpetuity calculations

Trans. 6.7

I. Symbols:

PV = Present value, what future cash flows are worth today
FV_t = Future value, what cash flows are worth in the future
r = Interest rate, rate of return, or discount rate per period—typically, but not always, one year
t = Number of periods—typically, but not always, the number of years
C = Cash amount

II. Future value of C per period for t periods at r percent per period:

$$FV_t = C \times \{(1 + r)^t\} - 1]/r$$

A series of identical cash flows is called an *annuity,* and the term $[(1 + r)^t - 1]/r$ is called the *annuity future value factor.*

III. Present value of C per period for t periods at r percent per period:

$$PV = C \times [1 - \{1/(1 + r)^t\}]/r$$

The term $[1 - \{1/(1 + r)^t\}]/r$ is called the *annuity present value factor.*

IV. Present value of a perpetuity of C per period:

$$PV = C/r$$

A *perpetuity* has the same cash flow every year forever.

petuity turns out to be the easiest possible case. The present value of a perpetuity is simply:

Concept Q Answer 6.2b

$$\text{PV for a perpetuity} = C/r \qquad [6.4]$$

For example, an investment offers a perpetual cash flow of $500 every year. The return you require on such an investment is 8 percent. What is the value of this investment? The value of this perpetuity is:

$$\text{Perpetuity PV} = C/r = \$500/.08 = \$6{,}250$$

This concludes our discussion of valuing investments with multiple cash flows. For future reference, Table 6.2 contains a summary of the annuity and perpetuity basic calculations we described.

EXAMPLE 6.7 Preferred Stock

Preferred stock (or preference stock) is an important example of a perpetuity. When a corporation sells preferred stock, the buyer is promised a fixed cash dividend every period (usually every quarter) forever. This dividend must be paid before any dividend can be paid to regular stockholders, hence the term *preferred.*

Suppose the Fellini Co. wants to sell preferred stock at $100 per share. A very similar issue of preferred stock already outstanding has a price of $40 per share and offers a dividend of $1 every quarter. What dividend will Fellini have to offer if the preferred stock is going to sell?

The issue that is already out has a present value of $40 and a cash flow of $1 every quarter forever. Since this is a perpetuity:

$$\text{Present value} = \$40 = \$1 \times (1/r)$$
$$r = 2.5\%$$

To be competitive, the new Fellini issue will also have to offer 2.5 percent *per quarter;* so, if the present value is to be $100, the dividend must be such that:

$$\text{Present value} = \$100 = C \times (1/.025)$$
$$C = \$2.5 \text{ (per quarter)} \quad \ldots$$

CONCEPT QUESTIONS

6.2a In general, what is the present value of an annuity of C dollars per period at a discount rate of r per period? The future value?

6.2b In general, what is the present value of a perpetuity?

6.3 COMPARING RATES: THE EFFECT OF COMPOUNDING PERIODS

Self-Test Problem 6.4
Problems 12–23, 31

The last issue we need to discuss has to do with the way interest rates are quoted. This subject causes a fair amount of confusion because rates are quoted in many different ways. Sometimes the way a rate is quoted is the result of tradition, and sometimes it's the result of legislation. Unfortunately, at times, rates are quoted in deliberately deceptive ways to mislead borrowers and investors. We will discuss these topics in this section.

Effective Annual Rates and Compounding

If a rate were quoted as 10 percent compounded semiannually, then what this means is that the investment actually pays 5 percent every six months. A natural question then arises: Is 5 percent every six months the same thing as 10 percent per year? It's easy to see that it is not. If you invest $1 at 10 percent per year, you will have $1.10 at the end of the year. If you invest at 5 percent every six months, then you'll have the future value of $1 at 5 percent for two periods, or:

$$\$1 \times (1.05)^2 = \$1.1025$$

Concept Q
Answers 6.3a, 6.3b

stated interest rate
The interest rate expressed in terms of the interest payment made each period. Also quoted interest rate.

effective annual rate (EAR)
The interest rate expressed as if it were compounded once per year.

Trans. 6.8
Effective Annual Rates and Compounding (Supplemental)

This is $.0025 more. The reason is very simple. What has occurred is that your account is credited with $\$1 \times .05 = 5$ cents in interest after 6 months. In the following six months, you earned 5 percent on that nickel, for an extra $5 \times .05 = .25$ cents.

As our example illustrates, 10 percent compounded semiannually is actually equivalent to 10.25 percent per year. Put another way, we would be indifferent between 10 percent compounded semiannually and 10.25 percent compounded annually. Anytime we have compounding during the year, we need to be concerned about what the rate really is.

In our example, the 10 percent is called a **stated** or **quoted interest rate**. Other names are used as well. The 10.25 percent, which is actually the rate that you will earn, is called the **effective annual rate (EAR)**. To compare different investments or interest rates, we will always need to convert to effective rates. Some general procedures for doing this are discussed next.

Calculating and Comparing Effective Annual Rates

To see why it is important to work only with effective rates, suppose you've shopped around and come up with the following three rates:

Bank A: 15%, compounded daily

Bank B: 15.5%, compounded quarterly

Bank C: 16%, compounded annually

Which of these is the best if you are thinking of opening a savings account? Which of these is best if they represent loan rates?

To begin, Bank C is offering 16 percent per year. Since there is no compounding during the year, this is the effective rate. Bank B is actually paying .155/4 = .03875 or 3.875 percent per quarter. At this rate, an investment of $1 for four quarters would grow to:

Trans. 6.9
Cheap Financing versus Rebate (Supplemental)

$$\$1 \times (1.03875)^4 = \$1.1642$$

The EAR, therefore, is 16.42 percent. For a saver, this is much better than the 16 percent rate Bank C is offering; for a borrower, it's worse.

Bank A is compounding every day. This may seem a little extreme, but it is very common to calculate interest daily. In this case, the daily interest rate is actually:

$$.15/365 = .000411$$

This is .0411 percent per day. At this rate, an investment of $1 for 365 periods would grow to:

$$\$1 \times (1.000411)^{365} = \$1.1618$$

The EAR is 16.18 percent. This is not as good as Bank B's 16.42 percent for a saver, and not as good as Bank C's 16 percent for a borrower.

This example illustrates two things. First, the highest quoted rate is not necessarily the best. Second, the compounding during the year can lead to a significant difference between the quoted rate and the effective rate. Remember that the effective rate is what you get or what you pay.

If you look at our examples, we computed the EARs in three steps. We first divided the quoted rate by the number of times that the interest is compounded. We then added 1 to the result and raised it to the power of the number of times the interest is compounded. Finally, we subtracted the 1. If we let m be the number of times the interest is compounded during the year, these steps can be summarized simply as:

Concept Q Answer 6.3c

$$\text{EAR} = [1 + (\text{Quoted rate})/m]^m - 1 \qquad [6.5]$$

For example, suppose you were offered 12 percent compounded monthly. In this case, the interest is compounded 12 times a year; so m is 12. You can calculate the effective rate as:

$$\begin{aligned} \text{EAR} &= [1 + (\text{Quoted rate})/m]^m - 1 \\ &= [1 + .12/12]^{12} - 1 \\ &= 1.01^{12} - 1 \\ &= 1.126825 - 1 \\ &= 12.6825\% \end{aligned}$$

Lecture Tip: See IM for a suggested class discussion to stimulate interest in the difference between EAR and APR.

EXAMPLE 6.8 What's the EAR?

A bank is offering 12 percent compounded quarterly. If you put \$100 in an account, how much will you have at the end of one year? What's the EAR? How much will you have at the end of two years?

The bank is effectively offering 12%/4 = 3% every quarter. If you invest \$100 for four periods at 3 percent per period, the future value is:

$$\begin{aligned}\text{Future value} &= \$100 \times (1.03)^4\\ &= \$100 \times 1.1255\\ &= \$112.55\end{aligned}$$

The EAR is 12.55 percent: \$100 × (1 + .1255) = \$112.55.

We can determine what you would have at the end of two years in two different ways. One way is to recognize that two years is the same as eight quarters. At 3 percent per quarter, after eight quarters, you would have:

$$\$100 \times (1.03)^8 = \$100 \times 1.2668 = \$126.68$$

Alternatively, we could determine the value after two years by using an EAR of 12.55 percent; so after two years you would have:

$$\$100 \times (1.1255)^2 = \$100 \times 1.2688 = \$126.68$$

Thus, the two calculations produce the same answer. This illustrates an important point. Anytime we do a present or future value calculation, the rate we use must be an actual or effective rate. In this case, the actual rate is 3 percent per quarter. The effective annual rate is 12.55 percent. It doesn't matter which one we use once we know the EAR. • • •

EXAMPLE 6.9 Quoting a Rate

Now that you know how to convert a quoted rate to an EAR, consider going the other way. As a lender, you know you want to actually earn 18 percent on a particular loan. You want to quote a rate that features monthly compounding. What rate do you quote?

In this case, we know the EAR is 18 percent, and we know this is the result of monthly compounding. Let q stand for the quoted rate. We thus have:

$$\begin{aligned}\text{EAR} &= [1 + (\text{Quoted rate})/\text{m}]^m - 1\\ .18 &= [1 + q/12]^{12} - 1\\ 1.18 &= [1 + q/12]^{12}\end{aligned}$$

We need to solve this equation for the quoted rate. This calculation is the same as the ones we did to find an unknown interest rate in Chapter 5:

$$\begin{aligned}1.18^{(1/12)} &= (1 + q/12)\\ 1.18^{.08333} &= 1 + q/12\\ 1.0139 &= 1 + q/12\\ q &= .0139 \times 12\\ &= 16.68\%\end{aligned}$$

Therefore, the rate you would quote is 16.68 percent, compounded monthly. • • •

EARs and APRs

Sometimes it's not altogether clear whether a rate is an effective annual rate or not. A case in point concerns what is called the **annual percentage rate** or **APR** on a loan. Truth-in-lending laws in the United States require that lenders disclose an APR on virtually all consumer loans. This rate must be displayed on a loan document in a prominent and unambiguous way.

annual percentage rate (APR) The interest rate charged per period multiplied by the number of periods per year.

Given that an APR must be calculated and displayed, an obvious question arises: Is an APR an effective annual rate? Put another way, if a bank quotes a car loan at 12 percent APR, is the consumer actually paying 12 percent interest? Surprisingly, the answer is no. There is some confusion over this point, which we discuss next.

Trans. 6.10
Ripov Retailing: An Example (Supplemental)

Concept Q Answer 6.3b

The confusion over APRs arises because lenders are required by law to compute the APR in a particular way. By law, the APR is simply equal to the interest rate per period multiplied by the number of periods in a year. For example, if a bank is charging 1.2 percent per month on car loans, then the APR that must be reported is $1.2\% \times 12 = 14.4\%$. So, an APR is in fact a quoted or stated rate in the sense we've been discussing. For example, an APR of 12 percent on a loan calling for monthly payments is really 1 percent per month. The EAR on such a loan is thus:

★ **Ethics Note:** See IM for an example that introduces the concept of usury while teaching the basics of annuities.

$$\begin{aligned} \text{EAR} &= (1 + \text{APR}/12)^{12} - 1 \\ &= 1.01^{12} - 1 = 12.6825\% \end{aligned}$$

EXAMPLE 6.10 What Rate Are You Paying?

Depending on the issuer, a typical credit card agreement quotes an interest rate of 18 percent APR. Monthly payments are required. What is the actual interest rate you pay on such a credit card?

Based on our discussion, an APR of 18 percent with monthly payments is really $.18/12 = .015$ or 1.5 percent per month. The EAR is thus:

$$\begin{aligned} \text{EAR} &= (1 + .18/12)^{12} - 1 \\ &= 1.015^{12} - 1 \\ &= 1.1956 - 1 \\ &= 19.56\% \end{aligned}$$

This is the rate you actually pay. • • •

The difference between an APR and an EAR probably won't be all that great, but it is somewhat ironic that truth-in-lending laws sometimes require lenders to be *un*truthful about the actual rate on a loan.

CONCEPT QUESTIONS

6.3a If an interest rate is given as 12 percent, compounded daily, what do we call this rate?

6.3b What is an APR? What is an EAR? Are they the same thing?

6.3c In general, what is the relationship between a stated interest rate and an effective interest rate? Which is more relevant for financial decisions?

6.4 LOAN TYPES AND LOAN AMORTIZATION

Whenever a lender extends a loan, some provision will be made for repayment of the principal (the original loan amount). A loan might be repaid in equal installments, for example, or it might be repaid in a single lump sum. Because the way that the principal and interest are paid is up to the parties involved, there is actually an unlimited number of possibilities.

In this section, we describe a few forms of repayment that come up quite often, and more complicated forms can usually be built up from these. The three basic types are: pure discount loans, interest-only loans, and amortized loans. Working with these loans is a very straightforward application of the present value principles that we have already developed.

Pure Discount Loans

The *pure discount loan* is the simplest form. With such a loan, the borrower receives money today and repays a single lump sum at some time in the future. A one-year, 10 percent pure discount loan, for example, would require the borrower to repay \$1.1 in one year for every dollar borrowed today.

Because a pure discount loan is so simple, we already know how to value one. Suppose a borrower was able to repay \$25,000 in five years. If we, acting as the lender, wanted a 12 percent interest rate on the loan, how much would we be willing to lend? Put another way, what value would we assign today to that \$25,000 to be repaid in five years? Based on our work in Chapter 5, we know the answer is just the present value of \$25,000 at 12 percent for five years:

$$\begin{aligned}\text{Present value} &= \$25{,}000/1.12^5 \\ &= \$25{,}000/1.7623 \\ &= \$14{,}186\end{aligned}$$

Pure discount loans are very common when the loan term is short, say, a year or less. In recent years, they have become increasingly common for much longer periods.

EXAMPLE 6.11 Treasury Bills

When the U.S. government borrows money on a short-term basis (a year or less), it does so by selling what are called *Treasury bills,* or *T-bills* for short. A T-bill is a promise by the government to repay a fixed amount at some time in the future, for example, 3 months or 12 months.

Treasury bills are pure discount loans. If a T-bill promises to repay \$10,000 in 12 months, and the market interest rate is 7 percent, how much will the bill sell for in the market?

Since the going rate is 7 percent, the T-bill will sell for the present value of \$10,000 to be paid in one year at 7 percent, or:

$$\text{Present value} = \$10{,}000/1.07 = \$9{,}345.79$$

...

Interest-Only Loans

A second type of loan repayment plan calls for the borrower to pay interest each period and to repay the entire principal (the original loan amount) at some point in the future. Such loans are called *interest-only loans.* Notice that if there is just one period, a pure discount loan and an interest-only loan are the same thing.

For example, with a three-year, 10 percent, interest-only loan of $1,000, the borrower would pay $1,000 × .10 = $100 in interest at the end of the first and second years. At the end of the third year, the borrower would return the $1,000 along with another $100 in interest for that year. Similarly, a 50-year interest-only loan would call for the borrower to pay interest every year for the next 50 years and then repay the principal. In the extreme, the borrower pays the interest every period forever and never repays any principal. As we discussed in the chapter, the result is a perpetuity.

Most corporate bonds have the general form of an interest-only loan. Because we will be considering bonds in some detail in the next chapter, we will defer a further discussion of them for now.

Amortized Loans

Self-Test Problems 6.5, 6.6
Problems 36–38

With a pure discount or interest-only loan, the principal is repaid all at once. An alternative is an *amortized loan,* where the lender may require the borrower to repay parts of the loan amount over time. The process of paying off a loan by making regular principal reductions is called *amortizing* the loan.

A simple way of amortizing a loan is to have the borrower pay the interest each period plus some fixed amount. This approach is common with medium-term business loans. For example, suppose a business takes out a $5,000, five-year loan at 9 percent. The loan agreement calls for the borrower to pay the interest on the loan balance each year and to reduce the loan balance each year by $1,000. Since the loan amount declines by $1,000 each year, it is fully paid in five years.

In the case we are considering, notice that the total payment each year will decline. The reason is that the loan balance goes down, resulting in a lower interest charge each year, while the $1,000 principal reduction is constant. For example, the interest in the first year will be $5,000 × .09 = $450. The total payment will be $1,000 + 450 = $1,450. In the second year, the loan balance is $4,000, so the interest is $4,000 × .09 = $360, and the total payment is $1,360. We can calculate the total payment in each of the remaining years by preparing a simple *amortization schedule* as follows:

Trans. 6.11
Amortization Schedule: Fixed Principal

Year	Beginning Balance	Total Payment	Interest Paid	Principal Paid	Ending Balance
1	$5,000	$1,450	$ 450	$1,000	$4,000
2	4,000	1,360	360	1,000	3,000
3	3,000	1,270	270	1,000	2,000
4	2,000	1,180	180	1,000	1,000
5	1,000	1,090	90	1,000	0
Totals		$6,350	$1,350	$5,000	

Notice that, in each year, the interest paid is just given by the beginning balance multiplied by the interest rate. Also notice that the beginning balance is given by the ending balance from the previous year.

Probably the most common way of amortizing a loan is for the borrower to make a single, fixed payment every period. Almost all consumer loans (such as car loans) and mortgages work this way. For example, suppose our five-year, 9 percent, $5,000 loan was amortized this way. How would the amortization schedule look?

We first need to determine the payment. From our discussion in the chapter, we know that this loan's cash flows are in the form of an ordinary annuity. In this case, we can solve for the payment as follows:

$$\begin{aligned}\$5{,}000 &= C \times (1 - 1/1.09^5)/.09 \\ &= C \times (1 - .6499)/.09\end{aligned}$$

This gives us:

$$\begin{aligned}C &= \$5{,}000/3.8897 \\ &= \$1{,}285.46\end{aligned}$$

The borrower will therefore make five equal payments of $1,285.46. Will this pay off the loan? We will check by filling in an amortization schedule.

In our previous example, we knew the principal reduction each year. We then calculated the interest owed to get the total payment. In this example, we know the total payment. We will thus calculate the interest and then subtract it from the total payment to calculate the principal portion in each payment.

In the first year, the interest is $450 as we calculated before. Since the total payment is $1,285.46, the principal paid in the first year must be:

$$\text{Principal paid} = \$1{,}285.46 - 450 = \$835.46$$

The ending loan balance is thus:

$$\text{Ending balance} = \$5{,}000 - 835.46 = \$4{,}164.54$$

The interest in the second year is $4,164.54 × .09 = $374.81, and the loan balance declines by $1,285.46 − 374.81 = $910.65. We can summarize all of the relevant calculations in the following schedule:

Trans. 6.12
Amortization Schedule: Fixed Payments

Year	Beginning Balance	Total Payment	Interest Paid	Principal Paid	Ending Balance
1	$5,000.00	$1,285.46	$ 450.00	$ 835.46	$4,164.54
2	4,164.54	1,285.46	374.81	910.65	3,253.88
3	3,253.88	1,285.46	292.85	992.61	2,261.27
4	2,261.27	1,285.46	203.51	1,081.95	1,179.32
5	1,179.32	1,285.46	106.14	1,179.32	0.00
Totals		$6,427.30	$1,427.31	$5,000.00	

Since the loan balance declines to zero, the five equal payments do pay off the loan. Notice that the interest paid declines each period. This isn't surprising since the loan balance is going down. Given that the total payment is fixed, the principal paid must be rising each period.

If you compare the two loan amortizations in this section, you will see the total interest is greater for the equal total payment case, $1,427.31 versus $1,350. The reason for this is that the loan is repaid more slowly early on, so the interest is somewhat higher. This doesn't mean that one loan is better than the other; it simply means that one is effectively paid off faster than the other. For example, the principal reduction in the first year is $835.46 in the equal total payment case compared to $1,000 in the first case.

6.5 SUMMARY AND CONCLUSIONS

This chapter rounds out your understanding of fundamental concepts related to the time value of money and discounted cash flow valuation. Several important topics were covered, including:

1. There are two ways of calculating present and future values when there are multiple cash flows. Both approaches are straightforward extensions of our earlier analysis of single cash flows.
2. A series of constant cash flows that arrive or are paid at the end of each period is called an ordinary annuity, and we describe some useful shortcuts for determining the present and future values of annuities.
3. Interest rates can be quoted in a variety of ways. For financial decisions, it is important that any rates being compared be first converted to effective rates. The relationship between a quoted rate, such as an annual percentage rate (APR), and an effective annual rate (EAR) is given by:

   $$\text{EAR} = (1 + \text{Quoted rate}/m)^m - 1$$

   where m is the number of times during the year the money is compounded or, equivalently, the number of payments during the year.
4. Many loans are annuities. The process of paying off a loan is called amortizing the loan, and we discuss how amortization schedules are prepared and interpreted.

Chapter Review Problems and Self-Test

6.1 **Present Values with Multiple Cash Flows** A first-round draft choice quarterback has been signed to a three-year, $10 million contract. The details provide for an immediate cash bonus of $1 million. The player is to receive $2 million in salary at the end of the first year, $3 million the next, and $4 million at the end of the last year. Assuming a 10 percent discount rate, is this package worth $10 million? How much is it worth?

6.2 **Future Value with Multiple Cash Flows** You plan to make a series of deposits in an interest-bearing account. You will deposit $1,000 today, $2,000 in two years, and $8,000 in five years. If you withdraw $3,000 in three years and $5,000 in seven years, how much will you have after eight years if the interest rate is 9 percent? What is the present value of these cash flows?

6.3 **Annuity Present Value** You are looking into an investment that will pay you $12,000 per year for the next 10 years. If you require a 15 percent return, what is the most you would pay for this investment?

6.4 **APR versus EAR** The going rate on student loans is quoted as 9 percent APR. The terms of the loan call for monthly payments. What is the effective annual rate (EAR) on such a student loan?

6.5 It's the Principal That Matters Suppose you borrow \$10,000. You are going to repay the loan by making equal annual payments for five years. The interest rate on the loan is 14 percent per year. Prepare an amortization schedule for the loan. How much interest will you pay over the life of the loan?

6.6 Just a Little Bit Each Month You've recently finished your MBA at the Darnit School. Naturally, you must purchase a new BMW immediately. The car costs about \$21,000. The bank quotes an interest rate of 15 percent APR for a 72-month loan with a 10 percent down payment. What will your monthly payment be? What is the effective interest rate on the loan?

Answers to Self-Test Problems

6.1 Obviously, the package is not worth \$10 million because the payments are spread out over three years. The bonus is paid today, so it's worth \$1 million. The present values for the three subsequent salary payments are:

$$\begin{aligned}\$2/1.1 + 3/1.1^2 + 4/1.1^3 &= \$2/1.1 + 3/1.21 + 4/1.331\\ &= \$7.3028\end{aligned}$$

The package is worth a total of \$8.3028 million.

6.2 We will calculate the future values for each of the cash flows separately and then add them up. Notice that we treat the withdrawals as negative cash flows:

$$\begin{aligned}\$1{,}000 \times 1.09^8 &= \$1{,}000 \times 1.9926 = \$\ 1{,}992.60\\ \$2{,}000 \times 1.09^6 &= \$2{,}000 \times 1.6771 = \$\ 3{,}354.20\\ -\$3{,}000 \times 1.09^5 &= -\$3{,}000 \times 1.5386 = -\$\ 4{,}615.87\\ \$8{,}000 \times 1.09^3 &= \$8{,}000 \times 1.2950 = \$10{,}360.23\\ -\$5{,}000 \times 1.09^1 &= -\$5{,}000 \times 1.0900 = -\$\ 5{,}450.00\\ &\text{Total future value} = \$\ 5{,}641.12\end{aligned}$$

This value includes a small rounding error.

To calculate the present value, we could discount each cash flow back to the present or we could discount back a single year at a time. However, since we already know that the future value in eight years is \$5,641.12, the easy way to get the PV is just to discount this amount back eight years:

$$\begin{aligned}\text{Present value} &= \$5{,}641.12/1.09^8\\ &= \$5{,}641.12/1.9926\\ &= \$2{,}831.03\end{aligned}$$

We again ignore a small rounding error. For practice, you can verify that this is what you get if you discount each cash flow back separately.

6.3 The most you would be willing to pay is the present value of \$12,000 per year for 10 years at a 15 percent discount rate. The cash flows here are in ordinary annuity form, so the relevant present value factor is:

$$\begin{aligned}\text{Annuity present value factor} &= [1 - (1/1.15^{10})]/.15\\ &= [1 - .2472]/.15\\ &= 5.0188\end{aligned}$$

The present value of the 10 cash flows is thus:

$$\begin{aligned}\text{Present value} &= \$12{,}000 \times 5.0188\\ &= \$60{,}225\end{aligned}$$

This is the most you would pay.

6.4 A rate of 9 percent APR with monthly payments is actually 9%/12 = .75% per month. The EAR is thus:

$$\text{EAR} = (1 + .09/12)^{12} - 1 = 9.38\%$$

6.5 We first need to calculate the annual payment. With a present value of \$10,000, an interest rate of 14 percent, and a term of five years, the payment can be determined from:

$$\begin{aligned}\$10{,}000 &= \text{Payment} \times (1 - 1/1.14^5)/.14\\ &= \text{Payment} \times 3.4331\end{aligned}$$

Therefore, the payment is \$10,000/3.4331 = \$2,912.84 (actually, it's \$2,912.8355; this will create some small rounding errors in the schedule below). We can now prepare the amortization schedule as follows:

Year	Beginning Balance	Total Payment	Interest Paid	Principal Paid	Ending Balance
1	\$10,000.00	\$ 2,912.84	\$1,400.00	\$ 1,512.84	\$8,487.16
2	8,487.16	2,912.84	1,188.20	1,724.63	6,762.53
3	6,762.53	2,912.84	946.75	1,966.08	4,796.45
4	4,796.45	2,912.84	671.50	2,241.33	2,555.12
5	2,555.12	2,912.84	357.72	2,555.12	0.00
Totals		\$14,564.17	\$4,564.17	\$10,000.00	

6.6 The cash flows on the car loan are in annuity form, so we only need to find the payment. The interest rate is 15%/12 = 1.25% per month, and there are 72 months. The first thing we need is the annuity factor for 72 periods at 1.25 percent per period:

$$\begin{aligned}\text{Annuity present value factor} &= (1 - \text{Present value factor})/r\\ &= [1 - (1/1.0125^{72})]/.0125\\ &= [1 - (1/2.4459)]/.0125\\ &= (1 - .4088)/.0125\\ &= 47.2925\end{aligned}$$

The present value is the amount we finance. With a 10 percent down payment, we will be borrowing 90 percent of \$21,000, or \$18,900.

So, to find the payment, we need to solve for C in the following:

$$\begin{aligned} \$18{,}900 &= C \times \text{Annuity present value factor} \\ &= C \times 47.2925 \end{aligned}$$

Rearranging things a bit, we have:

$$\begin{aligned} C &= \$18{,}900 \times (1/47.2925) \\ &= \$18{,}900 \times .02115 \\ &= \$399.64 \end{aligned}$$

Your payment is just under $400 per month.

The actual interest rate on this loan is 1.25 percent per month. Based on our work in the chapter, we can calculate the effective annual rate as:

$$\text{EAR} = (1.0125)^{12} - 1 = 16.08\%$$

The effective rate is about one point higher than the quoted rate.

Questions and Problems

Basic (Questions 1–24)

@10%: PV = $1,688.75
@14%: PV = $1,559.83
@20%: PV = $1,394.68

1. **Present Value and Multiple Cash Flows** Looking Good Co. has identified an investment project with the following cash flows. If the discount rate is 10 percent, what is the present value of these cash flows? What is the present value at 14 percent? At 20 percent?

Year	Cash Flow
1	$500
2	$700
3	$600
4	$300

@6%: FV = $3,312.79
@8%: FV = $3,422.86
@16%: FV = $3,893.29

2. **Future Value and Multiple Cash Flows** ABC Co. has identified an investment project with the following cash flows. If the discount rate is 6 percent, what is the future value of these cash flows in Year 4? What is the future value at a discount rate of 8 percent? At 16 percent?

Year	Cash Flow
1	$900
2	$800
3	$700
4	$600

12 years: PV = $9,291.56
35 years: PV = $12,263.26
60 years: PV = $12,486.07
Forever: PV = $12,500.00

3. **Calculating Annuity Present Value** An investment offers $1,500 per year for 12 years, with the first payment occurring one year from now. If the required return is 12 percent, what is the value of the investment? What would the value be if the payments occurred for 35 years? 60 years? Forever?

C = $10,927.98

4. **Calculating Annuity Cash Flows** If you put up $55,000 today in exchange for a 9 percent, 7-year annuity, what will the annual cash flow be?

PV = $161,225.06
Trans. 6.13

5. **Calculating Annuity Values** Your company will generate $27,000 annual payments each year for the next eight years from a new information database. The computer system needed to set up the database

costs $180,000. If you can borrow the money to buy the computer system at 7 percent annual interest, can you afford the new system?

6. **Annuity Values** If you deposit $600 at the end of the next 10 years into an account paying 9.5 percent interest, how much money will you have in the account in 10 years? How much will you have in 13 years?

@10 years: FV = $9,336.17
@13 years: FV = $12,257.77

7. **Annuity Values** You want to have $17,000 in your savings account six years from now, and you're prepared to make equal annual deposits into the account at the end of each year. If the account pays 8 percent interest, what amount must you deposit each year?

C = $2,317.36

8. **Annuity Values** Betty's Bank offers you a $7,000, six-year term loan at 10 percent annual interest. What will your annual loan payment be?

C = $1,607.25

9. **Present Value and Multiple Cash Flows** Investment X offers to pay you $2,000 per year for four years, while Investment Y offers to pay you $2,500 per year for three years. Which of these cash flow streams has the higher present value if the discount rate is 5 percent? If the discount rate is 20 percent?

@5% PV_x = $7,091.90
PV_y = $6,808.12
@20%: PV_x = $5,177.47
PV_y = $5,266.20

10. **Perpetuity Values** Bob's Life Insurance Co. is trying to sell you an investment policy that will pay you and your heirs $700 per year forever. If the required return on this investment is 12 percent, how much will you pay for the policy?

PV = $5,833.33

11. **Perpetuity Values** In the previous problem, suppose Bob told you the policy costs $8,500. At what interest rate would this be a fair deal?

8.24%

12. **Calculating EAR** Find the EAR in each of the cases below:

10.38%
17.23%
9.42%

Stated Rate (APR)	Compounding Period	Effective Rate (EAR)
10%	Quarterly	
16%	Monthly	
9%	Daily	

13. **Calculating APR** Find the APR or stated rate in each of the cases below:

7.85%
11.39%
15.72%

Stated Rate (APR)	Compounding Period	Effective Rate (EAR)
	Semiannually	8%
	Monthly	12%
	Weekly	17%

14. **Calculating EAR** Last National Bank charges 8 percent, compounded quarterly, on its business loans. Last United Bank charges 8.5 percent compounded semiannually. As a potential borrower, which bank would you go to for a new loan?

Last National: EAR = 8.24%
Last United: EAR = 8.68%

15. **Calculating APR** Colossus Banken Corp. wants to earn an effective annual return on its consumer loans of 9 percent per year. The bank uses monthly compounding on its loans. What interest rate is the bank required by law to report to potential borrowers? Explain why this rate is misleading to an uninformed borrower.

APR = 8.65%
EAR = 9%

16. **Calculating Future Value** What is the future value of $900 in 16 years assuming an interest rate of 11 percent compounded quarterly?

FV = $5,108.34

@3 years: FV = $338.25
@4 years: FV = $352.05
@20 years: FV = $667.63

17. **Calculating Future Value** Kommisar's Kredit Bank is offering 4 percent compounded daily on its savings accounts. If you deposit $300 today, how much will you have in the account in 3 years? In 4 years? In 20 years?

PV = $21,898.69

18. **Calculating Present Value** An investment will pay you $34,000 in four years. If the appropriate discount rate is 11 percent compounded daily, what is the present value?

APR = 300%
EAR = 1,355.19%

19. **EAR versus APR** Roger Ripov's Pawn Shop charges an interest rate of 25 percent per month on loans to its customers. Like all lenders, Roger Ripov must report an APR to consumers. What rate should the shop report? What is the effective annual rate?

C = $588.14
EAR = 12.57%;

20. **Calculating Loan Payments** You want to buy a new sports coupe for $26,500, and the finance office at the dealership has quoted you an 11.9 percent APR loan for 60 months to buy the car. What will your monthly payments be? What is the effective annual rate on this loan?

43 months

21. **Calculating Number of Periods** One of your customers is delinquent on his accounts payable balance. You've mutually agreed to a repayment schedule of $263 per month. You will charge 1.2 percent per month interest on the overdue balance. If the current balance is $8,794.29, how long will it take for the account to be paid off?

PV = $9,954.00

22. **Calculating Annuity Present Values** Beginning three months from now, you want to be able to withdraw $1,000 each quarter from your bank account to cover college expenses over the next three years. If the account pays 3 percent interest per quarter, how much do you need to have in your bank account today to meet your expense needs over the next three years?

PV = $10,405.23

23. **Discounted Cash Flow Analysis** If the appropriate discount rate for the following cash flows is 12 percent compounded quarterly, what is the present value of the cash flows?

Year	Cash Flow
1	$3,500
2	$4,900
3	$ 0
4	$5,500

PV = $1,515.74

24. **Discounted Cash Flow Analysis** If the appropriate discount rate for the following cash flows is 9.8 percent per year, what is the present value of the cash flows?

Year	Cash Flow
1	$800
2	$ 0
3	$450
4	$650

Intermediate (Questions 25–38)

PV_1 = $65,082.91
PV_2 = $62,541.45
Trans. 6.14

25. **Comparing Cash Flow Streams** You've just joined the investment banking firm of Godel, Esher, and Bock. They've offered you two different salary arrangements. You can have $40,000 per year for the next two years or $20,000 per year for the next two years, along with a $30,000 signing bonus today. If the interest rate is 14 percent compounded monthly, which do you prefer?

26. **Calculating Present Value of Annuities** Bill Broker wants to sell you an investment contract that pays equal $5,000 payments at the end of each of the next 8 years. If you require an effective annual return of 18 percent on this investment, how much will you pay for the contract today?

PV = $20,387.83

27. **Calculating Rates of Return** You're trying to choose between two different investments, both of which have up-front costs of $25,000. Investment G returns $40,000 in six years. Investment H returns $60,000 in 11 years. Which of these investments has the higher return?

G: 8.15%
H: 8.28%

28. **Present Value and Interest Rates** What is the relationship between the value of an annuity and the level of interest rates? Suppose you just bought an eight-year annuity of $400 per year when interest rates are 10 percent per year. What happens to the value of your investment if interest rates suddenly drop to 6 percent? What if interest rates suddenly rise to 14 percent?

@10%: PV = $2,133.97
@6%: PV = $2,483.92
@14%: PV = $1,855.55

29. **Calculating Annuity Future Values** You're prepared to make monthly payments of $75.21, beginning next month, into an account that pays 16 percent interest compounded monthly. How many payments will you have made when your account balance reaches $10,000?

77 payments

30. **Calculating Annuity Present Values** You want to borrow $12,000 from your local bank to buy a new sailboat. You can afford to make monthly payments of $325, but no more. Assuming monthly compounding, what is the highest 48-month APR loan you can afford to take out?

APR = 13.51%

31. **EAR versus APR** You have just purchased a new warehouse. To finance the purchase, you've arranged for a 20-year mortgage loan for 90 percent of the $700,000 purchase price. The monthly payment on this loan will be $5,500. What is the APR on this loan? The EAR?

APR = 8.58%
EAR = 8.93%

32. **Present Value and Interest Rates** You've just won the U.S. MegaLottery. Lottery officials offer you the choice of two alternative payouts: either $1 million today, or $2 million six years from now. Which payout will you choose if the relevant discount rate is 0 percent? 10 percent? 20 percent?

@0%: PV = $2 million
@10%: PV = $1.129 million
@20%: PV = $0.670 million

33. **Calculating Present Value of Annuities** Congratulations! You've just won the $10 million 1st prize in the Editor's Clearingworld Sweepstakes. Unfortunately, the sweepstakes will actually give you the $10 million in $250,000 annual installments over the next 40 years, beginning next year. If your appropriate discount rate is 7 percent per year, how much money did you really win?

PV = $3,332,927.21

34. **Calculating Annuities Due** As discussed in the text, an ordinary annuity assumes equal payments at the end of each period over the life of the annuity. An *annuity due* is the same thing except the payments occur at the beginning of each period instead. Thus a 3-year annual annuity due would have periodic payment cash flows occurring at Years 0, 1, and 2, while a 3-year annual ordinary annuity would have periodic payment cash flows occurring at Years 1, 2, and 3.

a. At a 7 percent annual discount rate, find the present value of a 4-year ordinary annuity contract of $500 payments.

b. Find the present value of the same contract if it is an annuity due.

a. PV = $1,693.61
b. PV = $1,812.16

C = $597.66

35. **Calculating Annuities Due** You want to lease a new car from Mary's Motorworks for $13,000. The lease contract is in the form of a 24-month annuity due at a 10.5 percent APR. What will your monthly lease payment be?

a. Third year = $368.49
b. Life of loan = $2,014.64

36. **Amortization with Equal Payments** Prepare an amortization schedule for a three-year loan of $6,000. The interest rate is 16 percent per year and the loan calls for equal annual payments. How much interest is paid in the third year? How much total interest is paid over the life of the loan?

a. Third year = $320.00
b. Life of loan = $1,920.00

37. **Amortization with Equal Principal Payments** Rework Problem 36 assuming that the loan agreement calls for a principal reduction of $2,000 every year instead of equal annual payments.

Balloon = $81,274.07

38. **Calculating a Balloon Payment** You have just arranged for a $100,000 mortgage to finance the purchase of a large tract of land. The mortgage has a 12 percent APR, and it calls for monthly payments over the next 10 years. However, the loan has a three-year balloon payment, meaning that the loan must be paid off then. How big will the balloon payment be?

Chapter Seven

7

Stock and Bond Valuation

• • •

After studying this chapter, you should have a good understanding of:

. . .

Features of corporate bonds and how their prices are quoted.

. . .

How bonds are valued.

. . .

Important features of common stock.

. . .

How shares of stock are valued.

In our previous chapters, we introduced you to the basic procedures used to value future cash flows. In this chapter, we show you how to use those procedures to value stocks and bonds. Along the way, we introduce you to some of the terminology that commonly appears in these areas, and we also describe how the prices for these assets are reported in the financial press.

Trans. 7.1
Chapter Outline

Throughout this and the next several chapters, we will generally assume that we know the appropriate discount rate. The question of what determines this discount rate and how we might go about measuring it is sufficiently important that we will devote several chapters to it later on. For now, we focus on the relevant cash flows from financial assets and how to value them, given a suitable discount rate.

Lecture Tip: In introducing the material in this chapter, it is useful to remind students that the value of any financial asset is a function of the size, timing, and the risk of its cash flows. Chapter 2 discussed cash flow size, and Chapters 5 and 6 discussed timing. The effect of risk is discussed in Chapter 11.

7.1 BONDS AND BOND VALUATION

When a corporation (or government) wishes to borrow money from the public on a long-term basis, it usually does so by issuing or selling debt securities that are generically called *bonds.* In this section, we describe the basic features of corporate bonds and some of the terminology associated with bonds. We then discuss the cash flows associated with a bond and how bonds can be valued using our discounted cash flow procedure. We conclude this section with a discussion of how bond prices are quoted in the financial press.

Self-Test Problems 1, 2
Problems 1–6

Bond Features and Prices

Concept Q Answer 7.1a, 7.1b

Trans. 7.2 Bond Features (Supplemental)

A bond is normally an interest-only loan, meaning that the borrower will pay the interest every period, but none of the principal will be repaid until the end of the loan. For example, suppose the TBA Corporation wants to borrow $1,000 for 30 years. The interest rate on similar debt issued by similar corporations is 12 percent. TBA will thus pay .12 × $1,000 = $120 in interest every year for 30 years. At the end of 30 years, TBA will repay the $1,000. As this example suggests, a bond is a fairly simple financing arrangement. There is, however, a rich jargon associated with bonds, so we will use this example to define some of the more important terms.

coupon
The stated interest payments made on a bond.

face value
The principal amount of a bond that is repaid at the end of the term. Also par value.

coupon rate
The annual coupon divided by the face value of a bond.

maturity
Specified date at which the principal amount of a bond is paid.

In our example, the $120 regular interest payments that TBA promises to make are called the bond's **coupons.** Because the coupon is constant and paid every year, the type of bond we are describing is sometimes called a *level coupon bond.* The amount that will be repaid at the end of the loan is called the bond's **face value** or **par value.** As in our example, this par value is usually $1,000 for corporate bonds, and a bond that sells for its par value is called a *par value bond.* Government bonds frequently have much larger face or par values. Finally, the annual coupon divided by the face value is called the **coupon rate** on the bond, which, in this case, is $120/1,000 = 12%; so the bond has a 12 percent coupon rate.

The number of years until the face value is paid is called the bond's time to **maturity.** A corporate bond will frequently have a maturity of 30 years when it is originally issued, but this varies. Once the bond has been issued, the number of years to maturity declines as time goes by.

Trans. 7.3 Bond Rates and Yields (Supplemental)

Bond Values and Yields

As time passes, interest rates change in the marketplace. The cash flows from a bond, however, stay the same. As a result, the value of the bond will fluctuate. When interest rates rise, the present value of the bond's remaining cash flows declines, and the bond is worth less. When interest rates fall, the bond is worth more.

To determine the value of a bond at a particular point in time, we need to know the number of periods remaining until maturity, the face value, the coupon, and the market interest rate for bonds with similar features. This interest rate required in the market on a bond is called the bond's **yield to maturity (YTM).** This rate is sometimes called the bond's *yield* for short. Given this information, we can calculate the present value of the cash flows as an estimate of the bond's current market value.

yield to maturity (YTM)
The rate required in the market on a bond.

Lecture Tip: To avoid confusion, you may wish to emphasize that "yield to maturity," "required return," and "market rate" are used synonymously; the "coupon rate," on the other hand, is set by the issuer at the time of issuance.

For example, suppose the Xanth (pronounced "zanth") Co. were to issue a bond with 10 years to maturity. The Xanth bond has an annual coupon of $80. Similar bonds have a yield to maturity of 8 percent. Based on our discussion above, the Xanth bond will pay $80 per year for the next 10 years in coupon interest. In 10 years, Xanth will pay $1,000 to the owner of the bond. The cash flows from the bond are shown in Figure 7.1. What would this bond sell for?

As illustrated in Figure 7.1, the Xanth bond's cash flows have an annuity component (the coupons) and a lump sum (the face value paid at maturity). We thus estimate the market value of the bond by calculating the present value of these two components separately and adding the results together.

FIGURE 7.1 Cash flows for Xanth Co. bond

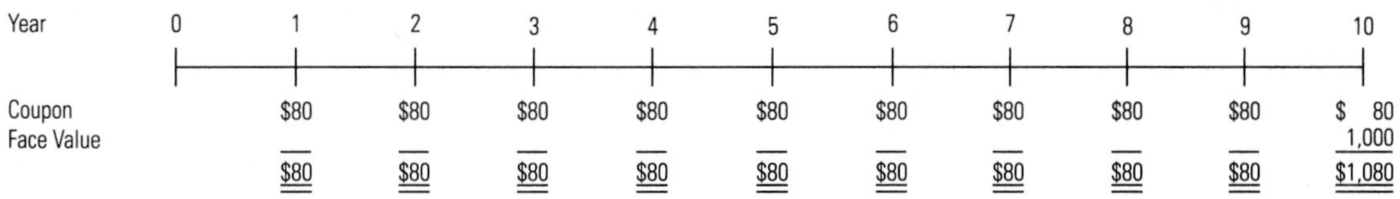

As shown, the Xanth bond has an annual coupon of $80 and a face or par value of $1,000 paid at maturity in 10 years.

First, at the going rate of 8 percent, the present value of the $1,000 paid in 10 years is:

$$\text{Present value} = \$1{,}000/1.08^{10} = \$1{,}000/2.1589 = \$463.19$$

Second, the bond offers $80 per year for 10 years, so the present value of this annuity stream is:

$$\begin{aligned}\text{Annuity present value} &= \$80 \times (1 - 1/1.08^{10})/.08\\ &= \$80 \times (1 - 1/2.1589)/.08\\ &= \$80 \times 6.7101\\ &= \$536.81\end{aligned}$$

We can now add the values for the two parts together to get the bond's value:

$$\text{Total bond value} = \$463.19 + 536.81 = \$1{,}000.00$$

This bond sells exactly for its face value. This is not a coincidence. The going interest rate in the market is 8 percent. Considered as an interest-only loan, what interest rate does this bond have? With an $80 coupon, this bond pays exactly 8 percent interest only when it sells for $1,000.

Trans. 7.4 Valuing a Bond (Supplemental)

To illustrate what happens as interest rates change, suppose a year has gone by. The Xanth bond now has nine years to maturity. If the interest rate in the market had risen to 10 percent, what would the bond be worth? To find out, we repeat the present value calculations above with 9 years instead of 10, and a 10 percent yield instead of an 8 percent yield. First, the present value of the $1,000 paid in nine years at 10 percent is:

Lecture Tip: See IM for added emphasis on the variables involved in bond valuation.

$$\text{Present value} = \$1{,}000/1.10^{9} = \$1{,}000/2.3579 = \$424.10$$

Second, the bond now offers $80 per year for nine years, so the present value of this annuity stream at 10 percent is:

$$\begin{aligned}\text{Annuity present value} &= \$80 \times (1 - 1/1.10^{9})/.10\\ &= \$80 \times (1 - 1/2.3579)/.10\\ &= \$80 \times 5.7590\\ &= \$460.72\end{aligned}$$

We can now add the values for the two parts together to get the bond's value:

$$\text{Total bond value} = \$424.10 + 460.72 = \$884.82$$

Trans. 7.5 A Discount Bond (Supplemental)

Therefore, the bond should sell for about $885. In the vernacular, we say that this bond, with its 8 percent coupon, is priced to yield 10 percent at $885.

The Xanth Co. bond now sells for less than its $1,000 face value. Why? The market interest rate is 10 percent. Considered as an interest-only loan of

$1,000, this bond only pays 8 percent, its coupon rate. Since this bond pays less than the going rate, investors are only willing to lend something less than the $1,000 promised repayment. Since the bond sells for less than face value, it is said to be a *discount bond.*

The only way to get the interest rate up to 10 percent is for the price to be less than $1,000 so that the purchaser, in effect, has a built-in gain. For the Xanth bond, the price of $885 is $115 less than the face value, so an investor who purchased and kept the bond would get $80 per year and would have a $115 gain at maturity as well. This gain compensates the lender for the below-market coupon rate.

Lecture Tip: See IM for a further exploration of this bond's value loss.

Another way to see why the bond is discounted by $115 is to note that the $80 coupon is $20 below the 10 percent coupon on a newly issued par value bond, based on current market conditions. By this we mean that the bond would be worth $1,000 only if it had a coupon of $100 per year. In a sense, an investor who buys and keeps the bond gives up $20 per year for nine years. At 10 percent, this annuity stream is worth:

$$\begin{aligned}\text{Annuity present value} &= \$20 \times (1 - 1/1.10^9)/.10 \\ &= \$20 \times 5.7590 \\ &= \$115.18\end{aligned}$$

This is just the amount of the discount.

What would the Xanth bond sell for if interest rates had dropped by 2 percent instead of rising by 2 percent? As you might guess, the bond will sell for more than $1,000. Such a bond is said to sell at a *premium* and is called a *premium bond.*

This case is just the opposite of a discount bond. The Xanth bond now has a coupon rate of 8 percent when the market rate is only 6 percent. Investors are willing to pay a premium to get this extra coupon. In this case, the relevant discount rate is 6 percent, and there are nine years remaining. The present value of the $1,000 face amount is:

$$\text{Present value} = \$1{,}000/1.06^9 = \$1{,}000/1.6895 = \$591.89$$

The present value of the coupon stream is:

$$\begin{aligned}\text{Annuity present value} &= \$80 \times (1 - 1/1.06^9)/.06 \\ &= \$80 \times (1 - 1/1.6895)/.06 \\ &= \$80 \times 6.8017 \\ &= \$544.14\end{aligned}$$

We can now add the values for the two parts together to get the bond's value:

Trans. 7.6
A Premium Bond
(Supplemental)

$$\text{Total bond value} = \$591.89 + 544.14 = \$1{,}136.03$$

Total bond value is therefore about $136 in excess of par value. Once again, we can verify this amount by noting that the coupon is now $20 too high, based on current market conditions. The present value of $20 per year for nine years at 6 percent is:

$$\begin{aligned}\text{Annuity present value} &= \$20 \times (1 - 1/1.06^9)/.06 \\ &= \$20 \times 6.8017 \\ &= \$136.03\end{aligned}$$

This is just as we calculated.

Based on our examples, we can now write the general expression for the value of a bond. If a bond has (1) a face value of F paid at maturity, (2) a coupon of C paid per period, (3) t periods to maturity, and (4) a yield of r per period, its value is:

Trans. 7.7 **General Expression for the Value of a Bond (Supplemental)**

$$\text{Bond value} = C \times [1 - 1/(1 + r)^t]/r + F/(1 + r)^t$$

$$\text{Bond value} = \text{Present value of the coupons} + \text{Present value of the face amount} \quad [7.1]$$

Concept Q Answer 7.1b

EXAMPLE 7.1 Semiannual Coupons

In practice, bonds issued in the United States usually make coupon payments twice a year. So, if an ordinary bond has a coupon rate of 14 percent, then the owner will get a total of $140 per year, but this $140 will come in two payments of $70 each. Suppose we were examining such a bond. The yield to maturity is quoted at 16 percent.

Bond yields are quoted like APRs; the quoted rate is equal to the actual rate per period multiplied by the number of periods. In this case, with a 16 percent quoted yield and semiannual payments, the true yield is 8 percent per six months. The bond matures in seven years. What is the bond's price? What is the effective annual yield on this bond?

Based on our discussion, we know the bond will sell at a discount because it has a coupon rate of 7 percent every six months when the market requires 8 percent every six months. So, if our answer exceeds $1,000, we know that we made a mistake.

To get the exact price, we first calculate the present value of the bond's face value of $1,000 paid in seven years. This seven-year period has 14 periods of six months each. At 8 percent per period, the value is:

$$\text{Present value} = \$1{,}000/1.08^{14} = \$1{,}000/2.9372 = \$340.46$$

The coupons can be viewed as a 14-period annuity of $70 per period. At an 8 percent discount rate, the present value of such an annuity is:

$$\begin{aligned}\text{Annuity present value} &= \$70 \times (1 - 1/1.08^{14})/.08 \\ &= \$70 \times (1 - .3405)/.08 \\ &= \$70 \times 8.2442 \\ &= \$577.10\end{aligned}$$

The total present value gives us what the bond should sell for:

$$\text{Total present value} = \$340.46 + 577.10 = \$917.56$$

To calculate the effective yield on this bond, note that 8 percent every six months is equivalent to:

$$\text{Effective annual rate} = (1 + .08)^2 - 1 = 16.64\%$$

The effective yield, therefore, is 16.64 percent. • • •

As we have illustrated in this section, bond prices and interest rates always move in opposite directions. When interest rates rise, a bond's value, like any other present value, will decline. Similarly, when interest rates fall, bond values rise. Even if we are considering a bond that is riskless in the sense that the borrower is certain to make all the payments, there is still risk in owning a bond. We discuss this next.

Trans. 7.8 **Bond Price Sensitivity to YTM (Supplemental)**

Concept Q Answer 7.1c

Interest Rate Risk

The risk that arises for bond owners from fluctuating interest rates is called *interest rate risk*. How much interest rate risk a bond has depends on how sensitive its price is to interest rate changes. This sensitivity directly depends on two things: the time to maturity and the coupon rate. As we will see momentarily, you should keep the following in mind when looking at a bond:

1. All other things being equal, the longer the time to maturity, the greater the interest rate risk.
2. All other things being equal, the lower the coupon rate, the greater the interest rate risk.

We illustrate the first of these two points in Figure 7.2. As shown, we compute and plot prices under different interest rate scenarios for 10 percent coupon bonds with maturities of 1 year and 30 years. Notice how the slope of the line connecting the prices is much steeper for the 30-year maturity than it is for the 1-year maturity. This tells us that a relatively small change in interest rates could lead to a substantial change in the bond's value. In comparison, the 1-year bond's price is relatively insensitive to interest rate changes.

Intuitively, the reason that longer-term bonds have greater interest rate sensitivity is that a large portion of a bond's value comes from the $1,000 face amount. The present value of this amount isn't greatly affected by a small change in interest rates if it is to be received in one year. If it is to be received in 30 years, however, even a small change in the interest rate can have a significant effect once it is compounded for 30 years. The present value of the face amount will be much more volatile with a longer-term bond as a result.

FIGURE 7.2
Interest rate risk and time to maturity

Trans. 7.9

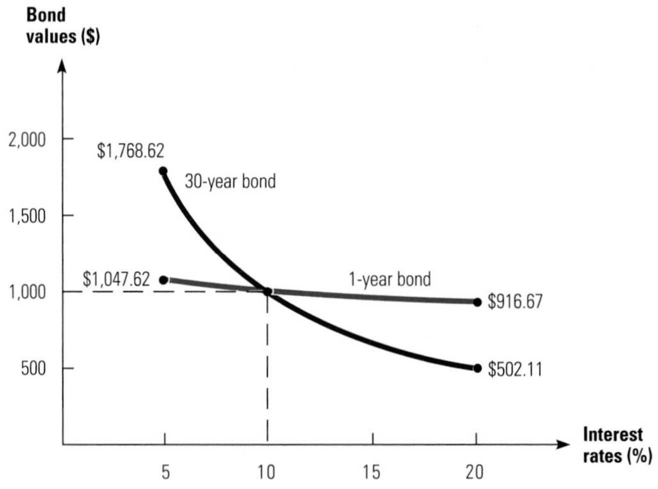

Value of a Bond with a 10% Coupon Rate for Different Interest Rates and Maturities

	Time to Maturity	
Interest Rate	**1 Year**	**30 Years**
5%	$1,047.62	$1,768.62
10	1,000.00	1,000.00
15	956.52	671.70
20	916.67	502.11

The reason that bonds with lower coupons have greater interest rate risk is essentially the same. As we discussed above, the value of a bond depends on the present value of its coupons and the present value of the face amount. If two bonds with different coupon rates have the same maturity, then the value of the one with the lower coupon is proportionately more dependent on the face amount to be received at maturity. As a result, all other things being equal, its value will fluctuate more as interest rates change. Put another way, the bond with the higher coupon has a larger cash flow early in its life, so its value is less sensitive to changes in the discount rate.

Lecture Tip: See IM for further discussion of reinvestment risk.

Finding the Yield to Maturity: More Trial and Error

Frequently, we will know a bond's price, coupon rate, and maturity date, but not its yield to maturity. For example, suppose we were interested in a six-year, 8 percent coupon bond. A broker quotes a price of \$955.14. What is the yield on this bond?

We've seen that the price of a bond can be written as the sum of its annuity and lump-sum components. With an \$80 coupon for six years and a \$1,000 face value, this price is:

$$\$955.14 = \$80 \times [1 - 1/(1 + r)^6]/r + \$1{,}000/(1 + r)^6$$

where r is the unknown discount rate or yield to maturity. We have one equation here and one unknown, but we cannot solve it for r explicitly. The only way to find the answer is to use trial and error.

This problem is essentially identical to the one we examined in the last chapter when we tried to find the unknown interest rate on an annuity. However, finding the rate (or yield) on a bond is even more complicated because of the \$1,000 face amount.

We can speed up the trial-and-error process by using what we know about bond prices and yields. In this case, the bond has an \$80 coupon and is selling at a discount. We thus know that the yield is greater than 8 percent. If we compute the price at 10 percent:

Lecture Tip: See IM for hints on solving for a bond's yield to maturity.

$$\begin{aligned}\text{Bond value} &= \$80 \times (1 - 1/1.10^6)/.10 + \$1{,}000/1.10^6\\ &= \$80 \times 4.3553 + \$1{,}000/1.7716\\ &= \$912.89\end{aligned}$$

At 10 percent, the value we calculate is lower than the actual price, so 10 percent is too high. The true yield must be somewhere between 8 percent and 10 percent. At this point, it's "plug and chug" to find the answer. You would probably want to try 9 percent next. If you do, you will see that this is in fact the bond's yield to maturity.[1]

Lecture Tip: See IM for a good formula for finding the approximate yield to maturity.

Our discussion of bond valuation is summarized in Table 7.1.

[1] Most financial calculators will find a bond's yield to maturity. A common procedure would involve entering \$80 (the coupon) as the payment (PMT), 6 as the number of periods (n), \$955.14 (the current price) as the present value (PV), and \$1,000 (the face value) as the future value (FV). If you solve for the interest rate (i), the answer should be 9 percent. On some calculators, the future value and/or the payment must be entered with a negative sign.

TABLE 7.1
Summary of bond valuation

Trans. 7.10

I. Finding the Value of a Bond

Bond value $= C \times [1 - 1/(1 + r)^t]/r + F/(1 + r)^t$

where

C = Coupon paid each period
r = Rate per period
t = Number of periods
F = Bond's face value

II. Finding the Yield on a Bond

Given a bond value, coupon, time to maturity, and face value, it is possible to find the implicit discount rate or yield to maturity by trial and error only. To do this, try different discount rates until the calculated bond value equals the given value. Remember that *increasing* the rate *decreases* the bond value.

Trans. 7.11
Bond Pricing Theorems (Supplemental)

EXAMPLE 7.2 Bond Yields

You're looking at two bonds identical in every way except for their coupons and, of course, their prices. Both have 12 years to maturity. The first bond has a 10 percent coupon rate and sells for $935.08. The second has a 12 percent coupon rate. What do you think it would sell for?

Since the two bonds are very similar, they will be priced to yield about the same rate. We first need to calculate the yield on the 10 percent coupon bond. Proceeding as before, the yield must be greater than 10 percent since the bond is selling at a discount. The bond has a fairly long maturity of 12 years. We've seen that long-term bond prices are relatively sensitive to interest rate changes, so the yield is probably close to 10 percent. A little trial and error reveals that the yield is actually 11 percent:

$$\begin{aligned}\text{Bond value} &= \$100 \times (1 - 1/1.11^{12})/.11 + \$1{,}000/1.11^{12}\\ &= \$100 \times 6.4924 + \$1{,}000/3.4985\\ &= \$649.24 + 285.84\\ &= \$935.08\end{aligned}$$

Lecture Tip: See IM for a discussion of the components of bond required returns.

Lecture Tip: See IM for some "Great Underlying Rules of Finance" pertaining to bond valuation.

With an 11 percent yield, the second bond will sell at a premium because of its $120 coupon. Its value is:

$$\begin{aligned}\text{Bond value} &= \$120 \times (1 - 1/1.11^{12})/.11 + \$1{,}000/1.11^{12}\\ &= \$120 \times 6.4924 + \$1{,}000/3.4985\\ &= \$779.08 + 285.84\\ &= \$1{,}064.92\end{aligned}$$

• • •

Bond Price Reporting

If you were to look in the *Wall Street Journal* (or similar financial newspaper), you would see information on various bonds issued by large corporations. Figure 7.3 reproduces a small section of the bond page from February 17, 1995. If you look down the list, you will come to an entry marked "ATT 6s00." This tells us that the bond was issued by ATT, and it will mature in '00, meaning the year 2000. The 6 is the bond's coupon rate, so the coupon is 6% of the face value. Assuming the face value is $1,000, the annual coupon on this bond is .06 × $1,000 = $60. The small "s" doesn't mean anything important.

The column marked "Close" gives us the last available price on the bond at close of business the day before. As with the coupon, the price is quoted as

NEW YORK EXCHANGE BONDS

Quotations as of 4 p.m. Eastern Time

CORPORATION BONDS
Volume, $29,064,000

Bonds	Cur Yld	Vol	Close	Net Chg.
AMR 9s16	9.1	36	98 3/4	+ 3/4
AMR 8.10s98	8.1	13	100 1/2	...
AMR 6 1/8 24	cv	43	87 1/2	− 1 1/8
ATT 7 1/2 06	7.7	179	98	+ 1/8
ATT 8.35s25	8.3	5	100 1/4	+ 5/8
ATT 4 3/4 98	5.1	12	92 1/2	− 1/2
ATT 6s00	6.5	89	92 1/8	− 3/8
ATT 5 1/8 01	5.9	37	87 1/4	+ 1/8
ATT 8 5/8 31	8.5	11	101 5/8	...
ATT 7 1/8 02	7.3	25	97	+ 1/2
ATT 8 1/8 22	8.2	30	98 5/8	+ 1/4
ATT 8 1/8 24	8.3	150	98 1/4	+ 1/4
Actava 9 1/2 98	10.1	99	93 3/4	− 1/4
AirbF 6 3/4 01	cv	10	95	− 1/2
AlskAr 6 7/8 14	cv	1	76 1/4	...
AlbnyInt 5s02	cv	53	85	− 3/4
AlldC zr98	...	15	75 1/8	− 3/4
AlldC zr2000	...	20	66 3/4	− 1/4
AlldC zr03	...	5	53 3/8	+ 7/8
Allwst 7 1/4 14	cv	41	89	+ 1/4
AmBrnd 9 1/8 16	8.9	20	102 7/8	− 1/8
AmBrnd 8 5/8 21	8.4	25	102 1/2	+ 1 1/4
AmBrnd 7 1/2 99	7.6	8	98 1/2	− 1
AmHme 6 7/8 97	7.0	49	98 3/8	− 1
AMedia 11 5/8 04	11.2	15	104 1/4	...
Amoco 8 5/8 16	8.4	10	103	− 1
Anhr 8 5/8 16	8.5	60	101 3/4	+ 1/4
AnnTaylr 8 3/4 00	9.0	95	97 1/4	+ 1/4
Arml 8 1/2 01	9.4	10	90	+ 5
Arml 11 3/8 99	11.2	5	102	+ 1
Arrow 5 3/4 02	cv	6	119 1/2	− 1 1/2
Ashlnd 6 3/4 14	cv	69	90 1/4	− 1/4
ARch 10 7/8 05	9.2	25	118 5/8	+ 5/8
AubrnHl 12 3/8 20f	...	4	134 1/2	+ 1/2

Source: Reprinted by permission of *The Wall Street Journal*, © 1995 Dow Jones & Company, Inc., February 17, 1995. All Rights Reserved Worldwide.

FIGURE 7.3 Sample Wall Street Journal bond quotation

Trans. 7.12

a percentage of face value; so, again assuming a face value of $1,000, this bond last sold for 92⅛ percent of $1,000 or $921.25. Since this bond is selling for about 92 percent of its par value, it is trading at a discount. The last column, marked "Net Chg.," indicates that yesterday's closing price was ⅜ of 1 percent lower than the previous day's closing price.

The bond's **current yield** (abbreviated as "Cur Yld") is given in the first column. The current yield is equal to the coupon payment divided by the bond's closing price. For this bond, assuming a face value of $1,000, this works out to be $60/$921.25 = 6.51%, or 6.5% rounded off to one decimal point. Notice that this is not equal to the bond's yield to maturity (unless the bond sells for par). Finally, the volume for the day (the number of bonds that were bought and sold) is reported in the second column ("Vol"). For this particular issue, 89 bonds changed hands during the day (in this market).

current yield
A bond's coupon payment divided by its closing price.

EXAMPLE 7.3 Current Yields

Below are several bond quotations for the Albanon Corporation. Assuming these are from *The Wall Street Journal*, supply the missing information for each.

Albanon 8s98	?.?	8	84.5	+½
Albanon ?s06	9.4	8	74.5	+⅛
Albanon 8s10	9.0	8	??.?	+¼

In each case, we need to recall that the current yield is equal to the *annual* coupon divided by the price (even if the bond makes semiannual payments). Also, remember that the price is expressed as a percentage of par. In the first case, the coupon rate is 8 percent and the price is 84.5, so the current yield must be 8/84.5 or 9.5 percent. In the second case, the current yield is 9.4 percent, so the coupon rate must be such that:

Coupon rate/74.5% = 9.4%

Therefore, the coupon rate must be about 7 percent. Finally, in the third case, the price must be such that:

8%/Price = 9%

Therefore, the price is 8/9 or 88.9% of par value. • • •

CONCEPT QUESTIONS

7.1a What are the cash flows associated with a bond?

7.1b What is the general expression for the value of a bond?

7.1c Is it true that the only risk associated with owning a bond is that the issuer will not make all the payments? Explain.

7.2 MORE ON BOND FEATURES

Bonds typically have a number of important features in addition to the ones we have discussed, including such things as security, call features, sinking funds, ratings, and protective covenants. The following table illustrates these features for a hypothetical bond. If these terms are unfamiliar, have no fear. We discuss them all next.

Trans. 7.13
Features of a Hypothetical Bond (Supplemental)

Features of a Hypothetical Bond

Terms		Explanations
Amount of issue	$100 million	The company will issue $100 million of bonds.
Date of issue	10/21/95	The bonds will be sold on 10/21/95.
Maturity	10/21/25	The principal will be paid in 30 years.
Face value	$1,000	The denomination of the bonds is $1,000.
Annual coupon	10.50	Each bondholder will receive $105 per bond per year (10.50% of face value).
Offer price	100	The offer price will be 100% of the $1,000 face value per bond.
Yield to maturity	10.50%	If the bond is held to maturity, bondholders will receive a stated annual rate of return equal to 10.50%.
Coupon payment dates	7/1, 1/1	Coupons of $105/2 = $52.50 will be paid on these dates.
Security	None	The bonds are debentures.
Sinking fund	Annual	The firm will make annual payments toward the sinking fund.
Call provision	Not callable before 12/31/05	The bonds have a deferred call feature.
Call price	$1,100	After 12/31/05, the company can buy back the bonds for $1,100 per bond.
Rating	Moody's Aaa	This is Moody's highest rating. The bonds have the lowest probability of default.

Many of these features will be detailed in the bond indenture, so we discuss this first.

The Indenture

The **indenture** is the written agreement between the corporation (the borrower) and its creditors. Usually, a trustee (a bank, perhaps) is appointed by the corporation to represent the bondholders. The trustee must (1) make sure the terms of the indenture are obeyed, (2) manage the sinking fund (described below), and (3) represent the bondholders in default, that is, if the company defaults on its payments to them.

indenture
Written agreement between the corporation and the lender detailing the terms of the debt issue.

Concept Q Answer 7.2b

Trans. 7.14 The Bond Indenture (Supplemental)

The bond indenture is a legal document. It can run several hundred pages and generally makes for very tedious reading. It is an important document, however, because it generally includes the following provisions:

1. The basic terms of the bonds.
2. The total amount of bonds issued.
3. A description of property used as security.
4. The repayment arrangements.
5. The call provisions.
6. Details of the protective covenants.

We discuss these features next.

Terms of a Bond Corporate bonds usually have a face value (that is, a denomination) of $1,000. This is called the *principal value* and it is stated on the bond certificate. So, if a corporation wanted to borrow $1 million, 1,000 bonds would have to be sold. The par value (that is, initial accounting value) of a bond is almost always the same as the face value, and the terms are used interchangeably in practice.

Lecture Tip: IM discusses "baby bonds"—i.e., bonds with face values less than $1000.

Concept Q Answer 7.2a

Corporate bonds are usually in **registered form.** For example, the indenture might read as follows:

registered form
Registrar of company records ownership of each bond; payment is made directly to the owner of record.

> Interest is payable semiannually on July 1 and January 1 of each year to the person in whose name the bond is registered at the close of business on June 15 or December 15, respectively.

This means that the company has a registrar who will record the ownership of each bond and record any changes in ownership. The company will pay the interest and principal by check mailed directly to the address of the owner of record. A corporate bond may be registered and have attached "coupons." To obtain an interest payment, the owner must separate a coupon from the bond certificate and send it to the company registrar (the paying agent).

Lecture Tip: See IM for a discussion of bearer bonds and the rationale behind the elimination of new bond issues in bearer form.

Security Debt securities are classified according to the collateral and mortgages used to protect the bondholder.

Collateral is a general term that, strictly speaking, means securities (for example, bonds and stocks) that are pledged as security for payment of debt. For example, collateral trust bonds often involve a pledge of common stock held by the corporation. However, the term *collateral* often is used much more loosely to refer to any form of security.

Mortgage securities are secured by a mortgage on the real property of the borrower. The property involved is usually real estate, for example, land or buildings. The legal document that describes the mortgage is called a *mortgage trust indenture* or *trust deed.*

debenture
Unsecured debt, usually with a maturity of 10 years or more.

note
Unsecured debt, usually with a maturity under 10 years.

Lecture Tip: See IM for factors affecting the yields of secured bonds vs. debentures.

Bonds frequently represent unsecured obligations of the company. A **debenture** is an unsecured bond, where no specific pledge of property is made. The term **note** is generally used for such instruments if the maturity of the unsecured bond is less than 10 or so years when it is originally issued. Debenture holders only have a claim on property not otherwise pledged, in other words, the property that remains after mortgages and collateral trusts are taken into account.

At the current time, almost all public bonds issued in the United States by industrial and financial companies are debentures. However, most utility and railroad bonds are secured by a pledge of assets.

Seniority In general terms, *seniority* indicates preference in position over other lenders, and debts are sometimes labeled as *senior* or *junior* to indicate seniority. Some debt is *subordinated,* as in, for example, a subordinated debenture.

In the event of default, holders of subordinated debt must give preference to other specified creditors. Usually, this means that the subordinated lenders will be paid off only after the specified creditors have been compensated. However, debt cannot be subordinated to equity.

sinking fund
Account managed by the bond trustee for early bond redemption.

Concept Q Answer 7.2c

call provision
Agreement giving the corporation the option to repurchase the bond at a specified price prior to maturity.

call premium
Amount by which the call price exceeds the par value of the bond.

deferred call
Call provision prohibiting the company from redeeming the bond prior to a certain date.

call protected
Bond during period in which it cannot be redeemed by the issuer.

protective covenant
Part of the indenture limiting certain actions that can be taken during the term of the loan, usually to protect the lender's interest.

Concept Q Answer 7.2b

Repayment Bonds can be repaid at maturity, at which time the bondholder will receive the stated or face value of the bond, or they may be repaid in part or in entirety before maturity. Early repayment in some form is more typical and is often handled through a sinking fund.

A **sinking fund** is an account managed by the bond trustee for the purpose of repaying the bonds. The company makes annual payments to the trustee, who then uses the funds to retire a portion of the debt. The trustee does this by either buying up some of the bonds in the market or calling in a fraction of the outstanding bonds. This second option is discussed below.

The Call Provision A **call provision** allows the company to repurchase or "call" part or all of the bond issue at stated prices over a specific period. Corporate bonds are usually callable.

Generally, the call price is above the bond's stated value (that is, the par value). The difference between the call price and the stated value is the **call premium.** The amount of the call premium usually becomes smaller over time. One arrangement is to initially set the call premium equal to the annual coupon payment and then make it decline to zero the closer the call date is to maturity.

Call provisions are not usually operative during the first part of a bond's life. This makes the call provision less of a worry for bondholders in the bond's early years. For example, a company might be prohibited from calling its bonds for the first 10 years. This is a **deferred call.** During this period, the bond is said to be **call protected.**

As explained in the accompanying *Principles in Action* box, some bonds have a "put" provision. This is a relatively new development in the bond market.

Protective Covenants A **protective covenant** is that part of the indenture or loan agreement that limits certain actions a company might otherwise wish to take during the term of the loan. Protective covenants can be classified into two types: negative covenants and positive (or affirmative) covenants.

Principles in Action

Putting the Bondholders' Interests First

Most corporations stack the deck against their bondholders, positioning themselves to benefit from falling interest rates. They do so by attaching a call feature to their bonds, giving them the right to repurchase the bonds from investors under certain conditions. However, there are some bonds designed to protect the interests of bondholders. They are called *put bonds,* and they are created when a corporation issues bonds with a "put" feature rather than a call feature. The put feature gives the bondholder the right, but not the obligation, to sell the bond back to the corporation prior to maturity for a specified price.

For a bondholder, buying a puttable bond is like owning two bonds in one. For example, if a bond with 20 years to maturity is puttable only in its tenth year, the investor effectively owns a bond with a put option for the first 10 years. Then, if the put option is not exercised during the tenth year, the investor owns a straight bond (no options attached) for the remaining 10 years to maturity.

If interest rates rise and bond prices fall, a bondholder may find it advantageous to put the bond back to the corporation at the stated put price. In the example of the 20-year bond, if, in the tenth year, the bond's market value is 95 percent of par, and the put option allows the holder to force the corporation to repurchase the bond for 100 percent of par, the bondholder should exercise the option. Often, this allows the investor to get rid of a bond paying a below-market coupon rate. There are, of course, other reasons an investor might wish to sell a bond prior to maturity, including changes in investment strategy or changes in bond quality, to name a couple. Owning a puttable bond gives the holder a way to liquidate the bond other than selling it in the open market at the going price.

Put bonds are obviously good for bondholders, but these bonds have some important quirks. First, most corporate bonds are callable and only a very few are puttable; however, most puttable bonds are not callable. Second, most put options can only be exercised for a short period of time, sometimes just one day. That is, in order for the put to work to the advantage of the bondholder, the price of the bond must be less than the put price during a very narrow period of time. Third, since a put option that has not expired has value for the investor, puttable bonds typically cost more, and thus offer a lower return on investment than otherwise identical bonds with no put option attached. Finally, for many puttable bonds, the put option can only be exercised after a change in corporate control. This is called a poison put and may really be designed to protect management, not the bondholder. Considering all of this, a put bond can place an investor in a position to exercise more control, but only at a price.

Source: "Power to the Creditors," *Forbes,* March 27, 1995, p. 148.

A *negative covenant* is a "thou shalt not." It limits or prohibits actions that the company may take. Here are some typical examples:

1. The firm must limit the amount of dividends it pays.
2. The firm cannot merge with another firm.
3. The firm cannot issue additional long-term debt.

A *positive* (or *affirmative*) *covenant* is a "thou shalt." It specifies an action that the company agrees to take or a condition the company must abide by. Here are some examples:

1. The company must maintain its working capital at or above some specified minimum level.
2. The company must periodically furnish audited financial statements to the lender.
3. The firm must maintain any collateral or security in good condition.

Lecture Tip: Bond indentures tend to be long, complex documents. Critical indenture terms are summarized in the publications of Moody's and Standard & Poor's Corporation.

This is only a partial list of covenants; a particular indenture may feature many different ones.

CONCEPT QUESTIONS

7.2a What is the typical principal amount of a corporate bond?

7.2b What is the indenture?

7.2c What is a sinking fund?

7.3 BOND RATINGS

Lecture Tip: See IM for a discussion of the practice of paying for bond ratings.

Firms frequently pay to have their debt rated. The two leading bond rating firms are Moody's and Standard & Poor's (S&P). The debt ratings are an assessment of the creditworthiness of the corporate issuer. The definitions of creditworthiness used by Moody's and S&P are based on how likely the firm is to default and the protection creditors have in the event of a default.

Concept Q Answer 7.3b

It is important to recognize that bond ratings *only* concern the possibility of default. Earlier in this chapter we discussed interest rate risk, which we defined as the risk of a change in the value of a bond from a change in interest rates. Bond ratings do not address this issue. As a result, the price of a highly rated bond can still be quite volatile.

Trans. 7.15 Bond Ratings (Supplemental)

Bond ratings are constructed from information supplied by the corporation. The rating classes and some information concerning them are shown in Table 7.2.

TABLE 7.2

	Investment-Quality Bond Ratings				Low-Quality, Speculative, and/or "Junk" Bond Ratings					
	High Grade		Medium Grade		Low Grade		Very Low Grade			
Standard & Poor's	AAA	AA	A	BBB	BB	B	CCC	CC	C	D
Moody's	Aaa	Aa	A	Baa	Ba	B	Caa	Ca	C	D

S&P	Moody's	
AAA	Aaa	Debt rated Aaa and AAA has the highest rating. Capacity to pay interest and principal is extremely strong.
AA	Aa	Debt rated Aa and AA has a very strong capacity to pay interest and repay principal. Together with the highest rating, this group comprises the high-grade bond class.
A	A	Debt rated A has a strong capacity to pay interest and repay principal, although it is somewhat more susceptible to the adverse effects of changes in circumstances and economic conditions than debt in high-rated categories.
BBB	Baa	Debt rated Baa or BBB is regarded as having an adequate capacity to pay interest and repay principal. Whereas it normally exhibits adequate protection parameters, adverse economic conditions or changing circumstances are more likely to lead to a weakened capacity to pay interest and repay principal for debt in this category than in higher-rated categories. These bonds are medium-grade obligations.
BB, B CCC CC	Ba, B Caa Ca	Debt rated in these categories is regarded, on balance, as predominantly speculative with respect to capacity to pay interest and repay principal in accordance with the terms of the obligation. Ba and BB indicate the lowest degree of speculation, and Ca and CC the highest degree of speculation. Although such debt will likely have some quality and protective characteristics, these are outweighed by large uncertainties or major risk exposures to adverse conditions.
C	C	This rating is reserved for income bonds on which no interest is being paid.
D	D	Debt rated D is in default, and payment of interest and/or repayment of principal is in arrears.

At times, both Moody's and S&P use adjustments to these ratings. S&P uses plus and minus signs: A+ is the strongest A rating and A− the weakest. Moody's uses a 1, 2, or 3 designation, with 1 being the highest.

The highest rating a firm can have is AAA or Aaa, and such debt is judged to be the best quality and to have the lowest degree of risk. This rating is not awarded very often; AA or Aa ratings indicate very good quality debt and are much more common. The lowest rating is D, for debt that is in default.

Lecture Tip: See IM for some other implications of bond ratings.

Video Note: See also the "Junk Bonds" video supplement.

Beginning in the 1980s, a growing part of corporate borrowing has taken the form of low-grade, or "junk," bonds. If they are rated at all, such low-grade bonds are corporate bonds rated below investment grade by the major rating agencies. Investment-grade bonds are bonds rated at least BBB by S&P or Baa by Moody's.

Concept Q Answer 7.3a

Lecture Tip: It is interesting to note that more wealth was lost by holders of IBM stock from 1991 to 1993 than was lost in the entire junk bond market from 1988 to 1993.

CONCEPT QUESTIONS

7.3a What is a junk bond?

7.3b What does a bond rating say about the risk of fluctuations in a bond's value from interest rate changes?

7.4 COMMON STOCK VALUATION

A share of common stock is more difficult to value in practice than a bond for at least three reasons. First, not even the promised cash flows are known in advance. Second, the life of the investment is essentially forever since common stock has no maturity. Third, there is no way to easily observe the rate of return that the market requires. Nonetheless, as we will see, there are cases under which we can come up with the present value of the future cash flows for a share of stock and thus determine its value.

Self-Test Problem 3

Problems 9, 11, 16–23

Lecture Tip: This is a good place to remind students that common stocks have no maturity because they represent shares of ownership in corporations, which have infinite lives in the eyes of the law.

Common Stock Cash Flows

Imagine that you were to buy a share of stock today. You plan to sell the stock in one year. You somehow know that the stock will be worth $70 at that time. You predict that the stock will also pay a $10 per share dividend at the end of the year. If you require a 25 percent return on your investment, what is the most you would pay for the stock? In other words, what is the present value of the $10 dividend along with the $70 ending value at 25 percent?

If you buy the stock today and sell it at the end of the year, you will have a total of $80 in cash. At 25 percent:

$$\text{Present value} = (\$10 + 70)/1.25 = \$64$$

Therefore, $64 is the value you would assign to the stock today.

More generally, let P_0 be the current price of the stock, and define P_1 to be the price in one period. If D_1 is the cash dividend paid at the end of the period, then:

Concept Q Answer 7.4a

$$P_0 = (D_1 + P_1)/(1 + r) \quad [7.2]$$

where r is the required return in the market on this investment.

Notice that we really haven't said much so far. If we wanted to determine the value of a share of stock today (P_0), we would first have to come up with the value in one year (P_1). This is even harder to do, so we've only made the problem more complicated.

Lecture Tip: You may wish to point out that, in equilibrium, "required return" and "expected return" must be equal.

What is the price in one period, P_1? We don't know in general. Instead, suppose we somehow knew the price in two periods, P_2. Given a predicted dividend in two periods, D_2, the stock price in one period would be:

$$P_1 = (D_2 + P_2)/(1 + r)$$

If we were to substitute this expression for P_1 into our expression for P_0, we would have:

$$P_0 = \frac{D_1 + P_1}{1 + r} = \frac{D_1 + \dfrac{D_2 + P_2}{1 + r}}{1 + r}$$

$$= \frac{D_1}{(1 + r)^1} + \frac{D_2}{(1 + r)^2} + \frac{P_2}{(1 + r)^2}$$

Now we need to get a price in two periods. We don't know this either, so we can procrastinate again and write:

$$P_2 = (D_3 + P_3)/(1 + r)$$

If we substitute this back in for P_2, we would have:

$$P_0 = \frac{D_1}{(1 + r)^1} + \frac{D_2}{(1 + r)^2} + \frac{P_2}{(1 + r)^2}$$

$$= \frac{D_1}{(1 + r)^1} + \frac{D_2}{(1 + r)^2} + \frac{\dfrac{D_3 + P_3}{1 + r}}{(1 + r)^2}$$

Trans. 7.16
Common Stock Cash Flows (Supplemental)

$$= \frac{D_1}{(1 + r)^1} + \frac{D_2}{(1 + r)^2} + \frac{D_3}{(1 + r)^3} + \frac{P_3}{(1 + r)^3}$$

You should start to notice that we can push the problem of coming up with the stock price off into the future forever. Importantly, no matter what the stock price is, the present value is essentially zero if we push it far enough away. What we would be left with is the result that the current price of the stock can be written as the present value of the dividends beginning in one period and extending out forever:

$$P_0 = \frac{D_1}{(1 + r)^1} + \frac{D_2}{(1 + r)^2} + \frac{D_3}{(1 + r)^3} + \frac{D_4}{(1 + r)^4} + \frac{D_5}{(1 + r)^5} + \cdots$$

Concept Q Answer 7.4b

We have illustrated here that the price of the stock today is equal to the present value of all of the future dividends. How many future dividends are there? In principle, there can be an infinite number. This means that we still can't compute a value for the stock because we would have to forecast an infinite number of dividends and then discount them all. In the next section, we consider some special cases where we can get around this problem.

EXAMPLE 7.4 Growth Stocks

You might be wondering about shares of stock in companies that currently pay no dividends. Small, growing companies frequently plow back everything and thus pay no dividends. Are such shares worth nothing? It depends. When we say that the value of the stock is equal to the present value of the future dividends, we don't rule out the possibility that some number of those dividends are zero. They just can't *all* be zero.

Imagine a company that had a provision in its corporate charter that prohibited the paying of dividends now or ever. The corporation never borrows any money, never pays out any money to stockholders in any form whatsoever, and never sells any assets. Such a corporation couldn't really exist because the IRS wouldn't like it, and the stockholders could always vote to amend the charter if they wanted to. If it did exist, however, what would the stock be worth?

The stock is worth absolutely nothing. Such a company is a financial "black hole." Money goes in, but nothing valuable ever comes out. Since nobody would ever get any return on this investment, the investment has no value. This example is a little absurd, but it illustrates that when we speak of companies that don't pay dividends, what we really mean is that they are not *currently* paying dividends. • • •

Common Stock Valuation: Some Special Cases

There are a few very useful special circumstances where we can come up with a value for the stock. What we have to do is make some simplifying assumptions about the pattern of future dividends. The two cases we consider are: (1) the dividend has a zero growth rate, and (2) the dividend grows at a constant rate.

Lecture Tip: Notice that common stock valuation models are analogous to the financial planning models discussed in Chapter 4; in this case, we are projecting dividend cash flows rather than financial statement variables.

Zero Growth The case of zero growth is one we've already seen. A share of common stock in a company with a constant dividend is much like a share of preferred stock. From the previous chapter, we know that the dividend on a share of preferred stock has zero growth and thus is constant through time. For a zero growth share of common stock, this implies that:

$$D_1 = D_2 = D_3 = D = \text{constant}$$

So, the value of the stock is:

$$P_0 = \frac{D}{(1 + r)^1} + \frac{D}{(1 + r)^2} + \frac{D}{(1 + r)^3} + \frac{D}{(1 + r)^4} + \frac{D}{(1 + r)^5} + \cdots$$

Since the dividend is always the same, the stock can be viewed as an ordinary perpetuity with a cash flow equal to D every period. The per share value is thus given by:

$$P_0 = D/r \qquad [7.3]$$

where r is the required return.

For example, suppose the Paradise Prototyping Company has a policy of paying a \$10 per share dividend every year. If this policy is to be continued indefinitely, what is the value of a share of stock if the required return is 20 percent? The stock in this case amounts to an ordinary perpetuity, so the stock is worth \$10/.20 = \$50 per share.

Constant Growth Suppose we know that the dividend for some company always grows at a steady rate. Call this growth rate g. If we let D_0 be the dividend just paid, then the next dividend, D_1, is:

$$D_1 = D_0 \times (1 + g)$$

The dividend in two periods is:

$$\begin{aligned} D_2 &= D_1 \times (1 + g) \\ &= [D_0 \times (1 + g)] \times (1 + g) \\ &= D_0 \times (1 + g)^2 \end{aligned}$$

We could repeat this process to come up with the dividend at any point in the future. In general, from our discussion of compound growth in the previous chapter, we know that the dividend t periods in the future, D_t, is given by:

$$D_t = D_0 \times (1 + g)^t$$

An asset with cash flows that grow at a constant rate forever is called a *growing perpetuity.* As we will see momentarily, there is a simple expression for determining the value of such an asset.

The assumption of steady dividend growth might strike you as peculiar. Why would the dividend grow at a constant rate? The reason is that, for many companies, steady growth in dividends is an explicit goal. This subject falls under the general heading of dividend policy, so we will defer further discussion of it to a later chapter.

EXAMPLE 7.5 Dividend Growth

The Hedless Corporation has just paid a dividend of $3 per share. The dividend grows at a steady rate of 8 percent per year. Based on this information, what will the dividend be in five years?

Here we have a $3 current amount that grows at 8 percent per year for five years. The future amount is thus:

$$\$3 \times (1.08)^5 = \$3 \times 1.4693 = \$4.41$$

The dividend will therefore increase by $1.41 over the coming five years. • • •

If the dividend grows at a steady rate, then we have replaced the problem of forecasting an infinite number of future dividends with the problem of coming up with a single growth rate, a considerable simplification. In this case, if we take D_0 to be the dividend just paid and g to be the constant growth rate, the value of a share of stock can be written as:

Trans. 7.17 Dividend Growth Model

Concept Q Answer 7.4c

$$\begin{aligned} P_0 &= \frac{D_1}{(1 + r)^1} + \frac{D_2}{(1 + r)^2} + \frac{D_3}{(1 + r)^3} + \cdots \\ &= \frac{D_0(1 + g)^1}{(1 + r)^1} + \frac{D_0(1 + g)^2}{(1 + r)^2} + \frac{D_0(1 + g)^3}{(1 + r)^3} + \cdots \end{aligned}$$

As long as the growth rate, g, is less than the discount rate, r, the present value of this series of cash flows can be written very simply as:

dividend growth model Model that determines the current price of a stock as its dividend next period divided by the discount rate less the dividend growth rate.

$$P_0 = \frac{D_0 \times (1 + g)}{r - g} = \frac{D_1}{r - g} \qquad [7.4]$$

This elegant result goes by a lot of different names. We will call it the **dividend growth model.** By any name, it is very easy to use. To illustrate, suppose D_0 is \$2.30, r is 13 percent, and g is 5 percent. The price per share in this case is:

$$\begin{aligned} P_0 &= D_0 \times (1 + g)/(r - g) \\ &= \$2.30 \times (1.05)/(.13 - .05) \\ &= \$2.415/(.08) \\ &= \$30.19 \end{aligned}$$

We can actually use the dividend growth model to get the stock price at any point in time, not just today. In general, the price of the stock as of time t is:

Self-Test Problem 7.3

$$P_t = \frac{D_t \times (1 + g)}{r - g} = \frac{D_{t+1}}{r - g} \qquad [7.5]$$

In our example, suppose we were interested in the price of the stock in five years, P_5. We first need the dividend at time 5, D_5. Since the dividend just paid is \$2.30 and the growth rate is 5 percent per year, D_5 is:

$$D_5 = \$2.30 \times (1.05)^5 = \$2.30 \times 1.2763 = \$2.935$$

From the dividend growth model, the price of stock in five years is:

$$P_5 = \frac{D_5 \times (1 + g)}{r - g} = \frac{\$2.935 \times (1.05)}{.13 - .05} = \frac{\$3.0822}{.08} = \$38.53$$

EXAMPLE 7.6 Gordon Growth Company

Trans. 7.18, 7.19
Stock Price Sensitivity (Supplemental)

The next dividend for the Gordon Growth Company will be \$4.00 per share. Investors require a 16 percent return on companies such as Gordon. Gordon's dividend increases by 6 percent every year. Based on the dividend growth model, what is the value of Gordon's stock today? What is the value in four years?

The only tricky thing here is that the next dividend, D_1, is given as \$4.00, so we won't multiply this by $(1 + g)$. With this in mind, the price per share is given by:

$$\begin{aligned} P_0 &= D_1/(r - g) \\ &= \$4.00/(.16 - .06) \\ &= \$4.00/(.10) \\ &= \$40.00 \end{aligned}$$

Since we already have the dividend in one year, the dividend in four years is equal to $D_1 \times (1 + g)^3 = \$4.00 \times (1.06)^3 = \$4.764$. The price in four years is therefore:

$$\begin{aligned} P_4 &= [D_4 \times (1 + g)]/(r - g) \\ &= [\$4.764 \times 1.06]/(.16 - .06) \\ &= \$5.05/(.10) \\ &= \$50.50 \end{aligned}$$

Notice in this example that P_4 is equal to $P_0 \times (1 + g)^4$.

$$P_4 = \$50.50 = \$40.00 \times (1.06)^4 = P_0 \times (1 + g)^4$$

To see why this is so, notice first that:

$$P_4 = D_5/(r - g)$$

However, D_5 is just equal to $D_1 \times (1 + g)^4$, so we can write P_4 as:

$$P_4 = D_1 \times (1 + g)^4/(r - g)$$
$$= [D_1/(r - g)] \times (1 + g)^4$$
$$= P_0 \times (1 + g)^4$$

This last example illustrates that the dividend growth model has the implicit assumption that the stock price will grow at the same constant rate as the dividend. This really isn't too surprising. What it tells us is that if the cash flows on an investment grow at a constant rate through time, so does the value of that investment. • • •

Trans. 7.20 More on Dividend Growth (Supplemental)

Lecture Tip: The constant growth model is derived in the IM.

Lecture Tip: See IM for further discussion of the constant growth model.

You might wonder what would happen with the dividend growth model if the growth rate, g, were greater than the discount rate, r. It looks like we would get a negative stock price because $r - g$ would be less than zero. This is not what would happen.

Instead, if the constant growth rate exceeds the discount rate, then the stock price is infinitely large. Why? If the growth rate is bigger than the discount rate, then the present value of the dividends keeps on getting bigger and bigger. Essentially, the same is true if the growth rate and the discount rate are equal. In both cases, the simplification that allows us to replace the infinite stream of dividends with the dividend growth model is "illegal," so the answers we get from the dividend growth model are nonsense unless the growth rate is less than the discount rate.

Components of the Required Return

Thus far, we have taken the required return or discount rate, r, as given. We will have quite a bit to say on this subject in Chapters 10 and 11. For now, we want to examine the implications of the dividend growth model for this required return. Earlier, we calculated P_0 as:

$$P_0 = D_1/(r - g)$$

If we rearrange this to solve for r, we get:

$$(r - g) = D_1/P_0$$
$$r = D_1/P_0 + g \qquad [7.6]$$

dividend yield
A stock's expected cash dividend divided by its current price.

This tells us that the total return, r, has two components. The first of these, D_1/P_0, is called the **dividend yield.** Since this is calculated as the expected cash dividend divided by the current price, it is conceptually similar to the current yield on a bond.

capital gains yield
The dividend growth rate or the rate at which the value of an investment grows.

The second part of the total return is the growth rate, g. We know that the dividend growth rate is also the rate at which the stock price grows (see Example 7.6). Thus, this growth rate can be interpreted as the **capital gains yield,** that is, the rate at which the value of the investment grows.[2]

To illustrate the components of the required return, suppose we observe a stock selling for $20 per share. The next dividend will be $1 per share. You

[2] Here and elsewhere, we use the term *capital gain* a little loosely. For the record, a capital gain (or loss) is, strictly speaking, something defined by the IRS. For our purposes, it would be more accurate (but less common) to use the term *price appreciation* instead of *capital gain.*

think that the dividend will grow by 10 percent more or less indefinitely. What return does this stock offer you if this is correct?

The dividend growth model calculates total return as:

$$r = \text{Dividend yield} + \text{Capital gains yield}$$
$$r = \quad D_1/P_0 \quad + \quad g$$

In this case, total return works out to be:

$$\begin{aligned} r &= \$1/\$20 + 10\% \\ &= 5\% + 10\% \\ &= 15\% \end{aligned}$$

This stock, therefore, has a return of 15 percent.

We can verify this answer by calculating the price in one year, P_1, using 15 percent as the required return. Based on the dividend growth model, this price is:

$$\begin{aligned} P_1 &= D_1 \times (1 + g)/(r - g) \\ &= \$1 \times (1.10)/(.15 - .10) \\ &= \$1.1/.05 \\ &= \$22 \end{aligned}$$

Notice that this \$22 is \$20 × (1.1), so the stock price has grown by 10 percent as it should. If you pay \$20 for the stock today, you will get a \$1 dividend at the end of the year, and you will have a \$22 − 20 = \$2 gain. Your dividend yield is thus \$1/\$20 = 5%. Your capital gains yield is \$2/\$20 = 10%, so your total return would be 5% + 10% = 15%.

Our discussion of stock valuation is summarized in Table 7.3.

Lecture Tip: See IM for the "four fundamentals of stock valuation" according to Malkiel's *A Random Walk Down Wall Street.*

International Note: See IM for a discussion of the relative importance of dividends and capital gains in valuing foreign stocks.

Stock Market Reporting

If you look through the pages of *The Wall Street Journal* (or other financial newspaper), you will find information on a large number of stocks in several different markets. Figure 7.4 reproduces a small section of the stock page for

TABLE 7.3
Summary of stock valuation

Trans. 7.21

I. The General Case

In general, the price today of a share of stock, P_0, is the present value of all of its future dividends, $D_1, D_2, D_3, \ldots$:

$$P_0 = \frac{D_1}{(1+r)^1} + \frac{D_2}{(1+r)^2} + \frac{D_3}{(1+r)^3} + \cdots$$

where r is the required return.

II. Constant Growth Case

If the dividend grows at a steady rate, g, then the price can be written as:

$$P_0 = \frac{D_1}{(r - g)}$$

This result is called the *dividend growth model.*

III. The Required Return

The required return, r, can be written as the sum of two things:

$$r = D_1/P_0 + g$$

where D_1/P_0 is the *dividend yield* and g is the *capital gains yield* (which is the same thing as the growth rate in dividends for the steady-growth case).

F I G U R E 7.4
Sample stock quotation from *The Wall Street Journal*

Trans. 7.22

NEW YORK STOCK EXCHANGE
COMPOSITE TRANSACTIONS

Quotations as of 5 p.m. Eastern Time
Friday, February 17, 1995

52 Weeks Hi	Lo	Stock	Sym	Div	Yld %	PE	Vol 100s	Hi	Lo	Close	Net Chg.
s 40¼	30	MellonBK	MEL	1.80	4.8	13	4435	37⅞	37½	37⅞	+⅜
27¾	25⅛	MellonBk pfI		2.40	9.3	...	41	26⅛	25⅞	25⅞	−¼
27	23⅜	MellonBk pfJ		2.13	8.5	...	18	25¼	25⅛	25⅛	+⅛
27	22⅝	MellonBk pfK		2.05	8.2	...	658	25¼	24⅞	24⅞	−¼
41⅝	29½	Melville	MES	1.52	4.6	11	1460	33¼	32½	32⅞	+⅜
s 39¼	29½	MercBcpMO	MTL	1.32f	3.6	10	132	36⅜	36⅛	36¼	−⅛
57	30½	MercStrs	MST	1.02	2.4	16	1197	44¼	43	43¼	−½
40¾	28⅛	Merck	MRK	1.20	3.0	17	25857	40⅝	40⅛	40½	−⅛
18⅞	11⅛	MercuryFin	MFN	.32	2.1	21	833	15½	15⅛	15⅜	...
49⅛	41⅝	Meredith	MDP	.80f	1.7	21	271	48	47½	47¾	−¼
44½	32¼	MerrillLynch	MER	.92	2.3	9	5274	40¼	39⅞	40⅛	−⅛
3⅝	⅝	vjMerryGoRnd	MGR		...	...	13315	1⅜	1⅛	1⅛	−¼
24½	16¼	MerryLdInv	MRY	1.40	6.8	18	343	20¾	20½	20½	−¼
7⅞	3⅝ ♣	Mesa	MXP		...	dd	647	5⅛	5	5	−⅛
3⅞	2⅝	MesabiTr	MSB	.24e	6.9	...	106	3⅝	3½	3½	−⅛
10¼	9	Mestek	MCC		...	11	1	9⅝	9⅝	9⅝	...
n 25⅛	23⅛	MetEdCap pfA		2.25	9.0	...	54	25	24⅞	25	...

Source: Reprinted by permission of *The Wall Street Journal,* ©1995 Dow Jones & Company, Inc., February 17, 1995. All Rights Reserved Worldwide.

the New York Stock Exchange (NYSE) from February 17, 1995. In Figure 7.4, locate the line for Merck. With the column headings, the line reads:

Lecture Tip: See IM for a suggested use of *The Wall Street Journal* in class.

52 Weeks Hi	Lo	Stock	Sym	Div	Yld %	PE	Vol 100s	Hi	Lo	Close	Net Chg
40¾	28⅛	Merck	MRK	1.20	3.0	17	25857	40⅝	40⅛	40½	−⅛

The first two numbers, 40¾ and 28⅛, are the high and low price for the last 52 weeks. The 1.20 is the annual dividend. Since Merck, like most companies, pays dividends quarterly, this $1.20 is actually the last quarterly dividend multiplied by 4. So, the last cash dividend paid was $1.20/4 = $.30.

Jumping ahead just a bit, the Hi(gh), Lo(w), and Close figures are the high, low, and closing prices during the day. The "Net Chg" of −⅛ tells us that the closing price of $40½ per share is −⅛ or $.125 lower than the closing price the day before; so we say that Merck was down ⅛ for the day.

The column marked "Yld %" gives the dividend yield based on the current dividend and the closing price. For Merck, this is $1.20/40½ = 3.0% as shown. The next column, labeled PE (short for price/earnings or P/E ratio), is the closing price of $40½ divided by annual earnings per share (based on the most recent four quarters). In the jargon of Wall Street, we might say that Merck "sells for 17 times earnings."

The remaining column, marked "Vol 100s," tells us how many shares traded during the day (in hundreds). For example, the 25857 for Merck tells us that 2,585,700 or about 2.6 million shares changed hands on this day alone. If the average price during the day was $40 or so, then the dollar volume of transactions was on the order of $40 × 2.6 million = $104 million worth of Merck stock alone. This was a somewhat active day of trading in Merck shares, so this amount is a little larger than is typical, but it serves to illustrate how active the market can be.

CONCEPT QUESTIONS

7.4a What are the relevant cash flows for valuing a share of common stock?

7.4b Does the value of a share of stock depend on how long you expect to keep it?

7.4c What is the value of a share of stock when the dividend grows at a constant rate?

7.5 SOME FEATURES OF COMMON AND PREFERRED STOCKS

In discussing common stock features, we focus on shareholder rights and dividend payments. For preferred stock, we explain what the "preferred" means, and we also debate whether preferred stock is really debt or equity.

Common Stock Features

The term **common stock** means different things to different people, but it is usually applied to stock that has no special preference either in dividends or in bankruptcy.

common stock
Equity without priority for dividends or in bankruptcy.

Shareholder Rights The conceptual structure of the corporation assumes that shareholders elect directors who, in turn, hire management to carry out their directives. Shareholders, therefore, control the corporation through the right to elect the directors. Generally, only shareholders have this right.

Concept Q Answer 7.5a

Directors are elected each year at an annual meeting. Although there are exceptions (discussed below), the general idea is "one share, one vote" (*not* one share*holder,* one vote). Corporate democracy is thus very different from our political democracy. With corporate democracy, the "golden rule" prevails absolutely.[3]

Lecture Tip: See IM for an additional comment on corporate democracy.

Directors are elected at an annual shareholders' meeting by a vote of the holders of a majority of shares who are present and entitled to vote. However, the exact mechanism for electing directors differs across companies. The most important difference is whether shares must be voted cumulatively or must be voted straight.

To illustrate the two different voting procedures, imagine that a corporation has two shareholders: Smith with 20 shares and Jones with 80 shares. Both want to be a director. Jones does not want Smith, however. We assume there are a total of four directors to be elected.

The effect of **cumulative voting** is to permit minority participation.[4] If cumulative voting is permitted, the total number of votes that each shareholder may cast is determined first. This is usually calculated as the number of shares (owned or controlled) multiplied by the number of directors to be elected.

cumulative voting
Procedure where a shareholder may cast all votes for one member of the board of directors.

With cumulative voting, the directors are elected all at once. In our example, this means that the top four vote getters will be the new directors. A shareholder can distribute votes however he or she wishes.

---

[3] The golden rule: Whosoever has the gold makes the rules.

[4] By minority participation, we mean participation by shareholders with relatively small amounts of stock.

Will Smith get a seat on the board? If we ignore the possibility of a five-way tie, then the answer is yes. Smith will cast 20 × 4 = 80 votes, and Jones will cast 80 × 4 = 320 votes. If Smith gives all his votes to himself, he is assured of a directorship. The reason is that Jones can't divide 320 votes among four candidates in such a way as to give all of them more than 80 votes, so Smith will finish fourth at worst.

In general, if there are N directors up for election, then $1/(N + 1)$ percent of the stock (plus one share) will guarantee you a seat. In our current example, this is $1/(4 + 1) = 20\%$. So the more seats that are up for election at one time, the easier (and cheaper) it is to win one.

straight voting
Procedure where a shareholder may cast all votes for each member of the board of directors.

With **straight voting,** the directors are elected one at a time. Each time, Smith can cast 20 votes and Jones can cast 80. As a consequence, Jones will elect all of the candidates. The only way to guarantee a seat is to own 50 percent plus one share. This also guarantees that you will win every seat, so it's really all or nothing.

EXAMPLE 7.7 Buying the Election

Stock in JRJ Corporation sells for $20 per share and features cumulative voting. There are 10,000 shares outstanding. If three directors are up for election, how much does it cost to ensure yourself a seat on the board?

The question here is how many shares of stock will it take to get a seat. The answer is 2,501, so the cost is 2,501 × $20 = $50,020. Why 2,501? Because there is no way the remaining 7,499 votes can be divided among three people to give all of them more than 2,501 votes. For example, suppose two people receive 2,502 votes and the first two seats. A third person can receive at most 10,000 − 2,502 − 2,502 − 2,501 = 2,495, so the third seat is yours. • • •

As we've illustrated, straight voting can "freeze out" minority shareholders; that is the reason many states have mandatory cumulative voting. In states where cumulative voting is mandatory, devices have been worked out to minimize its impact.

One such device is to stagger the voting for the board of directors. With staggered elections, only a fraction of the directorships are up for election at a particular time. Thus, if only two directors are up for election at any one time, it will take $1/(2 + 1) = 33.33\%$ of the stock (plus one share) to guarantee a seat.

Overall, staggering has two basic effects:

1. Staggering makes it more difficult for a minority to elect a director when there is cumulative voting because there are fewer to be elected at one time.
2. Staggering makes takeover attempts less likely to be successful because it is more difficult to vote in a majority of new directors.

We should note that staggering may serve a beneficial purpose. It provides "institutional memory," that is, continuity on the board of directors. This may be important for corporations with significant long-range plans and projects.

Proxy Voting A **proxy** is the grant of authority by a shareholder to someone else to vote his or her shares. For convenience, much of the voting in large public corporations is actually done by proxy.

proxy
Grant of authority by shareholder allowing for another individual to vote his or her shares.

As we have seen, with straight voting, each share of stock has one vote. The owner of 10,000 shares has 10,000 votes. Many companies, such as Anheuser-Busch, have hundreds of thousands or even millions of shareholders. Shareholders can come to the annual meeting and vote in person, or they can transfer their right to vote to another party.

Concept Q Answer 7.5b

Lecture Tip: See IM for a discussion of Carl Icahn's proxy fight against Texaco management.

Obviously, management always tries to get as many proxies transferred to it as possible. However, if shareholders are not satisfied with management, an "outside" group of shareholders can try to obtain votes via proxy. They can vote by proxy to replace management by electing enough directors. This is called a *proxy fight.*

Classes of Stock Some firms have more than one class of common stock. Often, the classes are created with unequal voting rights. The Ford Motor Company, for example, has Class B common stock, which is not publicly traded (it is held by Ford family interests and trusts). This class has about 40 percent of the voting power. However, these shares comprise only about 15 percent of the total outstanding stock.

There are many other cases of corporations with different classes of stock. For example, General Motors has its "GM Classic" shares (the original) and two more recently created classes, Class E ("GME") and Class H ("GMH"). These classes were created to help pay for two large acquisitions, Electronic Data Systems and Hughes Aircraft.

In principle, the New York Stock Exchange does not allow companies to create classes of publicly traded common stock with unequal voting rights. Exceptions (e.g., Ford) appear to have been made. In addition, many non-NYSE companies have dual classes of common stock.

A primary reason for creating dual or multiple classes of stock has to do with control of the firm. If such stock exists, management of a firm can raise equity capital by issuing nonvoting or limited-voting stock while maintaining control.

The subject of unequal voting rights is controversial in the United States, and the idea of one share, one vote has a strong following and a long history. Interestingly, however, shares with unequal voting rights are quite common in the United Kingdom and elsewhere around the world.

Other Rights The value of a share of common stock in a corporation is directly related to the general rights of shareholders. In addition to the right to vote for directors, shareholders usually have the following rights:

Concept Q Answer 7.5a

1. The right to share proportionally in dividends paid.
2. The right to share proportionally in assets remaining after liabilities have been paid in a liquidation.
3. The right to vote on stockholder matters of great importance, such as a merger, usually done at the annual meeting or a special meeting.

In addition, stockholders sometimes have the right to share proportionally in any new stock sold. This is called the *preemptive right.*

Principles in Action

One Share, One Vote

What is the value of a single vote in corporate decision-making? In the case of American Maize-Products Co., the one vote attached to a single $40 share of stock may ultimately stop a deal worth $430 million. The story is complicated, but it illustrates both the power and the value of a shareholder's voting rights.

When their father's estate was being settled in 1973, William Ziegler III and Helen Ziegler Steinkraus were supposed to receive equal shares. However, since their father owned an odd number of Class B voting shares in American Maize-Products Co., William was given one more share than Helen. Neither became aware of the disparity until the 1980s. The shares, which combined make up 47 percent of the American Maize Class B shares, are held in GIH Corp., a family trust. Because William owns one share more than his sister, it appears he owns 50.001 percent of the trust, and thus controls how the trust's shares are voted. But this story wouldn't be particularly interesting if it weren't more complicated than that.

After his father died, William took over the day-to-day operations of American Maize. The firm's stock underperformed the market averages while the firm was under his control, and the Steinkraus family and other shareholders grew restless. Under pressure from those stockholders, William agreed to step down as chief executive officer by 1993. In addition, during the early 1990s, several new outside directors were added to the board. Since then, the fortunes of the firm have rebounded.

In February 1995 the directors of American Maize voted to accept a French firm's offer to buy the company for $40 per share, a total acquisition price of $430 million. The price represents a 52 percent premium over the January 1995 share price. However, William is not in favor of the deal, preferring that the ownership of American Maize stay with the family. He personally owns 7 percent of the American Maize Class B stock, plus, by virtue of owning one share more than his sister, he effectively controls the voting decisions of GIH Corp. Thus, he apparently controls 54 percent of the votes. He has filed a lawsuit against the board of directors to halt the sale.

At present, the battle is at a standstill. The board is considering options to circumvent William's voting control, including issuing more shares of Class B stock. William has publicly acknowledged that he doesn't have the money to purchase additional shares, so a new stock issue could effectively dilute his voting majority to a minority. However, he claims that such a stock issue would be illegal. The future of the firm hangs in the balance, most likely to be determined in the courts. And all because of that one extra share William got from his father's estate.

Source: "Single Share Shapes Furor in the Family, Future of Firm," *The Wall Street Journal,* March 7, 1995, pp. C1, C11.

Essentially, a preemptive right means that a company that wishes to sell stock must first offer it to the existing stockholders before offering it to the general public. The purpose is to give a stockholder the opportunity to protect his or her proportionate ownership in the corporation.

The accompanying *Principles in Action* box gives an excellent example of the importance of classes of stock, voting power, and the rights of majority stockholders.

dividends
Payment by corporation to shareholders, made in either cash or stock.

Dividends A distinctive feature of corporations is that they have shares of stock on which they are authorized by law to pay dividends to their shareholders. **Dividends** paid to shareholders represent a return on the capital directly or indirectly contributed to the corporation by the shareholders. The payment of dividends is at the discretion of the board of directors.

Some important characteristics of dividends include the following:

1. Unless a dividend is declared by the board of directors of a corporation, it is not a liability of the corporation. A corporation cannot default on an undeclared dividend. As a consequence, corporations cannot become bankrupt because of nonpayment of dividends. The amount of the dividend and even whether it is paid are decisions based on the business judgment of the board of directors.
2. The payment of dividends by the corporation is not a business expense. Dividends are not deductible for corporate tax purposes. In short, dividends are paid out of the corporation's after tax profits.
3. Dividends received by individual shareholders are for the most part considered ordinary income by the IRS and are fully taxable. However, corporations that own stock in other corporations are permitted to exclude 70 percent of the dividend amounts they receive and are taxed only on the remaining 30 percent.[5]

Preferred Stock Features

Preferred stock differs from common stock because it has preference over common stock in the payment of dividends and in the distribution of corporation assets in the event of liquidation. *Preference* means only that the holders of the preferred shares must receive a dividend (in the case of an ongoing firm) before holders of common shares are entitled to anything.

preferred stock
Stock with dividend priority over common stock, normally with a fixed dividend rate, sometimes without voting rights.

Problems 9, 23

Concept Q Answer 7.5c

Trans. 7.23 Preferred Stock (Supplemental)

Preferred stock is a form of equity from a legal and tax standpoint. Importantly, however, holders of preferred stock sometimes have no voting privileges.

Stated Value Preferred shares have a stated liquidating value, usually $100 per share. The cash dividend is described in terms of dollars per share. For example, General Motors "$5 preferred" easily translates into a dividend yield of 5 percent of stated value.

Cumulative and Noncumulative Dividends A preferred dividend is *not* like interest on a bond. The board of directors may decide not to pay the dividends on preferred shares, and their decision may have nothing to do with the current net income of the corporation.

Dividends payable on preferred stock are either *cumulative* or *noncumulative;* most are cumulative. If preferred dividends are cumulative and are not paid in a particular year, they will be carried forward as an *arrearage.* Usually both the accumulated (past) preferred dividends plus the current preferred dividends must be paid before the common shareholders can receive anything.

[5] For the record, the 70 percent exclusion applies when the recipient owns less than 20 percent of the outstanding stock in a corporation. If a corporation owns more than 20 percent but less than 80 percent, the exclusion is 80 percent. If more than 80 percent is owned, the corporation can file a single "consolidated" return and the exclusion is effectively 100 percent.

Unpaid preferred dividends are *not* debts of the firm. Directors elected by the common shareholders can defer preferred dividends indefinitely. However, in such cases:

1. Common shareholders must also forgo dividends.
2. Holders of preferred shares are often granted voting and other rights if preferred dividends have not been paid for some time.

Because preferred stockholders receive no interest on the accumulated dividends, some have argued that firms have an incentive to delay paying preferred dividends.

Is Preferred Stock Really Debt? A good case can be made that preferred stock is really debt in disguise, a kind of equity bond. Preferred shareholders receive a stated dividend only, and, if the corporation is liquidated, preferred shareholders get a stated value. Often, preferreds carry credit ratings much like bonds. Furthermore, preferred stock is sometimes convertible into common stock, and preferred stocks are often callable.

In addition, in recent years, many new issues of preferred stock have had obligatory sinking funds. Such a sinking fund effectively creates a final maturity since the entire issue will ultimately be retired. For these reasons, preferred stock seems to be a lot like debt. However, for tax purposes, preferred dividends are treated like common stock dividends.

CONCEPT QUESTIONS

7.5a What rights do stockholders have?

7.5b What is a proxy?

7.5c Why is preferred stock called "preferred"?

7.6 SUMMARY AND CONCLUSIONS

This chapter has shown you how to extend the basic present value results of Chapter 6 in some important ways. In our discussion of bonds and stocks, we saw that:

1. Bonds are long-term corporate debts. We examined the cash flows from a corporate bond and found that the present value of the cash flows and, hence, the bond's value can be readily determined. We also introduced some of the terminology associated with bonds, and we discussed how bond prices are reported in the financial press.
2. The cash flows from owning a share of stock come in the form of future dividends. We saw that in certain special cases it is possible to calculate the present value of all the future dividends and thus come up with a value for the stock. We discussed some of the terms and features associated with common and preferred stock, and we also examined how common stock price information is reported.

This chapter completes Part 3 of our book. By now, you should have a good grasp of what we mean by present value. You should also be familiar with how to calculate present values, loan payments, and so on. In Part 4, we cover capital budgeting decisions. As you will see, the techniques you learned in Chapters 5, 6, and 7 form the basis for our approach to evaluating business investment decisions.

Chapter Review Problems and Self-Test

7.1 **Bond Values** A Cowles Industries bond has a 10 percent coupon rate and a $1,000 face value. Interest is paid semiannually, and the bond has 20 years to maturity. If investors require a 12 percent yield, what is the bond's value? What is the effective annual yield on the bond?

7.2 **Bond Yields** A Macrohard Corp. bond carries an 8 percent coupon, paid semiannually. The par value is $1,000, and the bond matures in six years. If the bond currently sells for $911.37, what is its yield to maturity? What is the effective annual yield?

7.3 **Dividend Growth and Stock Valuation** The Brigapenski Co. has just paid a cash dividend of $2 per share. Investors require a 16 percent return from investments such as this. If the dividend is expected to grow at a steady 8 percent per year, what is the current value of the stock? What will the stock be worth in five years?

Answers to Self-Test Problems

7.1 Since the bond has a 10 percent coupon yield while investors require a 12 percent return, we know that the bond must sell at a discount. Notice that, since the bond pays interest semiannually, the coupons amount to $100/2 = $50 every six months. The required yield is 12%/2 = 6% every six months. Finally, the bond matures in 20 years, so there are a total of 40 six-month periods.

The bond's value is thus equal to the present value of $50 every six months for the next 40 six-month periods plus the present value of the $1,000 face amount:

$$\begin{aligned}\text{Bond value} &= \$50 \times [1 - 1/(1.06)^{40}]/.06 + \$1{,}000/(1.06)^{40} \\ &= \$50 \times 15.04630 + \$1{,}000/10.2857 \\ &= \$849.54\end{aligned}$$

Notice that we discounted the $1,000 back 40 periods at 6 percent per period, rather than 20 years at 12 percent. The reason is that the effective annual yield on the bond is $1.06^2 - 1 = 12.36\%$, not 12%. We thus could have used 12.36 percent per year for 20 years when we calculated the present value of the $1,000 face amount, and the answer would have been the same.

7.2 The present value of the bond's cash flows is its current price, $911.37. The coupon is $40 every 6 months for 12 periods. The face value is $1,000, so the bond's yield is the unknown discount rate in the following:

$$\$911.37 = \$40 \times [1 - 1/(1 + r)^{12}]/r + \$1{,}000/(1 + r)^{12}$$

The bond sells at a discount. Since the coupon rate is 8 percent, the yield must be something in excess of that.

If we were to solve this by trial and error, we might try 12 percent (or 6 percent per six months):

$$\text{Bond value} = \$40 \times [1 - 1/(1.06)^{12}]/.06 + \$1{,}000/1.06^{12}$$
$$= \$832.32$$

This is less than the actual value, so our discount rate is too high. We now know that the yield is somewhere between 8 percent and 12 percent. With further trial and error (or a little machine assistance), the yield works out to be 10 percent, or 5 percent every six months.

By convention, the bond's yield to maturity would be quoted as $2 \times 5\% = 10\%$. The effective yield is thus $1.05^2 - 1 = 10.25\%$.

7.3 The last dividend, D_0, was \$2. The dividend is expected to grow steadily at 8 percent. The required return is 16 percent. Based on the dividend growth model, the current price is:

$$P_0 = D_1/(r - g) = D_0 \times (1 + g)/(r - g)$$
$$= \$2 \times (1.08)/(.16 - .08)$$
$$= \$2.16/(.08)$$
$$= \$27$$

We could calculate the price in five years by calculating the dividend in five years and then using the growth model again. Alternatively, we could recognize that the stock price will increase by 8 percent per year and calculate the future price directly. We'll do both. First, the dividend in five years will be:

$$D_5 = D_0 \times (1 + g)^5$$
$$= \$2 \times 1.08^5$$
$$= \$2.9387$$

The price in five years would therefore be:

$$P_5 = D_5 \times (1 + g)/(r - g)$$
$$= \$2.9387 \times (1.08)/.08$$
$$= \$3.1738/.08$$
$$= \$39.67$$

Once we understand the dividend model, however, it's easier to notice that:

$$P_5 = P_0 \times (1 + g)^5$$
$$= \$27 \times 1.08^5$$
$$= \$27 \times 1.4693$$
$$= \$39.67$$

Notice that both approaches yield the same price in five years.

Questions and Problems

Basic (Questions 1–23)

1. **Coupon Rates** How does a bond issuer decide the appropriate coupon rate to set on its bonds? Explain the difference between the coupon rate and the required return on a bond.

2. **Interpreting Bond Yields** Suppose you buy a 9 percent coupon, 15-year bond today when it's first issued. If interest rates suddenly rise to 15 percent, what happens to the value of your bond? Why?

3. **Bond Prices** CIR, Inc., has 7 percent coupon bonds on the market that have 11 years left to maturity. The bonds make annual payments. If the YTM on these bonds is 8.5 percent, what is the current bond price? $895.47

4. **Bond Yields** N&N Co. has 10.5 percent coupon bonds on the market with 8 years left to maturity. The bonds make annual payments. If the bond currently sells for $1,070, what is its YTM? 9.22%

5. **Coupon Rates** Merton Enterprises has bonds on the market making annual payments, with 14 years to maturity, and selling for $950. At this price, the bonds yield 7.5 percent. What must the coupon rate be on Merton's bonds? 6.91%

6. **Bond Prices** Jane's Pizzeria issued 10-year bonds one year ago at a coupon rate of 8.75 percent. The bonds make semiannual payments. If the YTM on these bonds is 7.25 percent, what is the current bond price? $1,097.91

7. **Bond Yields** Jerry's Spaghetti Factory issued 12-year bonds two years ago at a coupon rate of 9.5 percent. The bonds make semiannual payments. If these bonds currently sell for 96 percent of par value, what is the YTM? 10.15% **Trans. 7.24**

8. **Terms of Indentures** What is the effect of each of the following provisions on the coupon rate for a newly issued bond? Give a brief explanation in each case.
   a. A call provision.
   b. A put provision.
   c. A provision allowing the bond to be converted to stock at the owner's option.
   d. Real property collateral.
   e. A maximum dividend payout covenant.

9. **Valuing Preferred Stock** Bob's Bank just issued some new preferred stock. The issue will pay a $7.00 annual dividend in perpetuity, beginning four years from now. If the market requires a 6 percent return on this investment, how much does a share of preferred stock cost today? $97.96 **Trans. 7.25**

10. **Using Stock Quotes** You found the following stock quote for DRK Enterprises, Inc., in the financial pages of today's newspaper. What was the closing price for this stock that appeared in yesterday's paper? Close = 78⅝

52 wk.											
Hi	Lo	Stock	Sym	Div	Yld %	P/E	Vol 100s	Hi	Lo	Close	Net Chg
117	52½	DRK	DRK	3.60	4.6	16	7295	81¾	76	??	−⅜

11. **Stock Value Intuition** Suppose you buy some stock today with the intention of selling it in three years to your brother. Does your expected selling price enter into your valuation of the current stock

price? Draw a time line of your cash flows from the stock and a time line of your brother's cash flows to illustrate your answer.

a. 125,001
b. 375,001

12. **Voting for Directors** The shareholders of Vycom, Inc., need to elect five new directors to the board. There are 750,000 shares of common stock outstanding. How many shares do you need to own to guarantee yourself a seat on the board if:
    a. The company uses cumulative voting procedures?
    b. The company uses straight voting procedures?

13. **Dual Classes of Stock** What does it mean to say that a firm has dual classes of stock? What are some reasons that a firm might want to have more than one class of stock? What is a common objection to multiple classes of stock in the United States?

Close = 90

14. **Using Bond Quotes** Suppose the following bond quote for ISU Corporation appears on the financial page of today's newspaper. If this bond has a face value of $1,000, what closing price appeared in yesterday's newspaper?

Bonds	Cur Yld	Vol	Close	Net Chg
ISU 7⅞ s11	8.7	10	??	+½

7.82%

15. **Coupon Rates** Dunbar Corporation has bonds on the market with 10.5 years to maturity, a YTM of 10 percent, and a current price of $860. The bonds make semiannual payments. What must the coupon rate be on Dunbar's bonds?

P_0 = $30.29
P_3 = $36.07
P_{15} = $72.58

16. **Stock Values** MegaCapital, Inc., just paid a dividend of $2.00 per share on its stock. The dividends are expected to grow at a constant 6 percent per year indefinitely. If investors require a 13 percent return on MegaCapital stock, what is the current price? What will the price be in 3 years? In 15 years?

9.26%
Trans. 7.26

17. **Stock Values** SAF, Inc.'s next dividend payment will be $3.00 per share. The dividends are anticipated to maintain a 5 percent growth rate forever. If SAF stock currently sells for $70.50 per share, what is the required return?

Dividend yield = 4.26%
Capital gains yield = 5%

18. **Stock Values** For the company in the previous problem, what is the dividend yield? What is the expected capital gains yield?

$47.22

19. **Stock Values** Makin' Copies Corporation will pay a $4.25 per share dividend next year. The company pledges to increase its dividend by 9 percent per year indefinitely. If you require an 18 percent return on your investment, how much will you pay for the company's stock today?

10.5%

20. **Stock Valuation** Utopia Power Co. is expected to maintain a constant 5 percent growth rate in its dividends indefinitely. If the company has a dividend yield of 5.5 percent, what is the required return on the power company's stock?

$3.49

21. **Stock Valuation** Suppose you know that a company's stock currently sells for $50 per share and the required return on the stock is 15 percent. You also know that the total return on the stock is evenly divided between a capital gains yield and a dividend yield. If it's the

company's policy to always maintain a constant growth rate in its dividends, what is the current dividend per share?

22. **Stock Valuation** Jordan's Jalopies pays a constant $5.00 dividend on its stock. The company will maintain this dividend for the next 7 years, and then cease paying any more dividends forever. If the required return on this stock is 12 percent, what is the current share price? $22.82

23. **Valuing Preferred Stock** Always Tranquil, Inc., has an issue of preferred stock outstanding that pays an $8.50 dividend every year in perpetuity. If this issue currently sells for $115.00 per share, what is the required return? 7.39%

Intermediate (Questions 24–30)

24. **Bond Prices versus Yields**
    a. What is the relationship between the price of a bond and its YTM?
    b. Explain why some bonds sell at a premium to par value, and other bonds sell at a discount. What do you know about the relationship between the coupon rate and the YTM for premium bonds? What about for discount bonds? For bonds selling at par value?
    c. What is the relationship between the current yield and YTM for premium bonds? For discount bonds? For bonds selling at par value?

25. **Bond Price Movements** Bond X is a premium bond making annual payments. The bond pays a 9 percent coupon, has a YTM of 7 percent, and has 15 years to maturity. Bond Y is a discount bond making annual payments. This bond pays a 6 percent coupon, has a YTM of 9 percent, and also has 15 years to maturity. If interest rates remain unchanged, what do you expect the price of these bonds to be one year from now? In 5 years? In 10 years? In 14 years? In 15 years? What's going on here? Illustrate your answers by graphing bond prices versus time to maturity.

X: P_0 = $1,182.16
P_1 = $1,174.91
P_5 = $1,140.47
Y: P_0 = $758.18
P_1 = $766.42
P_5 = $807.47

26. **Interest Rate Risk** Both Bond A and Bond B have 8 percent coupons, make semiannual payments, and are priced at par value. Bond A has 2 years to maturity, while Bond B has 15 years to maturity. If interest rates suddenly rise by 2 percent, what is the percentage change in price of Bond A? Of Bond B? If rates were to suddenly fall by 2 percent instead, what would the percentage change in price of Bond A be now? Of Bond B? Illustrate your answers by graphing bond prices versus YTM. What does this problem tell you about the interest rate risk of longer-term bonds?

+2%: $\Delta P_A = -3.55\%$
$\Delta P_B = -15.37\%$
−2%: $\Delta P_A = +3.72\%$
$\Delta P_B = +19.60\%$

27. **Interest Rate Risk** Bond J is a 4 percent coupon bond. Bond K is a 10 percent coupon bond. Both bonds have 10 years to maturity, make semiannual payments, and have a YTM of 9 percent. If interest rates suddenly rise by 2 percent, what is the percentage price change of these bonds? What if rates suddenly fall by 2 percent instead? What does this problem tell you about the interest rate risk of lower-coupon bonds?

+2%: $\Delta P_J = -13.79\%$
$\Delta P_K = -11.72\%$
−2%: $\Delta P_J = +16.60\%$
$\Delta P_K = +13.91\%$

28. **Bond Yields** BrainDrain Software has 12 percent coupon bonds on the market with 9 years to maturity. The bonds make semiannual

Current yield = 10.91%
YTM = 10.27%
Effective yield = 10.53%

payments and currently sell for 110 percent of par. What is the current yield on BrainDrain's bonds? The YTM? The effective annual yield?

7.43%

29. **Bond Yields** DRK Co. wants to issue new 10-year bonds for some much-needed expansion projects. The company currently has 8 percent coupon bonds on the market that sell for $1,040, make semiannual payments, and mature in 10 years. What coupon rate should the company set on its new bonds if it wants them to sell at par?

12 years

30. **Finding the Bond Maturity** ABC Co. has 10 percent coupon bonds making annual payments with a YTM of 8.5 percent. The current yield on these bonds is 9.01 percent. How many years do these bonds have left until they mature?

Part Four

CAPITAL BUDGETING

In Part Four, we apply the basic valuation tools developed in our previous section to the capital budgeting decision. In Chapter 8, we evaluate various investment criteria. We compare and contrast net present value with other methods for selecting among alternative investment proposals and learn that the net present value approach is the superior procedure.

In Chapter 9, we show how to apply the net present value criterion to the question of project selection. We discuss the various cash flows that should and should not be considered in the analysis and also describe some techniques used to evaluate the quality of a net present value analysis.

OUTLINE

Chapter Eight

Net Present Value and Other Investment Criteria

After studying this chapter, you should have a good understanding of:

The payback rule and some of its shortcomings.

Accounting rates of return and some of the problems with them.

The internal rate of return criterion and its strengths and weaknesses.

Why the net present value criterion is the best way to evaluate proposed investments.

Trans. 8.1 Chapter Outline

In Chapter 1, we identified the three key areas of concern to the financial manager. The first of these was: "What fixed assets should we buy?" We called this the *capital budgeting decision.* In this chapter, we begin to deal with the issues that arise in answering this question.

The process of allocating or budgeting capital is usually more involved than just deciding on whether or not to buy a particular fixed asset. We will frequently face broader issues like whether or not we should launch a new product or enter a new market. Decisions such as these will determine the nature of a firm's operations and products for years to come, primarily because fixed asset investments are generally long-lived and not easily reversed once they are made.

Lecture Tip: You may wish to emphasize the point that firm value comes primarily from the asset side of the balance sheet—it's a good lead-in to the capital structure discussion in Chapter 14.

For the reasons we have discussed, the capital budgeting question is probably the most important issue in corporate finance. How a firm chooses to finance its operations (the capital structure question) and how a firm manages its short-term operating activities (the working capital question) are certainly issues of concern, but it is the fixed assets that define the business of the firm. Airlines, for example, are airlines because they operate airplanes, regardless of how they finance them.

Any firm possesses a huge number of possible investments. Each possible investment is an option available to the firm. Some options are valuable and some are not. The essence of successful financial management, of course, is learning to identify which are which. With this in mind, our goal in this chapter is to introduce you to the techniques used to analyze potential business ventures to decide which are worth undertaking.

We present and compare several different procedures used in practice. Our primary goal is to acquaint you with the advantages and disadvantages of the various approaches. As we shall see, the most important concept in this area is the idea of net present value. We consider this next.

8.1 NET PRESENT VALUE

In Chapter 1, we argued that the goal of financial management is to create value for the stockholders. The financial manager must therefore examine a potential investment in light of its likely effect on the price of the firm's shares. In this section, we describe a widely used procedure for doing this, the net present value approach.

Self-Test Problem 8.1
Problems 6, 9, 15, 21

The Basic Idea

An investment is worth undertaking if it creates value for its owners. In the most general sense, we create value by identifying an investment worth more in the marketplace than it costs us to acquire. How can something be worth more than it costs? It's a case of the whole being worth more than the cost of the parts.

For example, suppose you buy a run-down house for $25,000 and spend another $25,000 on painters, plumbers, and so on to get it fixed up. Your total investment is $50,000. When the work is completed, you place the house back on the market and find that it's worth $60,000. The market value ($60,000) exceeds the cost ($50,000) by $10,000. What you have done here is to act as a manager and bring together some fixed assets (a house), some labor (plumbers, carpenters, and others), and some materials (carpeting, paint, and so on). The net result is that you have created $10,000 in value. Put another way, this $10,000 is the *value added* by management.

Concept Q Answer 8.1b

With our house example, it turned out *after the fact* that $10,000 in value was created. Things thus worked out very nicely. The real challenge, of course, was to somehow identify *ahead of time* whether or not investing the necessary $50,000 was a good idea in the first place. This is what capital budgeting is all about, namely, trying to determine whether a proposed investment or project will be worth more than it costs once it is in place.

Lecture Tip: See IM 8.1 for an extension of this example and its links to the material in Chapter 1.

Lecture Tip: See IM for a tip on avoiding potential student confusion regarding NPV and PV.

For reasons that will be obvious in a moment, the difference between an investment's market value and its cost is called the **net present value** of the investment, abbreviated NPV. In other words, net present value is a measure of how much value is created or added today by undertaking an investment. Given our goal of creating value for the stockholders, the capital budgeting process can be viewed as a search for investments with positive net present values.

net present value (NPV)
The difference between an investment's market value and its cost.

With our run-down house, you can probably imagine how we would go about making the capital budgeting decision. We would first look at what comparable, fixed-up properties were selling for in the market. We would then get estimates of the cost of buying a particular property, fixing it up, and bringing it to market. At this point, we have an estimated total cost and an estimated market value. If the difference is positive, then this investment is worth undertaking because it has a positive estimated net present value. There is risk, of course, because there is no guarantee that our estimates will turn out to be correct.

As our example illustrates, investment decisions are greatly simplified when there is a market for assets similar to the investment we are considering. Capital budgeting becomes much more difficult when we cannot observe the market price for at least roughly comparable investments. The reason is that we are then faced with the problem of estimating the value of an investment using only indirect market information. Unfortunately, this is precisely the situation the financial manager usually encounters. We examine this issue next.

Estimating Net Present Value

Trans. 8.2 NPV Illustrated (Supplemental)

Imagine we are thinking of starting a business to produce and sell a new product, say, organic fertilizer. We can estimate the start-up costs with reasonable accuracy because we know what we will need to buy to begin production. Would this be a good investment? Based on our discussion, you know that the answer depends on whether or not the value of the new business exceeds the cost of starting it. In other words, does this investment have a positive NPV?

This problem is much more difficult than our "fixer-upper" house example, because entire fertilizer companies are not routinely bought and sold in the marketplace; so it is essentially impossible to observe the market value of a similar investment. As a result, we must somehow estimate this value by other means.

Based on our work in Chapters 5 and 6, you may be able to guess how we will go about estimating the value of our fertilizer business. We will first try to estimate the future cash flows we expect the new business to produce. We will then apply our basic discounted cash flow procedure to estimate the present value of those cash flows. Once we have this estimate, we then estimate NPV as the difference between the present value of the future cash flows and the cost of the investment. As we mentioned in Chapter 6, this procedure is often called **discounted cash flow (DCF) valuation.**

discounted cash flow (DCF) valuation
The process of valuing an investment by discounting its future cash flows.

To see how we might go about estimating NPV, suppose we believe the cash revenues from our fertilizer business will be $20,000 per year, assuming everything goes as expected. Cash costs (including taxes) will be $14,000 per year. We will wind down the business in eight years. The plant, property, and equipment will be worth $2,000 as salvage at that time. The project costs $30,000 to launch. We use a 15 percent discount rate on new projects such as this one. Is this a good investment? If there are 1,000 shares of stock outstanding, what will be the effect on the price per share from taking it?

From a purely mechanical perspective, we need to calculate the present value of the future cash flows at 15 percent. The net cash inflow will be $20,000 cash income less $14,000 in costs per year for eight years. These cash flows are illustrated in Figure 8.1. As Figure 8.1 suggests, we effectively have an eight-year annuity of $20,000 − 14,000 = $6,000 per year along with a single lump-sum inflow of $2,000 in eight years. Calculating the

Time (years)	0	1	2	3	4	5	6	7	8
Initial cost	−$30								
Inflows		$20	$20	$20	$20	$20	$20	$20	$20
Outflows		− 14	− 14	− 14	− 14	− 14	− 14	− 14	− 14
Net inflow		$ 6	$ 6	$ 6	$ 6	$ 6	$ 6	$ 6	$ 6
Salvage									2
Net cash flow	−$30	$ 6	$ 6	$ 6	$ 6	$ 6	$ 6	$ 6	$ 8

FIGURE 8.1
Project cash flows (000)

present value of the future cash flows thus comes down to the same type of problem we considered in Chapter 6. The total present value is:

$$\begin{aligned}\text{Present value} &= \$6{,}000 \times (1 - 1/1.15^8)/.15 + \$2{,}000/1.15^8 \\ &= \$6{,}000 \times 4.4873 + 2{,}000/3.0590 \\ &= \$26{,}924 + 654 \\ &= \$27{,}578\end{aligned}$$

When we compare this to the $30,000 estimated cost, the NPV is:

$$\text{NPV} = -\$30{,}000 + 27{,}578 = -\$2{,}422$$

Therefore, this is *not* a good investment. Based on our estimates, taking it would *decrease* the total value of the stock by $2,422. With 1,000 shares outstanding, our best estimate of the impact of taking this project is a loss of value of $2,422/1,000 = $2.422 per share.

Lecture Tip: See IM 8.1 for an alternative interpretation of the meaning of negative NPV.

Our fertilizer example illustrates how NPV estimates can be used to determine whether or not an investment is desirable. From our example, notice that, if the NPV is negative, the effect on share value will be unfavorable. If the NPV were positive, the effect would be favorable. As a consequence, all we need to know about a particular proposal for the purpose of making an accept/reject decision is whether the NPV is positive or negative.

Given that the goal of financial management is to increase share value, our discussion in this section leads us to the *net present value rule:*

An investment should be accepted if the net present value is positive and rejected if it is negative.

Concept Q Answer 8.1a

In the unlikely event that the net present value turned out to be exactly zero, we would be indifferent to taking the investment or not taking it.

Lecture Tip: See IM 8.1 for an alternative interpretation of "borderline" results, that is, cases where NPV = 0.

Two comments about our example are in order. First and foremost, it is not the rather mechanical process of discounting the cash flows that is important. Once we have the cash flows and the appropriate discount rate, the required calculations are fairly straightforward. The task of coming up with the cash flows and the discount rate in the first place is much more challenging. We will have much more to say about this in the next several chapters. For the remainder of this chapter, we take it as given that we have estimates of the cash revenues and costs and, where needed, an appropriate discount rate.

The second thing to keep in mind about our example is that the −$2,422 NPV is an estimate. Like any estimate, it can be high or low. The only way to find out the true NPV would be to place the investment up for sale and see what we could get for it. We generally won't be doing this, so it is important that our estimates be reliable. Once again, we will have more to say about this later. For the rest of this chapter, we will assume the estimates are accurate.

EXAMPLE 8.1 Using the NPV Rule

Suppose we are asked to decide whether or not a new consumer product should be launched. Based on projected sales and costs, we expect that the cash flows over the five-year life of the project will be $2,000 in the first two years, $4,000 in the next two, and $5,000 in the last year. It will cost about $10,000 to begin production. We use a 10 percent discount rate to evaluate new products. What should we do here?

Given the cash flows and discount rate, we can calculate the total value of the product by discounting the cash flows back to the present:

$$\begin{aligned}\text{Present value} &= \$2{,}000/1.1 + 2{,}000/1.1^2 + 4{,}000/1.1^3 + 4{,}000/1.1^4 \\ &\quad + 5{,}000/1.1^5 \\ &= \$1{,}818 + 1{,}653 + 3{,}005 + 2{,}732 + 3{,}105 \\ &= \$12{,}313\end{aligned}$$

The present value of the expected cash flows is $12,313, but the cost of getting those cash flows is only $10,000, so the NPV is $12,313 − 10,000 = $2,313. This is positive; so, based on the net present value rule, we should take on the project. • • •

As we have seen in this section, estimating NPV is one way of assessing the profitability of a proposed investment. It is certainly not the only way profitability is assessed, and we now turn to some alternatives. As we will see, when compared to NPV, each of the ways of assessing profitability that we examine is flawed in some key way; so NPV is the preferred approach in principle, if not always in practice.

CONCEPT QUESTIONS

8.1a What is the net present value rule?

8.1b If we say an investment has an NPV of $1,000, what exactly do we mean?

8.2 THE PAYBACK RULE

Problems 2, 3, 16, 18, 19

★ **Ethics Note:** See IM for an ethics problem involving the payback period.

Concept Q Answer 8.2a

It is very common in practice to talk of the payback on a proposed investment. Loosely, the *payback* is the length of time it takes to recover our initial investment or "get our bait back." Because this idea is widely understood and used, we will examine it in some detail.

Defining the Rule

We can illustrate how to calculate a payback with an example. Figure 8.2 shows the cash flows from a proposed investment. How many years do we have to wait until the accumulated cash flows from this investment equal or exceed the cost of the investment? As Figure 8.2 indicates, the initial investment is $50,000. After the first year, the firm has recovered $30,000, leaving $20,000. The cash flow in the second year is exactly $20,000, so this invest-

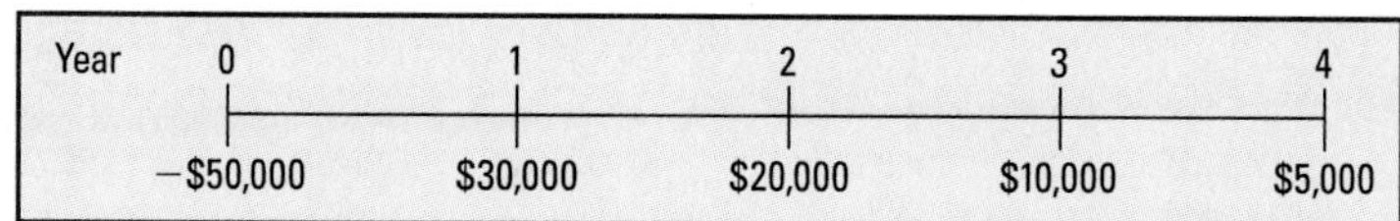

FIGURE 8.2
Net project cash flows

ment "pays for itself" in exactly two years. Put another way, the **payback period** (or just payback) is two years. If we require a payback of, say, three years or less, then this investment is acceptable. This illustrates the *payback period rule:*

payback period
The amount of time required for an investment to generate cash flows to recover its initial cost.

> **Based on the payback rule, an investment is acceptable if its calculated payback period is less than some prespecified number of years.**

In our example, the payback works out to be exactly two years. This won't usually happen, of course. When the numbers don't work out exactly, it is customary to work with fractional years. For example, suppose the initial investment is $60,000, and the cash flows are $20,000 in the first year and $90,000 in the second. The cash flows over the first two years are $110,000, so the project obviously pays back sometime in the second year. After the first year, the project has paid back $20,000, leaving $40,000 to be recovered. To figure out the fractional year, note that this $40,000 is $40,000/90,000 = 4/9 of the second year's cash flow. Assuming that the $90,000 cash flow is paid uniformly throughout the year, the payback would thus be 1$\frac{4}{9}$ years.

EXAMPLE 8.2 Calculating Payback

Trans. 8.3
Payback Rule Illustrated (Supplemental)

The projected cash flows from a proposed investment are:

Year	Cash Flow
1	$100
2	200
3	500

This project costs $500. What is the payback period for this investment?

The initial cost is $500. After the first two years, the cash flows total $300. After the third year, the total cash flow is $800, so the project pays back sometime between the end of Year 2 and the end of Year 3. Since the accumulated cash flows for the first two years are $300, we need to recover $200 in the third year. The third year cash flow is $500, so we will have to wait $200/500 = .40 of the year to do this. The payback period is thus 2.4 years, or about two years and five months. • • •

Now that we know how to calculate the payback period on an investment, using the payback period rule for making decisions is straightforward. A particular cutoff time is selected, say, two years, and all investment projects that have payback periods of two years or less are accepted, and all of those that pay back in more than two years are rejected.

Table 8.1 illustrates cash flows for five different projects. The figures shown as the Year 0 cash flows are the cost of the investment. We examine these to indicate some peculiarities that can, in principle, arise with payback periods.

The payback for the first project, A, is easily calculated. The sum of the cash flows for the first two years is $70, leaving us with $100 − 70 = $30 to

TABLE 8.1
Expected cash flows for Projects A through E

Year	A	B	C	D	E
0	−$100	−$200	−$200	−$200	−$ 50
1	30	40	40	100	100
2	40	20	20	100	− 50,000,000
3	50	10	10	− 200	
4	60		130	200	

go. Since the cash flow in the third year is \$50, the payback occurs sometime in that year. When we compare the \$30 we need to the \$50 that will be coming in, we get \$30/50 = .60; so, payback will occur 60 percent of the way into the year. The payback period is thus 2.6 years.

Project B's payback is also easy to calculate: It *never* pays back because the cash flows never total up to the original investment. Project C has a payback of exactly four years because it supplies the \$130 that B is missing in Year 4. Project D is a little strange. Because of the negative cash flow in Year 3, you can easily verify that it has two different payback periods, two years and four years. Which of these is correct? Both of them; the way the payback period is calculated doesn't guarantee a single answer. Finally, Project E is obviously unrealistic, but it does pay back in six months, thereby illustrating the point that a rapid payback does not guarantee a good investment.

Analyzing the Payback Period Rule

When compared to the NPV rule, the payback period rule has some rather severe shortcomings. First, the payback period is calculated by simply adding up the future cash flows. There is no discounting involved, so the time value of money is completely ignored. The payback rule also does not consider risk differences. The payback would be calculated the same way for both very risky and very safe projects.

Perhaps the biggest problem with the payback period rule is coming up with the right cutoff period, because we don't really have an objective basis for choosing a particular number. Put another way, there is no economic rationale for looking at payback in the first place, so we have no guide as to how to pick the cutoff. As a result, we end up using a number that is arbitrarily chosen.

Suppose we have somehow decided on an appropriate payback period, say two years or less. As we have seen, the payback period rule ignores the time value of money for the first two years. More seriously, cash flows after the second year are ignored entirely. To see this, consider the two investments, Long and Short, in Table 8.2. Both projects cost \$250. Based on our discussion, the payback on Long is 2 + \$50/100 = 2.5 years, and the payback on Short is 1 + \$150/200 = 1.75 years. With a cutoff of two years, Short is acceptable and Long is not.

Is the payback period rule giving us the right decisions? Maybe not. Suppose again that we require a 15 percent return on this type of investment. We can calculate the NPV for these two investments as:

$$\text{NPV(Short)} = -\$250 + 100/1.15 + 200/1.15^2 = -\$11.81$$
$$\text{NPV(Long)} = -\$250 + 100 \times (1 - 1/1.15^4)/.15 = \$35.50$$

Now we have a problem. The NPV of the shorter-term investment is actually negative, meaning that taking it diminishes the value of the shareholders' eq-

Year	Long	Short
0	−$250	−$250
1	100	100
2	100	200
3	100	0
4	100	0

TABLE 8.2
Investment projected cash flows

uity. The opposite is true for the longer-term investment—it increases share value.

Our example illustrates two primary shortcomings of the payback period rule. First, by ignoring time value, we may be led to take investments (like Short) that actually are worth less than they cost. Second, by ignoring cash flows beyond the cutoff, we may be led to reject profitable long-term investments (like Long). More generally, using a payback period rule will tend to bias us towards shorter-term investments.

Redeeming Qualities of the Payback Period Rule

Despite its shortcomings, the payback period rule is often used by large and sophisticated companies when making relatively minor decisions. There are several reasons for this. The primary reason is that many decisions simply do not warrant detailed analysis because the cost of the analysis would exceed the possible loss from a mistake. As a practical matter, an investment that pays back rapidly and has benefits extending beyond the cutoff period probably has a positive NPV.

Small investment decisions are made by the hundreds every day in large organizations. Moreover, they are made at all levels. As a result, it would not be uncommon for a corporation to require, for example, a two-year payback on all investments of less than $10,000. Investments larger than this are subjected to greater scrutiny. The requirement of a two-year payback is not perfect for reasons we have seen, but it does exercise some control over expenditures and thus has the effect of limiting possible losses.

In addition to its simplicity, the payback rule has two other positive features. First, because it is biased toward short-term projects, it is biased toward liquidity. In other words, a payback rule tends to favor investments that free up cash for other uses more quickly. This could be very important for a small business; it would be less so for a large corporation. Second, the cash flows that are expected to occur later in a project's life are probably more uncertain. Arguably, a payback period rule adjusts for the extra riskiness of later cash flows, but it does so in a rather draconian fashion—by ignoring them altogether.

We should note here that some of the apparent simplicity of the payback rule is an illusion. The reason is that we still must come up with the cash flows first, and, as we discuss above, this is not at all easy to do. Thus, it would probably be more accurate to say that the *concept* of a payback period is both intuitive and easy to understand.

Summary of the Payback Period Rule

To summarize, the payback period is a kind of "break-even" measure. Because time value is ignored, you can think of the payback period as the length of time it takes to break even in an accounting sense, but not in an economic

Concept Q Answer 8.2b

sense. The biggest drawback to the payback period rule is that it doesn't ask the right question. The relevant issue is the impact an investment will have on the value of our stock, not how long it takes to recover the initial investment.

Lecture Tip: See IM for another way of interpreting the payback period.

Nevertheless, because it is so simple, companies often use it as a screen for dealing with the myriad of minor investment decisions they have to make. There is certainly nothing wrong with this practice. Like any simple rule of thumb, there will be some errors in using it, but it wouldn't have survived all this time if it weren't useful. Now that you understand the rule, you can be on the alert for those circumstances under which it might lead to problems. To help you remember, the following table lists the pros and cons of the payback period rule.

International Note: See IM for a discussion of the use of the payback rule in making capital budgeting decisons in an international context.

Lecture Tip: Some analysts prefer to employ discounted cash flows to calculate the payback period—the "discounted payback" method is discussed in the IM and in *Fundamentals of Corporate Finance* by Ross, Westerfield, Jordan, Irwin Publishing.

Advantages and Disadvantages of the Payback Period Rule

Advantages	Disadvantages
1. Easy to understand.	1. Ignores the time value of money.
2. Adjusts for uncertainty of later cash flows.	2. Requires an arbitrary cutoff point.
3. Biased toward liquidity.	3. Ignores cash flows beyond the cutoff date.
	4. Biased against long-term projects, such as research and devleopment, and new projects.

CONCEPT QUESTIONS

8.2a In words, what is the payback period? The payback period rule?

8.2b Why do we say that the payback period is, in a sense, an accounting break-even?

8.3 THE AVERAGE ACCOUNTING RETURN

average accounting return (AAR)
An investment's average net income divided by its average book value.

Self-Test Problem 8.3
Problems 4, 20

Concept Q Answer 8.3a

Another attractive, but flawed, approach to making capital budgeting decisions is the **average accounting return (AAR).** There are many different definitions of the AAR. However, in one form or another, the AAR is always defined as:

$$\frac{\text{Some measure of average accounting profit}}{\text{Some measure of average accounting value}}$$

The specific definition we will use is:

$$\frac{\text{Average net income}}{\text{Average book value}}$$

To see how we might calculate this number, suppose we are deciding whether or not to open a store in a new shopping mall. The required investment in improvements is \$500,000. The store would have a five-year life because everything reverts to the mall owners after that time. The required investment would be 100 percent depreciated (straight-line) over five years, so the depreciation would be \$500,000/5 = \$100,000 per year. The tax rate is 25 percent. Table 8.3 contains the projected revenues and expenses. Based on these figures, net income in each year is also shown.

To calculate the average book value for this investment, we note that we started out with a book value of \$500,000 (the initial cost) and ended up at \$0. The average book value during the life of the investment is thus (\$500,000 +

	Year 1	Year 2	Year 3	Year 4	Year 5
Revenue	$433,333	$450,000	$266,667	$200,000	$133,333
Expenses	200,000	150,000	100,000	100,000	100,000
Earnings before depreciation	$233,333	$300,000	$166,667	$100,000	$ 33,333
Depreciation	100,000	100,000	100,000	100,000	100,000
Earnings before taxes	$133,333	$200,000	$ 66,667	$ 0	−$ 66,667
Taxes (T = 0.25)	33,333	50,000	16,667	0	− 16,667
Net income	$100,000	$150,000	$ 50,000	$ 0	−$ 50,000

$$\text{Average net income} = \frac{(\$100{,}000 + 150{,}000 + 50{,}000 + 0 - 50{,}000)}{5} = \$50{,}000$$

$$\text{Average book value} = \frac{\$500{,}000 + 0}{2} = \$250{,}000$$

TABLE 8.3
Projected yearly revenue and costs for average accounting return

0)/2 = $250,000. As long as we use straight-line depreciation, the average investment will always be one-half of the initial investment.[1]

Looking at Table 8.3, net income is $100,000 in the first year, $150,000 in the second year, $50,000 in the third year, $0 in Year 4, and −$50,000 in Year 5. The average net income, then, is:

Trans 8.4
Average Accounting Return Illustrated (Supplemental)

$$[\$100{,}000 + 150{,}000 + 50{,}000 + 0 + (-50{,}000)]/5 = \$50{,}000$$

The average accounting return is:

$$\text{AAR} = \frac{\text{Average net income}}{\text{Average book value}} = \frac{\$50{,}000}{\$250{,}000} = 20\%$$

If the firm has a target AAR less than 20 percent, then this investment is acceptable; otherwise not. The *average accounting return rule* is thus:

> **Based on the average accounting return rule, a project is acceptable if its average accounting return exceeds a target average accounting return.**

As we will see in the next section, this rule has a number of problems.

Analyzing the Average Accounting Return Method

Concept Q Answer 8.3b

You should recognize the chief drawback to the AAR immediately. Above all else, the AAR is not a rate of return in any meaningful economic sense. Instead, it is the ratio of two accounting numbers, and it is not comparable to the returns offered, for example, in financial markets.[2]

One of the reasons the AAR is not a true rate of return is that it ignores time value. When we average figures that occur at different times, we are treating the near future and the more distant future the same way. There was no discounting involved when we computed the average net income, for example.

---

[1] We could, of course, calculate the average of the six book values directly. In thousands, we would have ($500 + 400 + 300 + 200 + 100 + 0)/6 = $250.

[2] The AAR is closely related to the return on assets (ROA) discussed in Chapter 3. In practice, the AAR is sometimes computed by first calculating the ROA for each year, and then averaging the results. This produces a number that is similar, but not identical, to the one we computed.

The second problem with the AAR is similar to the problem we had with the payback period rule concerning the lack of an objective cutoff period. Since a calculated AAR is really not comparable to a market return, the target AAR must somehow be specified. There is no generally agreed upon way to do this. One way of doing it is to calculate the AAR for the firm as a whole and use this as a benchmark, but there are lots of other ways as well.

The third, and perhaps worst, flaw in the AAR is that it doesn't even look at the right things. Instead of cash flow and market value, it uses net income and book value. These are both poor substitutes. As a result, an AAR doesn't tell us what the effect on share price will be from taking an investment, so it doesn't tell us what we really want to know.

Does the AAR have any redeeming features? About the only one is that it almost always can be computed. The reason is that accounting information will almost always be available, both for the project under consideration and for the firm as a whole. We hasten to add that once the accounting information is available, we can always convert it to cash flows, so even this is not a particularly important fact. The AAR is summarized in the table below.

Lecture Tip: See IM for a discussion of the frequency of use of the payback and AAR techniques in practice.

Advantages and Disadvantages of the Average Accounting Return

Advantages	Disadvantages
1. Easy to calculate.	1. Not a true rate of return; time value of money is ignored.
2. Needed information will usually be available.	2. Uses an arbitrary benchmark cutoff rate.
	3. Based on accounting (book) values, not cash flows and market values.

CONCEPT QUESTIONS

8.3a What is an average accounting rate of return (AAR)?

8.3b What are the weaknesses of the AAR rule?

8.4 THE INTERNAL RATE OF RETURN

internal rate of return (IRR) The discount rate that makes the NPV of an investment zero.

Self-Test Problem 8.2
Problems 5, 7, 8, 10, 11, 22, 24

★ **Ethics Note:** See IM for an ethics example involving capital budgeting.

We now come to the most important alternative to NPV, the **internal rate of return,** universally known as the IRR. As we will see, the IRR is closely related to NPV. With the IRR, we try to find a single rate of return that summarizes the merits of a project. Furthermore, we want this rate to be an "internal" rate in the sense that it only depends on the cash flows of a particular investment, not on rates offered elsewhere.

To illustrate the idea behind the IRR, consider a project that costs \$100 today and pays \$110 in one year. Suppose you were asked "What is the return on this investment?" What would you say? It seems both natural and obvious to say that the return is 10 percent because, for every dollar we put in, we get \$1.10 back. In fact, as we will see in a moment, 10 percent is the internal rate of return or IRR on this investment.

Lecture Tip: The discussion of the interpretation of a zero-NPV in IM 8.1 also applies to the IRR rule.

Is this project with its 10 percent IRR a good investment? Once again, it would seem apparent that this is a good investment only if our required return is less than 10 percent. This intuition is also correct and illustrates the *IRR rule:*

Based on the IRR rule, an investment is acceptable if the IRR exceeds the required return. It should be rejected otherwise.

Imagine that we wanted to calculate the NPV for our simple investment. At a discount rate of r, the NPV is:

$$\text{NPV} = -\$100 + 110/(1 + r)$$

Now, suppose we didn't know the discount rate. This presents a problem, but we could still ask how high the discount rate would have to be before this project was unacceptable. We know that we are indifferent to taking or not taking this investment when its NPV is just equal to zero. In other words, this investment is *economically* a break-even proposition when the NPV is zero because value is neither created nor destroyed. To find the break-even discount rate, we set NPV equal to zero and solve for r:

$$\begin{aligned} \text{NPV} &= 0 = -\$100 + 110/(1 + r) \\ \$100 &= \$110/(1 + r) \\ 1 + r &= \$110/100 = 1.10 \\ r &= 10\% \end{aligned}$$

This 10 percent is what we already have called the return on this investment. What we have now illustrated is that the internal rate of return on an investment (or just "return" for short) is the discount rate that makes the NPV equal to zero. This is an important observation, so it bears repeating:

The IRR on an investment is the required return that results in a zero NPV when it is used as the discount rate.

The fact that the IRR is simply the discount rate that makes the NPV equal to zero is important because it tells us how to calculate the returns on more complicated investments. As we have seen, finding the IRR turns out to be relatively easy for a single period investment. However, suppose you were now looking at an investment with the cash flows shown in Figure 8.3. As illustrated, this investment costs \$100 and has a cash flow of \$60 per year for two years, so it's only slightly more complicated than our single period example. However, if you were asked for the return on this investment, what would you say? There doesn't seem to be any obvious answer (at least to us). However, based on what we now know, we can set the NPV equal to zero and solve for the discount rate:

$$\text{NPV} = 0 = -\$100 + 60/(1 + \text{IRR}) + 60/(1 + \text{IRR})^2$$

Trans. 8.5
Internal Rate of Return Illustrated (Supplemental)

Unfortunately, the only way to find the IRR in general is by trial and error, either by hand or by calculator. This is precisely the same problem that came up in Chapter 6 when we found the unknown rate for an annuity and in Chapter 7 when we found the yield to maturity on a bond. In fact, we now see that, in both of those cases, we were finding an IRR.

In this particular case, the cash flows form a two-period, \$60 annuity. To find the unknown rate, we can try some different rates until we get the an-

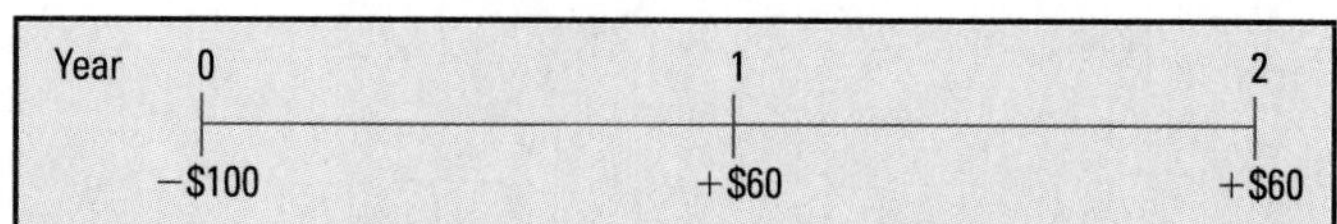

FIGURE 8.3
Project cash flows

TABLE 8.4
NPV at different discount rates

Discount Rate	NPV
0%	$20.00
5	11.56
10	4.13
15	− 2.46
20	− 8.33

swer. If we were to start with a 0 percent rate, the NPV would obviously be $\$120 - 100 = \$20$. At a 10 percent discount rate, we would have:

$$\text{NPV} = -\$100 + 60/1.1 + 60/(1.1)^2 = \$4.13$$

Trans. 8.6
NPV Profile
(Supplemental)

Now, we're getting close. We can summarize these and some other possibilities as shown in Table 8.4. From our calculations, the NPV appears to be zero between 10 percent and 15 percent, so the IRR is somewhere in that range. With a little more effort, we can find that the IRR is about 13.1 percent. So, if our required return is less than 13.1 percent, we would take this investment. If our required return exceeds 13.1 percent, we would reject it.

By now, you have probably noticed that the IRR rule and the NPV rule appear to be quite similar. In fact, the IRR is sometimes simply called the *discounted cash flow* or *DCF return.* The easiest way to illustrate the relationship between NPV and IRR is to plot the numbers we calculated in Table 8.4. We put the different NPVs on the vertical or y-axis and the discount rates on the horizontal or x-axis. If we had a very large number of points, the resulting picture would be a smooth curve called a **net present value profile.** Figure 8.4 illustrates the NPV profile for this project. Beginning with a 0 percent discount rate, we have $20 plotted directly on the y-axis. As the discount rate increases, the NPV declines smoothly. Where will the curve cut through the x-axis? This will occur where the NPV is just equal to zero, so it will happen right at the IRR of 13.1 percent.

net present value profile
A graphical representation of the relationship between an investment's NPVs and various discount rates.

In our example, the NPV rule and the IRR rule lead to identical accept/reject decisions. We will accept an investment using the IRR rule if the re-

FIGURE 8.4
An NPV profile

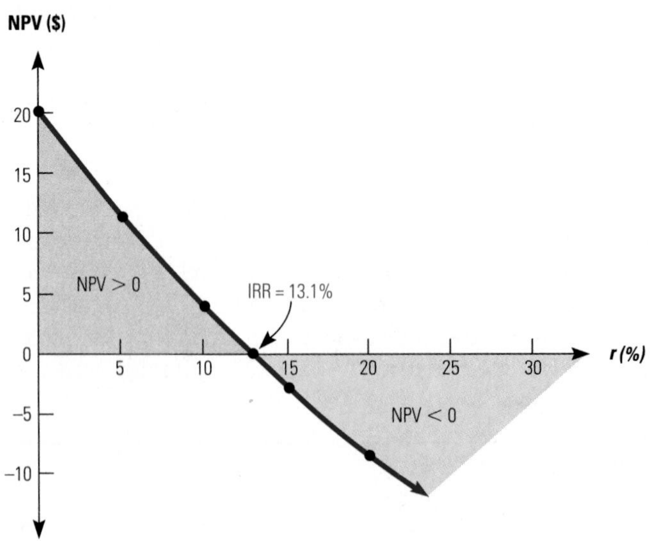

quired return is less than 13.1 percent. As Figure 8.4 illustrates, however, the NPV is positive at any discount rate less than 13.1 percent, so we would accept the investment using the NPV rule as well. The two rules are equivalent in this case.

EXAMPLE 8.3 Calculating the IRR

A project has a total up-front cost of $435.44. The cash flows are $100 in the first year, $200 in the second year, and $300 in the third year. What's the IRR? If we require an 18 percent return, should we take this investment?

We'll describe the NPV profile and find the IRR by calculating some NPVs at different discount rates. You should check our answers for practice. Beginning with 0 percent, we have:

Discount Rate	NPV
0%	$164.56
5	100.36
10	46.15
15	0.00
20	−39.61

The NPV is zero at 15 percent, so 15 percent is the IRR. If we require an 18 percent return, then we should not take the investment. The reason is that the NPV is negative at 18 percent (check that it is −$24.47). The IRR rule tells us the same thing in this case. We shouldn't take this investment because its 15 percent return is below our required 18 percent return. • • •

Lecture Tip: See IM for an example of mutually exclusive projects and multiple discount rates.

At this point, you may be wondering whether the IRR and the NPV rules always lead to identical decisions. The answer is yes as long as two very important conditions are met. First, the project's cash flows must be *conventional,* meaning that the first cash flow (the initial investment) is negative and all the rest are positive. Second, the project must be *independent,* meaning that the decision to accept or reject this project does not affect the decision to accept or reject any other. The first of these conditions is typically met, but the second often is not. In any case, when one or both of these conditions are not met, problems can arise. We discuss some of these next.

Concept Q Answer 8.4a

Problems with the IRR

Trans. 8.7 Multiple Rate of Return (Supplemental Problem)

The problems with the IRR come about when the cash flows are not conventional or when we are trying to compare two or more investments to see which is best. In the first case, surprisingly, the simple question "What's the return?" can become very difficult to answer. In the second case, the IRR can be a misleading guide.

Nonconventional Cash Flows Suppose we have a strip-mining project that requires a $60 investment. Our cash flow in the first year will be $155. In the second year, the mine is depleted, but we have to spend $100 to restore the terrain. As Figure 8.5 illustrates, both the first and third cash flows are negative.

To find the IRR on this project, we can calculate the NPV at various rates:

Discount Rate	NPV
0%	−$5.00
10	− 1.74
20	− 0.28
30	0.06
40	− 0.31

F I G U R E 8.5
Project cash flows

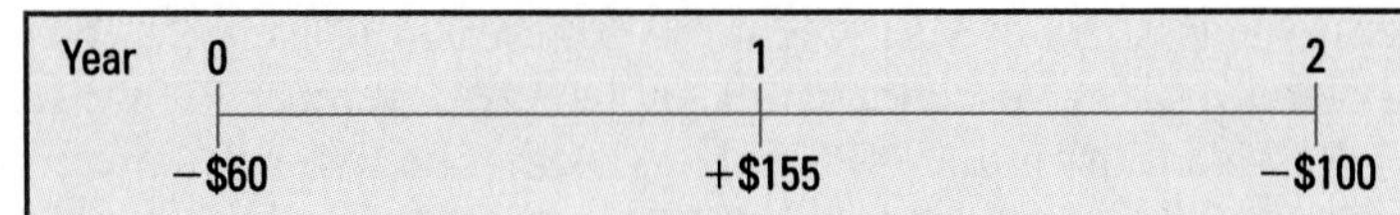

F I G U R E 8.6
NPV profile

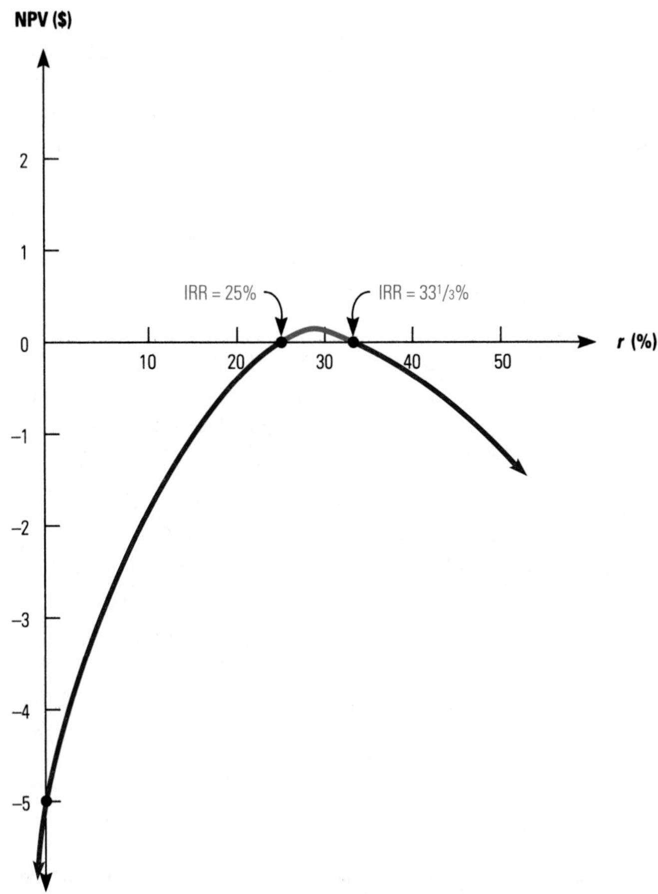

The NPV appears to be behaving in a very peculiar fashion here. First, as the discount rate increases from 0 percent to 30 percent, the NPV starts out negative and becomes positive. This seems backwards because the NPV is rising as the discount rate rises. It then starts getting smaller and becomes negative again. What's the IRR? To find out, we draw the NPV profile in Figure 8.6.

In Figure 8.6, notice that the NPV is zero when the discount rate is 25 percent, so this is the IRR. Or is it? The NPV is also zero at 33⅓ percent. Which of these is correct? The answer is both or neither; more precisely, there is no unambiguously correct answer. This is the **multiple rates of return** problem. Many financial computer packages aren't aware of this problem and just report the first IRR that is found. Others report only the smallest positive IRR, even though this answer is no better than any other.

multiple rates of return
The possibility that more than one discount rate makes the NPV of an investment zero.

In our current example, the IRR rule breaks down completely. Suppose our required return were 10 percent. Should we take this investment? Both IRRs are greater than 10 percent, so, by the IRR rule, maybe we should. However, as Figure 8.6 shows, the NPV is negative at any discount rate less than 25 percent, so this is not a good investment. When should we take it? Looking at Figure 8.6 one last time, the NPV is positive only if our required return is between 25 percent and 33⅓ percent.

The moral of the story is that when the cash flows aren't conventional, strange things can start to happen to the IRR. This is not anything to get upset about, however, because the NPV rule, as always, works just fine. This illustrates that, oddly enough, the obvious question—What's the rate of return?—may not always have a good answer.

EXAMPLE 8.4 What's the IRR?

You are looking at an investment that requires you to invest $51 today. You'll get $100 in one year, but you must pay out $50 in two years. What is the IRR on this investment?

You're on the alert now to the nonconventional cash flow problem, so you probably wouldn't be surprised to see more than one IRR. However, if you start looking for an IRR by trial and error, it will take you a long time. The reason is that there is no IRR. The NPV is negative at every discount rate, so we shouldn't take this investment under any circumstances. What's the return on this investment? Your guess is as good as ours. • • •

Mutually Exclusive Investments Even if there is a single IRR, another problem can arise concerning **mutually exclusive investment decisions.** If two investments, X and Y, are mutually exclusive, then taking one of them means that we cannot take the other. Two projects that are not mutually exclusive are said to be independent. For example, if we own one corner lot, then we can build a gas station or an apartment building, but not both. These are mutually exclusive alternatives.

mutually exclusive investment decisions
A situation where taking one investment prevents the taking of another.

Thus far, we have asked whether or not a given investment is worth undertaking. There is a related question, however, that comes up very often: Given two or more mutually exclusive investments, which one is the best? The answer is simple enough: The best one is the one with the largest NPV. Can we also say that the best one has the highest return? As we show, the answer is no.

To illustrate the problem with the IRR rule and mutually exclusive investments, consider the cash flows from the following two mutually exclusive investments:

Year	Investment A	Investment B
0	−$100	−$100
1	50	20
2	40	40
3	40	50
4	30	60
IRR	24%	21%

Since these investments are mutually exclusive, we can only take one of them. Simple intuition suggests that Investment A is better because of its higher return. Unfortunately, simple intuition is not always correct.

To see why Investment A is not necessarily the better of the two investments, we've calculated the NPV of these investments for different required returns:

Discount Rate	NPV(A)	NPV(B)
0%	$60.00	$70.00
5	43.13	47.88
10	29.06	29.79
15	17.18	14.82
20	7.06	2.31
25	−1.63	−8.22

The IRR for A (24%) is larger than the IRR for B (21%). However, if you compare the NPVs, you'll see that which investment has the higher NPV depends on our required return. B has greater total cash flow, but it pays back more slowly than A. As a result, it has a higher NPV at lower discount rates.

In our example, the NPV and IRR rankings conflict for some discount rates. If our required return is 10 percent, for instance, then B has the higher NPV and is thus the better of the two even though A has the higher return. If our required return is 15 percent, then there is no ranking conflict: A is better.

Trans. 8.8
IRR, NPV, and Mutually Exclusive Projects (Supplemental)

The conflict between the IRR and NPV for mutually exclusive investments can be illustrated by plotting their NPV profiles as we have done in Figure 8.7. In Figure 8.7, notice that the NPV profiles cross at about 11 percent. Notice also that at any discount rate less than 11.1 percent, the NPV for B is higher. In this range, taking B benefits us more than taking A, even though A's IRR is higher. At any rate greater than 11.1 percent, Investment A has the greater NPV.

FIGURE 8.7
NPV profiles for mutually exclusive investments

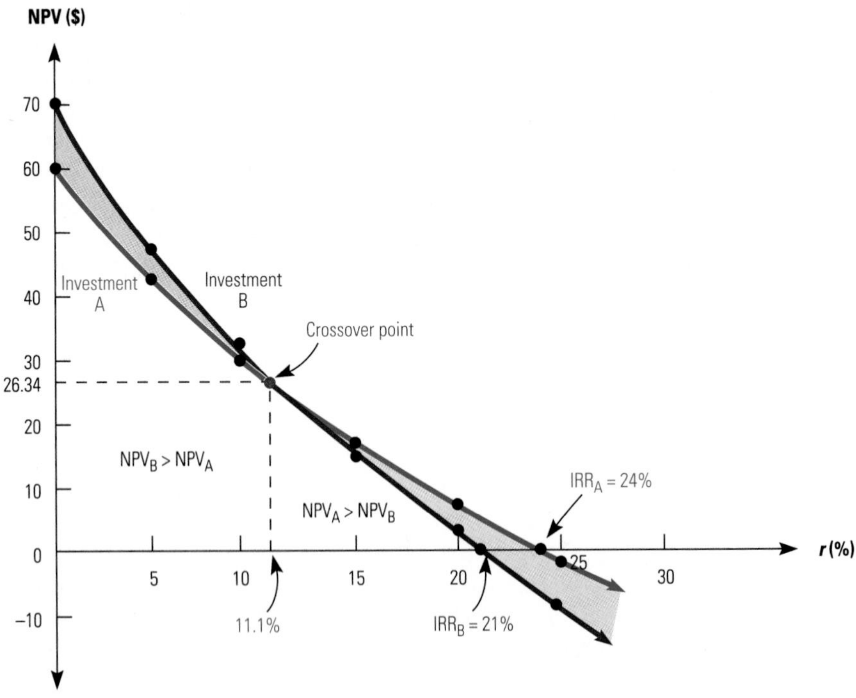

This example illustrates that whenever we have mutually exclusive projects, we shouldn't rank them based on their returns. More generally, anytime we are comparing investments to determine which is best, IRRs can be misleading. Instead, we need to look at the relative NPVs to avoid the possibility of choosing incorrectly. Remember, we're ultimately interested in creating value for the shareholders, so the option with the higher NPV is preferred, regardless of the relative returns.

If this seems counterintuitive, think of it this way. Suppose you have two investments. One has a 10 percent return and makes you $100 richer immediately. The other has a 20 percent return and makes you $50 richer immediately. Which one do you like better? We would rather have $100 than $50, regardless of the returns, so we like the first one better.

Redeeming Qualities of the IRR

Despite its flaws, the IRR is very popular in practice, more so than even the NPV. It probably survives because it fills a need that the NPV does not. In analyzing investments, people in general, and financial analysts in particular, seem to prefer talking about rates of return rather than dollar values.

In a similar vein, the IRR also appears to provide a simple way of communicating information about a proposal. One manager might say to another: "Remodeling the clerical wing has a 20 percent return." This may somehow be simpler than saying: "At a 10 percent discount rate, the net present value is $4,000."

Finally, under certain circumstances, the IRR may have a practical advantage over the NPV. We can't estimate the NPV unless we know the appropriate discount rate, but we can still estimate the IRR. Suppose we didn't know the required return on an investment, but we found, for example, that it had a 40 percent return. We would probably be inclined to take it since it is very unlikely that the required return is that high. The advantages and disadvantages of the IRR are summarized below.

Concept Q Answer 8.4b

Advantages and Disadvantages of the Internal Rate of Return

Advantages	Disadvantages
1. Closely related to NPV, often leading to identical decisions.	1. May result in multiple answers with nonconventional cash flows.
2. Easy to understand and communicate.	2. May lead to incorrect decisions in comparisons of mutually exclusive investments.

CONCEPT QUESTIONS

8.4a Under what circumstances will the IRR and NPV rules lead to the same accept/reject decisions? When might they conflict?

8.4b Is it generally true that an advantage of the IRR rule over the NPV rule is that we don't need to know the required return to use the IRR rule?

8.5 THE PROFITABILITY INDEX

Another method used to evaluate projects is called the **profitability index (PI)** or benefit/cost ratio. This index is defined as the present value of the future cash flows divided by the initial investment. So, if a project costs $200 and

profitability index (PI)
The present value of an investment's future cash flows divided by its initial cost. Also benefit/cost ratio.

the present value of its future cash flows is $220, the profitability index value would be $220/200 = 1.10. Notice that the NPV for this investment is $20, so it is a desirable investment.

Problems 12, 13, 19, 23

More generally, if a project has a positive NPV, then the present value of the future cash flows must be bigger than the initial investment. The profitability index would thus be bigger than 1.00 for a positive NPV investment and less than 1.00 for a negative NPV investment.

Concept Q Answers 8.5a, 8.5b

How do we interpret the profitability index? In our example, the PI was 1.10. This tells us that, per dollar invested, $1.10 in value or $.10 in NPV results. The profitability index thus measures "bang for the buck," that is, the value created per dollar invested. For this reason, it is often proposed as a measure of performance for government or other not-for-profit investments. Also, when capital is scarce, it may make sense to allocate it to those projects with the highest PIs.

The PI is obviously very similar to the NPV. However, consider an investment that costs $5 and has a $10 present value and an investment that costs $100 with a $150 present value. The first of these investments has an NPV of $5 and a PI of 2. The second has an NPV of $50 and a PI of 1.50. If these were mutually exclusive investments, then the second one is preferred even though it has a lower PI. This ranking problem is very similar to the IRR ranking problem we saw in the previous section. In all, there seems to be little reason to rely on the PI instead of the NPV. Our discussion of the PI is summarized below.

Advantages and Disadvantages of the Profitability Index

Advantages	Disadvantages
1. Closely related to NPV, generally leading to identical decisions.	1. May lead to incorrect decisions in comparisons of mutually exclusive investments
2. Easy to understand and communicate.	
3. May be useful when available investment funds are limited.	

CONCEPT QUESTIONS

8.5a What does the profitability index measure?

8.5b How would you state the profitability index rule?

8.6 THE PRACTICE OF CAPITAL BUDGETING

Given that NPV seems to be telling us directly what we want to know, you might be wondering why there are so many other procedures and why alternative procedures are commonly used. Recall that we are trying to make an investment decision and that we are frequently operating under considerable uncertainty about the future. We can only *estimate* the NPV of an investment in this case. The resulting estimate can be very "soft," meaning that the true NPV might be quite different.

Concept Q Answer 8.6b

Because the true NPV is unknown, the astute financial manager seeks clues to assess whether the estimated NPV is reliable. For this reason, firms would typically use multiple criteria for evaluating a proposal. For example, suppose we have an investment with a positive estimated NPV. Based on our experience with other projects, this one appears to have a short payback and a very high AAR. In this case, the different indicators seem to agree that it's "all systems go." Put another way, the payback and the AAR are consistent with the conclusion that the NPV is positive.

On the other hand, suppose we had a positive estimated NPV, a long payback, and a low AAR. This could still be a good investment, but it looks like we need to be much more careful in making the decision since we are getting conflicting signals. If the estimated NPV is based on projections in which we have little confidence, then further analysis is probably in order. We will consider how to go about this analysis in more detail in the next chapter.

Lecture Tip: See IM for additional reasons for using multiple criteria.

There have been a number of surveys conducted asking firms what types of investment criteria they actually use. Table 8.5 summarizes the results of several of these. The first part of the table examines large U.S. firms and large multinationals. For the large U.S. firms, the figure given is the percentage of firms that use each of the methods. One thing we see is that payback periods are very common; over 80 percent of the firms report using it. The least common approach is the AAR, but even so, 59 percent of these large firms report using it. For the multinational firms, we have the primary and secondary methods reported separately. Based on our discussion, we are not surprised to see that IRR is the most commonly used approach. About two-thirds of these firms use it as their primary method, and over 80 percent use either NPV or IRR. Payback is only rarely used as the primary criterion, but it is the most commonly used secondary method.

Concept Q Answer 8.6a

The second part of the table is an historical comparison looking at the primary capital budgeting technique used by large firms through time. In 1959, only 19 percent of the firms surveyed used either IRR or NPV, and 68 percent used either payback periods or accounting returns. Through time, it is clear that IRR and NPV have become the dominant criteria. In fact, these two approaches have become so commonplace today that surveys such as the

TABLE 8.5 Capital budgeting techniques in practice

A. Comparison of Capital Budgeting Practices of Large U.S. and Multinational Firms

	Large U.S. Firms	Multinationals	
	Percentage Using Each Method	Use as Primary Method	Use as Secondary Method
Payback Period	80.3%	5.0%	37.6%
Accounting Rate of Return (ARR)	59.0	10.7	14.6
Internal Rate of Return (IRR)	65.5	65.3	14.6
Net Present Value (NPV)	67.6	16.5	30.0
Other	—	2.5	3.2

B. Historical Comparison of the Primary Use of Various Capital Budgeting Techniques

	1959	1964	1970	1975	1977	1979	1981
Payback Period	34%	24%	12%	15%	9%	10%	5.0%
Accounting Rate of Return (ARR)	34	30	26	10	25	14	10.7
Internal Rate of Return (IRR)	19	38	57	37	54	60	65.3
Net Present Value (NPV)	—	—	—	26	10	14	16.5
IRR or NPV	19	38	57	63	64	74	81.8

Sources: J. S. Moore and A. K. Reichert, "An Analysis of the Financial Management Techniques Currently Employed by Large U.S. Corporations," *Journal of Business Finance and Accounting* (Winter 1983) pp. 623–45; M. T. Stanley and S. R. Block, "A Survey of Multinational Capital Budgeting," *The Financial Review* (March 1984) pp. 36–51.

TABLE 8.6 Summary of investment criteria

I. Discounted Cash Flow Criteria

A. *Net present value (NPV).* The NPV of an investment is the difference between its market value and its cost. The NPV rule is to take a project if its NPV is positive. NPV is frequently estimated by calculating the present value of the future cash flows (to estimate market value) and then subtracting the cost. NPV has no serious flaws; it is the preferred decision criterion.

B. *Internal rate of return (IRR).* The IRR is the discount rate that makes the estimated NPV of an investment equal to zero; it is sometimes called the *discounted cash flow (DCF) return.* The IRR rule is to take a project when its IRR exceeds the required return. IRR is closely related to NPV, and it leads to exactly the same decisions as NPV for conventional, independent projects. When project cash flows are not conventional, there may be no IRR or there may be more than one. More seriously, the IRR cannot be used to rank mutually exclusive projects; the project with the highest IRR is not necessarily the preferred investment.

C. *Profitability index (PI).* The PI, also called the *benefit/cost ratio,* is the ratio of present value to cost. The PI rule is to take an investment if the index exceeds 1. The PI measures the present value of an investment per dollar invested. It is quite similar to NPV, but, like IRR, it cannot be used to rank mutually exclusive projects. However, it is sometimes used to rank projects when a firm has more positive NPV investments than it can currently finance.

II. Payback Criteria

A. *Payback period.* The payback period is the length of time until the sum of an investment's cash flows equals its cost. The payback period rule is to take a project if its payback is *less* than some cutoff. The payback period is a flawed criterion primarily because it ignores risk, the time value of money, and cash flows beyond the cutoff point.

III. Accounting Criteria

A. *Average accounting return (AAR).* The AAR is a measure of accounting profit relative to book value. It is *not* related to the IRR, but it is similar to the accounting return on assets (ROA) measure in Chapter 3. The AAR rule is to take an investment if its AAR exceeds a benchmark AAR. The AAR is seriously flawed for a variety of reasons, and it has little to recommend it.

ones we have relied on in preparing Table 8.5 seem to have dried up, so our data end in 1981. For future reference, the various criteria we have discussed are summarized in Table 8.6.

CONCEPT QUESTIONS

8.6a What are the most commonly used capital budgeting procedures?

8.6b Since NPV is conceptually the best procedure for capital budgeting, why do you think multiple measures are used in practice?

8.7 SUMMARY AND CONCLUSIONS

This chapter has covered the different criteria used to evaluate proposed investments. The five criteria, in the order we discussed them, are:

1. Net present value (NPV).
2. Payback period.
3. Average accounting return (AAR).
4. Internal rate of return (IRR).
5. Profitability index (PI).

We illustrated how to calculate each of these and discussed the interpretation of the results. We also described the advantages and disadvantages of each of them. Ultimately, a good capital budgeting criterion must tell us two things. First, is a particular project a good investment? Second, if we have more than one good project, but we can only take one of them, which one should we take? The main point of this chapter is that only the NPV criterion can always provide the correct answer to both questions.

For this reason, NPV is one of the two or three most important concepts in finance, and we will refer to it many times in the chapters ahead. When we do, keep two things in mind: (1) NPV is always just the difference between the market value of an asset or project and its cost; and (2) the financial manager acts in the shareholders' best interests by identifying and taking positive NPV projects.

Finally, we noted that NPVs can't normally be observed in the market; instead, they must be estimated. Because there is always the possibility of a poor estimate, financial managers use multiple criteria for examining projects. These other criteria provide additional information about whether a project truly has a positive NPV.

Chapter Review Problems and Self-Test

8.1 Investment Criteria This problem will give you some practice calculating NPVs and paybacks. A proposed overseas expansion has the following cash flows:

Year	Cash Flow
0	−$100
1	50
2	40
3	40
4	15

Calculate the payback and NPV at a required return of 15 percent.

8.2 Mutually Exclusive Investments Consider the following two mutually exclusive investments. Calculate the IRR for each. Under what circumstances will the IRR and NPV criteria rank the two projects differently?

Year	Investment A	Investment B
0	−$100	−$100
1	50	70
2	70	75
3	40	10

8.3 Average Accounting Return You are looking at a three-year project with a projected net income of $1,000 in Year 1, $2,000 in Year 2, and $4,000 in Year 3. The cost is $9,000, which will be depreciated straight-line to zero over the three-year life of the project. What is the average accounting return (AAR)?

Answers to Self-Test Problems

8.1 In the table below, we have listed the cash flows and their discounted values (at 15%).

Cash Flows and Accumulated Cash Flows

	Cash Flow	
Year	Undiscounted	Discounted (at 15%)
1	$ 50	$ 43.5
2	40	30.2
3	40	26.3
4	15	8.6
Total	$145	$108.6

Recall that the initial investment is $100. Examining the undiscounted cash flows, we see that the payback occurs between

Years 2 and 3. The cash flows for the first two years are $90 total, so, going into the third year, we are short by $10. The total cash flow in Year 3 is $40, so the payback is 2 + $10/40 = 2.25 years.

Looking at the discounted cash flows, we see that the sum is $108.6, so the NPV is $8.6.

8.2 To calculate the IRR, we might try some guesses as in the following table:

Discount Rate	NPV(A)	NPV(B)
0%	$60.00	$55.00
10	33.36	33.13
20	13.43	16.20
30	− 1.91	2.78
40	− 14.01	− 8.09

Several things are immediately apparent from our guesses. First, the IRR on A must be just a little less than 30 percent (why?). With some more effort, we find that it's 28.61 percent. For B, the IRR must be a little more than 30 percent (again, why?); it works out to be 32.37 percent. Also, notice that at 10 percent, the NPVs are very close, indicating that the NPV profiles cross in that vicinity. Check that the NPVs are the same at 10.61 percent.

Now, the IRR for B is always higher. As we've seen, A has the larger NPV for any discount rate less than 10.61 percent, so the NPV and IRR rankings will conflict in that range. Remember, if there's a conflict, we will go with the higher NPV. Our decision rule is thus very simple: Take A if the required return is less than 10.61 percent, take B if the required return is between 10.61 percent and 32.37 percent (the IRR on B), and take neither if the required return is more than 32.37 percent.

8.3 Here we need to calculate the ratio of average net income to average book value to get the AAR. Average net income is:

$$\begin{aligned}\text{Average net income} &= (\$1{,}000 + 2{,}000 + 4{,}000)/3 \\ &= \$2{,}333.33\end{aligned}$$

Average book value is:

$$\text{Average book value} = \$9{,}000/2 = \$4{,}500$$

So the average accounting return is:

$$\text{AAR} = \$2{,}333.33/4{,}500 = 51.85\%$$

This is an impressive return. Remember, however, that it isn't really a rate of return like an interest rate or an IRR, so the size doesn't tell us a lot. In particular, our money is probably not going to grow at 51.85 percent per year, sorry to say.

Questions and Problems

Basic (Questions 1–17)

1. **Calculating Payback** What is the payback period for the following set of cash flows?

Year	Cash Flow
0	−$2,000
1	800
2	600
3	900
4	300

2.67 years

2. **Calculating Payback** An investment project provides annual cash inflows of $750 per year for eight years. What is the project payback period if the initial cost is $2,500? What if the initial cost is $5,000? $7,500?

a. 3.33 years
b. 6.67 years
c. Never

3. **Calculating Payback** John's Bakery Products, Inc., imposes a payback cutoff of 2.5 years for its investment projects. If the company has the following two projects available, should they accept either of them?

Payback A = 1.56 years
Payback B = 2.80 years
Trans. 8.9

Year	Cash Flows A	Cash Flows B
0	−$25,000	−$ 72,000
1	16,000	30,000
2	16,000	30,000
3	3,000	15,000
4	3,000	200,000

4. **Calculating AAR** You're trying to determine whether or not to expand your business by building a new manufacturing plant. The plant has an installation cost of $2 million, which will be depreciated straight-line to zero over its four-year life. If the project has projected net income of $417,000, $329,500, $216,200, and $48,000 over these four years, what is the project's average accounting return (AAR)?

AAR = 25.27%

5. **Calculating IRR** A firm evaluates all of its projects by applying the IRR rule. If the required return is 14 percent, should the firm accept the following project?

IRR = 16.11%

Year	Cash Flow
0	−$15,000
1	10,000
2	0
3	10,000

6. **Calculating NPV** For the cash flows in the previous problem, suppose the firm uses the NPV decision rule. At a required return of 14 percent, should the firm accept this project? What if the required return was 18 percent?

a. NPV = $521.64
b. NPV = −$439.12
Trans. 8.10

7. **Calculating NPV and IRR** A project that provides annual cash flows of $200 for seven years costs $1,000 today. Is this a good project if the required return is 7 percent? What if it's 15 percent?

@7%: NPV = $77.86
@15%: NPV = −$167.92

8. **Calculating IRR** What is the IRR of the following set of cash flows?

20.61%

Year	Cash Flow
0	−$600
1	200
2	300
3	400

a. \$300
b. \$130.28
c. \$6.48
d. −\$86.57

9. Calculating NPV For the cash flows in the previous problem, what is the NPV at a discount rate of zero percent? What if the discount rate is 10 percent? 20 percent? 30 percent?

a. IRR_L = 10.12%
IRR_S = 11.46%
b. NPV_L = \$336.67
NPV_S = \$377.54

10. NPV versus IRR The Heitman Group, Inc., has identified the following two mutually exclusive projects:

Year	Cash Flows L	Cash Flows S
0	−\$10,000	−\$10,000
1	200	5,000
2	500	6,000
3	8,200	500
4	4,800	500

a. What is the IRR for each of these projects? If you apply the IRR decision rule, which project should the company accept? Is this decision necessarily correct?
b. If the required return is 9 percent, what is the NPV for each of these projects? Which project will you choose if you apply the NPV decision rule?

a. NPV = \$25.62
b. IRR = +13.81%; −80.47%

11. Problems with IRR Friedlich Co. is trying to evaluate a project with the following cash flows:

Year	Cash Flow
0	−\$ 900
1	1,200
2	− 200

a. If the company requires a 10 percent return on its investments, should it accept this project? Why?
b. Compute the IRR for this project. How many IRRs are there? If you apply the IRR decision rule, should you accept the project or not? What's going on here?

a. 1.119
b. 1.049
c. 0.958

12. Calculating Profitability Index What is the profitability index for the following set of cash flows if the relevant discount rate is 8 percent? What if the discount rate is 12 percent? 18 percent?

Year	Cash Flow
0	−\$1,400
1	800
2	500
3	500

a. PI_X = 1.044
PI_Y = 1.201
b. NPV_X = \$1,018.31
NPV_Y = \$803.66

13. Problems with Profitability Index The Bundy Valve Corporation is trying to choose between the two mutually exclusive projects below.

Year	Cash Flows X	Cash Flows Y
0	−\$23,000	−\$4,000
1	10,000	2,000
2	10,000	2,000
3	10,000	2,000

a. If the required return is 12 percent and Bundy applies the profitability index decision rule, which project should the firm accept?
b. If the company applies the NPV decision rule, which project should it take?
c. Explain why your answers in (*a*) and (*b*) are different.

14. **Comparing Investment Criteria** Consider the following two mutually exclusive projects:

Year	Cash Flows A	Cash Flows B
0	−$260,000	−$40,000
1	5,000	45,000
2	15,000	5,000
3	15,000	500
4	425,000	500

Whichever project you choose, if any, you require a 15 percent return on your investment.

a. If you apply the payback criterion, which investment will you choose? Why?
b. If you apply the NPV criterion, which investment will you choose? Why?
c. If you apply the IRR criterion, which investment will you choose? Why?
d. If you apply the profitability index criterion, which investment will you choose? Why?
e. Based on your answers in (*a*) through (*d*), which project will you finally choose? Why?

a. Payback A = 3.53 years
Payback B = 0.89 years
b. NPV_A = $8,547.85
NPV_B = $3,525.79
c. IRR_A = 15.98%
IRR_B = 24.04%
d. PI_A = 1.033
PI_B = 1.088
Trans. 8.11

15. **NPV and Discount Rates** An investment has an installed cost of $176,515. The cash flows over the four-year life of the investment are projected to be $58,675, $63,116, $69,370, and $72,000. If the discount rate is zero, what is the NPV? If the discount rate is infinite, what is the NPV? At what discount rate is the NPV just equal to zero? Sketch the NPV profile for this investment based on these three points.

@0%: NPV = $86,646
@∞: NPV = −$176,515
@17.41%: NPV = 0

16. **Payback Intuition** If a project with conventional cash flows has a payback period less than the project's life, can you definitively state the algebraic sign of NPV? Why or why not? If you know that the discounted payback period is less than the project's life, what can you say about the NPV now? Explain.

17. **Investment Criteria and Their Relationships** Suppose a project has conventional cash flows and a positive NPV. What do you know about its payback? Its profitability index? Its IRR? Explain.

Intermediate (Questions 18–25)

18. **Interpreting Payback**
a. Describe how the payback period is calculated, and describe the information this measure provides about a sequence of cash flows. What is the payback criterion decision rule?
b. What are the problems associated with using the payback period as a means of evaluating cash flows?
c. What are the advantages of using the payback period to evaluate cash flows? Are there any circumstances where using payback might be appropriate? Explain.

19. **NPV and the Profitability Index** If we define the NPV index as the ratio of NPV to cost, what is the relationship between this index and the profitability index?

NPV index = PI − 1

20. **Interpreting AAR**
   a. Describe how the average accounting return is usually calculated, and describe the information this measure provides about a sequence of cash flows. What is the AAR criterion decision rule?
   b. What are the problems associated with using AAR as a means of evaluating a project's cash flows? What underlying feature of AAR is most troubling to you from a financial perspective? Does the AAR have any redeeming qualities?

21. **Interpreting NPV**
   a. Describe how NPV is calculated, and describe the information this measure provides about a sequence of cash flows. What is the NPV criterion decision rule?
   b. Why is NPV considered to be a superior method of evaluating the cash flows from a project? Suppose the NPV for a project's cash flows is computed to be $2,500. What does this number represent with respect to the firm's shareholders?

22. **Interpreting IRR**
   a. Describe how IRR is calculated, and describe the information this measure provides about a sequence of cash flows. What is the IRR criterion decision rule?
   b. What is the relationship between IRR and NPV? Are there any situations where you might prefer one method over the other? Explain.
   c. Despite its shortcomings in some situations, why do most financial managers use IRR along with NPV when evaluating projects? Can you think of a situation where IRR might be a more appropriate measure to use than NPV? Explain.

23. **Interpreting Profitability Index**
   a. Describe how the profitability index is calculated, and describe the information this measure provides about a sequence of cash flows. What is the profitability index decision rule?
   b. What is the relationship between the profitability index and NPV? Are there any situations where you might prefer one method over the other? Explain.

IRR = 1/payback

24. **Payback and IRR** A project has perpetual cash flows of $*C* per period, a cost of $*I*, and a required return of *r*. What is the relationship between the project's payback and its IRR? What implications does your answer have for long-lived projects with relatively constant cash flows?

IRR = 25%; 33.33%; 42.85%; 66.67%

25. **Multiple IRRs** This problem is useful for testing the ability of financial calculators and computer software. Consider the following cash flows. When should we take this project (Hint: Search for IRRs between 20 percent and 70 percent.)?

Year	Cash Flow
0	−$ 252
1	1,431
2	− 3,035
3	2,850
4	− 1,000

Chapter Nine

9

Making Capital Investment Decisions

• • •

After studying this chapter, you should have a good understanding of:

. . .

How to determine the relevant cash flows for a proposed investment.

. . .

How to analyze a project's projected cash flows.

. . .

How to evaluate an estimated NPV.

So far, we've covered various parts of the capital budgeting decision. Our task in this chapter is to start bringing these pieces together. In particular, we will show you how to "spread the numbers" for a proposed investment or project and, based on those numbers, make an initial assessment about whether or not the project should be undertaken.

Trans. 9.1
Chapter Outline

In the discussion that follows, we focus on the process of setting up a discounted cash flow analysis. From the last chapter, we know the projected future cash flows are the key element in such an evaluation. Accordingly, we emphasize working with financial and accounting information to come up with these figures.

In evaluating a proposed investment, we pay special attention to deciding what information is relevant to the decision at hand and what information is not. As we shall see, it is easy to overlook important pieces of the capital budgeting puzzle. We also describe how to go about evaluating the results of our discounted cash flow analysis.

Lecture Tip: We continue to assume that the required return on a capital budgeting project is known to the analyst. The estimation of required returns is discussed in later chapters.

9.1 PROJECT CASH FLOWS: A FIRST LOOK

The effect of taking a project is to change the firm's overall cash flows today and in the future. To evaluate a proposed investment, we must consider these changes in the firm's cash flows and then decide whether or not they add value to the firm. The first (and most important) step, therefore, is to decide which cash flows are relevant and which are not.

Relevant Cash Flows

Concept Q Answer 9.1a

Trans. 9.2 Relevant Cash Flows (Supplemental)

incremental cash flows
The difference between a firm's future cash flows with a project or without the project.

What is a relevant cash flow for a project? The general principle is simple enough: A relevant cash flow for a project is a change in the firm's overall future cash flow that comes about as a direct consequence of the decision to take that project. Because the relevant cash flows are defined in terms of changes in or increments to the firm's existing cash flow, they are called the **incremental cash flows** associated with the project.

The concept of incremental cash flow is central to our analysis, so we will state a general definition and refer back to it as needed:

> **The incremental cash flows for project evaluation consist of *any and all* changes in the firm's future cash flows that are a direct consequence of taking the project.**

Lecture Tip: See IM for more examples that facilitate consideration of incremental cash flows.

This definition of incremental cash flows has an obvious and important corollary: Any cash flow that exists regardless of whether or *not* a project is undertaken is *not* relevant.

The Stand-Alone Principle

Concept Q Answer 9.1b

stand-alone principle
Evaluation of a project based on the project's incremental cash flows.

In practice, it would be very cumbersome to actually calculate the future total cash flows to the firm with and without a project, especially for a large firm. Fortunately, it is not really necessary to do so. Once we identify the effect of undertaking the proposed project on the firm's cash flows, we need only focus on the project's resulting incremental cash flows. This is called the **stand-alone principle**.

What the stand-alone principle says is that, once we have determined the incremental cash flows from undertaking a project, we can view that project as a kind of "minifirm" with its own future revenues and costs, its own assets, and, of course, its own cash flows. We will then be primarily interested in comparing the cash flows from this minifirm to the cost of acquiring it. An important consequence of this approach is that we will be evaluating the proposed project purely on its own merits, in isolation from any other activities or projects.

CONCEPT QUESTIONS

9.1a What are the relevant incremental cash flows for project evaluation?

9.1b What is the stand-alone principle?

9.2 INCREMENTAL CASH FLOWS

Problems 2, 3, 10

We are concerned here only with those cash flows that are incremental to a project. Looking back at our general definition, it seems easy enough to decide whether a cash flow is incremental or not. Even so, there are a few situations when mistakes are easy to make. In this section, we describe some of these common pitfalls and how to avoid them.

Sunk Costs

sunk cost
A cost that has already been incurred and cannot be removed and therefore should not be considered in an investment decision.

A **sunk cost,** by definition, is a cost we have already paid or have already incurred the liability to pay. Such a cost cannot be changed by the decision today to accept or reject a project. Put another way, the firm will have to pay this cost no matter what. Based on our general definition of incremental cash flow, such a cost is clearly not relevant to the decision at hand. So, we will always be careful to exclude sunk costs from our analysis.

Concept Q Answer 9.2a

Lecture Tip: See IM for an example utilizing sunk costs to share in class.

That a sunk cost is not relevant seems obvious given our discussion. Nonetheless, it's easy to fall prey to the sunk cost fallacy. For example, suppose General Milk Company hires a financial consultant to help evaluate whether or not a line of chocolate milk should be launched. When the consultant turns in the report, General Milk objects to the analysis because the consultant did not include the hefty consulting fee as a cost to the chocolate milk project.

Who is correct? By now, we know that the consulting fee is a sunk cost, because the consulting fee must be paid whether or not the chocolate milk line is actually launched (this is an attractive feature of the consulting business).

Opportunity Costs

When we think of costs, we normally think of out-of-pocket costs, namely, those that require us to actually spend some amount of cash. An **opportunity cost** is slightly different; it requires us to give up a benefit. A common situation arises where a firm already owns some of the assets a proposed project will be using. For example, we might be thinking of converting an old rustic cotton mill we bought years ago for $100,000 into "upmarket" condominiums.

opportunity cost
The most valuable alternative that is given up if a particular investment is undertaken.

If we undertake this project, there will be no direct cash outflow associated with buying the old mill since we already own it. For purposes of evaluating the condo project, should we then treat the mill as "free"? The answer is no. The mill is a valuable resource used by the project. If we didn't use it here, we could do something else with it. Like what? The obvious answer is that, at a minimum, we could sell it. Using the mill for the condo complex thus has an opportunity cost: We give up the valuable opportunity to do something else with it.[1]

Concept Q Answer 9.2a

Lecture Tip: The use of current market value as the appropriate opportunity cost of an asset implies that the asset is routinely traded in the marketplace. The difficulties inherent in valuing unique assets make the estimation of opportunity costs more problematic.

There is another issue here. Once we agree that the use of the mill has an opportunity cost, how much should the condo project be charged? Given that we paid $100,000, it might seem that we should charge this amount to the condo project. Is this correct? The answer is no, and the reason is based on our discussion concerning sunk costs.

The fact that we paid $100,000 some years ago is irrelevant. It's sunk. At a minimum, the opportunity cost that we charge the project is what the mill would sell for today (net of any selling costs) because this is the amount that we give up by using it instead of selling it.

Side Effects

Remember that the incremental cash flows for a project include all the changes in the *firm's* future cash flows. It would not be unusual for a project to have side or spillover effects, both good and bad. For example, if the Innovative Motors Company (IMC) introduces a new car, some of the sales might come at the expense of other IMC cars. This is called **erosion,** and the same

erosion
The cash flows of a new project that come at the expense of a firm's existing projects.

[1] Economists sometimes use the acronym "TANSTAAFL," which is short for "There ain't no such thing as a free lunch," to describe the fact that only very rarely is something truly free.

Concept Q Answer 9.2b

★ **Ethics Note:** An ethical dilemma related to the side-effects issue is presented in IM 9.2.

general problem could occur for any multiline consumer producer or seller.[2] In this case, the cash flows from the new line should be adjusted downward to reflect lost profits on other lines.

In accounting for erosion, it is important to recognize that any sales lost as a result of our launching a new product might be lost anyway because of future competition. Erosion is only relevant when the sales would not otherwise be lost.

Net Working Capital

Normally, a project will require that the firm invest in net working capital in addition to long-term assets. For example, a project will generally need some amount of cash on hand to pay any expenses that arise. In addition, a project will need an initial investment in inventories and accounts receivable (to cover credit sales). Some of this financing will be in the form of amounts owed to suppliers (accounts payable), but the firm will have to supply the balance. This balance represents the investment in net working capital.

It's easy to overlook an important feature of net working capital in capital budgeting. As a project winds down, inventories are sold, receivables are collected, bills are paid, and cash balances can be drawn down. These activities free up the net working capital originally invested. So, the firm's investment in project net working capital closely resembles a loan. The firm supplies working capital at the beginning and recovers it towards the end.

Financing Costs

Concept Q Answer 9.2c

In analyzing a proposed investment, we will *not* include interest paid or any other financing costs such as dividends or principal repaid, because we are interested in the cash flow generated by the assets of the project. As we mentioned in Chapter 2, interest paid, for example, is a component of cash flow to creditors, not cash flow from assets.

More generally, our goal in project evaluation is to compare the cash flow from a project to the cost of acquiring that project in order to estimate NPV. The particular mixture of debt and equity a firm actually chooses to use in financing a project is a managerial variable and primarily determines how project cash flow is divided between owners and creditors. This is not to say financing arrangements are unimportant. They are just something to be analyzed separately. We will cover this in later chapters.

Other Issues

Lecture Tip: See IM for a discussion of some additional problems associated with cash flow estimation.

There are some other things to watch out for. First, we are only interested in measuring cash flow. Moreover, we are interested in measuring it when it actually occurs, not when it accrues in an accounting sense. Second, we are always interested in *aftertax* cash flow since taxes are definitely a cash outflow. In fact, whenever we write *incremental cash flows,* we mean aftertax incremental cash flows. Remember, however, that aftertax cash flow and accounting profit or net income are entirely different things.

[2] More colorfully, erosion is sometimes called *piracy* or *cannibalism*.

CONCEPT QUESTIONS

9.2a What is a sunk cost? An opportunity cost?

9.2b Explain what erosion is and why it is relevant.

9.2c Explain why interest paid is not a relevant cash flow for project evaluation.

9.3 PRO FORMA FINANCIAL STATEMENTS AND PROJECT CASH FLOWS

The first thing we need when we begin evaluating a proposed investment is a set of pro forma or projected financial statements. Given these, we can develop the projected cash flows from the project. Once we have the cash flows, we can estimate the value of the project using the techniques we described in the previous chapter.

Self-Test Problems 9.1, 9.2

Problems 4, 5

Getting Started: Pro Forma Financial Statements

Pro forma financial statements are a convenient and easily understood means of summarizing much of the relevant information for a project. To prepare these statements, we will need estimates of quantities such as unit sales, the selling price per unit, the variable cost per unit, and total fixed costs. We will also need to know the total investment required, including any investment in net working capital.

pro forma financial statements Financial statements projecting future years' operations.

To illustrate, suppose we think we can sell 50,000 cans of shark attractant per year at a price of $4.00 per can. It costs us about $2.50 per can to make the attractant, and a new product such as this one typically has only a three-year life (perhaps because the customer base dwindles rapidly). We require a 20 percent return on new products.

Trans. 9.3
Capital Budgeting: Pro Formas (Supplemental)

Fixed costs for the project, including such things as rent on the production facility, will run $12,000 per year. Further, we will need to invest a total of $90,000 in manufacturing equipment. For simplicity, we will assume that this $90,000 will be 100 percent depreciated over the three-year life of the project. Furthermore, the cost of removing the equipment will roughly equal its actual value in three years, so it will be essentially worthless on a market value basis as well. Finally, the project will require an initial $20,000 investment in net working capital. As usual, the tax rate is 34 percent.

In Table 9.1, we organize these initial projections by first preparing the pro forma income statement. Once again, notice that we have *not* deducted any interest expense. This will always be so. As we described earlier, interest paid is a financing expense, not a component of operating cash flow.

Lecture Tip: See IM for more regarding the rationale behind omitting interest expense in cash flow estimation.

TABLE 9.1
Projected income statement, shark attractant project

Sales (50,000 units at $4.00/unit)	$200,000
Variable costs ($2.50/unit)	125,000
	$ 75,000
Fixed costs	12,000
Depreciation ($90,000/3)	30,000
EBIT	$ 33,000
Taxes (34%)	11,220
Net income	$ 21,780

TABLE 9.2
Projected capital requirements, shark attractant project

	Year			
	0	1	2	3
Net working capital	$ 20,000	$20,000	$20,000	$20,000
Net fixed assets	90,000	60,000	30,000	0
Total investment	$110,000	$80,000	$50,000	$20,000

We can also prepare a series of abbreviated balance sheets that show the capital requirements for the project as we've done in Table 9.2. Here we have net working capital of $20,000 in each year. Fixed assets are $90,000 at the start of the project's life (Year 0), and they decline by the $30,000 in depreciation each year, ending up at zero. Notice that the total investment given here for future years is the total book or accounting value, not market value.

At this point, we need to start converting this accounting information into cash flows. We consider how to do this next.

Project Cash Flows

To develop the cash flows from a project, we need to recall (from Chapter 2) that cash flow from assets has three components: operating cash flow, capital spending, and additions to net working capital. To evaluate a project or minifirm, we need to arrive at estimates for each of these.

Once we have estimates of the components of cash flow, we will calculate cash flow for our minifirm just as we did in Chapter 2 for an entire firm:

$$\begin{aligned}\text{Project cash flow} = {} & \text{Project operating cash flow} \\ & - \text{Project additions to net working capital} \\ & - \text{Project capital spending}\end{aligned}$$

We consider these components next.

Trans. 9.4 Capital Budgeting: DCF Valuation (Supplemental)

Project Operating Cash Flow To determine the operating cash flow associated with a project, we first need to recall the definition of operating cash flow:

$$\begin{aligned}\text{Operating cash flow} = {} & \text{Earnings before interest and taxes (EBIT)} \\ & + \text{Depreciation} \\ & - \text{Taxes}\end{aligned}$$

Concept Q Answer 9.3a

To illustrate the calculation of operating cash flow, we will use the projected information from the shark attractant project. For ease of reference, Table 9.3 repeats the income statement.

Given the income statement in Table 9.3, calculating the operating cash flow is very straightforward. As we see in Table 9.4, projected operating cash flow for the shark attractant project is $51,780.

Concept Q Answer 9.3b

Lecture Tip: See IM for additional discussion of the components of capital spending.

Project Net Working Capital and Capital Spending We next need to take care of the fixed asset and net working capital requirements. Based on our balance sheets above, the firm must spend $90,000 up front for fixed assets and invest an additional $20,000 in net working capital. The immediate outflow is thus $110,000. At the end of the project's life, the fixed assets are

Sales	$200,000
Variable costs	125,000
Fixed costs	12,000
Depreciation	30,000
EBIT	$ 33,000
Taxes (34%)	11,220
Net income	$ 21,780

TABLE 9.3
Projected income statement, shark attractant project

EBIT	$ 33,000
Depreciation	+30,000
Taxes	−11,220
Operating cash flow	$ 51,780

TABLE 9.4
Projected operating cash flow, shark attractant project

	Year			
	0	1	2	3
Operating cash flow		$51,780	$51,780	$51,780
Additions to NWC	−$ 20,000			+ 20,000
Capital spending	− 90,000			
Total project cash flow	−$110,000	$51,780	$51,780	$71,780

TABLE 9.5
Projected total cash flows, shark attractant project

worthless (the salvage value is zero), but the firm will recover the $20,000 that was tied up in working capital. This will lead to a $20,000 cash *inflow* in the last year.

On a purely mechanical level, notice that whenever we have an investment in net working capital, that same investment has to be recovered; in other words, the same number needs to appear at some time in the future with the opposite sign.

Projected Total Cash Flow and Value

Given the information we've accumulated, we can finish the preliminary cash flow analysis as illustrated in Table 9.5.

Now that we have cash flow projections, we are ready to apply the various criteria we discussed in the last chapter. First, the NPV at the 20 percent required return is:

$$\begin{aligned} \text{NPV} &= -\$110{,}000 + \$51{,}780/1.2 + \$51{,}780/1.2^2 + \$71{,}780/1.2^3 \\ &= \$10{,}648 \end{aligned}$$

So, based on these projections, the project creates over $10,000 in value and should be accepted. Also, the return on this investment obviously exceeds 20 percent (since the NPV is positive at 20 percent). After some trial and error, we find that the IRR works out to be about 25.8 percent.

In addition, if required, we could go ahead and calculate the payback and the average accounting return (AAR). Inspection of the cash flows shows that the payback on this project is just a little over two years (check that it's about 2.1 years).

Lecture Tip: Observant students will notice that we routinely assume project cash flows occur at the end of the year. You may wish to point this out and indicate that, while traditional, the analysis can be modified to account for other cash flow patterns.

From the last chapter, the AAR is average net income divided by average book value. The net income each year is \$21,780. The average (in thousands) of the four book values (from Table 9.2) for total investment is (\$110 + 80 + 50 + 20)/4 = \$65, so the AAR is \$21,780/65,000 = 33.51 percent. We've already seen that the return on this investment (the IRR) is about 26 percent. The fact that the AAR is larger illustrates again why the AAR cannot be meaningfully interpreted as the return on a project.

CONCEPT QUESTIONS

9.3a What is the definition of project operating cash flow? How does this differ from net income?

9.3b In the shark attractant project, why did we add back the firm's net working capital investment in the final year?

9.4 MORE ON PROJECT CASH FLOW

Self-Test Problem 9.1
Problem 7

In this section, we take a closer look at some aspects of project cash flow. In particular, we discuss project net working capital in more detail. We then examine current tax laws regarding depreciation.

A Closer Look at Net Working Capital

Concept Q Answer 9.4a

In calculating operating cash flow, we did not explicitly consider the fact that some of our sales might be on credit. Also, we may not have actually paid some of the costs shown. In either case, the cash flow has not yet occurred. We show here that these possibilities are not a problem as long as we don't forget to include additions to net working capital in our analysis. This discussion thus emphasizes the importance and the effect of doing so.

Trans. 9.5
A Closer Look: NWC Spending (Supplemental)

Suppose during a particular year of a project we have the following simplified income statement:

Sales	\$500
Costs	310
Net income	\$190

Depreciation and taxes are zero. No fixed assets are purchased during the year. Also, to illustrate a point, we assume that the only components of net working capital are accounts receivable and payable. The beginning and ending amounts for these accounts are:

	Beginning of Year	End of Year	Change
Accounts receivable	\$880	\$910	+\$30
Accounts payable	550	605	+ 55
Net working capital	\$330	\$305	−\$25

Based on this information, what is total cash flow for the year? We can first just mechanically apply what we have been discussing to come up with the answer. Operating cash flow in this particular case is the same as EBIT since there are no taxes or depreciation and thus equals \$190. Also, notice that net working capital actually *declined* by \$25, so the "addition" to net working

Principles in Action

Samuel Weaver on Capital Budgeting at Hershey Foods Corporation

The capital program at Hershey Foods Corporation and most Fortune 500/1,000 companies involves a three-phase approach: planning/budgeting, evaluation, and post-completion reviews.

The first phase involves identification of likely projects at strategic planning time. These are selected to support the strategic objectives of the corporation. This identification is generally broad in scope with minimal financial evaluation attached. As the planning process focuses more closely on the short-term plans, major capital expenditures are scrutinized more rigorously. Project costs are more closely honed, and specific projects may be reconsidered.

Each project is then individually reviewed and authorized. Planning, developing, and refining cash flows underlie capital analysis at Hershey Foods. Once the cash flows have been determined, the application of capital evaluation techniques such as net present value, internal rate of return, and payback period is routine. Presentation of the results is enhanced using sensitivity analysis, which plays a major role for management in assessing the critical assumptions and resulting impact.

The final phase relates to post-completion reviews in which the original forecasts of the project's performance are compared to actual results and/or revised expectations.

Capital expenditure analysis is only as good as the assumptions that underlie the project. The old cliché of "GIGO" (Garbage In, Garbage Out) applies in this case. Incremental cash flows primarily result from incremental sales or margin improvements (cost savings). For the most part, a range of incremental cash flows can be identified from marketing research or engineering studies. However, for a number of projects, correctly discerning the implications and the relevant cash flows is analytically challenging. For example, when a new product is introduced and is expected to generate millions of dollars worth of sales, the appropriate analysis focuses on the incremental sales after accounting for cannibalization of existing products.

One of the problems that we face at Hershey Foods deals with the application of net present value (NPV) versus internal rate of return (IRR). NPV offers the correct investment indication when dealing with mutually exclusive alternatives. However, decision makers at all levels sometimes find it difficult to comprehend the result. Specifically, an NPV of, say, $535,000 needs to be interpreted. It is not enough to know that the NPV is positive or even more positive than an alternative. Decision makers seek a level of "comfort" of how profitable the investment is by relating it to other standards.

Although the IRR may provide a misleading indication of which project to select, the result is provided in a way that can be interpreted by all parties. The resulting IRR can be mentally compared to expected inflation, current borrowing rates, the cost of capital, an equity portfolio's return, and so on. An IRR of, say, 18 percent is readily interpretable by management. Perhaps this ease of understanding is why surveys indicate that most Fortune 500 or Fortune 1,000 companies use the IRR method as a primary evaluation technique.

In addition to the NPV versus IRR problem, there are a limited number of projects for which traditional and capital expenditure analysis is difficult to apply because the cash flows can't be determined. When new computer equipment is purchased, an office building is renovated, or a parking lot is repaved, it is essentially impossible to identify the cash flows, so the use of traditional evaluation techniques is limited. These types of "capital expenditure" decisions are made using other techniques that hinge on management's judgment.

Samuel Weaver, Ph.D., is Director, Corporate Financial Planning and Analysis for the Hershey Foods Corporation. He is a certified management accountant, and he currently serves on the board of directors of the Financial Management Association as Vice President, Practitioner Services. His current position combines the theoretical with the pragmatic and involves the analysis of many different facets of finance in addition to capital expenditure analysis.

capital is negative. This just means that \$25 was freed up during the year. There was no capital spending, so the total cash flow for the year is:

$$\begin{aligned}\text{Total cash flow} &= \text{Operating cash flow} - \text{Additions to NWC} \\ &\quad - \text{Capital spending} \\ &= \$190 - (-\$25) - \$0 \\ &= \$215\end{aligned}$$

Lecture Tip: See IM for the impact of NWC changes on total cash flow.

Now, we know that this \$215 total cash flow has to be "dollars in" less "dollars out" for the year. We could therefore ask a different question: What were cash revenues for the year? Also, what were cash costs?

To determine cash revenues, we need to look more closely at net working capital. During the year, we had sales of \$500. However, accounts receivable rose by \$30 over the same time period. What does this mean? The \$30 increase tells us that sales exceeded collections by \$30. In other words, we haven't yet received the cash from \$30 of the \$500 in sales. As a result, our cash inflow is \$500 − 30 = \$470. In general, cash income is sales minus the increase in accounts receivable.

Cash outflows can be similarly determined. We show costs of \$310 on the income statement, but accounts payable increased by \$55 during the year. This means that we have not yet paid \$55 of the \$310, so cash costs for the period are just \$310 − 55 = \$255. In other words, in this case, cash costs equal costs less the increase in accounts payable.

Putting this information together, cash inflows less cash outflows is \$470 − 255 = \$215, just as we had before. Notice that:

$$\begin{aligned}\text{Cash flow} &= \text{Cash inflow} - \text{Cash outflow} \\ &= (\$500 - 30) - (\$310 - 55) \\ &= (\$500 - \$310) - (30 - 55) \\ &= \text{Operating cash flow} - \text{Additions to NWC} \\ &= \$190 - (-25) \\ &= \$215\end{aligned}$$

More generally, this example illustrates that including net working capital changes in our calculations has the effect of adjusting for the discrepancy between accounting sales and costs and actual cash receipts and payments.

EXAMPLE 9.1 Cash Collections and Costs

For the year just completed, the Combat Wombat Telestat Co. (CWT) reports sales of \$998 and costs of \$734. You have collected the following beginning and ending balance sheet information:

	Beginning	Ending
Accounts receivable	\$100	\$110
Inventory	100	80
Accounts payable	100	70
Net working capital	\$100	\$120

Based on these figures, what are cash inflows? Cash outflows? What happened to each account? What is net cash flow?

Sales were \$998, but receivables rose by \$10. So cash collections were \$10 less than sales, or \$988. Costs were \$734, but inventories fell by \$20. This means that we didn't replace $20 worth of inventory, so costs are actually overstated by this amount. Also, payables fell by $30. This means that, on a net basis, we actually paid our suppliers $30 more than we received from them, resulting in a $30 understatement of costs. Adjusting for these events, cash costs are $734 − 20 + 30 = $744. Net cash flow is $988 − 744 = $244.

Finally, notice that net working capital increased by $20 overall. We can check our answer by noting that the original accounting sales less costs of $998 − 734 is $264. In addition, CWT spent $20 on net working capital, so the net result is a cash flow of $264 − 20 = $244, as we calculated. • • •

Depreciation

As we note elsewhere, accounting depreciation is a noncash deduction. As a result, depreciation has cash flow consequences only because it influences the tax bill. The way that depreciation is computed for tax purposes is thus the relevant method for capital investment decisions. Not surprisingly, the procedures are governed by tax law. We now discuss some specifics of the depreciation system enacted by the Tax Reform Act of 1986. This system is a modification of the **Accelerated Cost Recovery System (ACRS)** instituted in 1981.

Concept Q Answer 9.4b

Accelerated Cost Recovery System (ACRS)
Depreciation method under U.S. tax law allowing for the accelerated write-off of property under various classifications.

Modified ACRS Depreciation Calculating depreciation is normally very mechanical. While there are a number of ifs, ands, and buts involved, the basic idea is that every asset is assigned to a particular class. An asset's class establishes its life for tax purposes. Once an asset's tax life is determined, the depreciation for each year is computed by multiplying the cost of the asset by a fixed percentage. The expected salvage value (what we think the asset will be worth when we dispose of it) and the actual expected economic life (how long we expect the asset to be in service) are not explicitly considered in the calculation of depreciation.

Some typical depreciation classes are described in Table 9.6, and associated percentages (rounded to two decimal places) are shown in Table 9.7.

TABLE 9.6
Modified ACRS property classes

Trans. 9.6

Class	Examples
3-year	Equipment used in research
5-year	Autos, computers
7-year	Most industrial equipment

TABLE 9.7
Modified ACRS depreciation allowances

Trans. 9.6

	Property Class		
Year	3-Year	5-Year	7-Year
1	33.33%	20.00%	14.29%
2	44.44	32.00	24.49
3	14.82	19.20	17.49
4	7.41	11.52	12.49
5		11.52	8.93
6		5.76	8.93
7			8.93
8			4.45

A nonresidential real property, such as an office building, is depreciated over 31.5 years using straight-line depreciation. A residential real property, such as an apartment building, is depreciated straight-line over 27.5 years. Remember that land cannot be depreciated.

To illustrate how depreciation is calculated, we consider an automobile costing $12,000. Autos are normally classified as five-year property. Looking at Table 9.7, the relevant figure for the first year of a five-year asset is 20 percent. The depreciation in the first year is thus $12,000 × .20 = $2,400. The relevant percentage in the second year is 32 percent, so the depreciation in the second year is $12,000 × .32 = $3,840, and so on. We can summarize these calculations as follows:

Year	MACRS Percentage	Depreciation
1	20.00%	.2000 × $12,000 = $ 2,400.00
2	32.00	.3200 × 12,000 = 3,840.00
3	19.20	.1920 × 12,000 = 2,304.00
4	11.52	.1152 × 12,000 = 1,382.40
5	11.52	.1152 × 12,000 = 1,382.40
6	5.76	.0576 × 12,000 = 691.20
	100.00%	$12,000.00

Notice that the ACRS percentages sum up to 100 percent. As a result, we write off 100 percent of the cost of the asset, or $12,000 in this case.

Lecture Tip: See IM for a discussion of some potential advantages of accelerated (versus straight-line) depreciation.

Book Value versus Market Value In calculating depreciation under current tax law, the economic life and future market value of the asset are not an issue. As a result, the book value of an asset can differ substantially from its actual market value. For example, with our $12,000 car, book value after the first year is $12,000 less the first year's depreciation of $2,400, or $9,600. The remaining book values are summarized in Table 9.8. After six years, the book value of the car is zero.

Suppose we wanted to sell the car after five years. Based on historical averages, it will be worth, say, 25 percent of the purchase price or .25 × $12,000 = $3,000. If we actually sold it for this, then we would have to pay taxes at the ordinary income tax rate on the difference between the sale price of $3,000 and the book value of $691.20. For a corporation in the 34 percent bracket, the tax liability is .34 × $2,308.80 = $784.99.

Lecture Tip: See IM 9.4 for further discussion of the complexities involved in calculating depreciation and estimating the tax effects of asset sales.

The reason that taxes must be paid in this case is that the difference in market value and book value is "excess" depreciation, and it must be "recaptured" when the asset is sold. What this means is that, as it turns out, we overdepreciated the asset by $3,000 − 691.20 = $2,308.80. Since we deducted $2,308.80 too much in depreciation, we paid $784.99 too little in taxes, and we simply have to make up the difference.

Notice that this is *not* a tax on a capital gain. As a general (albeit rough) rule, a capital gain only occurs if the market price exceeds the original cost.

TABLE 9.8
MACRS book values

Year	Beginning Book Value	Depreciation	Ending Book Value
1	$12,000.00	$2,400.00	$9,600.00
2	9,600.00	3,840.00	5,760.00
3	5,760.00	2,304.00	3,456.00
4	3,456.00	1,382.40	2,073.60
5	2,073.60	1,382.40	691.20
6	691.20	691.20	0.00

However, what is and what is not a capital gain is ultimately up to taxing authorities, and the specific rules can be very complex. We will ignore capital gains taxes for the most part.

Finally, if the book value exceeds the market value, then the difference is treated as a loss for tax purposes. For example, if we sell the car after two years for $4,000, then the book value exceeds the market value by $1,760. In this case, a tax saving of .34 × $1,760 = $598.40 occurs.

EXAMPLE 9.2 MACRS Depreciation

Trans. 9.7
MACRS Depreciation: An Example (Supplemental)

The Staple Supply Co. has just purchased a new computerized information system with an installed cost of $160,000. The computer is treated as five-year property. What are the yearly depreciation allowances? Based on historical experience, we think that the system will be worth only $10,000 when we get rid of it in four years. What are the tax consequences of the sale? What is the total aftertax cash flow from the sale?

The yearly depreciation allowances are calculated by just multiplying $160,000 by the five-year percentages in Table 9.7:

Year	MACRS Percentage	Depreciation	Ending Book Value
1	20.00%	.2000 × $160,000 = $ 32,000	$128,000
2	32.00	.3200 × 160,000 = 51,200	76,800
3	19.20	.1920 × 160,000 = 30,720	46,080
4	11.52	.1152 × 160,000 = 18,432	27,648
5	11.52	.1152 × 160,000 = 18,432	9,216
6	5.76	.0576 × 160,000 = 9,216	0
	100.00%	$160,000	

Notice that we have also computed the book value of the system as of the end of each year. The book value at the end of Year 4 is $27,648. If we sell it for $10,000 at that time, we will have a loss of $17,648 (the difference) for tax purposes. This loss, of course, is like depreciation because it isn't a cash expense.

What really happens? Two things. First, we get $10,000 from the buyer. Second, we save .34 × $17,648 = $6,000 in taxes. So the total aftertax cash flow from the sale is a $16,000 cash inflow. • • •

An Example: The Majestic Mulch and Compost Company (MMCC)

At this point, we want to go through a somewhat more involved capital budgeting analysis. Keep in mind as you read that the basic approach here is exactly the same as that in the shark attractant example above. We have only added some more "real-world" detail (and a lot more numbers).

MMCC is investigating the feasibility of a new line of power mulching tools aimed at the growing number of home composters. Based on exploratory conversations with buyers for large garden shops, we project unit sales as follows:

Year	Unit Sales
1	3,000
2	5,000
3	6,000
4	6,500
5	6,000
6	5,000
7	4,000
8	3,000

The new power mulcher will be priced to sell at $120 per unit to start. When the competition catches up after three years, however, we anticipate that the price will drop to $110.

TABLE 9.9
Projected revenues, power mulcher project

Year	Unit Price	Unit Sales	Revenues
1	$120	3,000	$360,000
2	120	5,000	600,000
3	120	6,000	720,000
4	110	6,500	715,000
5	110	6,000	660,000
6	110	5,000	550,000
7	110	4,000	440,000
8	110	3,000	330,000

TABLE 9.10
Annual depreciation, power mulcher project

Year	MACRS Percentage	Depreciation	Ending Book Value
1	14.29%	.1429 × $800,000 = $114,320	$685,680
2	24.49	.2449 × 800,000 = 195,920	489,760
3	17.49	.1749 × 800,000 = 139,920	349,840
4	12.49	.1249 × 800,000 = 99,920	249,920
5	8.93	.0893 × 800,000 = 71,440	178,480
6	8.93	.0893 × 800,000 = 71,440	107,040
7	8.93	.0893 × 800,000 = 71,440	35,600
8	4.45	.0445 × 800,000 = $ 35,600	0
	100.00%	$800,000	

The power mulcher project will require $20,000 in net working capital at the start. Subsequently, total net working capital at the end of each year will be about 15 percent of sales for that year. The variable cost per unit is $60, and total fixed costs are $25,000 per year.

It will cost about $800,000 to buy the equipment necessary to begin production. This investment is primarily in industrial equipment and thus qualifies as seven-year MACRS property. The equipment will actually be worth about 20 percent of its cost in eight years, or .20 × $800,000 = $160,000. The relevant tax rate is 34 percent, and the required return is 15 percent. Based on this information, should MMCC proceed?

Operating Cash Flows There is a lot of information here that we need to organize. The first thing we can do is calculate projected sales. Sales in the first year are projected at 3,000 units at $120 apiece, or $360,000 total. The remaining figures are shown in Table 9.9.

Next, we compute the depreciation on the $800,000 investment in Table 9.10. With this information, we can prepare the pro forma income statements, as shown in Table 9.11 (on page 221). From here, computing the operating cash flows is straightforward. The results are illustrated in the first part of Table 9.13 (on page 222).

Additions to NWC Now that we have the operating cash flows, we need to determine the additions to NWC. By assumption, net working capital requirements change as sales change. In each year, we will generally either add to or recover some of our project net working capital. Recalling that NWC starts out at $20,000 and then rises to 15 percent of sales, we can calculate the amount of NWC for each year as illustrated in Table 9.12.

TABLE 9.11 Pro forma income statements, power mulcher project

	Year							
	1	2	3	4	5	6	7	8
Unit price	$ 120	$ 120	$ 120	$ 110	$ 110	$ 110	$ 110	$ 110
Unit sales	3,000	5,000	6,000	6,500	6,000	5,000	4,000	3,000
Revenues	$360,000	$600,000	$720,000	$715,000	$660,000	$550,000	$440,000	$330,000
Variable costs	180,000	300,000	360,000	390,000	360,000	300,000	240,000	180,000
Fixed costs	25,000	25,000	25,000	25,000	25,000	25,000	25,000	25,000
Depreciation	114,320	195,920	139,920	99,920	71,440	71,440	71,440	35,600
EBIT	$ 40,680	$ 79,080	$195,080	$200,080	$203,560	$153,560	$103,560	$ 89,400
Taxes (34%)	13,831	26,887	66,327	68,027	69,210	52,210	35,210	30,396
Net income	$ 26,849	$ 52,193	$128,753	$132,053	$134,350	$101,350	$ 68,350	$ 59,004

TABLE 9.12 Additions to net working capital, power mulcher project

Year	Revenues	Net Working Capital	Cash Flow
0		$20,000	−$20,000
1	$360,000	54,000	− 34,000
2	600,000	90,000	− 36,000
3	720,000	108,000	− 18,000
4	715,000	107,250	750
5	660,000	99,000	8,250
6	550,000	82,500	16,500
7	440,000	66,000	16,500
8	$330,000	49,500	16,500

As illustrated, during the first year, net working capital grows from \$20,000 to 0.15 × \$360,000 = \$54,000. The increase in net working capital for the year is thus \$54,000 − 20,000 = \$34,000. The remaining figures are calculated the same way.

Remember that an increase in net working capital is a cash outflow, so we use a negative sign in this table to indicate an additional investment that the firm makes in net working capital. A positive sign represents net working capital returning to the firm. Thus, for example, \$16,500 in NWC flows back to the firm in Year 6. Over the project's life, net working capital builds to a peak of \$108,000 and declines from there as sales begin to drop off.

We show the result for additions to net working capital in the second part of Table 9.13. Notice that at the end of the project's life there is \$49,500 in net working capital still to be recovered. Therefore, in the last year, the project returns \$16,500 of NWC during the year and then returns the remaining \$49,500 at the end of the year for a total of \$66,000.

Capital Spending Finally, we have to account for the long-term capital invested in the project. In this case, we invest \$800,000 at Year 0. By assumption, this equipment will be worth \$160,000 at the end of the project. It will have a book value of zero at that time. As we discussed above, this \$160,000 excess of market value over book value is taxable, so the aftertax proceeds will be \$160,000 × (1 − .34) = \$105,600. These figures are shown in the third part of Table 9.13.

TABLE 9.13 Projected cash flows, power mulcher project

	Year 0	1	2	3	4	5	6	7	8
					I. Operating Cash Flow				
EBIT		$ 40,680	$ 79,080	$195,080	$200,080	$203,560	$153,560	$103,560	$ 89,400
Depreciation		114,320	195,920	139,920	99,920	71,440	71,440	71,440	35,600
Taxes	—	− 13,831	− 26,887	− 66,327	− 68,027	− 69,210	− 52,210	− 35,210	− 30,396
Operating cash flow		$141,169	$248,113	$268,673	$231,973	$205,790	$172,790	$139,790	$ 94,604
					II. Net Working Capital				
Initial NWC	−$ 20,000								
Increases in NWC		−$ 34,000	−$ 36,000	−$ 18,000	$ 750	$ 8,250	$ 16,500	$ 16,500	$ 16,500
NWC recovery	—	—	—	—	—	—	—	—	49,500
Additions to NWC	−$ 20,000	−$ 34,000	−$ 36,000	−$ 18,000	$ 750	$ 8,250	$ 16,500	$ 16,500	$ 66,000
					III. Capital Spending				
Initial outlay	−$800,000								
Aftertax salvage	—	—	—	—	—	—	—	—	$105,600
Capital spending	−$800,000								$105,600

TABLE 9.14 Projected total cash flows, power mulcher project

	Year								
	0	1	2	3	4	5	6	7	8
Operating cash flow		$141,169	$248,113	$268,673	$231,973	$205,790	$172,790	$139,790	$ 94,604
Additions to NWC	−$ 20,000	− 34,000	− 36,000	− 18,000	750	8,250	16,500	16,500	66,000
Capital spending	− 800,000								105,600
Total project cash flow	−$820,000	$107,169	$212,113	$250,673	$232,723	$214,040	$189,290	$156,290	$266,204
Cumulative cash flow	−$820,000	−$712,831	−$500,718	−$250,045	−$ 17,322	$196,718	$386,008	$542,298	$808,502
Discounted cash flow @ 15%	− 820,000	93,190	160,388	164,821	133,060	106,416	81,835	58,755	87,023

Net present value (15%) = $65,488
Internal rate of return = 17.24%
Payback = 4.09 years

Total Cash Flow and Value We now have all the cash flow pieces, and we put them together in Table 9.14. In addition to the total project cash flows, we have calculated the cumulative cash flows and the discounted cash flows. At this point, it's essentially "plug and chug" to calculate the net present value, internal rate of return, and payback.

If we sum the discounted flows and the initial investment, the net present value (at 15 percent) works out to be $65,488. This is positive, so, based on these preliminary projections, the power mulcher project is acceptable. The internal or DCF rate of return is greater than 15 percent since the NPV is positive. It works out to be 17.24 percent, again indicating that the project is acceptable.

Looking at the cumulative cash flows, we see that the project has almost paid back after four years since the cumulative cash flow is almost zero at that time. As indicated, the fractional year works out to be $17,322/214,040 = 0.09, so the payback is 4.09 years. We can't say whether or not this is good since we don't have a benchmark for MMCC. This is the usual problem with payback periods.

This completes our preliminary DCF analysis. Where do we go from here? If we have a great deal of confidence in our projections, then there is no further analysis to be done. We should begin production and marketing immediately. It is unlikely that this will be the case. It is important to remember that the result of our analysis is an estimate of NPV, and we will usually have less than complete confidence in our projections. This means we have more work to do. In particular, we will almost surely want to spend some time evaluating the quality of our estimates. We will take up this subject in the next chapter. For now, we take a look at some alternative definitions of operating cash flow, and we illustrate some different cases that arise in capital budgeting.

Lecture Tip: See IM for an extension of the MMCC example demonstrating the effects of alternative depreciation methods.

CONCEPT QUESTIONS

9.4a Why is it important to consider additions to net working capital in developing cash flows? What is the effect of doing so?

9.4b How is depreciation calculated for fixed assets under current tax law? What effect do expected salvage value and estimated economic life have on the calculated depreciation deduction?

9.5 EVALUATING NPV ESTIMATES

Problem 17

Trans. 9.8 Evaluating NPV Estimates (Supplemental)

As we discussed in Chapter 8, an investment has a positive net present value if its market value exceeds its cost. Such an investment is desirable because it creates value for its owner. The primary problem in identifying such opportunities is that most of the time we can't actually observe the relevant market value. Instead, we estimate it. Having done so, it is only natural to wonder whether or not our estimates are at least close to the true values. We consider this question next.

The Basic Problem

Suppose we are working on a preliminary DCF analysis along the lines we described in previous sections. We carefully identify the relevant cash flows, avoiding such things as sunk costs, and we remember to consider working capital requirements. We add back any depreciation; we account for possible erosion; and we pay attention to opportunity costs. Finally, we double-check our calculations, and, when all is said and done, the bottom line is that the estimated NPV is positive.

Now what? Do we stop here and move on to the next proposal? Probably not. The fact that the estimated NPV is positive is definitely a good sign, but, more than anything, this tells us that we need to take a closer look.

If you think about it, there are two circumstances under which a discounted cash flow analysis could lead us to conclude that a project has a positive NPV. The first possibility is that the project really does have a positive NPV. That's the good news. The bad news is the second possibility: A project may appear to have a positive NPV because our estimate is inaccurate.

Notice that we could also err in the opposite way. If we conclude that a project has a negative NPV when the true NPV is positive, then we lose a valuable opportunity.

Forecasting Risk

The key inputs into a DCF analysis are projected future cash flows. If these projections are seriously in error, then we have a classic GIGO (garbage-in, garbage-out) system. In this case, no matter how carefully we arrange the numbers and manipulate them, the resulting answer can still be grossly misleading. This is the danger in using a relatively sophisticated technique like DCF. It is sometimes easy to get caught up in number crunching and forget the underlying nuts-and-bolts economic reality.

Lecture Tip: You may wish to emphasize that the "economic reality" is that we are forecasting uncertain cash flows. Carrying computations to six decimal places (i.e., specious accuracy) is a sure sign that one has lost track of this reality.

The possibility that we make a bad decision because of errors in the projected cash flows is called **forecasting risk** (or *estimation risk*). Because of forecasting risk, there is the danger that we think a project has a positive NPV when it really does not. How is this possible? It happens if we are overly optimistic about the future, and, as a result, our projected cash flows don't realistically reflect the possible future cash flows.

forecasting risk
The possibility that errors in projected cash flows lead to incorrect decisions. Also estimation risk.

Concept Q Answer 9.5a

So far, we have not explicitly considered what to do about the possibility of errors in our forecasts, so our goal is to develop some tools that are useful in identifying areas where potential errors exist and where they might be especially damaging. In one form or another, we will be trying to assess the economic "reasonableness" of our estimates. We will also be wondering how much damage will be done by errors in those estimates.

Lecture Tip: Making bad decisions due to forecasting risk is analogous to making bad decisons in statistical inference: specifically, rejecting a project (null hypothesis) that should have been accepted is a Type I error; accepting a project (null hypothesis) that should have been rejected is a Type II error.

Sources of Value

The first line of defense against forecasting risk is simply to ask: "What is it about this investment that leads to a positive NPV?" We should be able to point to something specific as the source of value. For example, if the proposal under consideration involved a new product, then we might ask questions such as: "Are we certain that our new product is significantly better than that of the competition? Can we truly manufacture at lower cost, or distribute more effectively, or identify undeveloped market niches, or gain control of a market?"

Concept Q Answer 9.5b

These are just a few of the potential sources of value. There are many others. A key factor to keep in mind is the degree of competition in the market. It is a basic principle of economics that positive NPV investments will be

Lecture Tip: See IM 9.5 for a discussion of monopoly rents—perhaps the single largest source of positive NPVs.

Lecture Tip: See IM 9.5 for a summary of an excellent article detailing the sources of value in capital budgeting projects.

rare in a highly competitive environment. Therefore, proposals that appear to show significant value in the face of stiff competition are particularly troublesome, and the likely reaction of the competition to any innovations must be closely examined.

The point to remember is that positive NPV investments are probably not all that common, and the number of positive NPV projects is almost certainly limited for any given firm. If we can't articulate some sound economic basis for thinking ahead of time that we have found something special, then the conclusion that our project has a positive NPV should be viewed with some suspicion.

CONCEPT QUESTIONS

9.5a What is forecasting risk? Why is it a concern for the financial manager?

9.5b What are some potential sources of value in a new project?

9.6 SCENARIO AND OTHER "WHAT-IF" ANALYSES

Self-Test Problem 9.3
Problems 15, 16, 19, 20, 21

Our basic approach to evaluating cash flow and NPV estimates involves asking "what-if" questions. Accordingly, we discuss some organized ways of going about a what-if analysis. Our goal in doing so is to assess the degree of forecasting risk and to identify those components most critical to the success or failure of an investment.

Getting Started

We are investigating a new project. Naturally, the first thing we do is estimate NPV based on our projected cash flows. We will call this the *base case.* Now, however, we recognize the possibility of error in those cash flow projections. After completing the base case, we thus wish to investigate the impact of different assumptions about the future on our estimates.

One way to organize this investigation is to put an upper and lower bound on the various components of the project. For example, suppose we forecast sales at 100 units per year. We know this estimate may be high or low, but we are relatively certain it is not off by more than 10 units in either direction. We would thus pick a lower bound of 90 and an upper bound of 110. We go on to assign such bounds to any other cash flow components we are unsure about.

When we pick these upper and lower bounds, we are not ruling out the possibility that the actual values could be outside this range. What we are saying, loosely speaking, is that it is unlikely the true average (as opposed to our estimated average) of the possible values is outside this range.

An example is useful to illustrate the idea here. The project under consideration costs $200,000, has a five-year life, and no salvage value. Depreciation is straight-line to zero. The required return is 12 percent, and the tax rate is 34 percent. In addition, we have compiled the following information:

	Base Case	Lower Bound	Upper Bound
Unit sales	6,000	5,500	6,500
Price per unit	$80	$75	$85
Variable costs per unit	$60	$58	$62
Fixed costs per year	$50,000	$45,000	$55,000

With this information, we can calculate the base-case NPV by first calculating net income:

Sales	$480,000
Variable costs	360,000
Fixed costs	50,000
Depreciation	40,000
EBIT	$ 30,000
Taxes (34%)	10,200
Net income	$ 19,800

Operating cash flow is thus $30,000 + 40,000 − 10,200 = $59,800 per year. At 12 percent, the five-year annuity factor is 3.6048, so the base-case NPV is:

$$\text{Base-case NPV} = -\$200{,}000 + \$59{,}800 \times 3.6048$$
$$= \$15{,}567$$

Thus, the project looks good so far.

Scenario Analysis

The basic form of what-if analysis is called **scenario analysis.** What we do is investigate the changes in our NPV estimates that result from asking questions like "What if unit sales realistically should be projected at 5,500 units instead of 6,000?"

scenario analysis
The determination of what happens to NPV estimates when we ask what-if questions.

Once we start looking at alternative scenarios, we might find that most of the plausible ones result in positive NPVs. In this case, we have some confidence in proceeding with the project. If a substantial percentage of the scenarios look bad, then the degree of forecasting risk is high and further investigation is in order.

Concept Q Answer 9.6a

There are a number of possible scenarios we could consider. A good place to start is the worst-case scenario. This will tell us the minimum NPV of the project. If this were positive, we would be in good shape. While we are at it, we will go ahead and determine the other extreme, the best case. This puts an upper bound on our NPV.

Lecture Tip: See IM for a helpful analogy regarding the ex ante nature of NPV analysis to share in class.

To get the worst case, we assign the least favorable value to each item. This means *low* values for items like units sold and price per unit and *high* values for costs. We do the reverse for the best case. For our project, these values would be:

	Worst Case	Best Case
Unit sales	5,500	6,500
Price per unit	$75	$85
Variable costs per unit	$62	$58
Fixed costs	$55,000	$45,000

With this information, we can calculate the net income and cash flows under each scenario (check these for yourself):

Scenario	Net Income	Cash Flow	Net Present Value	IRR
Base case	$19,800	$59,800	$ 15,567	15.1%
Worst case*	− 15,510	24,490	− 111,719	−14.4
Best case	59,730	99,730	159,504	40.9

*We assume a tax credit is created in our worst-case scenario.

What we learn is that under the worst scenario, the cash flow is still positive at $24,490. That's good news. The bad news is that the return is −14.4 percent in this case, and the NPV is −$111,719. Since the project costs $200,000, we stand to lose a little more than half of the original investment under the worst possible scenario. The best case offers an attractive 41 percent return.

The terms "best case" and "worst case" are very commonly used, and we will stick with them, but we should note they are somewhat misleading. The absolutely best thing that could happen would be something absurdly unlikely, such as launching a new diet soda and subsequently learning that our (patented) formulation also just happens to cure the common cold. Similarly, the true worst case would involve some incredibly remote possibility of total disaster. We're not claiming that these things don't happen; once in a while they do. Some products, such as personal computers, succeed beyond the wildest of expectations, and some, such as asbestos, turn out to be absolute catastrophes. Instead, our point is that in assessing the reasonableness of an NPV estimate, we need to stick to cases that are reasonably likely to occur.

Instead of *best* and *worst,* then, it is probably more accurate to say *optimistic* and *pessimistic.* In broad terms, if we were thinking about a reasonable range for, say, unit sales, then what we call the best case would correspond to something near the upper end of that range. The worst case would simply correspond to the lower end.

Lecture Tip: See IM 9.6 for tips on linking the alternative scenarios discussion to the issue of variability presented in Chapters 10 and 11.

As we have mentioned, there is an unlimited number of different scenarios that we could examine. At a minimum, we might want to investigate two intermediate cases by going halfway between the base amounts and the extreme amounts. This would give us five scenarios in all, including the base case.

Concept Q Answer 9.6b

Beyond this point, it is hard to know when to stop. As we generate more and more possibilities, we run the risk of "paralysis of analysis." The difficulty is that no matter how many scenarios we run, all we can learn are possibilities, some good and some bad. Beyond that, we don't get any guidance as to what to do. Scenario analysis is thus useful in telling us what can happen and in helping us gauge the potential for disaster, but it does not tell us whether or not to take the project.

Sensitivity Analysis

sensitivity analysis
Investigation of what happens to NPV when only one variable is changed.

Concept Q Answer 9.6a

Sensitivity analysis is a variation on scenario analysis that is useful in pinpointing the areas where forecasting risk is especially severe. The basic idea with a sensitivity analysis is to freeze all of the variables except one and then see how sensitive our estimate of NPV is to changes in that one variable. If our NPV estimate turns out to be very sensitive to relatively small changes in the projected value of some component of project cash flow, then the forecasting risk associated with that variable is high.

To illustrate how sensitivity analysis works, we go back to our base case for every item except unit sales. We can then calculate cash flow and NPV using the largest and smallest unit sales figures.

Scenario	Unit Sales	Cash Flow	Net Present Value	IRR
Base case	6,000	$59,800	$15,567	15.1%
Worst case	5,500	53,200	− 8,226	10.3
Best case	6,500	66,400	39,357	19.7

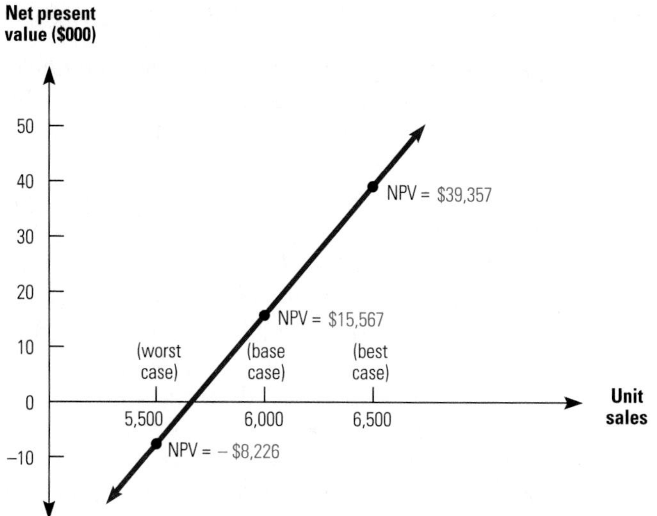

FIGURE 9.1
Sensitivity analysis for unit sales

The results of our sensitivity analysis for unit sales can be illustrated graphically as in Figure 9.1. Here we place NPV on the vertical axis and unit sales on the horizontal axis. When we plot the combinations of unit sales versus NPV, we see that all possible combinations fall on a straight line. The steeper the resulting line is, the greater the sensitivity of the estimated NPV to the projected value of the variable being investigated.

Lecture Tip: Students should be reminded that the purpose of isolating the most sensitive variables is to expend resources to acquire further information in the most effective manner.

By way of comparison, we now freeze everything except fixed costs and repeat the analysis:

Scenario	Fixed Costs	Cash Flow	Net Present Value	IRR
Base case	$50,000	$59,800	$15,567	15.1%
Worst case	55,000	56,500	3,670	12.7
Best case	45,000	63,100	27,461	17.4

What we see here is that, given our ranges, the estimated NPV of this project is more sensitive to projected unit sales than it is to projected fixed costs. In fact, under the worst case for fixed costs, the NPV is still positive.

As we have illustrated, sensitivity analysis is useful in pinpointing those variables that deserve the most attention. If we find that our estimated NPV is especially sensitive to a variable that is difficult to forecast (such as unit sales), then the degree of forecasting risk is high. We might decide that further market research would be a good idea in this case.

Lecture Tip: A third form of "What-if" analysis—simulation analysis—is described in *Fundamentals of Corporate Finance* by Ross, Westerfield, and Jordan.

Because sensitivity analysis is a form of scenario analysis, it suffers from the same drawbacks. Sensitivity analysis is useful for pointing out where forecasting errors will do the most damage, but it does not tell us what to do about possible errors.

Concept Q Answer 9.6b

CONCEPT QUESTIONS

9.6a What are scenario and sensitivity analyses?

9.6b What are the drawbacks to what-if analyses?

9.7 ADDITIONAL CONSIDERATIONS IN CAPITAL BUDGETING

Problem 18

Our final task for this chapter is a brief discussion of two additional considerations in capital budgeting: managerial options and capital rationing. Both of these can be very important in practice, but, as we will see, explicitly dealing with either of them is difficult.

Managerial Options and Capital Budgeting

Concept Q Answer 9.7a

Concept Q Answer 9.7b

Trans. 9.9 Managerial Options and Capital Budgeting

managerial options
Opportunities that managers can exploit if certain things happen in the future.

In our capital budgeting analysis thus far, we have more or less ignored the possibility of future managerial actions. Implicitly, we assumed that once a project is launched, its basic features cannot be changed. For this reason, we say that our analysis is *static* (as opposed to dynamic).

In reality, depending on what actually happens in the future, there will always be ways to modify a project. We will call these opportunities **managerial options.** There are a great number of these options. The way a product is priced, manufactured, advertised, and produced can all be changed, and these are just a few of the possibilities. We discuss some of the most important ones in the next few sections.

Contingency Planning The various what-if procedures in this chapter have another use. We can also view them as primitive ways of exploring the dynamics of a project and investigating managerial options. What we think about in this case are some of the possible futures that could come about and what actions we might take if they do.

For example, we might find that a project fails to break even when sales drop below 10,000 units. This is a fact that is interesting to know, but the more important thing is to then go on and ask: "What actions are we going to take if this actually occurs?" This is called **contingency planning,** and it amounts to an investigation of some of the managerial options implicit in a project.

contingency planning
Taking into account the managerial options implicit in a project.

There is no limit to the number of possible futures or contingencies that we could investigate. However, there are some broad classes, and we consider these next.

The Option to Expand One particularly important option we have not explicitly addressed is the option to expand. If we truly find a positive NPV project, then there is an obvious consideration. Can we expand the project or repeat it to get an even larger NPV? Our static analysis implicitly assumes that the scale of the project is fixed.

For example, if the sales demand for a particular product were to greatly exceed expectations, we might investigate increasing production. If this is not feasible for some reason, then we could always increase cash flow by raising the price. Either way, the potential cash flow is higher than we have indicated because we have implicitly assumed that no expansion or price increase is possible. Overall, because we ignore the option to expand in our analysis, we *underestimate* NPV (all other things being equal).

The Option to Abandon At the other extreme, the option to scale back or even abandon a project is also quite valuable. For example, if a project does not even cover its own expenses, we might be better off if we just abandoned it. Our DCF analysis implicitly assumes that we would keep operating even in this case.

In reality, if sales demand were significantly below expectations, we might be able to sell off some capacity or put it to another use. Maybe the product or service could be redesigned or otherwise improved. Regardless of the specifics, we once again *underestimate* NPV if we assume that the project must last for some fixed number of years, no matter what happens in the future.

The Option to Wait Implicitly, we have treated proposed investments as if they were "go or no-go" decisions. Actually, there is a third possibility. The project can be postponed, perhaps in hope of more favorable conditions. We call this the option to wait.

Lecture Tip: More extensive discussion of the option to wait can be found in IM 9.7.

For example, suppose an investment costs $120 and has a perpetual cash flow of $10 per year. If the discount rate is 10 percent, then the NPV is $10/.10 − 120 = −$20, so the project should not be undertaken now. However, this does not mean that we should forget about the project forever, because in the next period, the appropriate discount rate could be different. If it fell to, say, 5 percent, then the NPV would be $10/.05 − 120 = $80, and we would take the project.

More generally, as long as there is some possible future scenario under which a project has a positive NPV, then the option to wait is valuable.

Strategic Options Companies sometimes undertake new projects just to explore possibilities and evaluate potential future business strategies. This is a little like testing the water by sticking a toe in before diving. Such projects are difficult to analyze using conventional DCF because most of the benefits come in the form of **strategic options**, that is, options for future, related business moves. Projects that create such options may be very valuable, but that value is difficult to measure. Research and development, for example, is an important and valuable activity for many firms precisely because it creates options for new products and procedures.

strategic options
Options for future, related business products or strategies.

To give another example, a large manufacturer might decide to open a retail outlet as a pilot study. The primary goal is to gain some market insight. Because of the high start-up costs, this one operation won't break even. However, based on the sales experience from the pilot, we can then evaluate whether or not to open more outlets, to change the product mix, to enter new markets, and so on. The information gained and the resulting options for actions are all valuable, but coming up with a reliable dollar figure is probably not feasible.

Lecture Tip: See IM 9.7 for a discussion of some of the implications of strategic options for decision making.

We have seen that incorporating options into capital budgeting analysis is not easy. What can we do about them in practice? The answer is that we can only keep them in the back of our minds as we work with the projected cash flows. We will tend to underestimate NPV by ignoring options. The damage might be small for a highly structured, very specific proposal, but it might be great for an exploratory one.

Concept Q Answer 9.7c

capital rationing
The situation that exists if a firm has positive NPV projects but cannot obtain the necessary financing.

Capital Rationing

Capital rationing is said to exist when we have profitable (positive NPV) investments available but we can't get the needed funds to undertake them. For example, as division managers for a large corporation, we might identify $5 million in excellent projects, but find that, for whatever reason, we can spend only $2 million. Now what? Unfortunately, for reasons we will discuss, there may be no truly satisfactory answer.

soft rationing
The situation that occurs when units in a business are allocated a certain amount of financing for capital budgeting.

Soft Rationing The situation we have just described is **soft rationing.** This occurs when, for example, different units in a business are allocated some fixed amount of money each year for capital spending. Such an allocation is primarily a means of controlling and keeping track of overall spending. The important thing about soft rationing is that the corporation as a whole isn't short of capital; more can be raised on ordinary terms if management so desires.

If we face soft rationing, the first thing to do is try and get a larger allocation. Failing that, then one common suggestion is to generate as large a net present value as possible within the existing budget. This amounts to choosing those projects with the largest benefit/cost ratio (profitability index).

Strictly speaking, this is the correct thing to do only if the soft rationing is a one-time event; that is, it won't exist next year. If the soft rationing is a chronic problem, then something is amiss. The reason goes all the way back to Chapter 1. Ongoing soft rationing means we are constantly by-passing positive NPV investments. This contradicts our goal of the firm. If we are not trying to maximize value, then the question of which projects to take becomes ambiguous because we no longer have an objective goal in the first place.

hard rationing
The situation that occurs when a business cannot raise financing for a project under any circumstances.

Hard Rationing With **hard rationing,** a business cannot raise capital for a project under any circumstances. For large, healthy corporations, this situation probably does not occur very often. This is fortunate because with hard rationing our DCF analysis breaks down, and the best course of action is ambiguous.

The reason DCF analysis breaks down has to do with the required return. Suppose we say our required return is 20 percent. Implicitly, we are saying we will take a project with a return that exceeds this. However, if we face hard rationing, then we are not going to take a new project no matter what the return on that project is, so the whole concept of a required return is ambiguous. About the only interpretation we can give this situation is that the required return is so large that no project has a positive NPV in the first place.

Hard rationing can occur when a company experiences financial distress, meaning that bankruptcy is a possibility. Also, a firm may not be able to raise capital without violating a preexisting contractual agreement. We discuss these situations in greater detail in a later chapter.

CONCEPT QUESTIONS

9.7a Why do we say that our standard discounted cash flow analysis is static?

9.7b What are managerial options in capital budgeting? Give some examples.

9.7c What is capital rationing? What types are there? What problems does it create for discounted cash flow analysis?

9.8 SUMMARY AND CONCLUSIONS

This chapter describes how to go about putting together a discounted cash flow analysis and evaluating the results. In it, we covered:

1. The identification of relevant project cash flows. We discussed project cash flows and described how to handle some issues that often come up, including sunk costs, opportunity costs, financing costs, net working capital, and erosion.
2. Preparing and using pro forma or projected financial statements. We showed how such financial statement information is useful in coming up with projected cash flows.
3. The role of net working capital and depreciation in project cash flows. We saw that including the additions to net working capital was important because it adjusted for the discrepancy between accounting revenues (and costs) and cash revenues (and costs). We also went over the calculation of depreciation expense under current tax law.
4. The use of scenario and sensitivity analysis. These tools are widely used to evaluate the impact of assumptions made about future cash flows and NPV estimates.
5. Additional issues in capital budgeting. We examined the managerial options implicit in many capital budgeting situations. We also discussed the capital rationing problem.

The discounted cash flow analysis we've covered here is a standard tool in the business world. It is a very powerful tool, so care should be taken in its use. The most important thing is to get the cash flows identified in a way that makes economic sense. This chapter gives you a good start on learning to do this.

Chapter Review Problems and Self-Test

These problems will give you some practice with discounted cash flow analysis. The answers appear below.

9.1 Calculating Operating Cash Flow Mater Pasta, Inc., has projected a sales volume of $1,432 for the second year of a proposed expansion project. Costs normally run 70 percent of sales, or about $1,002 in this case. The depreciation expense will be $80, and the tax rate is 34 percent. What is the operating cash flow?

9.2 Capital Budgeting for Project X Based on the following information for Project X, should we undertake the venture? To answer, first prepare a pro forma income statement for each year. Next, calculate operating cash flow. Finish the problem by determining total cash flow and then calculating NPV assuming a 20 percent required return. Use a 34 percent tax rate throughout. For help, look back at our shark attractant and power mulcher examples.

Project X is a new type of audiophile-grade stereo amplifier. We think we can sell 500 units per year at a price of $10,000 each. Variable costs per amplifier will run about $5,000 per unit, and the project should have a four-year life.

Fixed costs for the project will run $610,000 per year. Further, we will need to invest a total of $1,100,000 in manufacturing equipment. This equipment is seven-year MACRS property for tax purposes. In four years, the equipment will be worth about half of what we paid for it. We will have to invest $900,000 in net working capital at the start. After that, net working capital requirements will be 30 percent of sales.

9.3 **Scenario Analysis** A project under consideration costs $500,000, has a five-year life, and has no salvage value. Depreciation is straight-line to zero. The required return is 15 percent, and the tax rate is 34 percent. Sales are projected at 400 units per year. Price per unit is $3,000, variable cost per unit is $1,900, and fixed costs are $250,000 per year. No net working capital is required.

Suppose you think the unit sales, price, variable cost, and fixed cost projections are accurate to within 5 percent. What are the upper and lower bounds for these projections? What is the base-case NPV? What are the best- and worst-case scenario NPVs?

Answers to Self-Test Problems

9.1 First, we can calculate the project's EBIT, its tax bill, and its net income.

$$\text{EBIT} = \$1{,}432 - 1{,}002 - 80 = \$350$$
$$\text{Taxes} = \$350 \times .34 = \$119$$
$$\text{Net income} = \$350 - 119 = \$231$$

With these numbers, operating cash flow is:

$$\begin{aligned} \text{OCF} &= \text{EBIT} + \text{Depreciation} - \text{Taxes} \\ &= \$350 + 80 - 119 \\ &= \$311 \end{aligned}$$

9.2 To develop the pro forma income statements, we need to calculate the depreciation for each of the four years. The relevant MACRS percentages, depreciation allowances, and book values for the first four years are (remember that this is seven-year property for tax purposes):

Year	MACRS Percentage	Depreciation	Ending Book Value
1	14.29%	.1429 × $1,100,000 = $157,190	$942,810
2	24.49	.2449 × 1,100,000 = 269,390	673,420
3	17.49	.1749 × 1,100,000 = 192,390	481,030
4	12.49	.1249 × 1,100,000 = 137,390	343,640

The projected income statements, therefore, are as follows:

	Year			
	1	2	3	4
Sales	$5,000,000	$5,000,000	$5,000,000	$5,000,000
Variable costs	2,500,000	2,500,000	2,500,000	2,500,000
Fixed costs	610,000	610,000	610,000	610,000
Depreciation	157,190	269,390	192,390	137,390
EBIT	$1,732,810	$1,620,610	$1,697,610	$1,752,610
Taxes (34%)	589,155	551,007	577,187	595,887
Net income	$1,143,655	$1,069,603	$1,120,423	$1,156,723

Based on this information, the operating cash flows are:

	Year 1	2	3	4
EBIT	$1,732,810	$1,620,610	$1,697,610	$1,752,610
Depreciation	157,190	269,390	192,390	137,390
Taxes	− 589,155	− 551,007	− 577,187	− 595,887
Operating cash flow	$1,300,845	$1,338,993	$1,312,813	$1,294,113

We now have to worry about the nonoperating cash flows. Net working capital starts out at $900,000 and then rises to 30 percent of sales, or $1,500,000. This is a $600,000 addition to net working capital.

Finally, we have to invest $1,100,000 to get started. In four years, the book value of this investment will be $343,640 compared to an estimated market value of $550,000 (half of the cost). The aftertax salvage is thus $550,000 − .34 × ($550,000 − 343,640) = $479,838.

When we combine all this information, the projected cash flows for Project X are:

	Year 0	1	2	3	4
Operating cash flow		$1,300,845	$1,338,993	$1,312,813	$1,294,113
Additions to NWC	−$ 900,000	− 600,000			1,500,000
Capital spending	− 1,100,000				479,838
Total cash flow	−$2,000,000	$ 700,845	$1,338,993	$1,312,813	$3,273,951

With these cash flows, the NPV at 20 percent is:

$$\begin{aligned} \text{NPV} &= -\$2{,}000{,}000 + 700{,}845/1.2 + 1{,}338{,}993/1.2^2 \\ &\quad + 1{,}312{,}813/1.2^3 + 3{,}273{,}951/1.2^4 \\ &= \$1{,}852{,}496 \end{aligned}$$

So this project appears quite profitable.

9.3 We can summarize the relevant information as follows:

	Base Case	Lower Bound	Upper Bound
Unit sales	400	380	420
Price per unit	$3,000	$2,850	$3,150
Variable costs per unit	$1,900	$1,805	$1,995
Fixed costs	$250,000	$237,500	$262,500

The depreciation is $100,000 per year and the tax rate is 34 percent, so we can calculate the cash flows under each scenario. Remember that we assign high costs and low prices and volume under the worst case and just the opposite for the best case.

Scenario	Unit Sales	Price	Variable Cost	Fixed Costs	Cash Flow
Base	400	$3,000	$1,900	$250,000	$159,400
Best	420	3,150	1,805	237,500	250,084
Worst	380	2,850	1,995	262,500	75,184

At 15 percent, the five-year annuity factor is 3.35216, so the NPVs are:

$$\text{Base-case NPV} = -\$500{,}000 + 3.35216 \times \$159{,}400 = \$\ 34{,}334$$

$$\text{Best-case NPV} = -\$500{,}000 + 3.35216 \times \$250{,}084 = \$338{,}320$$

$$\text{Worst-case NPV} = -\$500{,}000 + 3.35216 \times \$\ 75{,}184 = -\$247{,}972$$

Questions and Problems

Basic (Questions 1–18)

1. **Stand-Alone Principle** Suppose a financial manager is quoted as saying: "Our firm uses the stand-alone principle. Since we treat projects like a minifirm in our evaluation process, we include financing costs, because financing costs are relevant at the firm level." Critically evaluate this statement.

Investment = $7.7 million

2. **Relevant Cash Flows** Perfect Plexiglass, Inc., is looking at setting up a new manufacturing plant to produce surfboards. The company bought some land six years ago for $5 million in anticipation of using it as a warehouse and distribution site, but the company decided to rent facilities from a competitor instead. The land was appraised last week for only $200,000. The company wants to build its new manufacturing plant on this land; the plant will cost $7 million to build, and the site requires $500,000 in grading before it is suitable for construction. What is the proper cash flow amount to use as the initial investment in fixed assets when evaluating this project? Why?

Cash flow = $171 million

3. **Relevant Cash Flows** Stevinator Motorworks Corp. currently sells 10,000 compact cars per year at $8,000 each, and 25,000 luxury sedans per year at $20,000 each. The company wants to introduce a new mid-sized sedan to fill out its product line; they hope to sell 15,000 of the cars per year at $13,000 each. An independent consultant has determined that if Stevinator introduces the new cars, it will likely boost the sales of its existing compacts by 7,000 units per year, while reducing the unit sales of its luxury sedans by 4,000 units per year. What is the annual cash flow amount to use as the sales figure when evaluating this project? Why?

Net income = $43,875

4. **Calculating Projected Net Income** A proposed new investment has projected sales of $650,000. Variable costs are 55 percent of sales, and fixed costs are $125,000; depreciation is $100,000. Prepare a pro forma income statement assuming a tax rate of 35 percent. What is the projected net income?

OCF = $187,357

5. **Calculating OCF** Consider the following income statement:

Sales	$520,500
Costs	281,000
Depreciation	105,800
Taxes (39%)	?
Net income	?

Fill in the missing numbers and then calculate the OCF.

6. **Calculating OCF** A proposed new project has projected sales of $49,350, costs of $25,000, and depreciation of $6,175. The tax rate is 34 percent. Calculate operating cash flow.

OCF = $18,170.50
Trans. 9.10

7. **Calculating Depreciation** A piece of newly purchased industrial equipment costs $472,000 and is classified as seven-year property under modified ACRS. Calculate the annual depreciation allowances and end-of-the-year book values for this equipment.

Trans. 9.11

8. **Calculating Salvage Value** Consider an asset that costs $100,000 and is depreciated straight-line to zero over its eight-year tax life. The asset is to be used in a five-year project; at the end of the project, the asset can be sold for $20,000. If the relevant tax rate is 35 percent, what is the aftertax cash flow from the sale of this asset?

$26,125

9. **Calculating Salvage Value** An asset used in a four-year project falls in the five-year modified ACRS class life for tax purposes. The asset has an acquisition cost of $5 million and is sold for $2 million at the end of the project. If the tax rate is 34 percent, what is the aftertax salvage value of the asset?

$1,613,760

10. **Identifying Cash Flows** Last year, Stimpson and Renford Corporation reported sales of $52,775 and costs of $39,360. The following information was also reported for the same period:

NWC decreased $2,020
Net cash flow = $15,435

	Beginning	Ending
Accounts receivable	$42,100	$37,000
Inventory	61,750	66,330
Accounts payable	94,000	95,500

Based on this information, what was Stimpson and Renford's change in net working capital for last year? What was the net cash flow?

11. **Calculating Project OCF** Wilmot Industries is considering a new three-year expansion project that requires an initial fixed asset investment of $1.2 million. The fixed asset will be depreciated straight-line to zero over its three-year tax life, at which time it will be worthless. The project is estimated to generate $1 million in annual sales, with costs of $500,000. If the tax rate is 35 percent, what is the OCF for this project?

OCF = $465,000

12. **Calculating Project NPV** In the previous problem, suppose the required return on the project is 8 percent. What is the project's NPV?

NPV = −$1,649.90

13. **Calculating Project Cash Flow from Assets** In the previous problem, suppose the project requires an initial investment in net working capital of $100,000 and the fixed asset has a market value of $175,000 at the end of the project. What is the project's Year 0 net cash flow? Year 1? Year 2? Year 3? What is the new NPV?

NPV = $68,031.74

14. **NPV and Modified ACRS** In the previous problem, suppose the fixed asset actually falls into the three-year modified ACRS class life. All the other facts are the same. What is the project's Year 1 net cash flow now? Year 2? Year 3? What is the new NPV?

NPV = $70,992.35

15. **Scenario Analysis** Up-or-Down, Inc., has the following estimates for its new gear assembly project: price = $250 per unit; variable costs = $135 per unit; fixed costs = $8 million; quantity = 100,000

Trans. 9.12

units. Suppose the company believes all of its estimates are accurate only to within ±15 percent. What values should the company use for the four variables above when it performs its best-case scenario analysis? What about the worst-case scenario?

Trans. 9.13

16. **Sensitivity Analysis** For the company in the previous problem, suppose management is most concerned about the impact of its price estimate on the project's profitability. How could you answer this question for Up-or-Down? Describe how you would calculate your answer. What values would you use for the other forecast variables?

17. **Forecasting Risk** What is forecasting risk? In general, would the degree of forecasting risk be greater for a new product or a cost-cutting proposal? Why?

18. **Options and NPV** What is the option to abandon? The option to expand? Explain why we tend to underestimate NPV when we ignore these options.

Intermediate
(Questions 19–21)

OCF = \$343,625
NPV = \$452,782.34
$\Delta NPV/\Delta S = -\$21.246$

19. **Sensitivity Analysis** We are evaluating a project that costs \$960,000, has a six-year life, and no salvage value. Assume depreciation is straight-line to zero over the life of the project. Sales are projected at 150,000 units per year. Price per unit is \$19.95, variable cost per unit is \$12.00, and fixed costs are \$750,000 per year. The tax rate is 35 percent and we require a 12 percent return on this project.

Calculate the base-case cash flow and NPV. What is the sensitivity of NPV to changes in the sales figure? Explain what your answer tells you about a 500 unit decrease in projected sales.

Best case: NPV = \$2,380,729
Worst case: NPV = −\$1,219.014

20. **Scenario Analysis** In the previous problem, suppose the projections given for price, quantity, variable costs, and fixed costs are all accurate to within ±10 percent. Calculate the best-case and worst-case NPV figures.

a. Base case: NPV = \$80,706.66
Best case: NPV = \$545,987.62
Worst case: NPV = −\$319,471.13
b. $\Delta NPV/\Delta FC = -2.153$

21. **Project Analysis** You are considering a new product launch. It will cost \$720,000, have a four-year life, and have no salvage value; depreciation is straight-line to zero. Sales are projected at 75 units per year; price per unit will be \$20,000, variable cost per unit will be \$14,000, and fixed costs are \$175,000 per year. The required return on the project is 8 percent and the relevant tax rate is 35 percent.
   a. Based on your experience, you think the unit sales, variable cost, and fixed cost projections above are probably accurate to within ±12 percent. What are the upper and lower bounds for these projections? What is the base-case NPV? What are the best-case and worst-case scenarios?
   b. Evaluate the sensitivity of your base-case NPV to changes in fixed costs.

Challenge
(Questions 22–23)

a. OCF = \$436,000
NPV = \$235,767.34

22. **Scenario Analysis** Consider a project to supply the highway department of your state with 25,000 tons of rock salt annually to drop on winter roads in your county. You will need an initial \$1,250,000 investment in processing equipment to get the project started; the project will last for five years. The accounting

department estimates that annual fixed costs will be $200,000 and that variable costs should be $90 per ton; accounting will depreciate the initial fixed asset investment straight-line to zero over the five-year project life. It also estimates a salvage value of $100,000. The marketing department estimates that the state will let the contract at a selling price of $120 per ton. The engineering department estimates you will need an initial net working capital investment of $90,000. You require a 14 percent return and face a marginal tax rate of 38 percent on this project.

a. What is the estimated OCF for this project? The NPV? Should you pursue this project?

b. Suppose you believe the accounting department's cost and salvage value projections are only accurate to within ±15 percent; the marketing department's price estimate is accurate only to within ±10 percent; and the engineering department's net working capital estimate is accurate only to within ±5 percent. What is your worst-case scenario for this project? Your best-case scenario? Do you still want to pursue the project?

b. Worst-case:
NPV = −$1,192,006.19
Best-case:
NPV = $1,663,540.87

23. Project Evaluation Terminator Pest Control (TPC), Inc., projects unit sales for a new household-use laser-guided cockroach eradication system as follows:

NPV = −$723,161.25
IRR = 7.75%

Year	Unit Sales
1	80,000
2	90,000
3	95,000
4	99,000
5	75,000

The eradication system will require $875,000 in net working capital to start, and additional net working capital investments each year equal to 35 percent of the projected sales increase for the following year. (Since sales are expected to fall in Year 5, then there is no NWC cash flow occurring for Year 4.) Total fixed costs are $200,000 per year, variable production costs are $75 per unit, and the units are priced at $105 each. The equipment needed to begin production has an installed cost of $9,750,000. This equipment is mostly industrial machinery and thus qualifies as seven-year modified ACRS property. In five years, this equipment can be sold for about 28 percent of its acquisition cost. TPC is in the 38 percent marginal tax bracket and has a required return on all its projects of 10 percent. Based on these preliminary project estimates, what is the NPV of the project? What is the IRR?

Part Five

RISK AND RETURN

Almost all financial decisions are made under uncertainty, meaning that they involve decisions made today about events that will occur in the future. Consequently, an understanding of risk is crucial in financial decision making. In Chapter 10, we study the history of capital market risks and rewards to begin to understand the relation between risk and return. What we see is that the rewards obtained from bearing risk have, through time, been substantial. We also learn that the risks have been substantial.

Chapter 11 builds on the lessons from capital market history to develop a simple, but very powerful, understanding of how risks are priced in the capital markets. The key result is that only certain types of risks are rewarded.

OUTLINE

Chapter Ten

Some Lessons from Capital Market History

After studying this chapter, you should have a good understanding of:

How to calculate the return on an investment.

The relation between real and nominal returns.

The historical returns on various important types of investments.

The historical risks on various important types of investments.

Trans. 10.1
Chapter Outline

Thus far, we haven't had much to say about what determines the required return on an investment. In one sense, the answer is very simple: The required return depends on the risk of the investment. The greater the risk, the greater is the required return.

Lecture Tip: The maxim "The greater the risk, the greater the return" is another GURF (Great Underlying Rule of Finance).

Having said this, we are left with a somewhat more difficult problem. How can we measure the amount of risk present in an investment? Put another way, what does it mean to say that one investment is riskier than another? Obviously, we need to define what we mean by risk if we are going to answer these questions. This is our task in the next two chapters.

From the last several chapters, we know that one of the responsibilities of the financial manager is to assess the value of proposed investments. In doing this, it is important that we first look at what financial investments have to offer. At a minimum, the return we require from a proposed nonfinancial investment must be at least as large as what we can get from buying financial assets of similar risk.

Our goal in this chapter is to provide a perspective on what capital market history can tell us about risk and return. The most important thing to get out of this chapter is a feel for the numbers. What is a high return? What is a low one? More generally, what returns should we expect from financial assets and what are the risks from such investments? This perspective is essential for understanding how to analyze and value risky investment projects.

We start our discussion of risk and return by describing the historical experience of investors in U.S. financial markets. In 1931, for example, the stock market lost 43 percent of its value. Just two years later, the stock market gained 54 percent. In more recent memory, the market lost about 25 percent of its value on October 19, 1987, alone. What lessons, if any, can financial managers learn from such shifts in the stock market? We will explore the last half-century (and then some) of market history to find out.

Not everyone agrees on the value of studying history. On the one hand, there is philosopher George Santayana's famous comment, "Those who do not remember the past are condemned to repeat it." On the other hand, there is industrialist Henry Ford's equally famous comment, "History is more or less bunk." Nonetheless, perhaps everyone would agree with Mark Twain when he observed, "October. This is one of the peculiarly dangerous months to speculate in stocks in. The others are July, January, September, April, November, May, March, June, December, August, and February."

There are two central lessons that emerge from our study of market history. First, there is a reward for bearing risk. Second, the greater the potential reward is, the greater is the risk. To understand these facts about market returns, we devote much of this chapter to reporting the statistics and numbers that make up the modern capital market history of the United States. In the next chapter, these facts provide the foundation for our study of how financial markets put a price on risk.

10.1 RETURNS

We wish to discuss historical returns on different types of financial assets. The first thing we need to do, then, is to briefly discuss how to calculate the return from investing.

Problems 1–3

Dollar Returns

If you buy an asset of any sort, your gain (or loss) from that investment is called your *return on investment.* This return will usually have two components. First, you may receive some cash directly while you own the investment. This is called the *income component* of your return. Second, the value of the asset you purchase will often change. In this case, you have a capital gain or capital loss on your investment.[1]

Concept Q Answer 10.1a

To illustrate, suppose the Video Concept Company has several thousand shares of stock outstanding. You purchased some of these shares of stock in the company at the beginning of the year. It is now year-end, and you want to determine how well you have done on your investment.

First, over the year, a company may pay cash dividends to its shareholders. As a stockholder in Video Concept Company, you are a part owner of the company. If the company is profitable, it may choose to distribute some of its profits to shareholders (we discuss the details of dividend policy in

[1] As we mentioned in an earlier chapter, strictly speaking, what is and what is not a capital gain (or loss) is determined by the IRS. We thus use the terms loosely.

Chapter 15). So, as the owner of some stock, you will receive some cash. This cash is the income component from owning the stock.

In addition to the dividend, the other part of your return is the capital gain or capital loss on the stock. This part arises from changes in the value of your investment. For example, consider the cash flows illustrated in Figure 10.1. The stock is selling for \$37 per share. If you buy 100 shares, you have a total outlay of \$3,700. Suppose, over the year, the stock paid a dividend of \$1.85 per share. By the end of the year, then, you would have received income of:

$$\text{Dividend} = \$1.85 \times 100 = \$185$$

Also, the value of the stock rises to \$40.33 per share by the end of the year. Your 100 shares are worth \$4,033, so you have a capital gain of:

$$\text{Capital gain} = (\$40.33 - 37) \times 100 = \$333$$

On the other hand, if the price had dropped to, say, \$34.78, you would have a capital loss of:

$$\text{Capital loss} = (\$34.78 - 37) \times 100 = -\$222$$

Notice that a capital loss is the same thing as a negative capital gain.

The total dollar return on your investment is the sum of the dividend and the capital gain:

$$\text{Total dollar return} = \text{Dividend income} + \text{Capital gain (or loss)} \quad [10.1]$$

In our first example, the total dollar return is thus given by:

$$\text{Total dollar return} = \$185 + 333 = \$518$$

Notice that, if you sold the stock at the end of the year, the total amount of cash you would have would be your initial investment plus the total return. In the preceding example, then:

$$\begin{aligned} \text{Total cash if stock is sold} &= \text{Initial investment} + \text{Total return} \\ &= \$3{,}700 + 518 \quad [10.2] \\ &= \$4{,}218 \end{aligned}$$

FIGURE 10.1
Dollar returns

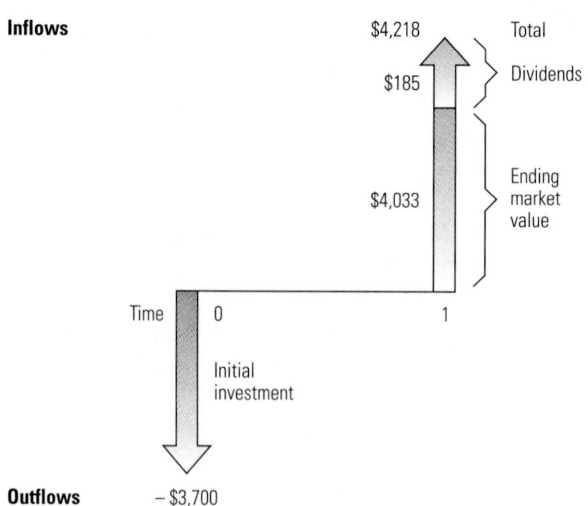

As a check, notice that this is the same as the proceeds from the sale of the stock plus the dividends:

$$\begin{aligned}\text{Proceeds from stock sale} + \text{Dividends} &= \$40.33 \times 100 + 185 \\ &= \$4{,}033 + 185 \\ &= \$4{,}218\end{aligned}$$

Suppose you hold on to your Video Concept stock and don't sell it at the end of the year. Should you still consider the capital gain as part of your return? Isn't this only a "paper" gain and not really a cash flow if you don't sell it?

Concept Q Answer 10.1b

The answer to the first question is a strong yes, and the answer to the second is an equally strong no. The capital gain is every bit as much a part of your return as the dividend, and you should certainly count it as part of your return. That you actually decided to keep the stock and not sell (you don't "realize" the gain) is irrelevant because you could have converted it to cash if you wanted to. Whether you choose to do so or not is up to you.

After all, if you insisted on converting your gain to cash, you could always sell the stock at year-end and immediately reinvest by buying the stock back. There is no net difference between doing this and just not selling (assuming, of course, that there are no tax consequences from selling the stock). Again, the point is that whether you actually cash out and buy sodas (or whatever) or reinvest by not selling doesn't affect the return you earn.

Lecture Tip: See IM 10.1 for points to consider in measuring a security's performance.

Percentage Returns

It is usually more convenient to summarize information about returns in percentage terms, rather than dollar terms, because that way your return doesn't depend on how much you actually invest. The question we want to answer is: How much do we get for each dollar we invest?

Concept Q Answer 10.1c

To answer this question, let P_t be the price of the stock at the beginning of the year and let D_{t+1} be the dividend paid on the stock during the year. Consider the cash flows in Figure 10.2. These are the same as those in Figure 10.1, except that we have now expressed everything on a per-share basis.

FIGURE 10.2 Percentage returns. Dollar return and per share return **Trans. 10.2**

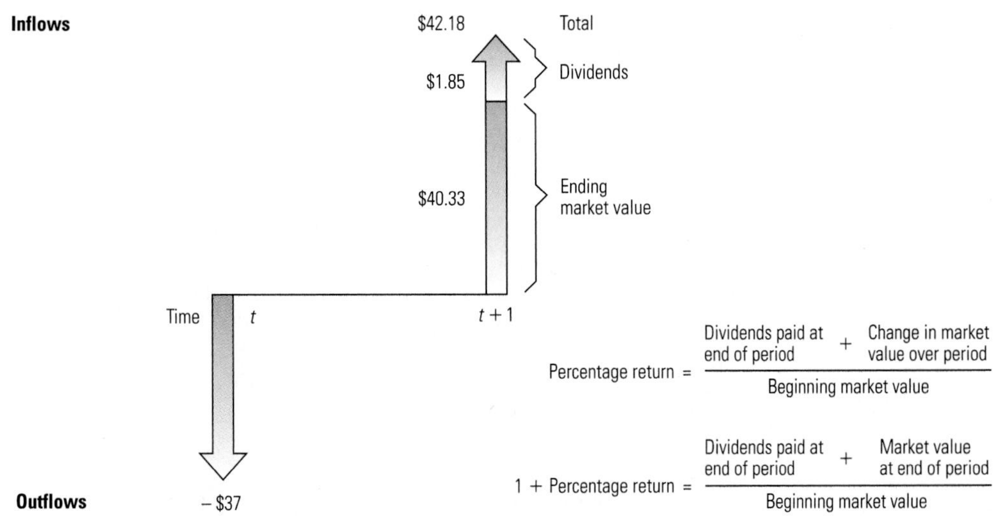

In our example, the price at the beginning of the year was \$37 per share and the dividend paid during the year on each share was \$1.85. As we discussed in Chapter 7, expressing the dividend as a percentage of the beginning stock price results in the dividend yield:

$$\begin{aligned} \text{Dividend yield} &= D_{t+1}/P_t \\ &= \$1.85/37 = .05 = 5\% \end{aligned}$$

This says that, for each dollar we invest, we get 5 cents in dividends.

The second component of our percentage return is the capital gains yield. Recall (from Chapter 7) that this is calculated as the change in the price during the year (the capital gain) divided by the beginning price:

$$\begin{aligned} \text{Capital gains yield} &= (P_{t+1} - P_t)/P_t \\ &= (\$40.33 - 37)/37 \\ &= \$3.33/37 \\ &= 9\% \end{aligned}$$

So, per dollar invested, we get 9 cents in capital gains.

Putting it together, per dollar invested, we get 5 cents in dividends and 9 cents in capital gains; so we get a total of 14 cents. Our percentage return is 14 cents on the dollar, or 14 percent.

To check this, notice that we invested \$3,700 and ended up with \$4,218. By what percentage did our \$3,700 increase? As we saw, we picked up \$4,218 − 3,700 = \$518. This is a \$518/3,700 = 14% increase.

EXAMPLE 10.1 Calculating Returns

Suppose you buy some stock for \$25 per share. At the end of the year, the price is \$35 per share. During the year, you got a \$2 dividend per share. This is the situation illustrated in Figure 10.3. What is the dividend yield? The capital gains yield? The percentage return? If your total investment was \$1,000, how much do you have at the end of the year?

Your \$2 dividend per share works out to a dividend yield of:

$$\begin{aligned} \text{Dividend yield} &= D_{t+1}/P_t \\ &= \$2/25 = .08 = 8\% \end{aligned}$$

FIGURE 10.3
Cash flow—an investment example

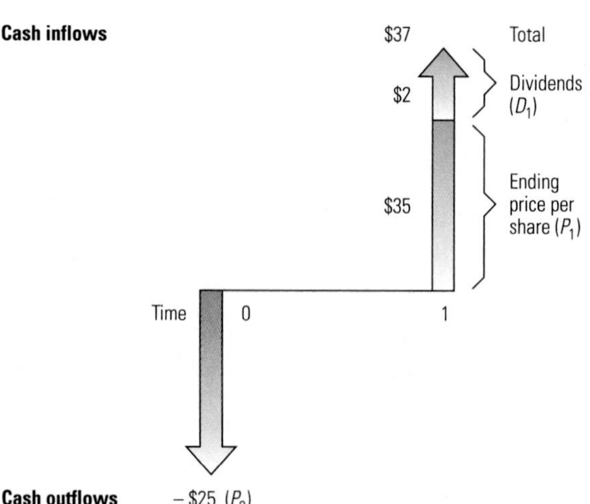

The per-share capital gain is \$10, so the capital gains yield is:

$$\begin{aligned}\text{Capital gains yield} &= (P_{t+1} - P_t)/P_t \\ &= (\$35 - 25)/25 \\ &= \$10/25 \\ &= 40\%\end{aligned}$$

The total percentage return is thus 48 percent.

If you had invested \$1,000, you would have \$1,480 at the end of the year, a 48 percent increase. To check this, note that your \$1,000 would have bought you \$1,000/25 = 40 shares. Your 40 shares would then have paid you a total of 40 × \$2 = \$80 in cash dividends. Your \$10 per-share gain would give you a total capital gain of \$10 × 40 = \$400. Add these together, and you get the \$480 increase. • • •

CONCEPT QUESTIONS

10.1a What are the two parts of total return?

10.1b Why are unrealized capital gains or losses included in the calculation of returns?

10.1c What is the difference between a dollar return and a percentage return? Why are percentage returns more convenient?

10.2 INFLATION AND RETURNS

So far, we haven't worried about inflation in calculating returns. Since this is an important consideration, we consider the impact of inflation next.

Problems 4–10, 15–17

Real versus Nominal Returns

The returns we calculated in the previous section are called **nominal returns** because they weren't adjusted for inflation. Returns that have been adjusted to reflect inflation are called **real returns.**

nominal return
Return on an investment not adjusted for inflation.

real return
Return adjusted for the effects of inflation.

To see the effect of inflation on returns, suppose prices are currently rising by 5 percent per year. In other words, the inflation rate is 5 percent. We are considering an investment that will be worth \$115.50 in one year. It costs \$100 today.

We start by calculating the percentage return. In this case, there is no income component, so the return is the capital gains yield of (\$115.50 − 100)/100 = 15.50%. Once again, we've ignored the effect of inflation, so this 15.50 percent is the nominal return.

Concept Q Answer 10.2a

Trans. 10.3 Inflation and Returns (Supplemental)

What is the impact of inflation here? To answer, suppose pizzas cost \$5 apiece at the beginning of the year. With \$100, we can buy 20 pizzas. Since the inflation rate is 5 percent, pizzas will cost 5 percent more, or \$5.25, at the end of the year. If we take the investment, how many pizzas can we buy at the end of the year? Measured in pizzas instead of dollars, what is our return?

Our \$115.50 from the investment will buy us \$115.50/5.25 = 22 pizzas. This is up from 20 pizzas, so our pizza return is (22 − 20)/20 = 10%. What this illustrates is that even though the nominal return on our investment is 15.5 percent, our buying power has only gone up by 10 percent because of inflation. Put another way, we are really only 10 percent richer. In this case, we say that the real return is 10 percent.

Lecture Tip: This example illustrates why it is often said that inflation encourages borrowing—loans are repaid in "cheaper" dollars.

Lecture Tip: See IM 10.2 for an example of the impact of taxes on real purchasing power.

Alternatively, with 5 percent inflation, each of the \$115.50 nominal dollars we get is worth 5 percent less in real terms, so the real dollar value of our investment in a year is:

$$\$115.50/1.05 = \$110$$

What we have done is to *deflate* the \$115.50 by 5 percent. Since we give up \$100 in current buying power to get the equivalent of \$110, our real return is again 10 percent. Because we have removed the effect of future inflation here, this \$110 is said to be measured in current dollars.

The difference between nominal and real returns is important and bears repeating:

> **Your nominal return on an investment is the percentage change in the number of dollars you have.**
>
> **Your real return on an investment is the percentage change in how much you can buy with your dollars, in other words, the percentage change in your buying power.**

The Fisher Effect

Fisher effect
Relationship between nominal returns, real returns, and inflation.

Concept Q Answer 10.2b

Our discussion of real and nominal returns illustrates a relationship often called the **Fisher effect** (after the great economist Irving Fisher). Since investors are ultimately concerned with what they can buy with their money, they require compensation for inflation. Let R stand for the nominal return and r stand for the real return. The Fisher effect tells us that the relationship between nominal returns, real returns, and inflation can be written as:

$$(1 + R) = (1 + r) \times (1 + h) \qquad [10.3]$$

where h is the inflation rate.

From the example above, the nominal return was 15.50 percent and the inflation rate was 5 percent. What was the real return? We can determine it by plugging in these numbers:

$$\begin{aligned}(1 + .1550) &= (1 + r) \times (1 + .05)\\ (1 + r) &= (1.1550)/(1.05) = 1.10\\ r &= 10\%\end{aligned}$$

This real return is the same as we had before. If we take another look at the Fisher effect, we can rearrange things a little as follows:

$$\begin{aligned}(1 + R) &= (1 + r) \times (1 + h)\\ R &= r + h + r \times h\end{aligned} \qquad [10.4]$$

What this tells us is that the nominal return has three components. First, there is the real return on the investment, r. Next, there is the compensation for the decrease in the value of the money originally invested because of inflation, h. The third component represents compensation for the fact that the dollars earned on the investment are also worth less because of the inflation.

This third component is usually small, so it is often dropped. The nominal rate is then approximately equal to the real rate plus the inflation rate:

$$R \approx r + h \qquad [10.5]$$

EXAMPLE 10.2 The Fisher Effect

If investors require a 10 percent real return, and the inflation rate is 8 percent, what must be the approximate nominal rate? The exact nominal rate?

First of all, the nominal rate is approximately equal to the sum of the real rate and the inflation rate: 10% + 8% = 18%. From the Fisher effect, we have:

$$\begin{aligned}(1 + R) &= (1 + r) \times (1 + h) \\ &= (1.10) \times (1.08) \\ &= 1.1880\end{aligned}$$

Therefore, the nominal rate will actually be closer to 19 percent. • • •

It is important to note that financial rates, such as interest rates, discount rates, and rates of return, are almost always quoted in nominal terms. To remind you of this, we will henceforth use the symbol R instead of r in most of our subsequent discussions about such rates.

International Note: This is a good point at which to discuss the response of financial markets to persistent inflation. IM 10.2 describes some instruments that became popular as a result of the inflation of the 1980s.

CONCEPT QUESTIONS

10.2a What is the difference between a nominal and a real return? Which is more important to a typical investor?

10.2b What is the Fisher effect?

10.3 THE HISTORICAL RECORD

Self-Test Problem 10.1
Problem 14

Roger Ibbotson and Rex Sinquefield conducted a famous set of studies dealing with rates of return in U.S. financial markets.[2] They presented year-to-year historical rates of return on five important types of financial investments. The returns can be interpreted as what you would have earned if you held portfolios of the following:

Lecture Tip: See IM 10.3 for a brief review of relevant statistics material.

1. Common stocks. The common stock portfolio is based on 500 of the largest companies (in terms of total market value of outstanding stock) in the United States.
2. Small stocks. This is a portfolio composed of smaller companies, where "small" corresponds to the smallest 20 percent of the companies listed on the New York Stock Exchange, again as measured by market value of outstanding stock.
3. Long-term corporate bonds. This is a portfolio of high-quality bonds with 20 years to maturity.
4. Long-term U.S. government bonds. This is a portfolio of U.S. government bonds with 20 years to maturity.
5. U.S. Treasury bills. This is a portfolio of Treasury bills (T-bills for short) with a three-month maturity.

These returns are not adjusted for inflation or taxes; thus, they are nominal, pretax returns.

In addition to the year-to-year returns on these financial instruments, the year-to-year percentage change in the Consumer Price Index (CPI) is also

[2] R. G. Ibbotson and R. A. Sinquefield, *Stocks, Bonds, Bills, and Inflation* [SBBI] (Charlottesville, Va.: Financial Analysis Research Foundation, 1982).

computed. This is a commonly used measure of inflation, so we can calculate real returns using this as the inflation rate.

A First Look

Before looking closely at the different portfolio returns, we take a look at the "big picture." Figure 10.4 shows what happened to $1 invested in these different portfolios at the beginning of 1925. The growth in value for each of the different portfolios over the 69-year period ending in 1994 is given separately (the long-term corporate bonds are omitted). Notice that to get everything on a single graph some modification in scaling is used. As is commonly done with financial series, the vertical axis is scaled such that equal distances measure equal percentage (as opposed to dollar) changes in values.

Looking at Figure 10.4, we see that the "small cap" (short for small capitalization) investment did the best overall. Every dollar invested grew to a

FIGURE 10.4
A $1 investment in different types of portfolios, 1926–1994 (Year-end 1925 = $1)

Trans. 10.4

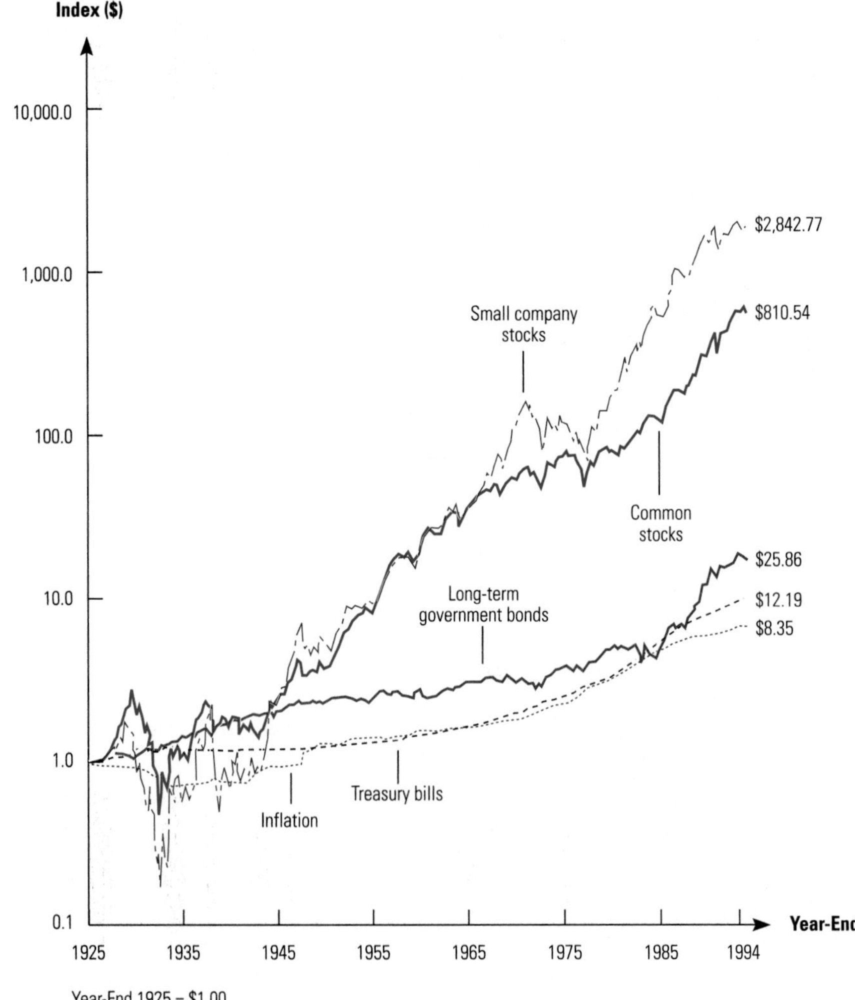

Source: © *Stocks, Bonds, Bills, and Inflation 1995 Yearbook*™, Ibbotson Associates, Inc., Chicago (annually updates work by Roger G. Ibbotson and Rex A. Sinquefield). All rights reserved.

remarkable \$2,842.77 over the 69 years. The larger common stock portfolio did less well; a dollar invested in it grew to \$810.54.

At the other end, the T-bill portfolio grew to only \$12.19. This is even less impressive when we consider the inflation over this period. As illustrated, the increase in the price level was such that \$8.35 is needed just to replace the original \$1.

Given the historical record, why would anybody buy anything other than small cap stocks? If you look closely at Figure 10.4, you will probably see the answer. The T-bill portfolio and the long-term government bond portfolio grew more slowly than did the stock portfolios, but they also grew much more steadily. The small stocks ended up on top, but as you can see, they grew quite erratically at times. For example, the small stocks were the worst performers for about the first 10 years and had a smaller return than long-term government bonds for almost 15 years.

Concept Q Answer 10.3a, 10.3b

A Closer Look

To illustrate the variability of the different investments, Figures 10.5 through 10.8 (on pages 251–253) plot the year-to-year percentage returns in the form of vertical bars drawn from the horizontal axis. The height of the bar tells us the return for the particular year. For example, looking at the long-term government bonds (Figure 10.7), we see the largest historical return (40.35 percent) occurred in 1982. This was a good year for bonds. In comparing these charts, notice the differences in the vertical axis scales. With this in mind, you can

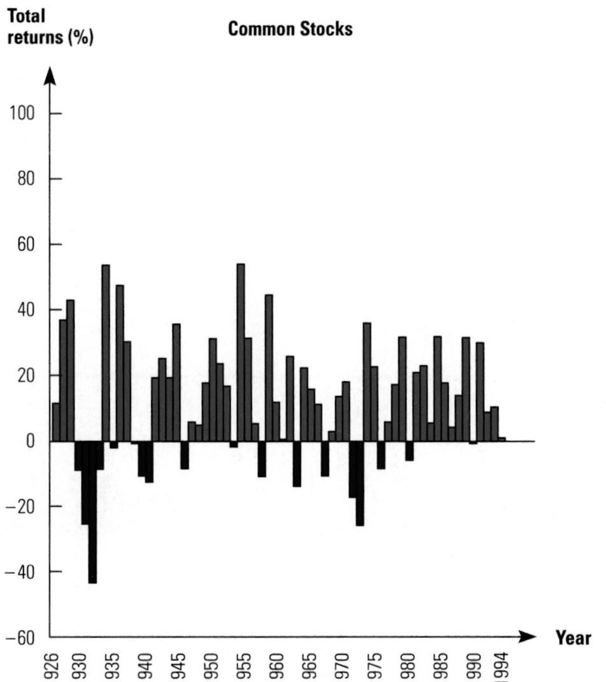

Source: © *Stocks, Bonds, Bills, and Inflation 1995 Yearbook*™, Ibbotson Associates, Inc., Chicago (annually updates work by Roger G. Ibbotson and Rex A. Sinquefield). All rights reserved.

FIGURE 10.5
Year-to-year total returns on common stocks: 1926–1994

Trans. 10.5

FIGURE 10.6
Year-to-year total returns on small-company stocks: 1926–1994

Trans. 10.6

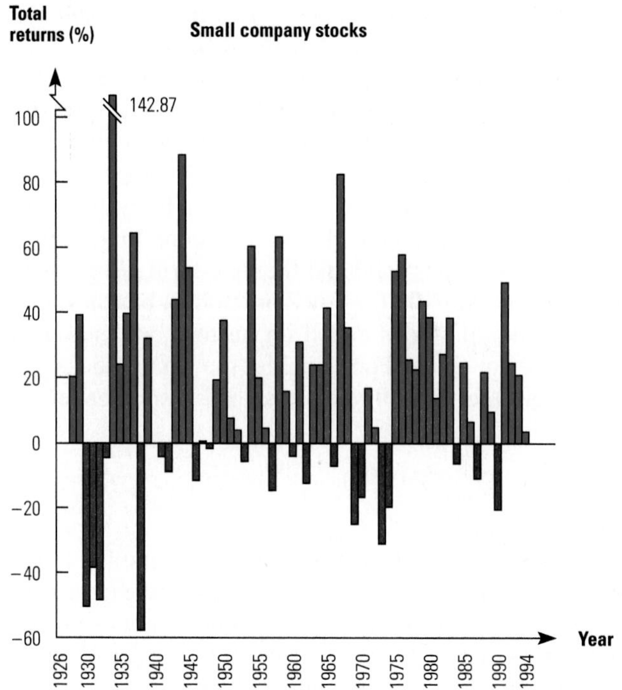

Source: © *Stocks, Bonds, Bills, and Inflation 1995 Yearbook*™, Ibbotson Associates, Inc., Chicago (annually updates work by Roger G. Ibbotson and Rex A. Sinquefield).

FIGURE 10.7 Year-to-year total returns on bonds and bills: 1926–1994 **Trans. 10.7**

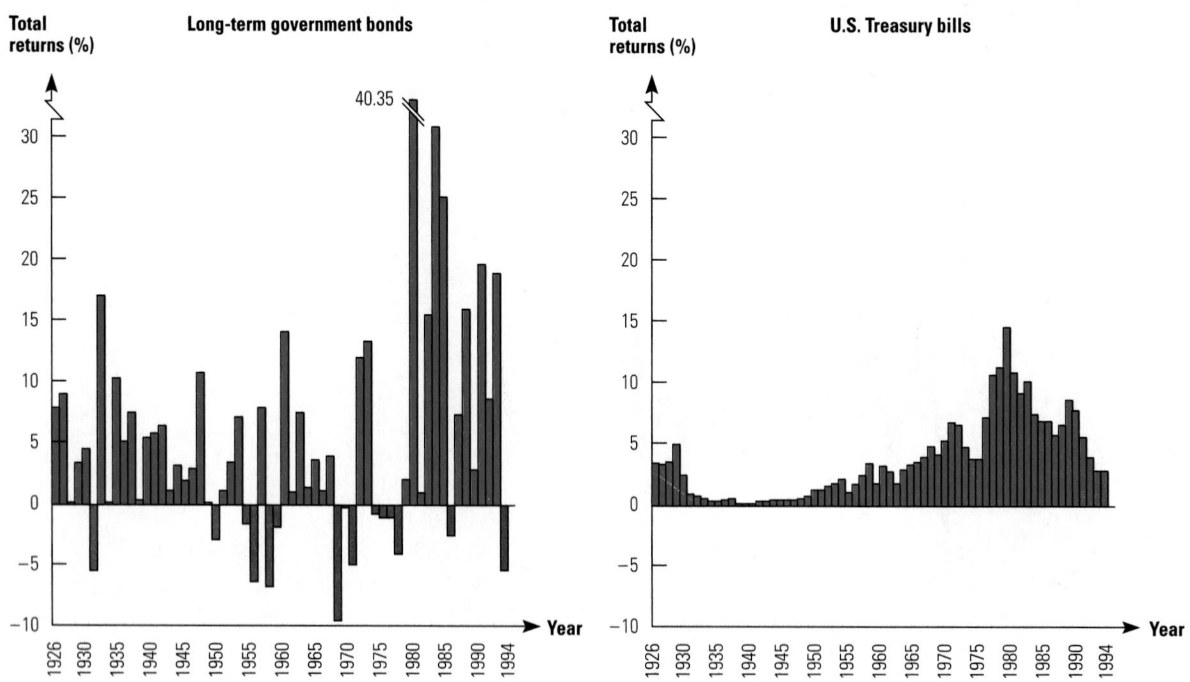

Source: © *Stocks, Bonds, Bills, and Inflation 1995 Yearbook*™, Ibbotson Associates, Inc., Chicago (annually updates work by Roger G. Ibbotson and Rex A. Sinquefield).

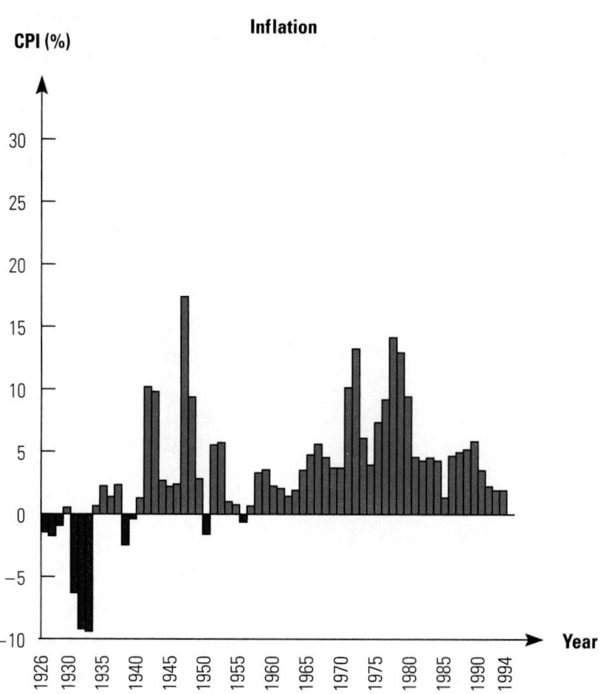

Source: © *Stocks, Bonds, Bills, and Inflation 1995 Yearbook*™, Ibbotson Associates, Inc., Chicago (annually updates work by Roger G. Ibbotson and Rex A. Sinquefield). All rights reserved.

FIGURE 10.8
Year-to-year inflation: 1926–1994

Trans. 10.8

see how predictably the Treasury bills (Figure 10.7) behaved compared to the small stocks (Figure 10.6).

The actual year-to-year returns used to draw these bar graphs are displayed in Table 10.1 (on pages 254–255). Looking at this table, we see, for example, that the largest single-year return is a remarkable 142.87 percent for the small cap stocks in 1933. In the same year, the large stocks (common stocks) "only" returned 53.99 percent. In contrast, the largest Treasury bill return was 14.71 percent in 1981.

Concept Q Answers 10.3c, 10.3d, 10.3e, 10.3f

CONCEPT QUESTIONS

10.3a With 20-20 hindsight, what was the best investment for the period 1926–35?

10.3b Why doesn't everyone just buy small stocks as investments?

10.3c What was the smallest return observed over the 69 years for each of these investments? When did it occur?

10.3d How many times did large stocks (common stocks) return more than 30 percent? How many times did they return less than −20 percent?

10.3e What was the longest "winning streak" (years without a negative return) for large stocks? For long-term government bonds?

10.3f How often did the T-bill portfolio have a negative return?

10.4 AVERAGE RETURNS: THE FIRST LESSON

Self-Test Problem 10.1
Problems 7, 10, 11

As you've probably begun to notice, the history of capital market returns is too complicated to be of much use in its undigested form. We need to begin

T A B L E 10.1
Year-to-year total returns: 1926–1994

Year	Common Stocks	Small Stocks	Long-Term Corporate Bonds	Long-Term Government Bonds	U.S. Treasury Bills	Consumer Price Index
1926	0.1162	0.0028	0.0737	0.0777	0.0327	−0.0149
1927	0.3749	0.2210	0.0744	0.0893	0.0312	−0.0208
1928	0.4361	0.3969	0.0284	0.0010	0.0324	−0.0097
1929	−0.0840	−0.5136	0.0327	0.0342	0.0475	0.0019
1930	−0.2490	−0.3815	0.0798	0.0466	0.0241	−0.0603
1931	−0.4334	−0.4975	−0.0185	−0.0531	0.0107	−0.0952
1932	−0.0819	−0.0539	0.1082	0.1684	0.0096	−0.1030
1933	0.5399	1.4287	0.1038	−0.0008	0.0030	0.0051
1934	−0.0144	0.2422	0.1384	0.1002	0.0016	0.0203
1935	0.4767	0.4019	0.0961	0.0498	0.0017	0.0299
1936	0.3392	0.6480	0.0674	0.0751	0.0018	0.0121
1937	−0.3503	−0.5801	0.0275	0.0023	0.0031	0.0310
1938	0.3112	0.3280	0.0613	0.0553	−0.0002	−0.0278
1939	−0.0041	0.0035	0.0397	0.0594	0.0002	−0.0048
1940	−0.0978	−0.0516	0.0339	0.0609	0.0000	0.0096
1941	−0.1159	−0.0900	0.0273	0.0093	0.0006	0.0972
1942	0.2034	0.4451	0.0260	0.0322	0.0027	0.0929
1943	0.2590	0.8837	0.0283	0.0208	0.0035	0.0316
1944	0.1975	0.5372	0.0473	0.0281	0.0033	0.0211
1945	0.3644	0.7361	0.0408	0.1073	0.0033	0.0225
1946	−0.0807	−0.1163	0.0172	−0.0010	0.0035	0.1817
1947	0.0571	0.0092	−0.0234	−0.0263	0.0050	0.0901
1948	0.0550	−0.0211	0.0414	0.0340	0.0081	0.0271
1949	0.1879	0.1975	0.0331	0.0645	0.0110	−0.0180
1950	0.3171	0.3875	0.0212	0.0006	0.0120	0.0579
1951	0.2402	0.0780	−0.0269	−0.0394	0.0149	0.0587
1952	0.1837	0.0303	0.0352	0.0116	0.0166	0.0088
1953	−0.0099	−0.0649	0.0341	0.0363	0.0182	0.0062
1954	0.5262	0.6058	0.0539	0.0719	0.0086	−0.0050
1955	0.3156	0.2044	0.0048	−0.0130	0.0157	0.0037
1956	0.0656	0.0428	−0.0681	−0.0559	0.0246	0.0286
1957	−0.1078	−0.1457	0.0871	0.0745	0.0314	0.0302
1958	0.4336	0.6489	−0.0222	−0.0610	0.0154	0.0176
1959	0.1195	0.1640	−0.0097	−0.0226	0.0295	0.0150

summarizing all these numbers. Accordingly, we discuss how to go about condensing the detailed data. We start out by calculating average returns.

Calculating Average Returns

Trans. 10.9
Average Returns and Volatility (Supplemental)

The obvious way to calculate the average returns on the different investments in Table 10.1 is simply to add up the yearly returns and divide by 69. The result is the historical average of the individual values.

For example, if you add up the returns for the common stocks for the 69 years, you will get about 8.36. The average annual return is thus 8.36/69 = 12.2%. You interpret this 12.2 percent just like any other average. If you picked a year at random from the 69-year history and you had to guess what the return in that year was, the best guess is 12.2 percent.

TABLE 10.1 *(concluded)*

Year	Common Stocks	Small Stocks	Long-Term Corporate Bonds	Long-Term Government Bonds	U.S. Treasury Bills	Consumer Price Index
1960	0.0047	−0.0329	0.0907	0.1378	0.0266	0.0148
1961	0.2689	0.3209	0.0482	0.0097	0.0213	0.0067
1962	−0.0873	−0.1190	0.0795	0.0689	0.0273	0.0122
1963	0.2280	0.2357	0.0219	0.0121	0.0312	0.0165
1964	0.1648	0.2352	0.0477	0.0351	0.0354	0.0119
1965	0.1245	0.4175	−0.0046	0.0071	0.0393	0.0192
1966	−0.1006	−0.0701	0.0020	0.0365	0.0476	0.0335
1967	0.2398	0.8357	−0.0495	−0.0919	0.0421	0.0304
1968	0.1106	0.3597	0.0257	−0.0026	0.0521	0.0472
1969	−0.0850	−0.2505	−0.0809	−0.0508	0.0658	0.0611
1970	0.0401	−0.1743	0.1837	0.1210	0.0653	0.0549
1971	0.1431	0.1650	0.1101	0.1323	0.0439	0.0336
1972	0.1898	0.0443	0.0726	0.0568	0.0384	0.0341
1973	−0.1466	−0.3090	0.0114	−0.0111	0.0693	0.0880
1974	−0.2647	−0.1995	−0.0306	0.0435	0.0800	0.1220
1975	0.3720	0.5282	0.1464	0.0919	0.0580	0.0701
1976	0.2384	0.5738	0.1865	0.1675	0.0508	0.0481
1977	−0.0718	0.2538	0.0171	−0.0067	0.0512	0.0677
1978	0.0656	0.2346	−0.0007	−0.0116	0.0718	0.0903
1979	0.1844	0.4346	−0.0418	−0.0122	0.1038	0.1331
1980	0.3242	0.3988	−0.0262	−0.0395	0.1124	0.1240
1981	−0.0491	0.1388	−0.0096	0.0185	0.1471	0.0894
1982	0.2141	0.2801	0.4379	0.4035	0.1054	0.0387
1983	0.2251	0.3967	0.0470	0.0068	0.0880	0.0380
1984	0.0627	−0.0667	0.1639	0.1543	0.0985	0.0395
1985	0.3216	0.2466	0.3090	0.3097	0.0772	0.0377
1986	0.1847	0.0685	0.1985	0.2444	0.0616	0.0113
1987	0.0523	−0.0930	−0.0027	−0.0269	0.0547	0.0441
1988	0.1681	0.2287	0.1070	0.0967	0.0635	0.0447
1989	0.3149	0.1018	0.1623	0.1811	0.0837	0.0465
1990	−0.0317	−0.2156	0.0678	0.0618	0.0781	0.0611
1991	0.3055	0.4463	0.1989	0.1930	0.0560	0.0306
1992	0.0767	0.2335	0.0939	0.0805	0.0351	0.0290
1993	0.0999	0.2098	0.1319	0.1824	0.0290	0.0275
1994	0.0131	0.0311	−0.0576	−0.0777	0.0390	0.0267

Source: © *Stocks, Bonds, Bills, and Inflation 1995 Yearbook*™, Ibbotson Associates, Inc., Chicago (annually updates work by Roger G. Ibbotson and Rex A. Sinquefield). All rights reserved.

Average Returns: The Historical Record

Table 10.2 (p. 256) shows the average returns computed from Table 10.1. As shown, in a typical year, the small stocks increased in value by 17.4 percent. Notice also how much larger the stock returns are than the bond returns.

These averages are, of course, nominal since we haven't worried about inflation. Notice that the average inflation rate was 3.2 percent per year over this 69-year span. The nominal return on U.S. Treasury bills was 3.7 percent per year. The average real return on Treasury bills was thus approximately .5 percent per year; so the real return on T-bills has been quite low historically.

Trans. 10.10
Average Annual Returns: 1926–1994

At the other extreme, small stocks had an average real return of about 17.4% − 3.2% = 14.2%, which is relatively large. If you remember the Rule

TABLE 10.2
Average annual returns: 1926–1994

Trans. 10.10

Investment	Average Return
Common stocks	12.2%
Small stocks	17.4
Long-term corporate bonds	5.7
Long-term government bonds	5.2
U.S. Treasury bills	3.7
Inflation	3.2

Source: © *Stocks, Bonds, Bills, and Inflation 1995 Yearbook*™, Ibbotson Associates, Inc., Chicago (annually updates work by Roger G. Ibbotson and Rex A. Sinquefield).

of 72 (Chapter 5), then a quick "back of the envelope" calculation tells us that 14.2 percent real growth doubles your buying power about every five years. Notice also that the real value of the common stock portfolio increased by 9 percent in a typical year.

Risk Premiums

Trans. 10.11
Using Capital Market History (Supplemental)

Now that we have computed some average returns, it seems logical to see how they compare with each other. Based on our discussion above, one such comparison involves government-issued securities. These are free of much of the variability we see in, for example, the stock market.

Concept Q Answer 10.4a

The government borrows money by issuing bonds. These bonds come in different forms. The ones we will focus on are the Treasury bills. These have the shortest time to maturity of the different government bonds. Because the government can always raise taxes to pay its bills, this debt is virtually free of any default risk over its short life. Thus, we will call the rate of return on such debt the *risk-free return,* and we will use it as a kind of benchmark.

Lecture Tip: See IM 10.4 for a look at the risk premiums of investments with longer horizons.

A particularly interesting comparison involves the virtually risk-free return on T-bills and the very risky return on common stocks. The difference between these two returns can be interpreted as a measure of the *excess return* on the average risky asset (assuming the stock of a large U.S. corporation has about average risk compared to all risky assets).

We call this the "excess" return since it is the additional return we earn by moving from a relatively risk-free investment to a risky one. Because it can be interpreted as a reward for bearing risk, we will call it a **risk premium.**

risk premium
The excess return required from an investment in a risky asset over a risk-free investment.

From Table 10.2, we can calculate the risk premiums for the different investments. We report only the nominal risk premium in Table 10.3 because there is only a slight difference between the historical nominal and real risk premiums.

The risk premium on T-bills is shown as zero in the table because we have assumed that they are riskless.

Concept Q Answers 10.4b, 10.4c

The First Lesson

Concept Q Answer 10.4d

Looking at Table 10.3, we see that the average risk premium earned by a typical large common stock is 12.2% − 3.7% = 8.5%. This is a significant reward. The fact that it exists historically is an important observation, and it is

Investment	Average Return	Risk Premium
Common stocks	12.2%	8.5%
Small stocks	17.4	13.7
Long-term corporate bonds	5.7	2.0
Long-term government bonds	5.2	1.5
U.S. Treasury bills	3.7	0.0

TABLE 10.3
Average annual returns and risk premiums 1926–1994

Source: © *Stocks, Bonds, Bills, and Inflation 1995 Yearbook*™, Ibbotson Associates, Inc., Chicago (annually updates work by Roger G. Ibbotson and Rex A. Sinquefield).

the basis for our first lesson: Risky assets, on average, earn a risk premium. Put another way, there is a reward for bearing risk.

Why is this so? Why, for example, is the risk premium for small stocks so much larger than the risk premium for large stocks? More generally, what determines the relative sizes of the risk premiums for the different assets? The answers to these questions are at the heart of modern finance, and the next chapter is devoted to them. For now, part of the answer can be found by looking at the historical variability of the returns of these different investments. So, to get started, we now turn our attention to measuring variability in returns.

CONCEPT QUESTIONS

10.4a What do we mean by excess return and risk premium?

10.4b What was the real (as opposed to nominal) risk premium on the common stock portfolio?

10.4c What was the nominal risk premium on corporate bonds? The real risk premium?

10.4d What is the first lesson from capital market history?

10.5 THE VARIABILITY OF RETURNS: THE SECOND LESSON

We have already seen that the year-to-year returns on common stocks tend to be more volatile than the returns on, say, long-term government bonds. We now discuss measuring this variability so we can begin examining the subject of risk.

Self-Test Problem 10.2
Problems 12–14, 22

Frequency Distributions and Variability

To get started, we can draw a *frequency distribution* for the common stock returns like the one in Figure 10.9. What we have done here is to count up the number of times the annual return on the common stock portfolio falls within each 10 percent range. For example, in Figure 10.9, the height of 11 in the range 30 percent to 40 percent means that 11 of the 69 annual returns were in that range. Notice also that the most frequent return is in the 10 percent to 20 percent range. The common stock portfolio had a return in this range 13 times in 69 years.

What we need to do now is to actually measure the spread in returns. We know, for example, the return on small stocks in a typical year was 17.4 per-

FIGURE 10.9
Frequency distribution of returns on common stocks: 1926–1994

Trans. 10.12

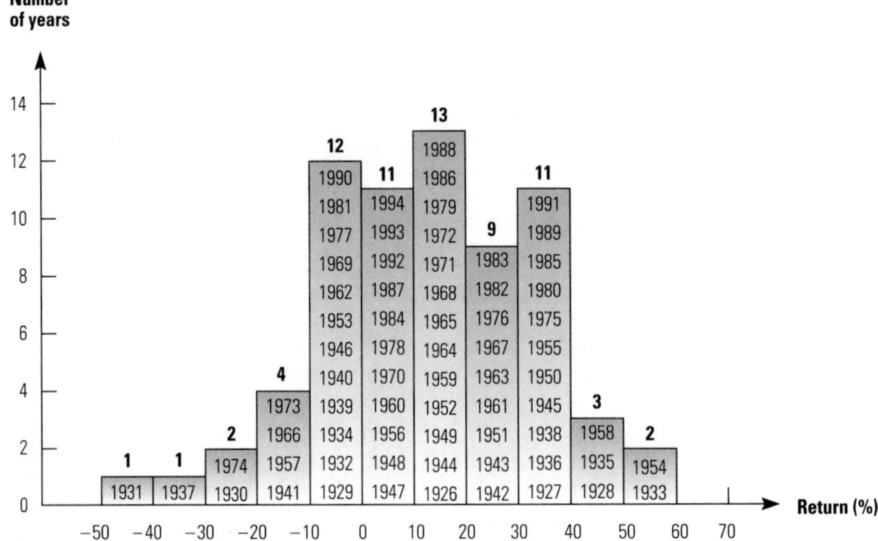

Source: © *Stocks, Bonds, Bills, and Inflation 1995 Yearbook*™, Ibbotson Associates, Inc., Chicago (annually updates work by Roger G. Ibbotson and Rex A. Sinquefield).

cent. We now want to know how far the actual return deviates from this average in a typical year. In other words, we need a measure of how volatile the return is. The **variance** and its square root, the **standard deviation,** are the most commonly used measures of volatility. We describe how to calculate them next.

variance
The average squared difference between the actual return and the average return.

standard deviation
The positive square root of the variance.

The Historical Variance and Standard Deviation

The variance essentially measures the average squared difference between the actual returns and the average return. The bigger this number is, the more the actual returns tend to differ from the average return. Also, the larger the variance or standard deviation is, the more spread out the returns will be.

The way we will calculate the variance and standard deviation depends on the specific situation. In this chapter, we are looking at historical returns; so the procedure we describe here is the correct one for calculating the *historical* variance and standard deviation. If we were examining projected future returns, then the procedure would be different. We describe this procedure in the next chapter.

To illustrate how we calculate the historical variance, suppose a particular investment had returns of 10 percent, 12 percent, 3 percent, and −9 percent over the last four years. The average return is $(.10 + .12 + .03 - .09)/4 = 4\%$. Notice that the return is never actually equal to 4 percent. Instead, the first return deviates from the average by $.10 - .04 = .06$, the second return deviates from the average by $.12 - .04 = .08$, and so on. To compute the variance, we square each of these deviations, add them up, and divide the result by the number of returns less one, or three in this case. This information is summarized in the following table.

Year	(1) Actual Return	(2) Average Return	(3) Deviation (1) − (2)	(4) Squared Deviation
1	.10	.04	.06	.0036
2	.12	.04	.08	.0064
3	.03	.04	−.01	.0001
4	−.09	.04	−.13	.0169
Totals	.16		.00	.0270

In the first column, we write down the four actual returns. In the third column, we calculate the difference between the actual returns and the average by subtracting out 4 percent. Finally, in the fourth column, we square the numbers in Column 3 to get the squared deviations from the average.

The variance can now be calculated by dividing .0270, the sum of the squared deviations, by the number of returns less one. Let Var(R) or σ^2 (read this as "sigma squared") stand for the variance of the return:

$$\text{Var}(R) = \sigma^2 = .027/(4 - 1) = .009$$

The standard deviation is the square root of the variance. So, if SD(R) or σ stands for the standard deviation of return:

$$\text{SD}(R) = \sigma = \sqrt{.009} = .09487$$

The square root of the variance is used because the variance is measured in "squared" percentages and thus is hard to interpret. The standard deviation is an ordinary percentage, so the answer here could be written as 9.487 percent.

In the table above, notice that the sum of the deviations is equal to zero. This will always be the case, and it provides a good way to check your work. In general, if we have T historical returns, where T is some number, we can write the historical variance as:

$$\text{Var}(R) = \frac{1}{T - 1}[(R_1 - \overline{R})^2 + \cdots + (R_T - \overline{R})^2] \quad [10.6]$$

Concept Q Answer 10.5a

This formula tells us to do just what we did above: Take each of the T individual returns ($R_1, R_2, \ldots$) and subtract the average return, $\overline{R}$; square the results, and add them all up; finally, divide this total by the number of returns less one ($T - 1$). The standard deviation is always the square root of Var(R).

EXAMPLE 10.3 Calculating the Variance and Standard Deviation

Suppose the Supertech Company and the Hyperdrive Company have experienced the following returns in the last four years:

Year	Supertech Returns	Hyperdrive Returns
1991	−.20	.05
1992	.50	.09
1993	.30	−.12
1994	.10	.20

What are the average returns? The variances? The standard deviations? Which investment was more volatile?

To calculate the average returns, we add up the returns and divide by four. The results are:

$$\text{Supertech average return} = \overline{R} = .70/4 = .175$$
$$\text{Hyperdrive average return} = \overline{R} = .22/4 = .055$$

Lecture Tip: See IM 10.5 for a discussion of the use of alternative dispersion measures.

To calculate the variance for Supertech, we can summarize the relevant calculations as follows:

Year	(1) Actual Return	(2) Average Return	(3) Deviation (1) − (2)	(4) Squared Deviation
1991	−.20	.175	−.375	.140625
1992	.50	.175	.325	.105625
1993	.30	.175	.125	.015625
1994	.10	.175	−.075	.005625
Totals	.70		.00	.267500

Since there are four years of returns, we calculate the variances by dividing .2675 by (4 − 1) = 3:

	Supertech	Hyperdrive
Variance (σ^2)	.2675/3 = .0892	.0529/3 = .0176
Standard deviation (σ)	$\sqrt{.0892}$ = .2987	$\sqrt{.0176}$ = .1327

For practice, check that you get the same answer as we do for Hyperdrive. Notice that the standard deviation for Supertech, 29.87 percent, is a little more than twice Hyperdrive's 13.27 percent; Supertech is thus the more volatile investment. • • •

The Historical Record

Figure 10.10 summarizes much of our discussion of capital market history so far. It displays average returns, standard deviations, and frequency distributions of annual returns on a common scale. In Figure 10.10, notice, for example, that the standard deviation for the small stock portfolio (34.6 percent per year) is more than 10 times larger than the T-bill portfolio's standard deviation (3.3 percent per year). We will return to these figures momentarily.

Normal Distribution

Concept Q Answer 10.5c

normal distribution
A symmetric, bell-shaped frequency distribution that is completely defined by its mean and standard deviation.

For many different random events in nature, a particular frequency distribution, the **normal distribution** (or *bell curve*), is useful for describing the probability of ending up in a given range. For example, the idea behind "grading on a curve" comes from the fact that exam scores often resemble a bell curve.

Figure 10.11 illustrates a normal distribution and its distinctive bell shape. As you can see, this distribution has a much cleaner appearance than the actual return distributions illustrated in Figure 10.10. Even so, like the normal distribution, the actual distributions do appear to be at least roughly mound-shaped and symmetrical. When this is true, the normal distribution is often a very good approximation.

Also, keep in mind that the distributions in Figure 10.10 are based on only 69 yearly observations while Figure 10.11 is, in principle, based on an infinite number. So, if we had been able to observe returns for, say, 1,000 years, we might have filled in a lot of the irregularities and ended up

FIGURE 10.10 Historical returns, standard deviations, and frequency distributions: 1926–1994 **Trans. 10.13**

Series	Average Return	Standard Deviation	Distribution
Large company stocks	12.2 %	20.3 %	
Small company stocks	17.4	34.6	*
Long-term corporate bonds	5.7	8.4	
Long-term government bonds	5.2	8.8	
Intermediate-term government bonds	5.2	5.7	
U.S. Treasury bills	3.7	3.3	
Inflation	3.2	4.6	
			−90% 0% +90%

*The 1993 Small Company Stock Total Return was 142.9 percent.

Source: © *Stocks, Bonds, Bills, and Inflation 1995 Yearbook*™, Ibbotson Associates, Inc., Chicago (annually updates work by Roger G. Ibbotson and Rex A. Sinquefield).

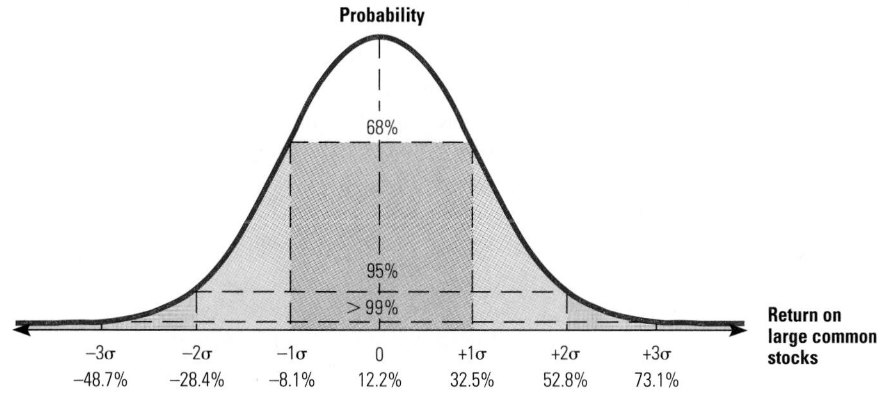

FIGURE 10.11 The normal distribution. Illustrated returns are based on the historical return and standard deviation for a portfolio of large common stocks.

Trans. 10.14

with a much smoother picture. For our purposes, it is enough to observe that the returns are at least roughly normally distributed.

Concept Q Answer 10.5b

The usefulness of the normal distribution stems from the fact that it is completely described by the average and the standard deviation. If you have these two numbers, then there is nothing else to know. For example, with a normal distribution, the probability that we end up within one standard deviation of the average is about 2/3. The probability that we end up within two standard deviations is about 95 percent. Finally, the probability of being more than three standard deviations away from the average is less than 1 percent. These ranges and the probabilities are illustrated in Figure 10.11.

To see why this is useful, recall from Figure 10.10 that the standard deviation of returns on the large common stocks is 20.3 percent. The average return is 12.2 percent. So, assuming the frequency distribution is at least approximately normal, the probability that the return in a given year is in the range −8.1 percent to 32.5 percent (12.2 percent plus or minus one standard deviation, 20.3 percent) is about 2/3. This range is illustrated in Figure 10.11. In other words, there is about one chance in three that the return will be *outside* this range. This literally tells you that, if you buy stocks in large companies, you should expect to be outside this range in one year out of every three. This reinforces our earlier observations about stock market volatility. However, there is only a 5 percent chance (approximately) that we would end up outside the range −28.4 percent to 52.8 percent (12.2 percent plus or minus 2 × 20.3%). These points are also illustrated in Figure 10.11.

The Second Lesson

Concept Q Answer 10.5d

Our observations concerning the year-to-year variability in returns are the basis for our second lesson from capital market history. On average, bearing risk is handsomely rewarded, but in a given year, there is a significant chance of a dramatic change in value. Thus, our second lesson is: The greater the potential reward, the greater is the risk.

Using Capital Market History

Lecture Tip: See IM 10.5 for an exercise that illustrates the risks involved in various securities investments.

Based on the discussion in this section, you should begin to have an idea of the risks and rewards from investing. For example, in 1995, Treasury bills were paying about 6 percent. Suppose we had an investment that we thought had about the same risk as a portfolio of large-firm common stocks. At a minimum, what return would this investment have to offer for us to be interested?

From Table 10.3, the risk premium on larger common stocks has been 8.5 percent historically, so a reasonable estimate of our required return would be this premium plus the T-bill rate, 6% + 8.5% = 14.5%. This may strike you as high, but, if we were thinking of starting a new business, then the risks of doing so might resemble investing in small-company stocks. In this case, the risk premium is 13.7 percent, so we might require as much as 19.7 percent from such an investment at a minimum.

We will discuss the relationship between risk and required return in more detail in the next chapter. For now, you should notice that a projected internal rate of return (IRR) on a risky investment in the 15 percent to 25 percent range isn't particularly outstanding. It depends on how much risk there is. This, too, is an important lesson from capital market history.

The discussion in this section shows that there is much to be learned from capital market history. As the accompanying *Principles in Action* box describes, capital market history also provides some unsolved mysteries.

EXAMPLE 10.4 Investing in Growth Stocks

The phrase *growth stock* is frequently a euphemism for small-company stock. Are such investments suitable for "widows and orphans"? Before answering, you should consider the historical volatility. For example, from the historical record, what is the approximate probability that you will actually lose 17 percent or more of your money in a single year if you buy a portfolio of such companies?

Principles in Action

January Is Open Season for Small Stocks

A December 1994 Wall Street Journal headline reads "January Effect to Disappoint" while a January 1995 Washington Post headline says "Waiting for the 'January Effect' to Take Effect." What they are talking about is the tendency for the prices of stock to, on average, increase in January. This type of pattern is known as a "seasonality" since it tends to reappear at regular intervals each year. Two of the more important of these patterns are the January and weekend effects, although the January effect captures more headlines.

The January effect refers to the tendency of stock prices, more specifically those of small company stocks, to increase in January and change little during the rest of the year. For example, a $1 investment in small company stocks in 1925 would have grown to about $3,000 in 1995. That same $1 investment would have grown to only $100 or so if all January returns are excluded. That's a loss of 97 percent in value from excluding only 8.3 percent of the observations. January returns are also viewed by some as a crystal ball. According to Yale Hirsch, publisher of *Stock Trader's Almanac,* from 1950 to 1993 the stock market has followed January returns 38 out of 43 times.

The January effect is generally viewed as resulting from tax-loss selling around the end of the calendar year. In December, investors sell stocks that have done poorly for the year to realize the capital losses for tax purposes. This money is then reinvested in the market in January. Small company stocks are popular buys in January, and the excess buying pressure pushes up share prices. While there is some evidence to support this hypothesis, many believe it is unlikely that this is the sole cause of the January effect.

A second seasonality, called the weekend effect or the day-of-the-week effect, refers to stock returns measured from Friday's market close to the market close on Monday. Since the stock market is not open over the weekend, Monday's return is actually a three-day return. Thus, one might expect the Monday return to be three times higher than that of other weekdays. Surprisingly, just the opposite is true. Monday is the only day on which the average return on stocks is negative. According to one study, the return on Monday averages about −0.134% while the average return on the other days of the week range from 0.002% to 0.096%. So far, no widely accepted explanation for this strange behavior has been found. While these returns are generally not large enough to overcome transaction costs and make a profit by trading on this pattern, they do suggest a simple trading rule: If you plan to sell stocks, sell them on Friday, and if you plan to buy, buy them late on Monday.

There are other so-called market regularities, and they exist in markets other than the stock market. In fact, they have been found in markets all around the world. As with the January and weekend effects, none occur with such certainty that traders can make easy money by implementing simple trading rules based on them. Still, savvy investors watch these patterns and try to use them to enhance returns.

Source: "Waiting for the 'January Effect' to Take Effect," *Washington Post,* January 8, 1995, p. H5; "January Effect to Disappoint," *The Wall Street Journal,* December 5, 1994, pp. C1–C2.

• • •

Looking back at Figure 10.10, the average return on small stocks is 17.4 percent and the standard deviation is 34.6 percent. Assuming the returns are approximately normal, there is about a 1/3 probability that you will experience a return outside the range −17.2 percent to 52.0 percent (17.4% ± 34.6%).

Because the normal distribution is symmetric, the odds of being above or below this range are equal. There is thus a 1/6 chance (half of 1/3) that you will lose more than 17.2 percent. So you should expect this to happen once in every six years, on average. Such investments can thus be *very* volatile, and they are not well-suited for those who cannot afford the risk. • • •

CONCEPT QUESTIONS

10.5a In words, how do we calculate a variance? A standard deviation?

10.5b With a normal distribution, what is the probability of ending up more than one standard deviation below the average?

10.5c Assuming that long-term corporate bonds have an approximately normal distribution, what is the approximate probability of earning 14 percent or more in a given year? With T-bills, approximately what is this probability?

10.5d What is the second lesson from capital market history?

10.6 CAPITAL MARKET EFFICIENCY

Problems 18–20, 23–26

Capital market history suggests that the market values of stocks and bonds can fluctuate widely from year to year. Why does this occur? At least part of the answer is that prices change because new information arrives, and investors reassess asset values based on that information.

Concept Q Answer 10.6a

efficient capital market Market in which security prices reflect available information.

The behavior of market prices has been extensively studied. A question that has received particular attention is whether prices adjust quickly and correctly when new information arrives. A market is said to be *efficient* if this is the case. To be more precise, in an **efficient capital market,** current market prices fully reflect available information. By this we simply mean that, based on available information, there is no reason to believe that the current price is too low or too high.

The concept of market efficiency is a rich one, and much has been written about it. A full discussion of the subject goes beyond the scope of our study of business finance. However, because the concept figures so prominently in studies of market history, we briefly describe the key points here.

Price Behavior in an Efficient Market

To illustrate how prices behave in an efficient market, suppose the F-Stop Camera Corporation (FCC) has, through years of secret research and development, developed a camera that will double the speed of the autofocusing systems now available. FCC's capital budgeting analysis suggests that launching the new camera is a highly profitable move; in other words, the NPV appears to be positive and substantial. The key assumption thus far is that FCC has not released any information about the new system; so, the fact of its existence is "inside" information only.

Now consider a share of stock in FCC. In an efficient market, its price reflects what is known about FCC's current operations and profitability, and it reflects market opinion about FCC's potential for future growth and profits. The value of the new autofocusing system is not reflected, however, because the market is unaware of its existence.

If the market agrees with FCC's assessment of the value of the new project, FCC's stock price will rise when the decision to launch is made public. For example, assume the announcement is made in a press release on Wednesday morning. In an efficient market, the price of shares in FCC will adjust quickly to this new information. Investors should not be able to buy the stock on Wednesday afternoon and make a profit on Thursday. This would

FIGURE 10.12 Reaction of stock price to new information in efficient and inefficient markets **Trans. 10.15**

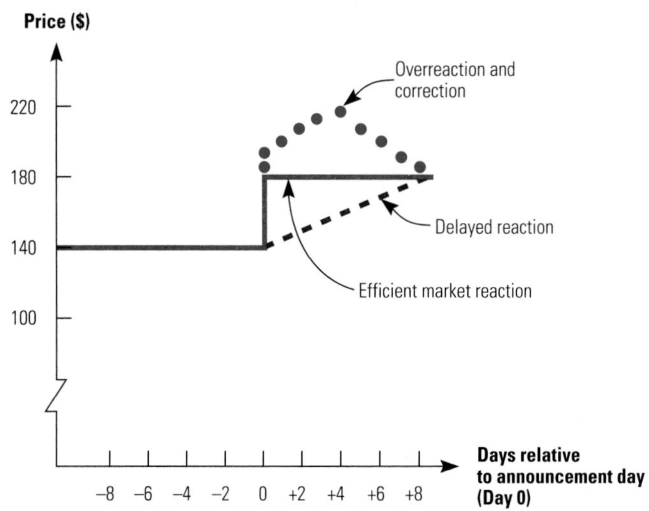

Efficient market reaction: The price instantaneously adjusts to and fully reflects new information; there is no tendency for subsequent increases and decreases.

Delayed reaction: The price partially adjusts to the new information; 8 days elapse before the price completely reflects the new information.

Overreaction: The price overadjusts to the new information; it "overshoots" the new price and subsequently corrects.

imply that it took the stock market a full day to realize the implication of the FCC press release. If the market is efficient, the price of shares of FCC stock on Wednesday afternoon will already reflect the information contained in the Wednesday morning press release.

Figure 10.12 presents three possible stock price adjustments for FCC. In Figure 10.12, Day 0 represents the announcement day. As illustrated, before the announcement, FCC's stock sells for $140 per share. The NPV per share of the new system is, say, $40, so the new price will be $180 once the value of the new project is fully reflected.

The solid line in Figure 10.12 represents the path taken by the stock price in an efficient market. In this case, the price adjusts immediately to the new information and no further changes in the price of the stock take place. The broken line in Figure 10.12 depicts a delayed reaction. Here it takes the market eight days or so to fully absorb the information. Finally, the dotted line illustrates an overreaction and subsequent adjustment to the correct price.

The broken line and the dotted line in Figure 10.12 illustrate paths that the stock price might take in an inefficient market. If, for example, stock prices don't adjust immediately to new information (the broken line), then buying stock immediately following the release of new information and then selling it several days later would be a positive NPV activity because the price is too low for several days after the announcement.

The Efficient Markets Hypothesis

The **efficient markets hypothesis (EMH)** asserts that well-organized capital markets, such as the NYSE, are efficient markets, at least as a practical matter. In other words, an advocate of the EMH might argue that while inefficiencies may exist, they are relatively small and not common.

efficient markets hypothesis (EMH)
The hypothesis that actual capital markets, such as the NYSE, are efficient.

If a market is efficient, then there is a very important implication for market participants: All investments in an efficient market are *zero* NPV investments. The reason is not complicated. If prices are neither too low nor too

Lecture Tip: See IM 10.6 for another example to use in explaining efficient markets.

high, then the difference between the market value of an investment and its cost is zero; hence, the NPV is zero. As a result, in an efficient market, investors get exactly what they pay for when they buy securities, and firms receive exactly what their stocks and bonds are worth when they sell them.

What makes a market efficient is competition among investors. Many individuals spend their entire lives trying to find mispriced stocks. For any given stock, they study what has happened in the past to the stock price and its dividends. They learn, to the extent possible, what a company's earnings have been, how much it owes to creditors, what taxes it pays, what businesses it is in, what new investments are planned, how sensitive it is to changes in the economy, and so on.

Not only is there a great deal to know about any particular company, there is a powerful incentive for knowing it, namely, the profit motive. If you know more about some company than other investors in the marketplace, you can profit from that knowledge by investing in the company's stock if you have good news and by selling it if you have bad news.

The logical consequence of all this information being gathered and analyzed is that mispriced stocks will become fewer and fewer. In other words, because of competition among investors, the market will become increasingly efficient. A kind of equilibrium comes into being where there is just enough mispricing around for those who are best at identifying it to make a living at it. For most other investors, the activity of information gathering and analysis will not pay.[3] Having said this, the accompanying *Principles in Action* box indicates just how hard it is for *anybody* to "beat the market."

Some Common Misconceptions about the EMH

★ **Ethics Note:** See IM 10.6 for a discussion of program trading vis-à-vis efficient markets.

No idea in finance has attracted as much attention as that of efficient markets, and not all of the attention has been flattering. Rather than rehash the arguments here, we will be content to observe that some markets are more efficient than others. For example, financial markets on the whole are probably much more efficient than real asset markets.

Having said this, it is the case that much of the criticism of the EMH is misguided because it is based on a misunderstanding of what the hypothesis says and what it doesn't say. For example, when the notion of market efficiency was first publicized and debated in the popular financial press, it was often characterized by words to the effect that "throwing darts at the financial page will produce a portfolio that can be expected to do as well as any managed by professional security analysts."

Confusion over statements of this sort has often led to a failure to understand the implications of market efficiency. For example, sometimes it is wrongly argued that market efficiency means it doesn't matter how you invest your money because the efficiency of the market will protect you from mak-

[3] The idea behind the EMH can be illustrated by the following short story: A student was walking down the hall with her finance professor when they both saw a $20 bill on the ground. As the student bent down to pick it up, the professor shook his head slowly and, with a look of disappointment on his face, said patiently to the student, "Don't bother. If it were really there, someone else would have picked it up already." The moral of the story reflects the logic of the efficient markets hypothesis: If you think you have found a pattern in stock prices or a simple device for picking winners, you probably have not.

Principles in Action

Of Money Managers and Efficient Markets . . .

Although the idea has been around for some time, there are still plenty of people who scoff at the hypothesis that the stock market is efficient. Perhaps the most skeptical group is made up of professional money managers, i.e., those in charge of managing the wide array of funds competing for the investing public's money. In general, the performance of these managers is measured against the market as a whole. If a manager's fund earns a greater return than the S&P 500 index, for example, the manager beat the market. A question of significance to the efficient markets hypothesis is how well professional money managers rate compared to the market. If they regularly beat the market, the hypothesis is in jeopardy.

One would expect money managers to at least be able to do better than random chance. *The Wall Street Journal* tests this in an ongoing contest between investment professionals and randomly chosen stocks. In each contest, four pros pick stocks, and their portfolio performance is compared to stocks chosen by *Journal* staffers throwing darts at a dart board. All investments are held for six months. By June 1995, the pros had a slight edge, having beaten the darts in 35 of 60 contests. However, they outperformed the Dow Jones Industrial Average only 31 to 29. The average returns make the pros look even better. The average six month gain for the pros for the 60 contests was 7.8 percent while the Dow increased 4.3 percent and the darts earned 3.5 percent. Random selection with darts did only slightly worse than the Dow Jones while the pros did slightly better. This contest suggests the pros can beat random chance and do at least as well as the market average, but it is a small sample of pros and a small portfolio of stocks. To realistically gauge money manager performance requires a broader study.

Performance Analytics, a pension consulting group in Chicago, analyzed the performance of over 2,700 equity managers for the first half of 1994. Surprisingly, of the 2,700 managers, 71 percent had a return lower that the S&P 500 index. The long-run performance of the group was even worse. Over the previous ten years, only 26 percent of the funds managed by these professionals earned a return in excess of the S&P 500 index. This suggests that, in 74 percent of the cases, investors would have earned a higher return by investing in a fund that mirrors the S&P 500 than by investing with this group of pros. They could do so by investing in an index fund, which is a mutual fund constructed to mirror a well known market index, requiring no active portfolio management. When an investor chooses an index fund, they accept the fate of performing as the market index does, no better and no worse.

None of this evidence proves that markets are efficient. Indeed, it is a hypothesis that is impossible to prove or disprove. It does, however, lend credence to the semi-strong form version of market efficiency. Plus, it adds to a growing body of evidence that tends to support a basic premise: While it may be possible to outperform the market for relatively short periods of time, it is very difficult to do so consistently over the long haul.

Source: "Pros Beat Darts in Picking Stocks, but Galloping Market Tops Both," *The Wall Street Journal,* June 7, 1995, pp. C1, C20; "The Coming Investor Revolt," *Fortune,* October 31, 1994, pp. 66–76.

• • •

ing a mistake. However, a random dart thrower might wind up with all of the darts sticking into one or two high-risk stocks that deal in genetic engineering. Would you really want all of your money in two such stocks?

What efficiency does imply is that the price a firm will obtain when it sells a share of its stock is a "fair" price in the sense that it reflects the value of that stock given the information available about the firm. Shareholders do not have to worry that they are paying too much for a stock with a low dividend or some other sort of characteristic because the market has already incorporated that characteristic into the price. We sometimes say the information has been "priced out."

The concept of efficient markets can be explained further by replying to a frequent objection. It is sometimes argued that the market cannot be efficient because stock prices fluctuate from day to day. If the prices are right, the argument goes, then why do they change so much and so often? From our discussion above, these price movements are in no way inconsistent with efficiency. Investors are bombarded with information every day. The fact that prices fluctuate is, at least in part, a reflection of that information flow. In fact, the absence of price movements in a world that changes as rapidly as ours would suggest inefficiency.

The Forms of Market Efficiency

Concept Q Answer 10.6b

It is common to distinguish between three forms of market efficiency. Depending on the degree of efficiency, we say that markets are either *weak form efficient, semistrong form efficient,* or *strong form efficient.* The difference between these forms relates to what information is reflected in prices.

★ **Ethics Note:** See IM 10.6 for a discussion of insider trading.

Video Note: The question of what is legal and what is not in the context of insider trading is discussed in "Test Your Insider IQ."

We start with the extreme case. If the market is strong form efficient, then *all* information of *every* kind is reflected in stock prices. In such a market, there is no such thing as inside information. Therefore, in our FCC example above, we apparently were assuming the market was not strong form efficient.

Casual observation, particularly in recent years, suggests inside information does exist and it can be valuable to possess. Whether it is lawful or ethical to use that information is another issue. In any event, we conclude that private information about a particular stock may exist that is not currently reflected in the price of the stock. For example, prior knowledge of a takeover attempt could be very valuable.

The second form of efficiency, semistrong efficiency, is the most controversial. If a market is semistrong form efficient, then all *public* information is reflected in the stock price. The reason this form is controversial is that it implies that a security analyst who tries to identify mispriced stocks using, for example, financial statement information is wasting his time because that information is already reflected in the current price.

The third form of efficiency, weak form efficiency, suggests that, at a minimum, the current price of a stock reflects its own past prices. In other words, studying past prices in an attempt to identify mispriced securities is futile if the market is weak form efficient. While this form of efficiency might seem rather mild, it implies that searching for patterns in historical prices that are useful in identifying mispriced stocks will not work (this practice is quite common).

What does capital market history say about market efficiency? Here again, there is great controversy. At the risk of going out on a limb, the evidence does seem to tell us three things. First, prices do appear to respond very rapidly to new information, and the response is at least not grossly different from what we would expect in an efficient market. Second, the future of market prices, particularly in the short run, is very difficult to predict based on publicly available information. Third, if mispriced stocks do exist, then there is no obvious means of identifying them. Put another way, simple-minded schemes based on public information will probably not be successful.

CONCEPT QUESTIONS

10.6a What is an efficient market?

10.6b What are the forms of market efficiency?

10.7 SUMMARY AND CONCLUSIONS

This chapter explores the subject of capital market history. Such history is useful because it tells us what to expect in the way of returns from risky assets. We summed up our study of market history with two key lessons:

1. Risky assets, on average, earn a risk premium. There is a reward for bearing risk.
2. The greater the potential reward from a risky investment, the greater is the risk.

These lessons have significant implications for the financial manager. We will be considering these implications in the chapters ahead.

We also discussed the concept of market efficiency. In an efficient market, prices adjust quickly and correctly to new information. Consequently, asset prices in efficient markets are rarely too high or too low. How efficient capital markets (such as the NYSE) are is a matter of debate, but, at a minimum, they are probably much more efficient than most real asset markets.

Chapter Review Problems and Self-Test

10.1 **Recent Return History** Use Table 10.1 to calculate the average return over the years 1990–1994 for common stocks, small stocks, and Treasury bills.

10.2 **More Recent Return History** Calculate the standard deviations using information from Problem 10.1. Which of the investments was the most volatile over this period?

Answers to Self-Test Problems

10.1 We calculate the averages as follows:

	Actual Returns and Averages		
Year	Common Stocks	Small Stocks	Treasury Bills
1990	−0.0317	−0.2156	0.0781
1991	0.3055	0.4463	0.0560
1992	0.0767	0.2335	0.0351
1993	0.0999	0.2098	0.0290
1994	0.0131	0.0311	0.0390
Average:	0.0927	0.1410	0.0474

10.2 We first need to calculate the deviations from the average returns. Using the averages from Problem 10.1, we get:

	Deviations from Average Returns		
Year	Common Stocks	Small Stocks	Treasury Bills
1990	−0.1244	−0.3566	0.0307
1991	0.2128	0.3053	0.0086
1992	−0.0160	0.0925	−0.0123
1993	0.0072	0.0688	−0.0184
1994	−0.0796	−0.1099	−0.0084
Total	0.0000	0.0000	0.0000

We square these deviations and calculate the variances and standard deviations:

	Squared Deviations from Average Returns		
Year	Common Stocks	Small Stocks	Treasury Bills
1990	0.0155	0.1272	0.0009
1991	0.0453	0.0932	0.0001
1992	0.0003	0.0086	0.0002
1993	0.0001	0.0047	0.0003
1994	0.0063	0.0121	0.0001
Variance:	0.0169	0.0614	0.0004
Standard deviation:	0.1298	0.2479	0.0199

To calculate the variances we added up the squared deviations and divided by four, the number of returns less one. Notice that the small stocks had substantially greater volatility with a smaller average return. Once again, such investments are risky, particularly over short periods of time.

Questions and Problems

Basic (Questions 1–20)

1. **Calculating Returns** Suppose a stock had an initial price of $54 per share, paid a dividend of $1.75 per share during the year, and had an ending share price of $46. Compute the percentage total return.

   −11.57%

2. **Calculating Yields** In Problem 1, what was the dividend yield? The capital gains yield?

   Dividend yield = 3.24%; Capital gains yield = −14.81%

3. **Return Calculations** Rework Problems 1 and 2 assuming the ending share price is $65.

   Total return = 23.61%; Dividend yield = 3.24%; Capital gain yield = 20.37%

4. **Calculating Real Rates of Return** If Treasury bills are currently paying 8 percent and the inflation rate is 6 percent, what is the approximate real rate of interest? The exact real rate?

   2%; 1.89%
   Trans. 10.16

5. **Inflation and Nominal Returns** Suppose the real rate is 2.5 percent and the inflation rate is 7 percent. What rate would you expect to see on a Treasury bill?

   9.68%

6. **Nominal and Real Returns** An investment offers an 18 percent total return over the coming year. Mary Moneybags thinks the total real return on this investment will only be 14 percent. What does Mary believe the inflation rate will be over the next year?

   3.51%

7. **Nominal versus Real Returns** Say you own an asset that had a total return last year of 14 percent. If the inflation rate last year was 5 percent, what was your real return?

   8.57%

8. **Inflation and Real Returns** In Problem 7, what was your real return if the inflation rate was 16 percent last year? Is your answer possible? Explain.

   −1.72%

9. **Calculating Returns** Suppose you bought an 11 percent coupon bond one year ago for $965.00. The bond sells for $925.00 today.
   a. What was your total dollar return on this investment over the past year?

   a. $70
   b. 7.25%
   c. 3.13%

b. What was your total nominal rate of return on this investment over the past year?
c. If the inflation rate last year was 4 percent, what was your total real rate of return on this investment?

10. **Nominal versus Real Returns** What was the average annual return on U.S. common stocks from 1926 through 1994:
a. In nominal terms?
b. In real terms?

11. **Bond Returns** What is the historical real return on long-term government bonds? On long-term corporate bonds?

12. **Calculating Returns and Variability** Using the following returns, calculate the average returns, the variances, and the standard deviations for X and Y.

X: Average return = 6.20%
Variance = .00627
Y: Average return = 9.40%
Variance = .03413
Trans. 10.19

	Returns	
Year	X	Y
1	14%	22%
2	3	− 5
3	− 6	−15
4	11	28
5	9	17

13. **Risk Premiums** Refer to Table 10.1 in the text and look at the period from 1980–1986.
a. Calculate the average returns for small stocks and T-bills over this time period.
b. Calculate the standard deviation of the returns for small stocks and T-bills over this time period.
c. Calculate the observed risk premium in each year for the small stocks versus the T-bills. What was the average risk premium over this period? What was the standard deviation of the risk premium over this period?
d. Is it possible for the risk premium to be negative before an investment is undertaken? Can the risk premium be negative after the fact? Explain.

14. **Calculating Returns and Variability** You've observed the following returns on Jayson Corporation's stock over the past 5 years: 5 percent, −11 percent, 2 percent, 27 percent, 7 percent.
a. What was the average return on Jayson's stock over this five-year period?
b. What was the variance of Jayson's returns over this period? The standard deviation?

a. 6%
b. Variance = .0187

15. **Calculating Real Returns and Risk Premiums** For Problem 14, suppose the average inflation rate over this period was 4.5 percent, and the average T-bill rate over the period was 4.8 percent.
a. What was the average real return on Jayson's stock?
b. What was the average nominal risk premium on Jayson's stock?

a. 1.44%
b. 1.20%

16. **Calculating Real Rates** Using the information in Problem 15, what was the average real risk-free rate over this time period? What was the average real risk premium?

0.29%; 1.15%

17. **Effects of Inflation** Look at Table 10.1 and Figure 10.7 in the text. When were T-bill rates at their highest over the period 1926–1994? Why do you think they were so high during this period? What relationship underlies your answer?

18. **EMH and NPV** Explain why a characteristic of an efficient market is that investments in that market have zero NPVs.

19. **EMH** A stock market analyst is able to identify mispriced stocks by comparing the average price for the last 10 days to the average price for the last 60 days. If this is true, what do you know about the market?

20. **Intuition and EMH** If a market is semistrong form efficient, is it also weak form efficient? Explain.

Intermediate (Questions 21–26)

a. ⅙
b. −12.4% to +22.8%
c. −21.2% to +31.6%

a. 0.1

21. **Using Return Distributions** Suppose the return on long-term government bonds is normally distributed. Based on the historical record, what is the approximate probability that your return will be less than −3.6 percent in a given year? What range of returns would you expect to see 95 percent of the time? 99 percent of the time?

22. **Using Return Distributions** Assuming the return from holding small-company stocks is normally distributed, what is the approximate probability that your money will double in value in a single year?

23. **EMH** What are the implications of the efficient markets hypothesis for investors who buy and sell stocks in an attempt to "beat the market"?

24. **EMH and Speculation** Critically evaluate the following statement: "Playing the stock market is like gambling. Such speculative investing has no social value, other than the pleasure people get from this form of gambling."

25. **Misconceptions about the EMH** There are several celebrated investors and stockpickers frequently mentioned in the financial press who have recorded huge returns on their investments over the past two decades. Is the success of these particular investors an invalidation of the EMH? Explain.

26. **Interpreting Efficient Markets** For each of the following scenarios, discuss whether profit opportunities exist from trading in the stock of the firm under the conditions that (1) the market is not weak form efficient, (2) the market is weak form but not semistrong form efficient, (3) the market is semistrong form but not strong form efficient, and (4) the market is strong form efficient.
    a. The stock price has risen steadily each day for the past 30 days.
    b. The financial statements for a company were released three days ago, and you believe you've uncovered some anomalies in the company's inventory and cost control reporting techniques that are understating the firm's true liquidity strength.
    c. You observe that the senior management of a company has been buying a lot of the company's stock on the open market over the past week.

Chapter Eleven

11

Risk and Return

After studying this chapter, you should have a good understanding of:

How to calculate expected returns.

The impact of diversification.

The systematic risk principle.

The security market line and the risk/return tradeoff.

Trans. 11.1 Chapter Outline

In our last chapter, we learned some important lessons from capital market history. Most importantly, there is a reward, on average, for bearing risk. We called this reward a *risk premium.* The second lesson is that this risk premium is larger for riskier investments. This chapter explores the economic and managerial implications of this basic idea.

Thus far, we have concentrated mainly on the return behavior of a few large portfolios. We need to expand our consideration to include individual assets. Specifically, we have two tasks to accomplish. First, we have to define risk and then discuss how to measure it. We then must quantify the relationship between an asset's risk and its required return.

When we examine the risks associated with individual assets, we find there are two types of risk: systematic and unsystematic. This distinction is crucial because, as we will see, systematic risk affects almost all assets in the economy, at least to some degree, while unsystematic risk affects at most a small number of assets. We then develop the principle of diversification, which shows that highly diversified portfolios will tend to have almost no unsystematic risk.

The principle of diversification has an important implication: To a diversified investor, only systematic risk matters. It follows that in deciding whether or not to buy a particular individual asset, a diversified investor will only be concerned with that asset's systematic risk. This is a key observation, and it allows us to say a great deal about the risks and returns on individual assets. In particular, it is the basis for a famous relationship between risk and return called the *security market line,* or SML. To develop the SML, we introduce the equally famous "beta" coefficient, one of the centerpieces of modern finance. Beta and the SML are key concepts because they supply us with at least part of the answer to the question of how to go about determining the required return on an investment.

11.1 EXPECTED RETURNS AND VARIANCES

Self-Test Problem 11.1
Problems 5, 6

In our previous chapter, we discussed how to calculate average returns and variances using historical data. We now begin to discuss how to analyze returns and variances when the information we have concerns future possible returns and their probabilities.

Expected Return

We start with a straightforward case. Consider a single period of time, say, a year. We have two stocks, L and U, which have the following characteristics: Stock L is expected to have a return of 25 percent in the coming year. Stock U is expected to have a return of 20 percent for the same period.

In a situation like this, if all investors agreed on the expected returns, why would anyone want to hold Stock U? After all, why invest in one stock when the expectation is that another will do better? Clearly, the answer must depend on the risk of the two investments. The return on Stock L, although it is *expected* to be 25 percent, could actually turn out to be higher or lower.

For example, suppose the economy booms. In this case, we think Stock L will have a 70 percent return. If the economy enters a recession, we think the return will be −20 percent. In this case, we say that there are two *states of the economy,* which means that these are the only two possible situations. This setup is oversimplified, of course, but it allows us to illustrate some key ideas without a lot of computation.

Suppose we think a boom and a recession are equally likely to happen, a 50–50 chance of each. Table 11.1 illustrates the basic information we have described and some additional information about Stock U. Notice that Stock U earns 30 percent if there is a recession and 10 percent if there is a boom.

Concept Q
Answer 11.1a

Obviously, if you buy one of these stocks, say Stock U, what you earn in any particular year depends on what the economy does during that year. However, suppose the probabilities stay the same through time. If you hold U

T A B L E 11.1
States of the economy and stock returns

State of Economy	Probability of State of Economy	Security Returns if State Occurs	
		L	U
Recession	0.5	−20%	30%
Boom	0.5	70	10
	1.0		

for a number of years, you'll earn 30 percent about half the time and 10 percent the other half. In this case, we say that your **expected return** on Stock U, $E(R_U)$, is 20 percent:

expected return
Return on a risky asset expected in the future.

$$E(R_U) = .50 \times 30\% + .50 \times 10\% = 20\%$$

In other words, you should expect to earn 20 percent from this stock, on average.

For Stock L, the probabilities are the same, but the possible returns are different. Here we lose 20 percent half the time, and we gain 70 percent the other half. The expected return on L, $E(R_L)$, is thus 25 percent:

$$E(R_L) = .50 \times -20\% + .50 \times 70\% = 25\%$$

Table 11.2 illustrates these calculations.

In our previous chapter, we defined the risk premium as the difference between the return on a risky investment and a risk-free investment, and we calculated the historical risk premiums on some different investments. Using our projected returns, we can calculate the *projected* or *expected risk premium* as the difference between the expected return on a risky investment and the certain return on a risk-free investment.

For example, suppose risk-free investments are currently offering 8 percent. We will say that the risk-free rate, which we label as R_f, is 8 percent. Given this, what is the projected risk premium on Stock U? On Stock L? Since the expected return on Stock U, $E(R_U)$, is 20 percent, the projected risk premium is:

$$\begin{aligned}\text{Risk premium} &= \text{Expected return} - \text{Risk-free rate} \\ &= E(R_U) - R_f \qquad [11.1] \\ &= 20\% - 8\% \\ &= 12\%\end{aligned}$$

Similarly, the risk premium on Stock L is 25% − 8% = 17%.

In general, the expected return on a security or other asset is simply equal to the sum of the possible returns multiplied by their probabilities. So, if we have 100 possible returns, we would multiply each one by its probability and then add the results up. The result would be the expected return. The risk premium would then be the difference between this expected return and the risk-free rate.

TABLE 11.2
Calculation of expected return

		Stock L		Stock U	
(1) State of Economy	(2) Probability of State of Economy	(3) Rate of Return if State Occurs	(4) Product (2) × (3)	(5) Rate of Return if State Occurs	(6) Product (2) × (5)
Recession	0.5	−.20	−.10	.30	.15
Boom	0.5	.70	.35	.10	.05
	1.0		$E(R_L)$ = 25%		$E(R_U)$ = 20%

TABLE 11.3
Calculation of expected return

Trans. 11.2

		Stock L		Stock U	
(1) State of Economy	(2) Probability of State of Economy	(3) Rate of Return if State Occurs	(4) Product (2) × (3)	(5) Rate of Return if State Occurs	(6) Product (2) × (5)
Recession	0.8	−.20	−.16	.30	.24
Boom	0.2	.70	.14	.10	.02
	1.0		$E(R_L) = -2\%$		$E(R_U) = 26\%$

Trans. 11.3
Calculating the Expected Return (Supplemental)

EXAMPLE 11.1 Unequal Probabilities

Look again at Tables 11.1 and 11.2. Suppose you thought a boom would only occur 20 percent of the time instead of 50 percent. What are the expected returns on Stocks U and L in this case? If the risk-free rate is 10 percent, what are the risk premiums?

The first thing to notice is that a recession must occur 80 percent of the time (1 − .20 = .80) since there are only two possibilities. With this in mind, Stock U has a 30 percent return in 80 percent of the years and a 10 percent return in 20 percent of the years. To calculate the expected return, we again just multiply the possibilities by the probabilities and add up the results:

$$E(R_U) = .80 \times 30\% + .20 \times 10\% = 26\%$$

Table 11.3 summarizes the calculations for both stocks. Notice that the expected return on L is −2 percent.

The risk premium for Stock U is 26% − 10% = 16% in this case. The risk premium for Stock L is negative: −2% − 10% = −12%. This is a little odd, but, for reasons we discuss later, it is not impossible. • • •

Calculating the Variance

Concept Q Answer 11.1b

Lecture Tip: You may wish to point out that the variance is also an expected value—it is the weighted average of the squared deviations from the mean.

Trans. 11.4
Calculating the Variance (Supplemental)

Lecture Tip: See IM for another example to use in class.

To calculate the variances of the returns on our two stocks, we first determine the squared deviations from the expected return. We then multiply each possible squared deviation by its probability. We add these up, and the result is the variance. The standard deviation, as always, is the square root of the variance.

To illustrate, Stock U above has an expected return of $E(R_U) = 20\%$. In a given year, it will actually return either 30 percent or 10 percent. The possible deviations are thus 30% − 20% = 10% or 10% − 20% = −10%. In this case, the variance is:

$$\text{Variance} = \sigma_u^2 = .50 \times (10\%)^2 + .50 \times (-10\%)^2 = .01$$

The standard deviation is the square root of this:

$$\text{Standard deviation} = \sigma_u = \sqrt{.01} = .10 = 10\%$$

Table 11.4 summarizes these calculations for both stocks. Notice that Stock L has a much larger variance.

TABLE 11.4
Calculation of variance

(1) State of Economy	(2) Probability of State of Economy	(3) Return Deviation from Expected Return	(4) Squared Return Deviation from Expected Return	(5) Product (2) × (4)
Stock L				
Recession	0.5	$-.20 - .25 = -.45$	$(-.45)^2 = .2025$	.10125
Boom	0.5	$.70 - .25 = .45$	$(.45)^2 = .2025$	.10125
	1.0			$\sigma_L^2 = .2025$
Stock U				
Recession	0.5	$.30 - .20 = .10$	$(.10)^2 = .01$	.005
Boom	0.5	$.10 - .20 = -.10$	$(-.10)^2 = .01$	.005
	1.0			$\sigma_U^2 = .010$

When we put the expected return and variability information for our two stocks together, we have:

	Stock L	Stock U
Expected return, E(R)	25%	20%
Variance, σ^2	.2025	.0100
Standard deviation, σ	45%	10%

Stock L has a higher expected return, but U has less risk. You could get a 70 percent return on your investment in L, but you could also lose 20 percent. Notice that an investment in U will always pay at least 10 percent.

Which of these two stocks should you buy? We can't really say; it depends on your personal preferences. We can be reasonably sure, however, that some investors would prefer L to U and some would prefer U to L.

You've probably noticed that the way we calculated expected returns and variances here is somewhat different from the way we did it in the last chapter. The reason is that, in Chapter 10, we were examining actual historical returns, so we estimated the average return and the variance based on some actual events. Here, we have projected *future* returns and their associated probabilities, so this is the information with which we must work.

Lecture Tip: See IM 11.1 for further discussion of this point.

EXAMPLE 11.2 More Unequal Probabilities

Going back to Example 11.1, what are the variances on the two stocks once we have unequal probabilities? The standard deviations?

We can summarize the needed calculations as follows:

Trans. 11.5 Expected Returns and Variances (Supplemental)

(1) State of Economy	(2) Probability of State of Economy	(3) Return Deviation from Expected Return	(4) Squared Return Deviation from Expected Return	(5) Product (2) × (4)
Stock L				
Recession	.80	$-.20 - (-.02) = -.18$	.0324	.02592
Boom	.20	$.70 - (-.02) = .72$	.5184	.10368
				$\sigma_L^2 = .12960$
Stock U				
Recession	.80	$.30 - .26 = .04$	.0016	.00128
Boom	.20	$.10 - .26 = -.16$	.0256	.00512
				$\sigma_U^2 = .00640$

Based on these calculations, the standard deviation for L is $\sigma_L = \sqrt{.1296} = 36\%$. The standard deviation for U is much smaller, $\sigma_U = \sqrt{.0064} = .08$ or 8%. • • •

CONCEPT QUESTIONS

11.1a How do we calculate the expected return on a security?

11.1b In words, how do we calculate the variance of the expected return?

11.2 PORTFOLIOS

portfolio
Group of assets such as stocks and bonds held by an investor.

Self-Test Problem 11.2
Problems 1–10, 28, 30

Thus far in this chapter, we have concentrated on individual assets considered separately. However, most investors actually hold a **portfolio** of assets. All we mean by this is that investors tend to own more than just a single stock, bond, or other asset. Given that this is so, portfolio return and portfolio risk are of obvious relevance. Accordingly, we now discuss portfolio expected returns and variances.

Portfolio Weights

portfolio weight
Percentage of a portfolio's total value in a particular asset.

There are many equivalent ways of describing a portfolio. The most convenient approach is to list the percentages of the total portfolio's value that are invested in each portfolio asset. We call these percentages the **portfolio weights.**

For example, if we have \$50 in one asset and \$150 in another, then our total portfolio is worth \$200. The percentage of our portfolio in the first asset is \$50/\$200 = .25. The percentage of our portfolio in the second asset is \$150/\$200, or .75. Our portfolio weights are thus .25 and .75. Notice that the weights have to add up to 1.00 since all of our money is invested somewhere.[1]

Concept Q
Answer 11.2a

Portfolio Expected Returns

Trans. 11.6
Portfolio Expected Returns (Supplemental)

Let's go back to Stocks L and U. You put half your money in each. The portfolio weights are obviously .50 and .50. What is the pattern of returns on this portfolio? The expected return?

Concept Q
Answer 11.2b

To answer these questions, suppose the economy actually enters a recession. In this case, half your money (the half in L) loses 20 percent. The other half (the half in U) gains 30 percent. Your portfolio return, R_P, in a recession will thus be:

$$R_P = .50 \times (-20\%) + .50 \times 30\% = 5\%$$

Table 11.5 summarizes the remaining calculations. Notice that when a boom occurs, your portfolio would return 40 percent:

$$R_P = .50 \times 70\% + .50 \times 10\% = 40\%$$

As indicated in Table 11.5, the expected return on your portfolio, $E(R_P)$, is 22.5 percent.

We can save ourselves some work by calculating the expected return more directly. Given these portfolio weights, we could have reasoned that we expect

[1] Some of it could be in cash, of course, but we would then just consider the cash to be one of the portfolio assets.

(1) State of Economy	(2) Probability of State of Economy	(3) Portfolio Return if State Occurs	(4) Product (2) × (3)
Recession	.50	$.50 \times (-20\%) + .50 \times (30\%) = 5\%$	.025
Boom	.50	$.50 \times (70\%) + .50 \times (10\%) = 40\%$	.200
	1.00		$E(R_P) = 22.5\%$

TABLE 11.5
Expected return on an equally weighted portfolio of Stock L and Stock U

half of our money to earn 25 percent (the half in L) and half of our money to earn 20 percent (the half in U). Our portfolio expected return is thus:

$$\begin{aligned} E(R_P) &= .50 \times E(R_L) + .50 \times E(R_U) \\ &= .50 \times 25\% + .50 \times 20\% \\ &= 22.5\% \end{aligned}$$

This is the same portfolio expected return we had before.

This method of calculating the expected return on a portfolio works no matter how many assets there are in the portfolio. Suppose we had n assets in our portfolio, where n is any number. If we let x_i stand for the percentage of our money in Asset i, then the expected return is:

$$E(R_P) = x_1 \times E(R_1) + x_2 \times E(R_2) + \ldots + x_n \times E(R_n) \quad [11.2]$$

This says that the expected return on a portfolio is a straightforward combination of the expected returns on the assets in that portfolio. This seems somewhat obvious, but, as we will examine next, the obvious approach is not always the right one.

EXAMPLE 11.3 Portfolio Expected Return

Suppose we have the following projections on three stocks:

State of Economy	Probability of State	Returns		
		Stock A	Stock B	Stock C
Boom	.40	10%	15%	20%
Bust	.60	8	4	0

We want to calculate portfolio expected returns in two cases. First, what would be the expected return on a portfolio with equal amounts invested in each of the three stocks? Second, what would be the expected return if half of the portfolio were in A, with the remainder equally divided between B and C?

From our earlier discussions, the expected returns on the individual stocks are (check these for practice):

$$\begin{aligned} E(R_A) &= 8.8\% \\ E(R_B) &= 8.4\% \\ E(R_C) &= 8.0\% \end{aligned}$$

If a portfolio has equal investments in each asset, the portfolio weights are all the same. Such a portfolio is said to be *equally weighted.* Since there are three stocks in this case, the weights are all equal to ⅓. The portfolio expected return is thus:

$$E(R_P) = (1/3) \times 8.8\% + (1/3) \times 8.4\% + (1/3) \times 8.0\% = 8.4\%$$

In the second case, check that the portfolio expected return is 8.5 percent. • • •

Portfolio Variance

Concept Q Answer 11.2c

Trans. 11.7 Portfolio Variance (Supplemental)

From our discussion above, the expected return on a portfolio that contains equal investment in Stocks U and L is 22.5 percent. What is the standard deviation of return on this portfolio? Simple intuition might suggest that half of the money has a standard deviation of 45 percent and the other half has a standard deviation of 10 percent, so the portfolio's standard deviation might be calculated as:

$$\sigma_P = .50 \times 45\% + .50 \times 10\% = 27.5\%$$

Lecture Tip: See IM 11.2 for discussion of portfolio variance utilizing the correlation coefficient.

Unfortunately, this approach is completely incorrect!

Let's see what the standard deviation really is. Table 11.6 summarizes the relevant calculations. As we see, the portfolio's variance is about .031, and its standard deviation is less than we thought—it's only 17.5 percent. What is illustrated here is that the variance on a portfolio is not generally a simple combination of the variances of the assets in the portfolio.

We can illustrate this point a little more dramatically by considering a slightly different set of portfolio weights. Suppose we put 2/11 (about 18 percent) in L and the other 9/11 (about 82 percent) in U. If a recession occurs, this portfolio will have a return of:

$$R_P = (2/11) \times (-20\%) + (9/11) \times (30\%) = 20.91\%$$

If a boom occurs, this portfolio will have a return of:

$$R_P = (2/11) \times (70\%) + (9/11) \times (10\%) = 20.91\%$$

Notice that the return is the same no matter what happens. No further calculations are needed: This portfolio has a zero variance. Apparently, combining assets into portfolios can substantially alter the risks faced by the investor. This is a crucial observation, and we will begin to explore its implications in the next section.

TABLE 11.6
Variance on an equally weighted portfolio of Stock L and Stock U

(1) State of Economy	(2) Probability of State of Economy	(3) Portfolio Return if State Occurs	(4) Squared Deviation from Expected Return	(5) Product (2) × (4)
Recession	.50	5%	$(.05 - .225)^2 = .030625$	.0153125
Boom	.50	40%	$(.40 - .225)^2 = .030625$	.0153125
	1.00			$\sigma_P^2 = .030625$
				$\sigma_P = \sqrt{.030625} = 17.5\%$

EXAMPLE 11.4 Portfolio Variance and Standard Deviation

Trans. 11.8
Portfolio Expected Returns and Variances (Supplemental)

In Example 11.3, what are the standard deviations on the two portfolios? To answer, we first have to calculate the portfolio returns in the two states. We will work with the second portfolio, which has 50 percent in Stock A and 25 percent in each of Stocks B and C. The relevant calculations can be summarized as follows:

State of Economy	Probability of State	Returns			
		Stock A	Stock B	Stock C	Portfolio
Boom	.40	10%	15%	20%	13.75%
Bust	.60	8	4	0	5.00

The portfolio return when the economy booms is calculated as:

$$.50 \times 10\% + .25 \times 15\% + .25 \times 20\% = 13.75\%$$

The return when the economy goes bust is calculated the same way. The expected return on the portfolio is 8.5 percent. The variance is thus:

$$\begin{aligned}\sigma^2 &= .40 \times (.1375 - .085)^2 + .60 \times (.05 - .085)^2 \\ &= .0018375\end{aligned}$$

The standard deviation is thus about 4.3 percent. For our equally weighted portfolio, check that the standard deviation is about 5.4 percent. • • •

CONCEPT QUESTIONS

11.2a What is a portfolio weight?

11.2b How do we calculate the expected return on a portfolio?

11.2c Is there a simple relationship between the standard deviation on a portfolio and the standard deviations of the assets in the portfolio?

11.3 ANNOUNCEMENTS, SURPRISES, AND EXPECTED RETURNS

Problems 12, 14

Trans. 11.9
Announcements, Surprises, and Expected Returns (Supplemental)

Now that we know how to construct portfolios and evaluate their returns, we begin to describe more carefully the risks and returns associated with individual securities. Thus far, we have measured volatility by looking at the differences between the actual returns on an asset or portfolio, R, and the expected return, $E(R)$. We now look at why those deviations exist.

Expected and Unexpected Returns

Concept Q
Answer 11.3a

To begin, for concreteness, we consider the return on the stock of a company called Flyers. What will determine this stock's return in, say, the coming year?

The return on any stock traded in a financial market is composed of two parts. First, the normal or expected return from the stock is the part of the return that shareholders in the market predict or expect. This return depends on the information shareholders have that bears on the stock, and it is based on the market's understanding today of the important factors that will influence the stock in the coming year.

The second part of the return on the stock is the uncertain or risky part. This is the portion that comes from unexpected information revealed within the year. A list of all possible sources of such information is endless, but here are a few examples:

News about Flyers' research.

Government figures released on gross domestic product (GDP).

The results from the latest arms control talks.

The news that Flyers' sales figures are higher than expected.

A sudden, unexpected drop in interest rates.

Based on this discussion, one way to write the return on Flyers' stock in the coming year would be:

$$\begin{aligned}\text{Total return} &= \text{Expected return} + \text{Unexpected return} \\ R &= \text{E}(R) + U\end{aligned} \qquad [11.3]$$

where R stands for the actual total return in the year, $\text{E}(R)$ stands for the expected part of the return, and U stands for the unexpected part of the return. What this says is that the actual return, R, differs from the expected return, $\text{E}(R)$, because of surprises that occur during the year. In any given year, the unexpected return will be positive or negative, but, through time, the average value of U will be zero. This simply means that, on average, the actual return equals the expected return.

Announcements and News

Lecture Tip: IM 11.3 discusses the use of recent news items to illustrate the effects of unanticipated announcements on market values.

We need to be careful when we talk about the effect of news items on the return. For example, suppose Flyers' business is such that the company prospers when GDP (gross domestic product) grows at a relatively high rate and suffers when GDP is relatively stagnant. In this case, in deciding what return to expect this year from owning stock in Flyers, shareholders either implicitly or explicitly must think about what GDP is likely to be for the year.

Concept Q Answer 11.3b

When the government actually announces GDP figures for the year, what will happen to the value of Flyers' stock? Obviously, the answer depends on what figure is released. More to the point, however, the impact depends on how much of that figure is *new* information.

At the beginning of the year, market participants will have some idea or forecast of what the yearly GDP will be. To the extent that shareholders had predicted GDP, that prediction will already be factored into the expected part of the return on the stock, $\text{E}(R)$. On the other hand, if the announced GDP is a surprise, then the effect will be part of U, the unanticipated portion of the return.

As an example, suppose shareholders in the market had forecast that the GDP increase this year would be 0.5 percent. If the actual announcement this year is exactly 0.5 percent, the same as the forecast, then the shareholders didn't really learn anything, and the announcement isn't news. There would be no impact on the stock price as a result. This is like receiving confirmation of something that you suspected all along; it doesn't reveal anything new.

A common way of saying that an announcement isn't news is to say that the market has already "discounted" the announcement. The use of the word *discount* here is different from the use of the term in computing present values, but the spirit is the same. When we discount a dollar in the future, we say it is worth less to us because of the time value of money. When we discount an announcement or a news item, we mean that it has less of an impact on the market because the market already knew much of it.

For example, going back to Flyers, suppose the government announced that the actual GDP increase during the year was 1.5 percent. Now shareholders have learned something, namely, that the increase is 1 percentage point higher than they had forecast. This difference between the actual result and the forecast, 1 percentage point in this example, is sometimes called the *innovation* or the *surprise*.

An announcement, then, can be broken into two parts, the anticipated or expected part and the surprise or innovation:

$$\text{Announcement} = \text{Expected part} + \text{Surprise} \qquad [11.4]$$

The expected part of any announcement is part of the information that the market uses to form the expectation, $E(R)$, of the return on the stock. The surprise is the news that influences the unanticipated return on the stock, U.

To take another example, if shareholders knew in January that the president of the firm was going to resign, the official announcement in February would be fully expected and would be discounted by the market. Because the announcement was expected before February, its influence on the stock would have taken place before February. The announcement itself will contain no surprise, and the stock's price shouldn't change at all when it is actually made.

Our discussion of market efficiency in the previous chapter bears on this discussion. We are assuming that relevant information known today is already reflected in the expected return. This is identical to saying that the current price reflects relevant publicly available information. We are thus implicitly assuming that markets are at least reasonably efficient in the semi-strong form sense.

Henceforth, when we speak of news, we will mean the surprise part of an announcement and not the portion that the market has expected and therefore already discounted.

Lecture Tip: It may be worthwhile to emphasize at this point that, since news (as defined here) is, by definition, not predictable, news-related changes in securities prices are likewise not predictable.

CONCEPT QUESTIONS

11.3a What are the two basic parts of a return?

11.3b Under what conditions will an announcement have no effect on common stock prices?

11.4 RISK: SYSTEMATIC AND UNSYSTEMATIC

Problems 11, 13, 14

The unanticipated part of the return, that portion resulting from surprises, is the true risk of any investment. After all, if we always receive exactly what we expect, then the investment is perfectly predictable and, by definition, risk-free. In other words, the risk of owning an asset comes from surprises—unanticipated events.

There are important differences, though, among various sources of risk. Look back at our previous list of news stories. Some of these stories are directed specifically at Flyers, and some are more general. Which of the news items are of specific importance to Flyers?

Announcements about interest rates or GDP are clearly important for nearly all companies, whereas the news about Flyers' president, its research, or its sales are of specific interest to Flyers. We will distinguish between these two types of events, because, as we shall see, they have very different implications.

Systematic and Unsystematic Risk

systematic risk
A risk that influences a large number of assets. Also *market risk.*

unsystematic risk
A risk that affects at most a small number of assets. Also *unique* or *asset-specific* risk.

Concept Q Answer 11.4a

Lecture Tip: See IM 11.4 for an expanded discussion of systematic and unsystematic risk.

The first type of surprise, the one that affects a large number of assets, we will label **systematic risk.** A systematic risk is one that influences a large number of assets, each to a greater or lesser extent. Because systematic risks are marketwide effects, they are sometimes called *market risks.*

The second type of surprise we will call **unsystematic risk.** An unsystematic risk is one that affects a single asset or a small group of assets. Because these risks are unique to individual companies or assets, they are sometimes called *unique* or *asset-specific risks.* We will use these terms interchangeably.

As we have seen, uncertainties about general economic conditions, such as GDP, interest rates, or inflation, are examples of systematic risks. These conditions affect nearly all companies to some degree. An unanticipated increase or surprise in inflation, for example, affects wages and the costs of the supplies that companies buy; it affects the value of the assets that companies own; and it affects the prices at which companies sell their products. Forces such as these, to which all companies are susceptible, are the essence of systematic risk.

In contrast, the announcement of an oil strike by a company will primarily affect that company and, perhaps, a few others (such as primary competitors and suppliers). It is unlikely to have much of an effect on the world oil market, however, or on the affairs of companies not in the oil business, so this is an unsystematic event.

Systematic and Unsystematic Components of Return

Concept Q Answer 11.4b

The distinction between a systematic risk and an unsystematic risk is never really as exact as we make it out to be. Even the most narrow and peculiar bit of news about a company ripples through the economy. This is true because every enterprise, no matter how tiny, is a part of the economy. It's like the tale of a kingdom that was lost because one horse lost a shoe. This is mostly hair-splitting, however. Some risks are clearly much more general than others. We'll see some evidence on this point in just a moment.

The distinction between the types of risk allows us to break down the surprise portion, U, of the return on Flyers' stock into two parts. From before, we had the actual return broken down into its expected and surprise components:

$$R = \text{E}(R) + U$$

We now recognize that the total surprise for Flyers, U, has a systematic and an unsystematic component, so:

$$R = \text{E}(R) + \text{Systematic portion} + \text{Unsystematic portion} \qquad [11.5]$$

Because it is traditional, we will use the Greek letter epsilon, ε, to stand for the unsystematic portion. Since systematic risks are often called market risks, we will use the letter m to stand for the systematic part of the surprise. With these symbols, we can rewrite the total return:

$$R = \text{E}(R) + U$$
$$= \text{E}(R) + m + \varepsilon$$

The important thing about the way we have broken down the total surprise, U, is that the unsystematic portion, ε, is more or less unique to Flyers. For this reason, it is unrelated to the unsystematic portion of return on most other assets. To see why this is important, we need to return to the subject of portfolio risk.

CONCEPT QUESTIONS

11.4a What are the two basic types of risk?

11.4b What is the distinction between the two types of risk?

11.5 DIVERSIFICATION AND PORTFOLIO RISK

We've seen earlier that portfolio risks can, in principle, be quite different from the risks of the assets that make up the portfolio. We now look more closely at the riskiness of an individual asset versus the risk of a portfolio of many different assets. We will once again examine some market history to get an idea of what happens with actual investments in U.S. capital markets. **Problem 11**

The Effect of Diversification: Another Lesson from Market History

In our previous chapter, we saw that the standard deviation of the annual return on a portfolio of 500 large common stocks has historically been about 20 percent per year (see Figure 10.10, for example). Does this mean that the standard deviation of the annual return on a typical stock in that group of 500 is about 20 percent? As you might suspect by now, the answer is *no.* This is an extremely important observation.

To examine the relationship between portfolio size and portfolio risk, Table 11.7 illustrates typical average annual standard deviations for portfolios that contain different numbers of randomly selected NYSE securities.

In Column 2 of Table 11.7, we see that the standard deviation for a "portfolio" of one security is about 49 percent. What this means is that, if you randomly selected a single NYSE stock and put all your money into it, your standard deviation of return would typically have been a substantial 49 percent per year. If you were to randomly select two stocks and invest half your money in each, your standard deviation would have been about 37 percent on average, and so on.

The important thing to notice in Table 11.7 is that the standard deviation declines as the number of securities is increased. By the time we have 100 randomly chosen stocks, the portfolio's standard deviation has declined by about 60 percent, from 49 percent to about 20 percent. With 500 securities, the standard deviation is 19.27 percent, similar to the 20 percent we saw in our previous chapter for the large common stock portfolio. The small difference exists because the portfolio securities and time periods examined are not identical. **Concept Q Answer 11.5a**

TABLE 11.7
Standard deviations of annual portfolio returns

Trans. 11.10

(1) Number of Stocks in Portfolio	(2) Average Standard Deviation of Annual Portfolio Returns	(3) Ratio of Portfolio Standard Deviation to Standard Deviation of a Single Stock
1	49.24%	1.00
2	37.36	0.76
4	29.69	0.60
6	26.64	0.54
8	24.98	0.51
10	23.93	0.49
20	21.68	0.44
30	20.87	0.42
40	20.46	0.42
50	20.20	0.41
100	19.69	0.40
200	19.42	0.39
300	19.34	0.39
400	19.29	0.39
500	19.27	0.39
1,000	19.21	0.39

These figures are from Table 1 in Meir Statman, "How Many Stocks Make a Diversified Portfolio?" *Journal of Financial and Quantitative Analysis* 22 (September 1987), pp. 353–64. They were derived from E. J. Elton and M. J. Gruber, "Risk Reduction and Portfolio Size: An Analytic Solution," *Journal of Business* 50 (October 1977), pp. 415–37.

The Principle of Diversification

Figure 11.1 illustrates the point we've been discussing. What we have plotted is the standard deviation of return versus the number of stocks in the portfolio. Notice in Figure 11.1 that the benefit in terms of risk reduction from adding securities drops off as we add more and more. By the time we have 10 securities, most of the effect is already realized, and by the time we get to 30 or so, there is very little remaining benefit.

Concept Q Answer 11.5b

Figure 11.1 illustrates two key points. First, some of the riskiness associated with individual assets can be eliminated by forming portfolios. The process of spreading an investment across assets (and thereby forming a portfolio) is called *diversification.* The **principle of diversification** tells us that spreading an investment across many assets will eliminate some of the risk. The blue shaded area in Figure 11.1, labeled "diversifiable risk," is the part that can be eliminated by diversification.

principle of diversification
Spreading an investment across a number of assets will eliminate some, but not all, of the risk.

International Note: Are there incremental benefits to be gained by diversifying across national borders? This issue is discussed in IM 11.5.

The second point is equally important. There is a minimum level of risk that cannot be eliminated simply by diversifying. This minimum level is labeled "nondiversifiable risk" in Figure 11.1. Taken together, these two points are another important lesson from capital market history: Diversification reduces risk, but only up to a point. Put another way, some risk is diversifiable and some is not.

Diversification and Unsystematic Risk

Concept Q Answer 11.5c

From our discussion of portfolio risk, we know that some of the risk associated with individual assets can be diversified away and some cannot. We are left with an obvious question: Why is this so? It turns out that the answer hinges on the distinction we made earlier between systematic and unsystematic risk.

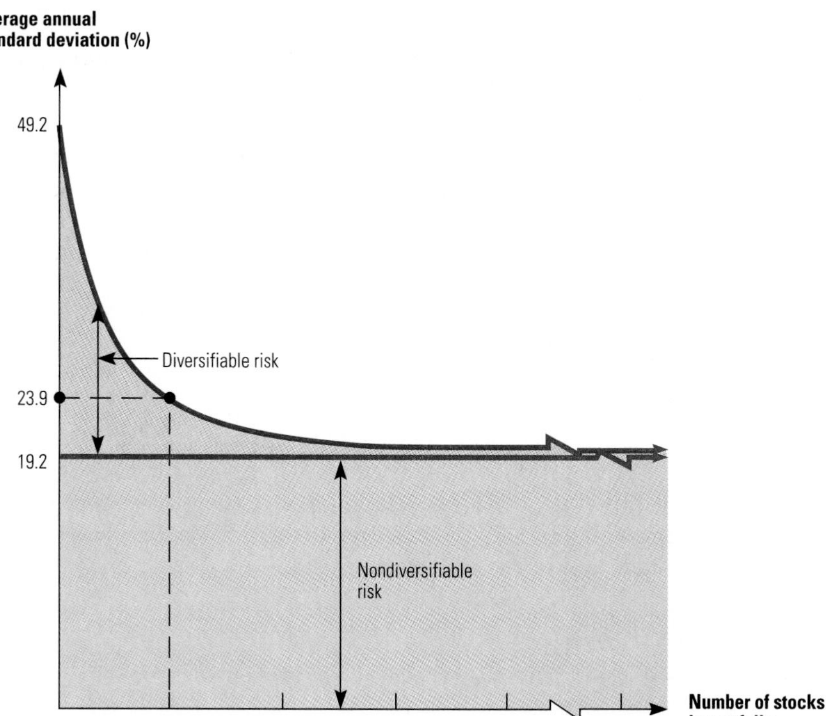

F I G U R E 11.1
Portfolio diversification

Trans. 11.11

By definition, an unsystematic risk is one that is particular to a single asset or, at most, a small group. For example, if the asset under consideration is stock in a single company, the discovery of positive NPV projects such as successful new products and innovative cost savings will tend to increase the value of the stock. Unanticipated lawsuits, industrial accidents, strikes, and similar events will tend to decrease future cash flows and thereby reduce share values.

Here is the important observation: If we only held a single stock, then the value of our investment would fluctuate because of company-specific events. If we hold a large portfolio, on the other hand, some of the stocks in the portfolio will go up in value because of positive company-specific events and some will go down in value because of negative events. The net effect on the overall value of the portfolio will be relatively small, however, as these effects will tend to cancel each other out.

Now we see why some of the variability associated with individual assets is eliminated by diversification. By combining assets into portfolios, the unique or unsystematic events—both positive and negative—tend to "wash out" once we have more than just a few assets.

This is an important point that bears restating:

Unsystematic risk is essentially eliminated by diversification, so a relatively large portfolio has almost no unsystematic risk.

In fact, the terms *diversifiable risk* and *unsystematic risk* are often used interchangeably.

Diversification and Systematic Risk

Concept Q Answer 11.5d

We've seen that unsystematic risk can be eliminated by diversifying. What about systematic risk? Can it also be eliminated by diversification? The answer is no because, by definition, a systematic risk affects almost all assets to some degree. As a result, no matter how many assets we put into a portfolio, the systematic risk doesn't go away. Thus, for obvious reasons, the terms *systematic risk* and *nondiversifiable risk* are used interchangeably.

Because we have introduced so many different terms, it is useful to summarize our discussion before moving on. What we have seen is that the total risk of an investment, as measured by the standard deviation of its return, can be written as:

$$\text{Total risk} = \text{Systematic risk} + \text{Unsystematic risk} \quad [11.6]$$

Systematic risk is also called *nondiversifiable risk* or *market risk.* Unsystematic risk is also called *diversifiable risk, unique risk,* or *asset-specific risk.* For a well-diversified portfolio, the unsystematic risk is negligible. For such a portfolio, essentially all of the risk is systematic.

CONCEPT QUESTIONS

11.5a What happens to the standard deviation of return for a portfolio if we increase the number of securities in the portfolio?

11.5b What is the principle of diversification?

11.5c Why is some risk diversifiable?

11.5d Why can't systematic risk be diversified away?

11.6 SYSTEMATIC RISK AND BETA

Problems 27, 31

The question that we now begin to address is: What determines the size of the risk premium on a risky asset? Put another way, why do some assets have a larger risk premium than other assets? The answer to these questions, as we discuss next, is also based on the distinction between systematic and unsystematic risk.

The Systematic Risk Principle

Thus far, we've seen that the total risk associated with an asset can be decomposed into two components: systematic and unsystematic risk. We have also seen that unsystematic risk can be essentially eliminated by diversification. The systematic risk present in an asset, on the other hand, cannot be eliminated by diversification.

systematic risk principle The expected return on a risky asset depends only on that asset's systematic risk.

Based on our study of capital market history, we know that there is a reward, on average, for bearing risk. However, we now need to be more precise about what we mean by risk. The **systematic risk principle** states that the reward for bearing risk depends only on the systematic risk of an investment. The underlying rationale for this principle is straightforward: Since unsystematic risk can be eliminated at virtually no cost (by diversifying), there is no reward for bearing it. Put another way, the market does not reward risks that are borne unnecessarily.

Lecture Tip: The role of mutual funds in achieving diversification is discussed in IM 11.6.

The systematic risk principle has a remarkable and very important implication:

Concept Q Answer 11.6a

The expected return on an asset depends only on that asset's systematic risk.

There is an obvious corollary to this principle: No matter how much total risk an asset has, only the systematic portion is relevant in determining the expected return (and the risk premium) on that asset.

Measuring Systematic Risk

Since systematic risk is the crucial determinant of an asset's expected return, we need some way of measuring the level of systematic risk for different investments. The specific measure we will use is called the **beta coefficient,** for which we will use the Greek symbol β. A beta coefficient, or beta for short, tells us how much systematic risk a particular asset has relative to an average asset. By definition, an average asset has a beta of 1.0 relative to itself. An asset with a beta of 0.50, therefore, has half as much systematic risk as an average asset; an asset with a beta of 2.0 has twice as much.

beta coefficient
Amount of systematic risk present in a particular risky asset relative to an average risky asset.

Table 11.8 contains the estimated beta coefficients for the stocks of some well-known companies. (This particular source rounds numbers to the nearest 0.05.) The range of betas in Table 11.8 is typical for stocks of large U.S. corporations. Betas outside this range occur, but they are less common.

Concept Q Answer 11.6b

The important thing to remember is that the expected return, and thus the risk premium, on an asset depends only on its systematic risk. Since assets with larger betas have greater systematic risks, they will have greater expected returns. Thus, in Table 11.8, an investor who buys stock in Exxon, with a beta of 0.60, should expect to earn less, on average, than an investor who buys stock in General Motors, with a beta of about 1.15.

Lecture Tip: Emphasize that the market does not reward *unnecessary* risks! For further discussion, see IM 11.6.

TABLE 11.8
Beta coefficients for selected companies

Trans. 11.12

Company	Beta Coefficient (β_i)
Exxon	0.60
AT&T	0.90
IBM	0.95
General Electric	1.10
General Motors	1.15
Wal-Mart	1.25
Microsoft	1.35
Harley-Davidson	1.60

Source: From Value Line *Investment Survey,* various issues, 1995.

EXAMPLE 11.5 Total Risk versus Beta

Consider the following information on two securities. Which has greater total risk? Which has greater systematic risk? Greater unsystematic risk? Which asset will have a higher risk premium?

	Standard Deviation	Beta
Security A	40%	0.50
Security B	20	1.50

Concept Q Answer 11.6d

From our discussion in this section, Security A has greater total risk, but it has substantially less systematic risk. Since total risk is the sum of systematic and unsystematic risk, Security A must have greater unsystematic risk. Finally, from the systematic risk principle, Security B will have a higher risk premium and a greater expected return, despite the fact that it has less total risk. • • •

Portfolio Betas

Concept Q Answer 11.6c

Earlier, we saw that the riskiness of a portfolio has no simple relationship to the risks of the assets in the portfolio. A portfolio beta, however, can be calculated just like a portfolio expected return. For example, looking again at Table 11.8, suppose you put half of your money in AT&T and half in General Electric. What would the beta of this combination be? Since AT&T has a beta of 0.90 and General Electric has a beta of 1.10, the portfolio's beta, β_P, would be:

$$\begin{aligned}\beta_P &= .50 \times \beta_{AT\&T} + .50 \times \beta_{GE}\\ &= .50 \times .90 + .50 \times 1.10\\ &= 1.00\end{aligned}$$

In general, if we had a large number of assets in a portfolio, we would multiply each asset's beta by its portfolio weight and then add the results up to get the portfolio's beta.

EXAMPLE 11.6 Portfolio Betas

Trans. 11.13 Portfolio Betas (Supplemental)

Suppose we had the following investments:

Security	Amount Invested	Expected Return	Beta
Stock A	$1,000	8%	0.80
Stock B	2,000	12	0.95
Stock C	3,000	15	1.10
Stock D	4,000	18	1.40

What is the expected return on this portfolio? What is the beta of this portfolio? Does this portfolio have more or less systematic risk than an average asset?

To answer, we first have to calculate the portfolio weights. Notice that the total amount invested is $10,000. Of this, $1,000/$10,000 = 10% is invested in Stock A. Similarly, 20 percent is invested in Stock B, 30 percent is invested in Stock C, and 40 percent is invested in Stock D. The expected return, $E(R_P)$, is thus:

$$\begin{aligned}E(R_P) &= .10 \times E(R_A) + .20 \times E(R_B) + .30 \times E(R_C) + .40 \times E(R_D)\\ &= .10 \times 8\% + .20 \times 12\% + .30 \times 15\% + .40 \times 18\%\\ &= 14.9\%\end{aligned}$$

Similarly, the portfolio beta, β_P, is:

$$\begin{aligned}\beta_P &= .10 \times \beta_A + .20 \times \beta_B + .30 \times \beta_C + .40 \times \beta_D \\ &= .10 \times .80 + .20 \times .95 + .30 \times 1.10 + .40 \times 1.40 \\ &= 1.16\end{aligned}$$

This portfolio thus has an expected return of 14.9 percent and a beta of 1.16. Since the beta is larger than 1.0, this portfolio has greater systematic risk than an average asset. • • •

CONCEPT QUESTIONS

11.6a What is the systematic risk principle?

11.6b What does a beta coefficient measure?

11.6c How do you calculate a portfolio beta?

11.6d True or false: The expected return on a risky asset depends on that asset's total risk. Explain.

11.7 THE SECURITY MARKET LINE

Self-Test Problems 11.3, 11.4
Problems 17–24, 29

We're now in a position to see how risk is rewarded in the marketplace. To begin, suppose that Asset A has an expected return of $E(R_A) = 20\%$ and a beta of $\beta_A = 1.6$. Furthermore, the risk-free rate is $R_f = 8\%$. Notice that a risk-free asset, by definition, has no systematic risk (or unsystematic risk), so a risk-free asset has a beta of 0.

Beta and the Risk Premium

Consider a portfolio made up of Asset A and a risk-free asset. We can calculate some different possible portfolio expected returns and betas by varying the percentages invested in these two assets. For example, if 25 percent of the portfolio is invested in Asset A, then the expected return is:

$$\begin{aligned}E(R_P) &= .25 \times E(R_A) + (1 - .25) \times R_f \\ &= .25 \times 20\% + .75 \times 8\% \\ &= 11.0\%\end{aligned}$$

Similarly, the beta on the portfolio, β_P, would be:

$$\begin{aligned}\beta_P &= .25 \times \beta_A + (1 - .25) \times 0 \\ &= .25 \times 1.6 \\ &= .40\end{aligned}$$

Notice that, since the weights have to add up to 1, the percentage invested in the risk-free asset is equal to 1 minus the percentage invested in Asset A.

Lecture Tip: See IM 11.7 for more on the use of a margin account on a portfolio's beta.

One thing that you might wonder about is whether it is possible for the percentage invested in Asset A to exceed 100 percent. The answer is yes. The way this can happen is for the investor to borrow at the risk-free rate. For example, suppose an investor has $100 and borrows an additional $50 at 8 percent, the risk-free rate. The total investment in Asset A would be $150, or 150 percent of the investor's wealth. The expected return in this case would be:

$$\begin{aligned}E(R_P) &= 1.50 \times E(R_A) + (1 - 1.50) \times R_f \\ &= 1.50 \times 20\% - .50 \times 8\% \\ &= 26.0\%\end{aligned}$$

The beta on the portfolio would be:

$$\begin{aligned}\beta_P &= 1.50 \times \beta_A + (1 - 1.50) \times 0 \\ &= 1.50 \times 1.6 \\ &= 2.4\end{aligned}$$

We can calculate some other possibilities as follows:

Trans. 11.14
Portfolio Expected Return and Beta
(Supplemental)

Percentage of Portfolio in Asset A	Portfolio Expected Return	Portfolio Beta
0%	8%	0.0
25	11	0.4
50	14	0.8
75	17	1.2
100	20	1.6
125	23	2.0
150	26	2.4

In Figure 11.2A, these portfolio expected returns are plotted against the portfolio betas. Notice that all the combinations fall on a straight line.

The Reward-to-Risk Ratio What is the slope of the straight line in Figure 11.2A? As always, the slope of a straight line is equal to the "rise over the run." In this case, as we move out of the risk-free asset into Asset A, the beta increases from zero to 1.6 (a "run" of 1.6). At the same time, the expected return goes from 8 percent to 20 percent, a "rise" of 12 percent. The slope of the line is thus 12%/1.6 = 7.50%.

Trans. 11.15
Return, Risk, and Equilibrium
(Supplemental)

Notice that the slope of our line is just the risk premium on Asset A, $E(R_A) - R_f$, divided by Asset A's beta, β_A:

$$\begin{aligned}\text{Slope} &= \frac{E(R_A) - R_f}{\beta_A} \\ &= \frac{20\% - 8\%}{1.6} = 7.50\%\end{aligned}$$

FIGURE 11.2A Portfolio expected returns and betas for Asset A

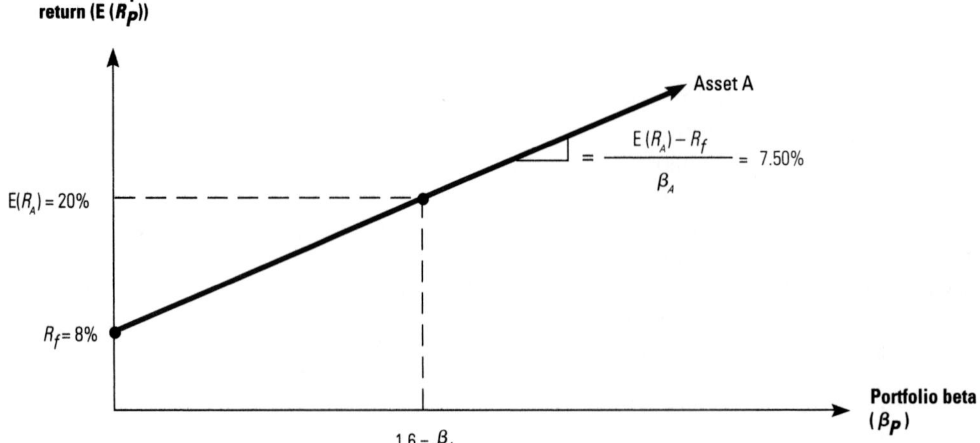

What this tells us is that Asset A offers a *reward-to-risk ratio* of 7.50 percent.[2] In other words, Asset A has a risk premium of 7.50 percent per "unit" of systematic risk.

The Basic Argument Now suppose we consider a second asset, Asset B. This asset has a beta of 1.2 and an expected return of 16 percent. Which investment is better, Asset A or Asset B? You might think that, once again, we really cannot say. Some investors might prefer A; some investors might prefer B. Actually, however, we can say: A is better because, as we shall demonstrate, B offers inadequate compensation for its level of systematic risk, at least relative to A.

To begin, we calculate different combinations of expected returns and betas for portfolios of Asset B and a risk-free asset just as we did for Asset A. For example, if we put 25 percent in Asset B and the remaining 75 percent in the risk-free asset, the portfolio's expected return would be:

$$\begin{aligned} E(R_P) &= .25 \times E(R_B) + (1 - .25) \times R_f \\ &= .25 \times 16\% + .75 \times 8\% \\ &= 10.0\% \end{aligned}$$

Similarly, the beta on the portfolio, β_P, would be:

$$\begin{aligned} \beta_P &= .25 \times \beta_B + (1 - .25) \times 0 \\ &= .25 \times 1.2 \\ &= .30 \end{aligned}$$

Some other possibilities are as follows:

Percentage of Portfolio in Asset B	Portfolio Expected Return	Portfolio Beta
0%	8%	0.0
25	10	0.3
50	12	0.6
75	14	0.9
100	16	1.2
125	18	1.5
150	20	1.8

When we plot these combinations of portfolio expected returns and portfolio betas in Figure 11.2B, we get a straight line just as we did for Asset A.

The key thing to notice is that when we compare the results for Assets A and B, as in Figure 11.2C, the line describing the combinations of expected returns and betas for Asset A is higher than the one for Asset B. What this tells us is that for any given level of systematic risk (as measured by β), some combination of Asset A and the risk-free asset always offers a larger return. This is why we were able to state that Asset A is a better investment than Asset B.

[2] This ratio is sometimes called the *Treynor index,* after one of its originators.

FIGURE 11.2B Portfolio expected returns and betas for Asset B

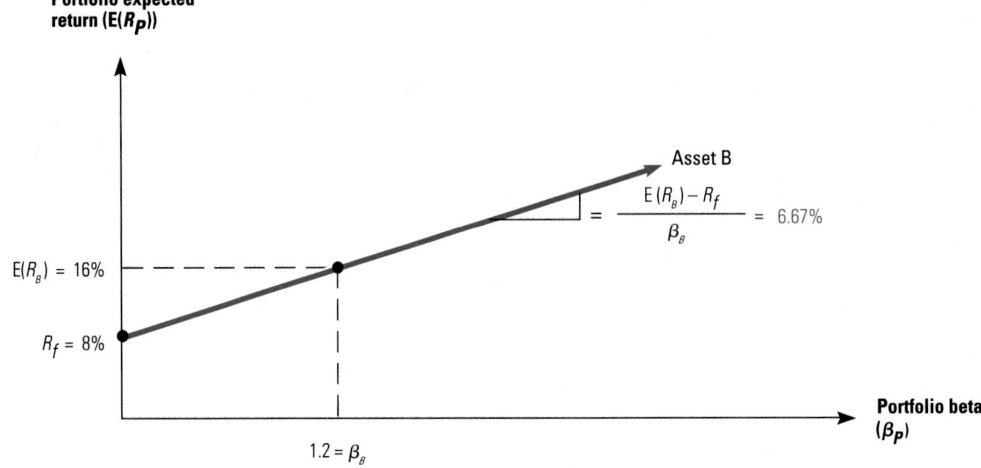

FIGURE 11.2C Portfolio expected returns and betas for both assets

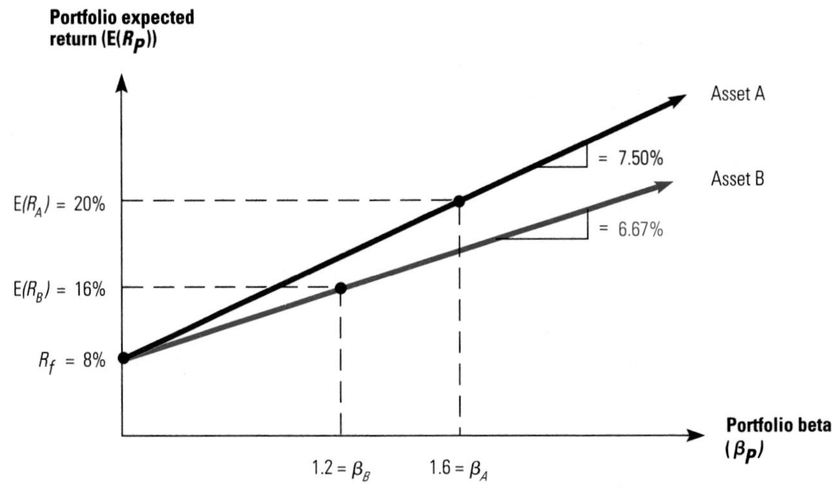

Another way of seeing that A offers a superior return for its level of risk is to note that the slope of our line for Asset B is:

$$\text{Slope} = \frac{E(R_B) - R_f}{\beta_B} = \frac{16\% - 8\%}{1.2} = 6.67\%$$

Thus, Asset B has a reward-to-risk ratio of 6.67 percent, which is less than the 7.5 percent offered by Asset A.

Concept Q Answer 11.7a

The Fundamental Result The situation we have described for Assets A and B cannot persist in a well-organized, active market, because investors would be attracted to Asset A and away from Asset B. As a result, Asset A's price would rise and Asset B's price would fall. Since prices and returns move in opposite directions, the result is that A's expected return would decline and B's would rise.

This buying and selling would continue until the two assets plotted on exactly the same line, which means they offer the same reward for bearing risk. In other words, in an active, competitive market, we must have that:

$$\frac{E(R_A) - R_f}{\beta_A} = \frac{E(R_B) - R_f}{\beta_B}$$

This is the fundamental relationship between risk and return.

Our basic argument can be extended to more than just two assets. In fact, no matter how many assets we had, we would always reach the same conclusion:

Lecture Tip: Emphasize here the issue of asset market equilibrium. The fundamental result stated here is essentially a "no-arbitrage" condition.

The reward-to-risk ratio must be the same for all the assets in the market.

This result is really not so surprising. What it says, for example, is that, if one asset has twice as much systematic risk as another asset, its risk premium will simply be twice as large.

Since all of the assets in the market must have the same reward-to-risk ratio, they all must plot on the same line. This argument is illustrated in Figure 11.3. As shown, Assets A and B plot directly on the line and thus have the same reward-to-risk ratio. If an asset plotted above the line, such as C in Figure 11.3, its price would rise, and its expected return would fall until it plotted exactly on the line. Similarly, if an asset plotted below the line, such as D in Figure 11.3, its expected return would rise until it too plotted directly on the line.

FIGURE 11.3 Expected returns and systematic risk

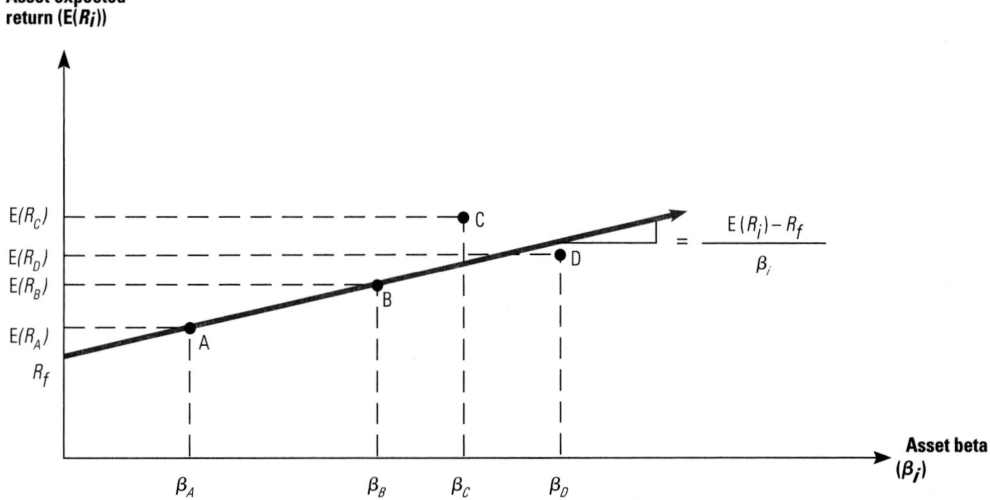

The fundamental relationship between beta and expected return is that all assets must have the same reward-to-risk ratio, $[E(R_i) - R_f]/\beta_i$. This means that they would all plot on the same straight line. Assets A and B are examples of this behavior. Asset C's expected return is too high; asset D's is too low.

The arguments we have presented apply to active, competitive, well-functioning markets. The financial markets, such as the NYSE, best meet these criteria. Other markets, such as real asset markets, may or may not. For this reason, these concepts are most useful in examining financial markets. We will thus focus on such markets here. However, as we discuss in a later section, the information about risk and return gleaned from financial markets is crucial in evaluating the investments that a corporation makes in real assets.

EXAMPLE 11.7 Buy Low, Sell High

An asset is said to be *overvalued* if its price is too high given its expected return and risk. Suppose you observe the following situation:

Security	Expected Return	Beta
SWMS Co.	14%	1.3
Insec Co.	10	0.8

The risk-free rate is currently 6 percent. Is one of the two securities above overvalued relative to the other?

To answer, we compute the reward-to-risk ratio for both. For SWMS, this ratio is (14% − 6%)/1.3 = 6.15%. For Insec, this ratio is 5 percent. What we conclude is that Insec offers an insufficient expected return for its level of risk, at least relative to SWMS. Since its expected return is too low, its price is too high. In other words, Insec is overvalued relative to SWMS, and we would expect to see its price fall relative to SWMS's. Notice that we could also say SWMS is *undervalued* relative to Insec. • • •

The Security Market Line

Concept Q Answer 11.7b

security market line (SML) Positively sloped straight line displaying the relationship between expected return and beta.

The line that results when we plot expected returns and beta coefficients is obviously of some importance, so it's time we gave it a name. This line, which we use to describe the relationship between systematic risk and expected return in financial markets, is usually called the **security market line (SML).** After NPV, the SML is arguably the most important concept in modern finance.

Market Portfolios It will be very useful to know the equation of the SML. There are many different ways we could write it, but one way is particularly common. Suppose we were to consider a portfolio made up of all of the assets in the market. Such a portfolio is called a market portfolio, and we will write the expected return on this market portfolio as $E(R_M)$.

Trans. 11.16 The Capital Asset Pricing Model (Supplemental)

Since all the assets in the market must plot on the SML, so must a market portfolio made up of those assets. To determine where it plots on the SML, we need to know the beta of the market portfolio, β_M. Since this portfolio is representative of all of the assets in the market, it must have average systematic risk. In other words, it has a beta of 1.0. We could therefore write the slope of the SML as:

market risk premium Slope of the SML, the difference between the expected return on a market portfolio and the risk-free rate.

$$\text{SML slope} = \frac{E(R_M) - R_f}{\beta_M} = \frac{E(R_M) - R_f}{1} = E(R_M) - R_f$$

The term $E(R_M) - R_f$ is often called the **market risk premium** since it is the risk premium on a market portfolio.

The Capital Asset Pricing Model To finish up, if we let $E(R_i)$ and β_i stand for the expected return and beta, respectively, on any asset in the market, then we know that it must plot on the SML. As a result, we know that its reward-to-risk ratio is the same as the overall market's:

Lecture Tip: See IM 11.7 for a discussion of the relationship between the historical risk premium and future risk premiums.

$$\frac{E(R_i) - R_f}{\beta_i} = E(R_M) - R_f$$

If we rearrange this, then we can write the equation for the SML as:

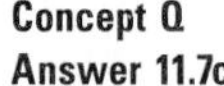
Concept Q Answer 11.7c

$$E(R_i) = R_f + [E(R_M) - R_f] \times \beta_i \qquad [11.7]$$

This result is identical to the famous **capital asset pricing model (CAPM).**

What the CAPM shows is that the expected return for a particular asset depends on three things:

capital asset pricing model (CAPM)
Equation of the SML showing relationship between expected return and beta.

1. *The pure time value of money.* As measured by the risk-free rate, R_f, this is the reward for merely waiting for your money, without taking any risk.
2. *The reward for bearing systematic risk.* As measured by the market risk premium, $[E(R_M) - R_f]$, this component is the reward the market offers for bearing an average amount of systematic risk in addition to waiting.
3. *The amount of systematic risk.* As measured by β_i, this is the amount of systematic risk present in a particular asset, relative to an average asset.

By the way, the CAPM works for portfolios of assets just as it does for individual assets. In an earlier section, we saw how to calculate a portfolio's β. To find the expected return on a portfolio, we simply use this β in the CAPM equation.

Figure 11.4 summarizes our discussion of the SML and the CAPM. As before, we plot expected return against beta. Now we recognize that, based on the CAPM, the slope of the SML is equal to the market risk premium, $[E(R_M) - R_f]$.

FIGURE 11.4
The security market line (SML)

Trans. 11.17

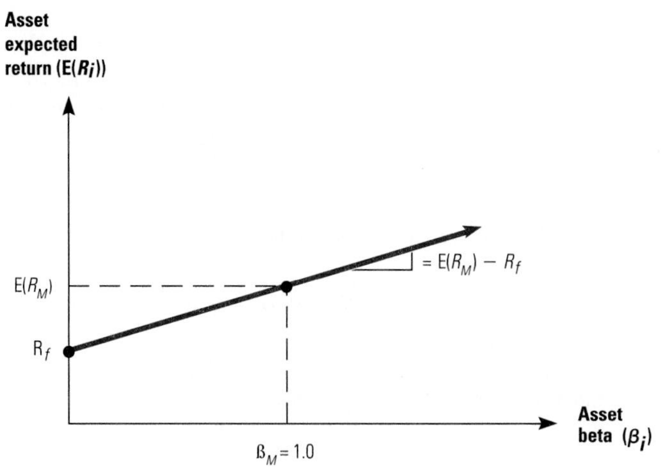

The slope of the security market line is equal to the market risk premium; i.e., the reward for bearing an average amount of systematic risk. The equation describing the SML can be written:

$$E(R_i) = R_f + [E(R_M) - R_f] \times \beta_i$$

which is the capital asset pricing model (CAPM).

TABLE 11.9 Summary of risk and return concepts **Trans. 11.18**

I. Total Return
The *total return* on an investment has two components: the expected return and the unexpected return. The unexpected return comes about because of unanticipated events. The risk from investing stems from the possibility of an unanticipated event.

II. Total Risk
The *total risk* of an investment is measured by the variance or, more commonly, the standard deviation of its return.

III. Systematic and Unsystematic Risks
Systematic risks (also called *market risks*) are unanticipated events that affect almost all assets to some degree because the effects are economywide. *Unsystematic risks* are unanticipated events that affect single assets or small groups of assets. Unsystematic risks are also called *unique* or *asset-specific risks.*

IV. The Effect of Diversification
Some, but not all, of the risk associated with a risky investment can be eliminated by diversification. The reason is that unsystematic risks, which are unique to individual assets, tend to wash out in a large portfolio, but systematic risks, which affect all of the assets in a portfolio to some extent, do not.

V. The Systematic Risk Principle and Beta
Because unsystematic risk can be freely eliminated by diversification, the *systematic risk principle* states that the reward for bearing risk depends only on the level of systematic risk. The level of systematic risk in a particular asset, relative to average, is given by the *beta* of that asset.

VI. The Reward-to-Risk Ratio and the Security Market Line
The *reward-to-risk ratio* for Asset i is the ratio of its risk premium, $E(R_i) - R_f$, to its beta, β_i:

$$\frac{E(R_i) - R_f}{\beta_i}$$

In a well-functioning market, this ratio is the same for every asset. As a result, when asset expected returns are plotted against asset betas, all assets plot on the same straight line, called the *security market line* (SML).

VII. The Capital Asset Pricing Model
From the SML, the expected return on Asset i can be written:

$$E(R_i) = R_f + [E(R_M) - R_f] \times \beta_i$$

This is the *capital asset pricing model* (CAPM). The expected return on a risky asset thus has three components. The first is the pure time value of money (R_f), the second is the market risk premium, $[E(R_M) - R_f]$, and the third is the beta for that asset, β_i.

This concludes our presentation of concepts related to the risk-return trade-off. For future reference, Table 11.9 summarizes the various concepts in the order we discussed them.

EXAMPLE 11.8 Risk and Return

Suppose the risk-free rate is 4 percent, the market risk premium is 8.6 percent, and a particular stock has a beta of 1.3. Based on the CAPM, what is the expected return on this stock? What would the expected return be if the beta were to double?

With a beta of 1.3, the risk premium for the stock would be 1.3 × 8.6%, or 11.18 percent. The risk-free rate is 4 percent, so the expected return is 15.18 percent. If the beta doubles to 2.6, the risk premium would double to 22.36 percent, so the expected return would be 26.36 percent. • • •

CONCEPT QUESTIONS

11.7a What is the fundamental relationship between risk and return in well-functioning markets?

11.7b What is the security market line? Why must all assets plot directly on it in a well-functioning market?

11.7c What is the capital asset pricing model (CAPM)? What does it tell us about the required return on a risky investment?

11.8 THE SML AND THE COST OF CAPITAL: A PREVIEW

Our goal in studying risk and return is twofold. First, risk is an extremely important consideration in almost all business decisions, so we want to discuss just what risk is and how it is rewarded in the market. Our second purpose is to learn what determines the appropriate discount rate for future cash flows. We briefly discuss this second subject now; we discuss it in more detail in Chapter 12.

The Basic Idea

The security market line tells us the reward for bearing risk in financial markets. At an absolute minimum, any new investment our firm undertakes must offer an expected return that is no worse than what the financial markets offer for the same risk. The reason for this is simply that our shareholders can always invest for themselves in the financial markets.

The only way we benefit our shareholders is by finding investments with expected returns that are superior to what the financial markets offer for the same risk. Such an investment will have a positive NPV. So, if we ask "What is the appropriate discount rate?" the answer is that we should use the expected return offered in financial markets on investments with the same systematic risk.

Concept Q Answer 11.8a

In other words, to determine whether or not an investment has a positive NPV, we essentially compare the expected return on that new investment to what the financial market offers on an investment with the same beta. This is why the SML is so important; it tells us the "going rate" for bearing risk in the economy.

Lecture Tip: See IM 11.8 for discussion of a common misconception about efficient markets vis-à-vis physical asset markets.

The Cost of Capital

The appropriate discount rate on a new project is the minimum expected rate of return an investment must offer to be attractive. This minimum required return is often called the **cost of capital** associated with the investment. It is called this because the required return is what the firm must earn on its capital investment in a project just to break even. It can thus be interpreted as the opportunity cost associated with the firm's capital investment.

cost of capital The minimum required return on a new investment.

Notice that when we say an investment is attractive if its expected return exceeds what is offered in financial markets for investments of the same risk, we are effectively using the internal rate of return (IRR) criterion that we developed and discussed in Chapter 8. The only difference is that now we have a much better idea of what determines the required return on an investment. This understanding will be critical when we discuss cost of capital and capital structure in Part 6 of our book.

Concept Q Answer 11.8b

CONCEPT QUESTIONS

11.8a If an investment has a positive NPV, would it plot above or below the SML? Why?

11.8b What is meant by the term *cost of capital?*

11.9 SUMMARY AND CONCLUSIONS

This chapter covers the essentials of risk. Along the way, we introduce a number of definitions and concepts. The most important of these is the security market line, or SML. The SML is important because it tells us the reward offered in financial markets for bearing risk. Once we know this, we have a benchmark against which we compare the returns expected from real asset investments to determine if they are desirable.

Because we cover quite a bit of ground, it's useful to summarize the basic economic logic underlying the SML as follows:

1. Based on capital market history, there is a reward for bearing risk. This reward is the risk premium on an asset.
2. The total risk associated with an asset has two parts: systematic risk and unsystematic risk. Unsystematic risk can be freely eliminated by diversification (this is the principle of diversification), so only systematic risk is rewarded. As a result, the risk premium on an asset is determined by its systematic risk. This is the systematic risk principle.
3. An asset's systematic risk, relative to average, can be measured by its beta coefficient, β_i. The risk premium on an asset is then given by its beta coefficient multiplied by the market risk premium, $[E(R_M) - R_f] \times \beta_i$.
4. The expected return on an asset, $E(R_i)$, is equal to the risk-free rate, R_f, plus the risk premium:

$$E(R_i) = R_f + [E(R_M) - R_f] \times \beta_i$$

This is the equation of the SML, and it is often called the *capital asset pricing model* (CAPM).

This chapter completes our discussion of risk and return and concludes Part 5 of our book. Now that we have a better understanding of what determines a firm's cost of capital for an investment, the next several chapters examine more closely how firms raise the long-term capital needed for investment.

Chapter Review Problems and Self-Test

11.1 Expected Return and Standard Deviation This problem will give you some practice calculating measures of prospective portfolio performance. There are two assets and three states of the economy:

(1) State of Economy	(2) Probability of State of Economy	(3) Stock A Rate of Return if State Occurs	(4) Stock B Rate of Return if State Occurs
Recession	.10	−.20	.30
Normal	.60	.10	.20
Boom	.30	.70	.50

What are the expected returns and standard deviations for these two stocks?

11.2 Portfolio Risk and Return In the previous problem, suppose you have \$20,000 total. If you put \$6,000 in Stock A and the remainder in Stock B, what will be the expected return and standard deviation on your portfolio?

11.3 Risk and Return Suppose you observe the following situation:

Security	Beta	Expected Return
Cooley, Inc.	1.6	19%
Moyer Co.	1.2	16

If the risk-free rate is 8 percent, are these securities correctly priced? What would the risk-free rate have to be if they are correctly priced?

11.4 **CAPM** Suppose the risk-free rate is 8 percent. The expected return on the market is 14 percent. If a particular stock has a beta of .60, what is its expected return based on the CAPM? If another stock has an expected return of 20 percent, what must its beta be?

Answers to Self-Test Problems

11.1 The expected returns are just the possible returns multiplied by the associated probabilities:

$$E(R_A) = .10 \times (-.20) + .60 \times (.10) + .30 \times (.70) = 25\%$$
$$E(R_B) = .10 \times (.30) + .60 \times (.20) + .30 \times (.50) = 30\%$$

The variances are given by the sums of the squared deviations from the expected returns multiplied by their probabilities:

$$\begin{aligned}
\sigma_A^2 &= .10 \times (-.20 - .25)^2 + .60 \times (.10 - .25)^2 \\
&\quad + .30 \times (.70 - .25)^2 \\
&= .10 \times (-.45)^2 + .60 \times (-.15)^2 + .30 \times (.45)^2 \\
&= .10 \times .2025 + .60 \times .0225 + .30 \times .2025 \\
&= .0945 \\
\sigma_B^2 &= .10 \times (.30 - .30)^2 + .60 \times (.20 - .30)^2 + .30 \\
&\quad \times (.50 - .30)^2 \\
&= .10 \times (.00)^2 + .60 \times (-.10)^2 + .30 \times (.20)^2 \\
&= .10 \times .00 + .60 \times .01 + .30 \times .04 \\
&= .0180
\end{aligned}$$

The standard deviations are thus:

$$\sigma_A = \sqrt{.0945} = 30.74\%$$
$$\sigma_B = \sqrt{.0180} = 13.42\%$$

11.2 The portfolio weights are \$6,000/20,000 = .30 and \$14,000/20,000 = .70. The expected return is thus:

$$\begin{aligned}
E(R_P) &= .30 \times E(R_A) + .70 \times E(R_B) \\
&= .30 \times 25\% + .70 \times 30\% \\
&= 28.50\%
\end{aligned}$$

Alternatively, we could calculate the portfolio's return in each of the states:

(1) State of Economy	(2) Probability of State of Economy	(3) Portfolio Return if State Occurs
Recession	.10	.30 × (−.20) + .70 × (.30) = .15
Normal	.60	.30 × (.10) + .70 × (.20) = .17
Boom	.30	.30 × (.70) + .70 × (.50) = .56

The portfolio's expected return is:

$$E(R_P) = .10 \times (.15) + .60 \times (.17) + .30 \times (.56) = 28.50\%$$

This is the same as we had before.

The portfolio's variance is:

$$\sigma_P^2 = .10 \times (.15 - .285)^2 + .60 \times (.17 - .285)^2 + .30 \times (.56 - .285)^2$$
$$= .03245$$

So the standard deviation is $\sqrt{.03245} = 18.01\%$.

11.3 If we compute the reward-to-risk ratios, we get $(19\% - 8\%)/1.6 = 6.875\%$ for Cooley versus 6.67% for Moyer. Relative to Cooley, Moyer's expected return is too low, so its price is too high.

If they are correctly priced, then they must offer the same reward-to-risk ratio. The risk-free rate would have to be such that:

$$(19\% - R_f)/1.6 = (16\% - R_f)/1.2$$

With a little algebra, we find that the risk-free rate must be 7 percent:

$$(19\% - R_f) = (16\% - R_f)(1.6/1.2)$$
$$19\% - 16\% \times (4/3) = R_f - R_f \times (4/3)$$
$$R_f = 7\%$$

11.4 Since the expected return on the market is 14 percent, the market risk premium is $14\% - 8\% = 6\%$ (the risk-free rate is 8 percent). The first stock has a beta of .60, so its expected return is $8\% + .60 \times 6\% = 11.6\%$.

For the second stock, notice that the risk premium is $20\% - 8\% = 12\%$. Since this is twice as large as the market risk premium, the beta must be exactly equal to 2. We can verify this using the CAPM:

$$E(R_i) = R_f + [E(R_M) - R_f] \times \beta_i$$
$$20\% = 8\% + (14\% - 8\%) \times \beta_i$$
$$\beta_i = 12\%/6\%$$
$$= 2.0$$

Questions and Problems

Basic (Questions 1–24)

1. **Determining Portfolio Weights** What are the portfolio weights for a portfolio that has 50 shares of stock that sells for \$30 per share and 20 shares of a stock that sells for \$45 per share? *(Margin: $Weight_1 = .625$, $Weight_2 = .375$)*
2. **Portfolio Expected Return** You own a portfolio that has \$500 invested in Stock A and \$1,000 invested in Stock B. If the expected returns on these stocks are 20 percent and 14 percent, respectively, what is the expected return on the portfolio? *(Margin: .16)*
3. **Portfolio Expected Return** You own a portfolio that is 40 percent invested in Stock X, 35 percent in Stock Y, and 25 percent in Stock Z. The expected returns on these three stocks are 8 percent, 15 percent, and 25 percent, respectively. What is the expected return on the portfolio? *(Margin: .147)*
4. **Portfolio Expected Return** You have \$100,000 to invest in a stock portfolio. Your choices are Stock H with an expected return of *(Margin: H: \$60,000; L: \$40,000)*

22 percent and Stock L with an expected return of 12 percent. If your goal is to create a portfolio with an expected return of 18 percent, how much money will you invest in Stock H? In Stock L?

5. **Calculating Expected Return** Based on the following information, calculate the expected return. .20

State of Economy	Probability of State of Economy	Rate of Return if State Occurs
Recession	0.25	0.05
Boom	0.75	0.25

6. **Calculating Expected Return** Based on the following information, calculate the expected return. .139

State of Economy	Probability of State of Economy	Rate of Return if State Occurs
Recession	0.10	−0.05
Normal	0.70	0.12
Boom	0.20	0.30

7. **Calculating Returns and Deviations** Based on the following information, calculate the expected return and standard deviation for the two stocks.

$E(R_A) = .1020$
$\sigma_A = .0511$
$E(R_B) = .2105$
$\sigma_B = .2025$

State of Economy	Probability of State of Economy	Stock A Rate of Return	Stock B Rate of Return
Recession	0.15	0.02	−0.15
Normal	0.60	0.09	0.18
Boom	0.25	0.18	0.50

8. **Calculating Expected Returns** A portfolio is invested 30 percent in Stock G, 50 percent in Stock J, and 20 percent in Stock K. The expected returns on these stocks are 10 percent, 20 percent, and 30 percent, respectively. What is the portfolio's expected return? How do you interpret your answer? .190

9. **Returns and Deviations** Consider the following information:

a. $E(R_p) = .1312$
b. $\sigma_p^2 = .00582$
Trans. 11.19

State of Economy	Probability of State of Economy	Stock A Rate of Return	Stock B Rate of Return	Stock C Rate of Return
Boom	0.65	0.12	0.16	0.25
Bust	0.35	0.10	0.04	0.00

a. What is the expected return on an equally-weighted portfolio of these three stocks?

b. What is the variance of a portfolio invested 25 percent in A and B, and 50 percent in C?

10. **Returns and Deviations** Consider the following information:

a. $E(R_p) = .0903$
b. $\sigma_p^2 = .0103$; $\sigma_p = .1015$

State of Economy	Probability of State of Economy	Stock A Rate of Return	Stock B Rate of Return	Stock C Rate of Return
Boom	0.20	0.10	0.35	0.20
Good	0.50	0.07	0.15	0.10
Poor	0.25	0.04	−0.05	0.00
Bust	0.05	0.00	−0.40	−0.08

a. Your portfolio is invested 30 percent in A and C, and 40 percent in B. What is the portfolio's expected return?

b. What is the variance of this portfolio? The standard deviation?

11. **Types of Risk** In broad terms, why is some risk diversifiable? Why are some risks nondiversifiable? Does it follow that an investor can control the level of unsystematic risk in a portfolio, but not the level of systematic risk?
12. **Announcements and Security Prices** Suppose the government announces that, based on a just-completed survey, the growth rate in the economy is likely to be 2 percent in the coming year as compared to 5 percent for the year just completed. Would security prices increase, decrease, or stay the same following this announcement? Does it make any difference whether the 2 percent figure was anticipated by the market or not? Explain.
13. **Systematic versus Unsystematic Risk** Classify the following events as mostly systematic or mostly unsystematic. Is the distinction clear in every case?
    a. Short-term interest rates increase unexpectedly.
    b. The interest rate a company pays on its short-term debt borrowing is increased by its bank.
    c. Oil prices unexpectedly decline.
    d. An oil tanker ruptures creating a large oil spill.
    e. A manufacturer loses a multimillion dollar product liability suit.
    f. A Supreme Court decision substantially broadens producer liability for injuries suffered by product users.
14. **Announcements and Risk** Classify the following events on whether they might cause stocks in general to change price, and whether they might cause Big Widget Corp.'s stock to change price.
    a. The government announces that inflation unexpectedly jumped by 2 percent last month.
    b. Big Widget's quarterly earnings report just issued generally fell in line with analysts' expectations.
    c. The government reports that economic growth last year was at 3 percent, which generally agreed with most economists' forecasts.
    d. The directors of Big Widget die in a plane crash.
    e. Congress approves changes to the tax code that will increase the top marginal corporate tax rate. The legislation had been debated for the previous six months.

$\beta_p = 1.06$

15. **Calculating Portfolio Betas** You own a stock portfolio invested 20 percent in Stock Q, 40 percent in Stock R, 25 percent in Stock S, and 15 percent in Stock T. The betas for these four stocks are 1.10, 0.95, 1.40, and 0.70, respectively. What is the portfolio beta?

$\beta_p = 1.80$

16. **Calculating Portfolio Betas** You own a portfolio equally invested in a risk-free asset and two stocks. If one of the stocks has a beta of 1.20 and the total portfolio is equally as risky as the market, what must the beta be for the other stock in your portfolio?

$E(R_s) = .142$

17. **Using CAPM** A stock has a beta of 0.9, the expected return on the market is 15 percent, and the risk-free rate is 7 percent. What must the expected return on this stock be?

$\beta_s = 1.20$

18. **Using CAPM** A stock has an expected return of 12 percent, the risk-free rate is 6 percent, and the market risk premium is 5 percent. What must the beta of this stock be?

19. **Using CAPM** A stock has an expected return of 15 percent, its beta is 1.25, and the risk-free rate is 5 percent. What must the expected return on the market be?

$E(R_M) = .13$

20. **Using CAPM** A stock has an expected return of 10 percent, a beta of 0.5, and the expected return on the market is 16 percent. What must the risk-free rate be?

$R_f = .04$

21. **Using CAPM** A stock has a beta of 0.80 and an expected return of 11 percent. A risk-free asset currently earns 8 percent.
   a. What is the expected return on a portfolio that is equally invested in the two assets?
   b. If a portfolio of the two assets has a beta of 0.45, what are the portfolio weights?
   c. If a portfolio of the two assets has an expected return of 10 percent, what is its beta?
   d. If a portfolio of the two assets has a beta of 1.75, what are the portfolio weights? How do you interpret the weights for the two assets in this case? Explain.

a. $E(R_p) = .095$
b. Weight $R_f = .4375$
c. $\beta_p = .533$
d. Weight $R_f = -1.1875$

22. **Using the SML** Asset W has an expected return of 20 percent and a beta of 1.25. If the risk-free rate is 6 percent, complete the following table for portfolios of Asset W and the risk-free asset. Illustrate the relationship between portfolio expected return and portfolio beta by plotting the expected returns against the betas. What is the slope of the line that results?

Slope = .112

Percentage of Portfolio in Asset W	Portfolio Expected Return	Portfolio Beta
0%		
25		
50		
75		
100		
125		
150		

23. **Reward-to-Risk Ratios** Stock M has a beta of 1.2 and an expected return of 20 percent. Stock N has a beta of 0.9 and an expected return of 16 percent. If the risk-free rate is 5 percent and the market risk premium is 12.3 percent, are these stocks correctly priced? Which one is undervalued? Overvalued?

$E(R_M) = .1976$
$E(R_N) = .1607$

24. **Reward-to-Risk Ratios** In the previous problem, what would the risk-free rate have to be for the two stocks to be correctly priced?

$R_f = .04$

Intermediate (Questions 25–33)

25. **Expected Portfolio Returns** If a portfolio has a positive investment in every asset, can the expected return on the portfolio be greater than that on every asset in the portfolio? Can it be less than that on every asset in the portfolio? If you answer yes to one or both of these questions, give an example to support your answer.

26. **Individual Asset Variance and Diversification** True or false: The most important characteristic in determining the variance of a well-diversified portfolio is the variances of the individual assets in the portfolio. Explain.

27. **Portfolio Risk** If a portfolio has a positive investment in every asset, can the standard deviation on the portfolio be less than that on every asset in the portfolio? What about the portfolio beta?

Trans. 11.20

28. **Portfolio Returns** Using information from the previous chapter on capital market history, what was the return on a portfolio that was equally invested in common stocks and long-term bonds? What was the return on a portfolio that was equally invested in small stocks and Treasury bills?

29. **CAPM** Using the CAPM, show that the ratio of the risk premiums on two assets is equal to the ratio of their betas.

a. $E(R_p) = .1875$
$\sigma_p^2 = .0588$; $\sigma_p = .2426$
b. .135
c. .1310; .1286

30. **Portfolio Returns and Deviations** Given the following information on a portfolio of three stocks:

State of Economy	Probability of State of Economy	Stock A Rate of Return	Stock B Rate of Return	Stock C Rate of Return
Boom	0.20	0.20	0.30	1.00
Normal	0.70	0.10	0.05	0.30
Bust	0.10	0.00	−0.20	−0.80

a. If your portfolio is invested 30 percent in A and B and 40 percent in C, what is the portfolio's expected return? The variance? The standard deviation?

b. If the expected T-bill rate is 5.25 percent, what is the expected risk premium on the portfolio?

c. If the expected inflation rate is 5 percent, what is the expected real return on the portfolio? What is the expected real risk premium on the portfolio?

C = Invest $55,000

31. **Analyzing a Portfolio** You want to create a portfolio equally as risky as the market, and you have $200,000 to invest. Given this information, fill in the rest of the table below.

Asset	Investment ($)	Beta
Stock A	$60,000	1.20
Stock B	$60,000	0.85
Stock C	??	1.40
Risk-free asset	??	??

Investment = $66,667

32. **Analyzing a Portfolio** You have $100,000 to invest in either Stock D, Stock F, or a risk-free asset. You must invest all of your money. Your goal is to create a portfolio that has an expected return of 10 percent and is only 60 percent as risky as the overall market. If D has an expected return of 20 percent and a beta of 1.50, F has an expected return of 15 percent and a beta of 1.15, and the risk-free rate is 5 percent, how much money will you invest in Stock F?

$\beta_A = 2.1875$
$\sigma_A = .0433$
$\beta_B = 0.9125$
$\sigma_B = .1821$

33. **Systematic versus Unsystematic Risk** Given the following information on stocks A and B:

State of Economy	Probability of State of Economy	Stock A Rate of Return	Stock B Rate of Return
Recession	0.15	0.14	−0.18
Normal	0.60	0.24	0.10
Boom	0.25	0.28	0.40

The market risk premium is 8 percent and the risk-free rate is 6 percent. Which stock has the most systematic risk? Which one has the most unsystematic risk? Which stock is "riskier"? Explain.

Part Six

LONG-TERM FINANCING

All firms have a need for financing. This part of our text examines how firms obtain financing, the costs associated with various types of financing, and the selection of different financing vehicles. Chapter 12 investigates the important subject of cost of capital. Capital is not free and to make financial decisions, firms must know the costs associated with the capital required.

Chapter 13 examines the process of raising capital. Two of the most interesting subjects covered deal with firms that are just getting started and raise funds in the venture capital market and firms that are contemplating "going public," i.e., selling stock to the public for the first time.

The capital used by firms consists of debt and equity. A natural question arises as to the optimal mixture, or capital structure. This mixture is the subject of Chapter 14, which considers the impact of capital structure on firm value.

Finally, a firm's dividend policy is a key component in its financing strategy. In Chapter 15 we examine dividends and dividend policies to evaluate the costs and benefits of paying dividends. We also examine an important alternative to dividends, stock repurchases.

OUTLINE

Chapter Twelve

Cost of Capital

After studying this chapter, you should have a good understanding of:

How to determine a firm's cost of equity capital.

How to determine a firm's cost of debt.

How to determine a firm's overall cost of capital.

Some of the pitfalls associated with a firm's overall cost of capital and what to do about them.

Trans. 12.1
Chapter Outline

Suppose you have just become the president of a large company and the first decision you face is whether to go ahead with a plan to renovate the company's warehouse distribution system. The plan will cost the company $50 million, and it is expected to save $12 million per year after taxes over the next six years.

This is a familiar problem in capital budgeting. To address it, you would determine the relevant cash flows, discount them, and, if the net present value is positive, take on the project; if the NPV is negative, you would scrap it. So far so good, but what should you use as the discount rate?

From our discussion of risk and return, you know that the correct discount rate depends on the riskiness of the warehouse distribution system. In particular, the new project will have a positive NPV only if its return exceeds what the financial markets offer on investments of similar risks. We called this minimum required return the *cost of capital* associated with the project.[1]

Thus, to make the right decision as president, you must examine what the capital markets have to offer and use this information to arrive at an estimate of the project's cost of capital. Our primary purpose in this chapter is to

[1] The term *cost of money* is also used.

describe how to go about doing this. There are a variety of approaches to this task, and a number of conceptual and practical issues arise.

One of the most important concepts we develop is the *weighted average cost of capital* (WACC). This is the cost of capital for the firm as a whole, and it can be interpreted as the required return on the overall firm. In discussing the WACC, we will recognize the fact that a firm will normally raise capital in a variety of forms and that these different forms of capital may have different costs associated with them.

We also recognize in this chapter that taxes are an important consideration in determining the required return on an investment, because we are always interested in valuing the aftertax cash flows from a project. We will therefore discuss how to incorporate taxes explicitly into our estimates of the cost of capital.

12.1 THE COST OF CAPITAL: SOME PRELIMINARIES

In Chapter 11, we developed the security market line (SML) and used it to explore the relationship between the expected return on a security and its systematic risk. We concentrated on how the risky returns from buying securities looked from the viewpoint of, for example, a shareholder in the firm. This helped us understand more about the alternatives available to an investor in the capital markets.

Trans. 12.2
Cost of Capital
(Supplemental)

In this chapter, we turn things around a bit and look more closely at the other side of the problem, which is how these returns and securities look from the viewpoint of the companies that issue them. The important fact to note is that the return an investor in a security receives is the cost of that security to the company that issued it.

Lecture Tip: *Why* we estimate the cost of capital is just as important as *how.* A list of reasons appears in IM 12.1.

Required Return versus Cost of Capital

When we say that the required return on an investment is, say, 10 percent, we usually mean that the investment will have a positive NPV only if its return exceeds 10 percent. Another way of interpreting the required return is to observe that the firm must earn 10 percent on the investment just to compensate its investors for the use of the capital needed to finance the project. This is why we could also say that 10 percent is the cost of capital associated with the investment.

To illustrate the point further, imagine we were evaluating a risk-free project. In this case, how to determine the required return is obvious: We look at the capital markets and observe the current rate offered by risk-free investments, and we use this rate to discount the project's cash flows. Thus, the cost of capital for a risk-free investment is the risk-free rate.

Concept Q
Answer 12.1b

If this project were risky, then, assuming that all the other information is unchanged, the required return is obviously higher. In other words, the cost of capital for this project, if it is risky, is greater than the risk-free rate, and the appropriate discount rate would exceed the risk-free rate.

We will henceforth use the terms *required return, appropriate discount rate,* and *cost of capital* more or less interchangeably because, as the discussion in this section suggests, they all mean essentially the same thing. The key fact to grasp is that the cost of capital associated with an investment depends on the risk of that investment. This is one of the most important lessons in corporate finance, so it bears repeating:

Concept Q Answer 12.1a

The cost of capital depends primarily on the use of the funds, not the source.

Lecture Tip: The instructor may wish to emphasize at this point that (a) the cost of capital is an opportunity rate, and (b) it is determined in the financial markets. It is a function of the risk of the firm's investments.

Lecture Tip: It is worthwhile to explain to students that the "target" capital structure is simply that combination of debt and equity which minimizes the firm's cost of capital and maximizes firm value.

It is a common error to forget this crucial point and fall into the trap of thinking that the cost of capital for an investment depends primarily on how and where the capital is raised.

Financial Policy and Cost of Capital

We know the particular mixture of debt and equity a firm chooses to employ—its capital structure—is a managerial variable. In this chapter, we will take the firm's financial policy as given. In particular, we will assume that the firm has a fixed debt/equity ratio that it maintains. This ratio reflects the firm's *target* capital structure. How a firm might choose that ratio is the subject of a later chapter.

From our discussion above, we know a firm's overall cost of capital will reflect the required return on the firm's assets as a whole. Given that a firm uses both debt and equity capital, this overall cost of capital will be a mixture of the returns needed to compensate its creditors and its stockholders. In other words, a firm's cost of capital will reflect both its cost of debt capital and its cost of equity capital. We discuss these costs separately in the sections below.

CONCEPT QUESTIONS

12.1a What is the primary determinant of the cost of capital for an investment?

12.1b What is the relationship between the required return on an investment and the cost of capital associated with that investment?

12.2 THE COST OF EQUITY

cost of equity
The return that equity investors require on their investment in the firm.

Self-Test Problem 12.1
Problems 1–4

Concept Q
Answer 12.2a, 12.2b

Trans. 12.3
Dividend Growth Approach (Supplemental)

We begin with the most difficult question on the subject of cost of capital: What is the firm's overall **cost of equity?** The reason this is a difficult question is that there is no way of directly observing the return that the firm's equity investors require on their investment. Instead, we must somehow estimate it. This section discusses two approaches to determining the cost of equity: the dividend growth model approach and the security market line (SML) approach.

The Dividend Growth Model Approach

The easiest way to estimate the cost of equity capital is to use the dividend growth model we developed in Chapter 7. Recall that, under the assumption that the firm's dividend will grow at a constant rate g, the price per share of the stock, P_0, can be written as:

$$P_0 = \frac{D_0 \times (1 + g)}{R_E - g} = \frac{D_1}{R_E - g}$$

where D_0 is the dividend just paid, and D_1 is the next period's projected dividend. Notice that we have used the symbol R_E (the E stands for equity) for the required return on the stock.

As we discussed in Chapter 7, we can rearrange this to solve for R_E as follows:

$$R_E = D_1/P_0 + g \qquad [12.1]$$

Since R_E is the return that the shareholders require on the stock, it can be interpreted as the firm's cost of equity capital.

Implementing the Approach To estimate R_E using the dividend growth model approach, we obviously need three pieces of information: P_0, D_0, and g. Of these, for a publicly traded, dividend-paying company, the first two can be observed directly, so they are easily obtained.[2] Only the third component, the expected growth rate in dividends, must be estimated.

To illustrate how we estimate R_E, suppose Greater States Public Service, a large public utility, paid a dividend of \$4 per share last year. The stock currently sells for \$60 per share. You estimate that the dividend will grow steadily at 6 percent per year into the indefinite future. What is the cost of equity capital for Greater States?

Using the dividend growth model, the expected dividend for the coming year, D_1, is:

$$\begin{aligned} D_1 &= D_0 \times (1 + g) \\ &= \$4 \times (1.06) \\ &= \$4.24 \end{aligned}$$

Given this, the cost of equity, R_E, is:

$$\begin{aligned} R_E &= D_1/P_0 + g \\ &= \$4.24/\$60 + .06 \\ &= 13.07\% \end{aligned}$$

The cost of equity is thus 13.07%.

Trans. 12.4
Estimating the Dividend Growth Rate (Supplemental)

Estimating *g* To use the dividend growth model, we must come up with an estimate for g, the growth rate. There are essentially two ways of doing this: (1) use historical growth rates, or (2) use analysts' forecasts of future growth rates. Analysts' forecasts are available from a variety of sources. Naturally, different sources will have different estimates, so one approach might be to obtain multiple estimates and then average them.

[2] Notice that if we have D_0 and g, we can simply calculate D_1 by multiplying D_0 by $(1 + g)$.

Lecture Tip: See IM 12.2 for other ways of computing *g*.

Alternatively, we might observe dividends for the previous, say, five years, calculate the year-to-year growth rates, and average them. For example, suppose we observe the following for some company:

Year	Dividend
1991	$1.10
1992	1.20
1993	1.35
1994	1.40
1995	1.55

We can calculate the percentage changes in the dividend for each year as follows:

Year	Dividend	Dollar Change	Percentage Change
1991	$1.10	—	—
1992	1.20	$.10	9.09%
1993	1.35	.15	12.50
1994	1.40	.05	3.70
1995	1.55	.15	10.71

Lecture Tip: See IM 12.2 for the valuation process for companies that do not pay dividends.

Lecture Tip: Some will wish to compute the average annually compounded growth rate rather than the simple average. In this example, the difference in using the two methods is approximately .05 percent.

Notice that we calculated the change in the dividend on a year-to-year basis and then expressed the change as a percentage. Thus, in 1992 for example, the dividend rose from $1.10 to $1.20, an increase of $.10. This represents a $.10/1.10 = 9.09% increase.

If we average the four growth rates, the result is (9.09 + 12.50 + 3.70 + 10.71)/4 = 9%, so we could use this as an estimate for the expected growth rate, *g*. There are other, more sophisticated, statistical techniques that could be used, but they all amount to using past dividend growth to predict future dividend growth.

Advantages and Disadvantages of the Approach The primary advantage of the dividend growth model approach is its simplicity. It is both easy to understand and easy to use. There are a number of associated practical problems and disadvantages.

First and foremost, the dividend growth model is obviously only applicable to companies that pay dividends. This means that the approach is useless in many cases. Furthermore, even for companies that do pay dividends, the key underlying assumption is that the dividend grows at a constant rate. As our example above illustrates, this will never be *exactly* the case. More generally, the model is really only applicable to cases where reasonably steady growth is likely to occur.

Lecture Tip: See IM 12.2 for articles discussing the effects of poor earnings performance on firm value and cost of capital.

A second problem is that the estimated cost of equity is very sensitive to the estimated growth rate. For a given stock price, an upward revision of g by just 1 percentage point, for example, increases the estimated cost of equity by at least a full percentage point. Since D_1 will probably be revised upwards as well, the increase will actually be somewhat larger than that.

Finally, this approach really does not explicitly consider risk. Unlike the SML approach (which we consider next), there is no direct adjustment for the riskiness of the investment. For example, there is no allowance for the degree of certainty or uncertainty surrounding the estimated growth rate in dividends. As a result, it is difficult to say whether or not the estimated return is commensurate with the level of risk.[3]

The SML Approach

In Chapter 11, we discussed the security market line (SML). Our primary conclusion was that the required or expected return on a risky investment depends on three things:

Trans. 12.5 SML Approach (Supplemental)

1. The risk-free rate, R_f.
2. The market risk premium, $E(R_M) - R_f$.
3. The systematic risk of the asset relative to average, which we called its beta coefficient, β.

Using the SML, the expected return on the company's equity, $E(R_E)$, can be written as:

$$E(R_E) = R_f + \beta_E \times [E(R_M) - R_f]$$

where β_E is the estimated beta for the equity. For the SML approach to be consistent with the dividend growth model, we will drop the *E*s denoting expectations and henceforth write the required return from the SML, R_E, as:

$$R_E = R_f + \beta_E \times (R_M - R_f) \qquad [12.2]$$

Implementing the Approach To use the SML approach, we need a risk-free rate, R_f, an estimate of the market risk premium, $R_M - R_f$, and an estimate of the relevant beta, β_E. In Chapter 10 (Table 10.3), we saw that one estimate of the market risk premium (based on large common stocks) is 8.5 percent. U.S. Treasury bills are paying about 5.6 percent as this is written, so we will use this as our risk-free rate. Beta coefficients for publicly traded companies are widely available.[4]

To illustrate, in Chapter 11, we saw that IBM had an estimated beta of .95 (Table 11.8). We could thus estimate IBM's cost of equity as:

$$\begin{aligned} R_{IBM} &= R_f + \beta_{IBM} \times (R_M - R_f) \\ &= 5.6\% + .95 \times (8.5\%) \\ &= 13.68\% \end{aligned}$$

Thus, using the SML approach, IBM's cost of equity is about 13.68 percent.

Advantages and Disadvantages of the Approach The SML approach has two primary advantages. First, it explicitly adjusts for risk. Second, it is applicable to companies other than just those with steady dividend growth. Thus, it may be useful in a wider variety of circumstances.

[3] There is an implicit adjustment for risk because the current stock price is used. All other things equal, the higher the risk, the lower is the stock price. Further, the lower the stock price, the greater is the cost of equity, again assuming all the other information is the same.

[4] Beta coefficients can be estimated directly by using historical data. For a discussion of how to do this, see Chapters 9, 10, and 11 in S. A. Ross, R.W. Westerfield, and J. J. Jaffe, *Corporate Finance,* 3rd ed. (Homewood, Ill.: Richard D. Irwin, 1993).

There are drawbacks, of course. The SML approach requires that two things be estimated, the market risk premium and the beta coefficient. To the extent that our estimates are poor, the resulting cost of equity will be inaccurate. For example, our estimate of the market risk premium, 8.5 percent, is based on about 70 years of returns on a particular portfolio of stocks. Using different time periods or different stocks could result in very different estimates.

Finally, as with the dividend growth model, we essentially rely on the past to predict the future when we use the SML approach. Economic conditions can change very quickly, so, as always, the past may not be a good guide to the future. In the best of all worlds, the two approaches (dividend growth model and SML) are both applicable and both result in similar answers. If this happens, we might have some confidence in our estimates. We might also wish to compare the results to those for other, similar companies as a reality check.

EXAMPLE 12.1 The Cost of Equity

Suppose stock in Alpha Air Freight has a beta of 1.2. The market risk premium is 8 percent, and the risk-free rate is 6 percent. Alpha's last dividend was $2 per share, and the dividend is expected to grow at 8 percent indefinitely. The stock currently sells for $30. What is Alpha's cost of equity capital?

We can start off by using the SML. Doing this, we find that the expected return on the common stock of Alpha Air Freight is:

$$\begin{aligned} R_E &= R_f + \beta_E \times (R_M - R_f) \\ &= 6\% + 1.2 \times 8\% \\ &= 15.6\% \end{aligned}$$

This suggests that 15.6 percent is Alpha's cost of equity. We next use the dividend growth model. The projected dividend is $D_0 \times (1 + g) = \$2 \times (1.08) = \$2.16$, so the expected return using this approach is:

$$\begin{aligned} R_E &= D_1/P_0 + g \\ &= \$2.16/30 + .08 \\ &= 15.2\% \end{aligned}$$

Lecture Tip: See IM for a discussion of differences in the output from the two approaches to cost of equity estimation.

Our two estimates are reasonably close, so we might just average them to find that Alpha's cost of equity is approximately 15.4 percent. • • •

CONCEPT QUESTIONS

12.2a What do we mean when we say that a corporation's cost of equity capital is 16 percent?

12.2b What are two approaches to estimating the cost of equity capital?

12.3 THE COSTS OF DEBT AND PREFERRED STOCK

Problems 5–8

In addition to ordinary equity, firms use debt and, to a lesser extent, preferred stock to finance their investments. As we discuss next, determining the costs of capital associated with these sources of financing is much easier than determining the cost of equity.

The Cost of Debt

The **cost of debt** is the return that the firm's creditors demand on new borrowing. In principle, we could determine the beta for the firm's debt and then use the SML to estimate the required return on debt just as we estimate the required return on equity. This isn't really necessary, however.

cost of debt
The return that lenders require on the firm's debt.

Unlike a firm's cost of equity, its cost of debt can normally be observed either directly or indirectly, because the cost of debt is simply the interest rate the firm must pay on new borrowing, and we can observe interest rates in the financial markets. For example, if the firm already has bonds outstanding, then the yield to maturity on those bonds is the market-required rate on the firm's debt.

Trans. 12.6
Costs of Debt and Preferred Stock (Supplemental)

Alternatively, if we knew that the firm's bonds were rated, say, AA, then we can simply find out what the interest rate on newly issued AA-rated bonds is. Either way, there is no need to actually estimate a beta for the debt since we can directly observe the rate we want to know.

There is one thing to be careful about, though. The coupon rate on the firm's outstanding debt is irrelevant here. That just tells us roughly what the firm's cost of debt was back when the bonds were issued, not what the cost of debt is today.[5] This is why we have to look at the yield on the debt in today's marketplace. For consistency with our other notation, we will use the symbol R_D for the cost of debt.

Concept Q Answer 12.3c

Lecture Tip: See IM for tips on emphasizing the distinction between coupon rate, current yield, and the yield to maturity.

EXAMPLE 12.2 The Cost of Debt

Suppose the General Tool Company issued a 30-year, 7 percent bond eight years ago. The bond is currently selling for 96 percent of its face value, or $960. What is General Tool's cost of debt?

Concept Q Answer 12.3a

Going back to Chapter 7, we need to calculate the yield to maturity on this bond. Since the bond is selling at a discount, the yield is apparently greater than 7 percent, but not much greater because the discount is fairly small. You can check that the yield to maturity is about 7.37 percent, assuming annual coupons. General Tool's cost of debt, R_D, is thus 7.37 percent. • • •

The Cost of Preferred Stock

Determining the *cost of preferred stock* is quite straightforward. As we discussed in Chapters 6 and 7, preferred stock has a fixed dividend paid every period forever, so a share of preferred stock is essentially a perpetuity. The cost of preferred stock, R_P, is thus:

$$R_P = D/P_0 \qquad [12.3]$$

Concept Q Answer 12.3b

where D is the fixed dividend and P_0 is the current price per share of the preferred stock. Notice that the cost of preferred stock is simply equal to the dividend yield on the preferred stock. Alternatively, preferred stocks are rated in much the same way as bonds, so the cost of preferred stock can be estimated by observing the required returns on other, similarly rated shares of preferred stock.

[5] The firm's cost of debt based on its historic borrowing is sometimes called the *embedded debt cost.*

EXAMPLE 12.3 Georgia Power's Cost of Preferred Stock

On March 8, 1995, Georgia Power had several issues of preferred stock that traded on the NYSE. One issue paid $7.80 annually per share and sold for $96½ per share. The other paid $2.13 per share annually and sold for $25⅞ per share. What is Georgia Power's cost of preferred stock?

Using the first issue, the cost of preferred stock is:

$$\begin{aligned} R_P &= D/P_0 \\ &= \$7.80/96.5 \\ &= 8.1\% \end{aligned}$$

Using the second issue, the cost is:

$$\begin{aligned} R_P &= D/P_0 \\ &= \$2.13/25.875 \\ &= 8.2\% \end{aligned}$$

So Georgia Power's cost of preferred stock appears to be in the 8.1–8.2 percent range. • • •

CONCEPT QUESTIONS

12.3a How can the cost of debt be calculated?

12.3b How can the cost of preferred stock be calculated?

12.3c Why is the coupon rate a bad estimate of a firm's cost of debt?

12.4 THE WEIGHTED AVERAGE COST OF CAPITAL

Self-Test Problem 12.2
Problems 9–17, 24

Now that we have the costs associated with the main sources of capital the firm employs, we need to worry about the specific mix. As we mentioned above, we will take this mix, which is the firm's capital structure, as given for now. Also, we will focus mostly on debt and ordinary equity in this discussion.

The Capital Structure Weights

Trans. 12.7
The Weighted Average Cost of Capital (Supplemental)

We will use the symbol E (for equity) to stand for the *market* value of the firm's equity. We calculate this by taking the number of shares outstanding and multiplying it by the price per share. Similarly, we will use the symbol D (for debt) to stand for the *market* value of the firm's debt. For long-term debt, we calculate this by multiplying the market price of a single bond by the number of bonds outstanding.

Lecture Tip: See IM for tips on emphasizing differences between book, target, and market value weights.

If there are multiple bond issues (as there normally would be), we repeat this calculation for each and then add up the results. If there is debt that is not publicly traded (because it is held by a life insurance company, for example), we must observe the yields on similar, publicly traded debt and then estimate the market value of the privately held debt using this yield as the discount rate. For short-term debt, the book (accounting) values and market values should be somewhat similar, so we might use the book values as estimates of the market values.

Finally, we will use the symbol V (for value) to stand for the combined market value of the debt and equity:

$$V = E + D \qquad [12.4]$$

If we divide both sides by V, we can calculate the percentages of the total capital represented by the debt and equity:

$$100\% = E/V + D/V \quad [12.5]$$

These percentages can be interpreted just like portfolio weights, and they are often called the *capital structure weights.*

For example, if the total market value of a company's stock were calculated as $200 million and the total market value of the company's debt were calculated as $50 million, then the combined value would be $250 million. Of this total, E/V = $200/250 = 80%, so 80 percent of the firm's financing is equity and the remaining 20 percent is debt.

We emphasize here that the correct way to proceed is to use the *market* values of the debt and equity. Under certain circumstances, such as a privately owned company, it may not be possible to get reliable estimates of these quantities. In this case, we might go ahead and use the accounting values for debt and equity. While this is probably better than nothing, we would have to take the answer with a grain of salt.

Taxes and the Weighted Average Cost of Capital

There is one final issue we need to discuss. Recall that we are always concerned with aftertax cash flows. If we are determining the discount rate appropriate to those cash flows, then the discount rate also needs to be expressed on an aftertax basis.

As we discussed previously in various places in this book (and as we will discuss later), the interest paid by a corporation is deductible for tax purposes. Payments to stockholders, such as dividends, are not. What this means, effectively, is that the government pays some of the interest. Thus, in determining an aftertax discount rate, we need to distinguish between the pretax and the aftertax cost of debt.

To illustrate, suppose a firm borrows $1 million at 9 percent interest. The corporate tax rate is 34 percent. What is the aftertax interest rate on this loan? The total interest bill will be $90,000 per year. This amount is tax deductible, however, so the $90,000 interest reduces our tax bill by .34 × $90,000 = $30,600. The aftertax interest bill is thus $90,000 − 30,600 = $59,400. The aftertax interest rate is thus $59,400/$1 million = 5.94%.

Trans. 12.8
Example: Water's Beginning Company's WACC (Supplemental)

Notice that, in general, the aftertax interest rate is simply equal to the pretax rate multiplied by one minus the tax rate. [If we use the symbol T_C to stand for the corporate tax rate, then the aftertax rate that we use can be written as $R_D \times (1 - T_C)$.] For example, using the numbers above, we find that the aftertax interest rate is 9% × (1 − .34) = 5.94%.

Concept Q Answer 12.4b

Collecting together the various topics we have discussed in this chapter, we now have the capital structure weights along with the cost of equity and the aftertax cost of debt. To calculate the firm's overall cost of capital, we multiply the capital structure weights by the associated costs and add them up. The result is the **weighted average cost of capital (WACC).**

Concept Q Answer 12.4a

weighted average cost of capital (WACC)
The weighted average of the cost of equity and the aftertax cost of debt.

$$\text{WACC} = (E/V) \times R_E + (D/V) \times R_D \times (1 - T_C) \quad [12.6]$$

This WACC has a very straightforward interpretation. It is the overall return the firm must earn on its existing assets to maintain the value of its

Principles in Action

EVA: The Financial Tool for the 1990s

What do AT&T, Coca-Cola, Quaker Oats, Briggs & Stratton and CSX have in common? Among other things, they have all linked their fortunes to a new way of managing corporate performance. It goes by many names, but Stern Stewart and Co. of New York City call it Economic Value Added, or EVA. According to Quaker CEO William Smithburg: "EVA makes managers act like shareholders. It's the true corporate faith of the 1990s." If that sounds suspiciously like maximizing shareholder wealth, there's a good reason. That is precisely the objective.

Simply stated, EVA is a method of measuring financial performance. So, how would you, as a corporate financial officer, implement the concept? First, you must identify who it is that supplies capital to your firm and measure the cost of that capital. Then, you identify how much capital is tied up in your corporate operation. Proponents of EVA say that adding up balance sheet assets such as working capital, plant and equipment, and the like is a good starting point. You should also account for other investments such as training employees or expenditures for research and development. These are not assets in an accounting sense, but they are investments that are expected to generate benefits that extend beyond the current year's operations. Finally, multiply the amount of capital from step two by the cost of capital from step one. This is the return, in dollars, you should be providing to your investors. Subtract this amount from operating income after taxes and you have EVA. If it's positive, then you generated value for your investors. If it's negative, then you are destroying the wealth of your investors.

Not surprisingly, EVA provides a link between a corporations's financial performance and its stock price. When AT&T computed its EVA back to 1984, they found an almost perfect correlation between their EVA and their stock price. The stock price rose with increases in EVA and vice versa even though they didn't use EVA extensively over that period. When CSX Intermodal began using EVA back in 1988, they found they had a negative EVA of $70 million. In 1992, Intermodal's EVA was a positive $10 million. Prior to instituting EVA, the price of a share of CSX stock was $28. By 1993 it had grown to $75. Other firms that have implemented EVA have discovered similar results: if a corporation creates value for its shareholders, its stock price rises!

EVA is a useful tool for monitoring a firm's financial performance. If EVA is too low, a firm can cut costs, find ways to generate more revenues while using less capital, or revise the ways in which new investment projects are evaluated. EVA can also be used as an incentive plan for managers or as a way to allocate capital among divisions in a large corporation. However, while the concept of EVA is sound in principle, the manner in which it is implemented has shortcomings. For one thing, EVA is typically computed using asset book values when market values would be preferred. For another, it is sometimes based on accounting measures of income although basing it on cash flow would paint a more accurate picture. Even with its problems, the concept of EVA focuses management attention on creating wealth for its investors. That, in itself, makes it a worthwhile tool.

Source: "The Real Key to Creating Wealth," *Fortune*, September 20, 1993, pp. 38–50.

• • •

stock. It is also the required return on any investments by the firm that have essentially the same risks as existing operations. So, if we were evaluating the cash flows from a proposed expansion of our existing operations, this is the discount rate we would use.

Lecture Tip: IM 12.4 extends the WACC formula to include preferred stock.

The WACC is increasingly being used by corporations to evaluate financial performance. The accompanying *Principles in Action* box provides some details on how this is being done.

EXAMPLE 12.4 Calculating the WACC

The B. B. Lean Co. has 1.4 million shares of stock outstanding. The stock currently sells for $20 per share. The firm's debt is publicly traded and was recently quoted at 93 percent of face value. It has a total face value of $5 million, and it is currently priced to yield 11 percent. The risk-free rate is 8 percent, and the market risk premium is 7 percent. You've estimated that Lean has a beta of .74. If the corporate tax rate is 34 percent, what is the WACC of Lean Co.?

We can first determine the cost of equity and the cost of debt. From the SML, the cost of equity is 8% + .74 × 7% = 13.18%. The total value of the equity is 1.4 million × \$20 = \$28 million. The pretax cost of debt is the current yield to maturity on the outstanding debt, 11 percent. The debt sells for 93 percent of its face value, so its current market value is .93 × \$5 million = \$4.65 million. The total market value of the equity and debt together is \$28 + 4.65 = \$32.65 million.

From here, we can calculate the WACC easily enough. The percentage of equity used by Lean to finance its operations is \$28/\$32.65 = 85.76%. Since the weights have to add up to 1.0, the percentage of debt is 1.0 − .8576 = 14.24%. The WACC is thus:

$$\begin{aligned} \text{WACC} &= (E/V) \times R_E + (D/V) \times R_D \times (1 - T_C) \\ &= .8576 \times 13.18\% + .1424 \times 11\% \times (1 - .34) \\ &= 12.34\% \end{aligned}$$

B. B. Lean thus has an overall weighted average cost of capital of 12.34 percent. • • •

Solving the Warehouse Problem and Similar Capital Budgeting Problems

Now we can use the WACC to solve the warehouse problem we posed at the beginning of the chapter. However, before we rush to discount the cash flows at the WACC to estimate NPV, we need to first make sure we are doing the right thing.

Concept Q Answer 12.4c

Going back to first principles, we need to find an alternative in the financial markets that is comparable to the warehouse renovation. To be comparable, an alternative must be of the same risk as the warehouse project. Projects that have the same risk are said to be in the same risk class.

The WACC for a firm reflects the risk and the target capital structure of the firm's existing assets as a whole. As a result, strictly speaking, the firm's WACC is the appropriate discount rate only if the proposed investment is a replica of the firm's existing operating activities.

In broader terms, whether or not we can use the firm's WACC to value the warehouse project depends on whether the warehouse project is in the same risk class as the firm. We will assume that this project is an integral part of the overall business of the firm. In such cases, it is natural to think that the cost savings will be as risky as the general cash flows of the firm, and the project will thus be in the same risk class as the overall firm. More generally, projects like the warehouse renovation that are intimately related to the firm's existing operations are often viewed as being in the same risk class as the overall firm.

We can now see what the president should do. Suppose the firm has a target debt/equity ratio of 1/3. From Chapter 3, we know that a debt/equity ratio of $D/E = 1/3$ implies that E/V is .75 and D/V is .25. The cost of debt is 10 percent, and the cost of equity is 20 percent. Assuming a 34 percent tax rate, the WACC will be:

$$\begin{aligned} \text{WACC} &= (E/V) \times R_E + (D/V) \times R_D \times (1 - T_C) \\ &= .75 \times 20\% + .25 \times 10\% \times (1 - .34) \\ &= 16.65\% \end{aligned}$$

Recall that the warehouse project had a cost of $50 million and expected aftertax cash flows (the cost savings) of $12 million per year for six years. The NPV is thus:

$$\text{NPV} = -\$50 + \frac{\$12}{(1 + \text{WACC})^1} + \cdots + \frac{\$12}{(1 + \text{WACC})^6}$$

Since the cash flows are in the form of an ordinary annuity, we can calculate this NPV using 16.65 percent (the WACC) as the discount rate as follows:

$$\begin{aligned} \text{NPV} &= -\$50 + \$12 \times \frac{1 - [1/(1 + 0.1665)^6]}{0.1665} \\ &= -\$50 + \$12 \times 3.6222 \\ &= -\$6.53 \end{aligned}$$

Lecture Tip: See IM 12.5 for a discussion of assumptions about the financing policy implicit in this example.

Should the firm take on the warehouse renovation? The project has a negative NPV using the firm's WACC. This means that the financial markets offer superior projects in the same risk class (namely, the firm itself). The answer is clear: The project should be rejected. For future reference, our discussion of the WACC is summarized in Table 12.1.

TABLE 12.1
Summary of capital cost calculations

Trans. 12.9

I. The Cost of Equity, R_E

A. Dividend growth model approach (from Chapter 7):

$$R_E = D_1/P_0 + g$$

where D_1 is the expected dividend in one period, g is the dividend growth rate, and P_0 is the current stock price.

B. SML approach (from Chapter 11):

$$R_E = R_f + \beta_E \times (R_M - R_f)$$

where R_f is the risk-free rate, R_M is the expected return on the overall market, and β_E is the systematic risk of the equity.

II. The Cost of Debt, R_D

A. For a firm with publicly held debt, the cost of debt can be measured as the yield to maturity on the outstanding debt. The coupon rate is irrelevant. Yield to maturity is covered in Chapter 7.

B. If the firm has no publicly traded debt, then the cost of debt can be measured as the yield to maturity on similarly rated bonds (bond ratings are discussed in Chapter 7).

III. The Weighted Average Cost of Capital, WACC

A. The firm's WACC is the overall required return on the firm as a whole. It is the appropriate discount rate to use for cash flows similar in risk to the overall firm.

B. The WACC is calculated as

$$\text{WACC} = (E/V) \times R_E + (D/V) \times R_D \times (1 - T_C)$$

where T_C is the corporate tax rate, E is the *market* value of the firm's equity, D is the *market* value of the firm's debt, and $V = E + D$. Note that E/V is the percentage of the firm's financing (in market value terms) that is equity, and D/V is the percentage that is debt.

CONCEPT QUESTIONS

12.4a How is the WACC calculated?

12.4b Why do we multiply the cost of debt by $(1 - T_C)$ when we compute the WACC?

12.4c Under what conditions is it correct to use the WACC to determine NPV?

12.5 DIVISIONAL AND PROJECT COSTS OF CAPITAL

As we have seen, using the WACC as the discount rate for future cash flows is only appropriate when the proposed investment is similar to the firm's existing activities. This is not as restrictive as it sounds. If we were in the pizza business, for example, and we were thinking of opening a new location, then the WACC is the discount rate to use. The same is true of a retailer thinking of a new store, a manufacturer thinking of expanding production, or a consumer products company thinking of expanding its markets.

Problem 23

Trans. 12.10
Divisional and Project Costs of Capital (Supplemental)

Nonetheless, despite the usefulness of the WACC as a benchmark, there will clearly be situations where the cash flows under consideration have risks distinctly different from those of the overall firm. We consider how to cope with this problem next.

The SML and the WACC

When we are evaluating investments with risks that are substantially different from the overall firm, the use of the WACC will potentially lead to poor decisions. Figure 12.1 illustrates why.

In Figure 12.1, we have plotted an SML corresponding to a risk-free rate of 7 percent and a market risk premium of 8 percent. To keep things simple, we consider an all-equity company with a beta of 1. As we have indi-

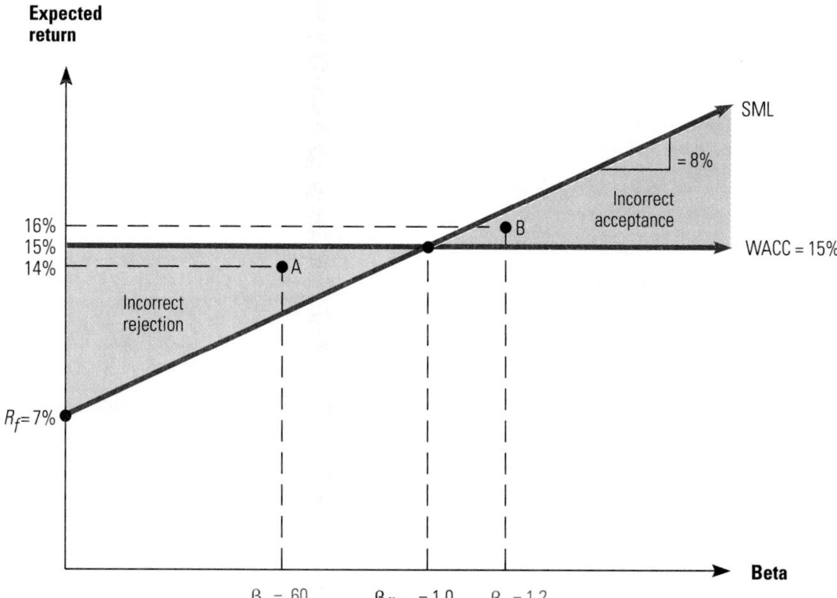

FIGURE 12.1
The security market line (SML) and the weighted average cost of capital (WACC)

Trans. 12.11
SML and the WACC

If a firm uses its WACC to make accept/reject decisions for all types of projects, it will have a tendency toward incorrectly accepting risky projects and incorrectly rejecting less risky projects.

cated, the WACC and the cost of equity are exactly equal to 15 percent for this company since there is no debt.

Concept Q Answer 12.5a

Suppose our firm uses its WACC to evaluate all investments. This means that any investment with a return of greater than 15 percent will be accepted and any investment with a return of less than 15 percent will be rejected. We know from our study of risk and return, however, that a desirable investment is one that plots above the SML. As Figure 12.1 illustrates, using the WACC for all types of projects can result in the firm incorrectly accepting relatively risky projects and incorrectly rejecting relatively safe ones.

For example, consider Point A. This project has a beta of $\beta_A = .60$ compared to the firm's beta of 1.0. It has an expected return of 14 percent. Is this a desirable investment? The answer is yes, because its required return is only:

$$\begin{aligned}\text{Required return} &= R_f + \beta_A \times (R_M - R_f)\\ &= 7\% + .60 \times 8\%\\ &= 11.8\%\end{aligned}$$

However, if we use the WACC as a cutoff, then this project will be rejected because its return is less than 15 percent. This example illustrates that a firm that uses its WACC as a cutoff will tend to reject profitable projects with risks less than those of the overall firm.

Lecture Tip: For tips on discussing the impact of marketable security investments on a firm's beta, see IM 12.5.

At the other extreme, consider Point B. This project has a beta of $\beta_B = 1.2$. It offers a 16 percent return, which exceeds the firm's cost of capital. This is not a good investment, however, because, given its level of systematic risk, its return is inadequate. Nonetheless, if we use the WACC to evaluate it, it will appear to be attractive. So the second error that will arise if we use the WACC as a cutoff is we will tend to make unprofitable investments with risks greater than the overall firm. As a consequence, through time, a firm that uses its WACC to evaluate all projects will have a tendency to both accept unprofitable investments and become increasingly risky.

Divisional Cost of Capital

Lecture Tip: See IM 12.5 for a look at average cost of capital and required return from the viewpoint of the individual investor.

The same type of problem with the WACC can arise in a corporation with more than one line of business. Imagine, for example, a corporation that has two divisions, a regulated telephone company and an electronics manufacturing operation. The first of these (the phone operation) has relatively low risk; the second has relatively high risk.

In this case, the firm's overall cost of capital is really a mixture of two different costs of capital, one for each division. If the two divisions were competing for resources, and the firm used a single WACC as a cutoff, which division would tend to be awarded greater funds for investment?

Lecture Tip: See IM 12.5 for more discussion of the use of published betas in estimating divisional costs of capital.

The answer is that the riskier division would tend to have greater returns (ignoring the greater risk), so it would tend to be the "winner." The less glamorous operation might have great profit potential that ends up being ignored. Large corporations in the United States are aware of this problem and many work to develop separate divisional costs of capital.

The Pure Play Approach

We've seen that using the firm's WACC inappropriately can lead to problems. How can we come up with the appropriate discount rates in such circumstances? Because we cannot observe the returns on these investments, there generally is no direct way of coming up with a beta, for example. Instead, what we must do is examine other investments outside the firm that are in the same risk class as the one we are considering and use the market-required returns on these investments as the discount rate. In other words, we will try to determine what the cost of capital is for such investments by trying to locate some similar investments in the marketplace.

For example, going back to our telephone division, suppose we wanted to come up with a discount rate to use for that division. What we can do is identify several other phone companies that have publicly traded securities. We might find that a typical phone company has a beta of .80, AA-rated debt, and a capital structure that is about 50 percent debt and 50 percent equity. Using this information, we could develop a WACC for a typical phone company and use this as our discount rate.

Alternatively, if we are thinking of entering a new line of business, we would try to develop the appropriate cost of capital by looking at the market-required returns on companies already in that business. In the language of Wall Street, a company that focuses only on a single line of business is called a *pure play*. For example, if you wanted to bet on the price of crude oil by purchasing common stocks, you would try to identify companies that dealt exclusively with this product since they would be the most affected by changes in the price of crude oil. Such companies would be called *pure plays* on the price of crude oil.

Concept Q Answer 12.5b

What we try to do here is to find companies that focus as exclusively as possible on the type of project in which we are interested. Our approach, therefore, is called the **pure play approach** to estimating the required return on an investment.

pure play approach
Use of a WACC that is unique to a particular project, based on companies in similar lines of business.

In Chapter 3, we discussed the subject of identifying similar companies for comparison purposes. The same problems we described there come up here. The most obvious one is that we may not be able to find any suitable companies. In this case, how to objectively determine a discount rate becomes a very difficult question. Even so, the important thing is to be aware of the issue so we at least reduce the possibility of the kinds of mistakes that can arise when the WACC is used as a cutoff on all investments.

The Subjective Approach

Because of the difficulties that exist in objectively establishing discount rates for individual projects, firms often adopt an approach that involves making subjective adjustments to the overall WACC. To illustrate, suppose a firm has an overall WACC of 14 percent. It places all proposed projects into four categories as follows:

Category	Examples	Adjustment Factor	Discount Rate
High risk	New products	+6%	20%
Moderate risk	Cost savings, expansion of existing lines	+0	14
Low risk	Replacement of existing equipment	−4	10
Mandatory	Pollution control equipment	n/a	n/a

n/a = Not applicable.

International Note: A variant of the subjective approach is frequently employed in international capital investment decisions. See IM 12.5 for further discussion.

F I G U R E 12.2
The security market line (SML) and the subjective approach

Trans. 12.12

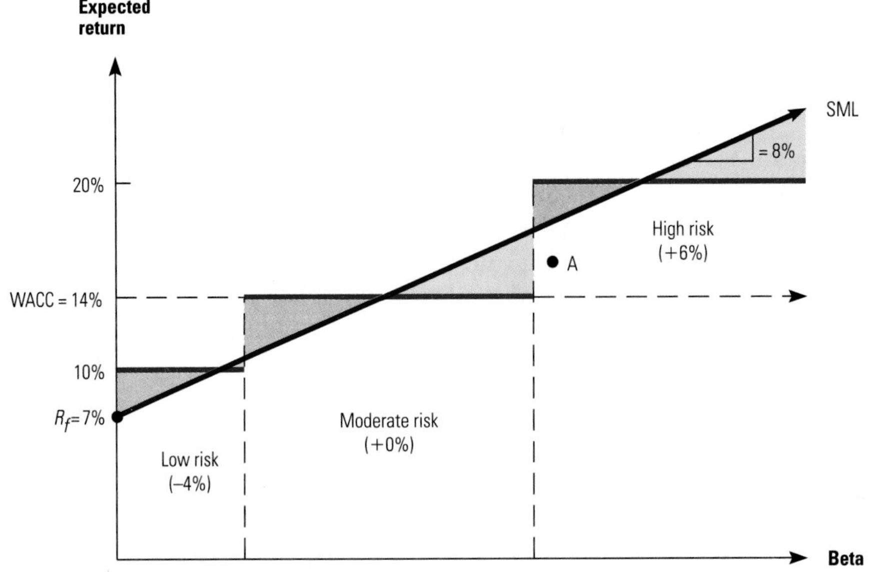

With the subjective approach, the firm places projects into one of several risk classes. The discount rate used to value the project is then determined by adding (for high risk) or subtracting (for low risk) an adjustment factor to or from the firm's WACC. This results in fewer incorrect decisions than if the firm simply used the WACC to make the decisions.

The effect of this crude partitioning is to assume that all projects either fall into one of three risk classes or else they are mandatory. In this last case, the cost of capital is irrelevant since the project must be taken. With the subjective approach, the firm's WACC may change through time as economic conditions change. As this happens, the discount rates for the different types of projects will also change.

Lecture Tip: See IM 12.5 for a look at how the definition of a risky investment varies across firms and markets.

Within each risk class, some projects will presumably have more risk than others, and the danger of incorrect decisions still exists. Figure 12.2 illustrates this point. Comparing Figures 12.1 and 12.2, we see that similar problems exist, but the magnitude of the potential error is less with the subjective approach. For example, the project labeled A would be accepted if the WACC were used, but it is rejected once it is classified as a high-risk investment. What this illustrates is that some risk adjustment, even if it is subjective, is probably better than no risk adjustment.

It would be better, in principle, to objectively determine the required return for each project separately. However, as a practical matter, it may not be possible to go much beyond subjective adjustments because either the necessary information is unavailable or else the cost and effort required are simply not worthwhile. These issues, along with some related considerations, are discussed in the accompanying *Principles in Action* box, which describes how one large company, Hershey Foods, evaluates its cost of capital.

CONCEPT QUESTIONS

12.5a What are the likely consequences if a firm uses its WACC to evaluate all proposed investments?

12.5b What is the pure play approach to determining the appropriate discount rate? When might it be used?

Principles in Action

Samuel Weaver on Cost of Capital and Hurdle Rates at Hershey Foods Corporation

At Hershey, we reevaluate our cost of capital annually or as market conditions warrant. The calculation of the cost of capital essentially involves three different issues, each with a few alternatives:

- *Capital structure weighting*
  Historical book value
  Target capital structure
  Market-based weights
- *Cost of debt*
  Historical book value
  Target capital structure
  Market-based interest rates
- *Cost of equity*
  Dividend growth model
  Capital asset pricing model (CAPM)

At Hershey, we calculate our cost of capital officially based upon the projected "target" capital structure at the end of our three-year intermediate planning horizon. This allows management to see the immediate impact of strategic decisions related to the planned composition of Hershey's capital pool. The cost of debt is calculated as the anticipated weighted average aftertax cost of debt in that final plan year based upon the coupon rates attached to that debt. The cost of equity is computed via the dividend growth model.

We recently conducted a survey of the 11 food processing companies that we consider our industry group competitors. The results of this survey indicated that the cost of capital for most of these companies was in the 10 to 12 percent range. Furthermore, without exception, all 11 of these companies employed the CAPM when calculating their cost of equity. Our experience has been that the dividend growth model works better for Hershey. We do pay dividends, and we do experience steady, stable growth in our dividends. This growth is also projected within our strategic plan. Consequently, the dividend growth model is technically applicable and appealing to management since it reflects their best estimate of the future long-term growth rate.

In addition to the calculation described above, the other possible combinations and permutations are calculated as barometers. Unofficially, the cost of capital is calculated using market weights, current marginal interest rates, and the CAPM cost of equity. For the most part, and due to rounding the cost of capital to the nearest whole percentage point, these alternative calculations yield approximately the same results.

From the cost of capital, individual project hurdle rates are developed using a subjectively determined risk premium based on the characteristics of the project. Projects are grouped into separate project categories, such as cost savings, capacity expansion, product line extension, and new products. For example, in general, a new product is more risky than a cost savings product. Consequently, each project category's hurdle rate reflects the level of risk and commensurate required return as perceived by senior management. As a result, capital project hurdle rates range from a slight premium over the cost of capital to the highest hurdle rate of approximately double the cost of capital.

Source: Samuel Weaver, Ph.D., is Director, Corporate Financial Planning and Analysis, for the Hershey Foods Corporation. He is a Certified Management Accountant, and he currently serves on the Board of Directors of the Financial Management Association as Vice President, Practitioner Services. His current position combines the theoretical with the pragmatic and involves the analysis of many different facets of finance in addition to capital expenditure analysis.

12.6 SUMMARY AND CONCLUSIONS

This chapter discussed cost of capital. The most important concept is the weighted average cost of capital (WACC), which we interpreted as the required rate of return on the overall firm. It is also the discount rate appropriate for cash flows that are similar in risk to the overall firm. We described how the WACC can be calculated, and we illustrated how it can be used in certain types of analyses.

We also pointed out situations in which it is inappropriate to use the WACC as the discount rate. To handle such cases, we described some alternative approaches to developing discount rates, such as the pure play approach.

Chapter Review Problems and Self-Test

12.1 **Calculating the Cost of Equity** Suppose stock in Boone Corporation has a beta of .90. The market risk premium is 7 percent, and the risk-free rate is 8 percent. Boone's last dividend was $1.80 per share, and the dividend is expected to grow at 7 percent indefinitely. The stock currently sells for $25. What is Boone's cost of equity capital?

12.2 **Calculating the WACC** In addition to the information in the previous problem, suppose Boone has a target debt/equity ratio of 50 percent. Its cost of debt is 8 percent, before taxes. If the tax rate is 34 percent, what is the WACC?

Answers to Self-Test Problems

12.1 We start off with the SML approach. Based on the information given, the expected return on Boone's common stock is:

$$\begin{aligned} R_E &= R_f + \beta_E \times (R_M - R_f) \\ &= 8\% + .9 \times 7\% \\ &= 14.3\% \end{aligned}$$

We now use the dividend growth model. The projected dividend is $D_0 \times (1 + g) = \$1.80 \times (1.07) = \$1.926$, so the expected return using this approach is:

$$\begin{aligned} R_E &= D_1/P_0 + g \\ &= \$1.926/25 + .07 \\ &= 14.704\% \end{aligned}$$

Since these two estimates, 14.3 percent and 14.7 percent, are fairly close, we will average them. Boone's cost of equity is approximately 14.5 percent.

12.2 Since the target debt/equity ratio is .50, Boone uses $.50 in debt for every $1.00 in equity. In other words, Boone's target capital structure is 1/3 debt and 2/3 equity. The WACC is thus:

$$\begin{aligned} \text{WACC} &= (E/V) \times R_E + (D/V) \times R_D \times (1 - T_C) \\ &= 2/3 \times 14.5\% + 1/3 \times 8\% \times (1 - .34) \\ &= 11.427\% \end{aligned}$$

Questions and Problems

Basic (Questions 1–17)

1. **Calculating Cost of Equity** The Chilton Oil Co. just issued a dividend of $2.50 per share on its common stock. The company is expected to maintain a constant 6 percent growth rate in its dividends indefinitely. If the stock sells for $50 a share, what is the company's cost of equity?

11.30%

2. **Calculating Cost of Equity** The Bedrock Corporation's common stock has a beta of 1.25. If the risk-free rate is 4 percent and the expected return on the market is 12 percent, what is Bedrock's cost of equity capital? 14.00%

3. **Calculating Cost of Equity** Stock in Eddy Industries has a beta of .90. The market risk premium is 9.5 percent, and T-bills are currently yielding 5 percent. Eddy's most recent dividend was $3.75 per share, and dividends are expected to grow at a 3 percent annual rate indefinitely. If the stock sells for $32.50 per share, what is your best estimate of Eddy's cost of equity? 14.22%

4. **Estimating the DCF Growth Rate** Suppose Winchell Broadcasting Company just issued a dividend of $0.90 per share on its common stock. The company paid dividends of $0.45, $0.58, $0.69, and $0.80 per share in the four previous years. If the stock currently sells for $17.50, what is your best estimate of the company's cost of equity capital? 25.20%

5. **Calculating Cost of Preferred Stock** Colossus Bank has an issue of preferred stock with a $5 stated dividend that just sold for $80 per share. What is the bank's cost of preferred stock? 6.25%

6. **Calculating Cost of Debt** DC Utilities, Inc., is trying to determine its cost of debt. The utility has a debt issue outstanding with 12 years to maturity that is quoted at 93 percent of face value. The issue makes semiannual payments and has an embedded cost of 6 percent annually. What is the utility's pretax cost of debt? If the tax rate is 35 percent, what is the aftertax cost of debt? Pretax cost = 6.87%; Aftertax cost = 4.46%

7. **Calculating Cost of Debt** Keefe Electronics issued a 20-year, 9 percent semiannual bond 7 years ago. The bond currently sells for 108 percent of its face value. The company's tax rate is 38 percent. a. 8.00%; b. 4.96%
   a. What is the pretax cost of debt?
   b. What is the aftertax cost of debt?
   c. Which is more relevant, the pretax or the aftertax cost of debt? Why?

8. **Calculating Cost of Debt** For the firm in Problem 7, suppose the book value of the debt issue is $50 million. In addition, the company has a second debt issue on the market, a zero coupon bond with nine years left to maturity; the book value of this issue is $30 million and the bonds sell for 48 percent of par. What is the company's total book value of debt? The total market value? What is your best estimate of the aftertax cost of debt now? Book value = $80 M; Market value = $68.4 M; Aftertax cost = 5.11%

9. **Calculating WACC** Corrado Construction Corporation has a target capital structure of 35 percent common stock, 10 percent preferred stock, and 55 percent debt. Its cost of equity is 18 percent, the cost of preferred stock is 8 percent, and the cost of debt is 10 percent. The relevant tax rate is 35 percent. a. 10.68%
   a. What is Corrado's WACC?
   b. The company president has approached you about Corrado's capital structure. He wants to know why the company doesn't use more preferred stock financing, since it costs less than debt. What would you tell the president?

15.47%

10. Taxes and WACC Merton Manufacturing has a target debt/equity ratio of .60. Its cost of equity is 20 percent and its cost of debt is 12 percent. If the tax rate is 34 percent, what is Merton's WACC?

D/E = 1.787

11. Finding the Target Capital Structure Gauss Corporation's weighted average cost of capital is 9.75 percent. The company's cost of equity is 16 percent and its cost of debt is 10.25 percent. The tax rate is 39 percent. What is Gauss Corporation's target debt/equity ratio?

a. $E/V = 0.568$
$D/V = 0.432$
b. $E/V = .700$
$D/V = .300$

12. Book Value versus Market Value Veetek Enterprises has 12.8 million shares of common stock outstanding. The current share price is $29, and the book value per share is $18. Veetek also has two bond issues outstanding. The first bond issue has a face value of $100 million, a 7 percent coupon, and sells for 94 percent of par. The second issue has a face value of $75 million, a 5.5 percent coupon, and sells for 87 percent of par. The first issue matures in 13 years, the second in 8 years.

a. What are Veetek's capital structure weights on a book value basis?

b. What are Veetek's capital structure weights on a market value basis?

c. Which are more relevant, the book or market value weights? Why?

12.32%

13. Calculating the WACC In Problem 12, suppose the most recent dividend was $2 and the dividend growth rate is 8 percent. Assume the overall cost of debt is the average of that implied by the two outstanding debt issues. Both bonds make semiannual payments. The tax rate is 35 percent. What is the company's WACC?

a. 8.46%
b. 16.00%

14. WACC Huesenberg Products has a target debt/equity ratio of 2. Its WACC is 10 percent and the tax rate is 35 percent.

a. If Huesenberg's cost of equity is 19 percent, what is its pretax cost of debt?

b. If instead you know that the aftertax cost of debt is 7 percent, what is the cost of equity?

7.82%

15. Finding the WACC Given the following information for Valley Power Co., find the WACC. Assume the company's tax rate is 35 percent.

Debt:	2,500 7.75 percent coupon bonds outstanding, $1,000 par value, eight years to maturity, selling for 103 percent of par; the bonds make annual payments.
Common stock:	75,000 shares outstanding selling for $50 per share; the beta is .85.
Preferred stock:	10,000 shares of 5 percent preferred stock outstanding, currently selling for $80 per share.
Market:	5 percent market risk premium and 6 percent risk-free rate.

a. $E/V = .4082$
$D/V = .4770$
$P/V = .1148$

16. Finding the WACC Bluefield Corporation has 5 million shares of common stock outstanding, 750,000 shares of 7 percent preferred stock outstanding, and 250,000 11 percent semiannual bonds outstanding, par value $1,000 each. The stock currently sells for $40 per share and has a beta of 1.2, the preferred stock currently sells for $75 per share, and the bonds have 15 years to maturity and sell for 93.5 percent of par. The market risk premium is 6 percent, T-bills are yielding 4 percent, and Bluefield's tax rate is 34 percent.

b. 9.40%
Trans. 12.13

a. What is the firm's market value capital structure?
b. If Bluefield is evaluating a new investment project that has the same risk as the firm's typical project, what rate should it use to discount the project's cash flows?

17. **SML and WACC** An all-equity firm is considering the following projects:

a. Y and Z
b. W and Y
Trans. 12.14

Project	Beta	Expected Return (%)
W	0.60	13
X	0.85	14
Y	1.15	18
Z	1.50	20

The T-bill rate is 6 percent, and the expected return on the market is 16 percent.
a. Which projects have a higher expected return than the firm's 16 percent cost of capital?
b. Which projects should be accepted?
c. Which projects would be incorrectly accepted or rejected if the firm's overall cost of capital is used as a hurdle rate?

Intermediate (Questions 18–24)

18. **DCF Cost of Equity Estimation** What are the advantages of using the DCF model for determining the cost of equity capital? What are the disadvantages? What specific piece of information needs to be estimated to find the cost of equity using this model? What are some of the ways in which you could get this estimate?

19. **SML Cost of Equity Estimation** What are the advantages of using the SML approach to finding the cost of equity capital? What are the disadvantages? What are the specific pieces of information needed to use this method? Are all of these variables observable, or do they need to be estimated? What are some of the ways in which you could get these estimates?

20. **Cost of Debt Estimation** How do you determine the appropriate cost of debt for a company? Does it make a difference if the company's debt is privately placed as opposed to being publicly traded? How would you estimate the cost of debt for a firm whose only debt issues are privately held by institutional investors?

21. **Cost of Capital** Suppose Tom O'Bedlam, president of Bedlam Products, Inc., has hired you to determine the firm's cost of debt and cost of equity capital.
a. The stock currently sells for $50 per share, and the dividend per share will probably be about $5. Tom argues: "It will cost us $5 per share to use the stockholders' money this year, so the cost of equity is equal to 10 percent ($5/$50)." What's wrong with this conclusion?

b. Based on the most recent financial statements, Bedlam Products' total liabilities are $8 million. Total interest expense for the coming year will be about $1 million. Tom therefore reasons: "We owe $8 million, and we will pay $1 million interest. Therefore, our cost of debt is obviously $1 million/$8 million = 12.5 percent." What's wrong with this conclusion?

c. Based on his own analysis, Tom is recommending that the company increase its use of equity financing, because "Debt costs 12.5 percent, but equity only costs 10 percent; thus equity is cheaper." Ignoring all the other problems, what do you think about the conclusion that the cost of equity is less than the cost of debt?

22. **SML and NPV** Both Dow Chemical Company, a large natural gas user, and Superior Oil, a major natural gas producer, are thinking of investing in natural gas wells near Houston. Both are all-equity financed companies. Dow and Superior are both looking at identical projects. They've analyzed their respective investments, which would involve a negative cash flow now and positive expected cash flows in the future. These cash flows would be the same for both firms. No debt would be used to finance the projects. Both companies estimate that their project would have a net present value of $1 million at an 18 percent discount rate and a −$1.1 million NPV at a 22 percent discount rate. Dow has a beta of 1.25, while Superior has a beta of 0.75. The expected risk premium on the market is 8 percent, and risk-free bonds are yielding 12 percent. Should either company proceed? Should both? Explain.

23. **Divisional Costs of Capital** Under what circumstances would it be appropriate for a firm to use different costs of capital for its different operating divisions? If the overall firm WACC is used as the hurdle rate for all divisions, would the riskier divisions or the more conservative divisions tend to get most of the investment projects? Why? If you were to try to estimate the appropriate cost of capital for different divisions, what problems might you encounter? What are two techniques you could use to develop a rough estimate for each division's cost of capital?

Breakeven cost = $85.91 M
Trans. 12.15

24. **WACC and NPV** A firm is considering a project that will result in initial aftertax cash savings of $9 million at the end of the first year, and these savings will grow at a rate of 5 percent per year indefinitely. The firm has a target debt/equity ratio of 3, a cost of equity of 22 percent, and an aftertax cost of debt of 10 percent. The cost-saving proposal is somewhat riskier than the usual project the firm undertakes; management uses the subjective approach and applies an adjustment factor of +3 percent to the cost of capital for such risky projects. Under what circumstances should the firm take on the project?

Chapter Thirteen

13

Raising Capital

After studying this chapter, you should have a good understanding of:

The venture capital market and its role in the financing of new, high-risk ventures.

How securities are sold to the public and the role of investment banks in the process.

Initial public offerings and some of the costs of going public.

Trans. 13.1 Chapter Outline

All firms must, at varying times, obtain capital. To do so, a firm must either borrow the money (debt financing), sell a portion of the firm (equity financing), or both. How a firm raises capital depends a great deal on the size of the firm, its life cycle stage, and its growth prospects.

In this chapter, we examine some of the ways firms actually raise capital. We begin by looking at companies early in their lives and the importance of venture capital for such firms. We then look at the process of going public and the role of investment banks. Along the way, we discuss many of the issues associated with selling securities to the public and their implications for all types of firms. We close the chapter with a discussion of sources of debt capital.[1]

13.1 THE FINANCING LIFE CYCLE OF A FIRM: EARLY STAGE FINANCING AND VENTURE CAPITAL

One day, you and a friend have a great idea for a new computer software product that helps users communicate using the Internet. Filled with entrepreneurial zeal, you christen the product "InterComm" and set about bringing it to market.[2]

[1] We are indebted to Jay R. Ritter of the University of Illinois for helpful comments and suggestions on this chapter.

[2] Neat name, don't you think?

Working nights and weekends, you are able to create a prototype of your product. It doesn't actually work, but at least you can show it around to illustrate your idea. To actually develop the product, you need to hire programmers, buy computers, rent office space, and so on. Unfortunately, since you are both college students, your combined assets are not sufficient to fund a pizza party, much less a "start-up" company. You need what is often referred to as OPM—other people's money.

Your first thought might be to approach a bank for a loan. You would probably discover, however, that banks are generally not interested in making loans to start-up companies with no assets (other than an idea) run by fledgling entrepreneurs with no track record. Instead, your search for capital would very likely lead you to the **venture capital (VC)** market.

venture capital
Financing for new, often high-risk ventures.

Venture Capital

Concept Q Answer 13.1a

The term *venture capital* does not have a precise meaning, but it generally refers to financing for new, often high-risk ventures. Individual venture capitalists invest their own money, while venture capital firms specialize in pooling funds from various sources and investing them. The underlying sources of funds for such firms include individuals, pension funds, insurance companies, large corporations, and even university endowment funds.

Concept Q Answer 13.2a

Venture capitalists and venture capital firms recognize that many or even most new ventures will not fly, but the occasional one will. The potential profits are enormous in such cases. To limit their risk, venture capitalists generally provide financing in stages. At each stage, enough money is invested to reach the next milestone or planning stage. For example, the *first-stage financing* might be enough to get a prototype built and a manufacturing plan completed. Based on the results, the *second-stage financing* might be a major investment needed to actually begin manufacturing, marketing, and distribution. There might be many such stages, each of which represents a key step in the process of growing the company.

Venture capital firms often specialize in different stages. Some specialize in very early "seed money" or "ground floor financing." In contrast, financing in the later stages might come from venture capitalists specializing in so-called mezzanine level financing, where "mezzanine level" refers to the level just above the ground floor.

The fact that financing is available in stages and is contingent on specified goals being met is a powerful motivating force for the firm's founders. Often, the founders receive relatively little in the way of salary and have substantial portions of their personal assets tied up in the business. At each stage of financing, the value of the founder's stake grows and the probability of success rises.

In addition to providing financing, venture capitalists often actively participate in running the firm, providing the benefit of experience with previous start-ups as well as general business expertise. This is especially true when the firm's founders have little or no hands-on experience in running a company.

Some Venture Capital Realities

Although there is a large venture capital market, the truth is that access to venture capital is really very limited. Venture capital companies receive huge numbers of unsolicited proposals, the vast majority of which end up in the circular file unread. Venture capitalists rely heavily on informal networks of lawyers, accountants, bankers, and other venture capitalists to help identify potential investments. As a result, personal contacts are important in gaining access to the venture capital market; it is very much an "introduction" market.

Another simple fact about venture capital is that it is incredibly expensive. In a typical deal, the venture capitalist will demand (and get) 40 percent or more of the equity in the company. The venture capitalist will frequently actually hold voting preferred stock, giving them various priorities in the event that the company is sold or liquidated. The venture capitalist will typically demand (and get) several seats on the company's board of directors and may even appoint one or more members of senior management.

Choosing a Venture Capitalist

Trans. 13.2
Choosing a Venture Capitalist

Some start-up companies, particularly those headed by experienced, previously successful entrepreneurs, will be in such demand that they have the luxury of looking beyond the money in choosing a venture capitalist. There are some key considerations in such a case, some of which can be summarized as follows:

1. Financial strength is important. The venture capitalist needs to have the resources and financial reserves for additional financing stages should they become necessary. This doesn't mean that bigger is necessarily better, however, because of our next consideration.
2. Style is important. Some venture capitalists will wish to be very involved in day-to-day operations and decision making, while others will be content with monthly reports. Which is better depends on the firm and also on the venture capitalist's business skills. In addition, a large venture capital firm may be less flexible and more bureaucratic than a smaller "boutique" firm.
3. References are important. Has the venture capitalist been successful with similar firms? Of equal importance, how has the venture capitalist dealt with situations that didn't work out?
4. Contacts are important. A venture capitalist may be able to help the business in ways other than financing and management by providing introductions to potentially important customers, suppliers, and other industry contacts. Venture capitalist firms frequently specialize in a few particular industries, and such specialization could prove quite valuable.
5. Exit strategy is important. Venture capitalists are generally not long-term investors. How and under what circumstances the venture capitalist will "cash out" of the business should be carefully evaluated.

If a start-up succeeds, the big payoff frequently comes when the company is sold to another company or goes public. Either way, investment bankers are often involved in the process. We discuss the process of selling securities to the public in the next several sections, paying particular attention to the process of going public.

CONCEPT QUESTIONS

13.1a What is venture capital?

13.1b Why is venture capital often provided in stages?

13.2 SELLING SECURITIES TO THE PUBLIC

Trans. 13.3
The Basic Procedure for a New Issue (Supplemental)

There are many rules and regulations surrounding the process of selling securities. The Securities Act of 1933 is the origin of federal regulations for all new interstate securities issues. The Securities Exchange Act of 1934 is the basis for regulating securities already outstanding. The Securities and Exchange Commission (SEC) administers both acts.

The Basic Procedure for a New Issue

Concept Q Answer 13.2a

There is a series of steps involved in issuing securities to the public. In general terms, the basic procedure is as follows:

Concept Q Answer 13.2b

1. Management's first step in issuing any securities to the public is to obtain approval from the board of directors. In some cases, the number of authorized shares of common stock must be increased. This requires a vote of the shareholders.

registration statement Statement filed with SEC that discloses all material information concerning the corporation making a public offering.

2. The firm must prepare and file a **registration statement** with the SEC. The registration statement is required for all public, interstate issues of securities, with two exceptions:
   a. Loans that mature within nine months.
   b. Issues that involve less than $1.5 million.

Regulation A SEC regulation that exempts public issues less than $1.5 million from most registration requirements.

The second exception is known as the *small-issues exemption.* In this case, simplified procedures are used. Under the basic small-issues exemption, issues of less than $1.5 million are governed by **Regulation A,** for which only a brief offering statement is needed. Normally, however, a registration statement contains many pages (50 or more) of financial information, including a financial history, details of the existing business, proposed financing, and plans for the future.

Lecture Tip: Humorous excerpts from an actual prospectus can be found in IM 13.2.

prospectus Legal document describing details of the issuing corporation and the proposed offering to potential investors.

red herring Preliminary prospectus distributed to prospective investors in a new issue of securities.

3. The SEC examines the registration statement during a waiting period. During this time, the firm may distribute copies of a preliminary **prospectus.** The prospectus contains much of the information put into the registration statement, and it is given to potential investors by the firm. The preliminary prospectus is sometimes called a **red herring,** in part because bold red letters are printed on the cover.

A registration statement becomes effective on the 20th day after its filing unless the SEC sends a *letter of comment* suggesting changes. After the changes are made, the 20-day waiting period starts again. Importantly, the SEC does not consider the economic merits of the proposed sale; it merely makes sure that various rules and regulations are followed. Also, the SEC generally does not check the accuracy or truthfulness of information in the prospectus.

The registration statement does not initially contain the price of the new issue. Usually, a price amendment is filed at or near the end of the waiting period, and the registration becomes effective in an accelerated way.

Lecture Tip: IM 13.2 discusses the absence of price information in the prospectus.

4. The company cannot sell these securities during the waiting period. However, oral offers can be made.
5. On the effective date of the registration statement, a price is determined and a full-fledged selling effort gets under way. A final prospectus must accompany the delivery of securities or confirmation of sale, whichever comes first.

Trans. 13.4
A Red Herring
(Supplemental)

tombstone
An advertisement announcing a public offering.

Tombstone advertisements are used by underwriters during and after the waiting period. An example is reproduced in Figure 13.1 (see page 340). The tombstone contains the name of issuer (the United States Government, in this case). It provides some information about the issue, and it lists the investment banks (the underwriters) who are involved with selling the issue. The role of the investment banks in selling securities is discussed more fully below.

Trans. 13.5
A Tombstone Ad

Lecture Tip: See IM 13.2 for a look at commercial paper maturity and SEC regulations.

The investment banks are divided into groups called *brackets* on the tombstone, based on their participation in the issue, and the names of the banks are listed alphabetically within each bracket. The brackets are often viewed as a kind of pecking order. In general, the higher the bracket, the greater is the underwriter's prestige.

★ **Ethics Note:** The prospectus doesn't always accomplish its intended task. See IM 13.2 for excerpts from *The Wall Street Journal* detailing such a case.

CONCEPT QUESTIONS

13.2a What are the basic procedures in selling a new issue?

13.2b What is a registration statement?

13.3 ALTERNATIVE ISSUE METHODS

When a company decides to issue a new security, it can sell it as a public issue or a private issue. If it is a public issue, the firm is required to register the issue with the SEC. However, if the issue is sold to fewer than 35 investors, it can be done privately. If so, a registration statement is not required.[3]

general cash offer
An issue of securities offered for sale to the general public on a cash basis.

For equity sales there are two kinds of public issues: a **general cash offer** and a **rights offer** (or *rights offering*). With a cash offer, securities are offered to the general public on a "first come, first served" basis. With a rights offer, securities are initially offered only to existing owners. Rights offers are fairly common in other countries, but they are relatively rare in the United States, particularly in recent years. We therefore focus on cash offers in this chapter.

rights offer
A public issue of securities in which securities are first offered to existing shareholders. Also a *rights offering.*

The first public equity issue that is made by a company is referred to as an **initial public offering (IPO)** or an *unseasoned new issue.* This occurs when a company decides to go public. Obviously, all initial public offerings are cash offers. If the firm's existing shareholders wanted to buy the shares, the firm wouldn't have to sell them publicly in the first place.

initial public offering
A company's first equity issue made available to the public. Also an *unseasoned new issue* or *IPO.*

[3] A variety of different arrangements can be made for private equity issues. Selling unregistered securities avoids the costs of complying with the Securities Exchange Act of 1934. Regulation significantly restricts the resale of unregistered equity securities. For example, the purchaser may be required to hold the securities for at least two years. Many of the restrictions were significantly eased in 1990 for very large institutional investors, however. The private placement of bonds is discussed in a later section.

TABLE 13.1
The methods of issuing new securities

Trans. 13.6
Methods of Issuing New Securities

Method	Type	Definition
Public		
Traditional negotiated cash offer	Firm commitment cash offer	Company negotiates an agreement with an investment banker to underwrite and distribute the new stocks. A specified number of shares is bought by underwriters and sold at a higher price.
	Best efforts cash offer	Company has investment bankers sell as many of the new shares as possible at the agreed-upon price. There is no guarantee concerning how much cash will be raised.
Privileged subscription	Direct rights offer	Company offers new stock directly to its existing shareholders.
	Standby rights offer	Like the direct rights offer, this contains a privileged subscription arrangement with existing shareholders. The net proceeds are guaranteed by the underwriters.
Nontraditional cash offer	Shelf cash offer	Qualifying companies can authorize all shares they expect to sell over a two-year period and sell them when needed.
	Competitive firm cash offer	Company can elect to award underwriting contract through a public auction instead of negotiation.
Private	Direct placement	Securities are sold directly to purchaser, who, at least until very recently, generally could not resell securities for at least two years.

seasoned new issue
A new equity issue of securities by a company that has previously issued securities to the public.

A **seasoned new issue** refers to a new issue for a company with securities that have been previously issued. A seasoned new issue of common stock can be made by using a cash offer or a rights offer.

These methods of issuing new securities are shown in Table 13.1. They are discussed in sections 13.4 through 13.6.

CONCEPT QUESTIONS

13.3a Why is an initial public offering necessarily a cash offer?

13.3b What is the difference between a rights offer and a cash offer?

13.4 THE CASH OFFER

underwriters
Investment firms that act as intermediaries between a company selling securities and the investing public.

Lecture Tip: See IM for a discussion of the omission of the offering price in the initial filing.

syndicate
A group of underwriters formed to share the risk and to help sell an issue.

If the public issue of securities is a cash offer, **underwriters** are usually involved. Underwriters perform services such as the following for corporate issuers:

1. Formulating the method used to issue the securities.
2. Pricing the new securities.
3. Selling the new securities.

Typically, the underwriter buys the securities for less than the offering price and accepts the risk of not being able to sell them. Because underwriting involves risk, underwriters combine to form an underwriting group called a **syndicate** to share the risk and to help sell the issue.

In a syndicate, one or more managers arrange or co-manage the offering. This manager is designated as the lead manager, or principal manager. The lead manager typically has the responsibility for pricing the securities. The other underwriters in the syndicate serve primarily to distribute the issue.

The difference between the underwriter's buying price and the offering price is called the **spread** or discount. It is the basic compensation received by the underwriter. Sometimes the underwriter will get noncash compensation in the form of warrants and stock in addition to the spread.[4]

Problems 1, 3, 8

spread
Compensation to the underwriter, determined by the difference between the underwriter's buying price and offering price.

Choosing an Underwriter

A firm can offer its securities to the highest bidding underwriter on a *competitive offer* basis, or it can negotiate directly with an underwriter. Except for a few large firms, new issues of debt and equity are usually done on a *negotiated offer* basis. The exception is public utility holding companies, which are essentially required to use competitive underwriting.

There is evidence that competitive underwriting is cheaper to use than negotiated underwriting, and the underlying reasons for the dominance of negotiated underwriting in the United States are the subject of ongoing debate.

Lecture Tip: See IM for empirical evidence on spread differences between competitive and negotiated issues.

Types of Underwriting

Two basic types of underwriting are involved in a cash offer: firm commitment and best efforts.

Firm Commitment Underwriting With **firm commitment underwriting,** the issuer sells the entire issue to the underwriters, who then attempt to resell it. This is the most prevalent type of underwriting in the United States. This is really just a purchase-resale arrangement, and the underwriter's fee is the spread. For a new issue of seasoned equity, the underwriters can look at the market price to determine what the issue should sell for, and 95 percent of all such new issues are firm commitments.

firm commitment underwriting
Underwriter buys the entire issue, assuming full financial responsibility for any unsold shares.

If the underwriter cannot sell all of the issue at the agreed-upon offering price, it may have to lower the price on the unsold shares. Nonetheless, with firm commitment underwriting, the issuer receives the agreed-upon amount, and all the risk associated with selling the issue is transferred to the underwriter.

Because the offering price usually isn't set until the underwriters have investigated how receptive the market is to the issue, this risk is usually minimal. Also, because the offering price usually is not set until just before selling commences, the issuer doesn't know precisely what its net proceeds will be until that time.

Best Efforts Underwriting With **best efforts underwriting,** the underwriter is legally bound to use "best efforts" to sell the securities at the agreed-upon offering price. Beyond this, the underwriter does not guarantee any particular amount of money to the issuer. This form of underwriting is more common with initial public offerings.

best efforts underwriting
Underwriter sells as much of the issue as possible, but can return any unsold shares to the issuer without financial responsibility.

[4] Warrants are essentially options to buy stock at a fixed price for some fixed period of time.

TABLE 13.2
Initial public offerings categorized by gross proceeds: 1977–1982

Trans. 13.7

Gross Proceeds	All Offerings	Firm Commitment	Best Efforts	Fraction Best Efforts
$ 100,000–1,999,999	243	68	175	0.720
2,000,000–3,999,999	311	165	146	0.469
4,000,000–5,999,999	156	133	23	0.147
6,000,000–9,999,999	137	122	15	0.109
10,000,000–120,174,195	180	176	4	0.022
All offerings	1,027	664	363	0.353

Source: J. R. Ritter, "The Costs of Going Public," *Journal of Financial Economics* 19 (1987). © Elsevier Science Publishers B.V. (North-Holland).

Concept Q Answer 13.4a

With best efforts underwriting, the underwriter essentially acts as an agent for the issuer and receives a commission. In practice, if the underwriter cannot sell the issue at the offer price, it is usually withdrawn. The issue might be repriced and/or reoffered at a later date.

Table 13.2 categorizes initial public offerings by size and type of underwriting. As indicated, best efforts offerings are very common with smaller issues. For issues under $2 million (which is quite small), 72 percent are best efforts. At the other end, for issues in excess of $10 million, firm commitment offerings are used almost exclusively.

The Aftermarket

The period after a new issue is initially sold to the public is referred to as the *aftermarket.* During this time, the members of the underwriting syndicate generally do not sell securities for less than the offering price.

The principal underwriter is permitted to buy shares if the market price falls below the offering price. The purpose would be to support the market and stabilize the price from temporary downward pressure. If the issue remains unsold after a time (for example, 30 days), members can leave the group and sell their shares at whatever price the market will allow.[5]

The Green Shoe Provision

Green Shoe provision
Contract provision giving the underwriter the option to purchase additional shares from the issuer at the offering price. Also the *overallotment option.*

Many underwriting contracts contain a **Green Shoe provision** (sometimes called the *overallotment option*), which gives the members of the underwriting group the option to purchase additional shares from the issuer at the offering price.[6] The stated reason for the Green Shoe option is to cover excess demand and oversubscriptions. Green Shoe options usually last for about 30 days and involve no more than 15 percent of the newly issued shares.

The Green Shoe option is a benefit to the underwriting syndicate and a cost to the issuer. If the market price of the new issue goes above the offering price within 30 days, the Green Shoe option allows the underwriters to buy shares from the issuer and immediately resell the shares to the public.

[5] Occasionally, the price of a security falls dramatically when the underwriter ceases to stabilize the price. In such cases, Wall Street humorists (the ones who didn't buy any of the stock) have referred to the period following the aftermarket as the aftermath.

[6] The term *Green Shoe provision* sounds quite exotic, but the origin is relatively mundane. It comes from the Green Shoe Company, which once granted such an option.

The Offering Price and Underpricing

Determining the correct offering price is the most difficult thing an underwriter must do for an initial public offering. The issuing firm faces a potential cost if the offering price is set too high or too low. If the issue is priced too high, it may be unsuccessful and have to be withdrawn. If the issue is priced below the true market value, the issuer's existing shareholders will experience an opportunity loss when they sell their shares for less than they are worth.

Video Note: You may wish to illustrate this process with the "Celtics IPO" video supplement.

Underpricing is fairly common. It obviously helps new shareholders earn a higher return on the shares they buy. However, the existing shareholders of the issuing firm are not helped by underpricing. To them, it is an indirect cost of issuing new securities.

Lecture Tip: See IM for empirical evidence on the long-run performance of IPOs.

Underpricing: The Case of Conrail The sale on March 26, 1987, of more than 58 million shares of Conrail, the previously U.S. government–owned railroad company, was the largest new issue of stock in U.S. history. A tombstone for this issue is shown in Figure 13.1.

At the end of the first day after the Conrail offering, the shares were more than 10 percent above their initial offering price level. This is a good example of underpricing. Two opposing views of the sale were prominent in the press after the offering:

1. The issue was hailed as a great success by underwriters and the U.S. Congress. By selling 100 percent of the railroad company, the government achieved its largest divestiture yet of state assets.
2. Others saw the sale as the largest commercial giveaway in U.S. government history. They asked how the government could get the price so wrong.

In passing, we note the Conrail issue raised a total of $1.65 billion. This is more than the $1.5 billion that AT&T obtained in 1983 in what had previously been the largest U.S. stock offering, but substantially less than, for example, the $4.76 billion raised when British Telecom (the British government–owned telephone company) went public in 1984. However, all of these issues pale in comparison to what NTT (Nippon Telephone and Telegraph, the Japanese telephone company) raised in 1987. In November of 1987, NTT sold 1.95 million shares at a price of 2.55 *million* yen *each.* At the then-prevailing exchange rate, this was roughly $19,000 per share. The total issue amount was thus on the order of $37 billion. What is even more remarkable is that NTT had already sold 1.95 million shares in February of the same year.

The Conrail issue was apparently underpriced, but, as we discuss next, the underpricing was not atypical (in percentage terms). Even so, underpricing a $1.65 *billion* issue by 10 percent or so means that the seller misses out on almost $200 million. Conrail's record for the largest IPO in U.S. history was broken in 1993 when Sears took its Allstate insurance subsidiary public and raised $2.4 billion. As originally structured, Sears sold 78.5 million shares at $27 per share for a total of $2.12 billion. However, the stock closed up 8.8 percent the first day, and the underwriters, led by Goldman Sachs, exercised their Green Shoe option and purchased an additional 11 million shares.

Evidence on Underpricing Figure 13.2 provides a more general illustration of the underpricing phenomenon. What is shown is the month-by-month his-

FIGURE 13.1 An example of a tombstone advertisement

58,750,000 Shares

Consolidated Rail Corporation

Common Stock

(par value $1.00 per share)

Price $28 Per Share

The shares are being sold by the United States Government pursuant to the Conrail Privatization Act. The Company will not receive any proceeds from the sale of the shares.

Upon request a copy of the Prospectus describing these securities and the business of the Company may be obtained within any State from any Underwriter who may legally distribute it within such State. The securities are offered only by means of the Prospectus, and this announcement is neither an offer to sell nor a solicitation of any offer to buy.

52,000,000 Shares

This portion of the offering is being offered in the United States and Canada by the undersigned.

Goldman, Sachs & Co.
The First Boston Corporation
Merrill Lynch Capital Markets
Morgan Stanley & Co. Incorporated
Salomon Brothers Inc.
Shearson Lehman Brothers Inc.

Alex Brown & Sons Incorporated — Dillon, Read & Co. Inc. — Donaldson, Lufkin & Jenrette Securities Corporation — Drexel Burnham Lambert Incorporated — Hambrecht & Quist Incorporated — E. F. Hutton & Company Inc.
Kidder, Peabody & Co. Incorporated — Lazard Frères & Co. — Montgomery Securities — Prudential-Bache Capital Funding — Robertson, Colman & Stephens
L. F. Rothschild, Unterberg, Towbin, Inc. — Smith Barney, Harris Upham & Co. Incorporated — Wertheim Schroder & Co. Incorporated — Dean Witter Reynolds Inc.
William Blair & Company — J. C. Bradford & Co. Incorporated — Dain Bosworth Incorporated — A. G. Edwards & Sons, Inc. — McDonald & Company Securities Inc. — Oppenheimer & Co., Inc.
Piper, Jaffray & Hopwood Incorporated — Prescott, Ball & Turben, Inc. — Thomson McKinnon Securities Inc. — Wheat, First Securities, Inc.
Advest, Inc. — American Securities Corporation — Arnhold and S. Bleichroeder, Inc. — Robert W. Baird & Co. Incorporated — Bateman Eichler, Hill Richards Incorporated
Sanford C. Bernstein & Co., Inc. — Blunt Ellis & Loewi Incorporated — Boettcher & Company, Inc. — Burns Fry and Timmins Inc. — Butcher & Singer Inc. — Cowen & Company
Dominion Securities Corporation — Eberstadt Fleming Inc. — Eppler, Guerin & Turner, Inc. — First of Michigan Corporation — First Southwest Company
Furman Selz Mager Dietz & Birney Incorporated — Gruntal & Co., Incorporated — Howard, Weil, Labouisse, Friedrichs Incorporated — Interstate Securities Corporation
Janney Montgomery Scott Inc. — Johnson, Lane, Smith & Co., Inc. — Johnston, Lemon & Co. Incorporated — Josephthal & Co. Incorporated — Ladenburg, Thalmann & Co. Inc.
Cyrus J. Lawrence Incorporated — Legg Mason Wood Walker Incorporated — Morgan Keegan & Company, Inc. — Moseley Securities Corporation — Needham & Company, Inc.
Neuberger & Berman — The Ohio Company — Rauscher Pierce Refsnes, Inc. — The Robinson-Humphrey Company, Inc. — Rothschild Inc. — Stephens Inc.
Stifel, Nicolaus & Company Incorporated — Sutro & Co. Incorporated — Tucker, Anthony & R. L. Day, Inc. — Underwood, Neuhaus & Co. Incorporated — Wood Grundy Corp.

This special bracket of minority-owned and controlled firms assisted the Co-Lead Managers in the United States Offering pursuant to the Conrail Privatization Act:

AIBC Investment Services Corporation — **Daniels & Bell, Inc.** — **Doley Securities, Inc.**
WR Lazard Securities Corporation — **Pryor, Govan Counts & Co., Inc.** — **Muriel Siebert & Co., Inc.**

6,750,000 Shares

This portion of the offering is being offered outside the United States and Canada by the undersigned

Goldman Sachs International Corp.
First Boston International Limited
Merrill Lynch Capital Markets
Morgan Stanley International
Salomon Brothers International Limited
Shearson Lehman Brothers International

Algemene Bank Nederland N.V. — Banque Bruxelles Lambert S.A. — Banque Nationale de Paris — Cazenove & Co. — The Nikko Securities Co., (Europe) Ltd.
Nomura International Limited — N.M. Rothschild & Sons Limited — J. Henry Schroder Wagg & Co. Limited — Société Générale — S. G. Warburg Securities
ABC International Ltd. — Banque Paribas Capital Markets Limited — Caisse Nationale de Crédit Agricole — Compagnie de Banque et d'investissements, CBI
Crédit Lyonnais — Daiwa Europe Limited — IMI Capital Markets (UK) Ltd. — Joh. Berenberg, Gossier & Co. — Leu Securities Limited
Morgan Greenfell & Co. Limited — Peterbroeck, van Campenhout & Cie SCS — Swiss Volksbank — Vereins-und Westbank Aktiengesellschaft
J. Vontobel & Co Ltd — M. M. Warburg-Brinckmann, Wirtz & Co. — Westdeutsche Landesbank Girozentrale — Yamaichi International (Europe) Limited

March 27, 1987

FIGURE 13.2 Average initial returns by month for SEC-registered initial public offerings: 1960–1992 **Trans. 13.8**

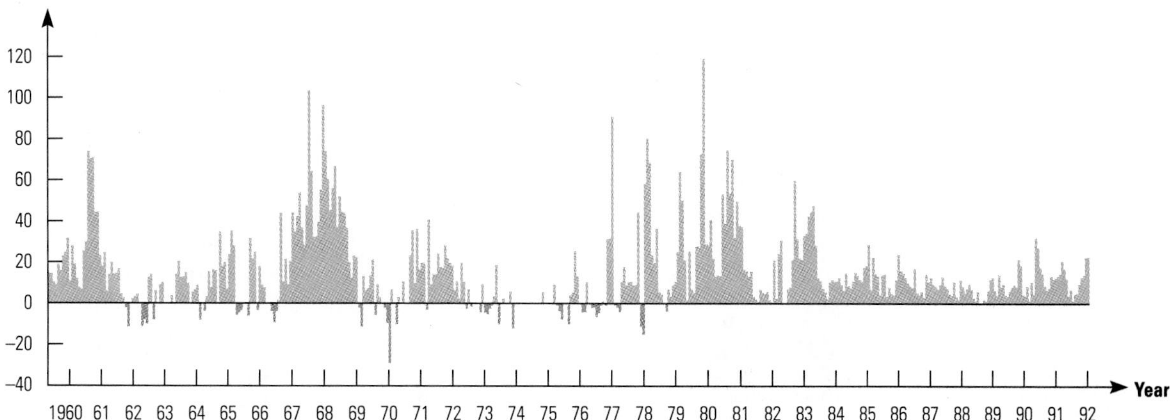

Sources: Roger G. Ibbotson, Jody L. Sindelar, and Jay R. Ritter, "Initial Public Offerings," *Journal of Applied Corporate Finance* 1 (Summer 1988), pp. 37–45, and Roger G. Ibbotson, Jody L. Sindelar, and Jay R. Ritter, "The Market's Problems with the Pricing of Initial Public Offerings," *Journal of Applied Corporate Finance* 7 (Spring 1994).

tory of underpricing for SEC-registered IPOs.[7] The period covered is 1960 through 1992. Figure 13.3 presents the number of offerings in each month for the same period.

Figure 13.2 shows that underpricing can be quite dramatic, exceeding 100 percent in some months. In such months, the average IPO more than doubled in value, sometimes in a matter of hours. Also, the degree of underpricing varies through time, and periods of severe underpricing (hot issue markets) are followed by periods of little underpricing (cold issue markets). For example, in the 1960s, the average IPO was underpriced by 21.25 percent. In the 1970s, the average was much smaller (8.95 percent), and it was actually very small or even negative for much of that time. Finally, for 1990–92, IPOs were underpriced by 10.85 percent on average.

In Figure 13.3, it is apparent that the number of IPOs is also highly variable through time. Further, there are pronounced cycles in both the degree of underpricing and the number of IPOs. Comparing Figures 13.2 and 13.3, increases in the number of new offerings tend to follow periods of significant underpricing by roughly 6 to 12 months. This probably occurs because companies decide to go public when they perceive that the market is highly receptive to new issues.

Table 13.3 contains a year-by-year summary of the information presented in Figures 13.2 and 13.3. As indicated, a grand total of 10,626 companies were included in this analysis. The degree of underpricing averaged 15.26 percent overall for the 33 years examined. Securities were overpriced on average in only 5 of the 33 years; the worst was 1973 when the average decrease in value was −17.82 percent. At the other extreme, in 1968, the 368 issues were underpriced, on average, by a remarkable 55.86 percent.

[7] The discussion in this section draws on Roger G. Ibbotson, Jody L. Sindelar, and Jay R. Ritter, "Initial Public Offerings," *Journal of Applied Corporate Finance* 1 (Summer 1988), pp. 37–45, and Roger G. Ibbotson, Jody L. Sindelar, and Jay R. Ritter, "Initial Public Offerings," *Journal of Applied Corporate Finance* (Spring 1994).

FIGURE 13.3 Number of offerings by month for SEC-registered initial public offerings: 1960–1992 **Trans. 13.9**

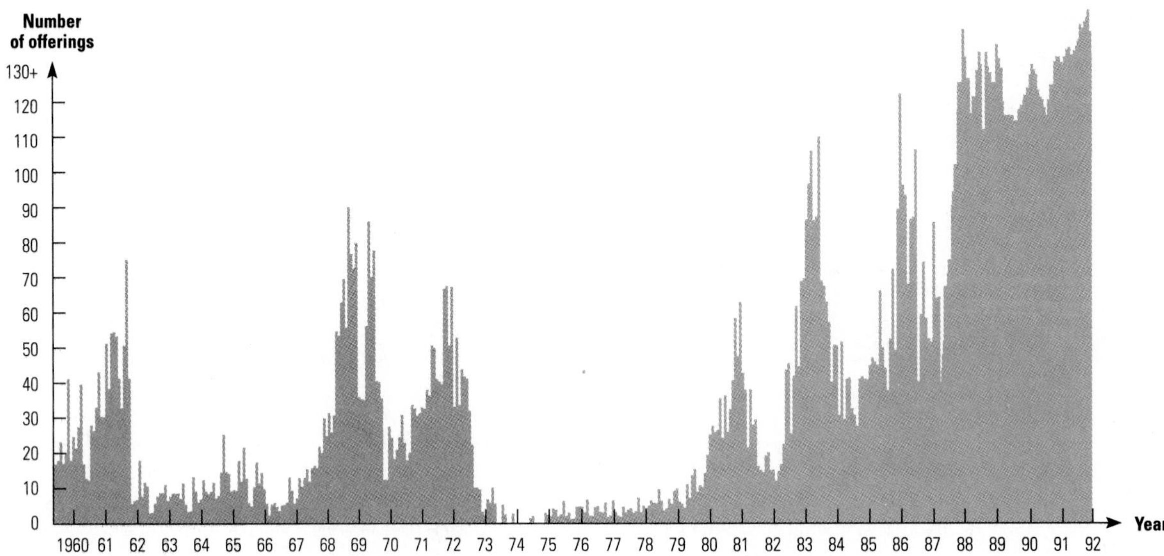

Sources: Roger G. Ibbotson, Jody L. Sindelar, and Jay R. Ritter, "Initial Public Offerings," *Journal of Applied Corporate Finance* 1 (Summer 1988), pp. 37–45, and Roger G. Ibbotson, Jody L. Sindelar, and Jay R. Ritter, "Initial Public Offerings," *Journal of Applied Corporate Finance* (Spring 1994).

Why Does Underpricing Exist? Based on the evidence we've examined, an obvious question is: Why does underpricing continue to exist? As we discuss, there are various explanations, but, to date, there is a lack of complete agreement among researchers as to which is correct.

We present some pieces of the underpricing puzzle by stressing two important caveats to our discussion above. First, the average figures we have examined tend to obscure the fact that much of the apparent underpricing is attributable to the smaller, more highly speculative issues. This point is illustrated in Table 13.4, which shows the extent of underpricing for 2,439 firms over the period 1975–84. Here, the firms are grouped based on their total sales in the 12 months prior to the IPO.

As illustrated in Table 13.4, the overall average underpricing is 20.7 percent for this sample; however, this underpricing is clearly concentrated in the firms with little to no sales in the previous year. These firms tend to have offering prices of less than $3 per share, and such *penny stocks* (as they are sometimes termed) can be very risky investments. Arguably, they must be significantly underpriced, on average, just to attract investors, and this is one explanation for the underpricing phenomenon. In fact, when the companies considered in Table 13.4 were grouped based on price per share instead of sales, the average degree of underpricing for those companies with initial offering prices of less than $3 per share was 42.8 percent. It averaged 8.6 percent for all the others.

The second caveat is that relatively few IPO buyers will actually get the initial high average returns observed in IPOs, and many will actually lose money. Although it is true that, on average, IPOs have positive initial returns, a significant fraction of them have price drops. Furthermore, when the price is too low, the issue is often "oversubscribed." This means investors will not be able to buy all of the shares they want, and the underwriters will allocate the shares among investors.

TABLE 13.3
Number of offerings, average initial return, and gross proceeds of initial public offerings: 1960–1992

Year	Number of Offerings*	Initial Return (percent)†	Average Gross Proceeds ($ in millions)
1960	269	17.83%	$ 553
1961	435	34.11	1,243
1962	298	−1.61	431
1963	83	3.93	246
1964	97	5.32	380
1965	146	12.75	409
1966	85	7.06	275
1967	100	37.67	641
1968	368	55.86	1,205
1969	780	12.53	2,605
1970	358	−0.67	780
1971	391	21.16	1,655
1972	562	7.51	2,724
1973	105	−17.82	330
1974	9	−6.98	51
1975	14	−1.86	264
1976	34	2.90	237
1977	40	21.02	151
1978	42	25.66	247
1979	103	24.61	429
1980	259	49.36	1,404
1981	438	16.76	3,200
1982	198	20.31	1,334
1983	848	20.79	13,168
1984	516	11.52	3,932
1985	507	12.36	10,450
1986	953	9.99	19,260
1987	630	10.39	16,380
1988	435	5.27	5,750
1989	371	6.47	6,068
1990	276	9.47	4,519
1991	367	11.83	16,420
1992	509	10.90	23,990
1960–69	2,661	21.25	7,988
1970–79	1,658	8.95	6,868
1980–89	5,155	15.18	80,946
1990–92	1,152	10.85	44,929
Total	10,626	15.26	140,731

*The number of offerings excludes Regulation A offerings (small issues, raising less than $1.5 million currently). The authors have excluded real estate investment trusts (REITs) and closed-end mutual funds.

†Initial returns are computed as the percentage return from the offering price to the end-of-the-calendar-month bid price, less the market return, for offerings in 1960–76. For 1977–92, initial returns are calculated as the percentage return from the offering price to the end-of-the-first-day bid price, without adjusting for market movements.

Sources: Roger G. Ibbotson, Jody L. Sindelar, and Jay R. Ritter, "Initial Public Offerings," *Journal of Applied Corporate Finance* 1 (Summer 1988), pp. 37–45, and Roger G. Ibbotson, Jody L. Sindelar, and Jay R. Ritter, "Initial Public Offerings," *Journal of Applied Corporate Finance* (Spring 1994).

Concept Q Answer 13.4b

The average investor will find it difficult to get shares in a "successful" offering (one where the price increases) because there will not be enough shares to go around. On the other hand, an investor blindly submitting orders for IPOs tends to get more shares in issues that go down in price.

To illustrate, consider this tale of two investors. Smith knows very accurately what the Bonanza Corporation is worth when its shares are offered. She is confident that they are underpriced. Jones knows only that prices usually rise one month after an IPO. Armed with this information, Jones decides

TABLE 13.4
Average initial returns categorized by annual sales of issuing firm: 1975–1984

Annual Sales of Issuing Firm ($)*	Number of Firms†	Average Initial Return (percent)‡
0	386	42.9%
1– 999,999	678	31.4
1,000,000– 4,999,999	353	14.3
5,000,000–14,999,999	347	10.7
15,000,000–24,999,999	182	6.5
25,000,000 and larger	493	5.3
All	2,439	20.7

*Annual sales are measured as the 12-month revenue for the year prior to going public. No adjustments for the effects of inflation have been made.

†Firms included are those using S-1 or S-18 registration forms, or with Federal Home Loan Bank Board approval, and listed in *Going Public: The IPO Reporter* for 1975–84. Issues not using an investment banker are excluded.

‡Initial returns are calculated as the percentage return from the offering price to the first recorded closing bid price. No adjustments for market movements have been made.

Source: Roger G. Ibbotson, Jody L. Sindelar, and Jay R. Ritter, "Initial Public Offerings," *Journal of Applied Corporate Finance* 1 (Summer 1988), pp. 37–45.

to buy 1,000 shares of every IPO. Does he actually earn an abnormally high return on the initial offering?

Lecture Tip: IM 13.4 includes the highlights of a recent *Business Week* article documenting the "winner's curse."

The answer is no, and at least one reason is Smith. Knowing about the Bonanza Corporation, Smith invests all her money in its IPO. When the issue is oversubscribed, the underwriters have to somehow allocate the shares between Smith and Jones. The net result is that when an issue is underpriced, Jones doesn't get to buy as much of it as he wanted.

Smith also knows that the Blue Sky Corporation IPO is overpriced. In this case, she avoids its IPO altogether, and Jones ends up with a full 1,000 shares. To summarize this tale, Jones gets fewer shares when more knowledgeable investors swarm to buy an underpriced issue and gets all he wants when the "smart money" avoids the issue.

Lecture Tip: It should also be pointed out that due diligence is performed prior to the offering, and investors have legal recourse against the underwriters if the prospectus has material omissions or misrepresentations of fact.

This is an example of a "winner's curse," and it is thought to be another reason why IPOs have such a large average return. When the average investor "wins" and gets her entire allocation, it may be because those who knew better avoided the issue. The only way underwriters can counteract the winner's curse and attract the average investor is to underprice new issues (on average) so that the average investor still makes a profit.

A final reason for underpricing is that the underpricing is a kind of insurance for the investment banks. Conceivably, an investment bank could be sued successfully by angry customers if it consistently overpriced securities. Underpricing guarantees that, at least on average, customers will come out ahead.

CONCEPT QUESTIONS

13.4a What is the difference between firm commitment and best efforts underwriting?

13.4b Suppose a stockbroker calls you up out of the blue and offers to sell you "all the shares you want" of a new issue. Do you think the issue will be more or less underpriced than average?

13.5 NEW EQUITY SALES AND THE VALUE OF THE FIRM

Concept Q Answer 13.5a

We now turn to a consideration of seasoned offerings, which, as we discussed above, are offerings by firms that already have outstanding securities. It seems reasonable to believe that new long-term financing is arranged by firms after positive net present value projects are put together. As a consequence, when the announcement of external financing is made, the firm's market value should go up. Interestingly, this is not what happens. Stock prices tend to decline following the announcement of a new equity issue, but they tend to not change much following a debt announcement. A number of researchers have studied this issue. Plausible reasons for this strange result include:

1. Managerial information. If management has superior information about the market value of the firm, it may know when the firm is overvalued. If it does, it will attempt to issue new shares of stock when the market value exceeds the correct value. This will benefit existing shareholders. However, the potential new shareholders are not stupid, and they will anticipate this superior information and discount it in lower market prices at the new issue date.
2. Debt usage. Issuing new equity may reveal that the company has too much debt or too little liquidity. One version of this argument is that the equity issue is a bad signal to the market. After all, if the new projects are favorable ones, why should the firm let new shareholders in on them? It could just issue debt and let the existing shareholders have all the gain.

Concept Q Answer 13.5b

3. Issue costs. As we discuss next, there are substantial costs associated with selling securities.

The drop in value of the existing stock following the announcement of a new issue is an example of an indirect cost of selling securities. This drop might typically be on the order of 3 percent for an industrial corporation (and somewhat smaller for a public utility), so, for a large company, it can be a substantial amount of money. We label this drop the *abnormal return* in our discussion of the costs of new issues below.

CONCEPT QUESTIONS

13.5a What are some possible reasons that the price of stock drops on the announcement of a new equity issue?

13.5b Explain why we might expect a firm with a positive NPV investment to finance it with debt instead of equity.

13.6 THE COSTS OF ISSUING SECURITIES

Self-Test Problem 1
Problems 4, 6

Issuing securities to the public isn't free, and the costs of different methods are important determinants of which is used. These costs associated with *floating* a new issue are generically called *flotation costs.* In this section, we take a closer look at the flotation costs associated with equity sales to the public.

Concept Q Answer 13.6a

The costs of selling stock are classified below and fall into six categories: (1) the spread, (2) other direct expenses, (3) indirect expenses, (4) abnormal returns (discussed above), (5) underpricing, and (6) the Green Shoe option.

The Costs of Issuing Securities

1. Spread	The spread consists of direct fees paid by the issuer to the underwriting syndicate—the difference between the price the issuer receives and the offer price.

2. Other direct expenses	These are direct costs, incurred by the issuer, that are not part of the compensation to underwriters. These costs include filing fees, legal fees, and taxes—all reported on the prospectus.
3. Indirect expenses	These costs are not reported on the prospectus and include the costs of management time spent working on the new issue.
4. Abnormal returns	In a seasoned issue of stock, the price of the existing stock drops on average by 3 percent upon the announcement of the issue. This drop is called the abnormal return.
5. Underpricing	For initial public offerings, losses arise from selling the stock below the true value.
6. Green Shoe option	The Green Shoe option gives the underwriters the right to buy additional shares at the offer price to cover overallotments.

Table 13.5 reports the direct costs of new equity issues in 1983 for publicly traded firms. These are all seasoned offerings; the percentages in Table 13.5 are as reported in the prospectuses of the issuing companies. These costs only include the spread (underwriter discount) and other direct costs, including legal fees, accounting fees, printing costs, SEC registration costs, and taxes. Not included are indirect expenses, abnormal returns, and the Green Shoe option.

As indicated in Table 13.5, the direct costs alone can be very large, particularly for smaller (less than $10 million) issues. For this group, the direct costs, as reported by the companies, average a little over 10 percent. This means that the company, net of costs, receives 90 percent of the proceeds of the sale on average. On a $10 million issue, this is $1 million in direct expenses—a substantial cost.

Table 13.5 only tells part of the story. For IPOs, the effective costs can be much greater because of the indirect costs. Table 13.6 reports both the direct costs of going public and the degree of underpricing based on IPOs that took place during 1977–82. Issues are classified by the type of underwriting (firm commitment or best efforts) and size of the issue.

TABLE 13.5
Flotation costs as a percentage of gross proceeds in 1983 for underwritten new issues of equity by publicly traded firms

Gross Proceeds ($ in millions)	Direct Costs Reported on Prospectus (percent)
$ 0– 10	10.10%
10– 20	7.02
20– 50	4.89
50–100	3.99
100–200	3.71
200+	3.30

Source: Robert Hansen, "Evaluating the Costs of a New Equity Issue," *Midland Corporate Finance Journal* 4, no. 1 (Spring 1986), p. 45.

TABLE 13.6 Costs of going public—total transactions costs as a percentage of gross proceeds: 1977–1982 **Trans. 13.10**

Gross Proceeds ($)	Firm Commitment Offerings					Best Efforts Offerings				
	(1) Under-writing Discount (percent)	(2) Other Expenses (percent)	(3) Total Direct Discount (percent) (1) + (2)	(4) Under-pricing (percent)	(5) Total Expenses (percent)	(6) Under-writing Discount (percent)	(7) Other Expenses (percent)	(8) Total Direct Discount (percent) (6) + (7)	(9) Under-pricing (percent)	(10) Total Expenses (percent)
1,000,000–1,999,999	9.84%	9.64%	19.48%	26.92%	31.73%	10.63%	9.52%	20.15%	39.62%	31.89%
2,000,000–3,999,999	9.83	7.60	17.43	20.70	24.93	10.00	6.21	16.21	63.41	36.28
4,000,000–5,999,999	9.10	5.67	14.77	12.57	20.90	9.86*	3.71*	13.57*	26.82*	14.49*
6,000,000–9,999,999	8.03	4.31	12.34	8.99	17.85	9.80*	3.42*	13.22*	40.79*	25.97*
10,000,000–120,174,195	7.24	2.10	9.34	10.32	16.27	8.03*	2.40*	10.43*	−5.42*	−0.17*
All offerings	8.67	5.36	14.03	14.80	21.22	10.26	7.48	17.74	47.78	31.87

The underpricing is computed as (p − OP)/OP, multiplied by 100 percent, where p is the closing bid price on the first day of trading and OP is the offering price. These are not annualized returns. Total costs are computed as 100 percent minus the net proceeds as a percentage of the market value of securities in the aftermarket. Consequently, total costs are not the sum of underwriting expenses and the average initial return. The underwriting discount is the commission paid by the issuing firm; this is listed on the front page of the firm's prospectus.

The other expenses figure comprises accountable and nonaccountable fees of the underwriters and cash expenses of the issuing firm for legal, printing, and auditing fees and other out-of-pocket costs. These other expenses are described in footnotes on the front page of the issuing firm's prospectus. None of the expense categories includes the value of warrants granted to the underwriter, a practice that is common with best efforts offerings.

Gross proceeds categories are nominal; no price-level adjustments have been made.

Also note that the −0.17% figure for the total expenses for best efforts offerings raising $10 million or more means that, on the average, these firms received net proceeds larger than the market value of the securities after the offering. It should be mentioned that there was less than one offering per year in the category.

*Based on fewer than 25 firms.

Source: Modified from J. R. Ritter, "The Costs of Going Public," *Journal of Financial Economics* 19 (1987). © Elsevier Science Publishers B.V. (North-Holland).

Columns (4) and (9) of Table 13.6 give some additional insight into the severity of underpricing. For example, with best efforts underwriting, the average price increase in the first full day of trading is 47.78 percent. This means that, on average, a stock offered at $10 per share sold for $14.78 at the end of the day. The underpricing was most severe for issues in the $2–3.99 million range, averaging 63.41 percent. The underpricing was much less severe with firm commitment underwriting; the worst average is 26.92 percent for the smallest offerings.

The total expenses of going public over these years averaged 21.22 percent for firm commitment and 31.87 percent for best efforts. Once again, we see that the costs of selling securities can be quite large.

Concept Q Answer 13.6b

Trans. 13.11 Five Conclusions on Flotation Costs (Supplemental)

Overall, five conclusions emerge from the various facts and figures we have discussed:

1. Substantial economies of size are evident. In percentage terms, the costs of selling securities decrease dramatically as the issue size grows.
2. The costs of selling securities are higher for best efforts offers.
3. The cost associated with underpricing can be substantial and can exceed the direct costs, particularly with smaller issues and best efforts underwriting.
4. Underpricing for best efforts offers is much greater than for firm commitment offers.
5. The direct issue costs are higher for an initial public offering than for a seasoned offering.

CONCEPT QUESTIONS

13.6a What are the different costs associated with security offerings?

13.6b What lessons do we learn from studying issue costs?

13.7 ISSUING DEBT SECURITIES

The general procedures followed in a public issue of bonds are the same as those for stocks. The issue must be registered with the SEC, there must be a prospectus, and so on. The registration statement for a public issue of bonds, however, is different from the one for common stock. For bonds, the registration statement must indicate an indenture.

Another important difference is that more than 50 percent of all debt is issued privately. There are two basic forms of direct, private long-term financing: term loans and private placement.

term loans
Direct business loans of, typically, one to five years.

private placements
Loans, usually long-term in nature, provided directly by a limited number of investors.

Term loans are direct business loans. These loans have maturities of between one year and five years. Most term loans are repayable during the life of the loan. The lenders include commercial banks, insurance companies, and other lenders that specialize in corporate finance. **Private placements** are very similar to term loans except that the maturity is longer.

The important differences between direct private, long-term financing and public issues of debt are:

Concept Q Answer 13.7a

1. A direct long-term loan avoids the cost of Securities and Exchange Commission registration.

Principles in Action

Red Herring Causes Red Alert

On November 8, 1994, 6.6 million shares of stock in First Alert Inc., a maker of smoke detecters, fire extinguishers, and carbon monoxide (CO) detectors, were sold to the public. Prior to the public issue, the firm filed the required registration statement with the SEC and circulated a red herring to potential investors. The prospectus, however, contained some questionable claims and information. Just two days later, in a highly unusual move, the stock offering was canceled and the purchasers' money was refunded. The story of First Alert's withdrawn offering emphasizes the care a company must take in the information it puts in its prospectus.

First Alert had been developing a CO detector for years before finally bringing it to market in late 1993. Early demand for the product was so strong that the company was forced to cancel a planned advertising campaign. Demand for CO detectors grew even stronger in September 1994 when tennis star Vitas Gerulaitis was found dead of carbon monoxide poisoning. First Alert's stock price climbed about fifty percent in the seven weeks following his death. The stock issue was designed to take advantage of the market potential for the new CO detector, and to take advantage of the recent runup in stock price. The day before the stock sale, the SEC questioned some of the company's claims in its prospectus. After overnight discussions, the SEC was satisfied by First Alert's answers, and the stock issue was allowed to proceed.

On November 9, 1994, an article in *The Wall Street Journal* raised more damaging questions about the accuracy of the stock prospectus. The article questioned the effectiveness of carbon monoxide detectors, including First Alert's claims about theirs, and prospectus claims that certain municipalities were considering mandating the use of CO detectors. On November 10th, First Alert withdrew the offering citing misinformation about its detectors, and announced the disputed claims in the prospectus would be fully investigated. The market price of the shares, which had been sold for $19 each, had fallen to just over $17.

In the end, the flawed prospectus was costly to First Alert and to the Thomas H. Lee Co., a Boston investment firm that had orchestrated a $92.5 million leveraged buyout of First Alert in 1992. The new owners pumped capital into First Alert to allow it to develop new products and grow and then took the company public with an initial public offering in the spring of 1994. The November stock offering would have further reduced their stake in the firm, but when it was canceled, Lee and the others involved in the LBO were forced to return the $125 million raised from the stock sale. Although First Alert itself wouldn't have received any of the proceeds from the stock issue, the company's name was tarnished by the affair, and the market for its CO detector was weakened. In addition, the company was sued by disgruntled investors who purchased stock around the time of the offering. As First Alert learned first hand, a prospectus provides information that investors rely on to make financial decisions. Errors or inflated claims in that prospectus can prove costly to everyone involved.

Sources: "Stockholder Lawsuits Put Firm on Alert," *Chicago Tribune,* November 28, 1994, sec. 4, pp. 1, 4; "Lee Co. Reaps Big First Alert Profit," *Boston Globe,* November 9, 1994, pp. 55, 65; "First Alert Cancels Sale of Stock," *Boston Globe,* November 11, 1994, pp. 63–64; "Thomas H. Lee Cashes In on a Fad and a Fear," *The Wall Street Journal,* November 9, 1994, sec. B, pp. 1–2; "First Alert withdraws Stock Offering following Reports Questioning Claims," *The Wall Street Journal,* November 11, 1994, sec. B, p. 2.

2. Direct placement is likely to have more restrictive covenants.
3. It is easier to renegotiate a term loan or a private placement in the event of a default. It is harder to renegotiate a public issue because hundreds of holders are usually involved.
4. Life insurance companies and pension funds dominate the private-placement segment of the bond market. Commercial banks are significant participants in the term-loan market.
5. The costs of distributing bonds are lower in the private market.

Concept Q Answer 13.7b

The interest rates on term loans and private placements are often higher than those on an equivalent public issue. This difference may reflect the trade-off between a higher interest rate and more flexible arrangements in the event of financial distress, as well as the lower costs associated with private placements.

International Note: The instructor may wish to supplement the material in this section with a discussion of the growing importance of foreign bond offerings. IM provides additional information.

An additional, and very important, consideration is that the flotation costs associated with selling debt are much less than the costs associated with selling equity.

CONCEPT QUESTIONS

13.7a What is the difference between private and public bond issues?

13.7b A private placement is likely to have a higher interest rate than a public issue. Why?

13.8 SHELF REGISTRATION

Concept Q Answer 13.8a

To simplify the procedures for issuing securities, in March 1982, the SEC adopted Rule 415 on a temporary basis, and it was made permanent in November 1983. Rule 415 allows shelf registration. Both debt and equity securities can be shelf registered.

shelf registration
SEC Rule 415 allowing a company to register all issues it expects to sell within two years at one time, with subsequent sales at any time within those two years.

Shelf registration permits a corporation to register an offering that it reasonably expects to sell within the next two years and then sell the issue whenever it wants over the next two years. Not all companies can use Rule 415. The primary qualifications are:

1. The company must be rated investment grade.
2. The firm cannot have defaulted on its debt in the past three years.
3. The aggregate market value of the firm's outstanding stock must be more than $150 million.
4. The firm must not have had a violation of the Securities Act of 1934 in the past three years.

Shelf registration allows firms to use a *dribble* method of new equity issuance. With dribbling, a company registers the issue and hires an underwriter as its selling agent. The company sells shares in "dribs and drabs" from time to time directly via a stock exchange (for example, the NYSE). Companies that have used dribble programs include Middle South Utilities, Niagara Mohawk, Pacific Gas and Electric, and The Southern Company.

Concept Q Answer 13.8b

The rule has been very controversial. Several arguments have been constructed against shelf registration:

1. The costs of new issues might go up because underwriters may not be able to provide as much current information to potential investors as would be true otherwise, so investors will pay less. The expense of selling the issue piece by piece might therefore be higher compared to selling it all at once.
2. Some investment bankers have argued that shelf registration will cause a "market overhang" that will depress market prices. In other words, the possibility that the company could increase the supply of stock at any time will have a negative impact on the current stock price. There is little evidence to support this position, however.

CONCEPT QUESTIONS

13.8a What is shelf registration?

13.8b What are the arguments against shelf registration?

13.9 SUMMARY AND CONCLUSIONS

This chapter looks at how corporate securities are issued. The following are the main points:

1. The venture capital market is a primary source of financing for new, high-risk companies.
2. The costs of issuing securities can be quite large. They are much lower (as a percentage) for larger issues.
3. Firm commitment underwriting is far more prevalent for large issues than best efforts underwriting. This is probably connected to the uncertainty of smaller issues. For a given size offering, the direct expenses of best efforts underwriting and firm commitment underwriting are of the same magnitude.
4. The direct and indirect costs of going public can be substantial. However, once a firm is public it can raise additional capital with much greater ease.

Chapter Review Problem and Self-Test

13.1 **Flotation Costs** The L5 Corporation is considering an equity issue to finance a new space station. A total of $10 million in new equity is needed. If the direct costs are estimated at 6 percent of the amount raised, how large does the issue need to be? What is the dollar amount of the flotation cost?

Answers to Self-Test Problem

13.1 The firm needs to net $10 million after paying the 6 percent flotation costs. So the amount raised is given by:

$$\text{Amount raised} \times (1 - .06) = \$10 \text{ million}$$

$$\text{Amount raised} = \$10/.94 = \$10.638 \text{ million}$$

The total flotation cost is thus $638,000.

Questions and Problems

Basic (Questions 1–8)

1. **IPO Investment and Underpricing** In 1980, a certain professor of finance bought 12 initial public offerings of common stock. He held each of these for approximately one month and then sold. The investment rule he followed was to submit a purchase order for every firm commitment initial public offering of oil and gas exploration companies. There were 22 of these offerings, and he submitted a purchase order for approximately $1,000 of stock for each of the companies. With 10 of these, no shares were allocated to this assistant professor. With 5 of the 12 offerings that were purchased, fewer than the requested number of shares were allocated.

The year 1980 was very good for oil and gas exploration company owners: on average, of the 22 companies that went public, the stocks were selling for 80 percent above the offering price a month after the initial offering date. The assistant professor looked at his performance record and found the $8,400 invested in the 12 companies had grown to $10,000, a return of only about 20 percent (commissions were negligible). Did he have bad luck, or should he have expected to do worse than the average initial public offering investor? Explain.

2. **IPO Underpricing** Analyze the following statement: Because initial public offerings of common stock are always underpriced, an investor can make money by purchasing shares in these offerings.

$2,000; $0
Trans. 13.12

3. **IPO Underpricing** The Bread Co. and the Butter Co. have both announced IPOs at $20 per share. One of these is undervalued by $4, the other is overvalued by $2, but you have no way of knowing which is which. You plan on buying 1,000 shares of each issue. If an issue is underpriced, it will be rationed, and only half your order will be filled. If you *could* get 1,000 shares in Bread and 1,000 shares in Butter, what would your profit be? What profit do you actually expect? What principle have you illustrated?

664,894

4. **Calculating Flotation Costs** The Beavis Corporation needs to raise $25 million to finance its expansion into new markets. The company will sell new shares of equity via a general cash offering to raise the needed funds. If the offer price is $40 per share and the company's underwriters charge a 6 percent spread, how many shares need to be sold?

674,202

5. **Calculating Flotation Costs** In the previous problem, if the SEC filing fee and associated administrative expenses of the offering are $350,000, how many shares need to be sold now?

34.85%
Trans. 13.13

6. **Calculating Flotation Costs** The Utopia Poultry Co. has just gone public. Under a firm commitment agreement, Utopia received $9 for each of the 2 million shares sold. The initial offering price was $10 per share, and the stock rose to $12 per share in the first few minutes of trading. Utopia paid $150,000 in direct legal and other costs, and $70,000 in indirect costs. What was the flotation cost as a percentage of funds raised?

7. **Venture Capital** What are some of the important considerations in choosing a venture capitalist for a start-up company?

8. **Analysis of an IPO** The following material contains the cover page and summary of the prospectus for the initial public offering of the Pest Investigation Control Corporation (PICC), which is going public tomorrow with a firm commitment initial public offering managed by the investment banking firm of Erlanger and Ritter. Answer the following questions:
   a. Assume that you know nothing about PICC other than the information contained in the prospectus. Based on your knowledge of finance, what is your prediction for the price of PICC tomorrow? Provide a short explanation of why you think this will occur.
   b. Assume that you have several thousand dollars to invest. When you get home from class tonight, you find that your stockbroker, whom you have not talked to for weeks, has called. She has left a message that PICC is going public tomorrow and that she can get

you several hundred shares at the offering price if you call her back first thing in the morning. Discuss the merits of this opportunity.

PROSPECTUS PICC

200,000 shares
PEST INVESTIGATION CONTROL CORPORATION

Of the shares being offered hereby, all 200,000 are being sold by the Pest Investigation Control Corporation, Inc. ("the Company"). Before the offering there has been no public market for the shares of PICC, and no guarantee can be given that any such market will develop.

These securities have not been approved or disapproved by the SEC nor has the commission passed upon the accuracy or adequacy of this prospectus. Any representation to the contrary is a criminal offense.

	Price to Public	Underwriting Discount	Proceeds to Company*
Per share	$11.00	$1.10	$9.90
Total	$2,200,000	$220,000	$1,980,000

*Before deducting expenses estimated at $27,000 and payable by the Company.

This is an initial public offering. The common shares are being offered, subject to prior sale, when, as, and if delivered to and accepted by the Underwriters and subject to approval of certain legal matters by their Counsel and by Counsel for the Company. The Underwriters reserve the right to withdraw, cancel, or modify such offer and to reject offers in whole or in part.

Erlanger and Ritter, Investment Bankers
July 12, 1994

Prospectus Summary

The Company	The Pest Investigation Control Corporation (PICC) breeds and markets toads and tree frogs as ecologically safe insect-control mechanisms.
The Offering	200,000 shares of common stock, no par value.
Listing	The Company will seek listing on NASDAQ and will trade over the counter.
Shares Outstanding	As of June 30, 1994, 400,000 shares of common stock were outstanding. After the offering, 600,000 shares of common stock will be outstanding.
Use of Proceeds	To finance expansion of inventory and receivables and general working capital, and to pay for country club memberships for certain finance professors.

Selected Financial Information
(amounts in thousands except per-share data)

	Fiscal Year Ended June 30		
	1992	1993	1994
Revenues	$60.00	$120.00	$240.00
Net earnings	3.80	15.90	36.10
Earnings per share	0.01	0.04	0.09

	As of June 30, 1994	
	Actual	As Adjusted for This Offering
Working capital	$ 8	$1,961
Total assets	511	2,464
Stockholders' equity	423	2,376

Chapter Fourteen

Leverage and Capital Structure

After studying this chapter, you should have a good understanding of:

. . .

The effect of financial leverage.

. . .

The impact of taxes and bankruptcy on capital structure choice.

. . .

The essentials of the bankruptcy process.

Trans. 14.1
Chapter Outline

Thus far, we have taken the firm's capital structure as given. Debt/equity ratios don't just drop on firms from the sky, of course, so now it's time to wonder where they do come from. Going back to Chapter 1, we call decisions about a firm's debt/equity ratio *capital structure decisions.*[1]

For the most part, a firm can choose any capital structure that it wants. If management so desired, a firm could issue some bonds and use the proceeds to buy back some stock, thereby increasing the debt/equity ratio. Alternatively, it could issue stock and use the money to pay off some debt, thereby reducing the debt/equity ratio. Activities, such as these, that alter the firm's existing capital structure are called capital *restructurings.* In general, such restructurings take place whenever the firm substitutes one capital structure for another while leaving the firm's assets unchanged.

Since the assets of a firm are not directly affected by a capital restructuring, we can examine the firm's capital structure decision separately from its other activities. This means that a firm can consider capital restructuring decisions in isolation from its investment decisions. In this chapter, then, we will ignore investment decisions and focus on the long-term financing, or capital structure, question.

[1] It is conventional to refer to decisions regarding debt and equity as *capital structure decisions.* However, the term *financial structure* would be more accurate, and we use the terms interchangeably.

What we will see in this chapter is that capital structure decisions can have important implications for the value of the firm and its cost of capital. We will also find that important elements of the capital structure decision are easy to identify, but precise measures of these elements are generally not obtainable. As a result, we are only able to give an incomplete answer to the question of what the best capital structure might be for a particular firm at a particular time.

Lecture Tip: Previously the term "GURF" was used to indicate a great underlying rule of finance; the question of optimal capital structure might be considered a "GUMF"—great unsolved mystery of finance. This point is discussed in IM 14.1.

14.1 THE CAPITAL STRUCTURE QUESTION

How should a firm go about choosing its debt/equity ratio? Here, as always, we assume that the guiding principle is to choose the course of action that maximizes the value of a share of stock. However, when it comes to capital structure decisions, this is essentially the same thing as maximizing the value of the whole firm, and, for convenience, we will tend to frame our discussion in terms of firm value.

Capital Structure and the Cost of Capital

In Chapter 12, we discussed the concept of the firm's weighted average cost of capital (WACC). You may recall that the WACC tells us that the firm's overall cost of capital is a weighted average of the costs of the various components of the firm's capital structure. When we described the WACC, we took the firm's capital structure as given. Thus, one important issue that we will want to explore in this chapter is what happens to the cost of capital when we vary the amount of debt financing or the debt/equity ratio.

Lecture Tip: See IM 14.1 for more on the link between optimal and target capital structure.

Trans. 14.2
Financial Leverage and Capital Structure Policy

A primary reason for studying the WACC is that the value of the firm is maximized when the WACC is minimized. To see this, recall that the WACC is the discount rate appropriate for the firm's overall cash flows. Since values and discount rates move in opposite directions, minimizing the WACC will maximize the value of the firm's cash flows.

Concept Q Answer 14.1a

Lecture Tip: A simple way of conceptualizing this idea is described in IM 14.1.

Thus, we will want to choose the firm's capital structure so that the WACC is minimized. For this reason, we will say that one capital structure is better than another if it results in a lower weighted average cost of capital. Further, we say that a particular debt/equity ratio represents the *optimal capital structure* if it results in the lowest possible WACC. This is sometimes called the firm's *target* capital structure as well.

Concept Q Answer 14.1b

CONCEPT QUESTIONS

14.1a What is the relationship between the WACC and the value of the firm?

14.1b What is an optimal capital structure?

14.2 THE EFFECT OF FINANCIAL LEVERAGE

In this section, we examine the impact of financial leverage on the payoffs to stockholders. As you may recall, financial leverage refers to the extent to which a firm relies on debt. The more debt financing a firm uses in its capital structure, the more financial leverage it employs.

Self-Test Problem 14.1
Problems 1, 4, 6

As we describe, financial leverage can dramatically alter the payoffs to shareholders in the firm. Remarkably, however, financial leverage may not affect the overall cost of capital. If this is true, then a firm's capital structure is irrelevant because changes in capital structure won't affect the value of the firm. We will return to this issue a little later.

The Impact of Financial Leverage

We start by illustrating how financial leverage works. For now, we ignore the impact of taxes. Also, for ease of presentation, we describe the impact of leverage in terms of its effects on earnings per share (EPS) and return on equity (ROE). These are, of course, accounting numbers, and, as such, are not our primary concern. Using cash flows instead of these accounting numbers would lead to precisely the same conclusions, but a little more work would be needed. We discuss the impact on market values in a subsequent section.

Trans. 14.3
Financial Leverage, EPS, and ROE: An Example (Supplemental)

Financial Leverage, EPS, and ROE: An Example The Trans Am Corporation currently has no debt in its capital structure. The CFO, Ms. Morris, is considering a restructuring that would involve issuing debt and using the proceeds to buy back some of the outstanding equity. Table 14.1 presents both the current and proposed capital structures. As shown, the firm's assets have a market value of \$8 million, and there are 400,000 shares outstanding. Because Trans Am is an all-equity firm, the price per share is \$20.

The proposed debt issue would raise \$4 million; the interest rate would be 10 percent. Since the stock sells for \$20 per share, the \$4 million in new debt would be used to purchase \$4 million/\$20 = 200,000 shares, leaving 200,000. After the restructuring, Trans Am would have a capital structure that was 50 percent debt, so the debt/equity ratio would be 1. Notice that, for now, we assume that the stock price will remain at \$20.

To investigate the impact of the proposed restructuring, Ms. Morris has prepared Table 14.2, which compares the firm's current capital structure to the proposed capital structure under three scenarios. The scenarios reflect different assumptions about the firm's EBIT. Under the expected scenario, the EBIT is \$1 million. In the recession scenario, EBIT falls to \$500,000. In the expansion scenario, it rises to \$1.5 million.

To illustrate some of the calculations in Table 14.2, consider the expansion case. EBIT is \$1.5 million. With no debt (the current capital structure) and no taxes, net income is also \$1.5 million. In this case, there are 400,000 shares worth \$8 million total. EPS is therefore \$1.5 million/400,000 = \$3.75

TABLE 14.1
Current and proposed capital structures for the Trans Am Corporation

	Current	Proposed
Assets	$8,000,000	$8,000,000
Debt	$ 0	$4,000,000
Equity	$8,000,000	$4,000,000
Debt/equity ratio	0	1
Share price	$20	$20
Shares outstanding	400,000	200,000
Interest rate	10%	10%

TABLE 14.2
Capital structure scenarios for the Trans Am Corporation

Current Capital Structure: No Debt			
	Recession	**Expected**	**Expansion**
EBIT	$500,000	$1,000,000	$1,500,000
Interest	0	0	0
Net income	$500,000	$1,000,000	$1,500,000
ROE	6.25%	12.50%	18.75%
EPS	$1.25	$2.50	$3.75
Proposed Capital Structure: Debt = $4 million			
	Recession	**Expected**	**Expansion**
EBIT	$500,000	$1,000,000	$1,500,000
Interest	400,000	400,000	400,000
Net income	$100,000	$ 600,000	$1,100,000
ROE	2.50%	15.00%	27.50%
EPS	$.50	$3.00	$5.50

per share. Also, since accounting return on equity (ROE) is net income divided by total equity, ROE is $1.5 million/$8 million = 18.75%.[2]

With $4 million in debt (the proposed capital structure), things are somewhat different. Since the interest rate is 10 percent, the interest bill is $400,000. With EBIT of $1.5 million, interest of $400,000, and no taxes, net income is $1.1 million. Now there are only 200,000 shares worth $4 million total. EPS is therefore $1.1 million/200,000 = $5.5 per share versus the $3.75 per share that we calculated above. Furthermore, ROE is $1.1 million/$4 million = 27.5 percent. This is well above the 18.75 percent we calculated for the current capital structure.

EPS versus EBIT The impact of leverage is evident when the effect of the restructuring on EPS and ROE is examined. In particular, the variability in both EPS and ROE is much larger under the proposed capital structure. This illustrates how financial leverage acts to magnify gains and losses to shareholders.

Concept Q Answer 14.2a

In Figure 14.1, we take a closer look at the effect of the proposed restructuring. This figure plots earnings per share (EPS) against earnings before interest and taxes (EBIT) for the current and proposed capital structures. The first line, labeled "No debt," represents the case of no leverage. This line begins at the origin, indicating that EPS would be zero if EBIT were zero. From there, every $400,000 increase in EBIT increases EPS by $1 (because there are 400,000 shares outstanding).

Lecture Tip: See IM for another example illustrating the relationship between ROE and ROA with leverage.

The second line represents the proposed capital structure. Here, EPS is negative if EBIT is zero. This follows because $400,000 of interest must be paid regardless of the firm's profits. Since there are 200,000 shares in this case, the EPS is −$2 per share as shown. Similarly, if EBIT were $400,000, EPS would be exactly zero.

Trans. 14.4 Break-Even EBIT: A Quick Note (Supplemental)

The important thing to notice in Figure 14.1 is that the slope of the line in this second case is steeper. In fact, for every $400,000 increase in EBIT,

[2] ROE is discussed in some detail in Chapter 3.

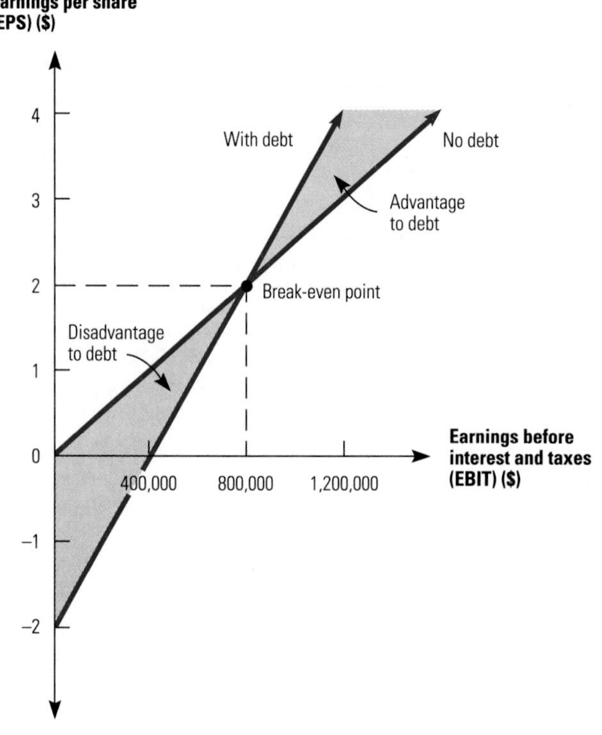

FIGURE 14.1
Financial leverage: EPS and EBIT for the Trans Am Corporation

EPS rises by \$2, so the line is twice as steep. This tells us that EPS is twice as sensitive to changes in EBIT because of the financial leverage employed.

Trans. 14.5
Financial Leverage, EPS, and EBIT (Supplemental)

Another observation to make in Figure 14.1 is that the lines intersect. At that point, EPS is exactly the same for both capital structures. To find this point, note that EPS is equal to EBIT/400,000 in the no-debt case. In the with-debt case, EPS is (EBIT − \$400,000)/200,000. If we set these equal to each other, EBIT is:

$$\text{EBIT}/400{,}000 = (\text{EBIT} - \$400{,}000)/200{,}000$$
$$\text{EBIT} = 2 \times (\text{EBIT} - \$400{,}000)$$
$$\text{EBIT} = \$800{,}000$$

When EBIT is \$800,000, EPS is \$2 per share under either capital structure. This is labeled as the break-even point in Figure 14.1; we could also call it the indifference point. If EBIT is above this level, leverage is beneficial; if it is below this point, it is not.

There is another, more intuitive, way of seeing why the break-even point is \$800,000. Notice that, if the firm has no debt and its EBIT is \$800,000, its net income is also \$800,000. In this case, the ROE is \$800,000/8,000,000 = 10%. This is precisely the same as the interest rate on the debt, so the firm earns a return that is just sufficient to pay the interest.

EXAMPLE 14.1 Break-Even EBIT

The MPD Corporation has decided in favor of a capital restructuring. Currently, MPD uses no debt financing. Following the restructuring, however, debt will be \$1 million. The interest rate on the debt will be 9 percent. MPD currently has 200,000 shares outstanding, and the price per share is $20. If the restructuring is expected to increase EPS, what is the minimum level for EBIT that MPD's management must be expecting? Ignore taxes in answering.

To answer, we calculate the break-even EBIT. At any EBIT above this the increased financial leverage will increase EPS, so this will tell us the minimum level for EBIT. Under the old capital structure, EPS is simply EBIT/200,000. Under the new capital structure, the interest expense will be $1 million × .09 = $90,000. Furthermore, with the $1 million proceeds, MPD will repurchase $1 million/$20 = 50,000 shares of stock, leaving 150,000 outstanding. EPS is thus (EBIT − $90,000)/150,000.

Lecture Tip: See IM for some insight into the relationship between break-even EPS and financial risk.

Now that we know how to calculate EPS under both scenarios, we set them equal to each other and solve for the break-even EBIT:

$$\text{EBIT}/200{,}000 = (\text{EBIT} - \$90{,}000)/150{,}000$$
$$\text{EBIT} = (4/3) \times (\text{EBIT} - \$90{,}000)$$
$$\text{EBIT} = \$360{,}000$$

Check that, in either case, EPS is $1.80 when EBIT is $360,000. Management at MPD is apparently of the opinion that EPS will exceed $1.80. • • •

Corporate Borrowing and Homemade Leverage

Based on Tables 14.1 and 14.2 and Figure 14.1, Ms. Morris draws the following conclusions:

1. The effect of financial leverage depends on the company's EBIT. When EBIT is relatively high, leverage is beneficial.
2. Under the expected scenario, leverage increases the returns to shareholders, as measured by both ROE and EPS.
3. Shareholders are exposed to more risk under the proposed capital structure since the EPS and ROE are much more sensitive to changes in EBIT in this case.
4. Because of the impact that financial leverage has on both the expected return to stockholders and the riskiness of the stock, capital structure is an important consideration.

The first three of these conclusions are clearly correct. Does the last conclusion necessarily follow? Surprisingly, the answer is no. As we discuss next, the reason is that shareholders can adjust the amount of financial leverage by borrowing and lending on their own. This use of personal borrowing to alter the degree of financial leverage is called **homemade leverage.**

Concept Q Answer 14.2b

homemade leverage
The use of personal borrowing to change the overall amount of financial leverage to which the individual is exposed.

We will now illustrate that it actually makes no difference whether or not Trans Am adopts the proposed capital structure, because any stockholder who prefers the proposed capital structure can simply create it using homemade leverage. To begin, the first part of Table 14.3 shows what would happen to an investor who buys $2,000 worth of Trans Am stock if the proposed capital structure were adopted. This investor purchases 100 shares of stock. From Table 14.2, EPS will either be $.50, $3, or $5.50, so the total earnings for 100 shares will either be $50, $300, or $550 under the proposed capital structure.

Concept Q Answer 14.2c

Trans. 14.6 Homemade Leverage: An Example (Supplemental)

Now, suppose Trans Am does not adopt the proposed capital structure. In this case, EPS will be $1.25, $2.50, or $3.75. The second part of Table 14.3 demonstrates how a stockholder who preferred the payoffs under the proposed structure can create them using personal borrowing. To do this, the stock-

TABLE 14.3
Proposed capital structure versus original capital structure with homemade leverage

Proposed Capital Structure			
	Recession	**Expected**	**Expansion**
EPS	$ .50	$ 3.00	$ 5.50
Earnings for 100 shares	50.00	300.00	550.00
Net cost = 100 shares at $20 = $2,000			
Original Capital Structure and Homemade Leverage			
	Recession	**Expected**	**Expansion**
EPS	$ 1.25	$ 2.50	$ 3.75
Earnings for 200 shares	250.00	500.00	750.00
Less: Interest on $2,000 at 10%	200.00	200.00	200.00
Net earnings	$ 50.00	$300.00	$550.00
Net cost = 200 shares at $20/share − Amount borrowed = $4,000 − 2,000 = $2,000			

holder borrows $2,000 at 10 percent on her own. Our investor uses this amount, along with her original $2,000, to buy 200 shares of stock. As shown, the net payoffs are exactly the same as those for the proposed capital structure.

How did we know to borrow $2,000 to create the right payoffs? We are trying to replicate Trans Am's proposed capital structure at the personal level. The proposed capital structure results in a debt/equity ratio of 1. To replicate it at the personal level, the stockholder must borrow enough to create this same debt/equity ratio. Since the stockholder has $2,000 in equity invested, borrowing another $2,000 will create a personal debt/equity ratio of 1.

This example demonstrates that investors can always increase financial leverage themselves to create a different pattern of payoffs. It thus makes no difference whether or not Trans Am chooses the proposed capital structure.

EXAMPLE 14.2 Unlevering the Stock

In our Trans Am example, suppose management adopts the proposed capital structure. Further suppose an investor who owned 100 shares preferred the original capital structure. Show how this investor could "unlever" the stock to recreate the original payoffs.

To create leverage, investors borrow on their own. To undo leverage, investors must loan out money. For Trans Am, the corporation borrowed an amount equal to half its value. The investor can unlever the stock by simply loaning out money in the same proportion. In this case, the investor sells 50 shares for $1,000 total and then loans out the $1,000 at 10 percent. The payoffs are calculated in the table below.

	Recession	Expected	Expansion
EPS (proposed structure)	$ .50	$ 3.00	$ 5.50
Earnings for 50 shares	25.00	150.00	275.00
Plus: Interest on $1,000 @ 10%	100.00	100.00	100.00
Total payoff	$125.00	$250.00	$375.00

These are precisely the payoffs the investor would have experienced under the original capital structure. • • •

CONCEPT QUESTIONS

14.2a What is the impact of financial leverage on stockholders?

14.2b What is homemade leverage?

14.2c Why is Trans Am's capital structure irrelevant?

14.3 CAPITAL STRUCTURE AND THE COST OF EQUITY CAPITAL

We have seen that there is nothing special about corporate borrowing because investors can borrow or lend on their own. As a result, whichever capital structure Trans Am chooses, the stock price will be the same. Trans Am's capital structure is thus irrelevant, at least in the simple world we examined.

Self-Test Problem 14.2
Problems 3, 5, 7

Our Trans Am example is based on a famous argument advanced by two Nobel Prize laureates, Franco Modigliani and Merton Miller, whom we will henceforth call M&M. What we illustrated for the Trans Am Corporation is a special case of **M&M Proposition I.** M&M Proposition I states that it is completely irrelevant how a firm chooses to arrange its finances.

M&M Proposition I
The value of the firm is independent of its capital structure.

M&M Proposition I: The Pie Model

One way to illustrate M&M Proposition I is to imagine two firms that are identical on the left-hand side of the balance sheet. Their assets and operations are exactly the same. The right-hand sides are different because the two firms finance their operations differently. In this case, we can view the capital structure question in terms of a "pie" model. Why we choose this name is apparent in Figure 14.2. Figure 14.2 gives two possible ways of cutting up this pie between the equity slice, E, and the debt slice, D: 40%–60% and 60%–40%. However, the size of the pie in Figure 14.2 is the same for both firms because the value of the assets is the same. This is precisely what M&M Proposition I states: The size of the pie doesn't depend on how it is sliced.

Trans. 14.7
M&M Propositions I and II (Supplemental)

Concept Q Answer 14.3a

The Cost of Equity and Financial Leverage: M&M Proposition II

Although changing the capital structure of the firm may not change the firm's *total* value, it does cause important changes in the firm's debt and equity. We now examine what happens to a firm financed with debt and equity when the debt/equity ratio is changed. To simplify our analysis, we will continue to ignore taxes.

Lecture Tip: See IM 14.3 for more on why we even consider a no-tax environment.

M&M Proposition II Based on our discussion in Chapter 12, if we ignore taxes, the weighted average cost of capital, WACC, is:

$$\text{WACC} = (E/V) \times R_E + (D/V) \times R_D$$

where $V = E + D$. We also saw that one way of interpreting the WACC is that it is the required return on the firm's overall assets. To remind us of this, we will use the symbol R_A to stand for the WACC and write:

$$R_A = (E/V) \times R_E + (D/V) \times R_D$$

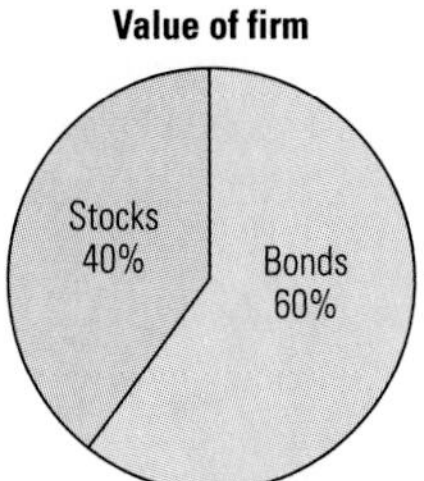

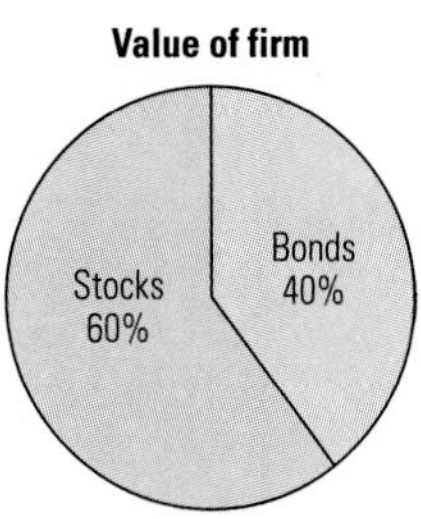

FIGURE 14.2
Two pie models of capital structure

FIGURE 14.3
The cost of equity and the WACC: M&M Propositions I and II with no taxes

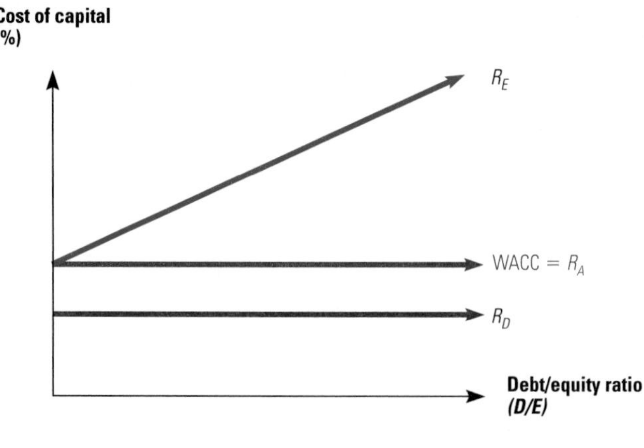

$R_E = R_A + (R_A - R_D) \times (D/E)$ by M&M Proposition II

$R_A = \text{WACC} = \left(\frac{E}{V}\right) \times R_E + \left(\frac{D}{V}\right) \times R_D$

where $V = D + E$

If we rearrange this to solve for the cost of equity capital, we see that:

$$R_E = R_A + (R_A - R_D) \times (D/E) \qquad [14.1]$$

M&M Proposition II
A firm's cost of equity capital is a positive linear function of its capital structure.

Concept Q Answer 14.3b

Trans. 14.8 M&M Proposition II (Supplemental)

Lecture Tip: See IM for an alternative interpretation of M&M Proposition II.

This is the famous **M&M Proposition II,** which tells us that the cost of equity depends on three things: the required rate of return on the firm's assets, R_A, the firm's cost of debt, R_D, and the firm's debt/equity ratio, D/E.

Figure 14.3 summarizes our discussion thus far by plotting the cost of equity capital, R_E, against the debt/equity ratio. As shown, M&M Proposition II indicates that the cost of equity, R_E, is given by a straight line with a slope of $(R_A - R_D)$. The y-intercept corresponds to a firm with a debt/equity ratio of zero, so $R_A = R_E$ in that case. Figure 14.3 shows that, as the firm raises its debt/equity ratio, the increase in leverage raises the risk of the equity and therefore the required return or cost of equity (R_E).

Notice in Figure 14.3 that the WACC doesn't depend on the debt/equity ratio; it's the same no matter what the debt/equity ratio is. This is another way of stating M&M Proposition I: The firm's overall cost of capital is unaffected by its capital structure. As illustrated, the fact that the cost of debt is lower than the cost of equity is exactly offset by the increase in the cost of equity from borrowing. In other words, the change in the capital structure weights (E/V and D/V) is exactly offset by the change in the cost of equity (R_E), so the WACC stays the same.

EXAMPLE 14.3 The Cost of Equity Capital

The Ricardo Corporation has a weighted average cost of capital (ignoring taxes) of 12 percent. It can borrow at 8 percent. Assuming that Ricardo has a target capital structure of 80 percent equity and 20 percent debt, what is its cost of equity? What is the cost of equity if the target capital structure is 50 percent equity? Calculate the WACC using your answers to verify that it is the same.

According to M&M Proposition II, the cost of equity, R_E, is:

$$R_E = R_A + (R_A - R_D) \times (D/E)$$

In the first case, the debt/equity ratio is .2/.8 = .25, so the cost of the equity is:

$$R_E = 12\% + (12\% - 8\%) \times (.25)$$
$$= 13\%$$

In the second case, check that the debt/equity ratio is 1.0, so the cost of equity is 16 percent.

We can now calculate the WACC assuming that the percentage of equity financing is 80 percent, the cost of equity is 13 percent, and the tax rate is zero:

$$\text{WACC} = (E/V) \times R_E + (D/V) \times R_D$$
$$= .80 \times 13\% + .20 \times 8\%$$
$$= 12\%$$

In the second case, the percentage of equity financing is 50 percent and the cost of equity is 16 percent. The WACC is:

$$\text{WACC} = (E/V) \times R_E + (D/V) \times R_D$$
$$= .50 \times 16\% + .50 \times 8\%$$
$$= 12\%$$

As we calculated, the WACC is 12 percent in both cases. • • •

Business and Financial Risk

M&M Proposition II shows that the firm's cost of equity can be broken down into two components. The first component, R_A, is the required return on the firm's assets overall, and it depends on the nature of the firm's operating activities. The risk inherent in a firm's operations is called the **business risk** of the firm's equity. Referring back to Chapter 11, this business risk depends on the systematic risk of the firm's assets. The greater a firm's business risk, the greater R_A will be, and, all other things the same, the greater will be its cost of equity.

business risk
The equity risk that comes from the nature of the firm's operating activities.

The second component in the cost of equity, $(R_A - R_D) \times (D/E)$, is determined by the firm's financial structure. For an all-equity firm, this component is zero. As the firm begins to rely on debt financing, the required return on equity rises. This occurs because the debt financing increases the risks borne by the stockholders. This extra risk that arises from the use of debt financing is called the **financial risk** of the firm's equity.

Trans. 14.9
More on Business and Financial Risk
(Supplemental)

financial risk
The equity risk that comes from the financial policy (i.e., capital structure) of the firm.

The total systematic risk of the firm's equity thus has two parts: business risk and financial risk. The first part (the business risk) depends on the firm's assets and operations and is not affected by capital structure. Given the firm's business risk (and its cost of debt), the second part (the financial risk) is completely determined by financial policy. As we have illustrated, the firm's cost of equity rises when it increases its use of financial leverage because the financial risk of the equity increases while the business risk remains the same.

Concept Q
Answer 14.3c

Lecture Tip: See IM 14.3 for additional hints on discussing financial risk.

CONCEPT QUESTIONS

14.3a What does M&M Proposition I state?

14.3b What are the three determinants of a firm's cost of equity?

14.3c The total systematic risk of a firm's equity has two parts. What are they?

14.4 CORPORATE TAXES AND CAPITAL STRUCTURE

Self-Test Problem 14.3
Problems 8–10

Debt has two distinguishing features that we have not taken into proper account. First, as we have mentioned in a number of places, interest paid on debt is tax deductible. This is good for the firm, and it may be an added benefit to debt financing. Second, failure to meet debt obligations can result in bankruptcy. This is not good for the firm, and it may be an added cost of debt financing. Since we haven't explicitly considered either of these two features of debt, we may get a different answer about capital structure once we do. Accordingly, we consider taxes in this section and bankruptcy in the next one.

Trans. 14.10
Debt, Taxes, and Bankruptcy (Supplemental)

We can start by considering what happens when we consider the effect of corporate taxes. To do this, we will examine two firms, Firm U (unlevered) and Firm L (levered). These two firms are identical on the left-hand side of the balance sheet, so their assets and operations are the same.

We assume that EBIT is expected to be $1,000 every year forever for both firms. The difference between them is that Firm L has issued $1,000 worth of perpetual bonds on which it pays 8 percent interest each year. The interest bill is thus .08 × $1,000 = $80 every year forever. Also, we assume that the corporate tax rate is 30 percent.

For our two firms, U and L, we can now calculate the following:

	Firm U	Firm L
EBIT	$1,000	$1,000
Interest	0	80
Taxable income	$1,000	$ 920
Taxes (30%)	300	276
Net income	$ 700	$ 644

The Interest Tax Shield

To simplify things, we will assume that depreciation is zero. We will also assume that capital spending is zero and that there are no additions to NWC. In this case, cash flow from assets is simply equal to EBIT − Taxes. For Firms U and L, we thus have:

Cash Flow from Assets	Firm U	Firm L
EBIT	$1,000	$1,000
− Taxes	300	276
Total	$ 700	$ 724

We immediately see that capital structure is now having some effect because the cash flows from U and L are not the same even though the two firms have identical assets.

To see what's going on, we can compute the cash flow to stockholders and bondholders.

Cash Flow	Firm U	Firm L
To stockholders	$700	$644
To bondholders	0	80
Total	$700	$724

What we are seeing is that the total cash flow to L is $24 more. This occurs because L's tax bill (which is a cash outflow) is $24 less. The fact that interest is deductible for tax purposes has generated a tax saving equal to the interest payment ($80) multiplied by the corporate tax rate (30 percent): $\$80 \times .30 = \$24$. We call this tax saving the **interest tax shield.**

interest tax shield
The tax saving attained by a firm from the tax deductibility of interest expense.

Taxes and M&M Proposition I

Since the debt is perpetual, the same $24 shield will be generated every year forever. The aftertax cash flow to L will thus be the same $700 that U earns plus the $24 tax shield. Since L's cash flow is always $24 greater, Firm L is worth more than Firm U by the value of this $24 perpetuity.

Because the tax shield is generated by paying interest, it has the same risk as the debt, and 8 percent (the cost of debt) is therefore the appropriate discount rate. The value of the tax shield is thus:

$$\text{PV} = \frac{\$24}{.08} = \frac{.30 \times \$1{,}000 \times .08}{.08} = .30 \times \$1{,}000 = \$300$$

As our example illustrates, the present value of the interest tax shield can be written as:

$$\begin{aligned}\text{Present value of the interest tax shield} &= (T_C \times D \times R_D)/R_D \qquad [14.2]\\ &= T_C \times D\end{aligned}$$

We have now come up with another famous result, M&M Proposition I with corporate taxes. We have seen that the value of Firm L, V_L, exceeds the value of Firm U, V_U, by the present value of the interest tax shield, $T_C \times D$. M&M Proposition I with taxes therefore states that:

Concept Q Answer 14.4a

$$V_L = V_U + T_C \times D \qquad [14.3]$$

Lecture Tip: See IM 14.4 for a comment regarding the impact of the corporate tax rate structure on financing decisions.

The effect of borrowing in this case is illustrated in Figure 14.4. We have plotted the value of the levered firm, V_L, against the amount of debt, D. M&M Proposition I with corporate taxes implies that the relationship is given by a straight line with a slope of T_C.

FIGURE 14.4
M&M Proposition I with taxes

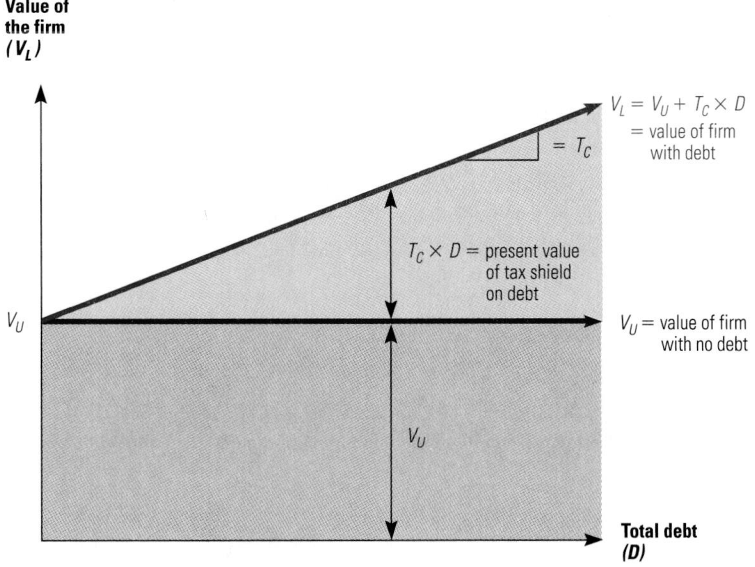

The value of the firm increases as total debt increases because of the interest tax shield. This is the basis of M&M Proposition I with taxes.

TABLE 14.4
Modigliani and Miller summary

Trans. 14.11

I. The No-Tax Case
   A. Proposition I: The value of the firm levered (V_L) is equal to the value of the firm unlevered (V_U):

$$V_L = V_U$$

   B. Implications of Proposition I:
      1. A firm's capital structure is irrelevant.
      2. A firm's weighted average cost of capital (WACC) is the same no matter what mixture of debt and equity is used to finance the firm.
   C. Proposition II: The cost of equity, R_E, is:

$$R_E = R_A + (R_A - R_D) \times D/E$$

   where R_A is the WACC, R_D is the cost of debt, and D/E is the debt/equity ratio.
   D. Implications of Proposition II:
      1. The cost of equity rises as the firm increases its use of debt financing.
      2. The risk of the equity depends on two things: the riskiness of the firm's operations (*business risk*) and the degree of financial leverage (*financial risk*). Business risk determines R_A; financial risk is determined by D/E.

II. The Tax Case
   A. Proposition I with taxes: The value of the firm levered (V_L) is equal to the value of the firm unlevered (V_U) plus the present value of the interest tax shield:

$$V_L = V_U + T_C \times D$$

   where T_C is the corporate tax rate and D is the amount of debt.
   B. Implications of Proposition I:
      1. Debt financing is highly advantageous, and, in the extreme, a firm's optimal capital structure is 100 percent debt.
      2. A firm's weighted average cost of capital (WACC) decreases as the firm relies more heavily on debt financing.

In Figure 14.4, we have also drawn a horizontal line representing V_U. As shown, the distance between the two lines is $T_C \times D$, the present value of the tax shield.

Lecture Tip: The IM discusses in more detail the notion of positive NPV financing opportunities.

As Figure 14.4 indicates, the value of the firm goes up by \$.30 for every \$1 in debt. In other words, the NPV *per dollar* of debt is \$.30. It is difficult to imagine why any corporation would not borrow to the absolute maximum under these circumstances.

Concept Q Answer 14.4b

The result of our analysis in this section is that, once we include taxes, capital structure definitely matters. However, we immediately reach the illogical conclusion that the optimal capital structure is 100 percent debt. Of course, we have not yet considered the impact of bankruptcy, so our story may change. For future reference, Table 14.4 contains a summary of the various M&M calculations and conclusions.

CONCEPT QUESTIONS

14.4a What is the relationship between the value of an unlevered firm and the value of a levered firm once we consider the effect of corporate taxes?

14.4b If we only consider the effect of taxes, what is the optimum capital structure?

14.5 BANKRUPTCY COSTS

One limit to the amount of debt a firm might use comes in the form of *bankruptcy costs*. As the debt/equity ratio rises, so too does the probability that the firm will be unable to pay its bondholders what was promised to them. When this happens, ownership of the firm's assets is ultimately transferred from the stockholders to the bondholders.

In principle, a firm becomes bankrupt when the value of its assets equals the value of its debt. When this occurs, the value of equity is zero and the stockholders turn over control of the firm to the bondholders. At this point, the bondholders hold assets whose value is exactly equal to what is owed on the debt. In a perfect world, there are no costs associated with this transfer of ownership, and the bondholders don't lose anything.

This idealized view of bankruptcy is not, of course, what happens in the real world. Ironically, it is expensive to go bankrupt. As we discuss, the costs associated with bankruptcy may eventually offset the tax-related gains from leverage.

Direct Bankruptcy Costs

When the value of a firm's assets equals the value of its debt, then the firm is economically bankrupt in the sense that the equity has no value. However, the formal means of turning over the assets to the bondholders is a *legal* process, not an economic one. There are legal and administrative costs to bankruptcy, and it has been remarked that bankruptcies are to lawyers what blood is to sharks.

Because of the expenses associated with bankruptcy, bondholders won't get all that they are owed. Some fraction of the firm's assets will "disappear" in the legal process of going bankrupt. These are the legal and administrative expenses associated with the bankruptcy proceeding. We call these costs **direct bankruptcy costs.**

Concept Q Answer 14.5a

direct bankruptcy costs
The costs that are directly associated with bankruptcy, such as legal and administrative expenses.

Indirect Bankruptcy Costs

Because it is expensive to go bankrupt, a firm will spend resources to avoid doing so. When a firm is having significant problems in meeting its debt obligations, we say that it is experiencing financial distress. Some financially distressed firms ultimately file for bankruptcy, but most do not because they are able to recover or otherwise survive.

Lecture Tip: Examples of real-world bankruptcy costs are described in IM 14.5.

Concept Q Answer 14.5b

The costs of avoiding a bankruptcy filing incurred by a financially distressed firm are called **indirect bankruptcy costs.** We use the term **financial distress costs** to refer generically to the direct and indirect costs associated with going bankrupt and/or avoiding a bankruptcy filing.

indirect bankruptcy costs
The costs of avoiding a bankruptcy filing incurred by a financially distressed firm.

financial distress costs
The direct and indirect costs associated with going bankrupt or experiencing financial distress.

The problems that come up in financial distress are particularly severe, and the financial distress costs are thus larger, when the stockholders and the bondholders are different groups. Until the firm is legally bankrupt, the stockholders control it. They, of course, will take actions in their own economic interests. Since the stockholders can be wiped out in a legal bankruptcy, they have a very strong incentive to avoid a bankruptcy filing.

The bondholders, on the other hand, are primarily concerned with protecting the value of the firm's assets and will try to take control away from stockholders. They have a strong incentive to seek bankruptcy to protect their interests and keep stockholders from further dissipating the assets of the firm. The net effect of all this fighting is that a long, drawn-out, and potentially quite expensive, legal battle gets started.

Meanwhile, as the wheels of justice turn in their ponderous way, the assets of the firm lose value because management is busy trying to avoid bankruptcy instead of running the business. Normal operations are disrupted, and sales are lost. Valuable employees leave, potentially fruitful programs are dropped to preserve cash, and otherwise profitable investments are not taken.

These are all indirect bankruptcy costs, or costs of financial distress. Whether or not the firm ultimately goes bankrupt, the net effect is a loss of value because the firm chose to use debt in its capital structure. It is this possibility of loss that limits the amount of debt that a firm will choose to use.

CONCEPT QUESTIONS

14.5a What are direct bankruptcy costs?

14.5b What are indirect bankruptcy costs?

14.6 OPTIMAL CAPITAL STRUCTURE

Our previous two sections have established the basis for an optimal capital structure. A firm will borrow because the interest tax shield is valuable. At relatively low debt levels, the probability of bankruptcy and financial distress is low, and the benefit from debt outweighs the cost. At very high debt levels, the possibility of financial distress is a chronic, ongoing problem for the firm, so the benefit from debt financing may be more than offset by the financial distress costs. Based on our discussion, it would appear that an optimal capital structure exists somewhere in between these extremes.

The Static Theory of Capital Structure

static theory of capital structure
Theory that a firm borrows up to the point where the tax benefit from an extra dollar in debt is exactly equal to the cost that comes from the increased probability of financial distress.

Concept Q Answer 14.6a

The theory of capital structure that we have outlined is called the **static theory of capital structure.** It says that firms borrow up to the point where the tax benefit from an extra dollar in debt is exactly equal to the cost that comes from the increased probability of financial distress. We call this the static theory because it assumes that the firm is fixed in terms of its assets and operations and it only considers possible changes in the debt/equity ratio.

The static theory is illustrated in Figure 14.5, which plots the value of the firm, V_L, against the amount of debt, D. In Figure 14.5, we have drawn lines corresponding to three different stories. The first is M&M Proposition I with no taxes. This is the horizontal line extending from V_U, and it indicates that the value of the firm is unaffected by its capital structure. The second case, M&M Proposition I with corporate taxes, is given by the upward-sloping straight line. These two cases are exactly the same as the ones we previously illustrated in Figure 14.4.

The third case in Figure 14.5 illustrates our current discussion: The value of the firm rises to a maximum and then declines beyond that point. This is the picture that we get from our static theory. The maximum value of the firm, V_L^*, is reached at a debt level of D^*, so this is the optimal amount of borrowing. Put another way, the firm's optimal capital structure is composed of D^*/V_L^* in debt and $(1 - D^*/V_L^*)$ in equity.

The final thing to notice in Figure 14.5 is that the difference between the value of the firm in our static theory and the M&M value of the firm with taxes is the loss in value from the possibility of financial distress. Also, the difference between the static theory value of the firm and the M&M value with no taxes is the gain from leverage, net of distress costs.

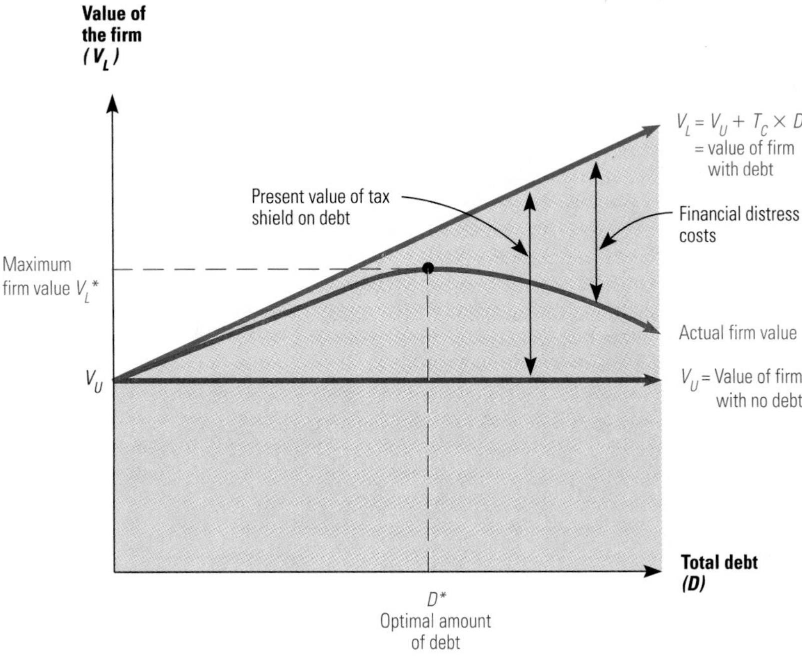

FIGURE 14.5
The static theory of capital structure: The optimal capital structure and the value of the firm

Trans. 14.12

According to the static theory, the gain from the tax shield on debt is offset by financial distress cost. An optimal capital structure exists which just balances the additional gain from leverage against the added financial distress cost.

Optimal Capital Structure and the Cost of Capital

As we discussed earlier, the capital structure that maximizes the value of the firm is also the one that minimizes the cost of capital. With the help of Figure 14.6, we can illustrate this point and tie together our discussion of capital structure and cost of capital. As we have seen, there are essentially three cases. We will use the simplest of the three cases as a starting point and then build up to the static theory of capital structure. Along the way, we will pay particular attention to the connection between capital structure, firm value, and cost of capital.

Figure 14.6 illustrates the original Modigliani and Miller (M&M) no-tax, no-bankruptcy argument in Case I. This is the most basic case. In the top part, we have plotted the value of the firm, V_L, against total debt, D. When there are no taxes, bankruptcy costs, or other real-world imperfections, we know that the total value of the firm is not affected by its debt policy, so V_L is simply constant. The bottom part of Figure 14.6 tells the same story in terms of the cost of capital. Here, the weighted average cost of capital, WACC, is plotted against the debt to equity ratio, D/E. As with total firm value, the overall cost of capital is not affected by debt policy in this basic case, so the WACC is constant.

Next, we consider what happens to the original M&M arguments once taxes are introduced. As Case II illustrates, we now see that the firm's value critically depends on its debt policy. The more the firm borrows, the more it is worth. From our earlier discussion, we know this happens because interest payments are tax deductible, and the gain in firm value is just equal to the present value of the interest tax shield.

FIGURE 14.6 The capital structure question

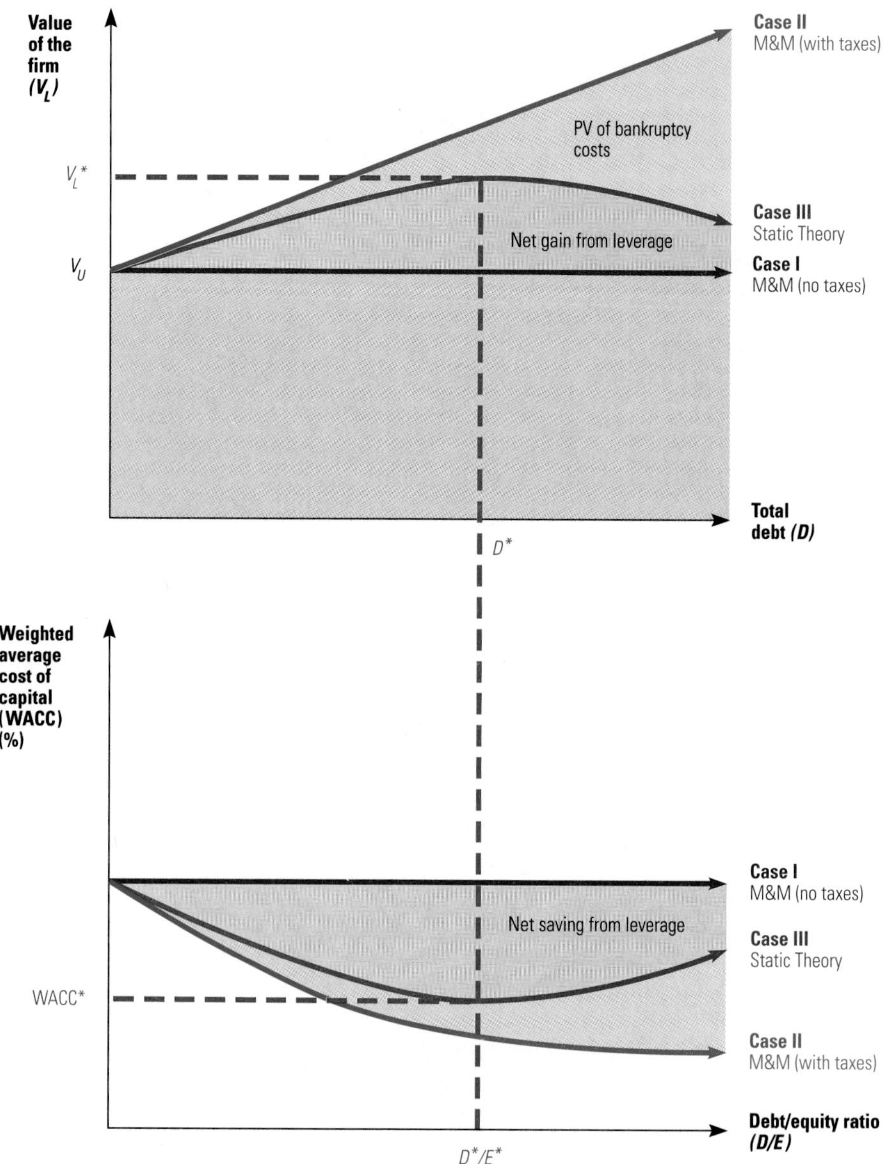

Case I
With no taxes or bankruptcy costs, the value of the firm and its weighted average cost of capital are not affected by capital structures.

Case II
With corporate taxes and no bankruptcy costs, the value of the firm increases and the weighted average cost of capital decreases as the amount of debt goes up.

Case III
With corporate taxes and bankruptcy costs, the value of the firm V_L^* reaches a maximum at D^*, the optimal amount of borrowing. At the same time, the weighted average cost of capital, WACC*, is minimized at D^*/E^*.

In the bottom part of Figure 14.6, notice how the WACC declines as the firm uses more and more debt financing. As the firm increases its financial leverage, the cost of equity does increase, but this increase is more than offset by the tax break associated with debt financing. As a result, the firm's overall cost of capital declines.

To finish our story, we include the impact of bankruptcy or financial distress costs to get Case III. As shown in the top part of Figure 14.6, the value of the firm will not be as large as we previously indicated. The reason is that the firm's value is reduced by the present value of the potential future bankruptcy costs. These costs grow as the firm borrows more and more, and they eventually overwhelm the tax advantage of debt financing. The optimal capital structure occurs at D^*, the point at which the tax saving from an additional dollar in debt financing is exactly balanced by the increased bankruptcy costs associated with the additional borrowing. This is the essence of the static theory of capital structure.

The bottom part of Figure 14.6 presents the optimal capital structure in terms of the cost of capital. Corresponding to D^*, the optimal debt level, is the optimal debt to equity ratio, D^*/E^*. At this level of debt financing, the lowest possible weighted average cost of capital, WACC*, occurs.

Capital Structure: Some Managerial Recommendations

The static model that we described is not capable of identifying a precise optimal capital structure, but it does point out two of the more relevant factors: taxes and financial distress. We can draw some limited conclusions concerning these.

Concept Q Answer 14.6b

Taxes First of all, the tax benefit from leverage is obviously only important to firms that are in a tax-paying position. Firms with substantial accumulated losses will get little value from the interest tax shield. Furthermore, firms that have substantial tax shields from other sources, such as depreciation, will get less benefit from leverage.

Also, not all firms have the same tax rate. The higher the tax rate, the greater the incentive to borrow.

Financial Distress Firms with a greater risk of experiencing financial distress will borrow less than firms with a lower risk of financial distress. For example, all other things being equal, the greater the volatility in EBIT, the less a firm should borrow.

In addition, financial distress is more costly for some firms than others. The costs of financial distress depend primarily on the firm's assets. In particular, financial distress costs will be determined by how easily ownership to those assets can be transferred.

International Note: IM includes discussion of the relevance of the static model for multinational firms.

For example, a firm with mostly tangible assets that can be sold without great loss in value will have an incentive to borrow more. For firms that rely heavily on intangibles, such as employee talent or growth opportunities, debt will be less attractive since these assets effectively cannot be sold.

CONCEPT QUESTIONS

14.6a Can you describe the trade-off that defines the static theory of capital structure?

14.6b What are the important factors in making capital structure decisions?

14.7 OBSERVED CAPITAL STRUCTURES

No two firms have identical capital structures. Nonetheless, there are some regular elements that we see when we start looking at actual capital structures. We discuss a few of these next.

Concept Q Answer 14.7a

The most striking thing we observe about capital structures, particularly in the United States, is that most corporations seem to have relatively low debt/equity ratios. In fact, most corporations use less debt than equity financing. This is true even though many of these corporations pay substantial taxes.

Given this, it is clear that corporations have not issued debt up to the point that tax shelters have been completely used up, and we conclude that there must be limits to the amount of debt corporations can issue.

Concept Q Answer 14.7b

A second regularity is apparent when we compare capital structures across industries. Table 14.5 shows debt/equity ratios in Japan and the United States by industry. As shown, there is wide variation in industry debt/equity ratios. For example, using market values, firms in the steel industry have a debt/equity ratio of 1.665 compared to .079 for firms in the pharmaceutical industry. In fact, despite what has appeared in the popular press, U.S. and Japanese companies have very similar capital structures on an industry-by-industry basis.

TABLE 14.5 Debt/equity ratios for different industries in the United States and Japan in 1983

	Net Debt to:		Number of Companies in the Sample		
Industry	Book Value Equity	Market Value Equity	Japan	United States	Total
Nonferrous metals	3.791	1.106	11	13	24
General chemicals	2.945	1.256	21	16	37
Steel	1.973	1.665	35	35	70
Paper	1.732	1.364	16	25	41
Paint	1.548	0.614	7	5	12
Petroleum refining	1.548	1.117	6	33	39
Audio equipment	1.539	0.631	7	10	17
Textiles	1.405	1.296	29	23	52
Cement	1.298	1.366	6	10	16
Glass	1.213	1.087	5	8	13
Soaps and detergents	1.143	0.683	6	8	14
Apparel	1.021	0.951	14	41	55
Tires and rubber	1.021	0.835	8	14	22
Motor vehicles	0.922	0.594	9	6	15
Plastics	0.843	0.792	18	25	43
Agricultural machinery	0.836	1.082	5	5	10
Electrical machinery	0.813	0.376	14	12	26
Construction machinery	0.688	0.810	6	12	18
Electronic parts	0.614	0.358	19	34	53
Motor vehicle parts	0.488	0.500	20	16	36
Machine tools	0.472	0.425	10	15	25
Photo equipment	0.468	0.222	7	7	14
Alcoholic beverages	0.427	0.284	8	10	18
Communication equipment	0.356	0.186	15	24	39
Confectionary	0.326	0.286	6	5	11
Pharmaceuticals	0.194	0.079	25	23	48
Household appliances	0.102	0.244	13	13	26

From W. C. Kester, "Capital and Ownership Structure: A Comparison of United States and Japanese Manufacturing Corporations," *Financial Management* 15 (Spring 1986).

Because different industries have different operating characteristics in terms of, for example, EBIT volatility and asset types, there does appear to be some connection between these characteristics and capital structure. Our story involving tax savings and financial distress costs is undoubtedly part of the reason, but, to date, there is no fully satisfactory theory that explains these regularities.

CONCEPT QUESTIONS

14.7a Do U.S. corporations rely heavily on debt financing?

14.7b What regularities do we observe in capital structures?

14.8 A QUICK LOOK AT THE BANKRUPTCY PROCESS

As we have discussed, one of the consequences of using debt is the possibility of financial distress, which can be defined in several ways:

1. *Business failure.* This is a term usually used to refer to a situation where a business has terminated with a loss to creditors, but even an all-equity firm can fail.
2. *Legal bankruptcy.* Firms or creditors bring petitions to a federal court for bankruptcy. **Bankruptcy** is a legal proceeding for liquidating or reorganizing a business.
3. *Technical insolvency.* Technical insolvency occurs when a firm defaults on a legal obligation; for example, it does not pay a bill.
4. *Accounting insolvency.* Firms with negative net worth are insolvent on the books. This happens when the total book liabilities exceed the book value of the total assets.

bankruptcy
A legal proceeding for liquidating or reorganizing a business. Also, the transfer of some or all of a firm's assets to its creditors.

Concept Q Answer 14.8a

For future reference, we will define *bankruptcy* as the transfer of some or all of the firm's assets to creditors. We now very briefly discuss some of the terms and more relevant issues associated with bankruptcy and financial distress.

Liquidation and Reorganization

Firms that cannot or choose not to make contractually required payments to creditors have two basic options: liquidation or reorganization. **Liquidation** means termination of the firm as a going concern, and it involves selling off the assets of the firm. The proceeds, net of selling costs, are distributed to creditors in order of established priority. **Reorganization** is the option of keeping the firm a going concern; it often involves issuing new securities to replace old securities. Liquidation or reorganization is the result of a bankruptcy proceeding. Which occurs depends on whether the firm is worth more "dead or alive."

liquidation
Termination of the firm as a going concern.

reorganization
Financial restructuring of a failing firm to attempt to continue operations as a going concern.

Bankruptcy Liquidation Chapter 7 of the Federal Bankruptcy Reform Act of 1978 deals with "straight" liquidation. The following sequence of events is typical:

1. A petition is filed in a federal court. Corporations may file a voluntary petition, or involuntary petitions may be filed against the corporation by several of its creditors.

Concept Q Answer 14.8b

Trans. 14.13 Bankruptcy Liquidation (Supplemental)

2. A trustee-in-bankruptcy is elected by the creditors to take over the assets of the debtor corporation. The trustee will attempt to liquidate the assets.
3. When the assets are liquidated, after payment of the bankruptcy administration costs, the proceeds are distributed among the creditors.
4. If any proceeds remain, after expenses and payments to creditors, they are distributed to the shareholders.

Trans. 14.14
Absolute Priority Rule (Supplemental)

The distribution of the proceeds of the liquidation occurs according to the following priority:

1. Administrative expenses associated with the bankruptcy.
2. Other expenses arising after the filing of an involuntary bankruptcy petition but before the appointment of a trustee.
3. Wages, salaries, and commissions.
4. Contributions to employee benefit plans.
5. Consumer claims.
6. Government tax claims.
7. Unsecured creditors.
8. Preferred stockholders.
9. Common stockholders.

absolute priority rule (APR) Rule establishing priority of claims in liquidation.

This priority rule in liquidation is called the **absolute priority rule (APR).** The higher a claim is on this list, the more likely it is to be paid. In many of these categories, there are various limitations and qualifications that we omit for the sake of brevity.

Two qualifications to this list are in order. The first concerns secured creditors. Such creditors are entitled to the proceeds from the sale of the security and are outside this ordering. However, if the secured property is liquidated and provides cash insufficient to cover the amount owed, the secured creditors join with unsecured creditors in dividing the remaining liquidated value. In contrast, if the secured property is liquidated for proceeds greater than the secured claim, the net proceeds are used to pay unsecured creditors and others. The second qualification to the APR is that, in reality, courts have a great deal of freedom in deciding what actually happens and who actually gets what in the event of bankruptcy, and, as a result, the APR is not always followed.

Trans. 14.15
Bankruptcy Reorganization (Supplemental)

Concept Q Answer 14.8b

Lecture Tip: A wonderful example of the reorganization process is found in the continuing saga of TransWorld Airlines in the post-Icahn era. IM 14.8 provides a brief history of TWA's recent travails in the bankruptcy process.

Bankruptcy Reorganization Corporate reorganization takes place under Chapter 11 of the Federal Bankruptcy Reform Act of 1978. The general objective of a proceeding under Chapter 11 is to plan to restructure the corporation with some provision for repayment of creditors. A typical sequence of events follows:

1. A voluntary petition can be filed by the corporation, or an involuntary petition can be filed by creditors.
2. A federal judge either approves or denies the petition. If the petition is approved, a time for filing proofs of claims is set.
3. In most cases, the corporation (the "debtor in possession") continues to run the business.
4. The corporation is required to submit a reorganization plan.
5. Creditors and shareholders are divided into classes. A class of creditors accepts the plan if a majority of the class agrees to the plan.
6. After acceptance by creditors, the plan is confirmed by the court.

Principles in Action

What Else Would You Expect from a Convenience Store?

In October 1990, Southland Corporation (better known as 7-Eleven) filed for Chapter 11 reorganization under the U. S. bankruptcy code. At the time of the filing, the company had in excess of $5 billion in liabilities including five classes of bonds plus bank loans. A firm with a financial structure this complex could reasonably expect to spend a year or longer in bankruptcy. But, true to its convenience store format where customers can get in and out fast, Southland did not stay in bankruptcy long. Less than four months later, the company emerged from Chapter 11 reorganized.

Firms typically file bankruptcy to seek protection from their creditors, essentially admitting that they cannot meet their financial obligations as presently structured. Once in bankruptcy, the firm attempts to reorganize its financial picture so that it can survive. A key to this process is that the creditors ultimately must give their approval of the restructuring plan. The time a firm spends in Chapter 11 depends on many things, but usually depends most heavily on the time it takes to get creditors to agree to a plan of reorganization.

Southland Corp. was able to expedite its bankruptcy by filing a presolicited, or "prepackaged" bankruptcy, often called a "prepack." The idea is simple. Prior to filing bankruptcy, the firm approaches its creditors with a plan for reorganization. The two sides negotiate a settlement and agree on the details of how the firm's finances will be restructured in bankruptcy. Then, the firm puts together the necessary paperwork for the bankruptcy court before filing for bankruptcy. A filing is a prepack if the firm essentially walks into court, files for bankruptcy, and, at the same time, files a reorganization plan complete with documentation of the approval of its creditors.

The key to the prepackaged reorganization process is that both sides have something to gain and something to lose. For the creditors, it is often the case that the firm is either in default on some of their obligations, or they are heading towards it. If bankruptcy is imminent, it may make sense for the creditors to expedite the process even though they are likely to take a financial loss in the restructuring. The faster the firm is reorganized, the faster it can concentrate on the business of making money to repay its obligations.

For the firm, operating in bankruptcy can be a difficult process. The bankruptcy court typically has a great deal of oversight over the firm's day-to-day operations, and the time it takes to put together a reorganization plan to emerge from bankruptcy can be a tremendous drain on management time, time better spent making the firm profitable again. Also, news that a firm is in bankruptcy can make skittish customers turn to competitors, endangering the future health of the firm. A prepack can't completely eliminate these problems, but, by speeding up the bankruptcy process, it can reduce the headaches involved.

Source: "Bankruptcy: No Longer a Dirty Word," *Management Review*, April 1992, pp. 22–27.

7. Payments in cash, property, and securities are made to creditors and shareholders. The plan may provide for the issuance of new securities.

The corporation may wish to allow the old stockholders to retain some participation in the firm. Needless to say, this may involve some protest by the holders of unsecured debt.

So-called prepackaged bankruptcies are a relatively new phenomenon. What happens is that the corporation secures the necessary approval of a bankruptcy plan by a majority of its creditors first, and then it files for bankruptcy. As a result, the company enters bankruptcy and reemerges almost immediately. The accompanying *Principles in Action* box describes one fairly recent prepackaged bankruptcy.

In some cases, the bankruptcy procedure is needed to invoke the "cram down" power of the bankruptcy court. Under certain circumstances, a class of creditors can be forced to accept a bankruptcy plan even if they vote not to approve it, hence the remarkably apt description "cram down."

☆ **Ethics Note:** An interesting development in bankruptcy cases is the use of the "cram-down," whereby bondholders (and other creditors) are forced to accept a less favorable settlement in order to get the reorganization plan approved. Recently, the bankruptcies of R. H. Macy, Interco, and Orion Pictures have all involved threatened cram-downs.

Agreements to Avoid Bankruptcy

When a firm defaults on an obligation, it can avoid bankruptcy. Because the legal process of bankruptcy can be lengthy and expensive, it is often in everyone's best interest to devise a "work out" that avoids a bankruptcy filing. Much of the time, creditors can work with the management of a company that has defaulted on a loan contract. Voluntary arrangements to restructure the company's debt can be and often are made. This may involve *extension,* which postpones the date of payment, or *composition,* which involves a reduced payment.

CONCEPT QUESTIONS

14.8a What is bankruptcy?

14.8b What is the difference between liquidation and reorganization?

14.9 SUMMARY AND CONCLUSIONS

The ideal mixture of debt and equity for a firm—its optimal capital structure—is the one that maximizes the value of the firm and minimizes the overall cost of capital. If we ignore taxes, financial distress costs, and any other imperfections, we find that there is no ideal mixture. Under these circumstances, the firm's capital structure is simply irrelevant.

If we consider the effect of corporate taxes, we find that capital structure matters a great deal. This conclusion is based on the fact that interest is tax deductible and thus generates a valuable tax shield. Unfortunately, we also find that the optimal capital structure is 100 percent debt, which is not something we observe for healthy firms.

We next introduced costs associated with bankruptcy, or, more generally, financial distress. These costs reduce the attractiveness of debt financing. We concluded that an optimal capital structure exists when the net tax saving from an additional dollar in interest just equals the increase in expected financial distress costs. This is the essence of the static theory of capital structure.

When we examine actual capital structures, we find two regularities. First, firms in the United States typically do not use great amounts of debt, but they pay substantial taxes. This suggests that there is a limit to the use of debt financing to generate tax shields. Second, firms in similar industries tend to have similar capital structures, suggesting that the nature of their assets and operations is an important determinant of capital structure.

Chapter Review Problems and Self-Test

14.1 **EBIT and EPS** Suppose the GNR Corporation has decided in favor of a capital restructuring that involves increasing its existing $5 million in debt to $25 million. The interest rate on the debt is 12 percent and is not expected to change. The firm currently has 1 million shares outstanding, and the price per share is $40. If the restructuring is expected to increase the ROE, what is the minimum level for EBIT that GNR's management must be expecting? Ignore taxes in your answer.

14.2 **M&M Proposition II (no taxes)** The Pro Bono Corporation has a WACC of 20 percent. Its cost of debt is 12 percent. If Pro Bono's debt/equity ratio is 2, what is its cost of equity capital? Ignore taxes in your answer.

14.3 **M&M Proposition I (with corporate taxes)** Suppose TransGlobal Co. currently has no debt and its equity is worth $20,000. If the corporate tax rate is 30 percent, what will the value of the firm be if TransGlobal borrows $6,000 and uses the proceeds to buy up stock?

Answers to Self-Test Problems

14.1 To answer, we can calculate the break-even EBIT. At any EBIT above this, the increased financial leverage will increase EPS. Under the old capital structure, the interest bill is $5 million × .12 = $600,000. There are 1 million shares of stock, so, ignoring taxes, EPS is (EBIT − $600,000)/1 million.

Under the new capital structure, the interest expense will be $25 million × .12 = $3 million. Furthermore, the debt rises by $20 million. This amount is sufficient to repurchase $20 million/$40 = 500,000 shares of stock, leaving 500,000 outstanding. EPS is thus (EBIT − $3 million)/500,000.

Now that we know how to calculate EPS under both scenarios, we set them equal to each other and solve for the break-even EBIT:

$$\begin{aligned}(\text{EBIT} - \$600{,}000)/1 \text{ million} &= (\text{EBIT} - \$3 \text{ million})/500{,}000\\ (\text{EBIT} - \$600{,}000) &= 2 \times (\text{EBIT} - \$3 \text{ million})\\ \text{EBIT} &= \$5{,}400{,}000\end{aligned}$$

Check that, in either case, EPS is $4.80 when EBIT is $5.4 million.

14.2 According to M&M Proposition II (no taxes), the cost of equity is:

$$\begin{aligned}R_E &= R_A + (R_A - R_D) \times (D/E)\\ &= 20\% + (20\% - 12\%) \times 2\\ &= 36\%\end{aligned}$$

14.3 After the debt issue, TransGlobal will be worth the original $20,000 plus the present value of the tax shield. According to M&M Proposition I with taxes, the present value of the tax shield is $T_C \times D$, or .30 × $6,000 = $1,800, so the firm is worth $20,000 + 1,800 = $21,800.

Questions and Problems

Basic (Questions 1–13)

1. **EBIT and Leverage** Debreu, Inc., has no debt outstanding and a total market value of $60,000. Earnings before interest and taxes (EBIT) are projected to be $5,000 if economic conditions are normal. If there is strong expansion in the economy, then EBIT will be 40 percent higher. If there is a recession, then EBIT will be 50 percent lower. Debreu is considering a $24,000 debt issue with a 10 percent interest rate. The proceeds will be used to buy up shares of stock. There are currently 1,000 shares outstanding. Ignore taxes for this problem.

a. EPS = $2.50; $5.00; $7.50
b. EPS = $0.17; $4.33; $7.67
Trans. 14.16

a. Calculate earnings per share (EPS) under each of the three economic scenarios before any debt is issued. Also, calculate the percentage changes in EPS when the economy expands or enters a recession.
b. Repeat part (*a*) assuming that Debreu goes through with recapitalization. What do you observe?

a. I: EPS = $3.00
II: EPS = $1.80
b. I: EPS = $7.00
II: EPS = $7.80
c. $1.62 M; $5.40

2. **Break-Even EBIT** Schwietzer Corporation is comparing two different capital structures, an all-equity plan (Plan I) and a levered plan (Plan II). Under Plan I, Schwietzer would have 300,000 shares of stock outstanding. Under Plan II, there would be 200,000 shares of stock outstanding and $6 million in debt outstanding. The interest rate on the debt is 9 percent and there are no taxes.
a. If EBIT is $900,000, which plan will result in the higher EPS?
b. If EBIT is $2.1 million, which plan will result in the higher EPS?
c. What is the break-even EBIT? What is EPS at this level of EBIT?

Price = $60 per share
I: Value = $18 M
II: Value = $18 M

3. **M&M and Stock Value** In Problem 2, use M&M Proposition I to find the price per share of equity under each of the two proposed plans. What is the value of the firm?

a. I: EPS = $2.40
II: EPS = $2.47
III: EPS = $2.50
b. I: $2,800
II: $2,800

4. **Break-Even EBIT and Leverage** The Milhone Co. is comparing two different capital structures. Plan I would result in 750 shares of stock and $8,750 in debt. Plan II would result in 900 shares of stock and $3,500 in debt. The interest rate on the debt is 8 percent.
a. Ignoring taxes, compare both of these plans to an all-equity plan assuming that EBIT will be $2,500. The all-equity plan would result in 1,000 shares of stock outstanding. Which of the three plans has the highest EPS? The lowest?
b. In part (*a*), what are the break-even levels of EBIT for each plan compared to an all-equity plan? Is one higher than the other? Why?
c. Ignoring taxes, when will EPS be identical for Plans I and II?

Price = $35 per share

5. **Leverage and Stock Value** Ignoring taxes in Problem 4, what is the price per share of equity under Plan I? Plan II? What principle is illustrated by your answers?

a. $200
b. $2.86

6. **Homemade Leverage** Buckner and Durham, Inc., a prominent waste management firm, is debating whether to convert its all-equity capital structure to one that is 30 percent debt. Currently, there are 400 shares outstanding and the price per share is $75. EBIT is expected to remain at $1,000 per year forever. The interest rate on new debt is 11 percent, and there are no taxes.
a. Mr. Smith, a shareholder of the firm, owns 80 shares of stock. What is his cash flow under the current capital structure, assuming the firm has a dividend payout rate of 100 percent?
b. What will Mr. Smith's cash flow be under the proposed capital structure of the firm? Assume that he keeps all 80 of his shares.
c. Suppose Buckner and Durham does convert, but Mr. Smith prefers the current all-equity capital structure. Show how he could unlever his shares of stock to recreate the original capital structure.
d. Using your answer in part (*c*), explain why Buckner and Durham's choice of capital structure is irrelevant.

7. **Business and Financial Risk** Explain what is meant by business and financial risk. Suppose Firm A has greater business risk than Firm B. Is it true that Firm A also has a higher cost of equity capital? Explain.

8. **Interest Tax Shield** Dibvig Co. has a 40 percent tax rate. Its total interest payment for the year just ended was $16 million. What is the interest tax shield? How do you interpret this amount? $6.4 million

9. **M&M** Corrado Corporation has no debt. Its current total value is $80 million. Ignoring taxes, what will Corrado's value be if it sells $40 million in debt? Suppose now that Corrado's tax rate is 35 percent. What will its overall value be if it sells $40 million in debt? $80 million; $94 million

10. **M&M** In the previous question, what is the debt/equity ratio in both cases? 1.0; 0.74

11. **M&M** Karry-Back Co. has no debt. Its cost of capital is 12 percent. Suppose Karry-Back converts to a debt/equity ratio of 1.0. The interest rate on the debt is 8 percent. Ignoring taxes, what is its new cost of equity? What is its new WACC? 16%, 12% **Trans. 14.17**

12. **M&M** Angel, Inc., has no debt. Its current value is $40 million. If Angel faces a 40 percent tax rate, how much does Angel have to borrow to create a total debt ratio (total debt divided by total value) of 0.50? $25 million

13. **Risk and Capital Costs** How would you answer in the following debate?

Q: Isn't it true that the riskiness of a firm's equity will rise if it increases its use of debt financing?

A: Yes, that's the essence of M&M Proposition II.

Q: And isn't it true that, as a firm increases its use of borrowing, the likelihood of default increases, thereby increasing the risk of the firm's debt?

A: Yes.

Q: In other words, increased borrowing increases the risk of the equity *and* the debt?

A: That's right.

Q: Well, given that the firm only uses debt and equity financing, and given that the risks of both are increased by increased borrowing, does it not follow that increasing debt increases the overall risk of the firm and therefore decreases the value of the firm?

A: ??

Chapter Fifteen

Dividends and Dividend Policy

After studying this chapter, you should have a good understanding of:

. . .

Dividend types and how dividends are paid.

. . .

The issues surrounding the dividend policy decision.

. . .

The difference between cash and stock dividends.

. . .

Why share repurchases are an alternative to dividends.

Trans. 15.1 Chapter Outline

Dividend policy is an important subject in corporate finance, and dividends are a major cash outlay for many corporations. At first glance, it may seem obvious that a firm would always want to give as much as possible back to its shareholders by paying dividends. It might seem equally obvious, however, that a firm can always invest the money for its shareholders instead of paying it out. The heart of the dividend policy question is just this: Should the firm pay out money to its shareholders, or should the firm take that money and invest it for its shareholders?

It may seem surprising, but much research and economic logic suggest that dividend policy doesn't matter. In fact, it turns out that the dividend policy issue is much like the capital structure question. The important elements are not difficult to identify, but the interactions between those elements are complex and no easy answer exists.

Lecture Tip: Some would suggest that the question of dividend policy relevance is another "GUMF"—great unsolved mystery of finance.

Dividend policy is controversial. Many implausible reasons are given for why dividend policy might be important, and many of the claims made about dividend policy are economically illogical. Even so, in the real world of corporate finance, determining the most appropriate dividend policy is considered an important issue. It could be that financial managers who worry about dividend policy are wasting time, but it could also be true that we are missing something important in our discussions.

In part, all discussions of dividends are plagued by the "two-handed lawyer" problem. President Truman, while discussing the legal implications of a possible presidential decision, asked his staff to set up a meeting with a lawyer. Supposedly Mr. Truman said, "But I don't want one of those two-handed lawyers." When asked what a two-handed lawyer was, he replied, "You know, a lawyer who says, 'On the one hand I recommend you do so and so because of the following reasons, but on the other hand I recommend that you don't do it because of these other reasons.' "

Unfortunately, any sensible treatment of dividend policy will appear to be written by a two-handed lawyer (or, in fairness, several two-handed financial economists). On the one hand, there are many good reasons for corporations to pay high dividends, but, on the other hand, there are also many good reasons to pay low dividends.

We will cover three broad topics that relate to dividends and dividend policy in this chapter. First, we describe the various kinds of dividends and how dividends are paid. Second, we consider an idealized case in which dividend policy doesn't matter. We then discuss the limitations of this case and present some real-world arguments for both high- and low-dividend payouts. Finally, we conclude the chapter by looking at some strategies that corporations might employ to implement a dividend policy, and we discuss share repurchases as an alternative to dividends.

15.1 CASH DIVIDENDS AND DIVIDEND PAYMENT

The term **dividend** usually refers to cash paid out of earnings. If a payment is made from sources other than current or accumulated retained earnings, the term **distribution** rather than dividend is used. However, it is acceptable to refer to a distribution from earnings as a dividend and a distribution from capital as a liquidating dividend. More generally, any direct payment by the corporation to the shareholders may be considered a dividend or a part of dividend policy.

dividend
Payment made out of a firm's earnings to its owners, either in the form of cash or stock.

distribution
Payment made by a firm to its owners from sources other than current or accumulated retained earnings.

Problems 3, 4

Concept Q Answer 15.1a

Trans. 15.2 Dividend Types (Supplemental)

Dividends come in several different forms. The basic types of cash dividends are:

1. Regular cash dividends.
2. Extra dividends.
3. Special dividends.
4. Liquidating dividends.

Later in the chapter, we discuss dividends paid in stock instead of cash, and we also consider an alternative to cash dividends, stock repurchase.

Cash Dividends

The most common type of dividend is a cash dividend. Commonly, public companies pay **regular cash dividends** four times a year. As the name suggests, these are cash payments made directly to shareholders, and they are made in the regular course of business. In other words, management sees nothing unusual about the dividend and no reason why it won't be continued.

regular cash dividend
Cash payment made by a firm to its owners in the normal course of business, usually made four times a year.

Lecture Tip: See IM for tips on teaching about various types of dividend payments.

Sometimes firms will pay a regular cash dividend and an *extra cash dividend.* By calling part of the payment "extra," management is indicating that it may or may not be repeated in the future. A *special dividend* is similar, but the name usually indicates that the dividend is viewed as a truly unusual or one-time event and won't be repeated. Finally, a *liquidating dividend* usually means that some or all of the business has been liquidated, that is, sold off.

However it is labeled, a cash dividend payment reduces corporate cash and retained earnings, except in the case of a liquidating dividend (where paid-in capital may be reduced).

Standard Method of Cash Dividend Payment

Lecture Tip: This is a crucial point: Prior to the declaration, the board is under no legal obligation to pay a cash dividend; hence, its size is uncertain. After the declaration, the uncertainty is resolved because the dividend is now a legal liability of the firm.

The decision to pay a dividend rests in the hands of the board of directors of the corporation. When a dividend has been declared, it becomes a liability of the firm and cannot be rescinded easily. Sometime after it has been declared, a dividend is distributed to all shareholders as of some specific date.

Commonly, the amount of the cash dividend is expressed in terms of the dollars per share (*dividends per share*). As we have seen in other chapters, it is also expressed as a percentage of the market price (the *dividend yield*) or as a percentage of net income or earnings per share (the *dividend payout*).

Dividend Payment: A Chronology

Concept Q Answer 15.1b

The mechanics of a cash dividend payment can be illustrated by the example in Figure 15.1 and the following description:

declaration date
Date on which the board of directors passes a resolution to pay a dividend.

ex-dividend date
Date two business days before the date of record, establishing those individuals entitled to a dividend.

Lecture Tip: The ex-dividend date went from 4 business days prior to the record day to 2 in June 1995 as a result of the "T + 3" change in settlement requirements.

1. **Declaration date.** On January 15, the board of directors passes a resolution to pay a dividend of $1 per share on February 16 to all holders of record as of January 30.
2. **Ex-dividend date.** To make sure that dividend checks go to the right people, brokerage firms and stock exchanges establish an *ex-dividend date.* This date is two business days before the date of record (discussed next). If you buy the stock before this date, then you are entitled to the dividend. If you buy on this date or after, then the previous owner will get it.

   In Figure 15.1, Wednesday, January 28, is the ex-dividend date. Before this date, the stock is said to trade "with dividend" or "cum dividend." Afterwards, the stock trades "ex dividend."

FIGURE 15.1
Example of procedure for dividend payment

Trans. 15.3

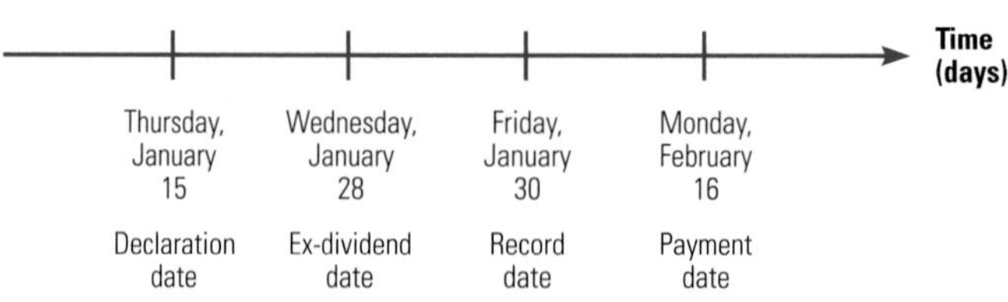

1. *Declaration date:* The board of directors declares a payment of dividends.
2. *Ex-dividend date:* A share of stock goes ex dividend on the date the seller is entitled to keep the dividend; under NYSE rules, shares are traded ex dividend on and after the second business day before the record date.
3. *Record date:* The declared dividends are distributable to shareholders of record on a specific date.
4. *Payment date:* The dividend checks are mailed to shareholders of record.

The ex-dividend date convention removes any ambiguity about who is entitled to the dividend. Since the dividend is valuable, the stock price will be affected when it goes "ex." We examine this effect below.

3. **Date of record.** Based on its records, the corporation prepares a list on January 30 of all individuals believed to be stockholders. These are the *holders of record* and January 30 is the *date of record* (or record date). The word "believed" is important here. If you buy the stock just before this date, the corporation's records may not reflect that fact because of mailing or other delays. Without some modification, some of the dividend checks will get mailed to the wrong people. This is the reason for the ex-dividend day convention.

date of record
Date on which holders of record are designated to receive a dividend.

4. **Date of payment.** The dividend checks are mailed on February 16.

date of payment
Date that the dividend checks are mailed.

More on the Ex-Dividend Date

Concept Q Answer 15.1c

The ex-dividend date is important and is a common source of confusion. We examine what happens to the stock when it goes ex, meaning that the ex-dividend date arrives. To illustrate, suppose we have a stock that sells for $10 per share. The board of directors declares a dividend of $1 per share, and the record date is Tuesday, June 12. Based on our discussion above, we know that the ex date will be two business (not calendar) days earlier on Friday, June 8.

If you buy the stock on Thursday, June 7, right as the market closes, you'll get the $1 dividend because the stock is trading cum dividend. If you wait and buy it right as the market opens on Friday, you won't get the $1 dividend. What will happen to the value of the stock overnight?

Lecture Tip: See IM 15.1 for more on the ex-dividend day behavior of stock prices.

If you think about it, the stock is obviously worth about $1 less on Friday morning, so its price will drop by this amount between close of business on Thursday and the Friday opening. In general, we expect that the value of a share of stock will go down by about the dividend amount when the stock goes ex dividend. The key word here is *about.* Since dividends are taxed, the actual price drop might be closer to some measure of the aftertax value of the dividend. Determining this value is complicated because of the different tax rates and tax rules that apply for different buyers.

International Note: The less-than-100 percent price drop in dividend-paying stocks was exploited by Japanese insurance companies in the late 1980s. Dividend recapture strategies are described in IM 15.1.

The series of events described here is illustrated in Figure 15.2.

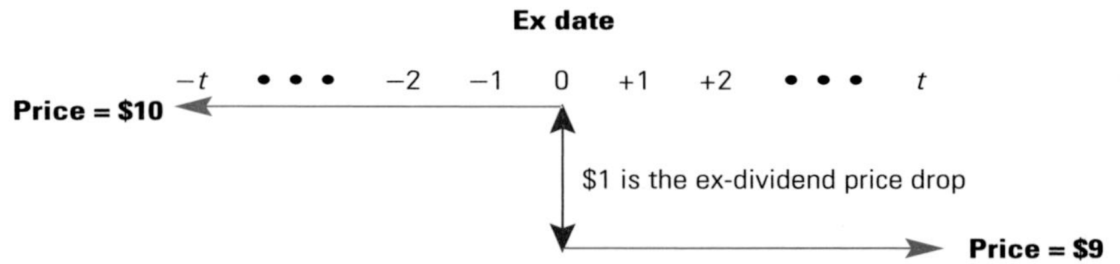

The stock price will fall by the amount of the dividend on the ex date (time 0). If the dividend is $1 per share, the price will be equal to $10 − $1 = $9 on the ex date:

Before ex date (time −1) dividend = 0	Price = $10
Ex-date (time 0) dividend = $1	Price = $9

FIGURE 15.2
Price behavior around ex-dividend date for a $1 cash dividend

EXAMPLE 15.1 "Ex" Marks the Day

The board of directors of Divided Airlines has declared a dividend of $2.50 per share payable on Tuesday, May 30, to shareholders of record as of Tuesday, May 9. Cal Icon buys 100 shares of Divided on Tuesday, May 2, for $150 per share. What is the ex date? Describe the events that will occur with regard to the cash dividend and the stock price.

The ex date is two business days before the date of record, Tuesday, May 9, so the stock will go ex on Friday, May 5. Cal buys the stock on Tuesday, May 2, so Cal has purchased the stock cum dividend. In other words, Cal will get $2.50 × 100 = $250 in dividends. The check will be mailed on Tuesday, May 30. When the stock does go ex on Friday, its value will drop overnight by about $2.50 per share. • • •

CONCEPT QUESTIONS

15.1a What are the different types of cash dividends?

15.1b What are the mechanics of the cash dividend payment?

15.1c How should the price of a stock change when it goes ex dividend?

15.2 DOES DIVIDEND POLICY MATTER?

Lecture Tip: See IM 15.2 for a comment on the "all else equal" nature of the irrelevance argument.

To decide whether or not dividend policy matters, we first have to define what we mean by dividend *policy.* All other things being the same, of course dividends matter. Dividends are paid in cash, and cash is something that everybody likes. The question we will be discussing here is whether the firm should pay out cash now or invest the cash and pay it out later. Dividend policy, therefore, is the time pattern of dividend payout. In particular, should the firm pay out a large percentage of its earnings now or a small (or even zero) percentage? This is the dividend policy question.

An Illustration of the Irrelevance of Dividend Policy

A powerful argument can be made that dividend policy does not matter. We illustrate this by considering the simple case of Wharton Corporation. Wharton is an all-equity firm that has existed for 10 years. The current financial managers plan to dissolve the firm in two years. The total cash flows the firm will generate, including the proceeds from liquidation, are $10,000 in each of the next two years.

Trans. 15.4 Does Dividend Policy Matter? (Supplemental)

Current Policy: Dividends Set Equal to Cash Flow At the present time, dividends at each date are set equal to the cash flow of $10,000. There are 100 shares outstanding, so the dividend per share will be $100. In Chapter 7, we showed that the value of the stock is equal to the present value of the future dividends. Assuming a 10 percent required return, the value of a share of stock today, P_0, is:

$$P_0 = \frac{D_1}{(1 + R)^1} + \frac{D_2}{(1 + R)^2}$$

$$= \frac{\$100}{1.10} + \frac{\$100}{1.10^2} = \$173.55$$

The firm as a whole is thus worth 100 × $173.55 = $17,355.

Several members of the board of Wharton have expressed dissatisfaction with the current dividend policy and have asked you to analyze an alternative policy.

Alternative Policy: Initial Dividend Is Greater than Cash Flow Another policy is for the firm to pay a dividend of $110 per share on the first date (Date 1), which is, of course, a total dividend of $11,000. Because the cash flow is only $10,000, an extra $1,000 must somehow be raised. One way to do it is to issue $1,000 of bonds or stock at Date 1. Assume that stock is issued. The new stockholders will desire enough cash flow at Date 2 so that they earn the required 10 percent return on their Date 1 investment.

What is the value of the firm with this new dividend policy? The new stockholders invest $1,000. They require a 10 percent return, so they will demand $1,000 × 1.10 = $1,100 of the Date 2 cash flow, leaving only $8,900 to the old stockholders. The dividends to the old stockholders will be:

	Date 1	Date 2
Aggregate dividends to old stockholders	$11,000	$8,900
Dividends per share	110	89

The present value of the dividends per share is therefore:

$$P_0 = \frac{\$110}{1.10} + \frac{\$89}{1.10^2} = \$173.55$$

This is the same value we had before.

The value of the stock is not affected by this switch in dividend policy even though we had to sell some new stock just to finance the dividend. In fact, no matter what pattern of dividend payout the firm chooses, the value of the stock will always be the same in this example. In other words, for the Wharton Corporation, dividend policy makes no difference. The reason is simple: Any increase in a dividend at some point in time is exactly offset by a decrease somewhere else, so the net effect, once we account for time value, is zero.

Lecture Tip: IM 15.2 provides an alternative approach using the constant growth model to illustrate this point.

A Test Our discussion to this point can be summarized by considering the following true/false test questions:

1. True or false: Dividends are irrelevant.
2. True or false: Dividend policy is irrelevant.

The first statement is surely false, and the reason follows from common sense. Clearly, investors prefer higher dividends to lower dividends at any single date if the dividend level is held constant at every other date. To be more precise regarding the first question, if the dividend per share at a given date is raised while the dividend per share at every other date is held constant, the stock price will rise. The reason is that the present value of the future dividends must go up if this occurs. This action can be accomplished by management decisions that improve productivity, increase tax savings, strengthen product marketing, or otherwise improve cash flow.

The second statement is true, at least in the simple case we have been examining. Dividend policy by itself cannot raise the dividend at one date while keeping it the same at all other dates. Rather, dividend policy merely establishes the trade-off between dividends at one date and dividends at another date. Once we allow for time value, the present value of the dividend stream is unchanged. Thus, in this simple world, dividend policy does not matter, because managers choosing either to raise or to lower the current dividend do not affect the current value of their firm. However, we have ignored several real-world factors that might lead us to change our minds; we pursue some of these in subsequent sections.

Lecture Tip: Some like to preface the following discussion with the apocryphal story about Harry Truman's disdain for two-handed lawyers. "They say, on the one hand, X is true; on the other hand, Y is true." Which hand do you believe?

Some Real-World Factors Favoring a Low Payout

The example we used to illustrate the irrelevance of dividend policy ignored taxes and flotation costs. We will now see that these factors might lead us to prefer a low dividend payout.

Trans. 15.5 Dividends and the Real World (Supplemental)

Ethics Note: The IM contains suggestions for generating class discussion on preferential treatment of capital gains income.

Taxes U.S. tax laws are complex, and they affect dividend policy in a number of ways. The key tax feature has to do with the taxation of dividend income and capital gains. For individual shareholders, *effective* tax rates on dividend income are higher than the tax rates on capital gains. Dividends received are taxed as ordinary income. Capital gains are taxed at somewhat lower rates, and the tax on a capital gain is deferred until the stock is sold. This second aspect of capital gains taxation makes the effective tax rate much lower because the present value of the tax is less.[1]

A firm that adopts a low dividend payout will reinvest the money instead of paying it out. This reinvestment increases the value of the firm and of the equity. All other things being equal, the net effect is that the expected capital gains portion of the return will be higher in the future. So the fact that capital gains are taxed favorably may lead us to prefer this approach.

Lecture Tip: As noted in Chapter 13, selling new stock will also decrease the value of existing stock if investors view the offering as a negative signal.

Flotation Costs In our example illustrating that dividend policy doesn't matter, we saw that the firm could sell some new stock if necessary to pay a dividend. As we mentioned in Chapter 13, selling new stock can be very expensive. If we include flotation costs in our argument, then we will find that the value of the stock decreases if we sell new stock.

More generally, imagine two firms identical in every way except that one pays out a greater percentage of its cash flow in the form of dividends. Since the other firm plows back more, its equity grows faster. If these two firms are to remain identical, then the one with the higher payout will have to periodically sell some stock to catch up. Since this is expensive, a firm might be inclined to have a low payout.

Lecture Tip: See IM 15.2 for reasons supporting bond contract restrictions on the level of dividend payments.

Dividend Restrictions In some cases, a corporation may face restrictions on its ability to pay dividends. For example, as we discussed in Chapter 7, a common feature of a bond indenture is a covenant prohibiting dividend payments above some level. Also, a corporation may be prohibited by state law from paying dividends if the dividend amount exceeds the firm's retained earnings.

[1] In fact, capital gains taxes can sometimes be avoided altogether. Although we do not recommend this particular tax-avoidance strategy, the capital gains tax may be avoided by dying. Your heirs are not considered to have a capital gain, so the tax liability dies when you do. In this instance, you can take it with you.

Some Real-World Factors Favoring a High Payout

In this section, we consider reasons why a firm might pay its shareholders higher dividends even if it means the firm must issue more shares of stock to finance the dividend payments.

Desire for Current Income It has been argued that many individuals desire current income. The classic example is the group of retired people and others living on a fixed income, the proverbial "widows and orphans." It is argued that this group is willing to pay a premium to get a higher dividend yield.

Lecture Tip: Kirk Kerkorian's recent attempts to force Chrysler to increase its dividend payout (under threat of takeover) illustrate an extreme case of (one investor's) desire for current income. A brief history of the struggle appears in IM 15.2.

It is easy to see, however, that this argument is not relevant in our simple case. An individual preferring high current cash flow but holding low-dividend securities could easily sell off shares to provide the necessary funds. Similarly, an individual desiring a low current cash flow but holding high-dividend securities can just reinvest the dividend. Thus, in a world of no transaction costs, a high current dividend policy would be of no value to the stockholder.

The current income argument may have relevance in the real world. Here the sale of low-dividend stocks would involve brokerage fees and other transaction costs. Such a sale might also trigger capital gains taxes. These direct cash expenses could be avoided by an investment in high-dividend securities. In addition, the expenditure of the stockholder's own time when selling securities and the natural (but not necessarily rational) fear of consuming out of principal might further lead many investors to buy high-dividend securities.

Tax and Legal Benefits from High Dividends Earlier we saw that dividends were taxed unfavorably for individual investors. This fact is a powerful argument for a low payout. However, there are a number of other investors who do not receive unfavorable tax treatment from holding high-dividend yield, rather than low-dividend yield, securities.

Corporate Investors A significant tax break on dividends occurs when a corporation owns stock in another corporation. A corporate stockholder receiving either common or preferred dividends is granted a 70 percent (or more) dividend exclusion. Since the 70 percent exclusion does not apply to capital gains, this group is taxed unfavorably on capital gains.

As a result of the dividend exclusion, high-dividend, low-capital-gains stocks may be more appropriate for corporations to hold. In fact, this is why corporations hold a substantial percentage of the outstanding preferred stock in the economy. This tax advantage of dividends also leads some corporations to hold high-yielding stocks instead of long-term bonds because there is no similar tax exclusion of interest payments to corporate bondholders.

Tax-Exempt Investors We have pointed out both the tax advantages and disadvantages of a low-dividend payout. Of course, this discussion is irrelevant to those in zero tax brackets. This group includes some of the largest investors in the economy, such as pension funds, endowment funds, and trust funds.

There are some legal reasons for large institutions to favor high-dividend yields. First, institutions such as pension funds and trust funds are often set up to manage money for the benefit of others. The managers of such institutions have a *fiduciary responsibility* to invest the money prudently. It has been considered imprudent in courts of law to buy stock in companies with no established dividend record.

Lecture Tip: Some promote high payouts as a means of uncertainty resolution—this "bird-in-the-hand" theory of dividend policy is discussed in the IM.

Second, institutions such as university endowment funds and trust funds are frequently prohibited from spending any of the principal. Such institutions might therefore prefer high-dividend yield stocks so they have some ability to spend. Like widows and orphans, this group thus prefers current income. Unlike widows and orphans, this group is very large in terms of the amount of stock owned.

Overall, individual investors (for whatever reason) may have a desire for current income and may thus be willing to pay the dividend tax. In addition, some very large investors such as corporations and tax-free institutions may have a very strong preference for high-dividend payouts.

Clientele Effects: A Resolution of Real-World Factors?

Concept Q Answer 15.2c

In our earlier discussion, we saw that some groups (wealthy individuals, for example) have an incentive to pursue low-payout (or zero-payout) stocks. Other groups (corporations, for example) have an incentive to pursue high-payout stocks. Companies with high payouts will thus attract one group and low-payout companies will attract another.

clientele effect
Argument that stocks attract particular groups based on dividend yield and the resulting tax effects.

Lecture Tip: See IM for another way of communicating the clientele effect.

These different groups are called *clienteles,* and what we have described is a **clientele effect.** The clientele effect argument states that different groups of investors desire different levels of dividends. When a firm chooses a particular dividend policy, the only effect is to attract a particular clientele. If a firm changes its dividend policy, then they just attract a different clientele.

What we are left with is a simple supply and demand argument. Suppose 40 percent of all investors prefer high dividends, but only 20 percent of the firms pay high dividends. Here the high-dividend firms will be in short supply; thus, their stock prices will rise. Consequently, low-dividend firms would find it advantageous to switch policies until 40 percent of all firms have high payouts. At this point, the *dividend market* is in equilibrium. Further changes in dividend policy are pointless because all of the clienteles are satisfied. The dividend policy for any individual firm is now irrelevant.

Lecture Tip: IM 15.2 relates the "leverage clientele" concept to that of dividend clienteles.

To see if you understand the clientele effect, consider the following statement: "In spite of the theoretical argument that dividend policy is irrelevant or that firms should not pay dividends, many investors like high dividends. Because of this fact, a firm can boost its share price by having a higher dividend payout ratio." True or false?

The answer is false if clienteles exist. As long as enough high-dividend firms satisfy the dividend-loving investors, a firm won't be able to boost its share price by paying high dividends. An unsatisfied clientele must exist for this to happen, and there is no evidence that this is the case.

CONCEPT QUESTIONS

15.2a Are dividends irrelevant?

15.2b What are some of the reasons for a low payout?

15.2c What are the implications of dividend clienteles for payout policies?

15.3 ESTABLISHING A DIVIDEND POLICY

In this section, we focus on a particular approach to establishing a dividend policy that reflects many of the attitudes and objectives of financial managers as well as observed corporate dividend policies.

Residual Dividend Approach

Trans. 15.6 Establishing a Dividend Policy (Supplemental)

Earlier, we noted that firms with higher dividend payouts will have to sell stock more often. As we have seen, such sales are not very common and they can be very expensive. Consistent with this, we will assume the firm wishes to minimize the need to sell new equity. We will also assume the firm wishes to maintain its current capital structure.

Concept Q Answer 15.3a

If a firm wishes to avoid new equity sales, then it will have to rely on internally generated cash flow to finance new, positive NPV projects.[2] Dividends can only be paid out of what is left over. This leftover is called the *residual,* and such a dividend policy is called a **residual dividend approach.**

residual dividend approach Policy under which a firm pays dividends only after meeting its investment needs while maintaining a desired debt/equity ratio.

With a residual dividend policy, the firm's objective is to meet its investment needs and maintain its desired debt/equity ratio before paying dividends. Given this objective, we expect those firms with many investment opportunities to pay a small percentage of their earnings as dividends and other firms with fewer opportunities to pay a high percentage of their earnings as dividends. This result appears to occur in the real world. Young, fast-growing firms commonly employ a low payout ratio, whereas older, slower-growing firms in more mature industries use a higher ratio.

Dividend Stability

Concept Q Answer 15.3b

The key point of the residual dividend approach is that dividends are paid only after all profitable investment opportunities are exhausted. Of course, a strict residual approach might lead to a very unstable dividend payout. If investment opportunities in one period are quite high, dividends would be low or zero. Conversely, dividends might be high in the next period if investment opportunities are considered less promising.

Consider the case of Big Department Stores, Inc., a retailer whose annual earnings are forecasted to be equal from year to year but whose quarterly earnings change throughout the year. They are low in each year's first quarter because of the post-Christmas business slump. Although earnings increase only slightly in the second and third quarters, they advance greatly in the fourth quarter as a result of the Christmas season. A graph of this firm's earnings is presented in Figure 15.3.

The firm can choose between at least two types of dividend policies. First, each quarter's dividend can be a fixed fraction of that quarter's earnings. Here, dividends will vary throughout the year. This is a *cyclical dividend policy.* Second, each quarter's dividend can be a fixed fraction of yearly earnings, implying that all dividend payments would be equal. This is a

[2] Our discussion of sustainable growth in Chapter 4 is relevant here. We assumed there that a firm has a fixed capital structure, profit margin, and capital intensity. If the firm raises no new external equity and wishes to grow at some target rate, then there is only one payout ratio consistent with these assumptions.

FIGURE 15.3
Earnings for Big Department Stores, Inc.

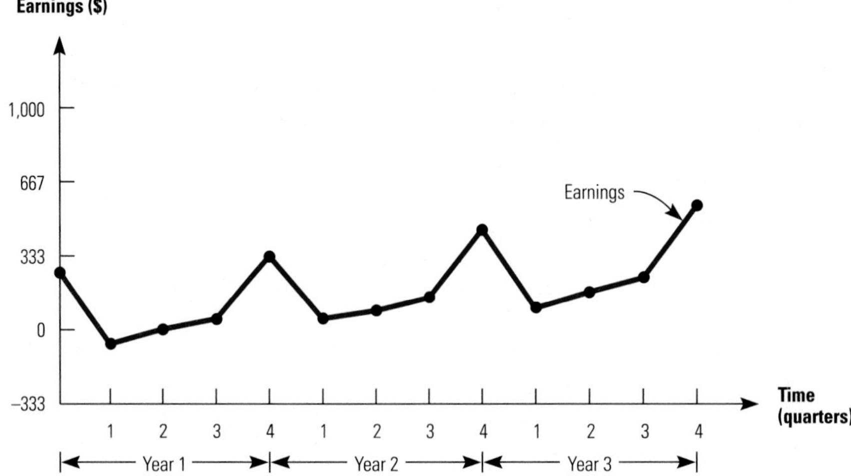

FIGURE 15.4
Alternative dividend policies for Big Department Stores, Inc.

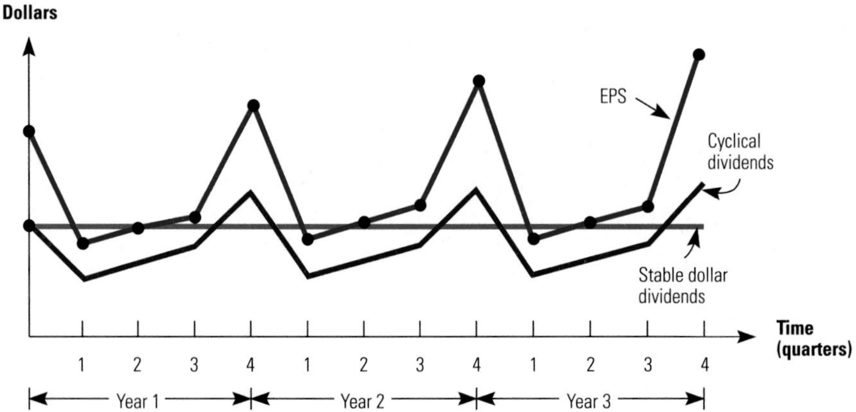

Cyclical dividend policy: Dividends are a constant proportion of earnings at each pay date.
Stable dividend policy: Dividends are a constant proportion of earnings over an earnings cycle.

stable dividend policy. These two types of dividend policies are displayed in Figure 15.4.

Most financial managers would agree that a stable dividend policy is in the best interests of the firm and its stockholders. Dividend cuts in particular are viewed as highly undesirable because such cuts are often interpreted as a sign of financial distress. Consequently, most companies will try to maintain a steady dividend through time, increasing the dividend only when management is confident the new dividend can be sustained indefinitely.

A Compromise Dividend Policy

In practice, many firms appear to follow what amounts to a compromise dividend policy. Such a policy is based on five main goals:

Trans. 15.7
A Compromise Dividend Policy

1. Avoid cutting back on positive NPV projects to pay a dividend.
2. Avoid dividend cuts.
3. Avoid the need to sell equity.

4. Maintain a target debt/equity ratio.
5. Maintain a target dividend payout ratio.

These goals are ranked more or less in order of their importance. In our strict residual approach, we assume that the firm maintains a fixed debt/equity ratio. Under the compromise approach, the debt/equity ratio is viewed as a long-range goal. It is allowed to vary in the short run if necessary to avoid a dividend cut or the need to sell new equity.

Lecture Tip: The instructor may wish to relate the following Wall Street aphorism: "Earnings declines are tolerable for a while, but the market never forgives a dividend cut."

In addition to a strong reluctance to cut dividends, financial managers tend to think of dividend payments in terms of a proportion of income, and they also tend to think investors are entitled to a "fair" share of corporate income. This share is the long-run **target payout ratio**, and it is the fraction of the earnings the firm expects to pay as dividends under ordinary circumstances. Again, this is viewed as a long-range goal, so it might vary in the short run if needed. As a result, in the long run, earnings growth is followed by dividend increases, but only with a lag.

target payout ratio
A firm's long-term desired dividend-to-earnings ratio.

One can minimize the problems of dividend instability by creating two types of dividends: regular and extra. For companies using this approach, the regular dividend would likely be a relatively small fraction of permanent earnings, so that it could be sustained easily. Extra dividends would be granted when an increase in earnings was expected to be temporary.

Since investors look on an extra dividend as a bonus, there is relatively little disappointment when an extra dividend is not repeated. Although the extra-dividend approach appears quite sensible, few companies use it in practice. One reason is that a share repurchase, which we discuss next, does much the same thing with some extra advantages.

Lecture Tip: An example of the effect of cutting dividends is provided in IM 15.3.

CONCEPT QUESTIONS

15.3a What is a residual dividend policy?

15.3b What is the chief drawback to a strict residual policy? What do many firms do in practice?

15.4 STOCK REPURCHASE: AN ALTERNATIVE TO CASH DIVIDENDS

When a firm wants to pay cash to its shareholders, it normally pays a cash dividend. Another way is to **repurchase** its own stock. Stock repurchasing has been a major financial activity in recent years, and it appears that it will continue to be one.

repurchase
Another method used to pay out a firm's earnings to its owners, which provides more preferable tax treatment than dividends.

Cash Dividends versus Repurchase

Self-Test Problem 15.1

Problems 5, 7

Trans. 15.8
Cash Dividends v. Repurchase

Imagine an all-equity company with excess cash of $300,000. The firm pays no dividends, and its net income for the year just ended is $49,000. The market value balance sheet at the end of the year is represented below.

Market Value Balance Sheet
(before paying out excess cash)

Excess cash	$ 300,000	$ 0	Debt
Other assets	700,000	1,000,000	Equity
Total	$1,000,000	$1,000,000	

There are 100,000 shares outstanding. The total market value of the equity is $1 million, so the stock sells for $10 per share. Earnings per share (EPS) were $49,000/100,000 = $.49, and the price/earnings ratio (P/E) is $10/$.49 = 20.4.

One option the company is considering is a $300,000/100,000 = $3 per share extra cash dividend. Alternatively, the company is thinking of using the money to repurchase $300,000/$10 = 30,000 shares of stock.

If commissions, taxes, and other imperfections are ignored in our example, the stockholders shouldn't care which option is chosen. Does this seem surprising? It shouldn't, really. What is happening here is that the firm is paying out $300,000 in cash. The new balance sheet is represented below.

Market Value Balance Sheet
(after paying out excess cash)

Excess cash	$ 0	$ 0	Debt
Other assets	700,000	700,000	Equity
Total	$ 700,000	$ 700,000	

If the cash is paid out as a dividend, there are still 100,000 shares outstanding, so each is worth $7.

The fact that the per-share value fell from $10 to $7 isn't a cause for concern. Consider a stockholder who owns 100 shares. At $10 per share before the dividend, the total value is $1,000.

After the $3 dividend, this same stockholder has 100 shares worth $7 each, for a total of $700, plus 100 × $3 = $300 in cash, for a combined total of $1,000. This just illustrates what we saw early on: A cash dividend doesn't affect a stockholder's wealth if there are no imperfections. In this case, the stock price simply fell by $3 when the stock went ex dividend.

Also, since total earnings and the number of shares outstanding haven't changed, EPS is still 49 cents. The price/earnings ratio (P/E), however, falls to $7/.49 = 14.3. Why we are looking at accounting earnings and P/E ratios will be apparent just below.

Alternatively, if the company repurchases 30,000 shares, there will be 70,000 left outstanding. The balance sheet looks the same.

Market Value Balance Sheet
(after share repurchase)

Excess cash	$ 0	$ 0	Debt
Other assets	700,000	700,000	Equity
Total	$ 700,000	$ 700,000	

The company is worth $700,000 again, so each remaining share is worth $700,000/70,000 = $10 each. Our stockholder with 100 shares is obviously unaffected. For example, if she were so inclined, she could sell 30 shares and end up with $300 in cash and $700 in stock, just as she has if the firm pays the cash dividend.

In this second case, EPS goes up since total earnings are the same while the number of shares goes down. The new EPS will be $49,000/70,000 = $.70 per share. However, the important thing to notice is that the P/E ratio is $10/$.70 = 14.3, just as it was following the dividend.

This example illustrates the important point that, if there are no imperfections, a cash dividend and a share repurchase are essentially the same thing. This is just another illustration of dividend policy irrelevance when there are no taxes or other imperfections.

Real-World Considerations in a Repurchase

The example we have just described shows that a repurchase and a cash dividend are the same thing in a world without taxes and transaction costs. In the real world, there are some accounting differences between a share repurchase and a cash dividend, but the most important difference is in the tax treatment.

Under current tax law, a repurchase has a significant tax advantage over a cash dividend. A dividend is fully taxed as ordinary income, and a shareholder has no choice about whether or not to receive the dividend. In a repurchase, a shareholder pays taxes only if (1) the shareholder actually chooses to sell and (2) the shareholder has a capital gain on the sale.

Concept Q Answer 15.4a

If this advantage strikes you as being too good to be true, you are quite likely right. The IRS does not allow a repurchase solely for the purpose of avoiding taxes. There must be some other business-related reason for doing it. Probably the most common reason is that "the stock is a good investment." The second most common is that "investing in the stock is a good use for the money" or that "the stock is undervalued," and so on.

Concept Q Answer 15.4b

Lecture Tip: Other benefits of stock repurchases are discussed in IM 15.4.

However it is justified, some corporations have engaged in massive repurchases in recent years. For example, despite an aggressive expansion campaign, Toys "R" Us still found itself with excess cash in 1994. It therefore announced a $1 billion share buy-back (another term for a repurchase); at the then-current share price of $39 per share, 12 percent of the outstanding stock would be repurchased. At about the same time, McDonald's also announced plans to repurchase $1 billion of its common stock over the next three years. Based on the share price on the announcement date, this repurchase amounted to about 5 percent of McDonald's 350 million shares outstanding. A cautionary note is in order, however. As the accompanying *Principles in Action* box indicates, many announced repurchases are never completed.

Share Repurchase and EPS

You may read in the popular financial press that a share repurchase is beneficial because earnings per share increase. As we have seen, this will happen. The reason is simply that a share repurchase reduces the number of outstanding shares, but it has no effect on total earnings. As a result, EPS rises.

However, the financial press may place undue emphasis on EPS figures in a repurchase agreement. In our example above, we saw that the value of the stock wasn't affected by the EPS change. In fact, the price/earnings ratio was exactly the same when we compared a cash dividend to a repurchase.

Since the increase in earnings per share is exactly tracked by the increase in the price per share, there is no net effect. Put another way, the increase in EPS is just an accounting adjustment that reflects (correctly) the change in the number of shares outstanding.

In the real world, to the extent that repurchases benefit the firm, we would argue that they do so primarily because of the tax considerations we discussed above.

Principles in Action

Talk Is Cheap!

In mid-1994, Philip Morris announced it would repurchase $6 billion of its own stock. By year-end, the company had repurchased only $1.6 billion in stock. In December of 1994, General Electric announced it would buy back about $5 billion in stock over the next two years. The last time GE announced a share repurchase was in 1989 when they set a target of buying back about $10 billion in stock. Ultimately, they repurchased about half that amount. Philip Morris and GE helped make 1994 a year in which publicly traded firms announced plans to repurchase a record $65 billion in stock. However, as many investors have discovered, a lot of firms are more talk than action. It is difficult to get accurate information on how many shares firms ultimately repurchase, but traders estimate that only about one-third of all share repurchases announced are ever completed.

Firms generally institute share repurchase programs when they have an excess amount of cash on hand. Rather than increase the quarterly dividend payout, which they might not be able to sustain in the future, they turn to the best alternative, a stock repurchase. When a firm repurchases shares of stock, it reduces the amount of equity outstanding. This increases earnings per share and is viewed by many investors as a positive signal regarding the firm's future prospects. Thus, the firm's stock price usually jumps when a share repurchase is announced as interest in the stock increases.

Often, the stated motivation for a repurchase is that the firm's management thinks its stock price is undervalued or that its stock is a good investment. If the stock price jumps before the share repurchase is completed, management may choose not to complete the repurchase at the higher price. While there is evidence that share repurchases do provide support for a firm's stock price, such price support can be short-lived if the firm fails to repurchase stock as announced. Investors who buy a company's stock based on an announced repurchase program may ultimately be disappointed in the performance of their investment if the buyback is not completed.

Share repurchase programs are often announced with open-ended language that does not require the firm to actually complete the repurchase. In GE's case, they announced their board had "authorized the repurchase of up to $5 billion of company stock over the next two years." Thus, they left the door open to repurchasing less stock than initially announced. Sometimes firms announce stock repurchase programs for no reason other than to prop up a sagging stock price. After the Dow Jones Industrial Average dropped 508 points on October 19, 1987, about 600 companies announced share repurchase programs. By six months following the crash, relatively few of the repurchases had been completed, giving the appearance that many of the firms made their announcements simply to give moral support to their stock price. One thing is clear: When investing in companies based on announced repurchase programs, it is definitely buyer beware.

Source: "Most Buybacks Are Stated, Not Completed," *The Wall Street Journal,* March 7, 1995, pp. C1-C2.

• • •

CONCEPT QUESTIONS

15.4a Why might a stock repurchase make more sense than an extra cash dividend?

15.4b Why don't all firms use stock repurchases instead of cash dividends?

15.5 STOCK DIVIDENDS AND STOCK SPLITS

stock dividend
Payment made by a firm to its owners in the form of stock, diluting the value of each share outstanding.

Another type of dividend is paid out in shares of stock. This type of dividend is called a **stock dividend.** A stock dividend is not a true dividend because it is not paid in cash. The effect of a stock dividend is to increase the number of shares that each owner holds. Since there are more shares outstanding, each is simply worth less.

A stock dividend is commonly expressed as a percentage; for example, a 20 percent stock dividend means that a shareholder receives one new share for every five currently owned (a 20 percent increase). Since every shareholder owns 20 percent more stock, the total number of shares outstanding rises by 20 percent. As we will see in a moment, the result would be that each share of stock is worth about 20 percent less.

Problem 2

A **stock split** is essentially the same thing as a stock dividend, except that a split is expressed as a ratio instead of a percentage. When a split is declared, each share is split up to create additional shares. For example, in a three-for-one stock split, each old share is split into three new shares.

stock split
An increase in a firm's shares outstanding without any change in owners' equity.

By convention, stock dividends of less than 20 to 25 percent are called *small stock dividends.* A stock dividend greater than this 20 to 25 percent is called a *large stock dividend.* Large stock dividends are not uncommon. For example, at one point, Walt Disney declared a 100 percent stock dividend, thereby doubling the number of outstanding shares. Except for some relatively minor accounting differences, this has the same effect as a two-for-one stock split.

Lecture Tip: See IM for more concerning the purchase of a stock that will undergo a stock split.

Value of Stock Splits and Stock Dividends

The laws of logic tell us that stock splits and stock dividends can (1) leave the value of the firm unaffected, (2) increase its value, or (3) decrease its value. Unfortunately, the issues are complex enough that one cannot easily determine which of the three relationships holds.

The Benchmark Case A strong case can be made that stock dividends and splits do not change either the wealth of any shareholder or the wealth of the firm as a whole. The reason is that they are just paper transactions and simply alter the number of shares outstanding. For example, if a firm declares a two-for-one split, all that happens is that the number of shares is doubled with the result that each share is worth half as much. The total value is not affected.

Lecture Tip: See IM for a discussion of the signalling issue in regard to a company's decision to announce a stock dividend.

Although this simple conclusion is relatively obvious, there are reasons that are often given to suggest that there may be some benefits to these actions. The typical financial manager is aware of many real-world complexities, and, for that reason, the stock split or stock dividend decision is not treated lightly in practice.

Popular Trading Range Proponents of stock dividends and stock splits frequently argue that a security has a proper **trading range.** When the security is priced above this level, many investors do not have the funds to buy the common trading unit of 100 shares, called a *round lot.* Although securities can be purchased in *odd-lot* form (fewer than 100 shares), the commissions are greater. Thus, firms will split the stock to keep the price in this trading range.

trading range
Price range between highest and lowest prices at which a stock is traded.

Although this argument is a popular one, its validity is questionable for a number of reasons. Mutual funds, pension funds, and other institutions have steadily increased their trading activity since World War II and now handle a sizable percentage of total trading volume (on the order of 80 percent of NYSE trading volume, for example). Because these institutions buy and sell in huge amounts, the individual share price is of little concern.

Furthermore, we sometimes observe share prices that are quite large without appearing to cause problems. To take an extreme case, the largest company in the world (in terms of the total market value of outstanding equity) is the Japanese telecommunications giant, NTT. In early 1994, NTT shares were selling for about $9,000 *each,* so a round lot would have cost a cool $.9 million. This is fairly expensive, but the stock has sold for more than $20,000 per share. Closer to home, Berkshire-Hathaway, a widely respected company, sold for about $16,000 per share at that time (it was selling for $22,000 per share in the spring of 1995).

Finally, there is evidence that stock splits may actually decrease the liquidity of the company's shares. Following a two-for-one split, the number of shares traded should more than double if liquidity is increased by the split. This doesn't appear to happen, and the reverse is sometimes observed.

Reverse Splits

reverse split
Stock split under which a firm's number of shares outstanding is reduced.

Concept Q Answer 15.5b

A less frequently encountered financial maneuver is the **reverse split.** In a one-for-three reverse split, each investor exchanges three old shares for one new share. The par value is tripled in the process. As mentioned previously with reference to stock splits and stock dividends, a case can be made that a reverse split changes nothing substantial about the company.

Given real-world imperfections, three related reasons are cited for reverse splits. First, transaction costs to shareholders may be less after the reverse split. Second, the liquidity and marketability of a company's stock might be improved when its price is raised to the popular trading range. Third, stocks selling below a certain level are not considered respectable, meaning that investors underestimate these firms' earnings, cash flow, growth, and stability. Some financial analysts argue that a reverse split can achieve instant respectability. As with stock splits, none of these reasons is particularly compelling, especially the third one.

There are two other reasons for reverse splits. First, stock exchanges have minimum price per share requirements. A reverse split may bring the stock price up to such a minimum. Second, companies sometimes perform reverse splits and, at the same time, buy out any stockholders who end up with less than a certain number of shares. This second tactic can be abusive if it is used to force out minority shareholders.

CONCEPT QUESTIONS

15.5a What is the effect of a stock split on stockholder wealth?

15.5b What is a reverse split?

15.6 SUMMARY AND CONCLUSIONS

In this chapter, we discussed the types of dividends and how they are paid. We then defined dividend policy and examined whether or not dividend policy matters. Next, we illustrated how a firm might establish a dividend policy and described an important alternative to cash dividends, a share repurchase.

In covering these subjects, we saw that:

1. Dividend policy is irrelevant when there are no taxes or other imperfections.
2. Individual shareholder income taxes and new issue flotation costs are real-world considerations that favor a low-dividend payout. With taxes and new issue costs, the firm should pay out dividends only after all positive NPV projects have been fully financed.
3. There are groups in the economy that may favor a high payout. These include many large institutions such as pension plans. Recognizing that some groups prefer a high payout and some prefer a low payout, the clientele effect supports the idea that dividend policy responds to the needs of stockholders. For example, if 40 percent of the stockholders prefer low dividends and 60 percent of the stockholders prefer high dividends, approximately 40 percent of companies will have a low-dividend payout, while 60 percent will have a high payout. This sharply reduces the impact of any individual firm's dividend policy on its market price.
4. A firm wishing to pursue a strict residual dividend payout will have an unstable dividend. Dividend stability is usually viewed as highly desirable. We therefore discussed a compromise strategy that provides for a stable dividend and appears to be quite similar to the dividend policies many firms follow in practice.
5. A stock repurchase acts much like a cash dividend, but has a significant tax advantage. Stock repurchases are therefore a very useful part of overall dividend policy.

To close out our discussion of dividends, we emphasize one last time the difference between dividends and dividend policy. Dividends are important, because the value of a share of stock is ultimately determined by the dividends that will be paid. What is less clear is whether or not the time pattern of dividends (more now versus more later) matters. This is the dividend policy question, and it is not easy to give a definitive answer to it.

Chapter Review Problem and Self-Test

15.1 Repurchase versus Cash Dividend Trantor Corporation is deciding whether to pay out \$300 in excess cash in the form of an extra dividend or a share repurchase. Current earnings are \$1.50 per share and the stock sells for \$15. The market value balance sheet before paying out the \$300 is as follows:

Market Value Balance Sheet
(before paying out excess cash)

Excess cash	\$ 300	\$ 400	Debt
Other assets	1,600	1,500	Equity
Total	\$1,900	\$1,900	

Evaluate the two alternatives in terms of the effect on the price per share of the stock, the EPS, and the P/E ratio.

Answer to Self-Test Problem

15.1 The market value of the equity is $1,500. The price per share is $15, so there are 100 shares outstanding. The cash dividend would amount to $300/100 = $3 per share. When the stock goes ex-dividend, the price will drop by $3 per share to $12. Put another way, the total assets decrease by $300, so the equity value goes down by this amount to $1,200. With 100 shares, the new stock price is $12 per share. After the dividend, EPS will be the same, $1.50, but the P/E ratio will be $12/1.50 = 8 times.

With a repurchase, $300/15 = 20 shares will be bought up, leaving 80. The equity will again be worth $1,200 total. With 80 shares, this is $1,200/80 = $15 per share, so the price doesn't change. Total earnings for Trantor must be $1.50 × 100 = $150. After the repurchase, EPS will be higher at $150/80 = $1.875. The P/E ratio, however, will still be $15/1.875 = 8 times.

Questions and Problems

Basic (Questions 1–10)

1. **Dividends and Taxes** The University of Pennsylvania pays no taxes on its capital gains nor on its dividend income and interest income. Would it be irrational to find low-dividend, high-growth stocks in its portfolio? Would it be irrational to find municipal bonds in its portfolio? Explain.

a. $28.57
b. $45.45
c. $36.36
d. $83.33

2. **Stock Splits and Stock Dividends** Cardassian Capital Corporation (CCC) currently has 250,000 shares of stock outstanding that sell for $50 per share. Assuming no market imperfections or tax effects exist, what will the share price be after:
   a. CCC has a 7-for-4 stock split?
   b. CCC has a 10 percent stock dividend?
   c. CCC has a 37.5 percent stock dividend?
   d. CCC has a 3-for-5 reverse stock split?
   e. Determine the new number of shares outstanding in parts (*a*)–(*d*).

3. **Determining the Ex-Dividend Date** On Tuesday, December 8, Lippincott Power Co.'s board of directors declares a dividend of 75 cents per share payable on Wednesday, January 17, to shareholders of record as of Wednesday, January 3. What is the ex-dividend date? If a shareholder buys stock before that date, who gets the dividends on those shares, the buyer or the seller?

P_0 = $25
P_x = $23.75
Trans. 15.9

4. **Regular Dividends** The balance sheet for Columbia Netware Corp. is shown below in market value terms. There are 4,000 shares of stock outstanding.

Assets		Liabilities and Equity	
Cash	$ 6,000	Equity	$100,000
Fixed assets	94,000		

The company has declared a dividend of $1.25 per share. The stock goes ex-dividend tomorrow. Ignoring any tax effects, what is the stock selling for today? What will it sell for tomorrow? What will the balance sheet above look like after the dividends are paid?

5. **Share Repurchase** In the previous problem, suppose Columbia Netware has announced it is going to repurchase $5,000 worth of stock. What effect will this transaction have on the equity of the firm? How many shares will be outstanding? What will the price per share be after the repurchase? Ignoring tax effects, show how the share repurchase is effectively the same as a cash dividend.

Shares outstanding = 3,800
Price = $25

6. **Stock Dividends** The market value balance sheet for Klein Manufacturing is shown below. Klein has declared a 10 percent stock dividend. The stock goes ex-dividend tomorrow (the chronology for a stock dividend is similar to a cash dividend). There are 5,000 shares of stock outstanding. What will the ex-dividend price be?

P_x = $36.36

Assets		Liabilities and Equity	
Cash	$100,000	Debt	$150,000
Fixed assets	250,000	Equity	200,000

7. **Stock Repurchase** Sleight Corporation is evaluating an extra dividend versus a share repurchase. In either case, $3,000 would be spent. Current earnings are $4 per share, and the stock currently sells for $40 per share. There are 250 shares outstanding. Ignore taxes and other imperfections in answering the first two questions.

Trans. 15.10

   a. Evaluate the two alternatives in terms of the effect on the price per share of the stock and shareholder wealth.
   b. What will be the effect on Sleight's EPS and P/E ratio under the two different scenarios?
   c. In the real world, which of these actions would you recommend? Why?

a. P_x = $28
b. EPS = $5.71

8. **Alternative Dividends** Some corporations, like one British company that offers its large shareholders free crematorium use, pay dividends in kind (that is, offer their services to shareholders at below-market cost). Should mutual funds invest in stocks that pay these dividends in kind? (The fundholders do not receive these services.)

9. **Dividend Policy** For initial public offerings of common stock, 1993 was a very big year, with over $43 billion raised in the process. Relatively few of these firms paid cash dividends. Why do you think that most chose not to pay cash dividends?

10. **Residual Policy versus a Compromise** What is the chief drawback to a strict residual dividend policy? Why is this a problem? How does a compromise policy work? How does it differ from a strict residual policy?

Part Seven

SHORT-TERM FINANCIAL MANAGEMENT

Short-term financial planning and working capital management are the related subjects we consider in this part of our text. We first examine a firm's operating and cash cycles and then show how a firm can anticipate and plan for short-term financing needs.

In Chapter 17, we focus on three key working capital areas: cash, accounts receivable, and inventory. We describe how firms manage each of these important activities and the tradeoffs that exist.

OUTLINE

Chapter Sixteen

Short-Term Financial Planning

After studying this chapter, you should have a good understanding of:

. . .

A firm's operating and cash flow cycles and why they are important.

. . .

The different types of short-term financial policies.

. . .

The essentials of short-term financial planning.

Trans. 16.1
Chapter Outline

To this point, we have described many of the decisions of long-term finance, for example, capital budgeting, dividend policy, and financial structure. In this chapter, we begin to discuss short-term finance. Short-term finance is primarily concerned with the analysis of decisions that affect current assets and current liabilities.

Frequently, the term *net working capital* is associated with short-term financial decision making. As we describe in Chapter 2 and elsewhere, net working capital is the difference between current assets and current liabilities. Often, short-term financial management is called *working capital management.* These mean the same thing.

There is no universally accepted definition of short-term finance. The most important difference between short-term and long-term finance is the timing of cash flows. Short-term financial decisions typically involve cash inflows and outflows that occur within a year or less. For example, short-term financial decisions are involved when a firm orders raw materials, pays in cash, and anticipates selling finished goods in one year for cash. In contrast, long-term financial decisions are involved when a firm purchases a special machine that will reduce operating costs over, say, the next five years.

What types of questions fall under the general heading of short-term finance? To name just a very few:

1. What is a reasonable level of cash to keep on hand (in a bank) to pay bills?

2. How much should the firm borrow short-term?
3. How much credit should be extended to customers?

This chapter introduces the basic elements of short-term financial decisions. First, we discuss the short-term operating activities of the firm. We then identify some alternative short-term financial policies. Finally, we outline the basic elements in a short-term financial plan and describe short-term financing instruments.

16.1 TRACING CASH AND NET WORKING CAPITAL

In this section, we examine the components of cash and net working capital as they change from one year to the next. We have already discussed various aspects of this subject in Chapters 2, 3, and 4. We briefly review some of that discussion as it relates to short-term financing decisions. Our goal is to describe the short-term operating activities of the firm and their impact on cash and working capital.

Problems 1–3

Lecture Tip: See IM for tips on motivating student interest in the study of short-term finance.

To begin, recall that *current assets* are cash and other assets that are expected to convert to cash within the year. Current assets are presented in the balance sheet in order of their accounting liquidity—the ease with which they can be converted to cash and the time it takes to do so. Four of the most important items found in the current asset section of a balance sheet are cash and cash equivalents, marketable securities, accounts receivable, and inventories.

Analogous to their investment in current assets, firms use several kinds of short-term debt, called *current liabilities.* Current liabilities are obligations that are expected to require cash payment within one year (or within the operating period if it is longer than one year). Three major items found as current liabilities are accounts payable, expenses payable, including accrued wages and taxes, and notes payable.

Because we want to focus on changes in cash, we start off by defining cash in terms of the other elements of the balance sheet. This lets us isolate the cash account and explore the impact on cash from the firm's operating and financing decisions. The basic balance sheet identity can be written as:

$$\text{Net working capital} + \text{Fixed assets} = \text{Long-term debt} + \text{Equity} \qquad [16.1]$$

Net working capital is cash plus other current assets, less current liabilities; that is,

Concept Q Answers 16.1a, 16.1b

$$\text{Net working capital} = (\text{Cash} + \text{Other current assets}) - \text{Current liabilities} \qquad [16.2]$$

If we substitute this for net working capital in the basic balance sheet identity and rearrange things a bit, cash is:

Lecture Tip: See IM 16.1 for more on the impact of a cash increase on net working capital.

$$\text{Cash} = \text{Long-term debt} + \text{Equity} + \text{Current liabilities} - \text{Current assets (other than cash)} - \text{Fixed assets} \qquad [16.3]$$

This tells us in general terms that some activities naturally increase cash and some activities decrease it. We can list these along with an example of each as follows:

Concept Q Answer 16.1c

Activities that Increase Cash

Increasing long-term debt (borrowing long-term).

Increasing equity (selling some stock).

Increasing current liabilities (getting a 90-day loan).

Decreasing current assets other than cash (selling some inventory for cash).

Decreasing fixed assets (selling some property).

Concept Q Answer 16.1d

Activities that Decrease Cash

Decreasing long-term debt (paying off a long-term debt).

Decreasing equity (repurchasing some stock).

Decreasing current liabilities (paying off a 90-day loan).

Increasing current assets other than cash (buying some inventory for cash).

Increasing fixed assets (buying some property).

Notice that our two lists are exact opposites. For example, floating a long-term bond issue increases cash (at least until the money is spent). Paying off a long-term bond issue decreases cash.

As we discussed in Chapter 3, those activities that increase cash are called *sources of cash.* Those activities that decrease cash are called *uses of cash.* Looking back at our list, sources of cash always involve increasing a liability (or equity) account or decreasing an asset account. This makes sense because increasing a liability means we have raised money by borrowing it or by selling an ownership interest in the firm. A decrease in an asset means that we have sold or otherwise liquidated an asset. In either case, there is a cash inflow.

Uses of cash are just the reverse. A use of cash involves decreasing a liability by paying it off, perhaps, or increasing assets by purchasing something. Both of these activities require that the firm spend some cash.

EXAMPLE 16.1 Sources and Uses

Here is a quick check of your understanding of sources and uses: If accounts payable go up by $100, is this a source or use? If accounts receivable go up by $100, is this a source or use?

Accounts payable are what we owe our suppliers. This is a short-term debt. If it rises by $100, we have effectively borrowed the money, so this is a *source* of cash. Receivables are what our customers owe to us, so an increase of $100 means that we loaned the money; this is a *use* of cash. • • •

CONCEPT QUESTIONS

16.1a What is the difference between net working capital and cash?

16.1b Will net working capital always increase when cash increases?

16.1c List five potential uses of cash.

16.1d List five potential sources of cash.

16.2 THE OPERATING CYCLE AND THE CASH CYCLE

The primary concern in short-term finance is the firm's short-run operating and financing activities. For a typical manufacturing firm, these short-run activities might consist of the following sequence of events and decisions:

Self-Test Problem 16.1
Problems 5, 6, 9

Events	Decisions
1. Buying raw materials	1. How much inventory to order?
2. Paying cash	2. Borrow or draw down cash balances?
3. Manufacturing the product	3. What choice of production technology?
4. Selling the product	4. Should credit be extended to a particular customer?
5. Collecting cash	5. How to collect?

These activities create patterns of cash inflows and cash outflows. These cash flows are both unsynchronized and uncertain. They are unsynchronized because, for example, the payment of cash for raw materials does not happen at the same time as the receipt of cash from selling the product. They are uncertain because future sales and costs cannot be precisely predicted.

Defining the Operating and Cash Cycles

We can start with a simple case. One day, call it Day 0, you purchase $1,000 worth of inventory on credit. You pay the bill 30 days later, and, after 30 more days, someone buys the $1,000 in inventory for $1,400. Your buyer does not actually pay for another 45 days. We can summarize these events chronologically as follows:

Day	Activity	Cash Effect
0	Acquire inventory	None
30	Pay for inventory	−$1,000
60	Sell inventory on credit	None
105	Collect on sale	+$1,400

Concept Q Answer 16.2b

The Operating Cycle There are several things to notice in our example. First, the entire cycle, from the time we acquire some inventory to the time we collect the cash, takes 105 days. This is called the **operating cycle.**

operating cycle
The time period between the acquisition of inventory and the collection of cash from receivables.

As we illustrate, the operating cycle is the length of time it takes to acquire inventory, sell it, and collect for it. This cycle has two distinct components. The first part is the time it takes to acquire and sell the inventory. This 60-day span in our example is called the **inventory period.** The second part is the time it takes to collect on the sale, 45 days in our example. This is called the **accounts receivable period.**

inventory period
The time it takes to acquire and sell inventory.

accounts receivable period
The time between sale of inventory and collection of the receivable.

Based on our definitions, the operating cycle is obviously just the sum of the inventory and receivables periods:

$$\begin{aligned}\text{Operating cycle} &= \text{Inventory period} \\ &\quad + \text{Accounts receivable period} \qquad [16.4] \\ 105 \text{ days} &= 60 \text{ days} + 45 \text{ days}\end{aligned}$$

What the operating cycle describes is how a product moves through the current asset accounts. It begins life as inventory, it is converted to a receivable when it is sold, and it is finally converted to cash when we collect from the sale. Notice that, at each step, the asset is moving closer to cash.

Concept Q Answer 16.2b

accounts payable period The time between receipt of inventory and payment for it.

cash cycle The time between cash disbursement and cash collection.

The Cash Cycle The second thing to notice is that the cash flows and other events that occur are not synchronized. For example, we didn't actually pay for the inventory until 30 days after we acquired it. This 30-day period is called the **accounts payable period.** Next, we spend cash on Day 30, but we don't collect until Day 105. Somehow, we have to arrange to finance the \$1,000 for 105 − 30 = 75 days. This period is called the **cash cycle.**

The cash cycle, therefore, is the number of days that pass until we collect the cash from a sale, measured from when we actually pay for the inventory. Notice that, based on our definitions, the cash cycle is the difference between the operating cycle and the accounts payable period:

$$\begin{aligned}\text{Cash cycle} &= \text{Operating cycle} - \text{Accounts payable period} \\ 75\text{ days} &= 105\text{ days} - 30\text{ days}\end{aligned} \qquad [16.5]$$

cash flow time line Graphical representation of the operating cycle and the cash cycle.

Lecture Tip: See IM 16.2 for a discussion of accounts payable and its impact on the cash cycle.

Figure 16.1 depicts the short-term operating activities and cash flows for a typical manufacturing firm by looking at the cash flow time line. As shown, the **cash flow time line** is made up of the operating cycle and the cash cycle. In Figure 16.1, the need for short-term financial management is suggested by the gap between the cash inflows and cash outflows. This is related to the length of the operating cycle and accounts payable period.

The gap between short-term inflows and outflows can be filled either by borrowing or by holding a liquidity reserve in the form of cash or marketable securities. Alternatively, the gap can be shortened by changing the inventory, receivable, and payable periods. These are all managerial options that we discuss below and in subsequent chapters.

The Operating Cycle and the Firm's Organizational Chart

Before we examine the operating and cash cycles in greater detail, it is useful to take a look at the people involved in managing a firm's current assets and

FIGURE 16.1 Cash flow time line and the short-term operating activities of a typical manufacturing firm

Trans. 16.2

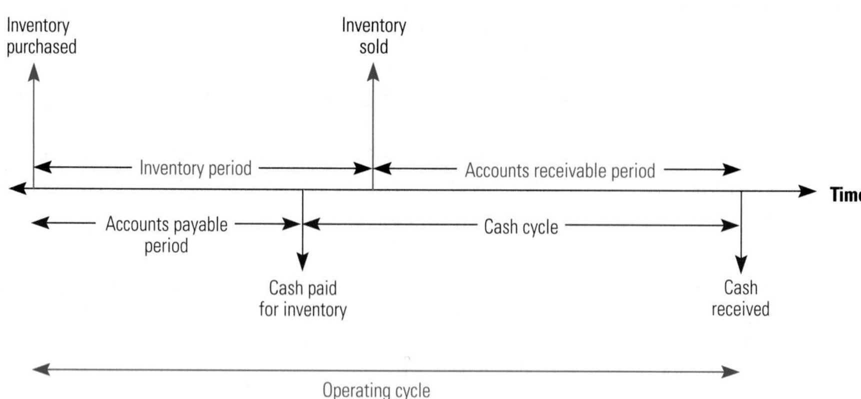

The operating cycle is the time period from inventory purchase until the receipt of cash. (Sometimes the operating cycle does not include the time from placement of the order until arrival of the stock.) The cash cycle is the time period from when cash is paid out to when cash is received.

liabilities. As Table 16.1 illustrates, short-term financial management in a large corporation involves a number of different financial and nonfinancial managers.[1] Examining Table 16.1, selling on credit involves at least three different individuals: the credit manager, the marketing manager, and the controller. Of these three, only two are responsible to the vice president of finance (the marketing function is usually associated with the vice president of marketing). Thus, there is the potential for conflict, particularly if different managers only concentrate on part of the picture. For example, if marketing is trying to land a new account, it may seek more liberal credit terms as an inducement. However, this may increase the firm's investment in receivables or its exposure to bad-debt risk, and conflict can result.

Lecture Tip: Table 16.1 illustrates a point made in Chapter 1—that financial decisions are made by nonfinancial managers, as well as those in "finance positions" (such as the CFO, treasurer, etc.).

Calculating the Operating and Cash Cycles

In our example, the lengths of time that made up the different periods were obvious. If all we have is financial statement information, we will have to do a little more work. We illustrate these calculations next.

To begin, we need to determine various things such as how long it takes, on average, to sell inventory and how long it takes, on average, to collect. We start by gathering some balance sheet information such as the following (in thousands):

Item	Beginning	Ending	Average
Inventory	$2,000	$3,000	$2,500
Accounts receivable	1,600	2,000	1,800
Accounts payable	750	1,000	875

TABLE 16.1 Managers who deal with short-term financial problems **Trans. 16.3**

Title of Manager	Duties Related to Short-Term Financial Management	Assets/Liabilities Influenced
Cash manager	Collection, concentration, disbursement; short-term investments; short-term borrowing; banking relations	Cash, marketable securities, short-term loans
Credit manager	Monitoring and control of accounts receivable; credit policy decisions	Accounts receivable
Marketing manager	Credit policy decisions	Accounts receivable
Purchasing manager	Decisions on purchases, suppliers; may negotiate payment terms	Inventory, accounts payable
Production manager	Setting of production schedules and materials requirements	Inventory, accounts payable
Payables manager	Decisions on payment policies and on whether to take discounts	Accounts payable
Controller	Accounting information on cash flows; reconciliation of accounts payable; application of payments to accounts receivable	Accounts receivable, accounts payable

Source: Ned C. Hill and William L. Sartoris, *Short-Term Financial Management*, 2nd ed. (New York: Macmillan, 1992), p. 15.

[1] The discussion draws on N. C. Hill and W. L. Sartoris, *Short-Term Financial Management*, 2nd ed. (New York: Macmillan, 1992), Chapter 1.

Also, from the most recent income statement, we might have the following figures (in thousands):

Net sales	$11,500
Cost of goods sold	8,200

We now need to calculate some financial ratios. We discussed these in some detail in Chapter 3; here we just define them and use them as needed.

Concept Q Answer 16.2a

Trans. 16.4 Hermetic, Inc., Operating Cycles (Supplemental)

Lecture Tip: The use of average values in the denominators of these ratios is discussed in IM 16.2.

Lecture Tip: The instructor may wish to digress here to point out that while some turnover ratios actually measure turnover, others (such as fixed asset turnover) simply measure the sales generated for each dollar of assets held.

The Operating Cycle First of all, we need the inventory period. We spent \$8.2 million on inventory (our cost of goods sold). Our average inventory was \$2.5 million. We thus turned our inventory over \$8.2/2.5 times during the year:[2]

$$\text{Inventory turnover} = \frac{\text{Cost of goods sold}}{\text{Average inventory}} = \frac{\$8.2 \text{ million}}{\$2.5 \text{ million}} = 3.28 \text{ times}$$

Loosely speaking, this tells us that we bought and sold off our inventory 3.28 times during the year. This means that, on average, we held our inventory for:

$$\text{Inventory period} = \frac{365 \text{ days}}{\text{Inventory turnover}} = \frac{365}{3.28} = 111.3 \text{ days}$$

So the inventory period is about 111 days. On average, in other words, inventory sat for about 111 days before it was sold.[3]

Similarly, receivables averaged \$1.8 million, and sales were \$11.5 million. Assuming that all sales were credit sales, the receivables turnover is:[4]

$$\text{Receivables turnover} = \frac{\text{Credit sales}}{\text{Average accounts receivable}} = \frac{\$11.5 \text{ million}}{\$1.8 \text{ million}} = 6.4 \text{ times}$$

If we turn over our receivables 6.4 times, then the receivables period is:

$$\text{Receivables period} = \frac{365 \text{ days}}{\text{Receivables turnover}} = \frac{365}{6.4} = 57 \text{ days}$$

The receivables period is also called the *days' sales in receivables* or the *average collection period.* Whatever it is called, it tells us that our customers took an average of 57 days to pay.

---

[2] Notice that in calculating inventory turnover here, we used the *average* inventory instead of the ending inventory as we did in Chapter 3. Both approaches are used in the real world. To gain some practice using average figures, we will stick with this approach in calculating various ratios throughout this chapter.

[3] This measure is conceptually identical to the days' sales in inventory we discussed in Chapter 3.

[4] If less than 100 percent of our sales are credit sales, then we would just need a little more information, namely, credit sales for the year. See Chapter 3 for more discussion of this measure.

The operating cycle is the sum of the inventory and receivables periods:

$$\begin{aligned}\text{Operating cycle} &= \text{Inventory period} + \text{Accounts receivables period} \\ &= 111 \text{ days} + 57 \text{ days} = 168 \text{ days}\end{aligned}$$

This tells us that, on average, 168 days elapse between the time we acquire inventory, sell it, and collect for the sale.

The Cash Cycle We now need the payables period. From the information given above, average payables were \$875,000, and cost of goods sold was again \$8.2 million. Our payables turnover is:

Trans. 16.5
Hermetic, Inc., Cash Cycle

$$\begin{aligned}\text{Payables turnover} &= \frac{\text{Cost of goods sold}}{\text{Average payables}} \\ &= \frac{\$8.2 \text{ million}}{\$.875 \text{ million}} = 9.4 \text{ times}\end{aligned}$$

The payables period is:

$$\begin{aligned}\text{Payables period} &= \frac{365 \text{ days}}{\text{Payables turnover}} \\ &= \frac{365}{9.4} = 39 \text{ days}\end{aligned}$$

Thus, we took an average of 39 days to pay our bills.

Finally, the cash cycle is the difference between the operating cycle and the payables period:

$$\begin{aligned}\text{Cash cycle} &= \text{Operating cycle} - \text{Accounts payable period} \\ &= 168 \text{ days} - 39 \text{ days} = 129 \text{ days}\end{aligned}$$

So, on average, there is a 129-day delay from the time we pay for merchandise and the time we collect on the sale.

EXAMPLE 16.2 The Operating and Cash Cycles

You have collected the following information for the Slowpay Company.

Item	Beginning	Ending
Inventory	\$5,000	\$7,000
Accounts receivable	1,600	2,400
Accounts payable	2,700	4,800

Credit sales for the year just ended were \$50,000, and cost of goods sold was \$30,000. How long does it take Slowpay to collect on its receivables? How long does merchandise stay around before it is sold? How long does Slowpay take to pay its bills?

We can first calculate the three turnover ratios:

$$\begin{aligned}\text{Inventory turnover} &= \$30{,}000/\$6{,}000 = 5 \text{ times} \\ \text{Receivables turnover} &= \$50{,}000/\$2{,}000 = 25 \text{ times} \\ \text{Payables turnover} &= \$30{,}000/\$3{,}750 = 8 \text{ times}\end{aligned}$$

We use these to get the various periods:

$$\begin{aligned}\text{Inventory period} &= 365/5 = 73 \text{ days} \\ \text{Receivables period} &= 365/25 = 14.6 \text{ days} \\ \text{Payables period} &= 365/8 = 45.6 \text{ days}\end{aligned}$$

Principles in Action

The Cycle of Life

In April 1994, Ameritech Corporation told its 70,000 suppliers that it would stretch out its bill payments to 45 days from 30 beginning on May 1. They did so, according to a company spokesperson, in an effort "to control costs and optimize cash flow." Ameritech was trying to lengthen its days accounts payable and shorten its cash cycle. Unfortunately for its suppliers, as a firm such as Ameritech shortens its cash cycle, the cash cycle of its suppliers lengthens.

Ameritech was not alone in its quest to conserve cash. In the first quarter of 1994, companies with 500 or more workers paid their bills more slowly than in any of the previous four years according to Dun & Bradstreet Corp. D&B, who also reported that payment performance had been declining since 1992, gets its data by surveying mostly small suppliers. Unfortunately for many small suppliers, a large customer can represent a significant proportion of annual sales, so they have little recourse but to accept the terms the big customer states. For some, it can be the kiss of death.

Earthly Elements, Inc., was one firm that could not survive its slow-paying big customer. Formed in March 1993, its owner rejoiced when the company received a $10,000 order from a national home-shopping service in November 1993. The order represented 20 percent of their total orders for the year. Unfortunately, it cost Earthly Elements, a maker of dried floral gifts and accessories, 25 percent more than expected to fill the order. Then, its customer was slow to pay the bill. By the end of February 1994, the payment was 30 days late and the company was running out of cash. By the time payment was received in April, the firm had already closed its doors in March, a victim of its cash cycle. Earthly Elements failed while, at precisely the same time, its home-shopping service customer was enjoying the benefits of holding onto its cash longer.

Managers of small firms may find life uncomfortable as larger firms begin paying slower, but they need not sit idly by and accept the deal. Caruthers Raisin Packing Co. stopped offering cash discounts for early payment when some of its large customers began cutting checks for the discounted amount and then waiting to mail the payment until more than a month later. Truck Brokers, Inc., another small firm, took a more proactive approach and began cracking down on potentially late-paying firms before the sale was completed. If the credit analysis of a customer indicated any potential for a late payment, the company did business on a cash-only basis, even if that meant losing a large customer. In the end, cash is the life's blood for any firm, and as many small firms discover, a lengthening cash cycle can mean a shortened life cycle.

Source: "Big Customers' Late Bills Choke Small Suppliers," *The Wall Street Journal,* June 22, 1994, p. B1.

Lecture Tip: See IM for some ideas on interpreting Slowpay's operating cycle.

All told, Slowpay collects on a sale in 14.6 days, inventory sits around for 73 days, and bills get paid after about 46 days. The operating cycle here is the sum of the inventory and receivables periods: 73 + 14.6 = 87.6 days. The cash cycle is the difference between the operating cycle and the payables period: 87.6 − 45.6 = 42 days. • • •

Interpreting the Cash Cycle

Our examples show that the cash cycle depends on the inventory, receivables, and payables periods. Taken one at a time, the cash cycle increases as the inventory and receivables periods get longer. It decreases if the company is able to defer payment of payables and thereby lengthen the payables period.

Most firms have a positive cash cycle, and they thus require financing for inventories and receivables. The longer the cash cycle, the more financing required. Also, changes in the firm's cash cycle are often monitored as an early warning measure. A lengthening cycle can indicate that the firm is having trouble moving inventory or collecting on its receivables. Such problems can be masked, at least partially, by an increased payables cycle, so both should be monitored. As the accompanying *Principles in Action* box illustrates, the cash cycle is especially important for smaller firms.

Lecture Tip: See IM 16.2 for a real-world example of actions taken to reduce the length of the cash cycle.

The link between the firm's cash cycle and its profitability can be easily seen by recalling that one of the basic determinants of profitability and growth for a firm is its total asset turnover, which is defined as sales/total assets. In Chapter 3, we saw that the higher this ratio is, the greater is the firm's accounting return on assets (ROA) and return on equity (ROE). Thus, all other things the same, the shorter the cash cycle is, the lower is the firm's investment in inventories and receivables. In this case, the firm's total assets are lower, and total turnover is higher as a result.

Concept Q Answer 16.2c

CONCEPT QUESTIONS

16.2a What does it mean to say that a firm has an inventory turnover ratio of 4?

16.2b Describe the operating cycle and cash cycle. What are the differences?

16.2c Explain the connection between a firm's accounting-based profitability and its cash cycle.

16.3 SOME ASPECTS OF SHORT-TERM FINANCIAL POLICY

The short-term financial policy that a firm adopts will be reflected in at least two ways:

Problems 4, 7

1. *The size of the firm's investment in current assets.* This is usually measured relative to the firm's level of total operating revenues. A *flexible* or accommodative short-term financial policy would maintain a relatively high ratio of current assets to sales. A *restrictive* short-term financial policy would entail a low ratio of current assets to sales.[5]
2. *The financing of current assets.* This is measured as the proportion of short-term debt (that is, current liabilities) and long-term debt used to finance current assets. A restrictive short-term financial policy means a high proportion of short-term debt relative to long-term financing, and a flexible policy means less short-term debt and more long-term debt.

If we take these two areas together, a firm with a flexible policy would have a relatively large investment in current assets. It would finance this investment with relatively less in short-term debt. The net effect of a flexible policy is thus a relatively high level of net working capital. Put another way, with a flexible policy, the firm maintains a larger overall level of liquidity.

[5] Some people use the term *conservative* in place of flexible and the term *aggressive* in place of restrictive.

The Size of the Firm's Investment in Current Assets

Trans. 16.6
The Size of the Firm's Investment in Current Assets

Flexible short-term financial policies with regard to current assets include such actions as:

1. Keeping large balances of cash and marketable securities.
2. Making large investments in inventory.
3. Granting liberal credit terms, which results in a high level of accounts receivable.

Restrictive short-term financial policies would be just the opposite of the ones above:

1. Keeping low cash balances and little investment in marketable securities.
2. Making small investments in inventory.
3. Allowing little or no credit sales, thereby minimizing accounts receivable.

Concept Q
Answer 16.3a

Determining the optimal investment level in short-term assets requires an identification of the different costs of alternative short-term financing policies. The objective is to trade off the cost of a restrictive policy against the cost of a flexible one to arrive at the best compromise.

Concept Q
Answer 16.3b

Current asset holdings are highest with a flexible short-term financial policy and lowest with a restrictive policy. So flexible short-term financial policies are costly in that they require a greater investment in cash and marketable securities, inventory, and accounts receivable. However, we expect that future cash inflows will be higher with a flexible policy. For example, sales are stimulated by the use of a credit policy that provides liberal financing to customers. A large amount of finished inventory on hand ("on the shelf") provides a quick delivery service to customers and may increase sales. Similarly, a large inventory of raw materials may result in fewer production stoppages because of inventory shortages.

A more restrictive short-term financial policy probably reduces future sales levels below those that would be achieved under flexible policies. It is also possible that higher prices can be charged to customers under flexible working capital policies. Customers may be willing to pay higher prices for the quick delivery service and more liberal credit terms implicit in flexible policies.

Managing current assets can be thought of as involving a trade-off between costs that rise and costs that fall with the level of investment. Costs that rise with increases in the level of investment in current assets are called **carrying costs**. The larger the investment a firm makes in its current assets, the higher its carrying costs will be. Costs that fall with increases in the level of investment in current assets are called **shortage costs.**

carrying costs
Costs that rise with increases in the level of investment in current assets.

shortage costs
Costs that fall with increases in the level of investment in current assets.

In a general sense, carrying costs are the opportunity costs associated with current assets. The rate of return on current assets is very low when compared to other assets. For example, the rate of return on U.S. Treasury bills is usually less than 10 percent. This is very low compared to the rate of return firms would like to achieve overall. (U.S. Treasury bills are an important component of cash and marketable securities.)

Shortage costs are incurred when the investment in current assets is low. If a firm runs out of cash, it will be forced to sell marketable securities. Of course, if a firm runs out of cash and cannot readily sell marketable securities, it may have to borrow or default on an obligation. This situation is called a *cash out.* A firm may lose customers if it runs out of inventory (a *stock out*) or if it cannot extend credit to customers.

Lecture Tip: See IM for a look at the trade-off between carrying and shortage costs in regard to JIT inventory.

More generally, there are two kinds of shortage costs:

1. *Trading or order costs.* Order costs are the costs of placing an order for more cash (brokerage costs, for example) or more inventory (production set-up costs, for example).
2. *Costs related to lack of safety reserves.* These are costs of lost sales, lost customer goodwill, and disruption of production schedules.

The top part of Figure 16.2 illustrates the basic trade-off between carrying costs and shortage costs. On the vertical axis, we have costs measured in dollars and, on the horizontal axis, we have the amount of current assets. Carrying costs start out at zero when current assets are zero and then climb steadily as current assets grow. Shortage costs start out very high and then decline as we add current assets. The total costs of holding current assets is the sum of the two. Notice how the combined costs reach a minimum at CA*. This is the optimal level of current assets.

Optimal current asset holdings are highest under a flexible policy. This policy is one in which the carrying costs are perceived to be low relative to shortage costs. This is Case A in Figure 16.2. In comparison, under restrictive current asset policies, carrying costs are perceived to be high relative to shortage costs, resulting in lower current asset holdings. This is Case B in Figure 16.2.

Alternative Financing Policies for Current Assets

In previous sections, we looked at the basic determinants of the level of investment in current assets, and we thus focused on the asset side of the balance sheet. Now we turn to the financing side of the question. Here we are concerned with the relative amounts of short-term and long-term debt, assuming the investment in current assets is constant.

A growing firm can be thought of as having a total asset requirement consisting of the current assets and long-term assets needed to run the business efficiently. The total asset requirement may exhibit change over time for many reasons, including (1) a general growth trend, (2) seasonal variation around the trend, and (3) unpredictable day-to-day and month-to-month fluctuations. This situation is depicted in Figure 16.3. (We have not tried to show the unpredictable day-to-day and month-to-month variations in the total asset requirement.)

The peaks and valleys in Figure 16.3 represent the firm's total asset needs through time. For example, for a lawn and garden supply firm, the peaks might represent inventory buildups prior to the spring selling season. The valleys come about because of lower off-season inventories. There are two strategies such a firm might consider to meet its cyclical needs. First, the firm could keep a relatively large pool of marketable securities. As the need for inventory and other current assets begins to rise, the firm sells off marketable securities and uses the cash to purchase whatever is needed. Once the

Lecture Tip: See IM 16.3 for a simple example demonstrating the alternative financing policies in Figures 16.2–16.5.

F I G U R E 16.2 Carrying costs and shortage costs **Trans. 16.7**

Short-term financial policy: the optimal investment in current assets.

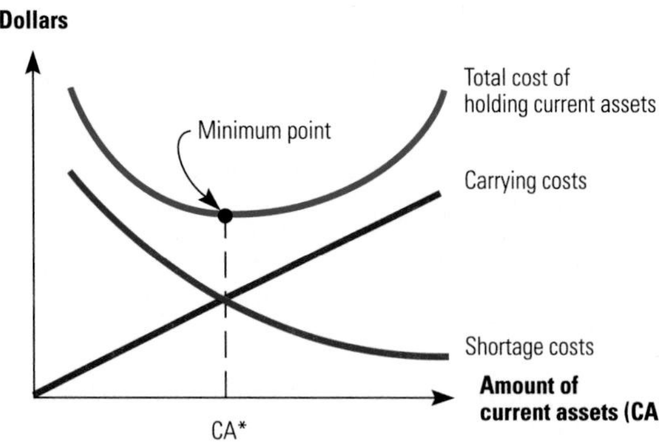

The optimal amount of current assets.
This point minimizes total costs.

Carrying costs increase with the level of investment in current assets. They include the costs of maintaining economic value and opportunity costs. Shortage costs decrease with increases in the level of investment in current assets. They include trading costs and the costs related to being short of the current asset (for example, being short of cash). The firm's policy can be characterized as flexible or restrictive.

A. Flexible policy

Dollars

Minimum point

Total cost

Carrying costs

Shortage costs

Amount of current assets (CA)

CA*

A flexible policy is most appropriate when carrying costs are low relative to shortage costs.

B. Restrictive policy

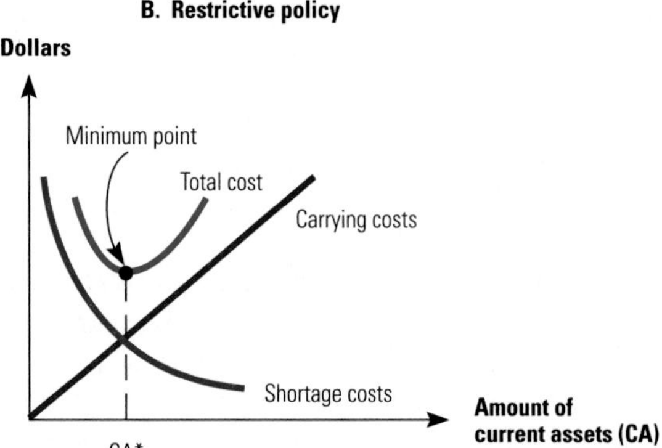

A restrictive policy is most appropriate when carrying costs are high relative to shortage costs.

F I G U R E 16.3
The total asset requirement over time

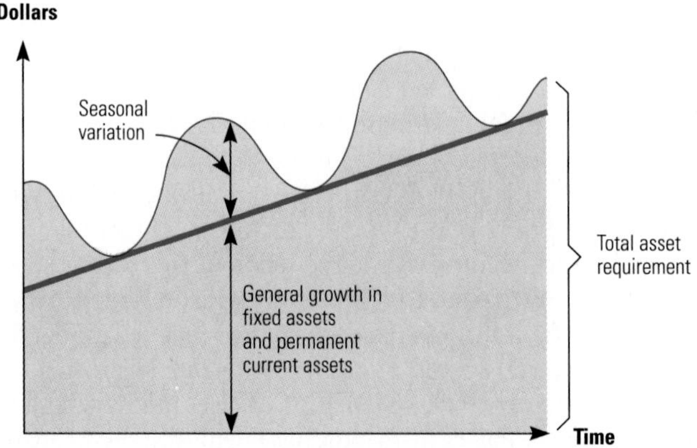

FIGURE 16.4 Alternative asset financing policies **Trans. 16.8**

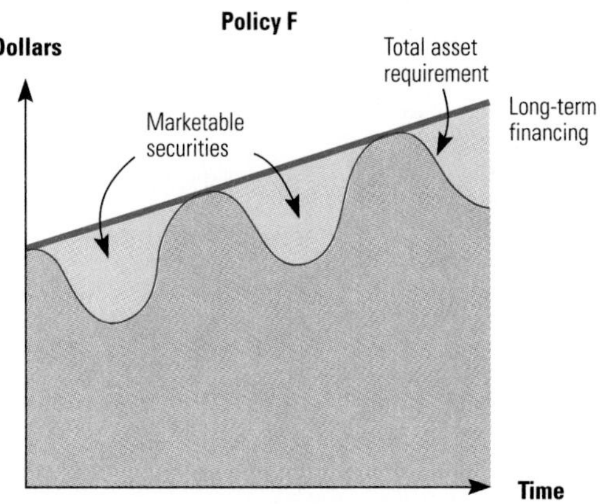

Policy F always implies a short-term cash surplus and a large investment in cash and marketable securities.

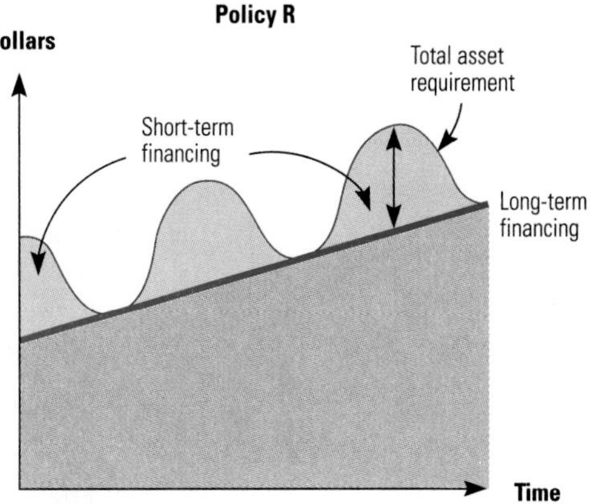

Policy R uses long-term financing for permanent asset requirements only and short-term borrowing for seasonal variations.

inventory is sold and inventory holdings begin to decline, the firm reinvests in marketable securities. This approach is the flexible policy illustrated in Figure 16.4 as Policy F. Notice that the firm essentially uses a pool of marketable securities as a buffer against changing current asset needs.

At the other extreme, the firm could keep relatively little in marketable securities. As the need for inventory and other assets begins to rise, the firm simply borrows the needed cash on a short-term basis. The firm repays the loans as the need for assets cycles back down. This approach is the restrictive policy illustrated in Figure 16.4 as Policy R.

In comparing the two strategies illustrated in Figure 16.4, notice that the chief difference is the way in which the seasonal variation in asset needs is financed. In the flexible case, the firm finances internally, using its own cash and marketable securities. In the restrictive case, the firm finances externally, borrowing the needed funds on a short-term basis. As we discussed above, all else the same, a firm with a flexible policy will have a greater investment in net working capital.

Which Financing Policy Is Best?

What is the most appropriate amount of short-term borrowing? There is no definitive answer. Several considerations must be included in a proper analysis:

1. *Cash reserves.* The flexible financing policy implies surplus cash and little short-term borrowing. This policy reduces the probability that a firm will experience financial distress. Firms may not have to worry as much about meeting recurring, short-run obligations. However, investments in cash and marketable securities are zero net present value investments at best.
2. *Maturity hedging.* Most firms attempt to match the maturities of assets and liabilities. They finance inventories with short-term bank loans and fixed assets with long-term financing. Firms tend to avoid financing long-lived assets with short-term borrowing.

Lecture Tip: An example of maturity hedging in personal financial management is provided in IM 16.8.

F I G U R E 16.5
A compromise financing policy

Trans. 16.9

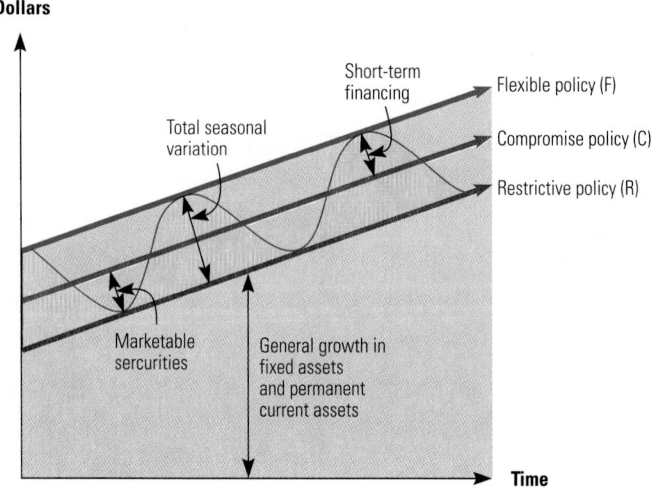

With a compromise policy, the firm keeps a reserve of liquidity which it uses to initially finance seasonal variations in current asset needs. Short-term borrowing is used when the reserve is exhausted.

This type of maturity mismatching would necessitate frequent refinancing and is inherently risky because short-term interest rates are more volatile than longer-term rates.

3. *Relative interest rates.* Short-term interest rates are usually lower than long-term rates. This implies that it is, on the average, more costly to rely on long-term borrowing as compared to short-term borrowing.

The two policies, F and R, we discuss above are, of course, extreme cases. With F, the firm never does any short-term borrowing, and, with R, the firm never has a cash reserve (an investment in marketable securities). Figure 16.5 illustrates these two policies along with a compromise, Policy C.

With this compromise approach, the firm borrows short-term to cover peak financing needs, but it maintains a cash reserve in the form of marketable securities during slow periods. As current assets build up, the firm draws down this reserve before doing any short-term borrowing. This allows for some run-up in current assets before the firm has to resort to short-term borrowing.

Current Assets and Liabilities in Practice

Short-term assets represent a significant portion of a typical firm's overall assets. For U.S. manufacturing, mining, and trade corporations, current assets were about 50 percent of total assets in the 1960s. Today, this figure is closer to 40 percent. Most of the decline is due to more efficient cash and inventory management. Over this same period, current liabilities rose from about 20 percent of total liabilities and equity to almost 30 percent. The result is that liquidity (as measured by net working capital to total assets) has declined, signaling a move to more restrictive short-term policies.

TABLE 16.2 Current assets and current liabilities as a percentage of total assets for selected industries, 1990

	Printing and Publishing	Industrial Chemicals	Iron and Steel	Aircraft and Missiles
Current assets				
Cash	3.2%	1.2%	3.7%	1.2%
Marketable securities	2.2	0.8	5.6	2.7
Accounts receivable	13.8	14.4	15.8	15.4
Inventory	7.1	11.2	18.9	40.2
Other current assets	4.5	3.5	1.6	1.5
Total current assets	30.8%	31.1%	45.6%	61.0%
Current liabilities				
Notes payable	3.7%	6.9%	3.7%	3.9%
Accounts payable	5.7	6.6	10.2	8.8
Accruals and other current liabilities	8.7	9.7	12.2	38.3
Total current liabilities	18.1%	23.2%	26.1%	51.0%

Source: Ned C. Hill and William L. Sartoris, *Short-Term Financial Management,* 2nd ed. (New York: Macmillan, 1992), p. 12.

The cash cycle is longer in some industries than others because of different products and industry practices.[6] Table 16.2 illustrates this point by comparing the current asset and liability percentages for four different industries. Of the four, the aircraft and missiles industry has more than twice the investment in inventories. Does this mean that aircraft and missile producers are less efficient? Probably not; instead, it is likely that the relatively high inventory levels consist largely of aircraft under construction. Because these are expensive products that take a long time to manufacture, inventories are naturally higher.

CONCEPT QUESTIONS

16.3a What considerations determine the optimal size of the firm's investment in current assets?

16.3b What considerations determine the optimal compromise between flexible and restrictive net working capital policies?

16.4 THE CASH BUDGET

The **cash budget** is a primary tool in short-run financial planning. It allows the financial manager to identify short-term financial needs and opportunities. Importantly, the cash budget will help the manager explore the need for short-term borrowing. The idea of the cash budget is simple: It records estimates of cash receipts (cash in) and disbursements (cash out). The result is an estimate of the cash surplus or deficit.

cash budget
A forecast of cash receipts and disbursements for the next planning period.

Self-Test Problem 16.2
Problems 8, 11–14

Sales and Cash Collections

We start with an example for the Fun Toys Corporation. We will prepare a quarterly cash budget. We could just as well use a monthly, weekly, or even

Trans. 16.10
A Cash Budget for Ajax Co. (Supplemental)

---

[6] This example is drawn from Chapter 1 of N. C. Hill and W. L. Sartoris, *Short-Term Financial Management,* 2nd ed. (New York: Macmillan, 1992).

daily basis. We choose quarters for convenience and also because a quarter is a common short-term business planning period.

All of Fun Toys' cash inflows come from the sale of toys. Cash budgeting for Fun Toys must therefore start with a sales forecast for the next year, by quarter:

	Q1	Q2	Q3	Q4
Sales (in millions)	$200	$300	$250	$400

Concept Q Answer 16.4a

Note that these are predicted sales, so there is forecasting risk here because actual sales could be more or less. Also, Fun Toys started the year with accounts receivable equal to $120.

Fun Toys has a 45-day receivables or average collection period. This means that half of the sales in a given quarter will be collected the following quarter. This happens because sales made during the first 45 days of a quarter will be collected in that quarter. Sales made in the second 45 days will be collected in the next quarter. Note we are assuming that each quarter has 90 days, so the 45-day collection period is the same as a half-quarter collection period.

Based on the sales forecasts, we now need to estimate Fun Toys' projected cash collections. First, any receivables that we have at the beginning of a quarter will be collected within 45 days, so all of them will be collected sometime during the quarter. Second, as we discussed, any sales made in the first half of the quarter will be collected, so total cash collections are:

$$\text{Cash collections} = \text{Beginning accounts receivable} + 1/2 \times \text{Sales} \qquad [16.6]$$

For example, in the first quarter, cash collections would be the beginning receivables of $120 plus half of sales, 1/2 × $200 = $100, for a total of $220.

Since beginning receivables are all collected along with half of sales, ending receivables for a particular quarter would be the other half of sales. First quarter sales are projected at $200, so ending receivables will be $100. This will be the beginning receivables in the second quarter. Cash collections in the second quarter will thus be $100 plus half of the projected $300 in sales, or $250 total.

Continuing this process, we can summarize Fun Toys' projected cash collections as shown in Table 16.3.

In Table 16.3, collections are shown as the only source of cash. Of course, this need not be the case. Other sources of cash could include asset sales, investment income, and receipts from planned long-term financing.

TABLE 16.3 Cash collections for Fun Toys (in millions)

	Q1	Q2	Q3	Q4
Beginning receivables	$120	→ $100	→ $150	→ $125
Sales	200	300	250	400
Cash collections	220	250	275	325
Ending receivables	100	150	125	200

Notes: Collections = Beginning receivables + 1/2 × Sales

Ending receivables = Beginning receivables + Sales − Collections

= 1/2 × Sales

Cash Outflows

Next, we consider the cash disbursements or payments. These come in four basic categories:

1. *Payments of accounts payable.* These are payments for goods or services rendered by suppliers, such as raw materials. Generally, these payments will be made sometime after purchases.
2. *Wages, taxes, and other expenses.* This category includes all other regular costs of doing business that require actual expenditures. Depreciation, for example, is often thought of as a regular cost of business, but it requires no cash outflow, and is not included.
3. *Capital expenditures.* These are payments of cash for long-lived assets.
4. *Long-term financing expenses.* This category, for example, includes interest payments on long-term debt outstanding and dividend payments to shareholders.

Fun Toys' purchases from suppliers (in dollars) in a quarter are equal to 60 percent of next quarter's predicted sales. Fun Toys' payments to suppliers are equal to the previous quarter's purchases, so the accounts payable period is 90 days. For example, in the quarter just ended, Fun Toys ordered $.60 \times \$200 = \$120$ in supplies. This will actually be paid in the first quarter (Q1) of the coming year.

Wages, taxes, and other expenses are routinely 20 percent of sales; interest and dividends are currently $20 per quarter. In addition, Fun Toys plans a major plant expansion (a capital expenditure) of $100 in the second quarter. If we put all this information together, the cash outflows are as shown in Table 16.4.

The Cash Balance

The predicted *net cash inflow* is the difference between cash collections and cash disbursements. The net cash inflow for Fun Toys is shown in Table 16.5.

TABLE 16.4
Cash disbursements for Fun Toys (in millions)

	Q1	Q2	Q3	Q4
Payment of accounts (60% of sales)	$120	$180	$150	$240
Wages, taxes, other expenses	40	60	50	80
Capital expenditures	0	100	0	0
Long-term financing expenses (interest and dividends)	20	20	20	20
Total cash disbursements	$180	$360	$220	$340

TABLE 16.5
Net cash inflow for Fun Toys (in millions)

	Q1	Q2	Q3	Q4
Total cash collections	$220	$250	$275	$325
Total cash disbursements	180	360	220	340
Net cash inflow	$ 40	−$110	$ 55	−$ 15

TABLE 16.6
Cash balance for Fun Toys (in millions)

	Q1	Q2	Q3	Q4
Beginning cash balance	$20	$ 60	−$50	$ 5
Net cash inflow	40	− 110	55	− 15
Ending cash balance	$60	−$ 50	$ 5	−$10
Minimum cash balance	− 10	− 10	− 10	− 10
Cumulative surplus (deficit)	$50	−$ 60	−$ 5	−$20

What we see immediately is that there is a cash surplus in the first and third quarters and a cash deficit in the second and fourth.

We will assume that Fun Toys starts the year with a $20 cash balance. Furthermore, Fun Toys maintains a $10 minimum cash balance to guard against unforeseen contingencies and forecasting errors. So we start the first quarter with $20 in cash. This rises by $40 during the quarter, and the ending balance is $60. Of this, $10 is reserved as a minimum, so we subtract it out and find that the first quarter surplus is $60 − 10 = $50.

Fun Toys starts the second quarter with $60 in cash (the ending balance from the previous quarter). There is a net cash inflow of −$110, so the ending balance is $60 − 110 = −$50. We need another $10 as a buffer, so the total deficit is −$60. These calculations and those for the last two quarters are summarized in Table 16.6.

Beginning in the second quarter, Fun Toys has a cash shortfall of $60. This occurs because of the seasonal pattern of sales (higher toward the end of the second quarter), the delay in collections, and the planned capital expenditure.

The cash situation at Fun Toys is projected to improve to a $5 deficit in the third quarter, but, by year's end, Fun Toys still has a $20 deficit. Without some sort of financing, this deficit will carry over into the next year. We explore this subject in the next section.

Concept Q Answer 16.4b

For now, we can make the following general comments on Fun Toys' cash needs:

1. Fun Toys' large outflow in the second quarter is not necessarily a sign of trouble. It results from delayed collections on sales and a planned capital expenditure (presumably a worthwhile one).
2. The figures in our example are based on a forecast. Sales could be much worse (or better) than the forecast.

CONCEPT QUESTIONS

16.4a How would you do a sensitivity analysis (discussed in Chapter 9) for Fun Toys' net cash balance?

16.4b What could you learn from such an analysis?

16.5 SHORT-TERM BORROWING

Problem 10

Fun Toys has a short-term financing problem. It cannot meet the forecasted cash outflows in the second quarter from internal sources. How it will finance that shortfall depends on its financial policy. With a very flexible policy, Fun Toys might seek up to $60 million in long-term debt financing.

In addition, much of the cash deficit comes from the large capital expenditure. Arguably, this is a candidate for long-term financing. Nonetheless, because we have discussed long-term financing elsewhere, we will concentrate here on two short-term borrowing options: (1) unsecured borrowing and (2) secured borrowing.

Concept Q Answer 16.5a

Trans. 16.11 Short-Term Borrowing (Supplemental)

Unsecured Loans

The most common way to finance a temporary cash deficit is to arrange a short-term, unsecured bank loan. Firms that use short-term bank loans often arrange a line of credit. A **line of credit** is an agreement under which a firm is authorized to borrow up to a specified amount. To ensure that the line is used for short-term purposes, the borrower will sometimes be required to pay the line down to zero and keep it there for some period during the year, typically 60 days (called a *clean-up period*).

line of credit
A formal (committed) or informal (noncommitted) prearranged, short-term bank loan.

Lecture Tip: See the IM for an example demonstrating various aspects of line-of-credit financing at the personal level.

Short-term lines of credit are classified as either *committed* or *noncommitted.* The latter is an informal arrangement that allows firms to borrow up to a previously specified limit without going through the normal paperwork (much like a credit card). A *revolving credit arrangement* (or just *revolver*) is similar to a line of credit, but it is usually open for two or more years whereas a line of credit would usually be evaluated on an annual basis.

Committed lines of credit are more formal legal arrangements and often involve a commitment fee paid by the firm to the bank. The interest rate on the line of credit will usually float. A firm that pays a commitment fee for a committed line of credit is essentially buying insurance to guarantee that the bank can't back out of the agreement (absent some material change in the borrower's status).

Secured Loans

Banks and other finance companies often require security for a short-term loan just as they do for a long-term loan. Security for short-term loans usually consists of accounts receivable, inventories, or both.

Lecture Tip: Another important source of unsecured financing, trade credit, is discussed in the IM.

Concept Q Answer 16.5b

Accounts Receivable Financing **Accounts receivable financing** involves either *assigning* receivables or *factoring* receivables. Under assignment, the lender has the receivables as security, but the borrower is still responsible if a receivable can't be collected. With *conventional factoring,* the receivable is discounted and sold to the lender (the factor). Once it is sold, collection is the factor's problem, and the factor assumes the full risk of default on bad accounts. With *maturity factoring,* the factor forwards the money on an agreed-upon future date.

accounts receivable financing
A secured short-term loan that involves either the assignment or factoring of receivables.

EXAMPLE 16.3 Cost of Factoring

For the year just ended, LuLu's Pies had an average of $50,000 in accounts receivable. Credit sales were $500,000. LuLu's factors its receivables by discounting them 3 percent, in other words, by selling them for 97 cents on the dollar. What is the effective interest rate on this source of short-term financing?

To determine the interest rate, we first have to know the accounts receivable or average collection period. During the year, LuLu's turned over its receivables \$500,000/\$50,000 = 10 times. The average collection period is therefore 365/10 = 36.5 days.

The interest paid here is a form of "discount interest." In this case, LuLu's is paying 3 cents in interest on every 97 cents of financing. The interest rate per 36.5 days is thus .03/.97 = 3.09%. The APR is 10 × 3.09% = 30.9%, but the effective annual rate is:

$$\text{EAR} = (1.0309)^{10} - 1 = 35.6\%$$

The factoring is a relatively expensive source of money in this case.

We should note that if the factor takes on the risk of default by a buyer, then the factor is providing insurance as well as immediate cash. More generally, the factor essentially takes over the firm's credit operations. This can result in a significant saving. The interest rate we calculated is therefore overstated, particularly if default is a significant possibility. • • •

inventory loan
A secured short-term loan to purchase inventory.

Lecture Tip: The use of inventory financing is discussed further in IM 16.5.

☆ **Ethics Note:** One of the biggest scams in modern finance involved the misuse of inventory financing. See IM 16.5 for a discussion of the exploits of Tino De Angelis, the "salad oil king."

Inventory Loans **Inventory loans,** short-term loans to purchase inventory, come in three basic forms: blanket inventory liens, trust receipts, and field warehouse financing:

1. *Blanket inventory lien.* A blanket lien gives the lender a lien against all the borrower's inventories (the blanket "covers" everything).
2. *Trust receipt.* A trust receipt is a device in which the borrower holds specific inventory in "trust" for the lender. Automobile dealer financing, for example, is done by trust receipts. This type of secured financing is also called *floor planning,* in reference to inventory on the showroom floor. However, it is somewhat cumbersome to use trust receipts for, say, wheat grain.
3. *Field warehouse financing.* In field warehouse financing, a public warehouse company (an independent company that specializes in inventory management) acts as a control agent to supervise the inventory for the lender.

Other Sources

There are a variety of other sources of short-term funds employed by corporations. Two of the most important are *commercial paper* and *trade credit.*

Lecture Tip: IM 16.5 provides additional considerations on the issuance of commercial paper.

Commercial paper consists of short-term notes issued by large and highly rated firms. Typically, these notes are of short maturity, ranging up to 270 days (beyond that limit, the firm must file a registration statement with the SEC). Because the firm issues these directly, the interest rate the firm obtains can be significantly below the rate a bank would charge for a direct loan.

Another option available to a firm is to increase the accounts payable period; in other words, it may take longer to pay its bills. This amounts to borrowing from suppliers in the form of trade credit. This is an extremely important form of financing for smaller businesses in particular. As we discuss in Chapter 17, a firm using trade credit may end up paying a much higher price for what it purchases, so this can be a very expensive source of financing.

CONCEPT QUESTIONS

16.5a What are the two basic forms of short-term financing?

16.5b Describe two types of secured loans.

16.6 A SHORT-TERM FINANCIAL PLAN

To illustrate a completed short-term financial plan, we will assume that Fun Toys arranges to borrow any needed funds on a short-term basis. The interest rate is 20 percent APR, and it is calculated on a quarterly basis. From Chapter 6, we know that the rate is 20%/4 = 5% per quarter. We will assume that Fun Toys starts the year with no short-term debt.

From Table 16.6, Fun Toys has a second quarter deficit of $60 million. We will have to borrow this amount. Net cash inflow in the following quarter is $55 million. We now have to pay $60 × .05 = $3 million in interest out of that, leaving $52 million to reduce the borrowing.

We still owe $60 − 52 = $8 million at the end of the third quarter. Interest in the last quarter will thus be $8 × .05 = $.4 million. In addition, net inflows in the last quarter are −$15 million, so we have to borrow a total of $15.4 million, bringing our total borrowing up to $15.4 + 8 = $23.4 million. Table 16.7 extends Table 16.6 to include these calculations.

Notice that the ending short-term debt is just equal to the cumulative deficit for the entire year, $20, plus the interest paid during the year, $3 + .4 = $3.4, for a total of $23.4.

Our plan is very simple. For example, we ignored the fact that the interest paid on the short-term debt is tax deductible. We also ignored the fact that the cash surplus in the first quarter would earn some interest (which would be taxable). We could add on a number of refinements. Even so, our plan highlights the fact that in about 90 days, Fun Toys will need to borrow $60 million or so on a short-term basis. It's time to start lining up the source of the funds.

Our plan also illustrates that financing the firm's short-term needs will cost about $3.4 million in interest (before taxes) for the year. This is a starting point for Fun Toys to begin evaluating alternatives to reduce this expense. For example, can the $100 million planned expenditure be postponed or spread out? At 5 percent per quarter, short-term credit is expensive.

Lecture Tip: You may wish to point out that Table 16.7 represents the combined results of Tables 16.3 through 16.6.

TABLE 16.7
Short-term financial plan for Fun Toys (in millions)

	Q1	Q2	Q3	Q4
Beginning cash balance	$20	$ 60	$10	$10.0
Net cash inflow	40	− 110	55	− 15.0
New short-term borrowing	—	60	—	15.4
Interest on short-term borrowing	—	—	− 3	− .4
Short-term borrowing repaid	—	—	− 52	—
Ending cash balance	$60	$ 10	$10	$10.0
Minimum cash balance	− 10	− 10	− 10	− 10.0
Cumulative surplus (deficit)	$50	$ 0	$ 0	$ 0.0
Beginning short-term borrowing	0	0	60	8.0
Change in short-term debt	0	60	− 52	15.4
Ending short-term debt	$ 0	$ 60	$ 8	$23.4

Also, if Fun Toys' sales are expected to keep growing, then the $20 million plus deficit will probably also keep growing, and the need for additional financing is permanent. Fun Toys may wish to think about raising money on a long-term basis to cover this need.

16.7 SUMMARY AND CONCLUSIONS

1. This chapter introduces the management of short-term finance. Short-term finance involves short-lived assets and liabilities. We trace and examine the short-term sources and uses of cash as they appear on the firm's financial statements. We see how current assets and current liabilities arise in the short-term operating activities and the cash cycle of the firm.
2. Managing short-term cash flows involves the minimizing of costs. The two major costs are carrying costs, the return forgone by keeping too much invested in short-term assets such as cash, and shortage costs, the cost of running out of short-term assets. The objective of managing short-term finance and doing short-term financial planning is to find the optimal trade-off between these two costs.
3. In an "ideal" economy, the firm could perfectly predict its short-term uses and sources of cash, and net working capital could be kept at zero. In the real world we live in, cash and net working capital provide a buffer that lets the firm meet its ongoing obligations. The financial manager seeks the optimal level of each of the current assets.
4. The financial manager can use the cash budget to identify short-term financial needs. The cash budget tells the manager what borrowing is required or what lending will be possible in the short run. The firm has available to it a number of possible ways of acquiring funds to meet short-term shortfalls, including unsecured and secured loans.

Chapter Review Problems and Self-Test

16.1 The Operating and Cash Cycles Consider the following financial statement information for the Glory Road Company:

Item	Beginning		Ending
Inventory	$1,543		$1,669
Accounts receivable	4,418		3,952
Accounts payable	2,551		2,673
Net sales		$11,500	
Cost of goods sold		8,200	

Calculate the operating and cash cycles.

16.2 **Cash Balance for Masson Corporation** The Masson Corporation has a 60-day average collection period and wishes to maintain a $5 million minimum cash balance. Based on this and the information below, complete the following cash budget. What conclusions do you draw?

MASSON CORPORATION
Cash Budget
(in millions)

	Q1	Q2	Q3	Q4
Beginning receivables	$120			
Sales	90	120	150	120
Cash collections				
Ending receivables				
Total cash collections				
Total cash disbursements	80	160	180	160
Net cash inflow				
Beginning cash balance	$ 5			
Net cash inflow				
Ending cash balance				
Minimum cash balance				
Cumulative surplus (deficit)				

Answers to Self-Test Problems

16.1 We first need the turnover ratios. Note that we use the average values for all balance sheet items and that we base the inventory and payables turnover measures on cost of goods sold.

$$\begin{aligned}\text{Inventory turnover} &= \$8{,}200/[(1{,}543 + 1{,}669)/2]\\ &= 5.11 \text{ times}\\ \text{Receivables turnover} &= \$11{,}500/[(4{,}418 + 3{,}952)/2]\\ &= 2.75 \text{ times}\\ \text{Payables turnover} &= \$8{,}200/[(2{,}551 + 2{,}673)/2]\\ &= 3.14 \text{ times}\end{aligned}$$

We can now calculate the various periods:

$$\begin{aligned}\text{Inventory period} &= 365 \text{ days}/5.11 \text{ times} = 71.43 \text{ days}\\ \text{Receivables period} &= 365 \text{ days}/2.75 \text{ times} = 132.73 \text{ days}\\ \text{Payables period} &= 365 \text{ days}/3.14 \text{ times} = 116.24 \text{ days}\end{aligned}$$

So the time it takes to acquire inventory and sell it is about 71 days. Collection takes another 133 days, and the operating cycle is thus $71 + 133 = 204$ days. The cash cycle is this 204 days less the payables period, $204 - 116 = 88$ days.

16.2 Since Masson has a 60-day collection period, only those sales made in the first 30 days of the quarter will be collected in the same quarter. Total cash collections in the first quarter will thus equal $30/90 = ⅓$ of sales plus beginning receivables, or $\$120 + ⅓ \times \$90 = \$150$. Ending receivables for the first quarter (and the second quarter beginning receivables) are the other ⅔ of sales, or ⅔ × \$90 = \$60. The remaining calculations are straightforward, and the completed budget follows.

MASSON CORPORATION
Cash Budget
(in millions)

	Q1	Q2	Q3	Q4
Beginning receivables	\$120	\$ 60	\$ 80	\$100
Sales	90	120	150	120
Cash collections	150	100	130	140
Ending receivables	\$ 60	\$ 80	\$100	\$ 80
Total cash collections	\$150	\$100	\$130	\$140
Total cash disbursements	80	160	180	160
Net cash inflow	\$ 70	−\$ 60	−\$ 50	−\$ 20
Beginning cash balance	\$ 5	\$ 75	\$ 15	−\$ 35
Net cash inflow	70	− 60	− 50	− 20
Ending cash balance	\$ 75	\$ 15	−\$ 35	−\$ 55
Minimum cash balance	−\$ 5	−\$ 5	−\$ 5	−\$ 5
Cumulative surplus (deficit)	\$ 70	\$ 10	−\$ 40	−\$ 60

The primary conclusion from this schedule is that, beginning in the third quarter, Masson's cash surplus becomes a cash deficit. By the end of the year, Masson will need to arrange for \$60 million in cash beyond what will be available.

Questions and Problems

Basic (Questions 1–14)

1. **Sources and Uses of Cash** For the year just ended, you have gathered the following information on the Holly Corporation:
   a. A \$200 dividend was paid.
   b. Accounts payable increased by \$500.
   c. Fixed asset purchases were \$900.
   d. Inventories increased by \$625.
   e. Long-term debt decreased by \$1,200.

   Label each as a source or use of cash and describe its effect on the firm's cash balance.

2. **Changes in the Cash Account** Indicate the impact of the following corporate actions on cash, using the letter I for an increase, D for a decrease, or N when no change occurs.
   a. A dividend is paid with funds received from a sale of common stock.
   b. A piece of machinery is purchased and paid for with long-term debt.
   c. Merchandise is sold on credit.
   d. A short-term bank loan is received.
   e. Last year's taxes are paid.
   f. Common stock is issued.
   g. Raw material is purchased for inventory on credit.
   h. Interest on long-term debt is paid.
   i. Payments for previous sales are collected.
   j. Payment is made for a previous purchase.

k. A dividend is paid.
l. A piece of office equipment is purchased and paid for with a short-term note.
m. Merchandise is sold on credit.
n. Cash is paid for raw materials purchased for inventory.
o. Marketable securities are purchased.

3. **Cash Equation** A. Rose & Company has a book net worth of $3,500. Long-term debt is $900. Net working capital, other than cash, is $1,400. Fixed assets are $2,000. How much cash does the company have? If current liabilities are $975, what are current assets?

Cash = $1,000
CA = $3,375

4. **Cost of Current Assets** Loftis Manufacturing, Inc., has recently installed a just-in-time (JIT) inventory system. Describe the likely effect on the company's carrying costs, shortage costs, and operating cycle.

5. **Changes in the Operating Cycle** Indicate the effect that the following company actions will have on the operating cycle. Use the letter I to show an increase, the letter D for a decrease, and the letter N for no change.
   a. Average receivables goes up.
   b. Credit repayment times for customers are increased.
   c. Inventory turnover goes from 5 times to 10 times.
   d. Payables turnover goes from 5 times to 10 times.
   e. Receivables turnover goes from 5 times to 10 times.
   f. Payments to suppliers are speeded up.

6. **Cycles** Is it possible for a firm's cash cycle to be longer than its operating cycle? Explain why or why not.

7. **Changes in the Cycles** Indicate the impact of the following company actions on the cash cycle and the operating cycle. Use the letter I to show an increase, the letter D for a decrease, and the letter N for no change.
   a. The terms of cash discounts offered to customers are made more favorable.
   b. The use of cash discounts offered by suppliers is decreased; thus, payments are made later.
   c. An increased number of customers pay on credit instead of with cash.
   d. Fewer raw materials than usual are purchased.
   e. A greater percentage of raw material purchases are paid for with cash.
   f. More finished goods are being produced for inventory instead of for order.

8. **Calculating Cash Collections** The Ace Turbine Company has projected the following quarterly sales amounts for the coming year:

	Q1	Q2	Q3	Q4
Sales	$575	$625	$700	$600

   a. Accounts receivable at the beginning of the year are $300. Ace Turbine has a 72-day collection period. Calculate cash

a. $415, $585, $640, $680

collections in each of the four quarters by completing the following:

	Q1	Q2	Q3	Q4
Beginning receivables	$	$	$	$
Sales				
Cash collections				
Ending receivables				

b. $530, $595, $655, $660
c. $645, $605, $670, $640

b. Rework (*a*) assuming a collection period of 54 days.
c. Rework (*a*) assuming a collection period of 36 days.

Operating cycle = 105.1 days
Cash cycle = −18.2 days
Trans. 16.12

9. **Calculating Cycles** Consider the following financial statement information for the Windbag Balloon Corporation:

Item	Beginning		Ending
Inventory	$4,925		$5,150
Accounts receivable	3,019		3,380
Accounts payable	7,516		7,952
Net sales		$47,115	
Cost of goods sold		22,893	

Calculate the operating and cash cycles. How do you interpret your answer?

26.06%

10. **Factoring Receivables** Your firm has an average collection period of 48 days. Current practice is to factor all receivables immediately at a 3 percent discount. What is the effective cost of borrowing in this case? Assume that default is extremely unlikely.

11. **Calculating Payments** Van Meter Products has projected the following sales for the coming year:

	Q1	Q2	Q3	Q4
Projected sales	$620	$550	$450	$600

Sales in the year following this one are projected to be 25 percent greater in each quarter.

a. Calculate payments to suppliers assuming that Van Meter places orders during each quarter equal to 45 percent of projected sales in the next quarter. Assume that Van Meter pays immediately. What is the payables period in this case?

	Q1	Q2	Q3	Q4
Payment of accounts	$	$	$	$

b. Rework (*a*) assuming a 90-day payables period.

	Q1	Q2	Q3	Q4
Payment of accounts	$	$	$	$

c. Rework (*a*) assuming a 60-day payables period.

	Q1	Q2	Q3	Q4
Payment of accounts	$	$	$	$

12. **Calculating Payments** The Kao-Teng Corporation's purchases from suppliers in a quarter are equal to 60 percent of the next quarter's forecasted sales. The payables deferral period is 60 days. Wages, taxes, and other expenses are 15 percent of sales, while interest and dividends are $30 per quarter. No capital expenditures are planned. $200, $231, $159 $168.50 **Trans. 16.13**

Projected quarterly sales are:

	Q1	Q2	Q3	Q4
Projected sales	$200	$300	$180	$150

Sales in the first quarter of the following year are projected at $280. Calculate Kao-Teng's cash outlays by completing the following:

	Q1	Q2	Q3	Q4
Payment of accounts	$	$	$	$
Wages, taxes, other expenses				
Long-term financing expenses (interest and dividends)				
Total	$	$	$	$

13. **Calculating Cash Collections** The following is the sales budget for Eazy Graphics Printers for the first quarter of 1995: a. $60,000 b. $50,666.67 c. $59,866.67 $80,383.33 $106,250.00

	January	February	March
Sales budget	$80,000	$105,000	$130,000

Credit sales are collected as follows:

25 percent in the month of the sale.
55 percent in the month after the sale.
20 percent in the second month after the sale.

The accounts receivable balance at the end of the previous quarter is $50,000 ($38,000 of which is uncollected December sales).

a. Compute the sales for November.
b. Compute the sales for December.
c. Compute the cash collections from sales for each month from January through March.

14. **Calculating the Cash Budget** Here are some important figures from the budget of Sturgis Products, Inc., for the second quarter of 1995:

	April	May	June
Credit sales	$240,000	$225,000	$276,000
Credit purchases	100,000	94,000	118,000
Cash disbursements			
Wages, taxes, and expenses	15,000	14,500	17,200
Interest	5,000	5,000	5,000
Equipment purchases	90,000	0	10,000

The company predicts that 10 percent of its sales will never be collected, 40 percent of its sales will be collected in the month of the sale, and the remaining 50 percent will be collected in the following month. Credit purchases will be paid in the month following the purchase.

In March 1995, credit sales were $250,000. Using this information, complete the following cash budget:

	April	May	June
Beginning cash balances	$300,000		
Cash receipts			
Cash collections from credit sales			
Total cash available			
Cash disbursements			
Purchases	95,000		
Wages, taxes, and expenses			
Interest			
Equipment purchases			
Total cash disbursements			
Ending cash balance			

Chapter Seventeen

Working Capital Management

After studying this chapter, you should have a good understanding of:

How firms manage their cash and some of the collection, concentration, and disbursement techniques used.

How firms manage their receivables and the basic components of a firm's credit policies.

The types of inventory and inventory management systems used by firms and what determines the optimal inventory level.

This chapter examines working capital management. Recall from Chapter 1 that working capital management deals with a firm's short-term, or current, assets and liabilities. A firm's current liabilities consist largely of short-term borrowing. We discussed short-term borrowing in our previous chapter, so this chapter mainly focuses on current assets, in particular, cash, accounts receivable, and inventory.

Trans. 17.1
Chapter Outline

17.1 FLOAT AND CASH MANAGEMENT

Trans. 17.2
Float and Cash Management (Supplemental)

Self-Test Problem 1
Problems 1–5

We begin our analysis of working capital management by looking at how firms manage cash.[1] The basic objective in cash management is to keep the investment in cash as low as possible while still operating the firm's activities efficiently and effectively. This goal usually reduces to the dictum: "Collect early and pay late." Accordingly, we discuss ways of accelerating collections and managing disbursements.

In addition, firms must invest temporarily idle cash in short-term marketable securities. As we discuss in various places, these securities can be

[1] We are indebted to Jarl Kallberg and David Wright for helpful comments and suggestions on this section.

bought and sold in the financial markets. As a group, they have very little default risk and most are highly liquid. There are different types of these so-called money market securities, and we discuss a few of the most important ones.

Reasons for Holding Cash

John Maynard Keynes, in his great work, *The General Theory of Employment, Interest, and Money,* identified three reasons why liquidity is important: the speculative motive, the precautionary motive, and the transaction motive. We discuss these next.

speculative motive
The need to hold cash to take advantage of additional investment opportunities, such as bargain purchases.

Lecture Tip: See IM 17.1 for a discussion of the importance of liquidity vis-à-vis financial slack.

Speculative and Precautionary Motives The **speculative motive** is the need to hold cash in order to be able to take advantage of, for example, bargain purchases that might arise, attractive interest rates, and (in the case of international firms) favorable exchange rate fluctuations.

For most firms, reserve borrowing ability and marketable securities can be used to satisfy speculative motives. Thus, for a modern firm, there might be a speculative motive for liquidity, but not necessarily for cash per se. Think of it this way: If you have a credit card with a very large credit limit, then you can probably take advantage of any unusual bargains that come along without carrying any cash.

precautionary motive
The need to hold cash as a safety margin to act as a financial reserve.

This is also true, to a lesser extent, for precautionary motives. The **precautionary motive** is the need for a safety supply to act as a financial reserve. Once again, there probably is a precautionary motive for liquidity. However, given that the value of money market instruments is relatively certain and that instruments such as T-bills are extremely liquid, there is no real need to hold substantial amounts of cash for precautionary purposes.

transaction motive
The need to hold cash to satisfy normal disbursement and collection activities associated with a firm's ongoing operations.

Concept Q Answer 17.1a

The Transaction Motive Cash is needed to satisfy the **transaction motive,** the need to have cash on hand to pay bills. Transaction-related needs come from the normal disbursement and collection activities of the firm. The disbursement of cash includes the payment of wages and salaries, trade debts, taxes, and dividends.

Cash is collected from sales, the selling of assets, and new financing. The cash inflows (collections) and outflows (disbursements) are not perfectly synchronized, and some level of cash holdings is necessary to serve as a buffer. Perfect liquidity is the characteristic of cash that allows it to satisfy the transaction motive.

As electronic funds transfers and other high-speed, "paperless" payment mechanisms continue to develop, even the transaction demand for cash may all but disappear. Even if it does, however, there will still be a demand for liquidity and a need to manage it efficiently.

Concept Q Answer 17.1b

Lecture Tip: See IM 17.1 for a personal cash management example to share in class.

Costs of Holding Cash When a firm holds cash in excess of some necessary minimum, it incurs an opportunity cost. The opportunity cost of excess cash (held in currency or bank deposits) is the interest income that could be earned in the next best use, such as investment in marketable securities.

Given the opportunity cost of holding cash, why would a firm hold excess cash? The answer is that a cash balance must be maintained to provide the liquidity necessary for transaction needs—paying bills. If the firm maintains too small a cash balance, it may run out of cash. If so, the firm may have to raise cash on a short-term basis. This could involve, for example, selling marketable securities or borrowing.

Activities such as selling marketable securities and borrowing involve various costs. As we've discussed, holding cash has an opportunity cost. To determine the appropriate cash balance, the firm must weigh the benefits of holding cash against these costs. We discuss this subject in more detail in the sections that follow.

Understanding Float

As you no doubt know, the amount of money you have according to your checkbook can be very different from the amount of money that your bank thinks you have. The reason is that some of the checks you have written haven't yet been presented to the bank for payment. The same thing is true for a business. The cash balance that a firm shows on its books is called the firm's *book* or *ledger balance.* The balance shown in its bank account as available to spend is called its *available* or *collected balance.* The difference between the available balance and the ledger balance is called the **float**, and it represents the net effect of checks in the process of *clearing* (moving through the banking system).

float
The difference between book cash and bank cash, representing the net effect of checks in the process of clearing.

Disbursement Float Checks written by a firm generate *disbursement float,* causing a decrease in its book balance but no change in its available balance. For example, suppose General Mechanics, Inc. (GMI), currently has $100,000 on deposit with its bank. On June 8, it buys some raw materials and pays with a check for $100,000. The company's book balance is immediately reduced by $100,000 as a result.

GMI's bank, however, will not find out about this check until it is presented to GMI's bank for payment on, say, June 14. Until the check is presented, the firm's available balance is greater than its book balance by $100,000. In other words, before June 8, GMI has a zero float:

$$\begin{aligned}\text{Float} &= \text{Firm's available balance} - \text{Firm's book balance}\\ &= \$100{,}000 - 100{,}000\\ &= \$0\end{aligned}$$

GMI's position from June 8 to June 14 is:

$$\begin{aligned}\text{Disbursement float} &= \text{Firm's available balance} - \text{Firm's book balance}\\ &= \$100{,}000 - 0\\ &= \$100{,}000\end{aligned}$$

During this period of time that the check is clearing, GMI has a balance with the bank of $100,000. It can obtain the benefit of this cash while the check is clearing. For example, the available balance could be temporarily invested in marketable securities and thus earn some interest. We will return to this subject a little later.

Collection Float and Net Float Checks received by the firm create *collection float.* Collection float increases book balances but does not immediately change available balances. For example, suppose GMI receives a check from a customer for $100,000 on October 8. Assume, as before, that the company has $100,000 deposited at its bank and a zero float. It deposits the check and increases its book balance by $100,000 to $200,000. However, the additional cash is not available to GMI until its bank has presented the check to the customer's bank and received $100,000. This will occur on, say, October 14. In the meantime, the cash position at GMI will reflect a collection float of $100,000. We can summarize these events. Before October 8, GMI's position is:

Concept Q Answer 17.1c

$$\begin{aligned} \text{Float} &= \text{Firm's available balance} - \text{Firm's book balance} \\ &= \$100{,}000 \qquad\qquad\quad - 100{,}000 \\ &= \$0 \end{aligned}$$

GMI's position from October 8 to October 14 is:

$$\begin{aligned} \text{Collection float} &= \text{Firm's available balance} - \text{Firm's book balance} \\ &= \$100{,}000 \qquad\qquad\quad - 200{,}000 \\ &= -\$100{,}000 \end{aligned}$$

In general, a firm's payment (disbursement) activities generate disbursement float, and its collection activities generate collection float. The net effect, that is, the sum of the total collection and disbursement floats, is the *net float.* The net float at a point in time is simply the overall difference between the firm's available balance and its book balance. If the net float is positive, then the firm's disbursement float exceeds its collection float and its available balance exceeds its book balance. If the available balance is less than the book balance, then the firm has a net collection float.

Lecture Tip: See IM 17.1 for a personal example of managing float.

A firm should be concerned with its net float and available balance more than its book balance. If a financial manager knows that a check written by the company will not clear for several days, she will be able to keep a lower cash balance at the bank than might be true otherwise. This can generate a great deal of money.

For example, take the case of Exxon. The average daily sales of Exxon are about $321 million. If Exxon's collections could be speeded up by a single day, then Exxon could free up $321 million for investing. At a relatively modest 0.015 percent daily rate, the interest earned would be on the order of $48,000 *per day.*

EXAMPLE 17.1 Staying Afloat

Suppose you have $5,000 on deposit. One day you write a check for $1,000 to pay for books, and you deposit $2,000. What are your disbursement, collection, and net floats?

After you write the $1,000 check, you show a balance of $4,000 on your books, but the bank shows $5,000 while the check is clearing. This is a disbursement float of $1,000.

After you deposit the $2,000 check, you show a balance of $6,000. Your available balance doesn't rise until the check clears. This is a collection float of −$2,000. Your net float is the sum of the collection and disbursement floats, or −$1,000.

Overall, you show $6,000 on your books. The bank shows a $7,000 balance, but only $5,000 is available because your deposit has not cleared. The discrepancy between your available balance and your book balance is the net float (−$1,000), and it is bad for you. If you write another check for $5,500, there may not be sufficient available funds to cover it, and it might bounce. This is the reason that the financial manager has to be more concerned with available balances than book balances. • • •

Float Management Float management involves controlling the collection and disbursement of cash. The objective in cash collection is to speed up collections and reduce the lag between the time customers pay their bills and the time the cash becomes available. The objective in cash disbursement is to control payments and minimize the firm's costs associated with making payments.

Total collection or disbursement times can be broken down into three parts: mailing time, processing delay, and availability delay:

1. *Mailing time* is the part of the collection and disbursement process where checks are trapped in the postal system.
2. *Processing delay* is the time it takes the receiver of a check to process the payment and deposit it in a bank for collection.
3. *Availability delay* refers to the time required to clear a check through the banking system.

Speeding up collections involves reducing one or more of these components. Slowing up disbursements involves increasing one or more of them. We will describe some procedures for managing collection and disbursement times below.

Concept Q Answer 17.1d

Ethical and Legal Questions The cash manager must work with collected bank cash balances and not the firm's book balance (which reflects checks that have been deposited but not collected). If this is not done, a cash manager could be drawing on uncollected cash as a source of funds for short-term investing. Most banks charge a penalty rate for the use of uncollected funds. However, banks may not have good enough accounting and control procedures to be fully aware of the use of uncollected funds. This raises some ethical and legal questions for the firm.

★ **Ethics Note:** See the IM for the source of a good discussion concerning cash management and the surrounding ethical issues.

For example, in May 1985, Robert Fomon, chairman of E. F. Hutton (a large investment bank), pleaded guilty to 2,000 charges of mail and wire fraud in connection with a scheme the firm had operated from 1980 to 1982. E. F. Hutton employees wrote checks totaling hundreds of millions of dollars against uncollected cash. The proceeds were then invested in short-term money market assets. This type of systematic overdrafting of accounts (or check *kiting* as it is sometimes called) is neither legal nor ethical and is apparently not a widespread practice among corporations. Also, the particular inefficiencies in the banking system that Hutton was exploiting have been largely eliminated.

For its part, E. F. Hutton paid a $2 million fine, reimbursed the government (the U.S. Department of Justice) $750,000, and reserved an additional $8 million for restitution to defrauded banks. We should note that the key issue in the case against Hutton was not its float management per se, but, rather, its practice of writing checks for no economic reason other than to exploit float.

Electronic Data Interchange: The End of Float? *Electronic data interchange* (EDI) is a general term that refers to the growing practice of direct, electronic information exchange between all types of businesses. One important use of EDI, often called financial EDI or FEDI, is to electronically transfer financial information and funds between parties, thereby eliminating paper invoices, paper checks, mailing, and handling. For example, it is now possible to arrange to have your checking account directly debited each month to pay

Lecture Tip: The availability of deposited funds is governed by the Expedited Funds Availability Act of 1990. Fund types and availability dates are detailed in the IM.

many types of bills, and corporations now routinely directly deposit paychecks into employee accounts. More generally, EDI allows a seller to send a bill electronically to a buyer, thereby avoiding the mail. The seller can then authorize payment, which also occurs electronically. Its bank then transfers the funds to the seller's account at a different bank. The net effect is that the length of time required to initiate and complete a business transaction is shortened considerably, and much of what we normally think of as float is sharply reduced or eliminated. As the use of FEDI increases (which it will), float management will evolve to focus much more on issues surrounding computerized information exchange and funds transfers.

CONCEPT QUESTIONS

17.1a What is the transaction motive for holding cash?

17.1b What is the cost to the firm of holding excess cash?

17.1c Which of these would a firm be most interested in reducing: collection or disbursement float? Why?

17.1d What is the benefit from reducing or eliminating float?

17.2 CASH MANAGEMENT: COLLECTION, DISBURSEMENT, AND INVESTMENT

As a part of managing its cash, a firm must make arrangements to collect from its customers, pay its suppliers, and invest any excess cash on hand. We begin by examining how firms collect and concentrate cash.

Cash Collection and Concentration

From our previous discussion, collection delays work against the firm. All other things the same, then, a firm will adopt procedures to speed up collections and thereby decrease collection times. In addition, even after cash is collected, firms need procedures to funnel, or concentrate, that cash to where it can be best used. We discuss some common collection and concentration procedures next.

Trans. 17.3
Check Clearing Illustrated (Supplemental)

Components of Collection Time Based on our discussion above, we can depict the basic parts of the cash collection process as follows: The total time in this process is made up of mailing time, check-processing delay, and the bank's availability delay.

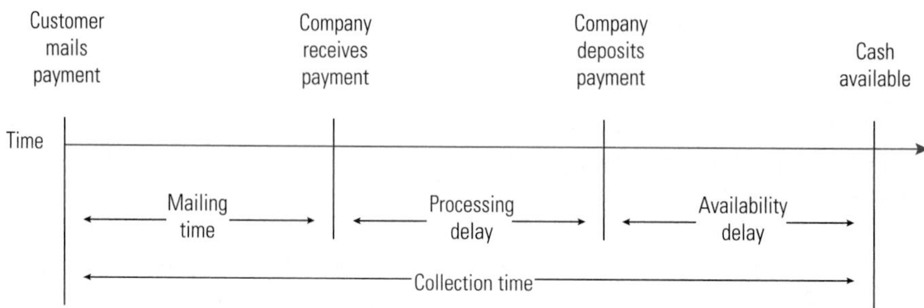

The amount of time that cash spends in each part of the cash collection process depends on where the firm's customers and banks are located and how efficient the firm is at collecting cash.

Cash Collection How a firm collects from its customers depends in large part on the nature of the business. The simplest case would be a business such as a restaurant chain. Most of its customers will pay with cash, check, or credit card at the point of sale (this is called *over-the-counter collection*), so there is no problem with mailing delay. Normally, the funds would be deposited in a local bank, and the firm would have some means (discussed below) of gaining access to the funds.

When some or all of the payments a company receives are checks that arrive through the mail, all three components of collection time become relevant. The firm may choose to have all the checks mailed to one location, or, more commonly, the firm might have a number of different mail collection points to reduce mailing times. Also, the firm may run its collection operation itself or might hire an outside firm that specializes in cash collection. We discuss these issues in more detail below.

Other approaches to cash collection exist. One that is becoming more common is the preauthorized payment. With this arrangement, the payment amounts and payment dates are fixed in advance. When the agreed-upon date arrives, the amount is automatically transferred from the customer's bank account to the firm's bank account, sharply reducing or even eliminating collection delays. The same approach is used by firms that have "on-line" terminals, meaning that when a sale is rung up, the money is immediately transferred to the firm's accounts.

Lockboxes When a firm receives its payments by mail, it must decide where the checks will be mailed and how the checks will be picked up and deposited. Careful selection of the number and locations of the collection points can greatly reduce collection times. Many firms use special post office boxes called **lockboxes** to intercept payments and speed cash collection.

Concept Q Answer 17.2a

lockboxes
Special post office boxes set up to intercept and speed up accounts receivable collections.

Figure 17.1 illustrates a lockbox system. The collection process is started by customers mailing their checks to a post office box instead of sending them to the firm. The lockbox is maintained by a local bank. A large corporation may actually maintain more than 20 lockboxes around the country.

In the typical lockbox system, the local bank collects the lockbox checks from the post office several times a day. The bank deposits the checks directly to the firm's account. Details of the operation are recorded (in some computer-usable form) and sent to the firm.

A lockbox system reduces mailing time because checks are received at a nearby post office instead of at corporate headquarters. Lockboxes also reduce the processing time because the corporation doesn't have to open the envelopes and deposit checks for collection. In all, a bank lockbox should enable a firm to get its receipts processed, deposited, and cleared faster than if it were to receive checks at its headquarters and deliver them itself to the bank for deposit and clearing.

Cash Concentration As we discussed earlier, a firm will typically have a number of cash collection points, and, as a result, cash collections may end up

FIGURE 17.1
Overview of lockbox processing

Trans. 17.4

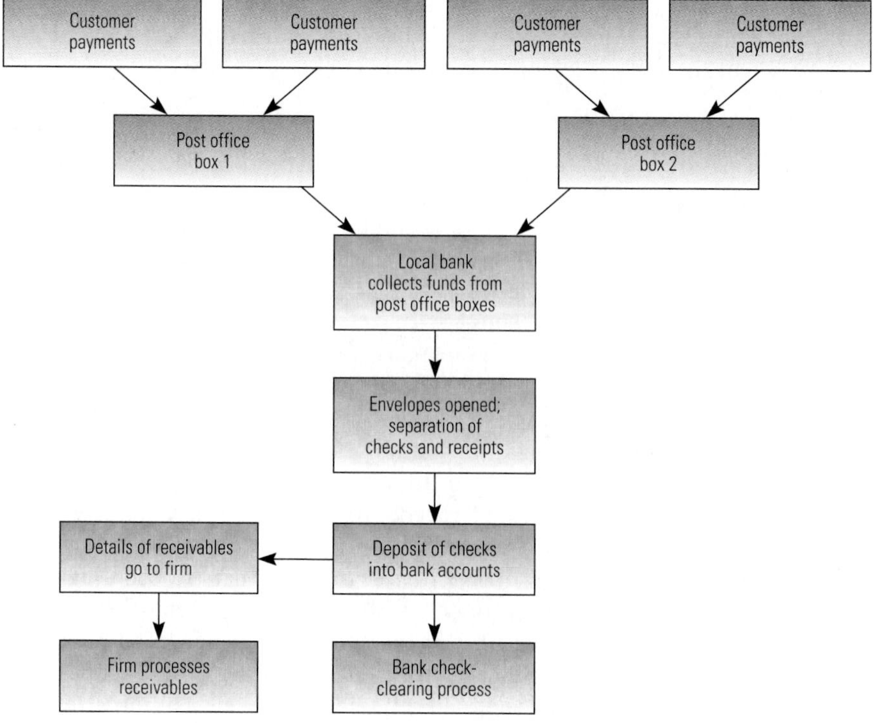

The flow starts when a customer mails remittances to a post office box instead of to the corporation. Several times a day the bank collects the lockbox receipts from the post office. The checks are then put into the company bank accounts.

cash concentration
The practice of and procedures for moving cash from multiple banks into the firm's main accounts.

Concept Q Answer 17.2b

in many different banks and bank accounts. From here, the firm needs procedures to move the cash into its main accounts. This is called **cash concentration.** By routinely pooling its cash, the firm's cash management is greatly simplified because only a small number of accounts must be tracked. Also, by having a larger pool of funds available, a firm may be able to negotiate or otherwise obtain a better rate on any short-term investments.

In setting up a concentration system, firms will typically use one or more *concentration banks.* A concentration bank pools the funds obtained from local banks contained within some geographic region. Concentration systems are often used in conjunction with lockbox systems. Figure 17.2 illustrates how an integrated cash collection and cash concentration system might look.

Managing Cash Disbursements

From the firm's point of view, disbursement float is desirable, so the goal in managing disbursement float is to slow down disbursements as much as possible. To do this, the firm may develop strategies to *increase* mail float, processing float, and availability float on the checks it writes. Beyond this, firms have developed procedures for minimizing cash held for payment purposes. We discuss the most common of these below.

Increasing Disbursement Float As we have seen, float in terms of slowing down payments comes from mail delivery, check-processing time, and collec-

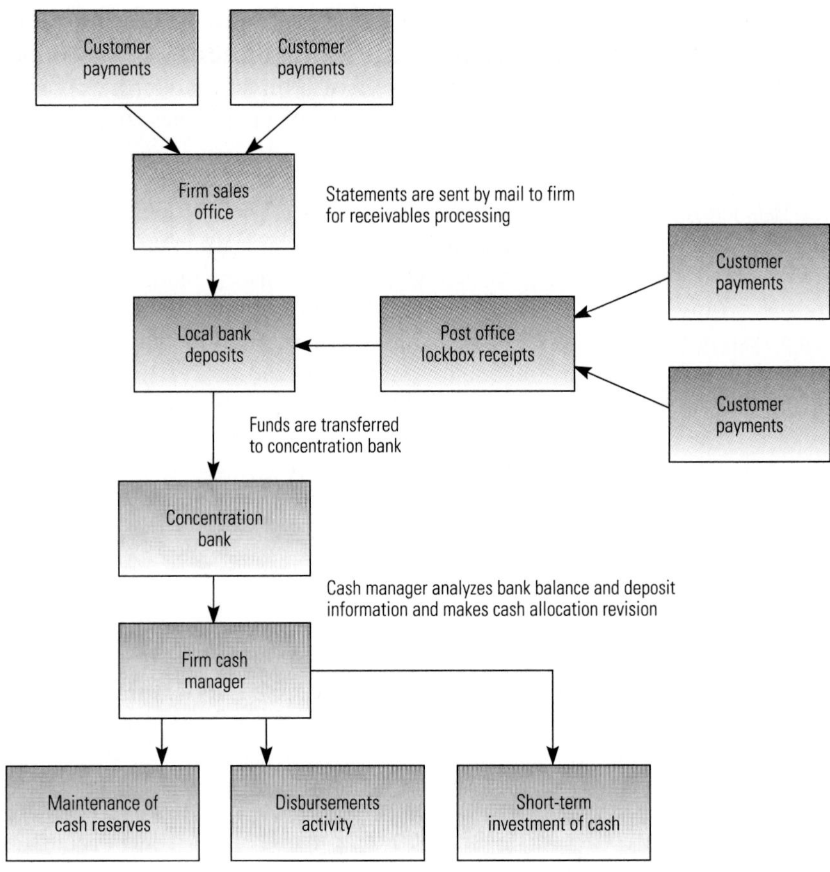

FIGURE 17.2
Lockboxes and concentration banks in a cash management system

Trans. 17.5

tion of funds. Disbursement float can be increased by writing a check on a geographically distant bank. For example, a New York supplier might be paid with checks drawn on a Los Angeles bank. This will increase the time required for the checks to clear through the banking system. Mailing checks from remote post offices is another way firms slow down disbursement.

Tactics for maximizing disbursement float are debatable on both ethical and economic grounds. First, as we discuss later, payment terms very frequently offer a substantial discount for early payment. The discount is usually much larger than any possible savings from "playing the float game." In such cases, increasing mailing time will be of no benefit if the recipient dates payments based on the date received (as is common) as opposed to the postmark date.

Concept Q Answer 17.2c

Beyond this, suppliers are not likely to be fooled by attempts to slow down disbursement. The negative consequences from poor relations with suppliers can be costly. In broader terms, intentionally delaying payments by taking advantage of mailing times or unsophisticated suppliers may amount to avoiding paying bills when they are due, an unethical business procedure.

★ **Ethics Note:** IM 17.2 provides additional real-world examples of cash management behavior for students to be on the lookout for.

Controlling Disbursements We have seen that maximizing disbursement float is probably poor business practice. However, a firm will still wish to tie up as little cash as possible in disbursements. Firms have therefore developed systems for efficiently managing the disbursement process. The general idea in such systems is to have no more than the minimum amount necessary to pay bills on deposit in the bank. We discuss some approaches to accomplish this goal next.

zero-balance account
A disbursement account in which the firm maintains a zero balance, transferring funds in from a master account only as needed to cover checks presented for payment.

Zero-Balance Accounts With a **zero-balance account,** the firm, in cooperation with its bank, maintains a master account and a set of subaccounts. When a check written on one of the subaccounts must be paid, the necessary funds are transferred in from the master account. Figure 17.3 illustrates how such a system might work. In this case, the firm maintains two disbursement accounts, one for suppliers and one for payroll. As shown, if the firm does not use zero-balance accounts, then each of these accounts must have a safety stock of cash to meet unanticipated demands. If the firm does use zero-balance accounts, then it can keep one safety stock in a master account and transfer the funds to the two subsidiary accounts as needed. The key is that the total amount of cash held as a buffer is smaller under the zero-balance arrangement, thereby freeing up cash to be used elsewhere.

controlled disbursement account
A disbursement practice under which the firm transfers an amount to a disbursing account that is sufficient to cover demands for payment.

Controlled Disbursement Accounts With a **controlled disbursement account,** almost all payments that must be made in a given day are known in the morning. The bank informs the firm of the total, and the firm transfers (usually by wire) the amount needed.

Investing Idle Cash

If a firm has a temporary cash surplus, it can invest in short-term securities. As we have mentioned at various times, the market for short-term financial assets is called the *money market.* The maturity of short-term financial assets that trade in the money market is one year or less.

Most large firms manage their own short-term financial assets, transacting through banks and dealers. Some large firms and many small firms use money market mutual funds. These are funds that invest in short-term fi-

FIGURE 17.3 Zero-balance accounts **Trans. 17.6**

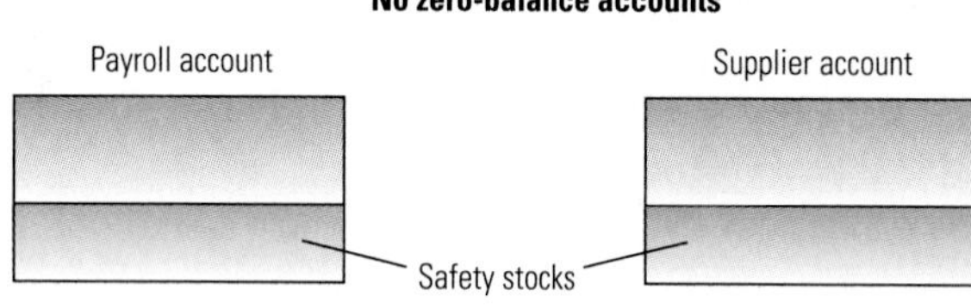

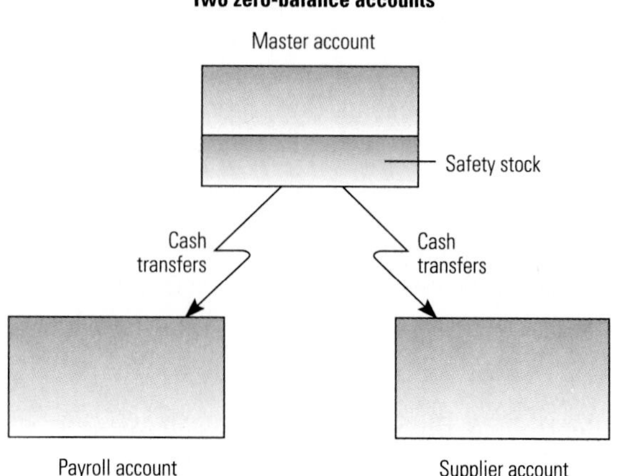

With no zero-balance accounts, separate safety stocks must be maintained, thereby tying up cash unnecessarily. With zero-balance accounts, the firm keeps a single safety stock of cash in a master account. Funds are transferred into disbursement accounts as needed.

nancial assets for a management fee. The management fee is compensation for the professional expertise and diversification provided by the fund manager.

Among the many money market mutual funds, some specialize in corporate customers. In addition, banks offer arrangements in which the bank takes all excess available funds at the close of each business day and invests them for the firm.

Temporary Cash Surpluses Firms have temporary cash surpluses for various reasons. Two of the most important are the financing of seasonal or cyclical activities of the firm and the financing of planned or possible expenditures.

Seasonal or Cyclical Activities Some firms have a predictable cash flow pattern. They have surplus cash flows during part of the year and deficit cash flows the rest of the year. For example, Toys "R" Us, a retail toy firm, has a seasonal cash flow pattern influenced by Christmas.

A firm such as Toys "R" Us may buy marketable securities when surplus cash flows occur and sell marketable securities when deficits occur. Of course, bank loans are another short-term financing device. The use of bank loans and marketable securities to meet temporary financing needs is illustrated in Figure 17.4. In this case, the firm is following a compromise working capital policy in the sense we discussed in the previous chapter.

Planned or Possible Expenditures Firms frequently accumulate temporary investments in marketable securities to provide the cash for a plant construction program, dividend payment, or other large expenditures. Thus, firms may issue bonds and stocks before the cash is needed, investing the proceeds in short-term marketable securities and then selling the securities to finance the expenditures. Also, firms may face the possibility of having to make a large cash outlay. An obvious example would be the possibility of losing a large lawsuit. Firms may build up cash surpluses against such a contingency.

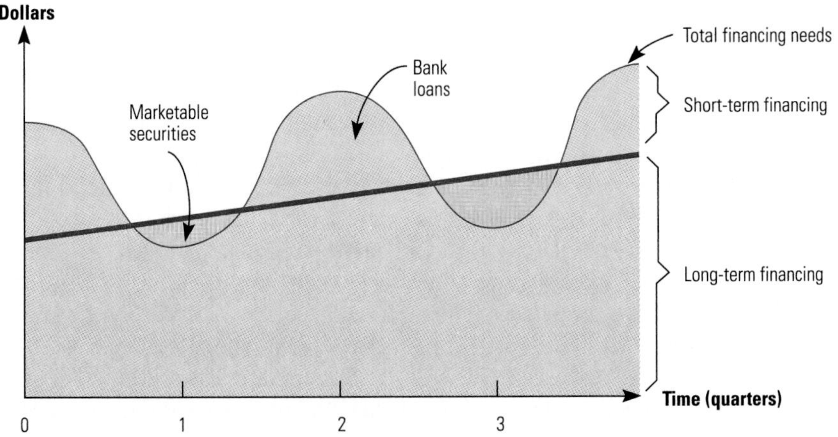

Time 1: A surplus cash position exists. Seasonal demand for current assets is low. The surplus cash is invested in short-term marketable securities.
Time 2: A deficit cash position exists. Seasonal demand for current assets is high. The financial deficit is financed by selling marketable securities and by bank borrowing.

FIGURE 17.4
Seasonal cash demands

Characteristics of Short-Term Securities Given that a firm has some temporarily idle cash, there are a variety of short-term securities available for investing. The most important characteristics of these short-term marketable securities are their maturity, default risk, marketability, and taxability.

Maturity Maturity refers to the time period over which interest and principal payments are made.

From Chapter 7, we know that for a given change in the level of interest rates, the prices of longer-maturity securities will change more than those of shorter-maturity securities. As a consequence, firms often limit their investments in marketable securities to those maturing in less than 90 days to avoid the risk of losses in value from changing interest rates.

Default Risk Default risk refers to the probability that interest and principal will not be paid in the promised amounts on the due dates (or not paid at all). Of course, some securities have negligible default risk, such as U.S. Treasury bills. Given the purposes of investing idle corporate cash, firms typically avoid investing in marketable securities with significant default risk.

Lecture Tip: Additional aspects of marketability are described in IM 17.2.

Marketability Marketability refers to how easy it is to convert an asset to cash; so marketability and liquidity mean much the same thing. Some money market instruments are much more marketable than others. At the top of the list are U.S. Treasury bills, which can be bought and sold very cheaply and very quickly.

Taxability Interest earned on money market securities that are not some kind of government obligation (either federal or state) are taxable at the local, state, and federal levels. U.S. Treasury obligations such as T-bills are exempt from state taxation, but other government-backed debt is not. Municipal securities are exempt from federal taxes, but they may be taxed at the state level.

Concept Q Answer 17.2d

Trans. 17.7 Money Market Securities (Supplemental)

Some Different Types of Money Market Securities Money market securities are generally highly marketable and short term. They usually have low risk of default. They are issued by the U.S. government (for example, U.S. Treasury bills), domestic and foreign banks (for example, certificates of deposit), and business corporations (for example, commercial paper). There are many types in all, and we only illustrate a few of the most common here.

U.S. Treasury bills are obligations of the U.S. government that mature in 90, 180, 270, or 360 days. The 90-day and 180-day bills are sold by auction every week, and 270-day and 360-day bills are sold every month.

Lecture Tip: See IM 17.2 for a tip on locating the daily money market rates in *The Wall Street Journal*.

Short-term tax-exempts are short-term securities issued by states, municipalities, and certain other agencies. Since these are all considered municipal securities, they are exempt from federal taxes. Short-term tax-exempts have more default risk than U.S. Treasury issues and are less marketable. Since the interest is exempt from federal income tax, the pretax yield on tax-exempts is lower than those on comparable securities such as U.S. Treasury bills. Also, corporations face some restrictions on holding tax-exempts as investments.

Commercial paper refers to short-term securities issued by finance companies, banks, and corporations. Typically, commercial paper is unsecured. Maturities range from a few weeks to 270 days.

There is no especially active secondary market in commercial paper. As a consequence, the marketability can be low; however, firms that issue commercial paper will often repurchase it directly before maturity. The default risk of commercial paper depends on the financial strength of the issuer.

Certificates of deposit (CDs) are short-term loans to commercial banks. These are normally jumbo CDs—those in excess of $100,000. There are active markets in CDs of 3-month, 6-month, 9-month, and 12-month maturities.

Because 70 to 80 percent of the dividends received by one corporation from another are exempt from taxation, the relatively high dividend yields on preferred stock provide a strong incentive for investment. The only problem is that the dividend is fixed with ordinary preferred stock, so the price can fluctuate more than is desirable in a short-term investment. So-called "money market" preferred stock is a recent innovation featuring a floating dividend. The dividend is reset fairly often (usually every 49 days), so this type of preferred has much less price volatility than ordinary preferred, and it has become a popular short-term investment.

CONCEPT QUESTIONS

17.2a What is a lockbox? What purpose does it serve?

17.2b What is a concentration bank? What purpose does it serve?

17.2c Is maximizing disbursement float a sound business practice?

17.2d What are some types of money market securities?

17.3 CREDIT AND RECEIVABLES: BACKGROUND

When a firm sells goods and services, it can demand cash on or before the delivery date or it can extend credit to customers and allow some delay in payment.

Trans. 17.8
Credit Management (Supplemental)

Why would firms grant credit? The obvious reason is that offering credit is a way of stimulating sales. The costs associated with granting credit are not trivial. First, there is the chance that the customer will not pay. Second, the firm has to bear the costs of carrying the receivables. The credit policy decision thus involves a trade-off between the benefits of increased sales versus the costs of granting credit.

From an accounting perspective, when credit is granted, an account receivable is created. These receivables include credit to other firms, called *trade credit,* and credit granted consumers, called *consumer credit* and they represent a major investment of financial resources by U.S. businesses. Furthermore, trade credit is a very important source of financing for corporations. However we look at it, receivables and receivables management are very important aspects of a firm's short-term financial policy.

Trans. 17.9
The Cash Flows from Granting Credit

Components of Credit Policy

If a firm decides to grant credit to its customers, then it must establish procedures for extending credit and collecting. In particular, the firm will have to deal with the following components of credit policy:

Concept Q Answer 17.3a

1. **Terms of sale.** The terms of sale establish how the firm proposes to sell its goods and services. If the firm grants credit to a customer, the terms of sale will specify (perhaps implicitly) the

terms of sale
Conditions under which a firm sells its goods and services for cash or credit.

credit period, the cash discount and discount period, and the type of credit instrument.

credit analysis
The process of determining the probability that customers will or will not pay.

2. **Credit analysis.** In granting credit, a firm determines how much effort to expend trying to distinguish between customers who will pay and customers who will not pay. Firms use a number of devices and procedures to determine the probability that customers will not pay, and, put together, these are called *credit analysis.*

collection policy
Procedures followed by a firm in collecting accounts receivable.

3. **Collection policy.** After credit has been granted, the firm has the potential problem of collecting the cash when it becomes due, for which it must establish a collection policy.

In the next several sections, we will discuss these components of credit policy that collectively make up the decision to grant credit.

Terms of the Sale

As we described above, the terms of a sale are made up of three distinct elements:

1. The period for which credit is granted (the credit period).
2. The cash discount and the discount period.
3. The type of credit instrument.

Lecture Tip: The instructor may wish to point out that, from an economist's viewpoint, the fact that these systems have survived for so long suggests that they are an efficient means of granting credit.

Within a given industry, the terms of sale are usually fairly standard, but these terms vary quite a bit across industries. In many cases, the terms of sale are remarkably archaic and literally date to previous centuries. Organized systems of trade credit that resemble current practice can be easily traced to the great fairs of medieval Europe, and they almost surely existed long before then.

The Basic Form The easiest way to understand the terms of sale is to consider an example. For bulk candy, terms of 2/10, net 60 might be quoted.[2] This means that customers have 60 days from the invoice date (discussed below) to pay the full amount. However, if payment is made within 10 days, a 2 percent cash discount can be taken.

Consider a buyer who places an order for $1,000, and assume that the terms of the sale are 2/10, net 60. The buyer has the option of paying $1,000 × (1 − .02) = $980 in 10 days, or paying the full $1,000 in 60 days. If the terms were stated as just net 30, then the customer has 30 days from the invoice date to pay the entire $1,000, and no discount is offered for early payment.

In general, credit terms are interpreted in the following way:

⟨take this discount off the invoice price⟩/⟨if you pay in this many days⟩,
⟨else pay the full invoice amount in this many days⟩

Thus, 5/10, net 45 means take a 5 percent discount from the full price if you pay within 10 days, or else pay the full amount in 45 days.

[2] The terms of sale cited from specific industries in this section and elsewhere are drawn from Theodore N. Beckman, *Credits and Collections: Management and Theory* (New York: McGraw-Hill, 1962).

The Credit Period The **credit period** is the basic length of time that credit is granted. The credit period varies widely from industry to industry, but it is almost always between 30 and 120 days. If a cash discount is offered, then the credit period has two components: the net credit period and the cash discount period.

credit period
The length of time that credit is granted.

The net credit period is the length of time the customer has to pay. The cash discount period, as the name suggests, is the time during which the discount is available. With 2/10, net 30, for example, the net credit period is 30 days and the cash discount period is 10 days.

The Invoice Date The invoice date is the beginning of the credit period. An **invoice** is a written account of merchandise shipped to the buyer. For individual items, by convention, the invoice date is usually the shipping date or the billing date, *not* the date that the buyer receives the goods or the bill.

invoice
Bill for goods or services provided by the seller to the purchaser.

Length of the Credit Period A number of factors influence the length of the credit period. One of the most important is the *buyer's* inventory period and operating cycle. All other things being equal, the shorter these are, the shorter the credit period will normally be.

Lecture Tip: Common invoice dating practices are described in the IM.

Trans. 17.10
Length of the Credit Period (Supplemental)

Based on our discussion in Chapter 16, the operating cycle has two components: the inventory period and the receivables period. The inventory period is the time it takes the buyer to acquire inventory (from us), process it, and sell it. The receivables period is the time it then takes the buyer to collect on the sale. Note that the credit period that we offer is effectively the buyer's payables period.

By extending credit, we finance a portion of our buyer's operating cycle and thereby shorten his or her cash cycle. If our credit period exceeds the buyer's inventory period, then we are not only financing the buyer's inventory purchases, but part of the buyer's receivables as well.

Furthermore, if our credit period exceeds our buyer's operating cycle, then we are effectively providing financing for aspects of our customer's business beyond the immediate purchase and sale of our merchandise. The reason is that the buyer effectively has a loan from us even after the merchandise is resold, and the buyer can use that credit for other purposes. For this reason, the length of the buyer's operating cycle is often cited as an appropriate upper limit to the credit period.

There are a number of other factors that influence the credit period. Many of these also influence our customers' operating cycles; so, once again, these are related subjects. Among the most important are:

1. *Perishability and collateral value.* Perishable items have relatively rapid turnover and relatively low collateral value. Credit periods are thus shorter for such goods.
2. *Consumer demand.* Products that are well established generally have more rapid turnover. Newer or slow-moving products will often have longer credit periods associated with them to entice buyers.
3. *Cost, profitability, and standardization.* Relatively inexpensive goods tend to have shorter credit periods. The same is true for relatively standardized goods and raw materials. These all tend to

have lower markups and higher turnover rates, both of which lead to shorter credit periods.

4. *Credit risk.* The greater the credit risk of the buyer, the shorter the credit period is likely to be (assuming that credit is granted at all).
5. *The size of the account.* If the account is small, the credit period may be shorter because small accounts are more costly to manage, and the customers are less important.
6. *Competition.* When the seller is in a highly competitive market, longer credit periods may be offered as a way of attracting customers.
7. *Customer type.* A single seller might offer different credit terms to different buyers. A food wholesaler, for example, might supply groceries, bakeries, and restaurants. Each group would probably have different credit terms. More generally, sellers often have both wholesale and retail customers, and they frequently quote different terms to the two types.

cash discount
A discount given to induce prompt payment. Also *sales discount.*

Cash Discounts As we have seen, **cash discounts** are often part of the terms of sale. The practice of granting discounts for cash purchases in the United States dates to the Civil War and is widespread today. One reason discounts are offered is to speed up the collection of receivables. This will have the effect of reducing the amount of credit being offered, and the firm must trade this off against the cost of the discount.

Notice that when a cash discount is offered, the credit is essentially free during the discount period. The buyer only pays for the credit after the discount expires. With 2/10, net 30, a rational buyer either pays in 10 days to make the greatest possible use of the free credit or pays in 30 days to get the longest possible use of the money in exchange for giving up the discount. So, by giving up the discount, the buyer effectively gets 30 − 10 = 20 days' credit.

Lecture Tip: See IM for further comments on the cost of trade credit.

Another reason for cash discounts is that they are a way of charging higher prices to customers that have had credit extended to them. In this sense, cash discounts are a convenient way of charging for the credit granted to customers.

Cost of the Credit In our examples, it might seem that the discounts are rather small. With 2/10, net 30, for example, early payment only gets the buyer a 2 percent discount. Does this provide a significant incentive for early payment? The answer is yes because the implicit interest rate is extremely high.

To see why the discount is important, we will calculate the cost to the buyer of not paying early. To do this, we will find the interest rate that the buyer is effectively paying for the trade credit. Suppose the order is for $1,000. The buyer can pay $980 in 10 days or wait another 20 days and pay $1,000. It's obvious that the buyer is effectively borrowing $980 for 20 days and that the buyer pays $20 in interest on the "loan." What's the interest rate?

Concept Q Answer 17.3b

With $20 in interest on $980 borrowed, the rate is $20/$980 = 2.0408%. This is relatively low, but remember that this is the rate per 20-day period. There are 365/20 = 18.25 such periods in a year, so, by not taking the discount, the buyer is paying an effective annual rate (EAR) of:

$$\text{EAR} = (1.020408)^{18.25} - 1 = 44.6\%$$

From the buyer's point of view, this is an expensive source of financing!

Given that the interest rate is so high here, it is unlikely that the seller benefits from early payment. Ignoring the possibility of default by the buyer, the decision by a customer to forgo the discount almost surely works to the seller's advantage.

EXAMPLE 17.2 What's the Rate?

Ordinary tiles are often sold 3/30, net 60. What effective annual rate does a buyer pay by not taking the discount? What would the APR be if one were quoted?

Here we have 3 percent discount interest on 60 − 30 = 30 days' credit. The rate per 30 days is .03/.97 = 3.093%. There are 365/30 = 12.17 such periods in a year, so the effective annual rate is:

$$\text{EAR} = (1.03093)^{12.17} - 1 = 44.9\%$$

The APR, as always, would be calculated by multiplying the rate per period by the number of periods:

$$\text{APR} = .03093 \times 12.17 = 37.6\%$$

An interest rate calculated like this APR is often quoted as the cost of the trade credit, and, as this example illustrates, can seriously understate the true cost. • • •

credit instrument
The evidence of indebtedness.

Credit Instruments The **credit instrument** is the basic evidence of indebtedness. Most trade credit is offered on *open account.* This means that the only formal instrument of credit is the invoice, which is sent with the shipment of goods and which the customer signs as evidence that the goods have been received. Afterward, the firm and its customers record the exchange on their books of account.

At times, the firm may require that the customer sign a *promissory note.* This is a basic IOU and might be used when the order is large or when the firm anticipates a problem in collections. Promissory notes are not common, but they can eliminate possible controversies later about the existence of debt.

One problem with promissory notes is that they are signed after delivery of the goods. One way to obtain a credit commitment from a customer before the goods are delivered is to arrange a *commercial draft.* Typically, the firm draws up a commercial draft calling for the customer to pay a specific amount by a specified date. The draft is then sent to the customer's bank with the shipping invoices.

International Note: The use of acceptances and letters of credit in international trade is discussed further in IM 17.3.

If immediate payment on the draft is required, it is called a *sight draft.* If immediate payment is not required, then the draft is a *time draft.* When the draft is presented and the buyer "accepts" it, meaning that the buyer promises to pay it in the future, then it is called a *trade acceptance* and is sent back to the selling firm. The seller can then keep the acceptance or sell it to someone else. If a bank accepts the draft, meaning that the bank is guaranteeing payment, then the draft becomes a *banker's acceptance.* This arrangement is common in international trade.

Optimal Credit Policy

In principle, the optimal amount of credit is determined where the incremental cash flows from increased sales are exactly equal to the incremental costs of carrying the increased investment in accounts receivable.

The Total Credit Cost Curve The trade-off between granting credit and not granting credit isn't hard to identify, but it is difficult to quantify precisely. As a result, we can only describe an optimal credit policy.

To begin, the carrying costs associated with granting credit come in three forms:

1. The required return on receivables.
2. The losses from bad debts.
3. The costs of managing credit and credit collections.

We have already discussed the first and second of these. The third cost, the costs of managing credit, is the expense associated with running the credit department. Firms that don't grant credit have no such department and no such expense. These three costs will all increase as credit policy is relaxed.

If a firm has a very restrictive credit policy, then all of the above costs will be low. In this case, the firm will have a "shortage" of credit, so there will be an opportunity cost. This opportunity cost is the extra potential profit from credit sales that is lost because credit is refused. This forgone benefit comes from two sources, the increase in quantity sold, and, potentially, a higher price. These costs go down as credit policy is relaxed.

credit cost curve
Graphical representation of the sum of the carrying costs and the opportunity costs of a credit policy.

The sum of the carrying costs and the opportunity costs of a particular credit policy is called the total **credit cost curve.** We have drawn such a curve in Figure 17.5. As Figure 17.5 illustrates, there is a point, C^*, where the total credit cost is minimized. This point corresponds to the optimal amount of credit or, equivalently, the optimal investment in receivables.

If the firm extends more credit than this amount, the additional net cash flow from new customers will not cover the carrying costs of the investment in receivables. If the level of receivables is below this amount, then the firm is forgoing valuable profit opportunities.

In general, the costs and benefits from extending credit will depend on characteristics of particular firms and industries. All other things being

FIGURE 17.5
The costs of granting credit

Trans. 17.11

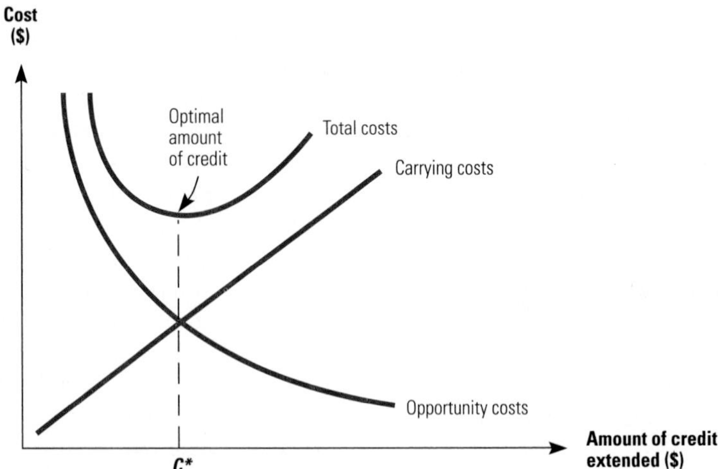

Carrying costs are the cash flows that must be incurred when credit is granted. They are positively related to the amount of credit extended.

Opportunity costs are the lost sales from refusing credit. These costs go down when credit is granted.

equal, for example, it is likely that firms with (1) excess capacity, (2) low variable operating costs, and (3) repeat customers will extend credit more liberally than otherwise. See if you can explain why each of these contributes to a more liberal credit policy.

Organizing the Credit Function Firms that grant credit have the expense of running a credit department. In practice, firms often choose to contract out all or part of the credit function to a factor, an insurance company, or a captive finance company. Chapter 16 discusses factoring, an arrangement in which the firm sells its receivables. Depending on the specific arrangement, the factor may have full responsibility for credit checking, authorization, and collection. Smaller firms may find such an arrangement cheaper than running a credit department.

Firms that manage internal credit operations are self-insured against default. An alternative is to buy credit insurance through an insurance company. The insurance company offers coverage up to a preset dollar limit for accounts. As you would expect, accounts with a higher credit rating merit higher insurance limits. This type of insurance is particularly important for exporters, and government insurance is available for certain types of exports.

Large firms often extend credit through a **captive finance company,** which is simply a wholly owned subsidiary that handles the credit function for the parent company. General Motors Acceptance Corporation (GMAC) is a well-known example. General Motors sells to car dealers who in turn sell to customers. GMAC finances the dealer's inventory of cars and also finances customers who buy the cars.

captive finance company
A wholly-owned subsidiary that handles the credit function for the parent company.

Credit Analysis

Thus far, we have focused on establishing credit terms. Once a firm decides to grant credit to its customers, it must then establish guidelines for determining who will and who will not be allowed to buy on credit. *Credit analysis* refers to the process of deciding whether or not to extend credit to a particular customer. It usually involves two steps: gathering relevant information and determining creditworthiness.

Credit Information If a firm does want credit information on customers, there are a number of sources. Information commonly used to assess creditworthiness includes the following:

Lecture Tip: The use of credit information to adjust borrowing costs is discussed via example in IM 17.3.

1. *Financial statements.* A firm can ask a customer to supply financial statement information such as balance sheets and income statements. Minimum standards and rules of thumb based on financial ratios like the ones we discussed in Chapter 3 can then be used as a basis for extending or refusing credit.
2. *Credit reports on the customer's payment history with other firms.* Quite a few organizations sell information on the credit strength and credit history of business firms. The best-known and largest firm of this type is Dun & Bradstreet, which provides subscribers with a credit reference book and credit reports on individual firms. TRW is another well-known credit reporting firm. Ratings and

information are available for a huge number of firms, including very small ones. Equifax, Transunion, and TRW are the major suppliers of consumer credit information.

3. *Banks.* Banks will generally provide some assistance to their business customers in acquiring information on the creditworthiness of other firms.
4. *The customer's payment history with the firm.* The most obvious way to obtain information about the likelihood of a customer not paying is to examine whether they have settled past obligations and how quickly they have met these obligations.

Credit Evaluation and Scoring There are no magical formulas for assessing the probability that a customer will not pay. In very general terms, the classic **five Cs of credit** are the basic factors to be evaluated:

five Cs of credit
The five basic credit factors to be evaluated: character, capacity, capital, collateral, and conditions.

Trans. 17.12
Five Cs of Credit

Concept Q
Answer 17.3c

Lecture Tip: Further discussion of the five Cs of credit is provided in IM 17.3.

1. *Character.* The customer's willingness to meet credit obligations.
2. *Capacity.* The customer's ability to meet credit obligations out of operating cash flows.
3. *Capital.* The customer's financial reserves.
4. *Collateral.* Assets pledged by the customer for security in case of default.
5. *Conditions.* General economic conditions in the customer's line of business.

credit scoring
The process of quantifying the probability of default when granting consumer credit.

Lecture Tip: You may wish to emphasize that the use of credit scoring models is most appropriate for firms that evaluate large numbers of potential borrowers annually, and would therefore, find it prohibitively costly to perform individual analyses manually.

★ **Ethics Note:** Some ethical considerations in the use of credit scoring models are discussed in IM 17.3.

Credit scoring refers to the process of calculating a numerical rating for a customer based on information collected and then granting or refusing credit based on the result. For example, a firm might rate a customer on a scale of 1 (very poor) to 10 (very good) on each of the five Cs of credit using all the information available about the customer. A credit score could then be calculated based on the total. From experience, a firm might choose to grant credit only to customers with a score above, say, 30.

Firms such as credit card issuers have developed elaborate statistical models for credit scoring. Usually, all of the legally relevant and observable characteristics of a large pool of customers are studied to find their historic relation to default rates. Based on the results, it is possible to determine the variables that best predict whether or not a customer will pay and then calculate a credit score based on those variables.

Because credit-scoring models and procedures determine who is and who is not creditworthy, it is not surprising that they have been the subject of government regulation. In particular, the kinds of background and demographic information that can be used in the credit decision are limited.

Collection Policy

Collection policy is the final element in credit policy. Collection policy involves monitoring receivables to spot trouble and obtaining payment on past-due accounts.

Monitoring Receivables To keep track of payments by customers, most firms will monitor outstanding accounts. First, a firm will normally keep track of its average collection period (ACP) through time. If a firm is in a seasonal business, the ACP will fluctuate during the year, but unexpected increases in the ACP are a cause for concern. Either customers in general are taking longer to pay, or some percentage of accounts receivable is seriously overdue.

The **aging schedule** is a second basic tool for monitoring receivables. To prepare one, the credit department classifies accounts by age.[3] Suppose a firm has $100,000 in receivables. Some of these accounts are only a few days old, but others have been outstanding for quite some time. The following is an example of an aging schedule.

aging schedule
A compilation of accounts receivable by the age of each account.

Aging Schedule

Age of Account	Amount	Percent of Total Value of Accounts Receivable
0–10 days	$ 50,000	50
11–60 days	25,000	25
61–80 days	20,000	20
Over 80 days	5,000	5
	$100,000	100

If this firm has a credit period of 60 days, then 25 percent of its accounts are late. Whether or not this is serious depends on the nature of the firm's collections and customers. It is often the case that accounts beyond a certain age are almost never collected. Monitoring the age of accounts is very important in such cases.

Lecture Tip: IM 17.3 references a seminal article describing improved tools for the management of accounts receivable.

Firms with seasonal sales will find the percentages on the aging schedule changing during the year. For example, if sales in the current month are very high, then total receivables will also increase sharply. This means that the older accounts, as a percentage of total receivables, become smaller and might appear less important. Some firms have refined the aging schedule so that they have an idea of how it should change with peaks and valleys in their sales.

Collection Effort A firm usually goes through the following sequence of procedures for customers whose payments are overdue:

1. It sends out a delinquency letter informing the customer of the past-due status of the account.
2. It makes a telephone call to the customer.
3. It employs a collection agency.
4. It takes legal action against the customer.

Lecture Tip: You may wish to point out that the lender's decision to implement these steps is taken with great care—procedures 3 and 4 virtually guarantee that the customer is lost, and are not inexpensive.

At times, a firm may refuse to grant additional credit to customers until arrearages are cleared up. This may antagonize a normally good customer, and it points to a potential conflict of interest between the collections department and the sales department.

CONCEPT QUESTIONS

17.3a What are the basic components of credit policy?

17.3b Explain what terms of "3/45, net 90" mean. What is the effective interest rate?

17.3c What are the five Cs of credit?

[3] Aging schedules are used elsewhere in business. For example, aging schedules are often prepared for inventory items.

17.4 INVENTORY MANAGEMENT

Like receivables, inventories represent a significant investment for many firms. For a typical manufacturing operation, inventories will often exceed 15 percent of assets. For a retailer, inventories could represent more than 25 percent of assets. From our discussion in Chapter 16, we know that a firm's operating cycle is made up of its inventory period and its receivables period. This is one reason for considering credit and inventory policy in the same chapter. Beyond this, both credit policy and inventory policy are used to drive sales, and the two must be coordinated to ensure that the process of acquiring inventory, selling it, and collecting on the sale proceeds smoothly. For example, changes in credit policy designed to stimulate sales must be simultaneously accompanied by planning for adequate inventory.

The Financial Manager and Inventory Policy

Despite the size of a typical firm's investment in inventories, the financial manager of a firm will not normally have primary control over inventory management. Instead, other functional areas such as purchasing, production, and marketing will usually share decision-making authority. Inventory management has become an increasingly important specialty in its own right, and financial management will often only have input into the decision. However, as the accompanying *Principles in Action* box describes, inventory policy can have dramatic financial effects. We will therefore survey some basics of inventory and inventory policy in the sections ahead.

Inventory Types

Concept Q Answer 17.4a

For a manufacturer, inventory is normally classified into one of three categories. The first category is *raw material.* This is whatever the firm uses as a starting point in its production process. Raw materials might be something as basic as iron ore for a steel manufacturer or something as sophisticated as disk drives for a computer manufacturer.

The second type of inventory is *work-in-progress,* which is just what the name suggests—unfinished product. How big this portion of inventory is depends in large part on the length of the production process. For an airframe manufacturer, for example, work-in-progress can be substantial. The third and final type of inventory is *finished goods,* that is, products ready to ship or sell.

Concept Q Answer 17.4b

There are three things to keep in mind concerning inventory types. First, the names for the different types can be a little misleading because one company's raw materials could be another's finished goods. For example, going back to our steel manufacturer, iron ore would be a raw material, and steel would be the final product. An auto body panel stamping operation will have steel as its raw material and auto body panels as its finished goods, and an automobile assembler will have body panels as raw materials and automobiles as finished products.

Lecture Tip: Interindustry differences on inventory holdings and inventory liquidity also explain the use of "industry norms" as benchmarks in financial analysis, as described in Chapter 3.

The second thing to keep in mind is that the various types of inventory can be quite different in terms of their liquidity. Raw materials that are commodity-like or relatively standardized can be easy to convert to cash. Work-in-progress, on the other hand, can be quite illiquid and have little more

Principles in Action

Zeroing in on Working Capital

American Standard is a privately-held producer of Trane air conditioners, American Standard plumbing supplies, and Wabco brakes for trucks. In the early 1990s, all three of the company's product markets went sour, throwing the company into a battle for survival. Management needed to make drastic changes to generate cash flow. Their answer? Raid working capital, which in 1988 amounted to $725 million, or about 25 cents for each dollar in sales. By comparison, in 1994, the average Fortune 500 company had about 20 cents in working capital for each dollar of sales. The key to the company's survival was to reduce working capital and the associated carrying costs without losing sales or increasing shortage costs.

To cut working capital, American Standard had to change its manufacturing practices. The company's production output was supply-based—it forecasted demand for its products and then generated a supply projected to meet that demand. In their Trane division, for example, it produced each of the many separate parts for their products in long production runs designed to keep their machines running. This built up inventories of many separate items, called work-in-process inventory, to later be assembled into finished products. Even though most of these parts were on the production machines for only minutes, they often sat as inventory for weeks, and sometimes months or even years.

The firm's new production system is demand-based—products are generated in response to actual customer orders, not demand forecasts, requiring the ability to produce finished goods very fast. To do this, the company reorganized the machines in its factories into clusters so that machines that produce parts for a particular product were located in close proximity to one another. It then began producing parts in shorter production runs, focusing on generating less work-in-process and more finished-goods inventory. Ultimately, American Standard managed to produce finished goods so much faster that it dramatically reduced the time it takes from when a customer order comes in to when the finished product is shipped to the customer. The firm's customers, many of whom resold the products, benefitted from the increased responsiveness to orders by having to carry less inventory themselves. As a result, they paid for the goods sooner, reducing the level of accounts receivable carried by American Standard. By the middle of 1994 the company had reduced its working capital investment by $200 million to $525 million, or about 14 cents for each dollar in sales, even as sales increased.

The benefits of reducing investment in net working capital are both immediate and long-term. In the short-term, each dollar working capital is reduced results in a one-time $1 contribution to cash flow. American Standard used the $200 million cash flow from working capital to pay down debt and fund capital expenditures. The long-term benefit of reducing net working capital is that it permanently raises earnings by decreasing carrying costs. Investment in working capital must be financed, and storing inventory requires warehouse space and people and equipment to move it around and keep track of it. Thus, as a firm reduces its investment in working capital, it reduces operating expenses and increases earnings. Since 1990, annual operating earnings of American Standard have increased by 33 percent. It's hardly surprising, then, that American Standard is not alone in its crusade to reduce working capital. General Electric, Whirlpool, Quaker Oats, and Campbell Soup all have stated a similar objective: zero net working capital.

Source: "Raiding a Company's Hidden Cash," *Fortune,* August 22, 1994, pp. 82–87.

than scrap value. As always, the liquidity of finished goods depends on the nature of the product.

Finally, a very important distinction between finished goods and other types of inventories is that the demand for an inventory item that becomes a part of another item is usually termed *derived* or *dependent demand* because the firm's need for these inventory types depends on its need for finished items. In contrast, the firm's demand for finished goods is not derived from demand for other inventory items, so it is sometimes said to be *independent.*

Inventory Costs

As we discussed in Chapter 16, there are two basic types of costs associated with current assets in general and with inventory in particular. The first of these are *carrying costs.* Here, carrying costs represent all of the direct and opportunity costs of keeping inventory on hand. These include:

1. Storage and tracking costs.
2. Insurance and taxes.
3. Losses due to obsolescence, deterioration, or theft.
4. The opportunity cost of capital on the invested amount.

The sum of these costs can be substantial, roughly ranging from 20 to 40 percent of inventory value per year.

The other types of costs associated with inventory are *shortage costs.* These are costs associated with having inadequate inventory on hand. The two components of shortage costs are restocking costs and costs related to safety reserves. Depending on the firm's business, restocking or order costs are either the costs of placing an order with suppliers or the cost of setting up a production run. The costs related to safety reserves are opportunity losses such as lost sales and loss of customer goodwill that result from having inadequate inventory.

Concept Q Answer 17.4c

A basic trade-off in inventory management exists because carrying costs increase with inventory levels while shortage or restocking costs decline with inventory levels. The basic goal of inventory management is thus to minimize the sum of these two costs. We consider ways to reach this goal in the next section.

Lecture Tip: The use of subcontractors can reduce inventory carrying costs. IM 17.4 describes a real-world example of this.

CONCEPT QUESTIONS

17.4a What are the different types of inventory?

17.4b What are three things to remember when examining inventory types?

17.4c What is the basic goal of inventory management?

17.5 INVENTORY MANAGEMENT TECHNIQUES

Self-Test Problem 2
Problems 17–21

As we described earlier, the goal of inventory management is usually framed as cost minimization. Three techniques are discussed in this section, ranging from the relatively simple to the very complex.

The ABC Approach

The ABC approach is a simple approach to inventory management where the basic idea is to divide inventory into three (or more) groups. The underlying rationale is that a small portion of inventory in terms of quantity might represent a large portion in terms of inventory value. For example, this situation would exist for a manufacturer that uses some relatively expensive, high-tech components and some relatively inexpensive basic materials in producing its products.

Figure 17.6 illustrates an ABC comparison of items in terms of the percentage of inventory value represented by each group versus the percentage of items represented. As Figure 17.6 shows, the A Group constitutes only 10 percent of inventory by item count, but it represents over half of the value of inventory. The A Group items are thus monitored closely, and inventory levels

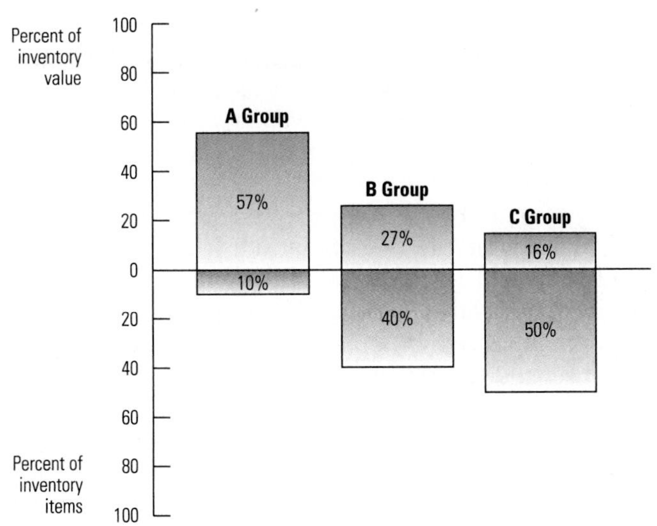

FIGURE 17.6
ABC inventory analysis

Trans. 17.13

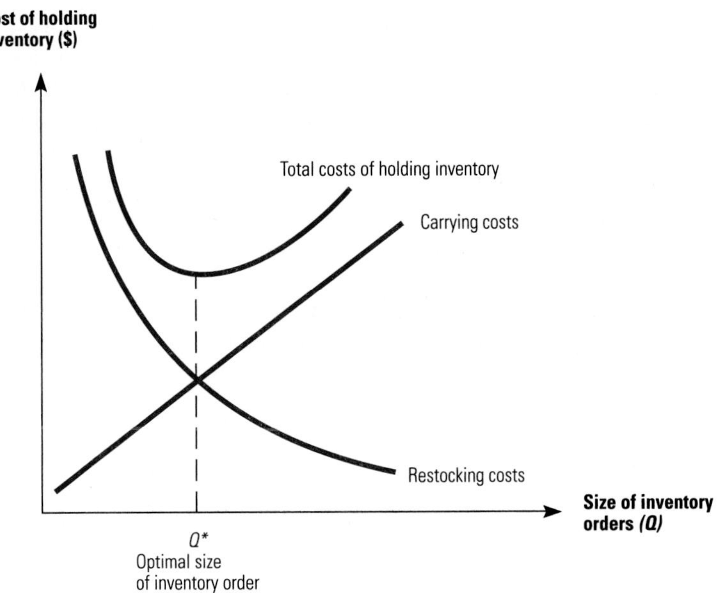

FIGURE 17.7
Costs of holding inventory

Trans. 17.14

Restocking costs are greatest when the firm holds a small quantity of inventory. Carrying costs are greatest when there is a large quantity of inventory on hand. Total costs are the sum of the carrying and restocking costs.

are kept relatively low. At the other end, basic inventory items, such as nuts and bolts, will also exist, but because these are crucial and inexpensive, large quantities are ordered and kept on hand. These would be C Group items. The B Group is made up of in-between items.

The Economic Order Quantity (EOQ) Model

The economic order quantity (EOQ) model is the best-known approach to explicitly establishing an optimal inventory level. The basic idea is illustrated in Figure 17.7, which plots the various costs associated with holding inventory (on the vertical axis) against inventory levels (on the horizontal axis). As shown, inventory carrying costs rise and restocking costs decrease as inventory levels increase. From our discussion of the total credit cost curve in this chapter, the general shape of the total inventory cost curve is familiar. With the EOQ model, we will attempt to specifically locate the minimum total cost point, Q^*.

Concept Q Answer 17.5a

In our discussion below, an important point to keep in mind is that the actual cost of the inventory itself is not included. The reason is that the *total* amount of inventory the firm needs in a given year is dictated by sales. What we are analyzing here is how much the firm should have on hand at any particular time. More precisely, we are trying to determine what order size the firm should use when it restocks its inventory.

Lecture Tip: See IM 17.5 for a variation of the EOQ model that takes seasonal sales into account.

Inventory Depletion To develop the EOQ, we will assume that the firm's inventory is sold off at a steady rate until it hits zero. At that point, the firm restocks its inventory back to some optimal level. For example, suppose the Eyssell Corporation starts out today with 3,600 units of a particular item in inventory. Annual sales of this item are 46,800 units, which is about 900 per week. If Eyssell sells off 900 units in inventory each week, then, after four weeks, all the available inventory will be sold, and Eyssell will restock by ordering (or manufacturing) another 3,600 and start over. This selling and restocking process produces a sawtooth pattern for inventory holdings; this pattern is illustrated in Figure 17.8. As the figure shows, Eyssell always starts with 3,600 units in inventory and ends up at zero. On average, then, inventory is half of 3,600, or 1,800 units.

The Carrying Costs As Figure 17.7 illustrates, carrying costs are normally assumed to be directly proportional to inventory levels. Suppose we let Q be the quantity of inventory that Eyssell orders each time (3,600 units); we will

FIGURE 17.8
Inventory holdings for the Eyssell Corporation

Trans. 17.15

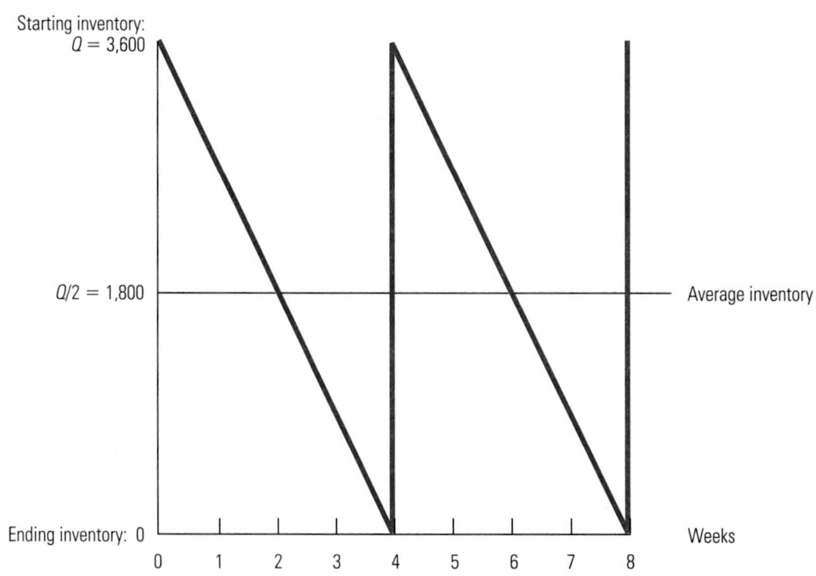

The Eyssell Corporation starts with inventory of 3,600 units. The quantity drops to zero by the end of the fourth week. The average inventory is $Q/2 = 3{,}600/2 = 1{,}800$ over the period.

call this the restocking quantity. Average inventory would then just be $Q/2$, or 1,800 units. If we let CC be the carrying cost per unit per year, Eyssell's total carrying costs will be:

$$\text{Total carrying costs} = \text{Average inventory} \times \text{Carrying costs per unit}$$
$$= (Q/2) \times \text{CC} \qquad [17.1]$$

In Eyssell's case, if carrying costs were $0.75 per unit per year, then total carrying costs would be the average inventory of 1,800 multiplied by $0.75, or $1,350 per year.

The Shortage Costs For now, we will focus only on the restocking costs. In essence, we will assume that the firm never actually runs short on inventory, so that costs relating to safety reserves are not important. We will return to this issue below.

Restocking costs are normally assumed to be fixed. In other words, every time we place an order, there are fixed costs associated with that order (remember the cost of the inventory itself is not considered here). Suppose we let T be the firm's total unit sales per year. If the firm orders Q units each time, then it will need to place a total of T/Q orders. For Eyssell, annual sales were 46,800, and the order size was 3,600. Eyssell thus places a total of $46,800/3,600 = 13$ orders per year. If the fixed cost per order is F, the total restocking cost for the year would be:

$$\text{Total restocking cost} = \text{Fixed cost per order} \times \text{Number of orders}$$
$$= F \times (T/Q) \qquad [17.2]$$

For Eyssell, order costs might be $50 per order, so the total restocking cost for 13 orders would be $50 × 13 = $650 per year.

The Total Costs The total costs associated with holding inventory are the sum of the carrying costs and the restocking costs:

$$\text{Total costs} = \text{Carrying costs} + \text{Restocking costs}$$
$$= (Q/2) \times \text{CC} + F \times (T/Q) \qquad [17.3]$$

Our goal is to find the value of Q, the restocking quantity, that minimizes this cost. To see how we might go about this, we can calculate total costs for some different values of Q. For the Eyssell Corporation, we had carrying costs (CC) of $0.75 per unit per year, fixed costs (F) of $50 per order, and total unit sales (T) of 46,800 units. With these numbers, some possible total costs are (check some of these for practice):

Restocking Quantity (Q)	Total Carrying Costs ($Q/2 \times$ CC)	+	Restocking Costs ($F \times T/Q$)	=	Total Costs
500	$ 187.5		$4,680.0		$4,867.5
1,000	375.0		2,340.0		2,715.0
1,500	562.5		1,560.0		2,122.5
2,000	750.0		1,170.0		1,920.0
2,500	937.5		936.0		1,873.5
3,000	1,125.0		780.0		1,905.0
3,500	1,312.5		668.6		1,981.1

Inspecting the numbers, we see that total costs start out at almost $5,000, and they decline to just under $1,900. The cost-minimizing quantity appears to be approximately 2,500.

To find the precise cost-minimizing quantity, we can take a look back at Figure 17.7. What we notice is that the minimum point occurs right where the two lines cross. At this point, carrying costs and restocking costs are the same. For the particular types of costs we have assumed here this will always be true, so we can find the minimum point just by setting these costs equal to each other and solving for Q^*:

$$\begin{aligned}&\text{Carrying costs} = \text{Restocking costs}\\&(Q^*/2) \times \text{CC} = F \times (T/Q^*)\end{aligned} \qquad [17.4]$$

With a little algebra, we get:

$$(Q^*)^2 = \frac{2T \times F}{\text{CC}} \qquad [17.5]$$

To solve for Q^*, we take the square root of both sides to find:

$$Q^* = \sqrt{\frac{2T \times F}{\text{CC}}} \qquad [17.6]$$

economic order quantity (EOQ) The restocking quantity that minimizes the total inventory costs.

This reorder quantity, which minimizes the total inventory cost, is called the **economic order quantity (EOQ).** For the Eyssell Corporation, the EOQ is:

$$\begin{aligned}Q^* &= \sqrt{\frac{2T \times F}{\text{CC}}} \qquad [17.7]\\&= \sqrt{\frac{(2 \times 46{,}800) \times \$50}{\$.75}}\\&= \sqrt{6{,}240{,}000}\\&= 2{,}498 \text{ units}\end{aligned}$$

Thus, for Eyssell, the economic order quantity is actually 2,498 units. At this level, check that the restocking costs and carrying costs are identical (they're both \$936.75).

EXAMPLE 17.3 Carrying Costs

Thiewes Shoes begins each period with 100 pairs of hiking boots in stock. This stock is depleted each period and reordered. If the carrying cost per pair of boots per year is \$3, what are the total carrying costs for the hiking boots?

Inventories always start at 100 items and end up at 0, so average inventory is 50 items. At an annual cost of \$3 per item, total carrying costs are \$150. • • •

EXAMPLE 17.4 Restocking Costs

In our previous example (Example 17.3), suppose Thiewes sells a total of 600 pairs of boots in a year. How many times per year does Thiewes restock? Suppose the restocking cost is \$20 per order. What are total restocking costs?

Thiewes orders 100 items each time. Total sales are 600 items per year, so Thiewes restocks six times per year, or about every two months. The restocking costs would be 6 orders × \$20 per order = \$120. • • •

EXAMPLE 17.5 The EOQ

Based on our previous two examples, what size orders should Thiewes place to minimize costs? How often will Thiewes restock? What are the total carrying and restocking costs? The total costs?

We have that the total number of pairs of boots ordered for the year (T) is 600. The restocking cost (F) is \$20 per order, and the carrying cost (CC) is \$3. We can calculate the EOQ for Thiewes as follows:

$$\begin{aligned}
\text{EOQ} &= \sqrt{\frac{2T \times F}{\text{CC}}} \\
&= \sqrt{\frac{(2 \times 600) \times \$20}{\$3}} \\
&= \sqrt{8{,}000} \\
&= 89.44 \text{ units}
\end{aligned}$$

Since Thiewes sells 600 pairs per year, it will restock 600/89.44 = 6.71 times. The total restocking costs will be \$20 × 6.71 = \$134.16. Average inventory will be 89.44/2 = 44.72. The carrying costs will be \$3 × 44.72 = \$134.16, the same as the restocking costs. The total costs are thus \$268.33. • • •

Extensions to the EOQ Model

Thus far, we have assumed that a company will let its inventory run down to zero and then reorder. In reality, a company will wish to reorder before its inventory goes to zero for two reasons. First, by always having at least some inventory on hand, the firm minimizes the risk of a stock-out and the resulting losses of sales and customers. Second, when a firm does reorder, there will be some time lag before the inventory arrives. Thus, to finish our discussion of the EOQ, we consider two extensions, safety stocks and reordering points.

Safety Stocks A *safety stock* refers to the minimum level of inventory that a firm keeps on hand. Inventories are reordered whenever the level of inventory falls to the safety stock level. Part A of Figure 17.9 illustrates how a safety stock can be incorporated into an EOQ model. Notice that adding a safety stock simply means that the firm does not run its inventory all the way down to zero. Other than this, the situation is identical to our earlier discussion of the EOQ.

Reorder Points To allow for delivery time, a firm will place orders before inventories reach a critical level. The *reorder points* are the times at which the firm will actually place its inventory orders. These points are illustrated in Part B of Figure 17.9. As shown, the reorder points simply occur some fixed number of days (or weeks or months) before inventories are projected to reach zero.

One of the reasons that a firm will keep a safety stock is to allow for uncertain delivery times. We can therefore combine our reorder point and safety stock discussions in Part C of Figure 17.9. The result is a generalized EOQ in which the firm orders in advance of anticipated needs and also keeps a safety stock of inventory to guard against unforeseen fluctuations in demand and delivery times.

FIGURE 17.9 Safety stocks and reorder points

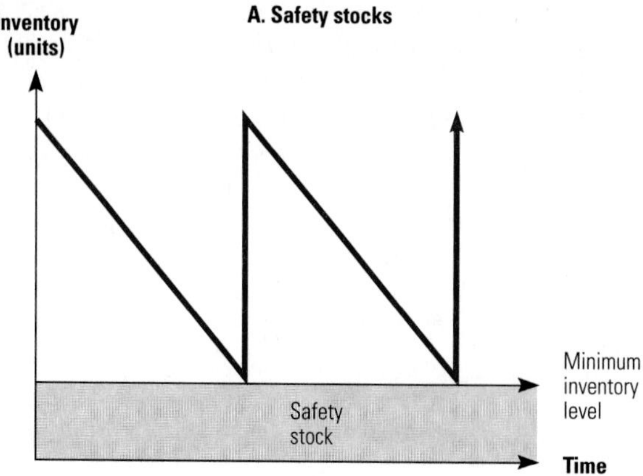

With a safety stock, the firm reorders when inventory reaches a minimum level.

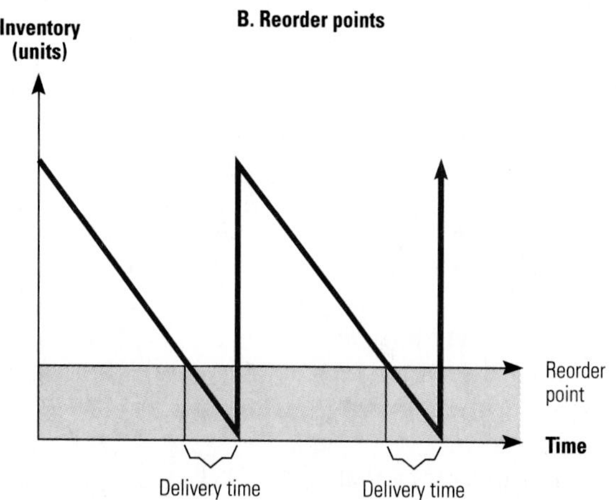

When there are lags in delivery or production times, the firm reorders when inventory reaches the reorder point.

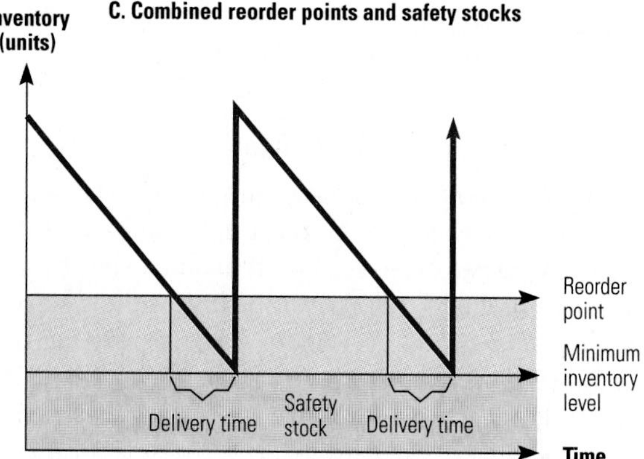

By combining safety stocks and reorder points, the firm maintains a buffer against unforeseen events.

Managing Derived-Demand Inventories

The third type of inventory management technique is used to manage derived-demand inventories. As we described above, demand for some inventory types is derived from or dependent on other inventory needs. A good example is an auto manufacturer where the demand for finished products derives from consumer demand, marketing programs, and other factors related to projected unit sales. The demand for inventory items such as tires, batteries, headlights, and other components is then completely determined by the number of autos planned. Materials requirements planning and just-in-time inventory management are two methods for managing demand-dependent inventories.

Materials Requirements Planning (MRP) Production and inventory specialists have developed computer-based systems for ordering and/or scheduling production of demand-dependent type inventories. These systems fall under the general heading of **materials requirements planning (MRP).** The basic idea behind MRP is that, once finished goods inventory levels are set, it is possible to determine what levels of work-in-progress inventories must exist to meet the need for finished goods. From there, it is possible to calculate the quantity of raw materials that must be on hand. This ability to schedule backward from finished goods inventories stems from the dependent nature of work-in-progress and raw materials inventories. MRP is particularly important for complicated products where a variety of components are needed to create the finished product.

materials requirements planning (MRP)
A set of procedures used to determine inventory levels for demand-dependent inventory types such as work-in-progress and raw materials.

Just-in-Time Inventory **Just-in-time (JIT) inventory** is a modern approach to managing dependent inventories. The goal of JIT is essentially to minimize such inventories, thereby maximizing turnover. The approach began in Japan, and it is a fundamental part of much of Japanese manufacturing philosophy. As the name suggests, the basic goal of JIT is to have only enough inventory on hand to meet immediate production needs.

just-in-time (JIT) inventory
A system for managing demand-dependent inventories that minimizes inventory holdings.

Concept Q Answer 17.5b

The result of the JIT system is that inventories are reordered and restocked frequently. Making such a system work and avoiding shortages requires a high degree of cooperation among suppliers. Japanese manufacturers often have a relatively small, tightly integrated group of suppliers with whom they work closely to achieve the needed coordination. These suppliers are a part of a large manufacturer's (such as Toyota's) industrial group, or *keiretsu.* Each large manufacturer tends to have its own *keiretsu.* It also helps to have suppliers located nearby, a situation that is common in Japan.

The *kanban* is an integral part of a JIT inventory system, and JIT systems are sometimes called *kanban systems.* The literal meaning of kanban is "card" or "sign," but, broadly speaking, a kanban is a signal to a supplier to send more inventory. For example, a kanban could literally be a card attached to a bin of parts. When a worker pulls that bin, the card is detached and routed back to the supplier who then supplies a replacement bin.

A JIT inventory system is an important part of a larger production planning process. A full discussion of it would necessarily shift our focus away from finance to production and operations management, so we will leave it here.

Lecture Tip: IM 17.5 discusses some of the pros and cons of JIT systems as utilized by American firms.

CONCEPT QUESTIONS

17.5a What does the EOQ model determine for the firm?

17.5b Which cost component of the EOQ model does JIT inventory minimize?

17.6 SUMMARY AND CONCLUSIONS

This chapter covers cash, receivables, and inventory management. Along the way, we touch on a large number of subjects. Some of the more important issues we examine are:

1. Firms seek to manage their cash by keeping no more than is needed on hand. The reason is that holding cash has an opportunity cost, namely, the returns that could be earned by investing the money.

2. Float is an important consideration in cash management, and firms seek to manage collections and disbursements in ways designed to minimize the firm's net float.
3. A firm's credit policy includes the terms of sale, credit analysis, and collection policy. The terms of sale cover three related subjects: the credit period, cash discount, and credit instrument.
4. The optimal credit policy for a firm depends on many specific factors, but generally involves trading off the costs of granting credit, such as the carrying costs of receivables and the possibility of nonpayment, with the benefits in terms of increased sales.
5. There are different types of inventories that differ greatly in their liquidity and management. The basic trade-off in inventory management is the cost of carrying inventory versus the cost of restocking. We develop the famous EOQ model, which explicitly balances these costs.
6. Firms use different inventory management techniques; we describe a few of the better known, including the ABC approach and just-in-time (JIT) inventory management

Chapter Review Problems and Self-Test

17.1 **Calculating Float** You have $10,000 on deposit with no outstanding checks or uncleared deposits. One day you write a check for $4,000 and then deposit a check for $3,000. What are your disbursement, collection, and net floats?

17.2 **The EOQ** Heusen Computer Manufacturing starts each period with 4,000 CPUs in stock. This stock is depleted each month and reordered. If the carrying cost per CPU is $1, and the fixed order cost is $10, is Heusen following an economically advisable strategy?

Answers to Self-Test Problems

17.1 First, after you write the check for $4,000, you show a balance of $6,000. However, while the check is clearing, your bank shows a balance of $10,000. This is a $4,000 disbursement float, and it is good for you. Next, when you deposit the $3,000, you show a balance of $9,000, but your account will not be credited for the $3,000 until it clears. This is a −$3,000 collection float, and it is bad for you.

The sum of the disbursement float and the collection float is your net float of $1,000. In other words, on a net basis, you show a balance of $9,000, but your bank shows a $10,000 balance, so, net, you are benefiting from the float.

17.2 We can answer by first calculating Heusen's carrying and restocking costs. The average inventory is 2,000 CPUs, and, since the carrying costs are $1 per CPU, total carrying costs are $2,000. Heusen restocks every month at a fixed order cost of $10, so the total restocking costs are $120. What we see is that carrying costs are large relative to reorder costs, so Heusen is carrying too much inventory.

To determine the optimal inventory policy, we can use the EOQ model. Because Heusen orders 4,000 CPUs 12 times per year, total needs (T) are 48,000 CPUs. The fixed order cost is \$10, and the carrying cost per unit (CC) is \$1. The EOQ is therefore:

$$\begin{aligned} \text{EOQ} &= \sqrt{\frac{2T \times F}{\text{CC}}} \\ &= \sqrt{\frac{(2 \times 48{,}000) \times \$10}{\$1}} \\ &= \sqrt{960{,}000} \\ &= 979.80 \text{ units} \end{aligned}$$

We can check this by noting that the average inventory is about 490 CPUs, so the carrying cost is \$490. Heusen will have to reorder 48,000/979.8 = 49 times. The fixed order cost is \$10, so the total restocking cost is also \$490.

Questions and Problems

Basic (Questions 1–21)

1. **Calculating Float** You have \$150,000 on deposit with no outstanding checks or uncleared deposits. One day you write a check for \$45,000. Does this create a disbursement or collection float? What is your available balance? Book balance? \$150,000; \$105,000
2. **Calculating Float** You have \$200,000 on deposit with no outstanding checks or uncleared deposits. If you deposit a check for \$200,000, does this create a disbursement or collection float? What is your available balance? Book balance? \$200,000; \$0
3. **Calculating Float** You have \$50,000 on deposit with no outstanding checks or uncleared deposits. One day you write a check for \$8,000 and then deposit a check for \$10,000. What are your disbursement, collection, and net floats? \$8,000; −\$10,000 −\$2,000
4. **Float** Which would a firm prefer: a net collection float or a net disbursement float? Why?
5. **Disbursement Float** Suppose a firm has a book balance of \$2 million. At the ATM (automatic teller machine), the cash manager finds out that the bank balance is \$2.5 million. What is the situation here? If this is an ongoing situation, what ethical dilemma arises?
6. **Marketable Securities** For each of the short-term marketable securities given below, provide an example of the potential disadvantages the investment has for meeting a corporation's cash management goals.
   a. U.S. Treasury bills
   b. Ordinary preferred stock
   c. Negotiable certificates of deposit (NCDs)
   d. Commercial paper
7. **Credit Policy Components** What are the three components of credit policy? Trans. 17.16
8. **Terms of Sale** The conditions under which a firm proposes to grant credit are called the *terms of sale.* What are the elements that make up the terms of sale?

a. 90 days; $24,000
b. 3%; 30 days; $23,280
c. $720; 60 days

9. **Cash Discounts** You place an order for 400 units of Good X at a unit price of $60. The supplier offers terms of 3/30, net 90.
   a. How long do you have to pay before the account is overdue? If you take the full period, how much should you remit?
   b. What is the discount being offered? How quickly must you pay to get the discount? If you do take the discount, how much should you remit?
   c. If you don't take the discount, how much interest are you paying implicitly? How many days' credit are you receiving?

10. **Credit Period Length** What are some of the factors that determine the length of the credit period? Why is the length of the buyer's operating cycle often considered an upper bound on the length of the credit period?

11. **Credit Period Length** In each of the following, indicate which firm would probably have a longer credit period and explain your reasoning.
   a. Firm A sells a miracle cure for baldness; Firm B sells toupees.
   b. Firm A specializes in products for landlords; Firm B specializes in products for renters.
   c. Firm A sells to customers with an inventory turnover of 10 times; Firm B sells to customers with an inventory turnover of 20 times.
   d. Firm A sells fresh fruit; Firm B sells canned fruit.
   e. Firm A sells and installs carpeting; Firm B sells rugs.

Trans. 17.17

12. **Credit Instruments** Describe each of the following:
   a. Sight draft
   b. Time draft
   c. Banker's acceptance
   d. Promissory note
   e. Trade acceptance

13. **Trade Credit Forms** In what form is trade credit most commonly offered? What is the credit instrument in this case?

14. **Credit Costs** What are the costs associated with carrying receivables? What are the costs associated with not granting credit? What do we call the sum of the costs for different levels of receivables?

15. **Five Cs of Credit** What are the five Cs of credit? Explain why each is important.

28.03%

16. **Terms of Sale** A firm offers terms of 3/15, net 60. What effective annual interest rate does the firm earn when a customer does not take the discount? Without doing any calculations, explain what will happen to this effective rate if:
   a. The discount is changed to 2 percent.
   b. The credit period is reduced to 30 days.
   c. The discount period is reduced to 10 days.

17. **Inventory Types** What are the different inventory types? How do the types differ? Why are some types said to have dependent demand whereas other types are said to have independent demand?

18. **Just-in-Time Inventory** If a company moves to a JIT inventory management system, what will happen to inventory turnover? What will happen to total asset turnover? What will happen to return on equity (ROE)? (Hint: remember the Du Pont equation from Chapter 3.)

19. **Inventory Costs** If a company's inventory carrying costs were $5 million per year and its fixed order costs were $8 million per year, do you think the firm keeps too much inventory on hand or too little? Why?

20. **EOQ** Brooks Manufacturing uses 8,000 subframes per week and then reorders another 8,000. If the relevant carrying cost per subframe is $25, and the fixed order cost is $1,500, is Brook's inventory policy optimal? Why or why not?

Carrying cost = $100,000
Order cost = $78,000
EOQ = 7,065
Trans. 17.18

21. **EOQ** The Hall Pottery Store begins each week with 250 pots in stock. This stock is depleted each week and reordered. If the carrying cost per pot is $12 per year and the fixed order cost is $900, what is the total carrying cost? What is the restocking cost? Should Hall increase or decrease its order size? Describe an optimal inventory policy for Hall in terms of order size and order frequency.

Carrying cost = $1,500
Order cost = $46,800
EOQ = 1,396
Orders = 9.3 per year

Part Eight

TOPICS IN BUSINESS FINANCE

In Parts One through Seven, we cover the basic core of business finance. Our job is not finished, however, without some coverage of the international aspects of financial management. We therefore conclude with a chapter on international financial management. We discuss the extra considerations, such as foreign exchange and exchange rate risk, that must be considered in international investing.

OUTLINE

Chapter Eighteen

International Aspects of Financial Management

After studying this chapter, you should have a good understanding of:

. . .

How exchange rates are quoted, what they mean, and the difference between spot and forward exchange rates.

. . .

Purchasing power parity and interest rate parity and their implications for exchange rate changes.

. . .

The different types of exchange rate risk and ways firms manage exchange rate risk.

. . .

The impact of political risk on international business investing.

Trans. 18.1
Chapter Outline

Companies with significant foreign operations are often called *international corporations* or *multinationals.* Such companies must consider many financial factors that do not directly affect purely domestic firms. These include foreign exchange rates, differing interest rates from country to country, complex accounting methods for foreign operations, foreign tax rates, and foreign government intervention.

The basic principles of corporate finance still apply to international corporations; like domestic companies, they seek to invest in projects that create more value for the shareholders (or owners) than they cost and to arrange financing that raises cash at the lowest possible cost. In other words, the net present value principle holds for both foreign and domestic operations, but it is usually more complicated to apply the NPV rule to foreign investments.

We won't have much to say here about the role of cultural and social differences in international business. We also will not be discussing the implications of differing political and economic systems. These factors are of great importance to international businesses, but it would take another book to do them justice. Consequently, we will focus only on some purely financial considerations in international finance and some key aspects of foreign exchange markets.

18.1 TERMINOLOGY

A common buzzword for the student of business finance is *globalization*. The first step in learning about the globalization of financial markets is to conquer the new vocabulary. As with any specialty, international finance is rich in jargon. Accordingly, we get started on the subject with a highly eclectic vocabulary exercise.

The terms that follow are presented alphabetically, and they are not all of equal importance. We choose these particular ones because they appear frequently in the financial press or because they illustrate some of the colorful language of international finance.

Trans. 18.2 International Finance Terminology

1. An **American Depository Receipt (ADR)** is a security issued in the United States that represents shares of a foreign stock, allowing that stock to be traded in the United States. Foreign companies use ADRs, which are issued in U.S. dollars, to expand the pool of potential U.S. investors. ADRs are available in two forms: company sponsored, which are listed on an exchange, and unsponsored, which usually are held by the investment bank that deals in the ADR. Both forms are available to individual investors, but only company-sponsored issues are quoted daily in newspapers.
2. The **cross-rate** is the implicit exchange rate between two currencies (usually non-U.S.) when both are quoted in some third currency, usually the U.S. dollar.
3. A **European Currency Unit (ECU)** is an index of European currencies devised in 1979 and intended to serve as a monetary unit for the European Monetary System (EMS).
4. A **Eurobond** is a bond issued in multiple countries, but denominated in a single currency, usually the issuer's home currency. Such bonds have become an important way to raise capital for many international companies and governments. Eurobonds are issued outside the restrictions that apply to domestic offerings and are syndicated and traded mostly from London. Trading can and does take place anywhere there is a buyer and a seller.
5. **Eurocurrency** is money deposited in a financial center outside of the country whose currency is involved. For instance, Eurodollars—the most widely used Eurocurrency—are U.S. dollars deposited in banks outside the U.S. banking system.
6. **Foreign bonds,** unlike Eurobonds, are issued in a single country and are usually denominated in that country's currency. Often, the country in which these bonds are issued will draw distinctions between them and bonds issued by domestic issuers, including different tax laws, restrictions on the amount issued, or tougher disclosure rules.

   Foreign bonds often are nicknamed for the country where they are issued: Yankee bonds (United States), Samurai bonds (Japan), Rembrandt bonds (the Netherlands), and Bulldog bonds (Britain). Partly because of tougher regulations and disclosure requirements, the foreign-bond market hasn't grown in past years with the vigor of the Eurobond market. A substantial portion of all foreign bonds are issued in Switzerland.

American Depository Receipt (ADR)
A security issued in the United States representing shares of a foreign stock and allowing that stock to be traded in the United States.

cross-rate
The implicit exchange rate between two currencies (usually non-U.S.) quoted in some third currency (usually the U.S. dollar).

European Currency Unit (ECU)
An index of European currencies intended to serve as a monetary unit for the European Monetary System (EMS).

Concept Q Answer 18.1a

Eurobonds
International bonds issued in multiple countries but denominated in a single currency (usually the issuer's currency).

Concept Q Answer 18.1b

Lecture Tip: Some background information on Eurodollars and Eurobonds is provided in IM 18.1.

Eurocurrency
Money deposited in a financial center outside of the country whose currency is involved.

foreign bonds
International bonds issued in a single country, usually denominated in that country's currency.

gilts
British and Irish government securities.

London Interbank Offer Rate (LIBOR)
The rate most international banks charge one another for overnight Eurodollar loans.

swaps
Agreements to exchange two securities or currencies.

Trans. 18.3
Global Capital Markets

7. **Gilts,** technically, are British and Irish government securities, although the term also includes issues of local British authorities and some overseas public-sector offerings.
8. The **London Interbank Offer Rate (LIBOR)** is the rate that most international banks charge one another for loans of Eurodollars overnight in the London market. LIBOR is a cornerstone in the pricing of money market issues and other debt issues by both government and corporate borrowers. Interest rates are frequently quoted as some spread over LIBOR, and they then float with the LIBOR rate.
9. There are two basic kinds of **swaps:** interest rate and currency. An interest rate swap occurs when two parties exchange a floating-rate payment for a fixed-rate payment or vice versa. Currency swaps are agreements to deliver one currency in exchange for another. Often both types of swaps are used in the same transaction when debt denominated in different currencies is swapped.

CONCEPT QUESTIONS

18.1a What are the differences between a Eurobond and a foreign bond?

18.1b What are Eurodollars?

18.2 FOREIGN EXCHANGE MARKETS AND EXCHANGE RATES

foreign exchange market
The market in which one country's currency is traded for another's.

Problems 1, 3, 6, 13

Video Note: International bond trading is described in the "Bond Buccaneers" video supplement.

The **foreign exchange market** is undoubtedly the world's largest financial market. It is the market where one country's currency is traded for another's. Most of the trading takes place in a few currencies: the U.S. dollar ($), the German deutsche mark (DM), the British pound sterling (£), the Japanese yen (¥), the Swiss franc (SF), and the French franc (FF). Table 18.1 lists some of the more common currencies and their symbols.

The foreign exchange market is an over-the-counter market, so there is no single location where traders get together. Instead, market participants are located in the major commercial and investment banks around the world. They communicate using computer terminals, telephones, and other telecommunications devices. For example, one communications network for foreign transactions is the Society for Worldwide Interbank Financial Telecommunications (SWIFT), a Belgian not-for-profit cooperative. Using data transmission lines, a bank in New York can send messages to a bank in London via SWIFT regional processing centers.

The many different types of participants in the foreign exchange market include the following:

1. Importers who pay for goods in foreign currencies.
2. Exporters who receive foreign currency and may want to convert to their domestic currency.
3. Portfolio managers who buy or sell foreign stocks and bonds.
4. Foreign exchange brokers who match buy and sell orders.
5. Traders who "make a market" in foreign currencies.
6. Speculators who try to profit from changes in exchange rates.

TABLE 18.1
International currency symbols

Trans. 18.4

Country	Currency	Symbol
Australia	Dollar	A$
Austria	Schilling	Sch
Belgium	Franc	BF
Canada	Dollar	Can$
Denmark	Krone	DKr
Finland	Markka	FM
France	Franc	FF
Germany	Deutsche mark	DM
Greece	Drachma	Dr
India	Rupee	Rs
Iran	Rial	RI
Italy	Lira	Lit
Japan	Yen	¥
Kuwait	Dinar	KD
Mexico	Peso	Ps
Netherlands	Guilder	FL
Norway	Krone	NKr
Saudi Arabia	Riyal	SR
Singapore	Dollar	S$
South Africa	Rand	R
Spain	Peseta	Pta
Sweden	Krona	Skr
Switzerland	Franc	SF
United Kingdom	Pound	£
United States	Dollar	$

Exchange Rates

An **exchange rate** is simply the price of one country's currency expressed in terms of another country's currency. In practice, almost all trading of currencies takes place in terms of the U.S. dollar. For example, both the French franc and the German mark are traded with their prices quoted in U.S. dollars.

exchange rate
The price of one country's currency expressed in terms of another country's currency.

Exchange Rate Quotations Figure 18.1 reproduces exchange rate quotations as they appear in *The Wall Street Journal.* The first column (labeled "U.S. $ equiv.") gives the number of dollars it takes to buy one unit of foreign currency. For example, the Australian dollar is quoted at .7236, which means that you can buy one Australian dollar with .7236 U.S. dollars.

Concept Q Answer 18.2c

The second column shows the amount of foreign currency per U.S. dollar. The Australian dollar is quoted here at 1.3821, so you can get 1.3821 Australian dollars for one U.S. dollar. Naturally, this second exchange rate is just the reciprocal of the first one, 1/.7236 = 1.3821, allowing for a rounding error.

EXAMPLE 18.1 On the Mark

Suppose you have $1,000. Based on the rates in Figure 18.1, how many Japanese yen can you get? Alternatively, if a Porsche costs DM 200,000, how many dollars will you need to buy it (DM is the abbreviation for deutsche marks)?

The exchange rate in terms of yen per dollar (second column) is 89.36. Your $1,000 will thus get you:

$1,000 × 89.36 yen per $1 = 89,360 yen

Since the exchange rate in terms of dollars per DM (first column) is .7126, you will need:

DM 200,000 × .7126 $ per DM = $142,520 • • •

FIGURE 18.1
Exchange rate quotations

Trans. 18.5

CURRENCY TRADING
EXCHANGE RATES

Monday, March 20, 1995

The New York foreign exchange selling rates below apply to trading among banks in amounts of $1 million and more, as quoted at 3 p.m. Eastern time by Bankers Trust Co., Dow Jones Telerate Inc. and other sources. Retail transactions provide fewer units of foreign currency per dollar.

Country	U.S. $ equiv. Mon.	Currency per U.S. $ Mon.
Argentina (Peso)	1.00	1.00
Australia (Dollar)	.7236	1.3821
Austria (Schilling)	.10160	9.84
Bahrain (Dinar)	2.6529	.3769
Belgium (Franc)	.03451	28.98
Brazil (Real)	1.0989011	.91
Britian (Pound)	1.5745	.6351
30-Day Forward	1.5743	.6352
90-Day Forward	1.5731	.6357
180-Day Forward	1.5697	.6371
Canada (Dollar)	.7107	1.4070
30-Day Forward	.7098	1.4089
90-Day Forward	.7076	1.4131
180-Day Forward	.7051	1.4181
Czech. Rep. (Koruna)		
Commercial Rate	.0382643	26.1340
Chile (Peso)	.002445	409.05
China (Renminbi)	.118662	8.4273
Colombia (Peso)	.001157	864.35
Denmark (Krone)	.1778	5.6235
Ecuador (Sucre)		
Floating Rate	.000417	2400.50
Finland (Markka)	.22750	4.3957
France (Franc)	.20066	4.9835
30-Day Forward	.20022	4.9945
90-Day Forward	.19947	5.0132
180-Day Forward	.19866	5.0338
Germany (Mark)	.7126	1.4033
30-Day Forward	.7133	1.4019
90-Day Forward	.7147	1.3991
180-Day Forward	.7171	1.3945
Greece (Drachma)	.004344	230.18
Hong Kong (Dollar)	.12936	7.7305
Hungary (Forint)	.0083063	120.3900
India (Rupee)	.03176	31.49
Indonesia (Rupiah)	.0004490	2227.00
Ireland (Punt)	1.5829	.6318
Israel (Shekel)	.3369	2.9678
Italy (Lira)	.0005767	1734.00
Japan (Yen)	.011191	89.36
30-Day Forward	.011233	89.02
90-Day Forward	.011311	88.41
180-Day Forward	.011444	87.38
Jordan (Dinar)	1.4535	.6880
Kuwait (Dinar)	3.3864	.2953
Lebanon (Pound)	.000611	1636.50
Malaysia (Ringgit)	.3922	2.5495
Malta (Lira)	2.8729	.3481
Mexico (Peso)		
Floating Rate	.1418440	7.0500
Netherland (Guilder)	.6358	1.5727
New Zealand (Dollar)	.6442	1.5524
Norway (Krone)	.1596	6.2670
Pakistan (Rupee)	.0324	30.85
Peru (New Sol)	.4423	2.26
Philippines (Peso)	.04002	24.99
Poland (Zloty)	.42553191	2.35
Portugal (Escudo)	.006739	148.40
Saudi Arabia (Riyal)	.26664	3.7504
Singapore (Dollar)	.7076	1.4133
Slovak Rep. (Koruna)	.0342583	29.1900
South Africa (Rand)	.2755	3.6301
South Korea (Won)	.0012912	774.45
Spain (Peseta)	.007756	128.92
Sweden (Krona)	.1378	7.2558
Switzerland (Franc)	.8573	1.1665
30-Day Forward	.8591	1.1640
90-Day Forward	.8626	1.1593
180-Day Forward	.8681	1.1519
Taiwan (Dollar)	.038511	25.97
Thailand (Baht)	.04044	24.72
Turkey (Lira)	.0000239	41889.03
United Arab (Dirham)	.2723	3.6723
Uruguay (New Peso)		
Financial	.167645	5.97
Venezuela (Bolivar)	.00589	169.78

SDR	1.53842	.65002
ECU	1.29370	. . . .

Special Drawing Rights (SDR) are based on exchange rates for the U.S., German, British, French and Japanese currencies. Source: International Monetary Fund

European Currency Unit (ECU) is based on a basket of community currencies.

Source: *The Wall Street Journal,* March 20, 1995. Reprinted by permission of *The Wall Street Journal,*

Cross-Rates and Triangle Arbitrage Using the U.S. dollar as the common denominator in quoting exchange rates greatly reduces the number of necessary cross-currency quotes. For example, with five major currencies, there would potentially be 10 exchange rates instead of just 4. Also, the fact that the dollar is used throughout cuts down on inconsistencies in the exchange rate quotations.

Earlier, we defined the cross-rate as the exchange rate for a non-U.S. currency expressed in terms of another non-U.S. currency. For example, suppose we observed the following:

$$\text{FF per } \$1 = 10.00$$

$$\text{DM per } \$1 = 2.00$$

Suppose the cross-rate is quoted as:

$$\text{FF per DM} = 4.00$$

What do you think?

The cross-rate here is inconsistent with the exchange rates. To see this, suppose you have \$100. If you convert this to deutsche marks, you will receive:

$$\$100 \times \text{DM } 2 \text{ per } \$1 = \text{DM } 200$$

If you convert this to francs at the cross-rate, you will have:

$$\text{DM } 200 \times \text{FF } 4 \text{ per DM } 1 = \text{FF } 800$$

However, if you just convert your dollars to francs without going through deutsche marks, you will have:

$$\$100 \times \text{FF } 10 \text{ per } \$1 = \text{FF } 1{,}000$$

What we see is that the franc has two prices, FF 10 per \$1 and FF 8 per \$1, depending on how we get them.

To make money, we want to buy low, sell high. The important thing to note is that francs are cheaper if you buy them with dollars because you get 10 francs instead of just 8. You should proceed as follows:

1. Buy 1,000 francs for \$100.
2. Use the 1,000 francs to buy deutsche marks at the cross-rate. Since it takes four francs to buy a deutsche mark, you will receive FF 1000/4 = DM 250.
3. Use the DM 250 to buy dollars. Since the exchange rate is DM 2 per dollar, you receive DM 250/2 = \$125, for a round-trip profit of \$25.
4. Repeat steps 1 through 3.

This particular activity is called *triangle arbitrage* because the arbitrage involves moving through three different exchange rates:

Concept Q Answer 18.2a

Trans. 18.6 Triangle Arbitrage

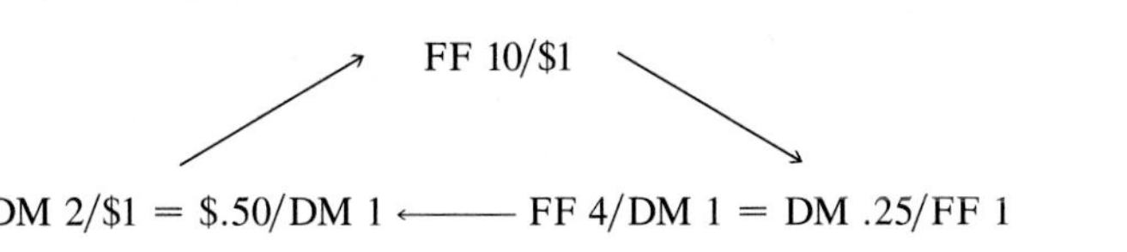

To prevent such opportunities, it is not difficult to see that since a dollar will buy you either 10 francs or 2 deutsche marks, the cross-rate must be:

$$(\text{FF } 10/\$1)/(\text{DM } 2/\$1) = \text{FF } 5/\text{DM } 1$$

That is, five francs per deutsche mark. If it were anything else, there would be a triangle arbitrage opportunity.

EXAMPLE 18.2 Shedding Some Pounds

Suppose the exchange rates for the British pound and German mark are:

Pounds per \$1 = 0.60

DM per \$1 = 2.00

The cross-rate is three marks per pound. Is this consistent? Explain how to go about making some money.

The cross-rate should be DM 2.00/£ .60 = DM 3.33 per pound. You can buy a pound for DM 3 in one market, and you can sell a pound for DM 3.33 in another. So we want to

Lecture Tip: See IM 18.2 for a comment on the small investor's ability to exploit a triangle arbitrage.

first get some marks, then use the marks to buy some pounds, and then sell the pounds. Assuming you have $100, you could:

1. Exchange dollars for marks: $100 × 2 = DM 200.
2. Exchange marks for pounds: DM 200/3 = £66.67.
3. Exchange pounds for dollars: £66.67/.60 = $111.12.

This would result in an $11.12 round-trip profit. • • •

Types of Transactions

spot trade
An agreement to trade currencies based on the exchange rate today for settlement within two business days.

spot exchange rate
The exchange rate on a spot trade.

forward trade
Agreement to exchange currency at some time in the future.

forward exchange rate
The agreed-upon exchange rate to be used in a forward trade.

Concept Q Answer 18.2b

There are two basic types of trades in the foreign exchange market: spot trades and forward trades. A **spot trade** is an agreement to exchange currency "on the spot," which actually means that the transaction will be completed or settled within two business days. The exchange rate on a spot trade is called the **spot exchange rate.** Implicitly, all of the exchange rates and transactions we have discussed so far have referred to the spot market.

Forward Exchange Rates A **forward trade** is an agreement to exchange currency at some time in the future. The exchange rate that will be used is agreed upon today and is called the **forward exchange rate.** A forward trade will normally be settled sometime in the next 12 months.

If you look back at Figure 18.1, you will see forward exchange rates quoted for some of the major currencies. For example, the spot exchange rate for the Swiss franc is SF 1 = $.8573. The 180-day forward exchange rate is SF 1 = $.8681. This means that you can buy a Swiss franc today for $.8573, or you can agree to take delivery of a Swiss franc in 180 days and pay $.8681 at that time.

Notice that the Swiss franc is more expensive in the forward market ($.8681 versus $.8573). Since the Swiss franc is more expensive in the future than it is today, it is said to be selling at a *premium* relative to the dollar. For the same reason, the dollar is said to be selling at a *discount* relative to the Swiss franc.

Why does the forward market exist? One answer is that it allows businesses and individuals to lock in a future exchange rate today, thereby eliminating any risk from unfavorable shifts in the exchange rate.

EXAMPLE 18.3 Looking Forward

Suppose you were expecting to receive a million British pounds in six months, and you agree to a forward trade to exchange your pounds for dollars. Based on Figure 18.1, how many dollars will you get in six months? Is the pound selling at a discount or a premium relative to the dollar?

In Figure 18.1, the spot exchange rate and the 180-day forward rate in terms of dollars per pound are $1.5745 = £1 and $1.5697 = £1, respectively. If you expect £1 million in 180 days, then you will get £1 million × $1.5697 per £ = $1.5697 million. Since it is cheaper to buy a pound in the forward market than in the spot market ($1.5697 versus $1.5745), the pound is selling at a discount relative to the dollar. • • •

As we mentioned earlier, it is standard practice around the world (with a few exceptions) to quote exchange rates in terms of the U.S. dollar. This means that rates are quoted as the amount of currency per U.S. dollar. For the remainder of this chapter, we will stick with this form. Things can get extremely confusing if you forget this. Thus, when we say things like "the exchange rate is expected to rise," it is important to remember that we are talking about the exchange rate quoted as units of foreign currency per U.S. dollar.

CONCEPT QUESTIONS

18.2a What is triangle arbitrage?

18.2b What do we mean by the 90-day forward exchange rate?

18.2c If we say that the exchange rate is DM 1.90, what do we mean?

18.3 PURCHASING POWER PARITY

Self-Test Problem 18.1
Problems 4, 5, 7, 12, 15

Now that we have discussed what exchange rate quotations mean, we can address an obvious question: What determines the level of the spot exchange rate? In addition, we know that exchange rates change through time. A related question is thus: What determines the rate of change in exchange rates? At least part of the answer in both cases goes by the name of **purchasing power parity (PPP),** the idea that the exchange rate adjusts to keep purchasing power constant among currencies. As we discuss next, there are two forms of PPP, *absolute* and *relative.*

purchasing power parity (PPP) The idea that the exchange rate adjusts to keep purchasing power constant among currencies.

Absolute Purchasing Power Parity

Concept Q Answer 18.3a

The basic idea behind *absolute purchasing power parity* is that a commodity costs the same regardless of what currency is used to purchase it or where it is selling. This is a very straightforward concept. If a beer costs £2 in London, and the exchange rate is £.60 per dollar, then a beer costs £2/.60 = \$3.33 in New York. In other words, absolute PPP says that \$1 will buy you the same number of, say, cheeseburgers, anywhere in the world.

More formally, let S_0 be the spot exchange rate between the British pound and the U.S. dollar today (Time 0), and remember that we are quoting exchange rates as the amount of foreign currency per dollar. Let P_{US} and P_{UK} be the current U.S. and British prices, respectively, on a particular commodity, say, apples. Absolute PPP simply says that:

$$P_{UK} = S_0 \times P_{US}$$

This tells us that the British price for something is equal to the U.S. price for that same something, multiplied by the exchange rate.

The rationale behind PPP is similar to that behind triangle arbitrage. If PPP did not hold, arbitrage would be possible (in principle) by moving apples from one country to another. For example, suppose apples in New York are selling for \$4 per bushel, while in London the price is £2.40 per bushel. Absolute PPP implies that:

$$P_{UK} = S_0 \times P_{US}$$

$$£2.40 = S_0 \times \$4$$

$$S_0 = £2.40/\$4 = £.60$$

That is, the implied spot exchange rate is £.60 per dollar. Equivalently, a pound is worth \$1/£.60 = \$1.67.

Suppose, instead, the actual exchange rate is £.50. Starting with \$4, a trader could buy a bushel of apples in New York, ship it to London, and sell it there for £2.40. Our trader then converts the £2.40 into dollars at the prevailing exchange rate, S_0 = £.50, yielding a total of £2.40/.50 = \$4.80. The round-trip gain is 80 cents.

Because of this profit potential, forces are set in motion to change the exchange rate and/or the price of apples. In our example, apples would begin moving from New York to London. The reduced supply of apples in New York would raise the price of apples there, and the increased supply in Britain would lower the price of apples in London.

In addition to moving apples around, apple traders would be busily converting pounds back into dollars to buy more apples. This activity increases the supply of pounds and simultaneously increases the demand for dollars. We would expect the value of a pound to fall. This means that the dollar is getting more valuable, so it will take more pounds to buy one dollar. Since the exchange rate is quoted as pounds per dollar, we would expect the exchange rate to rise from £.50.

For absolute PPP to hold absolutely, several things must be true:

1. The transactions costs of trading apples—shipping, insurance, spoilage, and so on—must be zero.
2. There must be no barriers to trading apples, such as tariffs, taxes, or other political barriers such as VRAs (voluntary restraint agreements).
3. Finally, an apple in New York must be identical to an apple in London. It won't do for you to send red apples to London if the English eat only green apples.

Given the fact that the transactions costs are not zero and that the other conditions are rarely exactly met, it is not surprising that absolute PPP is really applicable only to traded goods, and then only to very uniform ones.

For this reason, absolute PPP does not imply that a Mercedes costs the same as a Ford or that a nuclear power plant in France costs the same as one in New York. In the case of the cars, they are not identical. In the case of the power plants, even if they were identical, they are expensive and very difficult to ship. On the other hand, we would be very surprised to see a significant violation of absolute PPP for gold.

Relative Purchasing Power Parity

As a practical matter, a relative version of purchasing power parity has evolved. *Relative purchasing power parity* does not tell us what determines the absolute level of the exchange rate. Instead, it tells what determines the *change* in the exchange rate over time.

The Basic Idea Suppose the British pound/U.S. dollar exchange rate is currently S_0 = £.50. Further suppose that the inflation rate in Britain is predicted to be 10 percent over the coming year and (for the moment) the inflation rate in the United States is predicted to be zero. What do you think the exchange rate will be in a year?

If you think about it, a dollar currently costs .50 pounds in Britain. With 10 percent inflation, we expect prices in Britain to generally rise by 10 percent. So we expect that the price of a dollar will go up by 10 percent and the exchange rate should rise to £.50 × 1.1 = £.55.

If the inflation rate in the United States is not zero, then we need to worry about the *relative* inflation rates in the two countries. For example, suppose the U.S. inflation rate is predicted to be 4 percent. Relative to prices in the United States, prices in Britain are rising at a rate of 10% − 4% = 6% per year. So we expect the price of the dollar to rise by 6 percent, and the predicted exchange rate is £.50 × 1.06 = £.53.

The Result In general, relative PPP says that the change in the exchange rate is determined by the difference in the inflation rates between the two countries. To be more specific, we will use the following notation:

Concept Q Answer 18.3b

S_0 = Current (Time 0) spot exchange rate (foreign currency per dollar)

$E[S_t]$ = Expected exchange rate in t periods

h_{US} = Inflation rate in the United States

h_{FC} = Foreign country inflation rate

Based on our discussion just above, relative PPP says that the expected percentage change in the exchange rate over the next year, $(E[S_1] - S_0)/S_0$, is:

$$(E[S_1] - S_0)/S_0 = h_{FC} - h_{US} \quad [18.1]$$

In words, relative PPP simply says that the expected percentage change in the exchange rate is equal to the difference in inflation rates. If we rearrange this slightly, we get:

$$E[S_1] = S_0 \times [1 + (h_{FC} - h_{US})] \quad [18.2]$$

This result makes a certain amount of sense, but care must be used in quoting the exchange rate.

In our example involving Britain and the United States, relative PPP tells us that the exchange rate will rise by $h_{FC} - h_{US}$ = 10% − 4% = 6% per year. Assuming the difference in inflation rates doesn't change, the expected exchange rate in two years, $E[S_2]$, will therefore be:

$$\begin{aligned} E[S_2] &= E[S_1] \times (1 + .06) \\ &= .53 \times 1.06 \\ &= .562 \end{aligned}$$

Notice that we could have written this as:

$$\begin{aligned} E[S_2] &= .53 \times 1.06 \\ &= (.50 \times 1.06) \times 1.06 \\ &= .50 \times 1.06^2 \end{aligned}$$

In general, relative PPP says that the expected exchange rate at some time in the future, $E[S_t]$, is:

$$E[S_t] = S_0 \times [1 + (h_{FC} - h_{US})]^t \quad [18.3]$$

As we will see, this is a very useful relationship.

Because we don't really expect absolute PPP to hold for most goods, we will focus on relative PPP in our discussion below. Henceforth, when we refer to PPP without further qualification, we mean relative PPP.

EXAMPLE 18.4 It's All Relative

Suppose the Japanese exchange rate is currently 105 yen per dollar. The inflation rate in Japan over the next three years will run, say, 2 percent per year while the U.S. inflation rate will be 6 percent. Based on relative PPP, what will the exchange rate be in three years?

Since the U.S. inflation rate is higher, we expect that a dollar will become less valuable. The exchange rate change will be 2% − 6% = −4% per year. Over three years, the exchange rate will fall to:

$$\begin{aligned} \text{E}[S_3] &= S_0 \times [1 + (h_{FC} - h_{US})]^3 \\ &= 105 \times [1 + (-.04)]^3 \\ &= 92.90 \text{ yen per dollar} \end{aligned}$$

Lecture Tip: See IM 18.3 for further commentary and examples illustrating the effects of a strong or weak dollar.

Lecture Tip: See IM 18.3 for another example of the concept of relative PPP.

Currency Appreciation and Depreciation We frequently hear things like "the dollar strengthened (or weakened) in financial markets today" or "the dollar is expected to appreciate (or depreciate) relative to the pound." When we say the dollar strengthens or appreciates, we mean that the value of a dollar rises, so it takes more foreign currency to buy a dollar.

What happens to the exchange rates as currencies fluctuate in value depends on how exchange rates are quoted. Since we are quoting them as units of foreign currency per dollar, the exchange rate moves in the same direction as the value of the dollar: It rises as the dollar strengthens, and it falls as the dollar weakens.

Relative PPP tells us that the exchange rate will rise if the U.S. inflation rate is lower than the foreign country's. This happens because the foreign currency depreciates in value and therefore weakens relative to the dollar.

CONCEPT QUESTIONS

18.3a What does absolute PPP say? Why might it not hold for many types of goods?

18.3b According to relative PPP, what determines the change in exchange rates?

18.4 INTEREST RATE PARITY

Self-Test Problem 18.2

The next issue we need to address is the relationship between the spot exchange rates, forward exchange rates, and nominal interest rates. To get started, we need some additional notation:

$$\begin{aligned} F_t &= \text{Forward exchange rate for settlement at time } t \\ R_{US} &= \text{U.S. nominal risk-free interest rate} \\ R_{FC} &= \text{Foreign country nominal risk-free interest rate} \end{aligned}$$

As before, we will use S_0 to stand for the spot exchange rate. You can take the U.S. nominal risk-free rate, R_{US}, to be the T-bill rate.

Covered Interest Arbitrage

Suppose we observe the following information about U.S. and German currency in the market:

$$S_0 = \text{DM } 2.00 \qquad R_{US} = 10\%$$
$$F_1 = \text{DM } 1.90 \qquad R_G = 5\%$$

where R_G is the nominal risk-free rate in Germany. The period is one year, so F_1 is the 360-day forward rate.

Do you see an arbitrage opportunity here? There is one. Suppose you have \$1 to invest, and you want a riskless investment. One option you have is to invest the \$1 in a riskless U.S. investment such as a 360-day T-bill. We will call this Strategy 1. If you do this, then, in one period, your \$1 will be worth:

Strategy 1:

$$\begin{aligned}\$ \text{ value in 1 period} &= \$1 \times (1 + R_{US}) \\ &= \$1.10\end{aligned}$$

Alternatively, you can invest in the German risk-free investment. To do this, you need to convert your \$1 to deutsche marks and simultaneously execute a forward trade to convert marks back to dollars in one year. We will call this Strategy 2. The necessary steps would be as follows:

Strategy 2:

1. Convert your \$1 to \$1 × S_0 = DM 2.00.
2. At the same time, enter into a forward agreement to convert marks back to dollars in one year. Since the forward rate is DM 1.90, you get \$1 for every DM 1.90 that you have in one year.
3. Invest your DM 2.00 in Germany at R_G. In one year, you will have:

$$\begin{aligned}\text{DM value in 1 year} &= \text{DM } 2.00 \times (1 + R_G) \\ &= \text{DM } 2.00 \times 1.05 \\ &= \text{DM } 2.10\end{aligned}$$

4. Convert your DM 2.10 back to dollars at the agreed upon rate of DM 1.90 = \$1. You end up with:

$$\begin{aligned}\$ \text{ value in 1 year} &= \text{DM } 2.10/1.90 \\ &= \$1.1053\end{aligned}$$

Notice that the value in one year from this strategy can be written as:

$$\begin{aligned}\$ \text{ value in 1 year} &= \$1 \times S_0 \times (1 + R_G)/F_1 \\ &= \$1 \times 2.00 \times (1.05)/1.90 \\ &= \$1.1053\end{aligned}$$

The return on this investment is apparently 10.53 percent. This is higher than the 10 percent we get from investing in the United States. Since both investments are risk-free, there is an arbitrage opportunity.

To exploit the difference in interest rates, you need to borrow, say, \$5 million at the lower U.S. rate and invest it at the higher German rate. What is the round-trip profit from doing this? To find out, we can work through the steps above:

1. Convert the \$5 million at DM 2.00 = \$1 to get DM 10 million.
2. Agree to exchange marks for dollars in one year at DM 1.90 to the dollar.
3. Invest the DM 10 million for one year at $R_G = 5\%$. You end up with DM 10.5 million.
4. Convert the DM 10.5 million back to dollars to fulfill the forward contract. You receive DM 10.5 million/1.90 = \$5,526,316.
5. Repay the loan with interest. You owe \$5 million plus 10 percent interest, for a total of \$5.5 million. You have \$5,526,316, so your round-trip profit is a risk-free \$26,316.

The activity that we have illustrated here goes by the name of *covered interest arbitrage.* The term *covered* refers to the fact that we are covered in the event of a change in the exchange rate since we lock in the forward exchange rate today.

Interest Rate Parity (IRP)

Concept Q Answer 18.4a

If we assume that significant covered interest arbitrage opportunities do not exist, then there must be some relationship between spot exchange rates, forward exchange rates, and relative interest rates. To see what this relationship is, note that, in general, Strategy 1 above, investing in a riskless U.S. investment, gives us $(1 + R_{US})$ for every dollar we invest. Strategy 2, investing in a foreign risk-free investment, gives us $S_0 \times (1 + R_{FC})/F_1$ for every dollar we invest. Since these have to be equal to prevent arbitrage, it must be the case that:

$$(1 + R_{US}) = S_0 \times (1 + R_{FC})/F_1$$

interest rate parity (IRP) The condition stating that the interest rate differential between two countries is equal to the percentage difference between the forward exchange rate and the spot exchange rate.

Trans. 18.7 Prime Rates in Selected Countries (Supplemental)

Rearranging this a bit gets us the famous **interest rate parity (IRP)** condition:

$$F_1/S_0 = (1 + R_{FC})/(1 + R_{US}) \qquad [18.4]$$

There is a very useful approximation for IRP that illustrates very clearly what is going on and is not difficult to remember. If we define the percentage forward premium or discount as $(F_1 - S_0)/S_0$, then IRP says that this percentage premium or discount is *approximately* equal to the difference in interest rates:

$$(F_1 - S_0)/S_0 = R_{FC} - R_{US} \qquad [18.5]$$

Very loosely, what IRP says is that any difference in interest rates between two countries for some period is just offset by the change in the relative value of the currencies, thereby eliminating any arbitrage possibilities. Notice that we could also write:

$$F_1 = S_0 \times [1 + (R_{FC} - R_{US})] \qquad [18.6]$$

In general, if we have t periods instead of just one, the IRP approximation would be written as:

$$F_t = S_0 \times [1 + (R_{FC} - R_{US})]^t \qquad [18.7]$$

EXAMPLE 18.5 Parity Check

Suppose the exchange rate for Japanese yen, S_0, is currently ¥120 = $1. If the interest rate in the United States is R_{US} = 10% and the interest rate in Japan is R_J = 5%, then what must the one-year forward rate be to prevent covered interest arbitrage?

From IRP, we have:

$$\begin{aligned} F_1 &= S_0 \times [1 + (R_J - R_{US})] \\ &= ¥120 \times [1 + (.05 - .10)] \\ &= ¥120 \times .95 \\ &= ¥114 \end{aligned}$$

Notice that the yen will sell at a premium relative to the dollar (why?). • • •

Lecture Tip: Additional topics in this area—unbiased forward rates, uncovered interest parity, and the International Fisher Effect—are covered in *Fundamentals of Corporate Finance* by Ross, Westerfield, and Jordan.

CONCEPT QUESTIONS

18.4a What is interest rate parity?

18.4b Do you expect that interest rate parity will hold more closely than purchasing power parity? Why?

18.5 EXCHANGE RATE RISK

Exchange rate risk is the natural consequence of international operations in a world where relative currency values move up and down. As the accompanying *Principles in Action* box describes, managing exchange rate risk is an important part of international finance. As we discuss next, there are three different types of exchange rate risk or exposure: short-run exposure, long-run exposure, and translation exposure.

exchange rate risk
The risk related to having international operations in a world where relative currency values vary.

Concept Q Answer 18.5a

Short-Run Exposure

The day-to-day fluctuations in exchange rates create short-run risks for international firms. Most such firms have contractual agreements to buy and sell goods in the near future at set prices. When different currencies are involved, such transactions have an extra element of risk.

Lecture Tip: See IM 18.5 for a discussion of the advantage of a weak dollar currency to U.S. producers selling overseas.

For example, imagine that you are importing imitation pasta from Italy and reselling it in the United States under the Impasta brand name. Your largest customer has ordered 10,000 cases of Impasta. You place the order with your supplier today, but you won't pay until the goods arrive in 60 days. Your selling price is $6 per case. Your cost is 8,400 Italian lira per case, and the exchange rate is currently Lit 1,500, so it takes 1,500 lira to buy $1.

At the current exchange rate, your cost in dollars from filling the order is Lit 8,400/1,500 = $5.6 per case, so your pretax profit on the order is 10,000 × ($6 − $5.6) = $4,000. However, the exchange rate in 60 days will probably be different, so your profit will depend on what the future exchange rate turns out to be.

Lecture Tip: A recent *Wall Street Journal* article detailing the varied impacts of currency fluctuations on the residents of "Heartland America" is summarized in IM 18.5.

For example, if the rate goes to Lit 1,600, your cost is Lit 8,400/1,600 = $5.25 per case. Your profit goes to $7,500. If the exchange rate goes to, say, Lit 1,400, then your cost is Lit 8,400/1,400 = $6, and your profit is zero.

Principles in Action

Peso's Plunge Pinches Profits

The U.S. dollar/Mexican peso exchange rate stood at 0.2906977 dollars per peso on December 20, 1994. At this rate, $100 could be converted into 344 pesos. By January 4, 1995, just two weeks later, the exchange rate had dropped to 0.1805054, and those same 344 pesos could be converted into only $62.09, a decline in the value of roughly 38 percent. This devaluation of the peso resulted from a change in the Mexican government's policy toward managing the peso-dollar exchange rate. A decline in the value of the peso relative to the dollar makes U.S. imports to Mexico more expensive than before and also makes Mexican exports to the U.S. cheaper. The change created problems for many U.S. corporations doing business in Mexico, illustrating one of the major challenges of operating internationally.

U.S. firms that sell goods in Mexico must ultimately convert the pesos they receive as payment into dollars. As the value of the peso declines, so does the amount of dollars the firms receive in the exchange. What was unusual about December 1994 was that the peso declined in value so fast. It took only two weeks for its value to fall 38 percent, giving few U.S. firms operating in Mexico time to react. Some firms weren't immediately harmed by the change since they hedge their currency exchanges using forward trades and since Mexico is a relatively small international market. Still, for others, the peso's plunge meant substantial financial losses.

Ford Motor Company exported about 28,000 vehicles to Mexico in 1994, up from a few hundred in 1992. However, the peso's decline increased the price of each Ford vehicle enormously for Mexican buyers, dimming hopes for strong sales in 1995. Mattel Incorporated, a large U.S. toy maker, announced it would take an eight-cent-a-share charge for the fourth quarter of 1994 as the value of its inventory and receivables in Mexico declined with the value of the peso. The peso's plunge came at the peak of Mattel's shippling cycle, when its inventory and receivables in Mexico were relatively high. Pilgrim's Pride, a chicken producer, was expected to take a substantial write-down of its $120 million in assets in Mexico. Still, the firm was not scared out of the Mexican markets by the change. According to the firm's chief financial officer, they were still making money in Mexico and planned to futher expand their operations. Other firms weren't so optimistic.

Clorox Company and Tandem Computers, Incorporated, decided to put off plans to expand business in Mexico until the value of the peso stabilized. Price/Costco, Incorporated, and Price Enterprises, Incorporated, had to delay the sale of their stake in a joint venture to their Mexican partner in light of the peso's devaluation. Other firms were taking steps to structure sales to Mexican customers in a manner that protected their profits on those sales. Many firms are still optimistic about the Mexican market but realistically expect sales to fall as the decline in the value of the peso has dramatically increased the prices of U.S. goods sold in Mexico. Thus, whether a firm is concerned about its capital budgeting plans, the value of assets in place, or protecting profits on future transactions, the sudden devaluation of the peso reveals the exchange rate risk firms face when they do business in a foreign market.

Source: "Firms Feel the Pain of Peso's Change," *The Wall Street Journal,* January 5, 1995, p. A2.

Concept Q Answer 18.5b

Lecture Tip: The adverse effects of currency exposure on firm sales and profitability are illustrated in IM 18.5.

The short-run exposure in our example can be reduced or eliminated in several ways. The most obvious means of doing so is to enter into a forward exchange agreement to lock in an exchange rate. For example, suppose the 60-day forward rate is Lit 1,580. What will be your profit if you hedge?

If you hedge, you lock in an exchange rate of Lit 1,580. Your cost in dollars will thus be Lit 8,400/1,580 = $5.32 per case, so your profit will be 10,000 × ($6 − $5.32) = $6,800.

Long-Run Exposure

In the long run, the value of a foreign operation can fluctuate because of unanticipated changes in relative economic conditions. For example, imagine that we own a labor-intensive assembly operation located in another country to take advantage of lower wages. Through time, unexpected changes in economic conditions can raise the foreign wage levels to the point where the cost advantage is eliminated or even becomes negative.

Concept Q Answer 18.5b

Hedging long-run exposure is more difficult than hedging short-term risks. For one thing, organized forward markets don't exist for such long-term needs. Instead, the primary option that firms have is to try to match up foreign currency inflows and outflows. The same thing goes for matching foreign currency–denominated assets and liabilities. For example, a firm that sells in a foreign country might try to concentrate its raw material purchases and labor expense in that country. That way, the dollar value of its revenues and costs will move up and down together.

Similarly, a firm can reduce its long-run exchange risk by borrowing in the foreign country. Fluctuations in the value of the foreign subsidiary's assets will then be at least partially offset by changes in the value of the liabilities.

Translation Exposure

When a U.S. company calculates its accounting net income and EPS for some period, it must "translate" everything into dollars. This can create some problems for the accountants when there are significant foreign operations. In particular, two issues arise:

1. What is the appropriate exchange rate to use for translating each balance sheet account?
2. How should balance sheet accounting gains and losses from foreign currency translation be handled?

To illustrate the accounting problem, suppose we started a small foreign subsidiary in Lilliputia a year ago. The local currency is the gulliver, abbreviated GL. At the beginning of the year, the exchange rate was GL 2 = $1, and the balance sheet in gullivers looked like this:

Assets	GL 1,000	Liabilities	GL 500
		Equity	500

At 2 gullivers to the dollar, the beginning balance sheet in dollars was:

Assets	$500	Liabilities	$250
		Equity	250

Lilliputia is a quiet place, and nothing at all actually happened during the year. As a result, net income was zero (before consideration of exchange rate changes). However, the exchange rate did change to 4 gullivers = $1 purely because the Lilliputian inflation rate is much higher than the U.S. inflation rate.

Since nothing happened, the accounting ending balance sheet in gullivers is the same as the beginning one. However, if we convert it to dollars at the new exchange rate, we get:

Assets	$250	Liabilities	$125
		Equity	125

Notice that the value of the equity has gone down by $125, even though net income was exactly zero. Despite the fact that absolutely nothing really happened, there is a $125 accounting loss. How to handle this $125 loss has been a controversial accounting question.

One obvious and consistent way to handle this loss is simply to report the loss on the parent's income statement. During periods of volatile exchange rates, this kind of treatment can dramatically impact an international company's reported EPS. This is purely an accounting phenomenon, but, even so, such fluctuations are disliked by some financial managers.

The current approach to translation gains and losses is based on rules set out in Financial Accounting Standards Boards (FASB) Statement Number 52, issued in December 1981. For the most part, FASB 52 requires that all assets and liabilities be translated from the subsidiary's currency into the parent's currency using the exchange rate that currently prevails.

Any translation gains and losses that occur are accumulated in a special account within the shareholders' equity section of the balance sheet. This account might be labeled something like "unrealized foreign exchange gains (losses)." These gains and losses are not reported on the income statement. As a result, the impact of translation gains and losses will not be recognized explicitly in net income until the underlying assets and liabilities are sold or otherwise liquidated.

Managing Exchange Rate Risk

Video Note: The "European Currency Crisis" video supplement describes England's 1992 decision to withdraw support for the exchange rate mechanism of the European community.

For a large multinational firm, the management of exchange rate risk is complicated by the fact that there can be many different currencies involved in many different subsidiaries. It is very likely that a change in some exchange rate will benefit some subsidiaries and hurt others. The net effect on the overall firm depends on its net exposure.

For example, suppose a firm has two divisions. Division A buys goods in the United States for dollars and sells them in Britain for pounds. Division B buys goods in Britain for pounds and sells them in the United States for dollars. If these two divisions are of roughly equal size in terms of their inflows and outflows, then the overall firm obviously has little exchange rate risk.

In our example, the firm's net position in pounds (the amount coming in less the amount going out) is small, so the exchange rate risk is small. However, if one division, acting on its own, were to start hedging its exchange rate risk, then the overall firm's exchange rate risk would go up. The moral of the story is that multinational firms have to be conscious of the overall position that the firm has in a foreign currency. For this reason, management of exchange rate risk is probably best handled on a centralized basis.

CONCEPT QUESTIONS

18.5a What are the different types of exchange rate risk?

18.5b How can a firm hedge short-run exchange rate risk? Long-run exchange rate risk?

18.6 POLITICAL RISK

One final element of risk in international investing concerns **political risk.** Political risk refers to changes in value that arise as a consequence of political actions. This is not purely a problem faced by international firms. For example, changes in U.S. tax laws and regulations may benefit some U.S. firms and hurt others, so political risk exists nationally as well as internationally.

political risk
Risk related to changes in value that arise because of political actions.

Concept Q Answer 18.6a

Some countries do have more political risk than others, however. In such cases, the extra political risk may lead firms to require higher returns on overseas investments to compensate for the risk that funds will be blocked, critical operations interrupted, and contracts abrogated. In the most extreme case, the possibility of outright confiscation may be a concern in countries with relatively unstable political environments.

Political risk also depends on the nature of the business; some businesses are less likely to be confiscated because they are not particularly valuable in the hands of a different owner. An assembly operation supplying subcomponents that only the parent company uses would not be an attractive "takeover" target, for example. Similarly, a manufacturing operation that requires the use of specialized components from the parent is of little value without the parent company's cooperation.

Lecture Tip: A list of the riskiest countries in which to do business appears in IM 18.6.

Natural resource developments, such as copper mining or oil drilling, are just the opposite. Once the operation is in place, much of the value is in the commodity. The political risk for such investments is much higher for this reason. Also, the issue of exploitation is more pronounced with such investments, again increasing the political risk.

Political risk can be hedged in several ways, particularly when confiscation or nationalization is a concern. The use of local financing, perhaps from the government of the foreign country in question, reduces the possible loss because the company can refuse to pay on the debt in the event of unfavorable political activities. Based on our discussion above, structuring the operation such that it requires significant parent company involvement to function is another way to reduce political risk.

Concept Q Answer 18.6b

CONCEPT QUESTIONS

18.6a What is political risk?

18.6b What are some ways of hedging political risks?

18.7 SUMMARY AND CONCLUSIONS

The international firm has a more complicated life than the purely domestic firm. Management must understand the connection between interest rates, foreign currency exchange rates, and inflation, and it must become aware of a large number of different financial market regulations and tax systems. This chapter is intended to be a concise introduction to some of the financial issues that come up in international investing.

Our coverage was necessarily brief. The main topics we discussed include:

1. Some basic vocabulary. We briefly defined some exotic terms such as LIBOR and Eurodollar.
2. The basic mechanics of exchange rate quotations. We discussed the spot and forward markets and how exchange rates are interpreted.
3. The fundamental relationships between international financial variables:
   a. Absolute and relative purchasing power parity (PPP)
   b. Interest rate parity (IRP)

   Absolute purchasing power parity states that $1 should have the same purchasing power in each country. This means that an orange costs the same whether you buy it in New York or in Tokyo.

   Relative purchasing power parity means that the expected percentage change in exchange rates between the currencies of two countries is equal to the difference in their inflation rates.

   Interest rate parity implies that the percentage difference between the forward exchange rate and the spot exchange rate is equal to the interest rate differential. We showed how covered interest arbitrage forces this relationship to hold.
4. Exchange rate and political risk. We described the various types of exchange rate risk and discussed some commonly used approaches to managing the effect of fluctuating exchange rates on the cash flows and value of the international firm. We also discussed political risk and some ways of managing exposure to it.

Chapter Review Problems and Self-Test

18.1 Relative Purchasing Power Parity The inflation rate in the United States is projected at 6 percent per year for the next several years. The German inflation rate is projected to be 2 percent during that time. The exchange rate is currently DM 2.2. Based on relative PPP, what is the expected exchange rate in two years?

18.2 Covered Interest Arbitrage The spot and 360-day forward rates on the Swiss franc are SF 1.8 and SF 1.7, respectively. The risk-free interest rate in the United States is 8 percent, and the risk-free rate in Switzerland is 5 percent. Is there an arbitrage opportunity here? How would you exploit it?

Answers to Self-Test Problems

18.1 From relative PPP, the expected exchange rate in two years, $E[S_2]$ is:

$$E[S_2] = S_0 \times [1 + (h_G - h_{US})]^2$$

where h_G is the German inflation rate. The current exchange rate is DM 2.2, so the expected exchange rate is:

$$E[S_2] = \text{DM } 2.2 \times [1 + (.02 - .06)]^2$$
$$= \text{DM } 2.2 \times .96^2$$
$$= \text{DM } 2.03$$

18.2 From interest rate parity, the forward rate should be (approximately):

$$F_1 = S_0 \times [1 + (R_S - R_{US})]$$
$$= 1.8 \times [1 + .05 - .08]$$
$$= 1.75$$

Since the forward rate is actually SF 1.7, there is an arbitrage.

To exploit the arbitrage, we first note that dollars are selling for SF 1.7 each in the forward market. From IRP, this is too cheap because they should be selling for SF 1.75. So we want to arrange to buy dollars with Swiss francs in the forward market. To do this, we can:

1. Today: Borrow, say, $10 million for 360 days. Convert it to SF 18 million in the spot market, and forward contract at SF 1.7 to convert it back to dollars in 360 days. Invest the SF 18 million at 5 percent.
2. In one year: Your investment has grown to SF 18 × 1.05 = SF 18.9 million. Convert this to dollars at the rate of SF 1.7 = $1. You will have SF 18.9 million/1.7 = $11,117,647. Pay off your loan with 8 percent interest at a cost of $10 million × 1.08 = $10,800,000 and pocket the difference of $317,647.

Questions and Problems

Basic (Questions 1–15)

1. **Using Exchange Rates** Take a look back at Figure 18.1 to answer the following questions:
   a. If you have $100, how many Italian lira can you get?
   b. How much is one lira worth?
   c. If you have Lit 3 million (Lit stands for Italian lira), how many dollars do you have?
   d. Which is worth more: a New Zealand dollar or a Singapore dollar?
   e. Which is worth more: a Mexican peso or a Chilean peso?
   f. How many Swiss francs can you get for a Belgian franc? What do you call this rate?
   g. Per unit, what is the most valuable currency of the ones listed? The least valuable?

   a. Lit 173,400
   b. ¢ .05767
   c. $1,730.10
   f. SFr/BF = .04025

2. **Using the Cross-Rate** Use the information in Figure 18.1 to answer the following questions:
   a. Which would you rather have, $100 or £100? Why?
   b. Which would you rather have, FF 100 or £100? Why?
   c. What is the cross-rate for French francs in terms of British pounds? For British pounds in terms of French francs?

   c. FF/£ = 7.8468
   £/FF = .12744

Trans. 18.8

3. **Forward Exchange Rates** Use the information in Figure 18.1 to answer the following questions:
   a. What is the 180-day forward rate for the Japanese yen in yen per U.S. dollar? Is the yen selling at a premium or a discount? Explain.
   b. What is the 90-day forward rate for German deutsche marks in U.S. dollars per deutsche mark? Is the dollar selling at a premium or a discount? Explain.
   c. What do you think will happen to the value of the dollar relative to the yen and the deutsche mark, based on the information in the table? Explain.
4. **Using Spot and Forward Exchange Rates** Suppose the spot exchange rate for the Canadian dollar is Can$1.30 and the 180-day forward rate is Can$1.25.
   a. Which is worth more, a U.S. dollar or a Canadian dollar?
   b. Assuming absolute PPP holds, what is the cost in the United States of an Elkhead beer if the price in Canada is Can$1.95? Why might the beer actually sell at a different price in the United States from the price you found in (*a*)?
   c. Is the U.S. dollar selling at a premium or a discount relative to the Canadian dollar?
   d. Which currency is expected to appreciate in value?
   e. Which country do you think has higher interest rates—the United States or Canada? Explain.
5. **Spot versus Forward Rates** Suppose the exchange rate for the Swiss franc is quoted as SF 1.50 on the spot market and SF 1.53 in the 90-day forward market.
   a. Is the dollar selling at a premium or a discount relative to the franc?
   b. Does the financial market expect the Swiss franc to strengthen relative to the dollar? Explain.
   c. What do you suspect is true about relative economic conditions in the United States and Switzerland?

a. 180 ¥/£

6. **Cross-Rates and Arbitrage** Suppose the Japanese yen exchange rate is ¥120 = $1, and the British pound exchange rate is £1 = $1.50.
   a. What is the cross-rate in terms of ¥ per £?
   b. Suppose the cross-rate is ¥175 = £1. Is there an arbitrage opportunity here? If there is, explain how to take advantage of the mispricing.
7. **Inflation and Exchange Rates** Suppose the rate of inflation in Germany will run about 3 percent higher than the U.S. inflation rate over the next several years. All other things the same, what will happen to the deutsche mark versus dollar exchange rate? What relationship are you relying on in answering?
8. **Changes in Interest Rates and Inflation** The exchange rate for the Australian dollar is currently A$1.40. This exchange rate is expected to rise by 10 percent over the next year.
   a. Is the Australian dollar expected to get stronger or weaker?
   b. What do you think about the relative inflation rates in the United States and Australia?

c. What do you think about the relative nominal interest rates in the United States and Australia? Relative real rates?

9. **Foreign Bonds** Which of the following most accurately describes a Yankee bond?
   a. A bond issued by General Motors in Japan with the interest payable in U.S. dollars.
   b. A bond issued by General Motors in Japan with the interest payable in yen.
   c. A bond issued by Toyota in the United States with the interest payable in yen.
   d. A bond issued by Toyota in the United States with the interest payable in dollars.
   e. A bond issued by Toyota worldwide with the interest payable in dollars.

10. **Interest Rate Parity** Use Figure 18.1 to answer the following questions. Suppose interest rate parity holds, and the current 6-month risk-free rate in the United States is 4 percent. What must the 6-month risk-free rate be in France? In Japan? In Switzerland?

France: 5%
Japan: 1.8%
Switzerland: 2.7%

11. **Interest Rates and Arbitrage** The treasurer of a major U.S. firm has $12 million to invest for four months. The annual interest rate in the United States is 0.75 percent per month. The interest rate in Great Britain is 1 percent per month. The spot exchange rate is £0.60, and the three-month forward rate is £0.62. Ignoring transactions costs, in which country would the treasurer want to invest the company's funds? Why?

U.S.: $12,364,070
Britain: $12,084,434
Trans. 18.9

12. **Inflation and Exchange Rates** Suppose the current exchange rate for the French franc is FF 5. The expected exchange rate in four years is FF 4. What is the difference in the annual inflation rates for the United States and France over this period? Assume that the anticipated rate is constant for both countries. What relationship are you relying on in answering?

U.S. inflation 5.43% higher

13. **Exchange Rate Risk** Suppose your company imports computer modems from South Korea. The exchange rate is given in Figure 18.1. You have just placed an order for 60,000 modems at a cost to you of 121,245 won each. You will pay for the shipment when it arrives in 90 days. You can sell the modems for $170 each. Calculate your profit if the exchange rate goes up or down by 10 percent over the next 90 days. What is the break-even exchange rate? What percentage rise or fall does this represent in terms of the South Korean won versus the dollar?

Break-even rate = 713.21 W/$
Trans. 18.11

14. **Exchange Rates and Arbitrage** Suppose the spot and 180-day forward rates on the deutsche mark are DM 1.70 and DM 1.75, respectively. The annual risk-free rate in the United States is 7 percent, and the annual risk-free rate in Germany is 9 percent.
   a. Is there an arbitrage opportunity here? If so, how would you exploit it?
   b. What must the 180-day forward rate be to prevent arbitrage?

b. DM 1.7164

b. 3.69%

15. **Spot versus Forward Rates** Suppose the spot and 90-day forward rates for the yen are ¥110 and ¥109, respectively.
   a. Is the yen expected to get stronger or weaker?
   b. What would you estimate is the difference between the inflation rates of the United States and Japan?

Intermediate (Questions 16–17)

16. **Economic Conditions and Exchange Rates** Are the following statements true or false? Explain why.
   a. If the general price index in Great Britain rises faster than that in the United States, we would expect the pound to appreciate relative to the dollar.
   b. Suppose you are a German machine tool exporter and you invoice all of your sales in foreign currency. Further suppose that the German monetary authorities begin to undertake an expansionary monetary policy. If it is certain that the easy money policy will result in higher inflation rates in Germany relative to other countries, then you should use the forward markets to protect yourself against future losses resulting from the deterioration in the value of the deutsche mark.
   c. If you could accurately estimate differences in relative inflation rates between two countries over a long period of time, while other market participants were unable to do so, you could successfully speculate in spot currency markets.
17. **Economic Policy and Exchange Rates** Some countries often encourage movements in their exchange rate relative to some other country as a short-term means of addressing foreign trade imbalances. For each of the scenarios below, evaluate the impact the announced policy change would have on an American importer and an American exporter doing business with the foreign country.
   a. Officials in the administration of the United States government announce they are comfortable with a rising deutsche mark relative to the dollar.
   b. British monetary authorities announce they feel the pound has been driven too low by currency speculators relative to its value against the dollar.
   c. The Irish government announces it will devalue the punt in an effort to stay in line with the ECU.
   d. The Brazilian government announces it will print billions of new cruzeiros and inject them into the economy, in an effort to reduce the country's 40 percent unemployment rate.

Appendix

A

Mathematical Tables

TABLE A.1 Future value of $1 at the end of t periods $= (1 + r)^t$

Number of Periods	Interest Rate 1%	2%	3%	4%	5%	6%	7%	8%	9%
1	1.0100	1.0200	1.0300	1.0400	1.0500	1.0600	1.0700	1.0800	1.0900
2	1.0201	1.0404	1.0609	1.0816	1.1025	1.1236	1.1449	1.1664	1.1881
3	1.0303	1.0612	1.0927	1.1249	1.1576	1.1910	1.2250	1.2597	1.2950
4	1.0406	1.0824	1.1255	1.1699	1.2155	1.2625	1.3108	1.3605	1.4116
5	1.0510	1.1041	1.1593	1.2167	1.2763	1.3382	1.4026	1.4693	1.5386
6	1.0615	1.1262	1.1941	1.2653	1.3401	1.4185	1.5007	1.5869	1.6771
7	1.0721	1.1487	1.2299	1.3159	1.4071	1.5036	1.6058	1.7138	1.8280
8	1.0829	1.1717	1.2668	1.3686	1.4775	1.5938	1.7182	1.8509	1.9926
9	1.0937	1.1951	1.3048	1.4233	1.5513	1.6895	1.8385	1.9990	2.1719
10	1.1046	1.2190	1.3439	1.4802	1.6289	1.7908	1.9672	2.1589	2.3674
11	1.1157	1.2434	1.3842	1.5395	1.7103	1.8983	2.1049	2.3316	2.5804
12	1.1268	1.2682	1.4258	1.6010	1.7959	2.0122	2.2522	2.5182	2.8127
13	1.1381	1.2936	1.4685	1.6651	1.8856	2.1329	2.4098	2.7196	3.0658
14	1.1495	1.3195	1.5126	1.7317	1.9799	2.2609	2.5785	2.9372	3.3417
15	1.1610	1.3459	1.5580	1.8009	2.0789	2.3966	2.7590	3.1722	3.6425
16	1.1726	1.3728	1.6047	1.8730	2.1829	2.5404	2.9522	3.4259	3.9703
17	1.1843	1.4002	1.6528	1.9479	2.2920	2.6928	3.1588	3.7000	4.3276
18	1.1961	1.4282	1.7024	2.0258	2.4066	2.8543	3.3799	3.9960	4.7171
19	1.2081	1.4568	1.7535	2.1068	2.5270	3.0256	3.6165	4.3157	5.1417
20	1.2202	1.4859	1.8061	2.1911	2.6533	3.2071	3.8697	4.6610	5.6044
21	1.2324	1.5157	1.8603	2.2788	2.7860	3.3996	4.1406	5.0338	6.1088
22	1.2447	1.5460	1.9161	2.3699	2.9253	3.6035	4.4304	5.4365	6.6586
23	1.2572	1.5769	1.9736	2.4647	3.0715	3.8197	4.7405	5.8715	7.2579
24	1.2697	1.6084	2.0328	2.5633	3.2251	4.0489	5.0724	6.3412	7.9111
25	1.2824	1.6406	2.0938	2.6658	3.3864	4.2919	5.4274	6.8485	8.6231
30	1.3478	1.8114	2.4273	3.2434	4.3219	5.7435	7.6123	10.063	13.268
40	1.4889	2.2080	3.2620	4.8010	7.0400	10.286	14.974	21.725	31.409
50	1.6446	2.6916	4.3839	7.1067	11.467	18.420	29.457	46.902	74.358
60	1.8167	3.2810	5.8916	10.520	18.679	32.988	57.946	101.26	176.03

TABLE A.1 (concluded)

Interest Rate										
10%	12%	14%	15%	16%	18%	20%	24%	28%	32%	36%
1.1000	1.1200	1.1400	1.1500	1.1600	1.1800	1.2000	1.2400	1.2800	1.3200	1.3600
1.2100	1.2544	1.2996	1.3225	1.3456	1.3924	1.4400	1.5376	1.6384	1.7424	1.8496
1.3310	1.4049	1.4815	1.5209	1.5609	1.6430	1.7280	1.9066	2.0972	2.3000	2.5155
1.4641	1.5735	1.6890	1.7490	1.8106	1.9388	2.0736	2.3642	2.6844	3.0360	3.4210
1.6105	1.7623	1.9254	2.0114	2.1003	2.2878	2.4883	2.9316	3.4360	4.0075	4.6526
1.7716	1.9738	2.1950	2.3131	2.4364	2.6996	2.9860	3.6352	4.3980	5.2899	6.3275
1.9487	2.2107	2.5023	2.6600	2.8262	3.1855	3.5832	4.5077	5.6295	6.9826	8.6054
2.1436	2.4760	2.8526	3.0590	3.2784	3.7589	4.2998	5.5895	7.2058	9.2170	11.703
2.3579	2.7731	3.2519	3.5179	3.8030	4.4355	5.1598	6.9310	9.2234	12.166	15.917
2.5937	3.1058	3.7072	4.0456	4.4114	5.2338	6.1917	8.5944	11.806	16.060	21.647
2.8531	3.4785	4.2262	4.6524	5.1173	6.1759	7.4301	10.657	15.112	21.199	29.439
3.1384	3.8960	4.8179	5.3503	5.9360	7.2876	8.9161	13.215	19.343	27.983	40.037
3.4523	4.3635	5.4924	6.1528	6.8858	8.5994	10.699	16.386	24.759	36.937	54.451
3.7975	4.8871	6.2613	7.0757	7.9875	10.147	12.839	20.319	31.691	48.757	74.053
4.1772	5.4736	7.1379	8.1371	9.2655	11.974	15.407	25.196	40.565	64.359	100.71
4.5950	6.1304	8.1372	9.3576	10.748	14.129	18.488	31.243	51.923	84.954	136.97
5.0545	6.8660	9.2765	10.761	12.468	16.672	22.186	38.741	66.461	112.14	186.28
5.5599	7.6900	10.575	12.375	14.463	19.673	26.623	48.039	85.071	148.02	253.34
6.1159	8.6128	12.056	14.232	16.777	23.214	31.948	59.568	108.89	195.39	344.54
6.7275	9.6463	13.743	16.367	19.461	27.393	38.338	73.864	139.38	257.92	468.57
7.4002	10.804	15.668	18.822	22.574	32.324	46.005	91.592	178.41	340.45	637.26
8.1403	12.100	17.861	21.645	26.186	38.142	55.206	113.57	228.36	449.39	866.67
8.9543	13.552	20.362	24.891	30.376	45.008	66.247	140.83	292.30	593.20	1178.7
9.8497	15.179	23.212	28.625	35.236	53.109	79.497	174.63	374.14	783.02	1603.0
10.835	17.000	26.462	32.919	40.874	62.669	95.396	216.54	478.90	1033.6	2180.1
17.449	29.960	50.950	66.212	85.850	143.37	237.38	634.82	1645.5	4142.1	10143.
45.259	93.051	188.88	267.86	378.72	750.38	1469.8	5455.9	19427.	66521.	*
117.39	289.00	700.23	1083.7	1670.7	3927.4	9100.4	46890.	*	*	*
304.48	897.60	2595.9	4384.0	7370.2	20555.	56348.	*	*	*	*

*The factor is greater than 99.999.

TABLE A.2 Present value of $1 to be received after t periods $= 1/(1 + r)^t$

Number of Periods	Interest Rate 1%	2%	3%	4%	5%	6%	7%	8%	9%
1	0.9901	0.9804	0.9709	0.9615	0.9524	0.9434	0.9346	0.9259	0.9174
2	0.9803	0.9612	0.9426	0.9246	0.9070	0.8900	0.8734	0.8573	0.8417
3	0.9706	0.9423	0.9151	0.8890	0.8638	0.8396	0.8163	0.7938	0.7722
4	0.9610	0.9238	0.8885	0.8548	0.8227	0.7921	0.7629	0.7350	0.7084
5	0.9515	0.9057	0.8626	0.8219	0.7835	0.7473	0.7130	0.6806	0.6499
6	0.9420	0.8880	0.8375	0.7903	0.7462	0.7050	0.6663	0.6302	0.5963
7	0.9327	0.8706	0.8131	0.7599	0.7107	0.6651	0.6227	0.5835	0.5470
8	0.9235	0.8535	0.7894	0.7307	0.6768	0.6274	0.5820	0.5403	0.5019
9	0.9143	0.8368	0.7664	0.7026	0.6446	0.5919	0.5439	0.5002	0.4604
10	0.9053	0.8203	0.7441	0.6756	0.6139	0.5584	0.5083	0.4632	0.4224
11	0.8963	0.8043	0.7224	0.6496	0.5847	0.5268	0.4751	0.4289	0.3875
12	0.8874	0.7885	0.7014	0.6246	0.5568	0.4970	0.4440	0.3971	0.3555
13	0.8787	0.7730	0.6810	0.6006	0.5303	0.4688	0.4150	0.3677	0.3262
14	0.8700	0.7579	0.6611	0.5775	0.5051	0.4423	0.3878	0.3405	0.2992
15	0.8613	0.7430	0.6419	0.5553	0.4810	0.4173	0.3624	0.3152	0.2745
16	0.8528	0.7284	0.6232	0.5339	0.4581	0.3936	0.3387	0.2919	0.2519
17	0.8444	0.7142	0.6050	0.5134	0.4363	0.3714	0.3166	0.2703	0.2311
18	0.8360	0.7002	0.5874	0.4936	0.4155	0.3503	0.2959	0.2502	0.2120
19	0.8277	0.6864	0.5703	0.4746	0.3957	0.3305	0.2765	0.2317	0.1945
20	0.8195	0.6730	0.5537	0.4564	0.3769	0.3118	0.2584	0.2145	0.1784
21	0.8114	0.6598	0.5375	0.4388	0.3589	0.2942	0.2415	0.1987	0.1637
22	0.8034	0.6468	0.5219	0.4220	0.3418	0.2775	0.2257	0.1839	0.1502
23	0.7954	0.6342	0.5067	0.4057	0.3256	0.2618	0.2109	0.1703	0.1378
24	0.7876	0.6217	0.4919	0.3901	0.3101	0.2470	0.1971	0.1577	0.1264
25	0.7798	0.6095	0.4776	0.3751	0.2953	0.2330	0.1842	0.1460	0.1160
30	0.7419	0.5521	0.4120	0.3083	0.2314	0.1741	0.1314	0.0994	0.0754
40	0.6717	0.4529	0.3066	0.2083	0.1420	0.0972	0.0668	0.0460	0.0318
50	0.6080	0.3715	0.2281	0.1407	0.0872	0.0543	0.0339	0.0213	0.0134

TABLE A.2 (concluded)

Interest Rate										
10%	12%	14%	15%	16%	18%	20%	24%	28%	32%	36%
0.9091	0.8929	0.8772	0.8696	0.8621	0.8475	0.8333	0.8065	0.7813	0.7576	0.7353
0.8264	0.7972	0.7695	0.7561	0.7432	0.7182	0.6944	0.6504	0.6104	0.5739	0.5407
0.7513	0.7118	0.6750	0.6575	0.6407	0.6086	0.5787	0.5245	0.4768	0.4348	0.3975
0.6830	0.6355	0.5921	0.5718	0.5523	0.5158	0.4823	0.4230	0.3725	0.3294	0.2923
0.6209	0.5674	0.5194	0.4972	0.4761	0.4371	0.4019	0.3411	0.2910	0.2495	0.2149
0.5645	0.5066	0.4556	0.4323	0.4104	0.3704	0.3349	0.2751	0.2274	0.1890	0.1580
0.5132	0.4523	0.3996	0.3759	0.3538	0.3139	0.2791	0.2218	0.1776	0.1432	0.1162
0.4665	0.4039	0.3506	0.3269	0.3050	0.2660	0.2326	0.1789	0.1388	0.1085	0.0854
0.4241	0.3606	0.3075	0.2843	0.2630	0.2255	0.1938	0.1443	0.1084	0.0822	0.0628
0.3855	0.3220	0.2697	0.2472	0.2267	0.1911	0.1615	0.1164	0.0847	0.0623	0.0462
0.3505	0.2875	0.2366	0.2149	0.1954	0.1619	0.1346	0.0938	0.0662	0.0472	0.0340
0.3186	0.2567	0.2076	0.1869	0.1685	0.1372	0.1122	0.0757	0.0517	0.0357	0.0250
0.2897	0.2292	0.1821	0.1625	0.1452	0.1163	0.0935	0.0610	0.0404	0.0271	0.0184
0.2633	0.2046	0.1597	0.1413	0.1252	0.0985	0.0779	0.0492	0.0316	0.0205	0.0135
0.2394	0.1827	0.1401	0.1229	0.1079	0.0835	0.0649	0.0397	0.0247	0.0155	0.0099
0.2176	0.1631	0.1229	0.1069	0.0930	0.0708	0.0541	0.0320	0.0193	0.0118	0.0073
0.1978	0.1456	0.1078	0.0929	0.0802	0.0600	0.0451	0.0258	0.0150	0.0089	0.0054
0.1799	0.1300	0.0946	0.0808	0.0691	0.0508	0.0376	0.0208	0.0118	0.0068	0.0039
0.1635	0.1161	0.0829	0.0703	0.0596	0.0431	0.0313	0.0168	0.0092	0.0051	0.0029
0.1486	0.1037	0.0728	0.0611	0.0514	0.0365	0.0261	0.0135	0.0072	0.0039	0.0021
0.1351	0.0926	0.0638	0.0531	0.0443	0.0309	0.0217	0.0109	0.0056	0.0029	0.0016
0.1228	0.0826	0.0560	0.0462	0.0382	0.0262	0.0181	0.0088	0.0044	0.0022	0.0012
0.1117	0.0738	0.0491	0.0402	0.0329	0.0222	0.0151	0.0071	0.0034	0.0017	0.0008
0.1015	0.0659	0.0431	0.0349	0.0284	0.0188	0.0126	0.0057	0.0027	0.0013	0.0006
0.0923	0.0588	0.0378	0.0304	0.0245	0.0160	0.0105	0.0046	0.0021	0.0010	0.0005
0.0573	0.0334	0.0196	0.0151	0.0116	0.0070	0.0042	0.0016	0.0006	0.0002	0.0001
0.0221	0.0107	0.0053	0.0037	0.0026	0.0013	0.0007	0.0002	0.0001	*	*
0.0085	0.0035	0.0014	0.0009	0.0006	0.0003	0.0001	*	*	*	*

*The factor is zero to four decimal places.

T A B L E A.3 Present value of an annuity of \$1 per period for *t* periods $= [1 - 1/(1 + r)^t]/r$

	Interest Rate								
Number of Periods	**1%**	**2%**	**3%**	**4%**	**5%**	**6%**	**7%**	**8%**	**9%**
1	0.9901	0.9804	0.9709	0.9615	0.9524	0.9434	0.9346	0.9259	0.9174
2	1.9704	1.9416	1.9135	1.8861	1.8594	1.8334	1.8080	1.7833	1.7591
3	2.9410	2.8839	2.8286	2.7751	2.7232	2.6730	2.6243	2.5771	2.5313
4	3.9020	3.8077	3.7171	3.6299	3.5460	3.4651	3.3872	3.3121	3.2397
5	4.8534	4.7135	4.5797	4.4518	4.3295	4.2124	4.1002	3.9927	3.8897
6	5.7955	5.6014	5.4172	5.2421	5.0757	4.9173	4.7665	4.6229	4.4859
7	6.7282	6.4720	6.2303	6.0021	5.7864	5.5824	5.3893	5.2064	5.0330
8	7.6517	7.3255	7.0197	6.7327	6.4632	6.2098	5.9713	5.7466	5.5348
9	8.5660	8.1622	7.7861	7.4353	7.1078	6.8017	6.5152	6.2469	5.9952
10	9.4713	8.9826	8.5302	8.1109	7.7217	7.3601	7.0236	6.7101	6.4177
11	10.3676	9.7868	9.2526	8.7605	8.3064	7.8869	7.4987	7.1390	6.8052
12	11.2551	10.5753	9.9540	9.3851	8.8633	8.3838	7.9427	7.5361	7.1607
13	12.1337	11.3484	10.6350	9.9856	9.3936	8.8527	8.3577	7.9038	7.4869
14	13.0037	12.1062	11.2961	10.5631	9.8986	9.2950	8.7455	8.2442	7.7862
15	13.8651	12.8493	11.9379	11.1184	10.3797	9.7122	9.1079	8.5595	8.0607
16	14.7179	13.5777	12.5611	11.6523	10.8378	10.1059	9.4466	8.8514	8.3126
17	15.5623	14.2919	13.1661	12.1657	11.2741	10.4773	9.7632	9.1216	8.5436
18	16.3983	14.9920	13.7535	12.6593	11.6896	10.8276	10.0591	9.3719	8.7556
19	17.2260	15.6785	14.3238	13.1339	12.0853	11.1581	10.3356	9.6036	8.9501
20	18.0456	16.3514	14.8775	13.5903	12.4622	11.4699	10.5940	9.8181	9.1285
21	18.8570	17.0112	15.4150	14.0292	12.8212	11.7641	10.8355	10.0168	9.2922
22	19.6604	17.6580	15.9369	14.4511	13.1630	12.0416	11.0612	10.2007	9.4424
23	20.4558	18.2922	16.4436	14.8568	13.4886	12.3034	11.2722	10.3741	9.5802
24	21.2434	18.9139	16.9355	15.2470	13.7986	12.5504	11.4693	10.5288	9.7066
25	22.0232	19.5235	17.4131	15.6221	14.0939	12.7834	11.6536	10.6748	9.8226
30	25.8077	22.3965	19.6004	17.2920	15.3725	13.7648	12.4090	11.2578	10.2737
40	32.8347	27.3555	23.1148	19.7928	17.1591	15.0463	13.3317	11.9246	10.7574
50	39.1961	31.4236	25.7298	21.4822	18.2559	15.7619	13.8007	12.2335	10.9617

TABLE A.3 (concluded)

Interest Rate									
10%	12%	14%	15%	16%	18%	20%	24%	28%	32%
0.9091	0.8929	0.8772	0.8696	0.8621	0.8475	0.8333	0.8065	0.7813	0.7576
1.7355	1.6901	1.6467	1.6257	1.6052	1.5656	1.5278	1.4568	1.3916	1.3315
2.4869	2.4018	2.3216	2.2832	2.2459	2.1743	2.1065	1.9813	1.8684	1.7663
3.1699	3.0373	2.9137	2.8550	2.7982	2.6901	2.5887	2.4043	2.2410	2.0957
3.7908	3.6048	3.4331	3.3522	3.2743	3.1272	2.9906	2.7454	2.5320	2.3452
4.3553	4.1114	3.8887	3.7845	3.6847	3.4976	3.3255	3.0205	2.7594	2.5342
4.8684	4.5638	4.2883	4.1604	4.0386	3.8115	3.6046	3.2423	2.9370	2.6775
5.3349	4.9676	4.6389	4.4873	4.3436	4.0776	3.8372	3.4212	3.0758	2.7860
5.7590	5.3282	4.9464	4.7716	4.6065	4.3030	4.0310	3.5655	3.1842	2.8681
6.1446	5.6502	5.2161	5.0188	4.8332	4.4941	4.1925	3.6819	3.2689	2.9304
6.4951	5.9377	5.4527	5.2337	5.0286	4.6560	4.3271	3.7757	3.3351	2.9776
6.8137	6.1944	5.6603	5.4206	5.1971	4.7932	4.4392	3.8514	3.3868	3.0133
7.1034	6.4235	5.8424	5.5831	5.3423	4.9095	4.5327	3.9124	3.4272	3.0404
7.3667	6.6282	6.0021	5.7245	5.4675	5.0081	4.6106	3.9616	3.4587	3.0609
7.6061	6.8109	6.1422	5.8474	5.5755	5.0916	4.6755	4.0013	3.4834	3.0764
7.8237	6.9740	6.2651	5.9542	5.6685	5.1624	4.7296	4.0333	3.5026	3.0882
8.0216	7.1196	6.3729	6.0472	5.7487	5.2223	4.7746	4.0591	3.5177	3.0971
8.2014	7.2497	6.4674	6.1280	5.8178	5.2732	4.8122	4.0799	3.5294	3.1039
8.3649	7.3658	6.5504	6.1982	5.8775	5.3162	4.8435	4.0967	3.5386	3.1090
8.5136	7.4694	6.6231	6.2593	5.9288	5.3527	4.8696	4.1103	3.5458	3.1129
8.6487	7.5620	6.6870	6.3125	5.9731	5.3837	4.8913	4.1212	3.5514	3.1158
8.7715	7.6446	6.7429	6.3587	6.0113	5.4099	4.9094	4.1300	3.5558	3.1180
8.8832	7.7184	6.7921	6.3988	6.0442	5.4321	4.9245	4.1371	3.5592	3.1197
8.9847	7.7843	6.8351	6.4338	6.0726	5.4509	4.9371	4.1428	3.5619	3.1210
9.0770	7.8431	6.8729	6.4641	6.0971	5.4669	4.9476	4.1474	3.5640	3.1220
9.4269	8.0552	7.0027	6.5660	6.1772	5.5168	4.9789	4.1601	3.5693	3.1242
9.7791	8.2438	7.1050	6.6418	6.2335	5.5482	4.9966	4.1659	3.5712	3.1250
9.9148	8.3045	7.1327	6.6605	6.2463	5.5541	4.9995	4.1666	3.5714	3.1250

TABLE A.4 Future value of an annuity of $1 per period for t periods $= [(1 + r)^t - 1]/r$

	Interest Rate								
Number of Periods	1%	2%	3%	4%	5%	6%	7%	8%	9%
1	1.0000	1.0000	1.0000	1.0000	1.0000	1.0000	1.0000	1.0000	1.0000
2	2.0100	2.0200	2.0300	2.0400	2.0500	2.0600	2.0700	2.0800	2.0900
3	3.0301	3.0604	3.0909	3.1216	3.1525	3.1836	3.2149	3.2464	3.2781
4	4.0604	4.1216	4.1836	4.2465	4.3101	4.3746	4.4399	4.5061	4.5731
5	5.1010	5.2040	5.3091	5.4163	5.5256	5.6371	5.7507	5.8666	5.9847
6	6.1520	6.3081	6.4684	6.6330	6.8019	6.9753	7.1533	7.3359	7.5233
7	7.2135	7.4343	7.6625	7.8983	8.1420	8.3938	8.6540	8.9228	9.2004
8	8.2857	8.5830	8.8932	9.2142	9.5491	9.8975	10.260	10.637	11.028
9	9.3685	9.7546	10.159	10.583	11.027	11.491	11.978	12.488	13.021
10	10.462	10.950	11.464	12.006	12.578	13.181	13.816	14.487	15.193
11	11.567	12.169	12.808	13.486	14.207	14.972	15.784	16.645	17.560
12	12.683	13.412	14.192	15.026	15.917	16.870	17.888	18.977	20.141
13	13.809	14.680	15.618	16.627	17.713	18.882	20.141	21.495	22.953
14	14.947	15.974	17.086	18.292	19.599	21.015	22.550	24.215	26.019
15	16.097	17.293	18.599	20.024	21.579	23.276	25.129	27.152	29.361
16	17.258	18.639	20.157	21.825	23.657	25.673	27.888	30.324	33.003
17	18.430	20.012	21.762	23.698	25.840	28.213	30.840	33.750	36.974
18	19.615	21.412	23.414	25.645	28.132	30.906	33.999	37.450	41.301
19	20.811	22.841	25.117	27.671	30.539	33.760	37.379	41.446	46.018
20	22.019	24.297	26.870	29.778	33.066	36.786	40.995	45.762	51.160
21	23.239	25.783	28.676	31.969	35.719	39.993	44.865	50.423	56.765
22	24.472	27.299	30.537	34.248	38.505	43.392	49.006	55.457	62.873
23	25.716	28.845	32.453	36.618	41.430	46.996	53.436	60.893	69.532
24	26.973	30.422	34.426	39.083	44.502	50.816	58.177	66.765	76.790
25	28.243	32.030	36.459	41.646	47.727	54.865	63.249	73.106	84.701
30	34.785	40.568	47.575	56.085	66.439	79.058	94.461	113.28	136.31
40	48.886	60.402	75.401	95.026	120.80	154.76	199.64	259.06	337.88
50	64.463	84.579	112.80	152.67	209.35	290.34	406.53	573.77	815.08
60	81.670	114.05	163.05	237.99	353.58	533.13	813.52	1253.2	1944.8

T A B L E A.4 (concluded)

Interest Rate										
10%	12%	14%	15%	16%	18%	20%	24%	28%	32%	36%
1.0000	1.0000	1.0000	1.0000	1.0000	1.0000	1.0000	1.0000	1.0000	1.0000	1.0000
2.1000	2.1200	2.1400	2.1500	2.1600	2.1800	2.2000	2.2400	2.2800	2.3200	2.3600
3.3100	3.3744	3.4396	3.4725	3.5056	3.5724	3.6400	3.7776	3.9184	4.0624	4.2096
4.6410	4.7793	4.9211	4.9934	5.0665	5.2154	5.3680	5.6842	6.0156	6.3624	6.7251
6.1051	6.3528	6.6101	6.7424	6.8771	7.1542	7.4416	8.0484	8.6999	9.3983	10.146
7.7156	8.1152	8.5355	8.7537	8.9775	9.4420	9.9299	10.980	12.136	13.406	14.799
9.4872	10.089	10.730	11.067	11.414	12.142	12.916	14.615	16.534	18.696	21.126
11.436	12.300	13.233	13.727	14.240	15.327	16.499	19.123	22.163	25.678	29.732
13.579	14.776	16.085	16.786	17.519	19.086	20.799	24.712	29.369	34.895	41.435
15.937	17.549	19.337	20.304	21.321	23.521	25.959	31.643	38.593	47.062	57.352
18.531	20.655	23.045	24.349	25.733	28.755	32.150	40.238	50.398	63.122	78.998
21.384	24.133	27.271	29.002	30.850	34.931	39.581	50.895	65.510	84.320	108.44
24.523	28.029	32.089	34.352	36.786	42.219	48.497	64.110	84.853	112.30	148.47
27.975	32.393	37.581	40.505	43.672	50.818	59.196	80.496	109.61	149.24	202.93
31.772	37.280	43.842	47.580	51.660	60.965	72.035	100.82	141.30	198.00	276.98
35.950	42.753	50.980	55.717	60.925	72.939	87.442	126.01	181.87	262.36	377.69
40.545	48.884	59.118	65.075	71.673	87.068	105.93	157.25	233.79	347.31	514.66
45.599	55.750	68.394	75.836	84.141	103.74	128.12	195.99	300.25	459.45	700.94
51.159	63.440	78.969	88.212	98.603	123.41	154.74	244.03	385.32	607.47	954.28
57.275	72.052	91.025	102.44	115.38	146.63	186.69	303.60	494.21	802.86	1298.8
64.002	81.699	104.77	118.81	134.84	174.02	225.03	377.46	633.59	1060.8	1767.4
71.403	92.503	120.44	137.63	157.41	206.34	271.03	469.06	812.00	1401.2	2404.7
79.543	104.60	138.30	159.28	183.60	244.49	326.24	582.63	1040.4	1850.6	3271.3
88.497	118.16	158.66	184.17	213.98	289.49	392.48	723.46	1332.7	2443.8	4450.0
98.347	133.33	181.87	212.79	249.21	342.60	471.98	898.09	1706.8	3226.8	6053.0
164.49	241.33	356.79	434.75	530.31	790.95	1181.9	2640.9	5873.2	12941.	28172.3
442.59	767.09	1342.0	1779.1	2360.8	4163.2	7343.9	22729.	69377.	*	*
1163.9	2400.0	4994.5	7217.7	10436.	21813.	45497.	*	*	*	*
3034.8	7471.6	18535.	29220.	46058.	*	*	*	*	*	*

*The factor is greater than 99.999.

Appendix

Key Equations

Chapter 2

1. The balance sheet identity or equation:

$$\text{Assets} = \text{Liabilities} + \text{Shareholders' equity} \quad [2.1]$$

2. The income statement equation:

$$\text{Revenues} - \text{Expenses} = \text{Income} \quad [2.2]$$

3. The cash flow identity:

$$\text{Cash flow from assets} = \text{Cash flow to creditors} + \text{Cash flow to stockholders} \quad [2.3]$$

where

a. Cash flow from assets = Operating cash flow (OCF) − Net capital spending − Additions to net working capital (NWC)

(1) Operating cash flow = Earnings before interest and taxes (EBIT) + Depreciation − Taxes

(2) Net capital spending = Ending net fixed assets − Beginning net fixed assets + Depreciation

(3) Additions to net working capital = Ending NWC − Beginning NWC

b. Cash flow to creditors = Interest paid − Net new borrowing

c. Cash flow to stockholders = Dividends paid − Net new equity raised

Chapter 3

1. The current ratio:

$$\text{Current ratio} = \frac{\text{Current assets}}{\text{Current liabilities}} \quad [3.1]$$

2. The quick or acid-test ratio:

$$\text{Quick ratio} = \frac{\text{Current assets} - \text{Inventory}}{\text{Current liabilities}} \quad [3.2]$$

3. The cash ratio:

$$\text{Cash ratio} = \frac{\text{Cash}}{\text{Current liabilities}} \quad [3.3]$$

4. The total debt ratio:

$$\text{Total debt ratio} = \frac{\text{Total assets} - \text{Total equity}}{\text{Total assets}} \quad [3.4]$$

5. The debt/equity ratio:

$$\text{Debt/equity ratio} = \text{Total debt/Total equity} \quad [3.5]$$

6. The equity multiplier:

$$\text{Equity multiplier} = \text{Total assets/Total equity} \quad [3.6]$$

7. The times interest earned (TIE) ratio:

$$\text{Times interest earned ratio} = \frac{\text{EBIT}}{\text{Interest}} \quad [3.7]$$

8. The cash coverage ratio:

$$\text{Cash coverage ratio} = \frac{\text{EBIT} + \text{Depreciation}}{\text{Interest}} \quad [3.8]$$

9. The inventory turnover ratio:

$$\text{Inventory turnover} = \frac{\text{Cost of goods sold}}{\text{Inventory}} \quad [3.9]$$

10. The average days' sales in inventory:

$$\text{Days' sales in inventory} = \frac{365 \text{ days}}{\text{Inventory turnover}} \quad [3.10]$$

11. The receivables turnover ratio:

$$\text{Receivables turnover} = \frac{\text{Sales}}{\text{Accounts receivable}} \quad [3.11]$$

12. The days' sales in receivables:

$$\text{Days' sales in receivables} = \frac{365 \text{ days}}{\text{Receivables turnover}} \quad [3.12]$$

13. The total asset turnover ratio:

$$\text{Total asset turnover} = \frac{\text{Sales}}{\text{Total assets}} \quad [3.13]$$

14. Profit margin:

$$\text{Profit margin} = \frac{\text{Net income}}{\text{Sales}} \quad [3.14]$$

15. Return on assets (ROA):

$$\text{Return on assets} = \frac{\text{Net income}}{\text{Total assets}} \quad [3.15]$$

16. Return on equity (ROE):

$$\text{Return on equity} = \frac{\text{Net income}}{\text{Total equity}} \quad [3.16]$$

17. The price/earnings (P/E) ratio:

$$\text{P/E ratio} = \frac{\text{Price per share}}{\text{Earnings per share}} \quad [3.17]$$

18. The market-to-book ratio:

$$\text{Market-to-book ratio} = \frac{\text{Market value per share}}{\text{Book value per share}} \quad [3.18]$$

19. The Du Pont identity:

$$\text{ROE} = \underbrace{\frac{\text{Net income}}{\text{Sales}} \times \frac{\text{Sales}}{\text{Assets}}}_{\text{Return on assets}} \times \frac{\text{Assets}}{\text{Total equity}} \quad [3.19]$$

ROE = Profit margin
×Total asset turnover
×Equity multiplier

Chapter 4

1. The dividend payout ratio:

Dividend payout ratio = Cash dividends/Net income [4.1]

2. The internal growth rate:

$$\text{Internal growth rate} = \frac{\text{ROA} \times b}{1 - \text{ROA} \times b} \quad [4.2]$$

3. The sustainable growth rate:

$$\text{Sustainable growth rate} = \frac{\text{ROE} \times b}{1 - \text{ROE} \times b} \quad [4.3]$$

Chapter 5

1. The future value of $1 invested for t periods at rate of r per period:

Future value = $1 × $(1 + r)^t$ [5.1]

2. The present value of $1 to be received t periods in the future at a discount rate of r:

PV = $1 × $[1/(1 + r)^t]$ = $1/$(1 + r)^t$ [5.2]

3. The relationship between future value and present value (the basic present value equation):

$$\text{PV} \times (1 + r)^t = \text{FV}_t \quad [5.3]$$
$$\text{PV} = \text{FV}_t/(1 + r)^t = \text{FV}_t \times [1/(1 + r)^t]$$

Chapter 6

1. The present value of an annuity of C dollars per period for t periods when the rate of return or interest rate is r:

Annuity present value

$$= C \times \left[\frac{1 - \text{Present value factor}}{r}\right] = C \times \left[\frac{1 - \{1/(1 + r)^t\}}{r}\right] \quad [6.1]$$

2. The future value factor for an annuity:

Annuity FV factor
$= (\text{Future value factor} - 1)/r$ [6.2]
$= [\{(1 + r)^t\} - 1]/r$

3. Annuity due value
= Ordinary annuity value × $(1 + r)$ [6.3]

4. Present value for a perpetuity:

PV for a perpetuity = $C/r = C \times (1/r)$ [6.4]

5. Effective annual rate (EAR), where m is the number of times the interest is compounded during the year:

EAR = $[1 + (\text{Quoted rate})/m]^m - 1$ [6.5]

Chapter 7

1. Bond value if bond has (1) a face value of F paid at maturity, (2) a coupon of C paid per period, (3) t periods to maturity, and (4) a yield of r per period:

Bond value
$= C \times [1 - 1/(1 + r)^t]/r + F/(1 + r)^t$ [7.1]
Bond value
= Present value of the coupons + Present value of the face amount

2. $P_0 = (D_1 + P_1)/(1 + r)$ [7.2]
3. $P_0 = D/r$ [7.3]
4. The dividend growth model:

$$P_0 = \frac{D_0 \times (1 + g)}{r - g} = \frac{D_1}{r - g} \quad [7.4]$$

5. $$P_t = \frac{D_t \times (1 + g)}{r - g} = \frac{D_{t+1}}{r - g} \quad [7.5]$$

6. Required return:

$$(r - g) = D_1/P_0$$
$$r = D_1/P_0 + g \quad [7.6]$$

Chapter 8

1. Net present value (NPV):

NPV = Present value of future cash flows − Investment cost

2. Payback period:

Payback period = Number of years that pass before the sum of an investment's cash flows equal the cost of the investments

3. The average accounting return (AAR):

$$\text{AAR} = \frac{\text{Average net income}}{\text{Average book value}}$$

4. Internal rate of return (IRR):

IRR = Discount rate of required return such that the net present value of an investment is zero

6. Profitability index:

$$\text{Profitability index} = \frac{\text{PV of cash flows}}{\text{Cost of investment}}$$

Chapter 10

1. Total dollar return = Dividend income + Capital gain (or loss) [10.1]

2. Total cash if stock is sold = Initial investment + Total return
= $3,700 + 518 [10.2]
= $4,218

3. Fisher effect:

$$(1 + R) = (1 + r) \times (1 + h) \quad [10.3]$$

4. $$(1 + R) = (1 + r) \times (1 + h)$$
$$R = r + h + r \times h \quad [10.4]$$

5. $$R \approx r + h \quad [10.5]$$

6. Variance of returns, Var(R), or σ^2:

$$\text{Var}(R) = \frac{1}{T-1}[(R_1 - \overline{R})^2 + \cdots + (R_T - \overline{R})^2] \quad [10.6]$$

Chapter 11

1. Risk premium:

Risk premium = Expected return − Risk-free rate [11.1]
$= \text{E}(R_U) - R_f$

2. Expected return on a portfolio:

$$\text{E}(R_P) = x_1 \times \text{E}(R_1) + x_2 \times \text{E}(R_2) + \cdots + x_n \times \text{E}(R_n) \quad [11.2]$$

3. Total return = Expected return + Unexpected return

$$R = \text{E}(R) + U \quad [11.3]$$

4. Announcement = Expected part + Surprise [11.4]

5. $R = \text{E}(R)$ + Systematic portion + Unsystematic portion [11.5]

6. Total risk = Systematic risk + Unsystematic risk [11.6]

7. The capital asset pricing model (CAPM):

$$\text{E}(R_i) = R_f + [\text{E}(R_M) - R_f] \times \beta_i \quad [11.7]$$

Chapter 12

1. $R_E = D_1/P_0 + g$ [12.1]
2. $R_E = R_f + \beta_E \times (R_M - R_f)$ [12.2]
3. $R_P = D/P_0$ [12.3]
4. $V = E + D$ [12.4]
5. $100\% = E/V + D/V$ [12.5]
6. $\text{WACC} = (E/V) \times R_E + (D/V) \times R_D \times (1 - T_C)$ [12.6]

Chapter 14

1. Modigliani-Miller Propositions (no taxes):

Proposition II:

$$R_E = R_A + (R_A - R_D) \times (D/E) \quad [14.1]$$

2. Modigliani-Miller Propositions (with taxes):

a. Value of the interest tax shield:

Value of the interest tax shield
$= (T_C \times D \times R_D)/R_D$ [14.2]
$= T_C \times D$

3. Proposition I:

$$V_L = V_U + T_C \times D \quad [14.3]$$

Chapter 16

1. Net working capital + Fixed assets = Long-term debt + Equity [16.1]

2. Net working capital = (Cash + Other current assets) − Current liabilities [16.2]

3. Cash = Long-term debt + Equity + Current liabilities − Current assets (other than cash) − Fixed assets [16.3]

4. The operating cycle:
   Operating cycle = Inventory period + Accounts receivable period [16.4]
5. The cash cycle:
   Cash cycle = Operating cycle − Accounts payable period [16.5]
6. Cash collections = Beginning accounts receivable + 1/2 × Sales [16.6]

Chapter 17

1. The economic order quantity (EOQ) model:
   Total carrying costs:
   Total carrying costs = Average inventory × Carrying costs per unit = $(Q/2) \times \text{CC}$ [17.1]
2. Total restocking costs:
   Total restocking costs = Fixed cost per order × Number of orders = $F \times (T/Q)$ [17.2]
3. Total costs:
   Total costs = Carrying costs + Restocking costs = $(Q/2) \times \text{CC} + F \times (T/Q)$ [17.3]
4. Carrying costs = Restocking costs
   $(Q^*/2) \times \text{CC} = F \times (T/Q^*)$ [17.4]
5. $(Q^*)^2 = \dfrac{2T \times F}{\text{CC}}$ [17.5]
6. The optimal order size Q^*:
   $Q^* = \sqrt{\dfrac{2T \times F}{\text{CC}}}$ [17.6]

Chapter 18

1. $(\text{E}[S_1] - S_0)/S_0 = h_{FC} - h_{US}$ [18.1]
2. $\text{E}[S_1] = S_0 \times [1 + (h_{FC} - h_{US})]$ [18.2]
3. Purchasing power parity (PPP):
   $\text{E}[S_t] = S_0 \times [1 + (h_{FC} - h_{US})]^t$ [18.3]
4. Interest Rate Parity (IRP):
   Exact; single period:
   $F_t/S_0 = (1 + R_{FC})/(1 + R_{US})$ [18.4]
5. $(F_1 - S_0)/S_0 = R_{FC} - R_{US}$ [18.5]
6. $F_1 = S_0 \times [1 + (R_{FC} - R_{US})]$ [18.6]
7. Approximate; multi-period:
   $F_t = S_0 \times [1 + (R_{FC} - R_{US})]^t$ [18.7]

Appendix

Answers to Selected End-of-Chapter Problems

Chapter 2

2.1 Owners' equity = \$3,800; NWC = \$500

2.3 \$26,200

2.5 Book value assets = \$2.5 million
Market value assets = \$3.2 million

2.7 Average tax rate = 27.04%
Marginal tax rate = 39%

2.9 \$500,000

2.11 −\$325,000

2.13 \$500,000

2.15 \$1,000

2.17 Owners' equity = \$100 (assets = \$1,800)
Owners' equity = \$0 (assets = \$1,500)

2.19 *a.* −\$25,000
b. \$100,000

2.21 *a.* \$462
b. \$1,762
c. −\$338
d. Cash flow to creditors = \$300
Cash flow to stockholders = −\$638

Chapter 3

3.5 Current ratio = 1.28 times
Quick ratio = 0.94 times

3.7 Receivables turnover = 6.95 times
Days' sales in receivables = 52.51 days
Average collection period = 52.51 days

3.9 Debt/equity ratio = 1.50
Equity multiplier = 2.50

3.11 20%

3.13 Cash decreased by \$825

3.15 \$500; a use of cash

3.19 *a.* 1.183; 1.322
b. 0.474; 0.508
c. 0.113; 0.123
d. Debt/equity ratio: 0.621; 0.448
Equity multiplier: 1.621; 1.448
e. Total debt ratio: 0.383; 0.310

3.23 \$22.50

3.25 ROE = 14.67%

3.27 Cash coverage ratio = 8.33 times

3.29 Profit margin = 1.29%
Net income = \$9,937,000

3.31 ROE = 21.75%

3.33 P/E ratio = 9.85 times
Dividends/share = \$1.50
Market-to-book ratio = 2.14 times

Chapter 4

4.1 Pro forma net income = \$1,200
Pro forma equity = \$2,100
Dividends (the plug) = \$850

4.3 −\$572.50

4.5 \$692.80

4.7 g^* = 6.36%

4.9 \$837.78

4.13 ROA = 11.31%; ROE = 20.33%

4.15 g^* = 15.94%

4.17 g^* = 7.53%

4.19 12.28%

4.21 Total asset turnover = 1.887 times

4.23 g^* = 1.52%; additional borrowing = \$457
g_{int} = 0.86%

4.25 EFN = −\$10,788

Chapter 5

5.1 \$1,958.56

5.3 PV = \$260.79
PV = \$3,517.62
PV = \$3,363.82
PV = \$83,205.57

5.5 t = 9.79; 2.32; 28.66; 6.30 years

5.7 t = 8.04 years; t = 12.75 years

5.9 3.83 years

5.11 \$1.27; \$1.61

5.13 58.7% per six months

5.15 6.62 additional years

Chapter 6

6.1 PV@10% = $1,688.75
PV@14% = $1,559.83
PV@20% = $1,394.68

6.2 FV@6% = $3,312.79
FV@8% = $3,422.86
FV@16% = $3,893.29

6.5 PVA = $161,225.06

6.6 $9,336.17; $12,257.77

6.8 $1,607.25

6.11 8.24%

6.13 APR = 7.85%; 11.39%; 15.72%

6.15 APR = 8.65%

6.17 FV = $338.25; $352.05; $667.63

6.19 APR = 300%; EAR = 1,355.19%

6.21 43 months

6.23 $10,405.23

6.25 PVA_1 = $65,082.91
PVA_2 = $62,541.45

6.27 $r_G = 8.15\%$; $r_H = 8.28\%$

6.29 77 payments

6.31 8.58%; 8.93%

6.33 $3,332,927.21

6.35 $597.66

6.37 *a.* $320
b. $1,920

Chapter 7

7.3 P = $895.47

7.5 6.91%

7.7 10.15%

7.9 P_0 = $97.96

7.12 *a.* 125,001
b. 375,001

7.14 90

7.15 7.82%

7.17 9.26%

7.19 P_0 = $47.22

7.21 Dividends per share = $3.49

7.23 7.39%

Chapter 8

8.1 2.67 years

8.3 Payback: A = 1.56 years; B = 2.80 years

8.5 IRR = 16.11%

8.7 NPV@7% = $77.86; NPV@15% = −$167.92

8.9 $300; $130.28; $6.48; −$86.57

8.11 *a.* NPV = $25.62
b. IRR = 13.81%, −80.47%

8.14 *a.* A: 3.529 years; B: 0.889 years
b. A: $8,547.85; B: $3,525.79
c. A: 15.98%; B: 24.04%
e. A: 1.033; B: 1.088

8.15 NPV@0% = $86,646
NPV@∞ = −$176,515
NPV@17.41% = $0

Chapter 9

9.3 $171 million

9.5 Taxes = $52,143; Net income = $81,557
OCF = $187,357

9.6 OCF = $18,170.50

9.9 $1,613,760

9.11 $465,000

9.13 NPV = $68,031.74

9.19 OCF = $343,625; NPV = $452,782.34
$\Delta NPV/\Delta S$ = +$21.246

9.21 *a.* NPV_{worst} = −$319,471.13
NPV_{base} = $80,706.66
NPV_{best} = $545,987.62
b. $\Delta NPV/\Delta FC = -2.153$

9.23 NPV = −$723,161.25; IRR = 7.75%

Chapter 10

10.1 −11.57%

10.3 R = 23.61%; Dividend yield = 3.24%
Capital gains yield = 20.37%

10.5 9.68%

10.7 8.57%

10.9 *a.* $70
b. 7.25%
c. 3.13%

10.12 Average: X = 6.20%, Y = 9.40%
Standard deviation: $\sigma_X = 8.88\%$ $\sigma_Y = 18.47\%$

10.14 *a.* 6%
b. Variance = 0.0187
Standard deviation = 13.67%

10.15 *a.* 1.44%
b. 1.20%

10.21 The probability is about ⅙
@95%: R between −12.4% and +22.8%
@99%: R between −21.2% and +31.6%

Chapter 11

11.1 0.625; 0.375

11.3 14.7%

11.5 20.0%

11.7 $E(R_A) = 10.20\%$; $\sigma_A = 5.11\%$
$E(R_B) = 21.05\%$; $\sigma_B = 20.25\%$

11.9 *a.* 13.12%
b. 0.005824

11.15 1.055

11.17 14.2%

11.19 13%

11.21 *a.* 9.5%
b. Stock: 0.5625; risk-free asset: 0.4375
c. 0.533
d. Stock: 2.1875; risk-free asset: −1.1875

11.23 M is undervalued; N is overvalued

11.30 *a.* $E(R_P) = 18.75\%$; variance = 0.05884
Standard deviation = 24.26%
b. 13.50%
c. 13.10%; 12.86%

11.31 Investment in C = $55,000
Investment in risk-free asset = $25,000
$\beta_{rf} = 0$

11.33 $\beta_A = 2.1875$; $\beta_B = 0.9125$
$\sigma_A = 4.33\%$; $\sigma_B = 18.21\%$

Chapter 12

12.1 11.30%

12.3 14.22%

12.5 6.25%

12.7 *a.* 8.00%
b. 4.96%

12.9 *a.* 10.68%
b. Aftertax cost of debt = 6.50%

12.11 1.787

12.13 12.32%

12.15 7.82%

12.17 *a.* Y and Z
b. W and Y
c. W would be incorrectly rejected
Z would be incorrectly accepted

12.24 Breakeven cost = $885.909M

Chapter 13

13.3 $2,000; $0

13.5 674,202

13.6 flotation cost = 34.85%

Chapter 14

14.1 *a.* EPS = $2.50; $5.00; $7.00
b. EPS = $0.17; $4.33; $7.67

14.3 P = $60 per share; V = $18 million

14.5 P = $35 per share. This is M&M Proposition I without taxes.

14.8 $5.4 million

14.9 $80 million; $94 million

14.11 16%; 12%

Chapter 15

15.2 *a.* $28.57
b. $45.45
c. $36.36
d. $83.33
e. 437,500; 275,000; 343,750; 150,000

15.4 P_0 = $25; P_x = $23.75 The equity and cash accounts will both decline by $5,000.

15.6 $36.36

Chapter 16

16.3 Cash = $1,000; Current assets = $3,375

16.9 Operating cycle = 105.10 days
Cash cycle = −18.21 days

16.13 *a.* $60,000
b. $50,666.67
c. January: $59,866.67
February: $80,383.33
March: $106,250.00

Chapter 17

17.9 *a.* 90 days; $24,000
b. 3%; 30 days; $23,280
c. $720; 60 days

17.16 EAR = 28.03%
a. EAR = 17.81%
b. EAR = 109.84%
c. EAR = 24.90%

17.21 Carrying cost = $1,500
Restocking cost = $46,800
EOQ = 1,396.42 units
Order frequency = 9.31 times per year

Chapter 18

18.1 *a.* Lit 173,400
b. .05767¢
c. $1,730.10
d. Singapore dollar
e. Mexican peso
f. SFr .04025/BF; this is the cross rate

18.3 *a.* ¥104.24; premium
b. DM 1.7351; premium
c. It will probably fall; rise

18.10 5.0%; 1.8%; 2.7%

18.11 US: $12,364,070
Great Britain; $12,084,434; invest in US

18.13 No change: profit = $1.2 million
If the rate rises: profit = $2,018,182
If the rate falls: profit = $200,000
Break-even rate = W 713.21

Glossary

A–B

Absolute priority rule (APR) Rule establishing priority of claims in liquidation.

Accelerated Cost Recovery System (ACRS) Depreciation method under U.S. tax law allowing for the accelerated write-off of property under various classifications.

Accounts receivable financing A secured short-term loan that involves either the assignment or factoring of receivables.

Accounts payable period The time between receipt of inventory and payment for it.

Accounts receivable period The time between sale of inventory and collection of the receivable.

Agency problem The possibility of conflict of interest between the owners and management of a firm.

Aging schedule A compilation of accounts receivable by the age of each account.

American Depository Receipt (ADR) A security issued in the United States representing shares of a foreign stock and allowing that stock to be traded in the United States.

Annual percentage rate (APR) The interest rate charged per period multiplied by the number of periods per year.

Annuity due An annuity for which the cash flows occur at the beginning of the period.

Annuity A level stream of cash flows for a fixed period of time.

Applications of cash A firm's activities in which cash is spent. Also *uses of cash.*

Asset specific risk A risk that affects at most a small number of assets. Also *unique* or *unsystematic risks.*

Average accounting return (AAR) An investment's average net income divided by its average book value.

Average tax rate Total taxes paid divided by total taxable income.

Balance sheet Financial statement showing a firm's accounting value on a particular date.

Bankruptcy A legal proceeding for liquidating or reorganizing a business. Also, the transfer of some or all of a firm's assets to its creditors.

Benefit/cost ratio The present value of an investment's future cash flows divided by its initial cost. Also *profitability index.*

Best efforts underwriting Underwriter sells as much of the issue as possible, but can return any unsold shares to the issuer without financial responsibility.

Beta coefficient Amount of systematic risk present in a particular risky asset relative to an average risky asset.

Business risk The equity risk that comes from the nature of the firm's operating activities.

C

Call provision Agreement giving the corporation the option to repurchase a bond at a specified price prior to maturity.

Call protected Bond during period in which it cannot be redeemed by the issuer.

Call premium Amount by which the call price exceeds the par value of the bond.

Capital intensity ratio A firm's total assets divided by its sales, or the amount of assets needed to generate $1 in sales.

Capital structure The mixture of debt and equity maintained by a firm.

Capital rationing The situation that exists if a firm has positive net present value projects but cannot find the necessary financing.

Capital gains yield The dividend growth rate or the rate at which the value of an investment grows.

Capital asset pricing model (CAPM) Equation of the security market line showing the relationship between expected return and beta.

Capital budgeting The process of planning and managing a firm's long-term investments.

Captive finance company A wholly-owned subsidiary that handles the credit function for the parent company.

Carrying costs Costs that rise with increases in the level of investment in current assets.

Cash concentration The practice of and procedures for moving cash from multiple banks into the firm's main accounts.

Cash discount A discount given to induce prompt payment. Also *sales discount.*

Cash cycle The time between cash disbursement and cash collection.

Cash flow to stockholders Dividends paid out by a firm less net new equity raised.

Cash flow to creditors A firm's interest payments to creditors less net new borrowings.

Cash flow from assets The total of cash flow to creditors and cash flow to stockholders, consisting of the following: operating cash flow, capital spending, and additions to net working capital.

Cash flow time line Graphical representation of the operating cycle and the cash cycle.

Cash budget A forecast of cash receipts and disbursements for the next planning period.

Clientele effect Argument that stocks attract particular groups based on dividend yield tax brackets.

Collection policy Procedures followed by a firm in collecting accounts receivable.

Common stock Equity without priority for dividends or in bankruptcy.

Common-size statement A standardized financial statement presenting all items in percentage terms. Balance sheet items are shown as a percentage of assets and income statement items as a percentage of sales.

Compound value The amount an investment is worth after one or more periods. Also *future value.*

Compound interest Interest earned on both the initial principal and the interest reinvested from prior periods.

Compounding The process of accumulating interest in an investment over time in order to earn more interest.

Consol A type of perpetuity.

Contingency planning Taking into account the managerial options implicit in a project.

Controlled disbursement account A disbursement practice under which the firm transfers an amount to a disbursing account that is sufficient to cover demands for payment.

Corporation A business created as a distinct legal entity composed of one or more individuals or entities.

Cost of equity The return that equity investors require on their investment in the firm.

Cost of capital The minimum required return on a new investment.

Cost of debt The return that lenders require on the firm's debt.

Coupon The stated interest payments made on a bond.

Coupon rate The annual coupon divided by the face value of a bond.

Credit period The length of time that credit is granted.

Credit scoring The process of quantifying the probability of default when granting consumer credit.

Credit analysis The process of determining the probability that customers will or will not pay.

Credit instrument The evidence of indebtedness.

Credit cost curve Graphical representation of the sum of the carrying costs and the opportunity costs of a credit policy.

Cross-rate The implicit exchange rate between two currencies (usually non-U.S.) quoted in some third currency (usually the U.S. dollar).

Cumulative voting Procedure where a shareholder may cast all votes for one member of the board of directors.

Current yield A bond's coupon payment divided by its closing price.

D–E

Date of record Date on which holders of record are designated to receive a dividend.

Date of payment Date that dividend checks are mailed.

Debenture Unsecured debt, usually with a maturity of 10 years or more.

Declaration date Date on which the board of directors passes a resolution to pay a dividend.

Deferred call Bond call provision prohibiting the company from redeeming the bond prior to a certain date.

Direct bankruptcy costs The costs that are directly associated with bankruptcy, such as legal and administrative expenses.

Discount Calculate the present value of some future amount.

Discount rate The rate used to calculate the present value of future cash flows.

Discounted cash flow (DCF) valuation The process of valuing an investment by discounting its future cash flows.

Distribution Payment made by a firm to its owners from sources other than current or accumulated retained earnings.

Dividend growth model Model that determines the current price of a stock as its dividend next period divided by the discount rate less the dividend growth rate.

Dividend payout ratio Amount of cash paid out to shareholders divided by net income.

Dividend yield A stock's expected cash dividend divided by its current price.

Dividend Payment made out of a firm's earnings to its owners, either in the form of cash or stock.

Dividends Payment by corporation to shareholders, made in either cash or stock.

Du Pont identity Popular expression breaking ROE into three parts: operating efficiency, asset use efficiency, and financial leverage.

Economic order quantity (EOQ) The restocking quantity that minimizes the total inventory costs.

Effective annual rate (EAR) The interest rate expressed as if it were compounded once per year.

Efficient capital market Market in which security prices reflect available information.

Efficient markets hypothesis (EMH) The hypothesis that actual capital markets, such as the New York Stock Exchange, are efficient.

Erosion The cash flows of a new project that come at the expense of a firm's existing projects.

Estimation risk The possibility that errors in projected cash flows lead to incorrect decisions. Also *forecasting risk.*

Eurobonds International bonds issued in multiple countries but denominated in a single currency (usually the issuer's currency).

Eurocurrency Money deposited in a financial center outside of the country whose currency is involved.

European Currency Unit (ECU) An index of European currencies intended to serve as a monetary unit for the European Monetary System (EMS).

Ex-dividend date Date two business days before the date of record, establishing those individuals entitled to a dividend.

Exchange rate The price of one country's currency expressed in terms of another country's currency.

Exchange rate risk The risk related to having international operations in a world where relative currency values vary.

Expected return Return on a risky asset expected in the future.

F–H

Face value The principal amount of a bond that is repaid at the end of the term. Also *par value.*

Financial risk The equity risk that comes from the financial policy (i.e., capital structure) of the firm.

Financial distress costs The direct and indirect costs associated with going bankrupt or experiencing financial distress.

Financial ratios Relationships determined from a firm's financial information and used for comparison purposes.

Firm commitment underwriting Underwriter buys the entire issue, assuming full financial responsibility for any unsold shares.

Fisher effect Relationship between nominal returns, real returns, and inflation.

Five Cs of credit The five basic factors to be evaluated: character, capacity, capital, collateral, and conditions.

Float The difference between book cash and bank cash, representing the net effect of checks in the process of clearing.

Forecasting risk The possibility that errors in projected cash flows lead to incorrect decisions. Also *estimation risk.*

Foreign bonds International bonds issued in a single country, usually denominated in that country's currency.

Foreign exchange market The market in which one country's currency is traded for another's.

Forward exchange rate The agreed-upon exchange rate to be used in a forward trade.

Forward trade Agreement to exchange currency at some time in the future.

Future value (FV) The amount an investment is worth after one or more periods. Also *compound value.*

General cash offer An issue of securities offered for sale to the general public on a cash basis.

Generally Accepted Accounting Principles (GAAP) The common set of standards and procedures by which audited financial statements are prepared.

Gilts British and Irish government securities.

Green Shoe provision Contract provision giving the underwriter the option to purchase additional shares from the issuer at the offering price. Also *overallotment option.*

Hard rationing The situation that occurs when a business cannot raise financing for a project under any circumstances.

Homemade leverage The use of personal borrowing to change the overall amount of financial leverage to which an individual is exposed.

I–M

Income statement Financial statement summarizing a firm's performance over a period of time.

Incremental cash flows The difference between a firm's future cash flows with a project or without the project.

Indenture Written agreement between the corporation and the lender detailing the terms of the debt issue.

Indirect bankruptcy costs The costs of avoiding a bankruptcy filing incurred by a financial distressed firm.

Initial public offering (IPO) A company's first equity issue made available to the public. Also *unseasoned new issue.*

Interest rate parity (IRP) The condition stating that the interest rate differential between two countries is equal to the percentage difference between the forward exchange rate and the spot exchange rate.

Interest tax shield The tax saving attained by a firm from interest expense.

Interest on interest Interest earned on the reinvestment of previous interest payments.

Internal rate of return (IRR) The discount rate that makes the net present value of an investment zero.

Internal growth rate The maximum growth rate a firm can achieve without external financing of any kind.

Inventory period The time it takes to acquire and sell inventory.

Inventory loan A secured short-term loan to purchase inventory.

Invoice Bill for goods or services provided by the seller to the purchaser.

Just-in-time (JIT) inventory A system for managing demand-dependent inventories that minimizes inventory holdings.

Line of credit A formal (committed) or informal (non-committed) prearranged, short-term bank loan.

Liquidation Termination of the firm as a going concern.

Lockboxes Special post office boxes set up to intercept and speed up accounts receivable payments.

London Interbank Offer Rate (LIBOR) The rate most international banks charge one another for overnight Eurodollar loans.

M&M Proposition I The value of the firm is independent of its capital structure.

M&M Proposition II A firm's cost of equity capital is a positive linear function of its capital structure.

Managerial options Opportunities that managers can exploit if certain things happen in the future.

Marginal tax rate Amount of tax payable on the next dollar earned.

Market risk premium Slope of the security market line, the difference between the expected return on a market portfolio and the risk-free rate.

Market risk A risk that influences a large number of assets. Also *systematic risk.*

Materials requirements planning (MRP) A set of procedures used to determine inventory levels for demand-dependent inventory types, such as work-in-progress and raw materials.

Maturity Specified date at which the principal amount of a bond is paid.

Multiple rates of return The possibility that more than one discount rate makes the net present value of an investment zero.

Mutually exclusive investment decisions A situation where taking one investment prevents the taking of another.

N–P

Net present value profile A graphical representation of the relationship between an investment's net present values and various discount rates.

Net present value (NPV) The difference between an investment's market value and its cost.

Net working capital Current assets less current liabilities.

Nominal return Return on an investment not adjusted for inflation.

Noncash items Expenses charged against revenues that do not directly affect cash flow.

Normal distribution A symmetric, bell-shaped frequency distribution that is completely defined by its mean and standard deviation.

Note Unsecured debt, usually with a maturity of under 10 years.

Operating cash flow Cash generated from a firm's normal business activities.

Operating cycle The time period between the acquisition of inventory and the collection of cash from receivables.

Opportunity cost The most valuable alternative that is given up if a particular investment is undertaken.

Overallotment option Contract provision giving the underwriter the option to purchase additional shares from the issuer at the offering price. Also *Green Shoe provision.*

Par value The principal amount of a bond that is repaid at the end of the term. Also *face value.*

Partnership A business formed by two or more individuals or entities.

Payback period The amount of time required for an investment to generate cash flows sufficient to recover its initial cost.

Percentage of sales approach Financial planning method in which accounts are varied depending on a firm's predicted sales level.

Perpetuity An annuity in which the cash flows continue forever.

Plowback ratio Addition to retained earnings divided by net income. Also *retention ratio.*

Political risk Risk related to changes in value that arise because of political actions.

Portfolio weight Percentage of a portfolio's total value in a particular asset.

Portfolio Group of assets, such as stocks and bonds, held by an investor.

Precautionary motive The need to hold cash as a safety margin to act as a financial reserve.

Preferred stock Stock with dividend priority over common stock, normally with a fixed dividend rate, sometimes without voting rights.

Present value (PV) The current value of future cash flows discounted at the appropriate discount rate.

Principle of diversification Spreading an investment across a number of assets will eliminate some, but not all, of the risk.

Private placements Loans, usually long-term in nature, provided directly by a limited number of investors.

Pro forma financial statements Financial statements projecting future years' operations.

Profitability index (PI) The present value of an investment's future cash flows divided by its initial cost. Also *benefit/cost ratio.*

Prospectus Legal document describing details of the issuing corporation and the proposed offering to potential investors.

Protective covenant Part of the indenture limiting certain actions that can be taken during the term of the loan, usually to protect the lender's interest.

Proxy Grant of authority by shareholder allowing for another individual to vote his or her shares.

Purchasing power parity (PPP) The idea that the exchange rate adjusts to keep purchasing power constant among currencies.

Pure play approach Use of a weighted average cost of capital that is unique to a particular project, based on companies in similar lines of business.

Q–R

Quoted interest rate The interest rate expressed in terms of the interest payment made each period. Also *stated interest rate.*

Real return Return adjusted for the effects of inflation.

Red herring Preliminary prospectus distributed to prospective investors in a new issue of securities.

Registered form The registrar of a company records who owns each bond and bond payments are made directly to the owner of record.

Registration statement Statement filed with SEC that discloses all material information concerning the corporation making a public offering.

Regular cash dividend Cash payment made by a firm to its owners in the normal course of business, usually made four times a year.

Regulation A SEC regulation that exempts public issues less than $1.5 million from most registration requirements.

Reorganization Financial restructuring of a failing firm to attempt to continue operations as a going concern.

Repurchase Refers to a firm's purchases of its own stock; an alternative to a cash dividend.

Residual dividend approach Policy under which a firm pays dividends only after meeting its investment needs while maintaining a desired debt/equity ratio.

Retention ratio Addition to retained earnings divided by net income. Also *plowback ratio.*

Reverse split Stock split under which a firm's number of shares outstanding is reduced.

Rights offer A public issue of securities in which securities are first offered to existing shareholders. Also *rights offering.*

Rights offering A public issue of securities in which securities are first offered to existing shareholders. Also *rights offer.*

Risk premium The excess return required from an investment in a risky asset over a risk-free investment.

S

Sales discount A discount given to induce prompt payment. Also *cash discount.*

Scenario analysis The determination of what happens to net present value estimates when we ask "what-if" questions.

Seasoned new issue A new equity issue of securities by a company that has previously issued securities to the public.

Security market line (SML) Positively shaped straight line displaying the relationship between expected return and beta.

Sensitivity analysis Investigation of what happens to net present value when only one variable is changed.

Shelf registration SEC Rule 415 allowing a company to register all issues it expects to sell within two years at one time, with subsequent sales at any time within those two years.

Shortage costs Costs that fall with increases in the level of investment in current assets.

Simple interest Interest earned only on the original principal amount invested.

Sinking fund Account managed by the bond trustee for early bond redemption.

Soft rationing The situation that occurs when units in a business are allocated a certain amount of financing for capital budgeting.

Sole proprietorship A business owned by a single individual.

Sources of cash A firm's activities that generate cash.

Speculative motive The need to hold cash to take advantage of additional investment opportunities, such as bargain purchases.

Spot exchange rate The exchange rate on a spot trade.

Spot trade An agreement to trade currencies based on the exchange rate today for settlement within two business days.

Spread Compensation to the underwriter, determined by the difference between the underwriter's buying price and offering price.

Stakeholder Someone other than a stockholder or creditor who potentially has a claim on the cash flows of the firm.

Stand-alone principle Evaluation of a project based on the project's incremental cash flows.

Standard deviation The positive square root of the variance.

Standard Industry Classification (SIC) code U.S. government code used to classify a firm by its type of business operations.

Stated interest rate The interest rate expressed in terms of the interest payment made each period. Also *quoted interest rate.*

Statement of cash flows A firm's financial statement that summarizes its sources and uses of cash over a specified period.

Static theory of capital structure Theory that a firm borrows up to the point where the tax benefit from an extra dollar in debt is exactly equal to the cost that comes from the increased probability of financial distress.

Stock split An increase in a firm's shares outstanding without any change in owners' equity.

Stock dividend Payment made by a firm to its owners in the form of stock, diluting the value of each share outstanding.

Straight voting Procedure where a shareholder may cast all votes for each member of the board of directors.

Strategic options Options for future, related business products or strategies.

Sunk cost A cost that has already been incurred and cannot be removed and therefore should not be considered in an investment decision.

Sustainable growth rate The maximum growth rate a firm can achieve without external equity financing while maintaining a constant debt/equity ratio.

Swaps Agreements to exchange two securities or currencies.

Syndicate A group of underwriters formed to share the risk and to help sell an issue.

Systematic risk A risk that influences a large number of assets. Also *market risk.*

Systematic risk principle The expected return on a risky asset depends only on that asset's systematic risk.

T–Z

Target payout ratio A firm's long-term desired dividend-to-earnings ratio.

Term loans Direct business loans of, typically, one to five years.

Terms of sale Conditions under which a firm sells its goods and services for cash or credit.

Tombstone An advertisement announcing a public offering.

Trading range Price range between highest and lowest prices at which a stock is traded.

Transaction motive The need to hold cash to satisfy normal disbursement and collection activities associated with a firm's ongoing operations.

Underwriters Investment firms that act as intermediaries between a company selling securities and the investing public.

Unique risk A risk that affects at most a small number of assets. Also *unsystematic* or *asset-specific risks.*

Unseasoned new issue A company's first equity issue made available to the public. Also *initial public offering.*

Unsystematic risk A risk that affects at most a small number of assets. Also *unique* or *asset-specific risks.*

Uses of cash A firm's activities in which cash is spent. Also *applications of cash.*

Variance The average squared difference between the actual return and the average return.

Venture capital Financing for new, often high-risk ventures.

Weighted average cost of capital (WACC) The weighted average of the cost of equity and the aftertax cost of debt.

Working capital A firm's short-term assets and liabilities.

Yield to maturity (YTM) The rate required in the market on a bond.

Zero-balance account A disbursement account in which the firm maintains a zero balance, transferring funds in from a master account only as needed to cover checks presented for payment.

Name Index

Equation Index

Subject Index

THE FUNCTIONAL USE OF COLOR

Throughout **Essentials of Corporate Finance**, by Ross/Westerfield/Jordan, we make color a functional dimension of the discussion. In many chapters, color plays an extensive nonschematic and largely self-evident role. Color in these chapters alerts students to the relationship between numbers in a discussion and an accompanying table or figure.

Whenever appropriate, color is used schematically, to distinguish between items. For example, in Chapters 3 and 4 the colors teal and purple represent the income statement and balance sheet, respectively. As discussion progresses, numbers corresponding to each financial statement are highlighted in these same colors, helping students readily identify the origin of each.

Below we list chapters where colors are used schematically.

Chapter 2	*Section 2.4 (See examples U.S. Corp and Dole Cola)*	
	Teal:	Identifies cash flow numbers.
Chapters 3 and 4	*Throughout the chapter*	
	Teal:	Identifies income statement data.
	Purple:	Identifies balance sheet data. (Also see all 19 ratios in Chapter 3)
Chapter 7	*Section 7.1*	
	Teal:	Identifies key numbers that combine to determine the value of a bond.
	Purple:	Identifies the bond value.
Chapter 8	*Section 8.4*	
	Teal:	Identifies Investment A.
	Purple:	Identifies Investment B.
Chapter 10	*Section 10.5 (See Figure 10.11)*	
	Teal, Purple, & Burgundy:	Identifies the three normal distribution ranges and uses them to illustrate from which range each number has been derived.
Chapter 11	*Sections 11.1 and 11.2*	
	Teal:	Identifies Stock L.
	Purple:	Identifies Stock U.